V&R unipress

Mamluk Studies

Volume 17

Edited by Stephan Conermann and Bethany J. Walker

ANNEMARIE SCHIMMEL KOLLEG

History and Society during the Mamluk Era (1250 - 1517)

Editorial Board: Thomas Bauer (Münster, Germany), Albrecht Fuess (Marburg, Germany), Thomas Herzog (Bern, Switzerland), Konrad Hirschler (Berlin, Germany), Anna Paulina Lewicka (Warsaw, Poland), Linda Northrup (Toronto, Canada), Jo Van Steenbergen (Gent, Belgium)

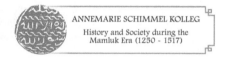

Reuven Amitai / Stephan Conermann (eds.)

The Mamluk Sultanate from the Perspective of Regional and World History

Economic, Social and Cultural Development in an Era of Increasing International Interaction and Competition

With 14 figures

V&R unipress

Bonn University Press

UNIVERSITÄT BONN

MIX
Papier aus verantwortungsvollen Quellen
FSC www.fsc.org FSC® C083411

Bibliographic information published by the Deutsche Nationalbibliothek
The Deutsche Nationalbibliothek lists this publication in the Deutsche Nationalbibliografie; detailed bibliographic data are available online: http://dnb.d-nb.de.

Publications of Bonn University Press are published by V&R unipress GmbH.

Sponsored by the DFG-funded Annemarie Schimmel Institute for Advanced Study "History and Society during the Mamluk Era, 1250–1517" and the Minerva Foundation.

Cover image: Daniel Hopfer (ca 1470–1536), Etching, Three Mamelukes with lances on horseback. Quelle: Wikimedia.org
Printed and bound by CPI books GmbH, Birkstraße 10, 25917 Leck, Germany
Printed in the EU.

Vandenhoeck & Ruprecht Verlage | www.vandenhoeck-ruprecht-verlage.com

ISSN 2198-5375
ISBN 978-3-8471-0411-7

Contents

Preface 9

A Note on Citations, Transliteration and Dates 13

I. General Considerations on the International Context of the Mamluk Sultanate

Stephan Conermann (University of Bonn)
The Mamluk Empire. Some Introductory Remarks on a Perspective of Mediterranean History 17

Yehoshua Frenkel (University of Haifa)
The Mamlūk Sultanate and its Neighbours: Economic, Social and Cultural Entanglements 39

Albrecht Fuess (Philipps University, Marburg)
How to Cope with the Scarcity of Commodities? The Mamluks' Quest for Metal 61

Jo Van Steenbergen (Ghent University)
Revisiting the Mamlūk Empire. Political Action, Relationships of Power, Entangled Networks, and the Sultanate of Cairo in Late Medieval Syro-Egypt 75

II. Local Concerns with Wider Implications

Robert Irwin (London)
How Circassian Were the Circassian Mamluks? 109

Nimrod Luz (Kinneret College on the Sea of Galilee)
Reconstructing the Urban Landscape of Mamluk Jerusalem: Spatial and Socio-political Implications . . . 123

Koby Yosef (Bar-Ilan University, Ramat Gan)
Cross-Boundary Hatred: (Changing) Attitudes towards Mongol and "Christian" *mamlūks* in the Mamluk Sultanate . . . 149

Georg Christ (University of Manchester)
The Sultans and the Sea: Mamluk Coastal Defence, Dormant Navy and Delegation of Maritime Policing (14th and Early 15th Centuries) . . . 215

Bethany J. Walker (University of Bonn)
The "Liquid Landscapes" of the Late Mamluk Mediterranean: Rural Perspectives on the Ever-Evolving Sultanate . . . 257

III. Mediterranean Connections

Amar S. Baadj (Bonn and Trier Universities)
Travel by Sea and Land between the Maghrib and the Mamluk Empire . . . 279

Nikolas Jaspert (Heidelberg University)
The Crown of Aragon and the Mamluk Sultanate: Entanglements of Mediterranean Politics and Piety . . . 307

IV. Looking North and East

Marie Favereau (University of Oxford)
The Mamluk Sultanate and the Golden Horde. Tension and Interaction During the Mongol Peace . . . 345

Michal Biran (The Hebrew University of Jerusalem)
The Mamluks and Mongol Central Asia . . . 367

Cihan Yüksel Muslu (University of Houston)
Patterns of Mobility between Ottoman and Mamluk Lands . . . 391

Albrecht Fuess (Philipps University, Marburg)
Three's a Crowd. The Downfall of the Mamluks in the Near Eastern Power Struggle, 1500–1517 . . . 431

V. The Red Sea and Beyond

John Meloy (American University of Beirut)
Mecca Entangled 453

Anne Regourd (CNRS, UMR 7192, Paris)
with the collaboration of Fiona Handley (University of Brighton)
Late Ayyubid and Mamluk Quṣayr al-Qadīm: What the Primary Sources Tell Us 479

Contributors 501

List of Illustrations 509

Index 511

Preface

By its very being, Mamluk studies should have an international orientation. The Mamluks themselves were brought from far-away, usually from the steppes north of the Black Sea or the Caucasus. Over the many decades of its existence, the Mamluks dealt with a series of external challenges: Ilkhanid Mongols, Franks, Cilician Armenia, Turkmans, Timurids, Ottomans, Safavids and more. At the same time, the Sultanate maintained relations, often warm, with various powers far away from its borders: the Mongol Golden Horde, Venice, Genoa, the Byzantine Empire, the Hohenstaufens in Sicily (and conversely, the Capetian Angevin empire), west African Muslim kingdoms, Ceylon, etc. Its commercial connections stretched across the Mediterranean, to the south of the Sahara, to the Crimea, to India and elsewhere.

The Mamluk sultans, formally governing in the name of the ʿAbbasid caliphs (and referred to as "Partner of the Commander of the Faithful"), claimed rule over all Muslims wherever they might be. Mamluk-controlled Mecca, Medina and Jerusalem were the focus of pilgrimage from all the Muslim world; the last named was also a center of Jewish and Christian religious tourism. The major cities of the Sultanate: Cairo and Alexandria in Egypt, and Damascus and Aleppo in Syria, were the foci of international traders, Muslim scholars and mystics, refugees, immigrants and other sundry visitors from afar. And it was the scholars and mystics who left these cities to head elsewhere or were in contact with other religious figures throughout the Muslim oecumene.

The wider geographic, political, economic and cultural context of the Sultanate found expression in the works of several of the earlier luminaries of Mamluk Studies. David Ayalon, the founder of the systematic study of the Mamluk state and its military-political elite, wrote about the larger Eurasian context of the phenomenon of military slavery, as well as the relations with the Mongols. His fellow Jerusalemite, Eliyahu Ashtor, certainly had a Mediterranean perspective (and beyond) when examining the economic life of the Sultanate. Another important historian of their generation was Peter M. Holt, remembered for his studies of Mamluk-Frankish relations. Perhaps the most prominent representative of the next generation of Mamlukists was Ulrich Haarmann, who with his interest in the Eurasian and Turkish background of Mamluk society, as well as European sources for the history of the Sultanate, clearly had wide perspectives.

Yet, in spite of these efforts and others, one might say that most of the work on the Mamluks in the post-WWII era was somewhat inwardly looking: the editing and translation of Arabic texts; the analysis of Mamluk politics and the culture (mostly of the elites), art history and archeology; intellectual and social history, again mainly of the elites; urban studies, etc. With the almost endless sources, and the far-flung Sultanate with its multi-varied population, there was certainly lots to do examining its internal history. In the last decade or two, however, this seems to have begun to change, and more emphasis is now placed on the myriad connections between the Mamluk Sultanate on its various levels, and the surrounding world: Muslim, Mediterranean, Indian Ocean, Eurasian, and more. This may be partially due to a growing interest in global and comparative history, but also to the increasing awareness that indeed, the Sultanate was a focus of different ongoing and changing regional and international links. Finally, perhaps Mamlukists are ever more aware that a dichotomy between internal and external relations never really holds, and in order to understand developments within the Sultanate, one needs constantly to look at the larger picture, and vice versa: the study of foreign connections facilitates a comprehension of interior aspects.

Many of these aspects of the relations of the Sultanate and its elites (and to a lesser extent, its overall population) with the wider regional and global arena find expression in this present volume. The majority of the papers had their origins at a conference held on 18–20 December 2015 by the Annemarie Schimmel-Kolleg for Mamluk Studies at the University of Bonn on the "The Mamluk Sultanate and its Neighbors: Economic, Social and Cultural Entanglements," co-convened by the two editors of this volume. Several other papers (by N. Luz, B. Walker and K. Yosef) were originally presented at a Minerva Gentner Symposium, held in Jerusalem in June 2014, also convened by the co-editors, who are grateful to the Minerva Foundation of Germany for its support. Finally, two papers (by R. Irwin and one of two by A. Fuess) were first delivered at a conference organized by Amalia Levanoni and R. Amitai in 2006 in Jerusalem and Haifa. That conference did not spawn a collective work as originally thought, and the editors were happy to invite these two authors to join the present volume with their pertinent papers.

The editors are grateful to the team at the Annemarie Schimmel-Kolleg for its assistance at various stages, and also to Mr. Or Amir of the Hebrew University for his assistance with the 2014 symposium in Jerusalem. We are appreciative of the support and advice of our colleague Prof. Amalia Levanoni. Finally, we wish to express our thanks to the authors of the papers for their cooperation and patience.

Reuven Amitai
Jerusalem

Stephan Conermann
Bonn

August 2018

A Note on Citations, Transliteration and Dates

This volume is a collection of papers from different specializations and disciplines, based on various scholarly approaches and methodologies. It was thus decided to give the authors a certain amount of leeway regarding both their citations methods and transliteration systems from non-Latin alphabets, as a reflection of their individual scholarly background. Overall, we have eschewed abbreviations for journals, encyclopedias and standard reference works, in the interest of clarity for a (hopefully) wide readership; not everyone is familiar with the abbreviations of all the journals in a neighboring discipline or in all the cited languages. Overall Common Era dates are used, but when Hijrī dates are also employed, the latter generally comes first; in any case, the distinction should be clear from the context.

I. General Considerations on the International Context of the Mamluk Sultanate

Stephan Conermann (University of Bonn)

The Mamluk Empire. Some Introductory Remarks on a Perspective of Mediterranean History[1]

From a classical, phenomenological point of view, space is envisaged as the (terrestrial) ground of human actions.[2] In the last two decades, however, it has become an established viewpoint in the systematic disciplines like sociology, anthropology and geography to think of space as a constructed reference value – and thus no longer a mere physical-material category. The *spatial turn* therefore stresses a more rational understanding of space: the processual spatial references of social interaction, so to speak.[3] Following the tradition of classical social theory (especially Georg Simmel),[4] action-theoretical approaches in the social sciences became more and more important, compared to a territorial, physical spatial determinism. Culture is accordingly no longer conceived of as a territorial fixed habitat, as implicitly propagated by the *area studies*, but rather as a process of exchange and acquisition.[5] The pre-modern Mediterranean is understood and studied in this context as a space of interaction.

In what follows, I present approaches to a global history, before turning to other theoretical considerations on how to analyze interactions between individuals, groups, and political organizations. Recent studies on the Mediterranean region eventually lead us to highlight four research works on the relations of the Mamluk Empire with associates in the North; they give a very incisive overview of contemporary studies and research questions in this field. As it turns out, we are just commencing on an interdisciplinary, theoretically profound and methodically precise research of the Mediterranean.

1 This is a shortened version of Conermann 2013. I thank the Stämpfli Verlag for giving me the permission to publish the modified text in this volume of collected articles.
2 Cf. Günzel 2006.
3 Cf. Simmel1903. For Simmel's theoretical approach, see Glauser 2006.
4 For the *spatial turn*, see Bachmann-Medick 2009 and Döring and Thielmann 2008.
5 See on this Ferguson and Gupta 1997.

Global History

Today, upholding the supremacy and dominance of national history has become just as untenable as considering only the history of single cultures. Global history lies less at the center of the clash of civilizations than it does at the intersection of the interactions; or – if you like – of the conflict between global, long-range developments and local and regional reactions.[6] Of course, there are typical spaces of interaction – the Indian Ocean, the Atlantic, the Mediterranean, the Baltic Sea. Global history focuses on the apprehension and description of the dialectic between spacious, external relations and spatial processes of integration (which inevitably lead to the drawing of boundaries and fragmentation) as well as between densification and differentiation. It is no longer a matter of tracing the Europeanization of the world but of understanding the interaction among different parts of the world in a process of constructing the present age. Just as a look at non-European history is presumed to widen the analytical circumscribed nature of national histories, global history is presumed to put the universalism of European history into perspective. Looking at the *longue durée* of processes of global history inevitably shakes up the well-established epochal structuring and the underlying parameters of modernization deduced from European development. The time is ripe to allot non-European parts of the world their very own historical existence and to stop locating them within the historiographical periphery of the European or national center.

Our special interest in the countless discussions on global history and phenomena of global history lies in the global dimensions before 1492, the so-called "early modern capitalistic world system."[7] "Global" here does not refer to any notion of "worldwide" in a physical sense, but rather to the interconnectedness and interlacing of Eurasian-African spaces. Some might want to generalize this to be the "Old World," but in fact it refers to the *human web* of the Old World[8] in times of an "archaic globalization"[9] or to an *Eurasian connectedness*[10] in the 13th and 14th centuries. To be more specific, it is concerned with the idea (developed especially by Janet Abu Lughod) of a *Pax Mongolica*, evoked, on the one hand, by the Mongols along the Silk Road, and of a space of communication established by Islamic traders and networks across the Indian Ocean, on the other hand.[11]

6 For global history, the following introductions are helpful: Kossock 1992; Mazlish 1993; Mazlish 2002; Osterhammel 2005; Grandner, Rothermund and Schwentker 2005; Hausberger 2007 and Osterhammel 2008.
7 Wallerstein 1986 which is based on Braudel 1986. For Wallerstein, see Nolte 2005.
8 McNeill and McNeill 2003.
9 Bayly 2007.
10 Darwin 2007.
11 Abu Lughod 1989; Abu Lughod 1993; Abu Lughod 1994.

The world of Islam, which once covered vast areas of Africa and Asia, was precisely not just a religious entity, but rather also conducive to a commercial and cultural cohesion of the space from Seville to Samarkand. This is the beginning of a "process of densification"[12] that is connected to keywords like nationalization, population growth, world-spanning navigation, a permanently interconnected world economy, the intensification of agriculture, and the global diffusion of culture, religion, and technology.

It has to be stated that a sweeping shift occurred between the 13th and the 15th centuries which led to the integration of the Mediterranean region into the global system of transportation and communication as well as the trans-regional processes of exchange.[13] Even though the Crusaders had once and for all been expelled from the Levant at the end of the 13th century, Europe had by no means been excluded from the Eastern Mediterranean. On the contrary, seen from the perspective of the Mamluk Empire, which from that time on held a pivotal function in global activities, Genoa, Venice, and Barcelona were fully integrated into the trade network.[14] Major disturbances of this pre-modern global exchange system were precipitated by the disastrous plague epidemic in mid-14th century[15] and the Hundred Years' War (1337–1453)[16] raging in Europe. Not until the "long" 16th century, which stretched from 1420 to 1620,[17] was this crisis in the North overcome. But from a global perspective, what followed in the 17th century was a period of massive changes with far-reaching impacts: In France, India, China, and England, processes of political and social reform started which, over the course of time, were to permanently change the face of the Earth.[18] Large amounts of capital were being released through the emerging European trade companies that increasingly exerted local power.[19] Furthermore, migration movements were taking place on a huge scale between Africa, America, and parts of Asia.[20] A main feature of the era lay in the remarkable exchange processes evolving on many levels – even though Europe as well as the Islamic realm were still politically largely fragmented (e.g., Mamluks, Ilkhanate, Golden Horde, Timurids, Hafsids, Merinids), a circumstance John Bayly calls a "Warrior Globalization."[21] These were, first and foremost, economic relations. Mamluk Syria and Egypt became the hub between East and West as well as between North and South. An in-

12 Ertl and Limberger 2009.
13 Cf. Jaspert 2009.
14 An overview gives North 2007.
15 An excellent account is Bergdolt 2011.
16 Cf. Curry 2012.
17 Braudel 1974.
18 Cf. Parker 2008.
19 Cf. Chaudhuri 1985; Tracy 1990; Nagel 2007 and Ertl 2008.
20 Cf. Lucassen and Lucassen 1997 and the relevant parts of Oltmer and Schuber.
21 Cf. Bayly 2007.

creasingly circular exchange of commodities, foodstuff, spices, and craft products arose on the Eurasian continent under the influence of various sub-cycles – and Africa was included in these activities:[22] (1) the European trade area covering the Atlantic Ocean and the Mediterranean sea; (2) the Middle East, which was connected to Central Asia and Africa via land bridges and was able to make use of sea connections to Europe and India; and, (3) the East Asian trade area extending from China via South Asia all the way to India. The corner marks were China and Western Europe, with the Arabic-Persian region at its core. The main transport routes consisted of the caravan routes through Central Asia and the shipping routes via the Indian Ocean;[23] Europe became a factor in those transcontinental linkages via the Mediterranean. Around 1300, a certain peak of this first world system may be registered. Besides trade goods, religious ideas also came to be circulated; shamanistic and animistic religions blended, were overlaid, and syncretized with Arabic and Turkish-Persian Islam, Buddhism, and Christianity, which had a strong influence on the North and East through the idea of the Crusades.[24] The idea of *travelling concepts*, that is, not only the transfer of culture and technology,[25] but also intellectual interlacing, played a significant role that has to date been studied only insufficiently.[26] *Knowledge flows* occurred not only in fields like astronomy, mathematics, and medicine, but also concerning business practices (commercial and financial techniques), military strategies and nautical knowledge. According to John Darwin, this Eurasian *connectedness* lasted until 1750. Only after that year did the global-imperial world of European hegemony came into being on winding paths. Jürgen Osterhammel very aptly calls this process, which arose against great resistance and much contingency, the "transformation of the world" ("Verwandlung der Welt").[27]

Theoretical and Methodological Approaches to the Study of Spaces of Interaction

The identification of the Mediterranean as a space of interaction leads us to questions on the categories we must apply to capture processes of exchange and interlacing, and on which method we should use to work with our material in order to get answers about the *connectedness* of the space and the different

22 Cf. Abu Lughod 1989.
23 Cf. Conermann 1998 and Conermann 2001.
24 Cf. Riley-Smith 1992.
25 Cf. Agius and Hitchkock 1994.
26 Cf. Neumann and Nünning 2012.
27 Osterhammel 2009.

agents.[28] Let us use a specific example to illustrate the problems encountered here.

For a long time, it was considered ideal to construct a "comparison" to answer historical social-scientific questions.[29] A comparative study in its traditional form compared two or more entities independent from each other, the goal being to determine similarities and differences of certain phenomena, which in turn could help to enlighten them both. So, even though they were related in many ways, they continued to be separate from each other – their existence and identity lay prior to their encounter on a temporal and a systematic level. A comparison was thus only desired – and even possible – when it concerned two communities that were located as far apart as possible from each other on a spatial level.[30]

Methodological problems also should be mentioned: Distinct units of comparison, which in reality do not exist as such, first have to be constructed in order to be compared.[31] Exponents of cultural transfer studies also criticize the fact that any comparison ignores the relations between the units of comparison and could hardly capture developments over time.[32] Against this backdrop the spaces of interaction became the center of attention. Transfer history, dealing predominantly with the movement of goods, people, and ideas in coinciding perspectives of the country of origin and the destination, experienced a revival.[33] Its exponents advocated the argument that societies are not given entities, but that they come into existence through communicative practices and are thus subject to constant change. First and foremost, however, communities should no longer be conceived of as existing prior to the processes of transfer and exchange, in the sense that two communities that were already identifiable and describable contacted each other in a second step. Rather, such a transfer should be understood as *constitutive* because it in fact brought forth the communities. If a definition of differences were the focal point of each comparison, then the term "transfer" (also as opposed to the concept of interlacing) allows the process to be grasped and operationalized more precisely in numerous aspects: First, the reasons for the transfer – specific situations, specific agents, specific motivations – have to be identified; second, the criteria of selection have to be defined, as only certain

28 The following paragraph is mainly based on Pernau 2011.

29 See Pernau 2011, 30–35 and 153–154. See Kaelble 1999a; Kaelble 1999b; Kaelble 2003; Kaelble 2005; Haupt and Kocka 1996 and Kocka 2003. For transcultural comparisons, see Osterhammel 2003; Höfert 2008a; Höfert 2008b; Drews 2008; Drews 2009; Oesterle 2008 and Oesterle 2009.

30 Cf. Galtung 2000.

31 Cf. Lorenz 1999 and Welskopp 1995.

32 Cf. Borgolte, Schiel; Schneidmüller 2008; Borgolte and Schneidmüller 2010; Borgolte, Dücker, Müllerburg and Schneidmüller 2011.

33 See Pernau 2011, 43–49 and 156–157.

aspects are transferred and never an entire culture; and finally, the results of the transfer have to be discussed.

Exponents and pioneers of a *connected history*[34] followed a similar approach, concentrating on the interconnection between the four world religions in the Early Modern Age. Serge Gruzinski, who emerged from the École des Hautes Études en Sciences Sociales (EHESS), especially concerned himself with the cultural processes that evolved in Latin America in the wake of the Spanish conquest.[35]According to his research, cultural hybrids (*métissages*) evolved from an encounter that essentially featured violence (conquest, slave trade with Africa, revolts, natural disasters, and diseases) and was by no means a "happy hybridity."[36] The approach of connected history inevitably fragmented the concept of culture and made it problematic. In his works, Sanjay Subrahmanya mindicates that we should not assume that precolonial societies were static and only developed their dynamic *vis-à-vis* the West.[37] In fact, tight connections and processes of exchange originating from different hubs always existed – in all directions and throughout all time. He argues the case for a fundamental openness of history, which should by no means be interpreted and read from its alleged terminal point: European world domination.

Another standpoint opposite to transfer research is the concept of "histoire croisée," as shaped by Michael Werner and Bénèdicte Zimmerman.[38] They also oppose the method of comparison and call for an elaboration of the theoretical presuppositions of research in order to make them significantly more precise. They are especially concerned with the circulation of ideas, people, institutions, and objects from one social context into another and in different directions, while including the point of view of the researcher. In their view, the scholar cannot immediately interpret the facts, but can only make a second-category interpretation that reflects the preexisting interpretation of the actors themselves. Recently, comparative history and transfer history underwent a rapprochement by changing the objective of the comparison: It is now all about displaying the specific and no longer about showing general causalities and developing historical macro prototypes. Galtung's objection that a proper comparison can be conducted only between entities that have not been related to each other before and that do not have a common origin becomes less important.[39] Transfer history actually *needs* the comparison (as a method). De-

34 See Pernau 2011, 37–43 and 145–146.
35 Cf. Gruzinski 2004.
36 Ahuja 2006, 112 (quoted after Pernau 2011, 38).
37 Cf. Subrahmanyam 1997; Subrahmanyam 2005a and Subrahmanyam 2005b.
38 Cf. Werner and Zimmermann 2002; Werner and Zimmermann 2004; Werner and Zimmermann 2006. See Pernau 2011, 49–56 and 157–159.
39 Cf. Galtung 2000.

termining differences by contemporary actors is the beginning of each and every process of transformation. Transfer leads to changes, not only in the cultures of origin and reception, but also in the object of transfer itself. These modifications can only be conceived properly by utilizing a temporal and geographical comparison. The presumption that a comparison leads to an essentialization is no longer accurate in any comprehensive way. Multipolar exchange must be managed methodologically and through practical research.

One last approach that intrigues our interest concerning the premodern Mediterranean is represented by the idea of "translocality," as developed by Ulrike Freitag, Achim von Oppen, and Nora Lafi from the Zentrum Moderner Orient (ZMO) in Berlin.[40] In the course of the *cultural turn*, history and the social sciences abandoned structural history and the quantifying methods, looking at "culture" in a more general sense.[41] This includes a preoccupation not only with products of the so-called "high culture," but with all kinds of social interaction to which actors attribute a meaning. Space too became a cultural construct – created through ideas, practices, and symbols. It is a matter of a new segmentation and structuring of space, of regulating the relationship between places. Various fields of action (economic, religious, political, etc.) can lead to different hierarchies between places in this case, though they can also partially overlap. This interaction between the dynamics of trans-local movements and what has been called "establishment," that is, the (not always successful) attempt of the agents to convert this dynamic into stable systems and structures, may be observed.

Mediterranean Studies

The Mediterranean region has long been the subject of countless essays, especially since Fernand Braudel's (1902–1985) publication of his professorial dissertation *La Méditerranée et le monde méditeranéen à l'epoque de Philippe II* in 1949.[42] There, Braudel creates a universal history of the *Méditerranée* at the time of Philip II of Spain (lived 1527–1598).[43] The work has three parts: He starts with an elaboration on the history of humans and their relationship to a geographical milieu and then deals with structures like states, societies, and cultures. The focus of the third part lies on political and military events. This outline corresponds to Braudel's general notion of history, which always moves in three different tempi: *longue durée* (geography, climate), *conjuncture* (economy, social

40 Cf. Freitag and von Oppen 2005; Freitag and von Oppen 2010. See Pernau 2011, 67–75 and 162–164.

41 Pernau 2011, 67. Fort the *cultural turn*, see Bachmann-Medick 2016.

42 Braudel 1949. For the reception of his theses, see Marino 2004; Molho 2001.

43 Helpful introductions are Horden and Purcell 2005; Balard 2006; Abulafia 2011.

cycles), *événements* (events). Eventually, Braudel's research directs itself against the thesis put forth by Henri Pirenne (1862–1935), arguing that the unity of the Mediterranean created through the Roman Empire as apolitical union was destroyed by the Arabs in the 7th century.[44] Braudel, on the other hand, assumes that not until the 16th century did fundamental global changes occur. Even though Braudel's approach has had great impact to this day, some have remarked that his research fails to sufficiently take the historical agents into account, and that he conceived of and described the three civilizations of the Mediterranean (Roman Christianity, Orthodox Christianity, Islam) in a way that was too essentialist.[45]

This is not the place to present an extensive research report on the history of the Mediterranean.[46] Nevertheless, two studies should be mentioned here which arose in the context of the 8-volume global history "Die Welt 1000–2000" (The World 1000–2000), edited by the historians Peter Feldbauer, Bernd Hausberger, and Jean-Paul Lehners. In his essay "Austausch-, Transfer- und Abgrenzungsraum. Das Mittelmeer"[47] (Space of Exchange, Transfer, and Demarcation. The Mediterranean), Nikolas Jaspert points to the ambiguity of Mediterranean Studies: "An unreflecting approach that misjudges the peculiarities of individual areas and the small-scale division of the Mediterranean risks evening out singularities and making the case for 'Mediterraneanism.'"[48] The small-scale division of the Mediterranean area with its multifaceted internal segmentation led to the fact that "communication and exchange in the Mediterranean area […] – whether on an economic, cultural, or political level – were essentially shaped regionally."[49]

Besides the spatial, there was also religious segmentation, especially in Christianity: Besides the Roman and the Greek-Orthodox Church, the Armenians, Nestorians, Syrians, and Copts were home to bigger enclaves, and indeed in many regions, multi-religiosity was the norm. Also, there was strong political fragmentation around the Mediterranean. This includes for the Islamic realm the Ottoman Empire in Anatolia, the Mamluk Empire in Egypt and Syria as well as the authoritative unions of the Hafsids, Abdalwadids, Merinids, and Nasrids in the Maghreb and Spain. The North was even more heterogeneous: Apart from the kingdoms of Castile, Aragon, France, Sicily, and Hungary, the Byzantine Empire and the Papal States, city-states like Pisa, Genoa, Venice, and Ragusa struggled for power.

44 Pirenne 1937. See for the reception of his thesis, Kölzer 1998.
45 See Pernau 2011, 98–101.
46 Cf. Oesterle 2012.
47 Jaspert 2009.
48 Jaspert 2009, 139–140.
49 Jaspert 2009, 143.

On the other hand, scholars have started to understand and research the Mediterranean Sea as a space of communication and therefore to focus on the trans-Mediterranean and transcontinental connections. It is increasingly being interpreted as a social space once characterized by various forms of mobility (migration, traveling, emigration, forced displacement). Furthermore, we find an unmistakable series of technical and cultural interlacing as well as economic interactions. There is some discordance concerning the classification of the era. In his article, Gottfried Liedl argues the case for the above-mentioned global history to be a "formative period of European Modernity" from 1348 to 1648.[50] He thinks many critical changes were characteristic of that time, especially the shift of external "occidental" aggression (think: Crusades) to an internal event that was a "veritable revolution in the way of thinking" in combination with the phenomena "Renaissance" and "Humanism" as well as a rapid development in military technology and seafaring. It should be added that this seems to be a very Eurocentric interpretation of the development because the date 1348, which roughly coincides with the catastrophe of the plague, cannot be interpreted only as a new beginning, but also as a depression in a process of development that was very dynamic and began in the 13th century.

The Mamluk Empire as a Node for Global Interaction

According to Birgit Schäbler, a main feature of a global history lies in conceptualizing interpretations polycentrically, including regional differences or asynchrony, and focusing on them.[51] Existing spatial interconnections and interactions were not subject to continual historical development, but rather evolved in waves of intensity including regressive phases. One such era of accelerated densification was, as already stated, the age of the Mongols. In the 13th and 14th century, global transportation and communication emerged, putting into motion far reaching processes that included political and military reactions as well as commercial changes, cultural and technological transfer. Only at the end of the late Middle Ages was Europe finally connected with this trans-regional network. By establishing useful bilateral relations with Genoa and Venice (and to a lesser degree also with Barcelona), the Mamluks had a great influence along the Eastern Mediterranean areas, as well as in the Black Sea. A decisive event of global dimension occurred in mid-14th century, when the plague spread from Central Asia via the above-mentioned seas to Europe and eventually claimed the lives of

50 Liedl 2008.
51 Cf. Schäbler 2007.

25 million people.[52] The end of the Mongol Empire complicated European access to the markets of East Asia and even of Persia and Turkestan.[53] The quest for other access possibilities to the treasures of the East led to the discovery of the sea routes around Africa and America.[54] The retreat of the Chinese from maritime trade facilitated the establishment of the Portuguese in the Indian Ocean.[55] Throughout the course of the entire era, the Mamluk Empire served as an interface between Eurasia, North Africa, and Sub-Saharan Africa.

That the Mamluk Empire had a pivotal function in a global trade network stems from the results of two studies presented by Peter Feldbauer and Gottfried Liedl.[56] In the first study, Feldbauer succeeded in writing a standard reference of the economic and social history of the Islamic world up to the 13th century. He adapted the research literature in an exemplary manner and was able to show the continuity of social productivity and economic performance of Muslim societies far beyond the 10th century. This contradicts the opinion still prevalent among many Orientalists today, namely, that the alleged golden age of the Islamic culture merely lasted up to the year 1000. The 11th century (but at latest the 13th century) are then thought of as consisting of a very long-lasting social, political, and economic crisis– as the beginning of a century-long decline. This incident is said to have been of such a fundamental nature that the development could not even have been stopped by consolidation through the establishment of great empires by the Ottomans, Safavids, and the Moguls. This phase model persists today, even though the Islamic Studies scholar Aziz al-Azmeh has long since very feasibly proven that the multifaceted stereotypes of decadence and decline used to describe the history of economy, society, and culture in the Islamic realm were exceedingly constructed as an antithesis to the civil-capitalist order that increasingly came to be seen as natural in modern era Europe.[57] However, as al-Azmeh states, a Eurocentric perspective on European development, eventually leading to national states, civic societies, the rise of capitalism, and the establishment of a world economy and international division of labor, results in a completely inappropriate search for factors that could obstruct capitalism with respect to non-European societies. With good reason, Feldbauer and Liedl point out that the intentionally naive question put forth by Michael Cook as to why the Islamic world should actually have been anticipating the capitalist development of Western Europe,[58] highlights the Eurocentric perspective of many of these

52 For the Muslim world, see Dols 1977.
53 Cf. Kauz 2009.
54 Cf. Hausberger 2008.
55 Cf. Dahm, Feldbauer and Rothermund 2008.
56 Feldbauer 1995; Feldbauer and Liedl 2008. The paragraph follows Conermann 2009.
57 Cf. Al-Azmeh 1996.
58 Cf. Cook 1993.

problematic comparisons. The (anti-)thesis of an (on average) rather favorable economic, sociopolitical, and cultural development extending beyond the time of the Crusades is – unfortunately – advocated only by a minority of modern Islamic historians. In this context, Maxime Rodinson, Michael Cook, Subhi Labib, Marshall G. S. Hodgson, and – to a lesser extent – also Gudrun Krämer and Reinhard Schulze should be mentioned.[59] It is very remarkable that the Islamic world comes off much better in the concepts of "regular" historians, such as Ferdinand Braudel, who assumes an economic, political, and cultural strength and creativity of the Islamic societies in the East and South of the Mediterranean lasting at least until the 16th century.[60] Feldbauer and Liedl correctly point out that especially exponents of the World Systems Theory, like Samir Amin, Christopher Chase-Dunn, Andre Gunder Frank, Barry K. Gills, Thomas D. Halland and Stephen K. Sanderson, who started to modify the concepts of Wallerstein's World Systems Theory in the 1970s, consider the position of the Islamic world at least until the 14th century as essentially positive and dominant.[61] In her study *Before European Hegemony. The World System A.D. 1250–1350*, Janet Abu Lughod in particular argued convincingly that it was basically the complementary phenomena of crisis during the second quarter of the 14th century (the plague and the aggressive trade policy of Venice and Genoa) along with severe changes in East Asia, India and Western Europe which changed the structures of the pre-modern world system, leading to crucial shifts in the global distribution of power.[62] Feldbauer and Liedl emphasize that "it was just in this period of time that an interesting congruence can be observed in the developments of – on the one hand – the 'European' cultural and economic area in the narrow sense of the word, and the wider unity called 'Euro-Méditerrannée,' on the other hand. To us, this means not only the aspiring and history-charged regions of the northern coasts of the Mediterranean, but at the same time – and we could not insist on this more – the so-called South and East which are closely entangled with their Northern, respectively Western 'counterparts,' the 'Levant' and the 'Orient': It is the area which has been called the European counter-coast or its Mediterranean 'façade.'"[63] Thus, the global dominion of the cultural sphere shaped by Islam is prolonged even up to the 16th century: "Combining the long-term tendency of the development of agriculture, industry and trade with the estimate of the Mediterranean expansion of the Crusaders and the Italian merchants, the boom years

59 See Labib 1965; Rodinson 1971, Cook 1993, Hodgson 1974; Hodgson 1993; Krämer 2005; Schulze 2008.

60 Cf. Braudel 1986.

61 Cf. Amin 1991; Chase-Dunn and Hall 1991; Chase-Dunn and Hall 1997; Frank and Gills 1993; Sanderson and Frank 1998.

62 Cf. Abu-Lughod 1989.

63 Feldbauer and Liedl 2008, 9–10.

of trade under the banner of the *Pax Mongolica* and the subsequent crisis of the 14th century, the beginning offensive of Iberian colonialism in the Maghreb as well as the Portuguese circumnavigation of the Cape and their venture into the Indian Ocean, it all results in the notion of productive, adaptive and innovative economies in the states and societies of the overall Arabic-Iranian region from the 11th up to the early 16th century."[64] There were certainly various crises in the Islamic world as well, but they were always compensated for and averted by equally influential phases of prosperity. The so-called "European wonder" remained in its early stages until the 17th century. Concerning economic development, the formerly popular model of stagnation is nowadays rejected to have extended far beyond the 16th century. In general, agriculture, trade, industry, and the financial system experienced a positive development, at least until the crisis occurred in the early 17th century. The Mamluk period therefore has to be reassessed against this backdrop and integrated into the overall economic context. Because we are still at the beginning of developing an interdisciplinary, premodern global history in which the Mediterranean constitutes one of the central spaces of interaction, no synthesis can be offered here. Instead, we present four path breaking studies shall be presented that discuss different facets of the interrelations.

Study 1: "Quelle etait la nature du pouvoir qui gouverna le Moyen Orient depuis la fin du XIVe siècle jusqu'aux debuts de l'âge moderne? Est-il justifié d'y voir des traits origineaux? Sur quels genres d'acteurs peut-on deconstruire le deuxieme Etat mamlouk?" These are the questions asked by Francisco Javier Appelániz Ruiz de Galarretain his study *Pouvoir et finance en Méditerranée pré-moderne. Le deuxième etat mamlouk et le commerce de épices (1382–1517)*, submitted in 2009.[65] The book focuses on the spice trade and the fiscal and economic measures the sultans took in this respect. The author questions conventional wisdom according to which the Islamic rulers deeply damaged free trade and the indigenous groups of merchants by establishing a state monopoly and by forcefully integrating the merchants into the apparatus of the state. Appelániz offers a new interpretation of politics and the decline of the Mamluk Empire in the Circassian period (1382–1517), thereby highlighting the financial constraints and shortages caused by the dependence on the profits of the spice trade.

Study 2: The next study was submitted by the French historian Damien Coulon, his doctoral thesis entitled *Barcelone et le grand commerce d'Orient au Moyen*

64 Feldbauer and Liedl, 2008, 167.
65 Appelániz 2009.

Âge. Un siècle de relations avec l'Égypte et la Syrie-Palestine (ca. 1330–ca. 1430), published in 2004.[66] Venice and Genoa have long been the main focus of the ever-expanding literature on the Levant trade of the 14th and 15th century. This led to the fact that other important agents, such as the merchants from Barcelona, are basically ignored. With his thesis, Damien Coulon fills this academic void by analyzing a remarkable number of largely unedited documents in order to understand how the subjects of the House of Aragon participated in the trade with the Orient between 1330 and 1430. His main sources are 15 notarial registers from the archives of Barcelona, containing several thousand documents that he closely analyzes. The author certainly understands the limits of such a documentation, which, by itself, could lead to making mistakes in perspective, ignoring the fact that the corpus is tied to a particular period and deducing general statements from it. Yet the author elegantly and easily circumvents these difficulties by also referring to documents found elsewhere: the archives of the Crown of Aragon, the citizenry of Barcelona, and of the church. The dioceses of Barcelona own many very interesting documents, for example, sermons prepared for shipowners who profited from a pontifical license allowing them to carry on free trade in the Levant between 1347 and 1418. The overall corpus offers a very solid base for the interpretation of trading between the Iberian Peninsula and the Levant, using the example of Barcelona. Not only can the quality and quantity of the transported goods be identified, also the growth of investment capital, the geographical and social origin of the investors, and the customers can be reconstructed with astounding precision.

Study 3: Georg Christ, currently working and teaching at the University of Manchester, in his dissertation examines the conflicts between Egypt and the Venetians in Alexandria between 1418 and 1420 against the backdrop of the two "civilizations" involved.[67] Large parts of the legacy of the Venetian merchants, especially that of the consul Biagio Dolfin (ca. 1370–1420), are in the state archives of Venice. They concern a time of crisis: Egypt was suffering from pandemics, swift changes of government, and economic recession, and the intrusion of European products and currencies into the Egyptian economy had created a series of problems. Many Venetian merchants were living in Alexandria, part of society but without thoroughly integrating themselves. Established networks and long-standing connections failed to prevent regular conflicts – also among the Venetians themselves. The various agents tried to stabilize their own interests by establishing far-reaching contacts, above all based on family ties. The consul of Alexandria played a central role in avoiding and solving such conflicts, mediating

66 Coulon 2004.
67 Christ 2012.

between Venetians, local and foreign merchants, Mamluk officials, and the Venetian administration – and occasionally operating at the verge of different legal systems. He made secret agreements with officials and merchants to prevent conflicts or to end them, of course always keeping his own interests in mind.

Being economic powers, the Mamluks, Genoa, and Venice (and to a lesser extent Barcelona) controlled the area around the Mediterranean and the Black Sea. But Egypt and Syria also served as transshipment point for numerous products that found their way to the port cities of the Persian Gulf and the Red Sea via the Indian Ocean, and which from there were transported overland to the Middle East. Furthermore, goods were transported to the Levant via the Silk Road and via the Mediterranean Sea to Europe. Thus, the Mamluk Empire served as a node between Europe, North Africa, Central Asia, Sub-Saharan Africa, and South Asia over the course of the entire era. After 1350, however, it became more complicated to transport goods from East to West and vice versa using the overland routes. Sea voyages via the Indian Ocean, on the other hand, went astonishingly well. Egypt remained important as a country in which transit trade took place, although the Red Sea was slowly becoming the hub of mercantile activities. Mecca and the Sharifs of the Hejaz also participated in the Red Sea trade. The port city of Jidda discharged and taxed most of the cargo from ships coming from the Indian Ocean. From there, the precious goods came to Alexandria and then via the Mediterranean Sea to Europe. From Jidda, ships sailed back to Calicut, carrying large amounts of copper, mercury, verdigris, saffron, rosewater, scarlet cloth, silk, camlet, and taffeta fabrics as well as gold and silver. The extensive and intense maritime traffic in the Mediterranean Sea and the Red Sea inevitably expanded to include the port cities of Aden, Alexandria, and Damietta. But the two oceans were not the only trade routes of Egypt. The land route from Egypt to Syria and the Middle East in general as well as to North Africa and Bilād al-Takrūr had a major stake in the prosperity of Egyptian trade. Eventually, Mecca also became an important center for trans-regional trade due to the annual pilgrimage.

Study 4: Even though the Mamluk period is fairly well studied, it is remarkable that there are almost no essays on Mecca, the central place of pilgrimage of the Muslims in that era. Only recently did John L. Meloy publish an excellent monograph on this topic, focusing not on locating Mecca as central node in the network of trans-regional pilgrimage activities, but rather emphasizing the political and economic parameters of the ruling Sharifs.[68] This family, who traced their ancestors back to the Prophet himself, had been ruling on a local level since the late 12th century. Its power was based on their control of the main places of

68 Meloy 2010.

pilgrimage, but also on the strategically favorable position of their sphere of influence – particularly in their port Jidda did trade from the Indian Ocean and the Mediterranean Sea meet via the Red Sea. The Red Sea trade continuously increased from the late 14th up to the 16th century, when the Portuguese intervened in the Asian trade and secured the basis of Mecca prosperity. However, the premise for the rule of the Sharifs in the Hejaz had always been their ability to maintain a *modus vivendi* in accordance with the Mamluk sultans in Cairo. In light of the massive crises that occurred during the 15th century, the Mamluk rulers in Cairo made use of their favorable geopolitical position and took control over the import and export of certain profitable goods in the oversea trade. The rulers of Mecca could not escape these attempts at monopolization. John L. Meloy portrays the history of the city amid these conflicting priorities: on the one hand, the prosperity connected to the commodity flows and, on the other hand, the hegemonic claims of the sultans, who always wanted to take their share in the revenues of long-distance trade. The local social-economic conditions were based predominantly on the synergy of the pilgrimage, breeding cattle, patronage, and systems of protection. Politics were very risky for the Sharifs–Mamluk ambitions had to be satisfied, as did various demands of local families, tribal alliances, and local notables. Meloy paraphrases a quotation from C. Snouck Hurgronje in describing the history of Mecca in the 15th century as "the loss of Mecca's isolation within the context of Mediterranean-Indian Ocean trade."

Conclusion

In the academic canon of disciplines that developed in the 19th century, Western universities established an extensive separation of cultures within research: While such universal subjects as history, sociology, and national economy were concerned above all with Western Europe and North America, preoccupation with non-Western cultures was "outsourced" to disciplines such as Islamic Studies, Sinology, Indology, etc. In combination with other factors, this led to the history of Western Europe being perceived and displayed as exemplary – and in many ways exclusive – describing the development toward Western modernity as stretching from Antiquity to Recent History. Accordingly, structures and lines of development of non-European history that did not resemble the analytical categories unilaterally established according to Western European history were only marginally noticed – often being referred to as stagnant and integrated into a story of decline contrasting the European ascent to modernity.[69] Any transcultural comparison thus runs against the presumed dis-

69 See Bayly 2004.

similarity of cultures;[70] it shifts the parameters by rejecting *a priori* the initial thesis of the exclusiveness of historical phenomena in two cultures and by looking for phenomena and categories that assume fundamental similarities instead. Only then are the differences between case studies determined. This backdrop means the history of the Mediterranean has to be rewritten. Even though many studies on this area of interaction have already been submitted, to date the non-European perspective has rarely, and especially much less equitably, been pursued and integrated into the overall interpretation. This can likely be achieved only through interdisciplinary research.[71] Such disciplinary modules, as shown in the examples of the four studies presented above, already exist.

Demonstrating historical alternatives reveals the diversity of historical development models, which contrasts the diversity of modernity with a diversity of the pre-modern period.[72] Between 1250 and 1500 a certain degree of economic, political, religious, and culturally-technical interlacing processes occurred that included not only the Mediterranean, but also large parts of the Eurasia as well as parts of Africa. The networks resulting from these processes of interlacing were complementary and influenced each other. The impacts of historical events like political power change, the closure of trade roads, the introduction of new technologies, or the outbreak of epidemics were felt via the various systems of interaction and affect remote world religions considerably. That is where we have to locate the Mamluk Empire.

Bibliography

Abu Lughod, J.L. (1989): *Before European Hegemony. The World System A.D. 1250–1350.* Oxford et al.

Abu Lughod, J.L. (1993): "Discontinuities and Persistence. One World System or a Succession of Systems?" In: A.B. Frank and B.K. Gills (eds.): *The World System. Five Hundred Years or Five Thousand?* London and New York, 278–293.

Abu Lughod, J.L. (1994): "The World System in the Thirteenth Century. Dead End or Precursor?" In: M. Adas (ed.), *Islamic and European Expansion. The Forging of a Global Order.* Washington, 75–102.

Abulafia, D. (2011): *The Great Sea. A Human History of the Mediterranean.* Oxford.

Agius, D.A.and R. Hitchkock (1994): *The Arab Influence in Medieval Europe.* Reading.

Ahuja, R. (2006): "Mobility and Containment. The Voyages of South Asian Seamen, c. 1900–1960." In: *International Review of Social History* 51, 111–141.

Al-Azmeh, A. (1996): *Die Islamisierung des Islam. Imaginäre Welten einer politischen Theologie.* Frankfurt.

70 Cf. Drews and Osterle 2008.

71 Cf. Meier 1989.

72 Cf. Eisenstadt 2007.

Amin, S. (1991): *The Ancient World-Systems versus the Modern Capitalist World-System.* In: *Review* (Fernand Braudel Center) 14/3, 349–385.

Apellániz Ruiz de Galarreta, F.J. (2009): *Pouvoir et finance en Méditerranée pré-moderne: le deuxième état mamelouk et le commerce des épices (1382–1517).* Barcelona.

Bachmann-Medick, D. (2009): "Spatial Turn." In: D. Bachmann-Medick: *Cultural Turns. Neuorientierungen in den Kulturwissenschaften,* 3rd ed. Reinbek, 284–328.

Bachmann-Medick, D. (2016): *Cultural Turns. New Orientations in the Study of Culture.* Berlin and Boston.

Balard, M. (2006): *La Méditerranée médiévale. Espaces, itinéraires, comptoirs.* Paris.

Bayly, C.A. (2007): "'Archaische' und 'moderne' Globalisierung in Eurasien und Afrika." In: S. Conrad, A. Eckert, and U. Freitag (eds.): *Globalgeschichte. Theorien, Ansätze, Themen.* Frankfurt am Main, 81–108.

Bayly, C.C. (2004): *The Birth of the Modern World, 1780–1914.* Oxford.

Bergdolt, K. (2011): *Der schwarze Tod in Europa.* 3rd ed. Munich.

Borgolte, M., J. Dücker, M. Müllerburg and B. Schneidmüller (eds.) (2011): *Integration und Desintegration der Kulturen im europäischen Mittelalter.* Berlin.

M. Borgolte, J. Schiel and B. Schneidmüller (eds.) (2008): *Mittelalter im Labor. Die Mediävistik testet Wege zu einer transkulturellen Europawissenschaft.* Berlin.

M. Borgolte and B. Schneidmüller (eds.) (2010): *Hybride Kulturen im mittelalterlichen Europa. Vorträge und Workshops einer internationalen Frühlingsschule.* Berlin.

Braudel, F. (1949): *La Méditerranée et le monde méditeranéen à l'epoque de Philippe II.* Paris.

Braudel, F. (1974): "Europäische Expansion und Kapitalismus 1450–1650." In: E. Schulin (ed.): *Universalgeschichte.* Cologne, 255–294.

Braudel, F. (1986): *Sozialgeschichte des 15. bis 18. Jahrhundert.* Bd. 3: *Aufbruch zur Weltwirtschaft.* Munich.

Chase-Dunn, Ch. and Th.D. Hall (eds.) (1991): *Core/Periphery Relations in Pre-capitalist Worlds.* Boulder, San Francisco and Oxford.

Chase-Dunn, Ch. and Th.D. Hall (eds.) (1997): *Rise and Demise. Comparing World-systems.* Boulder and Oxford.

Chaudhuri, K.N. (1985): *Trade and Civilisation in the Indian Ocean. An Economic History from the Rise of Islam to 1750.* Cambridge.

Christ, G. (2012): *Trading Conflicts: Venetian Merchants and Mamluk Officials in Late Medieval Alexandria.* Leiden.

Conermann, S. (1998): "Muslimische Seefahrt auf dem Indischen Ozean vom 14. bis zum 16. Jahrhundert." In: S. Conermann (ed.), *Der Indische Ozean in historischer Perspektive.* Hamburg, 143–180.

Conermann, S. (2001): "Politik, Diplomatie und Handel entlang der Seidenstraße im 15. Jahrhundert." In: U. Hübner, J. Kamlah and L. Reinfandt, L. (eds.): *Die Seidenstraße. Handel und Kulturaustausch in einem eurasiatischen Wegenetz.* Hamburg, 186–236.

Conermann, S. (2009): [Review of] Peter Feldbauer and Gottfried Liedl: *Die islamische Welt 1000 bis 1517. Wirtschaft. Gesellschaft. Staat.* Wien 2008, in: *sehepunkte* 10 (2009), Nr. 7/8 [15.7.2009], URL http://www.sehepunkte.de/2009/07/16514.html.

Conermann, S. (2013): "Das Mittelmeer zur Zeit der Mamlukenherrschaft in Ägypten und Syrien (1250–1517) – Vorbemerkungen zu einer globalgeschichtlichen Perspektive," in: M. Stolz (ed.), *Randgänge der Mediävistik.* Bd. 3, Bern 2013, 21–60.

Cook, M. (1993): "Wirtschaftliche Entwicklungen." In: J. Schacht and C.E. Bosworth (eds.): *Das Vermächtnis des Islam* 1. Munich, 254–292 and 306–308.

Coulon, D. (2004): *Barcelone et le grand commerce d'Orient au Moyen Âge. Un siècle de relations avec l'Égypte et la Syrie-Palestine (ca. 1330–ca. 1430)*, Madrid and Barcelona.

Curry, A. (2012): *Der Hundertjährige Krieg (1337–1453).* Darmstadt.

Dahm, B., P. Feldbauer and D. Rothermund (2008): "Agrarzivilisationen, Hafenfürstentümer, Kolonialsiedlungen. Indischer Ozean, Süd- und Südostasien." In: P. Feldbauer and J.-P. Lehners (eds.): *Die Welt im 16. Jahrhundert.* Vienna, 210–264.

Darwin, J. (2007): *After Tamerlane. The Global History of Empire Since 1405.* London.

Dols, M.W. (1977): *The Black Death in the Middle East.* Princeton.

Döring, J.and T. Thielmann (eds.) (2008): *Spatial Turn. Das Raumparadigma in den Kultur- und Sozialwissenschaften.* Bielefeld.

Drews, W. (2008): "Die 'Gleichzeitigkeit des Ungleichzeitigen' als Problem transkultureller historischer Komparatistik am Beispiel frühmittelalterlicher Herrschaftslegitimation." In: *Comparativ* 18/3–4, 41–56.

Drews, W. (2009): *Die Karolinger und die Abbasiden von Bagdad. Legitimationsstrategien frühmittellaterlicher Herrscherdynastien im transkulturellen Vergleich.* Berlin.

Drews, W. and J.R. Oesterle, (2008): "Vormoderne Globalgeschichten. Eine Einführung," in: *Comparativ* 18/3–4, 8–14.

Eisenstadt, S.N. (2007): *Vielfalt der Moderne.* Weilerswist.

Ertl, T. (2008): *Seide, Pfeffer und Kanonen. Globalisierung im Mittelalter.* Darmstadt.

Ertl, T. and M. Limberger (2009): "Vormoderne Verflechtungen von Dschingis Khan bis Christoph Columbus. Eine Einleitung." In: T. Ertl and M. Limberger (eds.): *Die Welt 1250–1500.* Vienna, 11–28.

Feldbauer, P. (1995): *Die islamische Welt 600–1250. Ein Frühfall von Unterentwicklung?* Vienna.

Feldbauer, P. and G. Liedl (2008): *Die islamische Welt 1000 bis 1517. Wirtschaft, Gesellschaft, Staat.* Vienna.

Ferguson, J. and A. Gupta (1997): *Culture, Power, Place. Explorations in Critical Anthropology.* Durham/London.

Frank, A.G. (1998), *ReORIENT. Global Economy in the Asian Age.* Berkeley/Los Angeles.

Frank, A.G. and B.K. Gills (1993), "World System, Economical Cycles and Hegemonial Shift to Europe 100 BC to 1500 AD." In: *The Journal of European Economic History* 22/1, 155–183.

Freitag, U. and A. von Oppen (eds.) (2010): *Translocality. The Study of Globalising Processes from a Southern Perspective.* Leiden.

Freitag, U./von Oppen, Achim (2005): "Translokalität als ein Zugang zur Geschichte globaler Verflechtungen." In: H-Soz-u-Kult, 10.06.2005, <http://hsozkult.geschichte.hu-berlin.de/forum/2005-06-001>

Galtung, J. (2000): Welt-, Global-, "Universalgeschichte und die heutige Historiographie." In: *Zeitschrift für Weltgeschichte* 1, 9–34.

Glauser, A. (2006): "Pionierarbeit mit paradoxen Folgen? Zur neueren Rezeption der Raumsoziologie von Georg Simmel." In: *Zeitschrift für Soziologie* 35,4, 250–268.

M. Grandner, D. Rothermund and W. Schwentker (eds.) (2005): *Globalisierung und Globalgeschichte.* Vienna.

Gruzinski, S. (2004): *Les quatre parties du monde. Histoire d'une mondialisation.* Paris.

Günzel, S. (2006): "Phänomenologie der Räumlichkeit." In: J. Dünne and S. Günzel: *Raumtheorie. Grundlagentexte aus Philosophie und Kulturwissenschaften.* Frankfurt/ Main, 8th ed., 105–128.

Harris, W. V. (ed.) (2005): *Rethinking the Mediterranean.* Oxford.

Haupt, H.-G. and J. Kocka, J. (eds.) (1996): *Geschichte im Vergleich. Ansätze und Ergebnisse international vergleichender Geschichtsschreibung.* Frankfurt.

Hausberger, B. (2007): "Wann und wo passiert Globalgeschichte?" In: *Zeitschrift für Weltgeschichte* 8/1, 11–36.

Hausberger, B. (2008): "Das Reich, in dem die Sonne nicht unterging. Die iberische Welt." In: P. Feldbauer and J.-P. Lehners (eds.): *Die Welt im 16. Jahrhundert.* Vienna, 335–372.

Hodgson, M. G. S. (1974): The Venture of Islam. Vol. 2: *The Expansion of Islam in the Middle Periods.* Chicago and London.

Hodgson, M. G. S. (1993): *Rethinking World History.* Edited, with an introduction and a conclusion, by E. Burke III. Cambridge.

Höfert, A. (2008a): "Anmerkungen zum Konzept einer 'transkulturellen' Geschichte in der deutschsprachigen Forschung." In: *Comparativ* 18/3–4, 15–27.

Höfert, A. (2008b): "Europa und der Nahe Osten. Der transkulturelle Vergleich in der Vormoderne und die Meistererzählung über den Islam." In: *Historische Zeitschrift* 287, 561–597.

Horden, P. and N. Purcell (2005): *The Corrupting Sea. A Study of Mediterranean History.* Oxford 2000,

Jaspert, N. (2009): "Austausch-, Transfer- und Abgrenzungsprozesse. Das Mittelmeer." In: T. Ertl and M. Limberger (eds.), *Die Welt 1250–1500.* Vienna, 138–174.

Kaelble, H. (1999a): *Der historische Vergleich. Eine Einführung zum 19. und 20. Jahrhundert.* Frankfurt and New York.

Kaelble, H. (1999b): "Der historische Zivilisationsvergleich." In: H. Kaelble and J. Schriewer (eds.): *Diskurse und Entwicklungspfade. Der Gesellschaftsvergleich in den Geschichts- und Sozialwissenschaften.* Frankfurt am Main, 29–52.

Kaelble, H. (2003): "Die interdisziplinären Debatten über Vergleich und Transfer." In: J. Schriewer (ed.): *Vergleich und Transfer. Komparatistik in den Sozial-, Geschichts- und Kulturwissenschaften.* Frankfurt am Main, 469–493.

Kaelble, H. (2005): "Die Debatte über Vergleich und Transfer und was jetzt? In: H-Soz-u-Kult," 08.02.2005, <http://hsozkult.geschichte.hu-berlin.de/forum/id=574&type=artikel>.

Kauz, R. (2009): "Zerstörung, Eroberung, politische Umstrukturierung. Zentralasien." In: T. Ertl and M. Limberger (eds.): *Die Welt 1250–1500.* Vienna, 297–324.

Kocka, J. (2003): "Comparison and Beyond." In: *History and Theory* 43, 39–44.

Kölzer, T. (1998): "Kulturbruch oder Kulturkontinuität? Europa zwischen Antike und Mittelalter – Die Pirenne-These nach 60 Jahren." In: K. Rosen (ed.): *Das Mittelmeer – die Wiege der europäischen Kultur.* Bonn, 208–227.

Kossock, M. (1992): "Von der Universal- zur Globalgeschichte." In: *Comparativ* 2/1, 92–104.

Krämer, G. (2005): *Geschichte des Islam.* Munich.

Labib, S. (1965): *Handelsgeschichte Ägyptens im Spätmittelalter, 1171–1517.* Wiesbaden.

Liedl, G. (2008): "Vernunft und Utopie. Die Méditerranée (1350–1650)." In: P. Feldbauer and J.-P.Lehners (eds): *Die Welt im 16. Jahrhundert.* Vienna, 116–152.

Lorenz, C. (1999): "Comparative Historiography: Problems and Perspectives." In: *History and Theory* 38, 25–39.

Lucassen, J. and L. Lucassen (eds.) (1997): *Migration, Migration History, History. Old Paradigms and New Perspectives.* Bern.

Marino, J. A. (2004): "The Exile and His Kingdom: The Reception of Braudel's *Mediterranean*," in: *The Journal of Modern History* 76, 622–652.

Mazlish, B. (1993); "An Introduction to Global History." In: B. Mazlisch and R. Buultjens, (eds.): *Conceptualizing Global History.* Boulder, Col. 1993, 1–24.

Mazlish, B. (2002): "Die neue Globalgeschichte." In: *Zeitschrift für Weltgeschichte* 3/1, 9–22.

McNeill, J.R. and W.H. McNeill (2003): *The Human Web. A Birds-Eye View of World History.* New York.

Meier, Ch. (1989): *Die Welt der Geschichte und die Provinz des Historikers. Drei Überlegungen.* Berlin.

Meloy, J.L. (2010): *Imperial Power and Maritime Trade. Mecca and Cairo in the Later Middle Ages.* Chicago.

Molho, A. (2001): "Like Ships Passing in the Dark. Reflections on the Reception of *La Méditerranée* in the U.S." In: *Review* (Fernand Braudel Center) 24, 139–162.

Nagel, J.G. (2007): *Abenteuer Fernhandel. Die Ostindienkompanien.* Darmstadt.

Neumann, B. and A. Nünning (eds.) (2012): *Travelling Concepts for the Study of Culture.* Berlin and New York.

Nolte, H.-H. (2005): "Das Weltsystem-Konzept – Debatte und Forschung." In: M. Grandner, D. Rothermund and W. Schwentker (eds.): *Globalisierung und Globalgeschichte. Vienna*, 115–138.

North, M. (2007): *Europa expandiert, 1250–1500.* Stuttgart.

Oesterle, J.R. (2008): "Papst – Kalif – König. Vergleich sakraler Herrschaftsformen im Spiegel islamischer und christlicher Quellen des Mittelalters und moderner Forschung." In: *Comparativ* 18/3–4, 57–72.

Oesterle, J.R. (2009): *Kalifat und Königtum. Herrschaftsrepräsentation der Fatimiden, Ottonen und frühen Salier an religiösen Hochfesten.* Darmstadt.

Oesterle, J.R. (2012): "Das Mittelmeer und die Mittelmeerwelt. Annäherungen an einen 'Gegenstand der Geschichte' in der neueren deutschen Mediävistik." In: *Construire la Méditerranée, penser les transferts culturels. Approches historiographiques et perspectives de recherche*, Munich, 72–92.

Oltmer, J. and M. Schuber: "Migration und Integration in Europa seit der Frühen Neuzeit. Eine Bibliographie zur Historischen Migrationsforschung" = http://www.imis.uni-osnabrueck.de/BibliographieMigration.pdf.

Osterhammel, J. (2003): "Transkulturell vergleichende Geschichtswissenschaft." In: Osterhammel, J.: *Geschichtswissenschaft jenseits des Nationalstaats. Studien zu Beziehungsgeschichte und Zivilisationsvergleich.* 2nd ed. Göttingen, 11–45.

Osterhammel, J. (2005): "'Weltgeschichte'. Ein Propädeutikum." In: *Geschichte in Wissenschaft und Unterricht* 56, 452–479.

Osterhammel, J. (2008): "Alte und neue Zugänge zur Weltgeschichte." In: J. Osterhammel, (ed.), *Weltgeschichte.* Stuttgart, 9–32.

Osterhammel, J. (2009): *Die Verwandlung der Welt. Eine Geschichte des 19. Jahrhunderts.* Munich.

Parker, G. (2008): "Crisis and Catastrophe: The Global Crisis of the Seventeenth Century Reconsidered." In: *American Historical Review* 113, 1053–1079.

Pernau, M. (2011): *Transnationale Geschichte.* Göttingen.

Pirenne, H. (1937): *Mahomet et Charlemagne.* Paris and Bruxelles.

Riley-Smith, J. (ed.) (1992): *Großer Bildatlas der Kreuzzüge. Sechs Jahrhunderte abendländischer Kultur- und Glaubensgeschichte.* Freiburg/B.

Rodinson, M. (1971): *Islam und Kapitalismus.* Frankfurt am Main.

Sanderson, S.K. (ed.) (1995): *Civilizations and World-Systems. Studying World-Historical Change.* Walnut Creek, London and New Delhi.

Schäbler, B. (2007): "Vorwort." In: B. Schäbler(ed.), *Area Studies und die Welt. Weltregionen und neue Globalgeschichte.* Vienna, 7–10.

Schulze, R. (2008): "Reiche und Reichskulturen. Die Frühe Neuzeit in der islamischen 152–176.Welt." In: P. Feldbauer and J.-P. Lehners (eds.). *Die Welt im 16. Jahrhundert.* Vienna,

Simmel, G. (1903): "Soziologie des Raumes (1903)." In: *Schriften zur Soziologie. Eine Auswahl.* Frankfurt am Main 1983, 221–242.

Subrahmanyam, S. (2005a): *Explorations in Connected History. From the Tagus to the Ganges.* Delhi.

Subrahmanyam, S. (2005b): *Explorations in Connected History. Mughals and Franks.* Delhi.

Subrahmanyam, S. (1977): "Connected Histories. Notes towards a Reconfiguration of Early Modern Eurasia." In: *Modern Asian Studies* 31, 735–762.

Tracy, J. D. (1990) (ed.): *The Rise of Merchant Empires. Long Distance Trade in the Early Modern World, 1350–1750.* Cambridge.

Wallerstein, I. (1986): *Das moderne Weltsystem. Die Anfänge kapitalistischer Landwirtschaft und die europäische Weltökonomie im 16. Jahrhundert.* Frankfurt am Main.

Welskopp, T. (1995): "Methodenkritische Anmerkungen zum internationalen Vergleich in der Gesellschaftsgeschichte." In: *Archiv für Sozialgeschichte* 35 (1995), 339–367.

Werner, M. and B. Zimmermann (2002): "Vergleich, Transfer, Verflechtung. Der Ansatz der Histoire croisée und die Herausforderung des Transnationalen." In: *Geschichte und Gesellschaft* 28, 607–636.

Werner, M. and B. Zimmermann. (2004): "Penser l'histoire croisée: entre empirie et réflexivité." In: M. Werner and B. Zimmermann (eds.): *De la comparaison à l'histoire croisée*, Paris, 15–49.

Werner, M. and B. Zimmermann (2006): "Beyond Comparison. Historie Croisée and the Challenge of Reflexivity." In: *History and Theory* 46, 30–50.

Yehoshua Frenkel (University of Haifa)

The Mamlūk Sultanate and its Neighbours: Economic, Social and Cultural Entanglements*

The Mamlūk Sultanate negotiated with distant forces and commercial partners and exchanged dispatches and embassies with competitors and rivals. These research topics attracted historians' attention already during the nineteenth century. Their studies illuminated the visible position of Cairo's Citadel in the world and the diplomatic histories of the 13th–16th centuries.[1] This article, based on literary evidence, is the first chapter in a research enterprise that deals with the diplomatic communications between the Mamlūk Sultanate and Muslim and non-Muslims governments.[2] A planned second chapter will focus on an investigation of archival materials.[3] How did the Mamlūk elite, both its civilian and military echelons, perceive the world around it? Several directions can be chosen in search for answer(s). The careful scrutiny of diverse literary genres, as well as the investigation of artefacts, certainly is a possible first one.[4] This article is based primarily on the inspection of 15th-century literary sources. It will concentrate primarily on three genres: 1) legal writings; 2) slave trade guides; and 3) geographical texts. These texts cast light on the juridical division employed by the religious establishment, on communications with foreign markets and on the image of these remote lands in the collective imagination of the texts' consumers. Certainly, the three literary genres mentioned above are not the only type of

* I would like to thank Prof. Reuven Amitai and Dr Julia Rubanovich for their help and advice.

1 For earlier works of mine on this topic, see Y. Frenkel, "Animals and Otherness in Mamluk Egypt and Syria," in Francisco de Asís García García, Mónica Ann Walker Vadillo and María Victoria Chico Picazabar (eds.), *Animals and Otherness in the Middle Ages: Perspectives across Disciplines* (Oxford, 2013), 52–55; Y. Frenkel, "Embassies and Ambassadors in Mamluk Cairo," in Frédéric Bauden (convener), *Mamluk Cairo: A Crossroad for Embassies* (Université de Liège, September 2012) (in preparation for publication).

2 The history of the Mamlūks and the Italian merchant republics is excluded.

3 One document was presented in Y. Frenkel, "Mamlūk Embassies and Diplomats in 15th-century Mediterranean – The Mamlūk Sultanate in the Days of Qāʾit-Bāy and the al-Ifranj," a talk at the Second Conference of the School of Mamlūk Studies, Liége, June 2015 (Panel: The Mamlūks and Distant Realms).

4 Doris Behrens-Abouseif, *Practising Diplomacy in the Mamluk Sultanate: Gifts and Material Culture in the Medieval Islamic World* (London, 2014).

sources at our disposal. Chronicles and biographical dictionaries also cast light on the world vision that prevailed among the Mamlūk elite. These sources also narrate Cairo's diplomatic ties with Muslim and non-Muslim powers in the Mediterranean, Africa, Central Asia and in India. In addition, these sources report on military operations against close and remote Muslim and non-Muslim forces. Biographical writings inform us of Muslim travellers, including merchants, who visited lands far from Cairo and Damascus.[5] A case in point is a reference to merchants from Mamlūk Egypt and Syria who called at the port of Hormuz (Jarun/Zarun) in the Persian Gulf.[6] Yet since my main concern is the Mamlūk elite's worldview (*die Weltanschauung*),[7] I will refrain from dwelling upon the history of events or political developments.[8]

Opposing Abodes

First, I will concentrate on selected findings taken from Mamlūk juridical compendia. Although quotations from earlier works are a salient feature of the methodology employed by the compilers of these texts, nevertheless the legal compositions produced by these jurists are not merely a transmission of frozen Abbasid traditions. The savants of the Mamlūk period carefully selected earlier generations' works and updated them to suit the contemporaneous interpretation of power struggles and negotiations. Their bulky production provides rich information on the reception of the past and on the mental vision of both the

5 On early Mamluk seafaring to Aden and India, see *Nūr al-maʿārif fī nuẓum wa-qawānīn wa-aʿrāf al-Yaman fī al-ʿahd al-Muẓaffarī al-wārif* [Lumière de la connaissance: règles, lois et coutumes du Yémen sous le règne du sultan rasoulide al-Muzaffar (fl. 647–694/1249–1295)], ed. Muḥammad ʿAbd al-Raḥīm Jāzim (Sanaa, 2003–5), 1: 175, 260–262, 265 (the currency of India and the ocean's islands), 492–494 (Kārimi merchants, who sail to Egypt, and slaves); on the contribution of this source to the study of the communication of Yemen with India see Elizabeth Lambourn, "India from Aden: *Khutba* and Muslim Urban Networks in Late Thirteenth-Century India," in Kenneth Hall (ed.), *Secondary Cities and Urban Networking in the Indian Ocean Realm, c. 1400–1800* (Lanham, Md., 2008), 60–63.

6 Kamāl al-Dīn ʿAbd al-Razzāq al-Samarqandī, *Maṭāliʿ-i saʿdayn va majmaʿ al-baḥrayn* [Kamaluddin Abdul-Razzaq Samarqandi's Mission to Calicut and Vijayanagara], in W. M. Thackston, (trans.) *A Century of Princes: Sources on Timurid History and Art* (Cambridge, Mass., 1989), 300; On Sūq al-Harāmiza in Mamluk Cairo see Muḥammad b. Aḥmad Ibn Iyās al-Ḥanafī (852–930/1448–1524), *Badāʾiʿ al-zuhūr fī waqāʾiʿ al-duhūr* [Die Chronik des Ibn Ijas (The Amazing Flowers about the Events of the Times)] ed. M. Mustafa (Wiesbaden: F. Steiner, 1975; reprinted Cairo: Dār al-Kutub, 1429/2008), 3: 434 (905/1500).

7 To use Kant's terminology. See Karl Mannheim, *Essays on the Sociology of Knowledge*, ed. Paul Kecskemeti (London, 1952), 33–83 [originally published in 1923].

8 Y. Frenkel, "The Mamluks among the Nations: A Medieval Sultanate in its Global Context," in Stephan Conermann (ed.), *Everything is on the Move: The Mamluk Empire as a Node in (Trans-)Regional Networks* (Bonn, 2014), 61–79.

authors who expounded earlier legal traditions and the consumers of these late Middle Islamic writings. Muslim jurists of the Middle Islamic period divided the planet into two "ideal"[9] abodes: Dār al-Islām versus Dār al-Ḥarb.[10] These two legal tags appear again and again in Mamlūk-period jurists' writings. From their legal compendia, we can safely argue that the immediate consequences of this bipolar world vision were not a declaration of war or military expeditions to subdue the infidels. Considering the relations between Muslims and non-Muslims they did not envision armed conflict as the sole option. Sultans adopted a similar attitude and devoted considerable efforts to negotiating political deals with competitors and even with religious adversaries. Quite often they favoured truces rather than taking to the field. That the Mamlūk military aristocracy demonstrated restraint and caution, preferring diplomacy to combat, we may deduce from various sources. Cairo sent diplomatic missions to Italy,[11] to the Golden Horde, to the Ilkhanid Mongols (e.g., Baybars, in 660–665/1262–1267)[12] and to additional ruling courts.[13] Other historical documents shed light on ceasefire agreements. This policy is reflected clearly in the Mamlūks' treaties with the Latins[14] and with the rulers of the Nile valley (*baqṭ*).[15] From al-Maqrīzī's account we learn that this early Islamic and Fatimid diplomatic arrangement with Nubia was known in 15th-century Cairo. Several juridical works can be construed as compositions showing that the religious establishment backed these diplomatic measures. Using the tag "the imam" (i.e. the sultan), al-ʿAynī, for example, creates an ideal and timeless picture of Islamic history and law. He states that if an armistice promises financial benefit, the Muslim leader (i.e. the Mamlūk

9 To use the Weberian terminology.

10 During the Mamluk period additional terms, such as *Dār kufr, Dār imān, balad silm, bilād murakkaba (qism thālith)*. Taqī al-Dīn Aḥmad b. ʿAbd al-Ḥalīm Ibn Taymiyya al-Ḥaranī (661–728/1263–1328), *Majmūʿ fatāwá* ed. ʿAbd al-Raḥmān b. Muḥammad b. Qāsim al-ʿĀṣimī al-Najdī al-Ḥanbalī (al-Madīna: wizārat al-shuʾūn al-islāmiyya, 1425/2004), 27: 248–49, 28: 240–241. I would like to thank Dr. Ashraf Abū Zarqa for this reference.

11 Konrad Hirschler, "Ibn Wāṣil: An Ayyūbid Perspective on Frankish Lordships and Crusades," in Alex Mallett (ed.), *Medieval Muslim Historians and the Franks in the Levant* (Leiden, 2015), 142; John Wansbrough, "A Mamluk Ambassador to Venice in 913/1507," *Bulletin of the School of Oriental and African Studies* 26 (1963): 503–530.

12 Reuven Amitai-Preiss, *Mongols and Mamluks: The Mamluk-Ilkhanid War, 1260–1281* (Cambridge, 1995), 81–84.

13 Mercè Viladrich, "Solving the 'Accursed Riddle' of the Diplomatic Relations between Catalonia and Egypt around 1430," *Al-Masaq* 14/1 (2002): 25–31; Leonard Patrick Harvey, *Muslims in Spain, 1500 to 1614* (Chicago, 2005), 84–85.

14 Peter Malcolm Holt, *Early Mamluk Diplomacy, 1260–1290* (Leiden, 1995).

15 Martin Hinds and H. Sakkout, "A Letter from the Governor of Egypt to the King of Nubia and Muqurra concerning Egyptian-Nubian Relations in 141/758," in W. Al-Qadi (ed.), *Studia Arabica et Islamica. Festschrift for Ihsan Abbas* (Beirut, 1981), 209–229; Jay Spaulding, "Medieval Christian Nubia and the Islamic World: A Reconsideration of the Baqt Treaty," *The International Journal of African Historical Studies* 28/3 (1995): 577–594.

sultan) is authorized to conclude a ceasefire truce (*muwādaʿah*) with non-Muslim powers (*ahl al-ḥarb*).[16] The Mamlūk jurists' discussion regarding the duty of Muslims to migrate from lands governed by non-Muslims fortifies this conclusion. A prevailing view among them was that Muslims can, in certain circumstances, live in territories governed by Christians and by other non-Muslim rulers.[17]

Another example of the adjustment of earlier legal discourse to new condition in the Near East are the works of Sharaf al-Dīn al-Ḥujāwī, who wrote during the closing days of the Mamlūk Sultanate and the incorporation of the Arab lands within the Ottomans' domains. Classifying the People of the Book (*ahl al-kitāb*), he brings the Mediterranean Europeans (*al-franj*) under the canopy of the safety pact (*ʿaqd al-dhimmah*).[18] In another case, al-Ḥujāwī classifies the monastic military orders. He maintains that even Franks who are members of the religious orders can continue, as long as they are not soldiers in the ranks of the fighting battalions, but rather depend on trade or make their livelihood by working in farms, to remain dwelling in the Abode of Islam. By paying the poll tax (*jizyah*) they obtain the protection of Islam. Women living in the Frankish castles are, according to his opinion, exempted from paying the *jizyah*. He does not even exclude taxation of illicit food (*ḥaram*) like wine and swine.[19] Moreover, he advises victorious Muslim conquerors to catalogue books seized following successful offensives. Books that contain useful knowledge that can enrich the Muslims might be preserved, according to al-Ḥujāwī, and used as intellectual *spolia*.[20] Al-Ḥujāwī's endeavour to update his legal manual to the new conditions in the Mediterranean and the Arabian Sea is also reflected by his statement that a Muslim who fights as a mariner obtains better merits than his co-religionist who serves as an infantryman.[21]

Based on this documentation and additional evidence, I argue that jurists' writings and ambassadorial accords support the assumption that, in addition to its military dimension, *jihād* served also a diplomatic tool. While jurists com-

16 Badr al-Dīn Maḥmūd b. Aḥmad al-ʿAynī al-Ḥanafī (762–855/1361–1451), *al-Bināyah fī sharḥ al-hidāyah* (Beirut, 1411/1990), 6: 518 [= Beirut, 1420/2000, 7: 117].

17 Abou El Fadl Khaled. "Islamic Law and Muslim Minorities: The Juristic Discourse on Muslim Minorities," *Islamic Law and Society* 1 (1994): 141–187.

18 Sharaf al-Dīn Abū al-Najā Mūsá b. Aḥmad b. Sālim b. ʿĪsá bn Sālim al-Ḥujāwī al-Maqdisī al-Ḥanbalī (895–968/1490–1560), *al-Iqnāʿ li-ṭālib al-intifāʿ [fī fiqh al-imām al-mubajjal Abī ʿAbd Allāh Aḥmad Ibn Ḥanbal]*, ed. Turkī (Riyadh, 1419/1999), 2: 127; on the presence of Frankish merchants in Damascus see ʿAlā al-Dīn ʿAlī b. Yūsuf al-Buṣrawī (842–905/1438–1500), *Taʾrīkh al-Buṣrawī*, ed. Ḥasan al-ʿUlabī (Beirut, 1498/1988), 137.

19 Sharaf al-Dīn al-Ḥujāwī, *al-Iqnāʿ li-ṭālib al-intifāʿ*, 2: 129–130.

20 Sharaf al-Dīn al-Ḥujāwī, *al-Iqnāʿ li-ṭālib al-intifāʿ*, 2: 91.

21 Sharaf al-Dīn al-Ḥujāwī, *al-Iqnāʿ li-ṭālib al-intifāʿ*, 2: 66; indeed from *ḥadīth* collections we can deduce that prophetic traditions on the significance of fighting at sea circulated among Muslims in the early Abbasid period.

posed several treatises on the merits of *jihād*, and encouraged Muslims to join the defensive forces that guarded the sultanate's shores,[22] sultans hesitated to lunch naval operations or to send military incursions into enemies' territories.[23] Although the term *jihād* was no stranger to Mamlūk propaganda and the armies of the sultanate penetrated deep into Anatolia and operated in the Sudan, they hardly led a religious war to spread the call of Islam. Naval and military expeditions aimed primarily to achieve strategic goals, to strengthen the Sultanate's positions at its edges or to deter enemies.[24]

The Fabric of Mamlūk Society and Culture

It is well established that Mamlūk society was multi-lingual and multi-ethnic.[25] Biographies of Sufis and religious scholars clearly reflect this social reality. Many among them were known by a *nisbah* that indicated Turkish or Persian origin. Furthermore, the very use of the term *mamlūk* signifies that soldiers and emirs were, ideally, outsiders in the Abode of Islam. They were supposed to be infidels recruited in the Abode of War.[26] Administrative titles and accounts of the sultans' court in the Citadel of Cairo support this characterization of the sultanate. Many of the terms used there originated from the Saljuq courts in Iran and attested to an earlier Persian background. The history of the communications among Muslim scholars is vast one, and promises new evidence to support a holistic picture of the Islamicate regions (to use Marshal Hodgson's terminology). The sources reveal that jurists and savants established contacts with colleagues and students who lived in regions outside the Mamlūk realm, in addition to their communications with those who dwelled within the boundaries of the sultanate. There is plenty of evidence to support the historical paradigm that depicts Cairo

22 Shihāb al-Dīn Aḥmad b. ʿAlī Ibn Ḥajar al-ʿAsqalānī al-Shāfiʿī (773–852/1372–1449), *[Risālah fī] al-Khiṣāl al-mukaffira lil-dhunūb al-mutaqaddimah wal-mutaʾakhirah* [The Good Qualities that Help Achieving God's Forgiveness], ed. A. A. Salīm (Jeddah, 1422/2001), 64 (citing al-Rabaʿī).

23 Y. Frenkel, "Al-Biqāʿī's Naval War-Report," in Stephan Conermann (ed.), *History and Society during the Mamlūk Period (1250–1517)* (Bonn, 2014), 9–20.

24 Shams al-Dīn Muḥammad b. ʿAbd al-Raḥmān al-Sakhāwī (831–902/1424–1497), *al-Dhayl al-tāmm ʿalá duwal al-islām lil-dhahabī*, ed. Ḥasan Ismāʿīl Marwah and Maḥmūd al-Arnāʾūṭ (Beirut, 1992–1998), 2: 141 (on the capture by Mamluk forces of a Genoese consul in the Aegean in 864/October 1459).

25 Zayn al-Dīn Abū Ḥafs ʿUmar b. al-Muẓaffar Ibn al-Wardī al-Maʿarrī (691–749/1292–1349), *Tatimmat al-mukhtaṣar fī akhbār al-bashar* [*taʾrīkh Ibn al-Wardī*] (Cairo, 1285/1868), 2: 269 (720/); al-Buṣrawī, *Taʾrīkh*, 60 (878/1474, *tawajjaha al-bāsh yashbak*).

26 On this, see the recent study by Amir Mazor, *The Rise and Fall of a Muslim Regiment: The Mansuriyya in the First Mamluk Sultanates 678/1279–741/1341* (Bonn, 2015), esp. appendixes 1 and 5.

of the Late Middle Islamic Period as the centre of Islamic learning. The capital of the Mamlūk sultanate, and to a lesser extent also Damascus, attracted students of Islamic sciences and Sufis from remote lands.[27]

A legal compendium composed by the famous Badr al-Dīn al-ʿAynī, who originated from the ethnically diverse region of southwest Anatolia, sheds light on this reality. The work is entitled *Masāʾil al-Badrīyyah al-muntakhabah min al-fatāwá al-ẓahīrīyah.*[28] This title transmits two details: 1) that it is a choice of legal responsa selected from an earlier work; and 2) that the author of this earlier work was a *muḥtasib* from Bukhara named Ẓahīr al-Dīn Muḥammad b. Aḥmad (d. 619/1222). I assume that al-ʿAynī transmitted the information presented below because his audience in Cairo were familiar with the Persian language and that they received willingly data from the "East," with which the great savant provided them.[29] This deduction is supported by a later work. The Shafiʿite jurist Ibn Ḥajar al-Haytamī, whose works reflect the state of production of Islamic scholarship in the post-Mamlūk era, brings in his responsa a question from a convert in Malabar (southern India) who reports his fear of followers of his former religion who, he claims, are brutally threatening him.[30] Al-ʿAynī's synopsis of the legal response from Bukhara contains relics of Persian. In the *Kitāb al-jihād* chapter he provides a list of "words that project infidelity (*alfāẓ al-kufr*)." He opens this list with the sentence: "It is a serious sin to say to someone: 'a bad judgment was given (*qaḍāʾ-ī bad rasīd*)'." The saying "the hand of God is long (*dast-i khudā dirāz-ast*)" is, according to al-ʿAynī, an additional case of wrong saying. The great majority of Muslim scholars consider this expression blasphemy.[31] A third example of a prevalent Persian saying is: "There is God but there is nothing good (*khudā bāshad va-hīch khayr nabāshad*')."[32] Because the person who says these words plays down, according to al-ʿAynī, the very real

27 Yet questions regarding how the *Fatāwá al-Ẓahīrīyah* reached Cairo from Central Asia are beyond the limits of present study.

28 Badr al-Dīn Maḥmūd Ibn Aḥmad al-ʿAynī al-ʿAyntabī al-Qāhirī al-Ḥanafī (762–855/1361–1451), *Masāʾil al-Badrīyyah al-muntakhabah min al-fatāwá al-ẓahīrīyah* ed. Aḥmad al-Ghāmidī (Mecca, 1423/2012) [= al-Riyāḍ, 2014; 2 vol.].

29 On al-Taftazānī see Walī al-Dīn ʿAbd al-Raḥmān Ibn Khaldūn al-Mālikī (732–808/1332–1406), *al-Muqaddimah*, trans. Franz Rosenthal (Princeton: Princeton University Press, 1967), 3: 117; Earl Edgar Elder (trans.), *Commentary on the Creed of Islam: Saʿd al-Din al-Taftazani on the Creed of Najm al-Din al-Nasafi* (New York, 1950), introduction, xxi.

30 Abū al-ʿAbbās Shihāb al-Dīn Aḥamd b. Muḥammad Ibn Ḥajar al-Haytamī (909–973/1503–66), *al-Fatāwá al-kubrá al-fiqahiyyah* ed. ʿAbd al-Ḥamīd Aḥmad Ḥanafī (Cairo, 1357/1938), 4: 249.

31 Al-ʿAynī, *Masāʾil al-Badrīyyah al-muntakhabah min al-fatāwá al-ẓahīrīyah*, 427.

32 The difference between *hast/nīst* is discussed in the Ḥurūfiyya's writings. Their ideas spread in the Mamlūk Sultanate in al-ʿAynī's day. Shahzad Bashir, *Fazlallah Astarabadi and the Hurufis* (Oxford, 2005), 73, 100–101.

existence of Heaven, Hell and their inhabitants, he judges him an infidel.[33] The saying: "do not be afraid of God (*az khudā namītarsī*)" contains double meanings, al-ʿAynī argues: "If it was said in a state of oppression than it is unfaithfulness, yet if the speaker believes that his partner is a truthful person than thesewords should not be considered blasphemy."[34] The last example is of a father who says to his son: "O you, an infidel son (*ya kāfir bachcha*)." According to al-ʿAynī's verdict this father "should not be regarded as a heretic."[35] In his work, al-ʿAynī mentions Abū al-Manṣūr al-Māturīdī (282–333/893–944). This reference to the theologian seems to be a rhetorical device used by an author whose agenda included calling for the reform of some practices common in the Mamlūk court in Cairo during the second half of the 15th century. Bowing to the sultan, al-ʿAynī maintains, should not be tagged as faithlessness. This, he says, is a common practice of his days and should not be interpreted as praying to the royal person. Rather, the wrongdoer is the person who claims that the current ruler is a righteous sultan, this is a wrong assumption since we, al-ʿAynī continues, "certainly know that he is a tyrant," adding that the ruler who substitutes justice with oppression is an unbeliever.[36]

Ethnicity

The major source of slaves who served the households and the armies of the Mamlūk Sultanate were lands in Dār al-Ḥarb. From these regions, girls and boys were recruited and transferred to the slave markets of Egypt and Syria. Textual sources reflect the rich ethnic variety that inhabited the mansions of affluent civilians and the military aristocracy. A point in case is the biography of Ibn Mibrad. In his writings this prolific Damascene writer sheds light on the social reality of his day. In his *samāʿāt*, he names Armenian and Turkish slave girls. He is particularly proud of his *umm-walad* Bulbul bint ʿAbd Allāh.[37] Slave-dealers and buyers could consult shoppers' manuals. Prominent among the authors of these shopping manuals were surgeons, a fact that Helmut Ritter mentioned already a hundred years ago.[38] Self-advice texts are another genre that illuminates the

33 Al-ʿAynī, *Masāʾil al-Badrīyyah al-muntakhabah min al-fatāwá al-ẓahīrīyah*, 429.
34 Al-ʿAynī, *Masāʾil al-Badrīyyah al-muntakhabah min al-fatāwá al-ẓahīrīyah*, 429.
35 al-ʿAynī, *Masāʾil al-Badrīyyah al-muntakhabah min al-fatāwá al-ẓahīrīyah*, 439.
36 al-ʿAynī, *Masāʾil al-Badrīyyah al-muntakhabah min al-fatāwá al-ẓahīrīyah*, 434.
37 Abū Yaʿlá Muḥammad b. al-Ḥusayn al-Farrāʾ al-Ḥanbalī (380–458/990–1066), *Kitāb al-Iʿtiqād* (Riyadh, 1423/2002), 20 (*samāʿāt*); cf. Ṣāliḥ Ibn Muḥammad Ibn ʿAbd al-Khāliq al-Azharī, *al-Fihris al-waṣfī lil-nusakh al-khaṭṭiyyah li-muʾalifāt Yūsuf b. ʿAbd al-Hādī Ibn al-Mibrad* (Kuwait, 1433/2012), 17, 24, 27, 30, 39, 42, 46.
38 Hellmut Ritter, "Ein arabisches Handbuch der Handelswissenschaft," *Der Islam* 7 (1916): 24 (Ibn al-Akfānī).

sultanate's slave markets. They were written for audiences who did not turn a blind eye to the advice of physiognomy manuals and who agreed with the "scientific" suggestion that the inspection of physical symptoms, such as colour, are a valuable tool. We can learn from various sources about the reception of this theory. We learn from Shams al-Dīn Muḥammad al-Ṣūfī al-Dimashqī, known by the nick name Shaykh al-Rabwah, that the categorization of mankind suggested by the authors of these guidebooks was well received in Mamlūk Damascus. One of his works is *al-Maʿāqid al-jammah min al-kiyāsah fī ʿilm al-firāsah wa-ḥasan al-siyāsah* ("The numerous divans of cleverness: about the sciences of physiognomy and the accurate control").[39]

Indeed, Shaykh al-Rabwah's originality is limited. His work is a compilation of materials available in earlier writings.[40] Like other Mamlūk authors, he also depends heavily on Abbasid-period sources.[41] This fact clearly illuminates the practices of the Mamlūk reading public, its reception of past works and the popularity of these past achievements. No doubt, this is a point of interest for students of Arabic literature. But assuming that Shaykh al-Rabwah's aim was not to demonstrate his academic achievements or to express nostalgia for a glorious and remote past, and that he was primarily interested in the reception of his work by his contemporaries, as well as with amusing them, we can safely assume that this audience's response shaped his literary production. He made accessible to them highly esteemed traditional accepted writings. In his chapters on the characters and qualities of human groups he makes wide use of Fakhr al-Dīn al-Rāzī as a source.[42] Yet his composition is not without value.[43] It reflects the prevailing images of the Other among his audience, images that as we well know are slow to change or disappear. His geography book is another source that reflects this world view. In it he informs his readers of the lands of origins of the

39 Shams al-Dīn Abū ʿAbd Allāh Muḥammad b. Abī Ṭālib al-Sūfī al-Dimashqī al-Anṣārī (654–737/1256–1327), *al-Siyāsah fī ʿilm al-firāsah* (Beirut, 1426/2005).

40 Cf. the note on al-Ibshīhī by Ulrich Marzolph, "Medieval Knowledge in Modern Reading: A Fifteenth-Century Arabic Encyclopaedia of *Omnire Scibili*," in Peter Binkley (ed.), *Pre-Modern Encyclopaedic Texts. Proceedings of the Second COMERS Congress* (Groningen, 1–4 July 1996) (Leiden: Brill, 1997).

41 Abū al-Fatḥ Shihāb al-Dīn Muḥammad b. Aḥmad al-Ibshīhī (790–850/1388–1466), *al-Mustaṭraf fī kulli fanni mustaẓraf*, ed. Ibrāhīm Ṣāliḥ (Beirut: Dar Ṣādir, 1419/1999), 2: 531 (*dhakara* al-Masʿūdī), 532 (al-Gharnāṭī, *Tuḥfat al-albāb*), 536 (al-Qazwīnī), 537 (Ibn Zūlāq), 549–553.

42 This might be an explanation why we do not have at our disposal a scientific edition of this work. I used the manuscripts from UCLA and Mecca, beside the volume printed by ʿAbd al-Amīr Muhannā, who based his publication on a single privately-owned manuscript.

43 On this, see Antonella Ghersetti, "The Semiotic Paradigm: Physiognomy and Medicine in Islamic Culture," in Simon Swain (ed.), *Seeing the Face, Seeing the Soul: Polemon's Physiognomy from Classical Antiquity to Medieval Islam* (Oxford, 2007), 301 (she used a Bursa MS.).

ethnic groups that he mentioned in his book on the *firāsah*. I will returnto Shaykh al-Rabwah's work below.

Another writer on *firāsah* is Ibn al-Akfānī (d. 749/1348). The values of these earlier works on physiognomy are high, he says. The data in them illuminates the circumstances of those people who mingle with friends, slaves and women to be married. Physiognomy is, according to him, a legal and accepted Muslim discipline. And, as man is a political creature (*al-insān madanī bil-tab*ʿ), he will benefit from the enunciation of ethnic qualities and the characterization of different people.[44] This, Ibn al-Akfānī claims, led him to compose a short tractate on the art of facial assessment.[45]

The Mamlūk Egyptian author al-Amshāṭī is another contributor to the genre that occupies us here.[46] This author produced, among other works, a guidebook entitled *al-Qawl al-sadīd* ("The Correct account of choosing slaves").[47] His point of departure is Ibn al-Akfānī's work on the characterization of slaves. "It is a good work," al-Amshāṭī notes," but lacking in contents and does not provide enough information. My aim is to append it with useful data."[48] In chapter one of this treatise, he provides a register of the ethnic groups that populate the world (*fī dhikr ajnās al-ʿālam*). Following it he provides an anachronistic catalogue of races: Turks, Circassians, Franks, Indians, Berbers, and Blacks.[49] Like other composers of treatises on issues such as race, colour and human geography, al-Amshāṭī does not go beyond the literary limits of the genre. An example of his fictional conservatism is his use of a maximum that Aristotle is supposed to have said to Alexander: "use the Armenians as slaves, employ the Greeks and seal with the Arabs."[50] The prevalence of these deeply entrenched representations of human races in the Mamlūk world vision, which combined ethnic images with ideas on the effects of world geography and climate, is seen by the popularity of Galen's theory. A case in point is al-Amshāṭī's negative picture of the Africans. He

44 Muḥammad b. Ibrāhīm Ibn al-Akfānī (ca. 1286–749/1348), *Kitāb Irshād al-qāṣid ilá asná al-maqāṣid*, ed. ʿAbd al-Munʿim Muḥammad ʿUmar (Cairo, 1990), 176.

45 Yet the manuscript that reached us is a damaged unicum, copied in the 15th century and preserved in Paris, and hence is of little value. William McGuckin de Slane, *Catalogue des manuscrits arabes* (Paris, Bibliothèque nationale – Département des manuscrits Arabes, 1883–1895), 392 no. 2234/3 (fol. 148–151); it was translated by Hans Müller, *Die Kunst des Sklavenkaufs* (Freiburg, 1980).

46 Cf. Ghersetti, "The Semiotic Paradigm" 295.

47 Maḥmūd b. Aḥmad al-ʿAyntābī al-Amshāṭī (812–903/1409–1496), *al-Qawl al-sadīd fī ikhtiyār al-imāʾ wal-ʿabīd: [risālah nādirah fī shará wa-taqlīb al-ʿabīd]*, ed. Muḥammad ʿĪsá Ṣāliḥīyah (Beirut, 1996).

48 Al-Amshāṭī, *al-Qawl al-sadīd*, 31–32.

49 Al-Amshāṭī, *al-Qawl al-sadīd*, 41–42.

50 Al-Amshāṭī, *al-Qawl al-sadīd*, 43.

argued, as did Ibn Khaldūn[51] and Ibn al-Nafīs,[52] that the distance from the sun affects people's qualities.

Mamlūk Imaginative World Geography

The previous sections presented a condensed account of the Mamlūk Sultanate's intensive contacts with Dār al-Ḥarb and Cairo's communications with neighbouring and remote lands as well as the political geography that Muslim jurists of the time espoused. The sultans established direct communication with the Mediterranean and the Black Sea as well as with the Horn of Africa and Ethiopia. This explains the Bahri-period (648–784/1250–1382) sources' description of territories and forces that were beyond the Mamlūks' boundaries. The colossal encyclopaedia of Ibn Faḍl Allāh al-ʿUmarī (700–750/1301–1349) serves as an example of the achievements of these sources.[53] In it he transmits valuable reports on foreign lands, from Anatolia to India.[54] He describes methods of government, languages of political legitimacy, coinages in use, agricultural systems and Islamic institutions of learning. In line with the Islamic mirror of princes genre, al-ʿUmarī also compares the court etiquette of a Muslim sultan with the ideal court of Alexander the Great. Using this narrative strategy helps him to introduce Islamic India to world history and particularly into the orbit of civilized nations.[55]

Yet, if al-ʿUmarī's writing provided knowledge that sultans in Cairo of his day could use to obtain data that supported their efforts to comprehend the world around them, the literary production from the Circassian regime (784–922/1382–1517) reveals a different picture.[56] I assume that this reflects the fact that in the second half of the 15th century, only a handful of embassies from Islamic India,[57]

51 El-Bushra El-Sayed, "Perspectives on the Contribution of Arabs and Muslims to Geography," *Geo Journal* 26/2 (1992): 161.

52 Max Meyerhof and J. Schacht (eds. and trans.), *The Theologus Autodidactus (Al-Risala al-Kamila) of Ibn Nafis* (Oxford, 1968), 71–74.

53 I would like to thank Professor Michal Biran for her remarks.

54 Ibn Faḍl Allāh Shihāb al-Dīn Aḥmad b. Yaḥyá al-ʿUmarī (700–750/1301–1349), *Masālik al-abṣār fī mamālik al-amṣār*, ed. K. Jabūrī (Beirut, 2010), 3: 35–87 (quoting Indian and Arab informants); Lambourn, "India from Aden," 56.

55 Aziz Al-Azmeh, "Barbarians in Arab Eyes," *Past & Present* 134 (1992): 7–8; Joan-Pau Rubiés, *Travel and Ethnology in the Renaissance. South India through European Eyes, 1250–1625* (Cambridge, 2000), 23–34, 147–149.

56 Moreover, I do not recall any Circassian Mamlūk emissary similar to the embassy of Kamāl al-Dīn ʿAbd al-Razzāq who was sent by the Timurids to India (845/1442).

57 Presumably Arabic and Persian were the languages of communication. But see the verses by Amīr Khusraw (1253–1325) "I have no Egyptian sugar with which to talk to an Arab, I am an

or from the islands of the Indian Ocean and the South China Sea, arrived in Cairo,[58] although these regions, which are already mentioned in Abbasid travel literature, served as important trade partners of the sultanate.[59] This is in sharp contrast to the accounts of Ethiopian and Mediterranean embassies that ascended to the Citadel or called at Damascus,[60] let alone other Muslim governments in the Mediterranean basin and Central Asia.[61] The maritime routes even gained even more importance in the years that experienced the decline of land traffic from Central Asia to the Near East. During the second half of the 15th century the Red Sea became more closely tied to the economy of the sultanate and the political scene in Cairo.[62] Contacts between the sultan's agents and a Chinese fleet, which sailed from India to the Red Sea, illuminates this new reality. Despite this, it seems that the first official delegation that Cairo dispatched to regions beyond the Hijaz was recorded only during the last decades of the 15th century. This was in response to reports that reached Cairo and informed the local governing elite that Portuguese flotillas were challenging the old naval order in the Indian Ocean. In response to this defiance of Islam's maritime superiority in that corner of the world, the sultan Qānṣūh al-Ghawrī sent a fleet commanded by the governor of Jeddah to protect the shores of the Indian Ocean. In the face of

Indian Turk, I respond in Hindi." Muzaffar Alam, *The Language of Political Islam in India c. 1200–1800* (New Delhi, 2010), 148.

58 Ibn Iyās, *Badā'iʿ al-zuhūr fī waqā'iʿ al-duhūr*, 3: 65 (876/1471), 212 (889/1484), 215 (890/1455, an ambassador from India to the Ottomans); al-Sakhāwī, *al-Dhayl al-tāmm*, 3: 46 (898/1493, on the arrival to Jeddah of three ships, that originated from Diu and Kanbāyah in India), 83 (reports reached Egypt on fighting among Muslims in India), 109, 153, 197.

59 On India as a remote heaven for Mamlūk refugees see al-Sakhāwī, *al-Dhayl al-tāmm*, 2: 55–56 (854/1450).

60 Ibn Iyās, *Badā'iʿ al-zuhūr fī waqā'iʿ al-duhūr*, 3: 145 (883/1478 on a naval mission to Anatolia and Cyprus), 150 (883/1479 the dispatch of an ambassador to Catalonia), 179–180 (886/1481 Ethiopia), 183, 185, 192 (886–7/1481–2 Ottomans), 206, 215 (890/1485); Shihāb al-Dīn Aḥmad b. Muḥammad Ibn al-Ḥimṣī (841–934/1458–1528), *Ḥawādith al-zamān wa-wafiyyāt al-shuyūkh wal-aqrān*, ed. ʿAbd al-ʿAzīz Ḥarfush (Beirut, 1421/2000), 235 (897/1492); Shams al-Dīn Muḥammad b. ʿAlī Ibn Ṭūlūn al-Ṣāliḥī (1473–1546/880–953), *Mufākahat al-khullān fī ḥawādith al-zamān* [The Joyful Stories of Close Friends Concerning Recent Events], ed. Kh. al-Mansur (Beirut, 1998), 10.

61 A case in point is the report of the plea that reached Cairo from al-Andalus. In response, the sultan instructed that the monks of the Holy Sepulchre be presented with an ultimatum. They should send an envoy to the king of Naples who should write to the king of Castile. Ibn Iyās, *Badā'iʿ al-zuhūr fī waqā'iʿ al-duhūr*, 3: 244–45 (892/1487), 316 (901/1495). Another account that illuminates the flow of information from Western Europe to the lands of the sultanate are the account of the Ottoman prince Cem. Al-Sakhāwī, *al-Dhayl al-tāmm*, 3: 223–224 (900/1494).

62 Patrick Wing, "Indian Ocean Trade and Sultanic Authority: The nāẓir of Jeddah and the Mamluk Political Economy," *Journal of the Economic and Social History of the Orient* 57 (2014): 56–62.

the intruders, another expedition was sent to Kamrān Island in the Red Sea, off the coast of Yemen.[63]

Geographical data from the last century of the Mamlūks' rule elucidate an incursion of imaginative elements into what should be a practical geographical discourse. The data do not represent the topography of Muslim settlements, but rather provide a map of locations populated by fabulous beast, mysterious and hybrid creatures and sites visited by mythological figures. These imaginary locations served to define the norms of Islamic world. The lack of direct communication between the sultans of Cairo and south-east Asia explains the quality of the Arabic accounts of these parts of the world. In the mind of the Mamlūk elite and in their *mappa mundi*, the Indian Ocean was depicted as a zone of exotic *mirabilia* (*ʿajāʾib*, accounts of the fantastic). It was an invented imaginary archipelago. This was in sharp contrast to reports on the "civilized" districts of Earth, namely regions that were governed by familiar systems of administration or by established religions.[64] Without considering these components our picture of the Mamlūk *Weltanschauung* will be a partial one. Following earlier Persian and Arab writers, Ibn al-Wardī's and Shaykh al-Rabwah's accounts contain a mix of "real facts" and "imaginary world."[65] The salient presentation of naked men and women in their accounts of the Indian Ocean support this deduction. Reports of people with faces resembling trees or beasts are illuminating examples of the legendary components that make up a considerable part of their narratives.[66] A case in point is the "account" of the Wāq-Wāq Island:

> On this island are trees that bear as fruit women: shapely, with bodies,eyes, hands, feet, hair, breasts, and vulvas like the vulvas of women.Their faces are exceptionally beautiful and they hang by their hair. They come out of cases like big swords, and when they feel the wind and sun, they shout Wāq Wāq until their hair tears.[67]

63 Aḥmad Ibn Muḥammad Ibn al-Mallá al-Ḥaṣkafī al-Ḥalabī al-Shāfiʿī (937–1003/1530–1595), *Mutʿat al-adhhān min al-tamattuʿ bil-iqrān bayna tarājim al-shuyūkh wal-aqrān* (Beirut: Dār Ṣādir, 1999), 1: 322, 323 (918/1512). On the India trade in these years see Francisco Apellániz, "News on the Bulaq: a Mamluk-Venetian Memorandum on Asian Trade, AD 1503," European University Institute Department of History and Civilization. *EUI Working Paper HEC* 2016/01.

64 Mark J. P. Wolf (ed.), *The Routledge Companion to Imaginary Worlds* (New York, 2018).

65 Sarāj al-Dīn Ibn al-Wardī al-Shāfiʿī (861/1457), *Kharīdat al-ʿajāʾib wa-fariḍat al-gharāʾib* [The Pearl of Wonders and the Uniqueness of Strange Things], ed. M. Fākhūrī (Beirut, 1411/1991). This pseudo-geographical and cosmographical summery of early sources is merely a plagiarism of the *Jāmiʿ al-funūn wa-salwat al-maḥzūn* of Naḏjm al-Dīn Aḥmad b. Ḥamdān b. Shabīb al-Ḥarrānī al-Ḥanbalī, who lived in Egypt *circa* 732/1332.

66 Ibn al-Wardī, *Kharīdat al-ʿajāʾib*, 73, 74, 78, 84, 85, 88, 94.

67 Shawkat M. Toorawa, "Waqwaq: Fabulous, Fabular, Indian Ocean (?) Island(s)," *Emergences* 10/2 (2000): 393.

Neither author limits his accounts to names of locations, religions or people, but rather both seek to place them on the borders of a geographical and historical picture, in an imaginative world map with which their audiences were familiar. References to Biblical fables, names of legendary patriarchs, stories taken from the Qur'ān and Persian legends are employed by both in an effort to elucidate prevailing images of "others" and of remote countries and to establish the ties of these people and lands with Islamic history. After all, goods from those mysterious destinations turned up in the markets of the Sultanate. Several examples sustain this interpretation. At the southern end of the Indian Ocean, in the island of Sarandīb, is said to be the mountain of al-Rāhūn. There the armchair geographer identifies the site where Adam fell, after his expulsion from the Garden.[68] His footprint is visible also in the island of Beljera/Balqaram [Rhinoceros].[69] A comparable function can be identified in the legend of the prophet al-Khiḍr.[70] Al-Manūfī provides additional data that supports this interpretation. His history of the equatorial Nile is entangled with biblical legends.[71]

Alexander the Great is prominent among the celebrated figures that played a role in combining past and present, local and general.[72] During the Middle Islamic Period the legend of "The One with Two Horns" (*Dhū al-Qarnayn*) spread far beyond the Arab-Islamic world.[73] It was well received in India and beyond. Arab authors located him in isolated islands and in remote lands. These were mysterious places that seized the imagination of Mamlūk audiences.[74] The story of Alexander's adventures has several functions.[75] One of them was to bridge the

68 Shams al-Dīn Abū ʿAbd Allāh Muḥammad Ibn Abī Ṭālib al-Ṣūfī Shaykh al-Rabwah al-Dimashqī al-Anṣārī (654–737/1256–1327), *Nukhbat al-dahr fī ajāʾib al-barr wal-baḥar* (Choice of the Time of Wonders of Land and Sea), ed. A. F. M. von Mehern (St. Petersburg, 1865), 152, 160 [= Shems ed-Din Abou Abdallah Mohammed de Damas, *Manuel de la Cosmographie du Moyen age*, trad. M.A.F. Mehren (Saint-Pe´tersbourg, 1874), 204].

69 Shaykh al-Rabwah, *Nukhbat al-dahr*, 157 [= Fr., 210]; Ibn al-Wardī, *Kharīdat al-ʿajāʾib*, 86–88.

70 In some exegeses of Qurʾān 18:60 the junction of the two seas is located at the edges of the Persian Gulf. I. Friedlaender, *Die Chadhirlegende und der Alexanderroman: Eine sagengeschichtliche und literarhistorische Untersuchung* (Leipzig, 1913), 303–304.

71 Shihāb al-Dīn Aḥmad b. Muḥammad al-Manūfī (1443–1521), "Les sources du Nil: Extrait d'un manuscrit arabe intitulé Kitāb al-Fayḍ al-Madīd fī Akhbār al-Nīl al-Saʿīd [Bargès (ed. et trans.), le Livre du courant étendu, traitant de tout ce qui a rapport à l'heureux Nil," *Journal Asiatique* (3rd ser.) 3, (1837): 145–165.

72 Shaykh al-Rabwah, *Nukhbat al-dahr*, 159–160 [= Fr., 214–215].

73 Cf. the report on the Mamlūk army commanders' headgear and the popular verses that were chanted in Cairo. Ibn Iyās, *Badāʾiʿal-zuhūr*, 3: 340 (902/1496); Although it should be added that in some exegeses of Q. 18: 83–101 he is not identified with Alexander, but rather with a South Arabian king. See Brannon M. Wheeler, *Moses in the Qur'an and Islamic Exegesis* (London, 2002), 16.

74 Ibn al-Wardī, *Kharīdat al-ʿajāʾib*, 73, 84.

75 The encounter between this mythological king and the sages of the south is told already in the

gap that separates the perfect days of the past and banal contemporary reality. An additional function was to bind remote territories to the central Islamic lands. The following story sheds light on this literary device. It is narrated that Alexander (Iskandar) had besieged a mountainous region in Tannīn (serpent or monster), an island in the Comoro Islands group.[76] On that island is a city which is also named Tannīn. The local population maintains that Alexander conquered the place and built the city.[77] The reason for his expedition was that in that location lived a huge and malicious monster. Alexander sent hunters who manufactured sacks from goats' hides and filled them with calcium and sulphur. The monster swallowed the bait and died. Following this achievement, Alexander decided to commemorate his success and founded the city.[78] By using the name of a mythologized Hellenic king and his legendary fame, the account served to join the Islands of the Moon (*al-qamar*) with the history of Mamlūk Egypt and Syria.[79]

Stories about the jinn (*jānn*) are another visible element in late Mamlūk-period accounts of remote lands.[80] So are stories of the Anti-Christ (*al-dajjāl*) and the adventures of Tamīm al-Dārī.[81] Mamlūk audiences believed that this companion of the Prophet had visited a remote island, which they located in the ocean that separates their land from India.[82] On its soil they believed Tamīm encountered the she-spy and the *dajjāl*.[83] These popular fables play a role in bringing together legendary histories and remote people, of connecting the Muslims of the sultanate with isolated and mysterious regions of the world. A common literary device for combining remote lands with the world known to the author's audiences is to populate these lands with people that these imaginative audiences were familiar with. Hence they report on Arabs and Muslims in

Talmud. On this and on adventures see Aleksandra Klęczar, "The Kingship of Alexander the Great in the Jewish Versions of the Alexander Narrative," in Richard Stoneman, Kyle Erickson and Ian Netton (eds.), *The Alexander Romance in Persia and the East* (Groningen, 2012), 61–79, and Faustina C.W. Doufikar-Aerts, "King Midas' Ears on Alexander's Head: In Search of the Afro-Asiatic Alexander Cycle," in ibid., 339–334.

76 Shaykh al-Rabwah, *Nukhbat al-dahr*, 148 [*Baleine* (whale) in the French translation, 198 but I assume that the name refers to the Bible, Genesis 1:21, Exodus 7: 9 and other verses.]

77 Read *malakaha.*

78 Ibn al-Wardī, *Kharīdat al-ʿalīda*, 73–74; Shaykh al-Rabwah, *Nukhbat al-dahr*, 159–160 [= Fr., 214–215].

79 On Baybars as "Iskandar al-zamān" see Denise Aigle. "Les inscriptions de Baybars dans le Bilad al-Šam. Une expression de la légitimité du pouvoir," *Studia Islamica* 97 (2003): 73–77.

80 Shaykh al-Rabwah, *Nukhbat al-dahr*, 149, 166; Ibn al-Wardī, *Kharīdat al-ʿajāʾib*, 85, 89. On the belief in these creatures see Ibn al-Mallá al-Ḥaṣkafī, *Mutʿat al-adhhān*, 1: 101–102.

81 Y. Frenkel, "*Volksroman* under the Mamluks: The Case of Tamīm ad-Dārī Popular Sira," in Conermann (ed.), *History and Society during the Mamlūk Period (1250–1517)* (Bonn, 2014), 21–36.

82 Shaykh al-Rabwah, *Nukhbat al-dahr*, 149 [= Fr., 198].

83 Ibn al-Wardī, *Kharīdat al-ʿajāʾib*, 91–92.

country far beyond the boundaries of the Middle East.[84] The population of the largest city of Sarandīb (Ceylon)[85] is depicted as a rich mosaic of religious communities: Muslims, Christians, Jews, Zoroastrians and infidels who do not hold with any belief system. Every group has its own governor. They do not offend each other and all of them depend on the Muslim king who leads them.[86] The Barṭāʾīl Island is populated by people resembling the Turks with long hair that looks like horses' tails. From a mountain on that island strange sounds are heard. Some say that this is the voice of the anti-Christ, other claim that it is the devil's voice.[87] A similar vision of ethnic and geographical images can also be identified in an account of the sources of the Nile. It tells that the Muslims of the Sudan are civilized and urbanized while the polytheists are said to be barbarians.[88] The people far remote from Islam's frontiers are not counted as belonging to the civilized world. Wild black people are equated to animals (*mutawaḥḥishūn*)[89] who eat what other people hand them, while the Nubians, who are Christians, are part of the civilized world (*al-ʿāmira bil-mudun wa-qurá*):[90]

> They are Christians and follow the law (do not sleep with their wife during the days of menstruation). The polytheistic Africans have no religion and no culture. They walk around naked. They are the offspring of Ham whom his father Noah cursed.[91] Some among these people are said to be cannibals.[92] They are lawless, and no prophet was born among them.[93]

The criteria explained above were also used to categorize other people, including the inhabitants of Central Asia and the remote northern corners of that continent. Shaykh al-Rabwah's description of Eurasia is based mainly on earlier sources.[94] Narrating in line with the genre's literary codes, he transmits the tradition that Gog and Magog are Turkish people. He is also familiar with the story of the Mamlūks' origin (*wa-aqam alān min hādhī al-ṭāʾifa bi-miṣr wal-*

84 Shaykh al-Rabwah, *Nukhbat al-dahr,* 160 (Arabs populate the island of al-Diba) [= Fr., 215: les Laquedives et les Maledives]; Joseph Toussaint Reinaud, *Relation des voyages faits par les Arabes et les Persans dans l'Inde et à la Chine dans le IXe siècke de l'ére chrétienne* (Paris, 1845), 55 (Arabs populate the island of al-Diba).

85 Shaykh al-Rabwah, *Nukhbat al-dahr*, 158,160 (on giraffes in Serendib/Sarandīb?!), [= Fr., 9 n. 3, 212, 215,].

86 Shaykh al-Rabwah, *Nukhbat al-dahr*, 160 [= Fr., 215].

87 Shaykh al-Rabwah, *Nukhbat al-dahr*, 158 [= Fr., 213].

88 Shaykh al-Rabwah, *Nukhbat al-dahr*, 268 [= Fr., 388].

89 Al-Manūfī, "Les sources du Nil," 148.

90 Al-Manūfī, "Les sources du Nil," 157.

91 Al-Manūfī, "Les sources du Nil," 266, 269.

92 Al-Manūfī, "Les sources du Nil," 269.

93 Al-Manūfī, "Les sources du Nil," 273.

94 Shaykh al-Rabwah, *Nukhbat al-dahr,* 261 (quoting al-Masʿūdī and al-Idrīsī), 261, 262, 263 (quoting Ibn al-Athīr), 265 (quoting Ibn ʿAbd al-Barr, *Ansāb al-umam*), 275.

shām).[95] These accounts bring remote lands into the shared civilization of Middle Eastern Muslims. They all believe in recognized and legitimate beliefs and behave according to the rules of tolerance, in contradiction to the cannibals.[96] The interpretation of these Mamlūk geographical works springs from the assumption that the accounts that were presented above reveal the Mamlūk elite's shared views. This research paradigm is supported by stories from the *One Thousand and One Nights*. The conclusion that these stories circulated in the Mamlūk territory is shared by many scholars. They base their view on several findings, which include the mentioning of *ashrafī* coins in the tales.[97] The details in the descriptions of the mysterious remote regions that compose the narratives of these tales agree with elements in the non-fictional accounts of our Damascene author. A case to the point is the frame story, that opens with the line: "It is related that long ago, during the time (*fī mulk*) of the Banū Sāsān dynasty in the island of India and Indo-China (*jazā'ir al-hind wa-ṣīn al-ṣīn*), there lived two kings who were brothers."[98] Another example can be traced in the story of Jullanār, where she says: "When I left you, I came out from the sea and sat on the shore of the island, where a man from the Islands of the Moon (*jazā'ir al-qamar*) apprehended me and sold me to a merchant who sold me to the king of this city for ten thousand dinars. I have had a happy life with him." She continues her tale and describes the king as a "pious, generous, and honourable man (*rajul dīn karīm wa-ṣāḥib muruwwa*)."[99] The story of night 102 opens with the line: "It is related, O King, that there lived once in the town of China and Kashgar (*madīnat al-ṣīn wa-qajqār*) a tailor who had a pretty, compatible and loyal wife."[100] This city is also named in one of the great love stories of the Arabian Nights, the tale of Qamar al-Zamān and his Two Sons. A sub-story in it tells of Maymūnah the she-demon (*'ifrīt*) and her encounters with Danhash.[101] She is the daughter of al-Dimiryāṭ, a descendant of Iblīs the Devil and one of the well-known kings of the jinn, and he is the son of Shamhursh (or Shārūkh), the chief judge (*qāḍī*) of the jinn. This jinni presents himself and tells Maymūnah that he comes from the

95 Shaykh al-Rabwah, *Nukhbat al-dahr*, 264 , 265 [= Fr., 381, 383].
96 Shaykh al-Rabwah, *Nukhbat al-dahr*, 159,[= Fr., 214].
97 Muhsin Mahdi (ed.), *The Thousand and One Nights (Alf Layla wa-Layla) from the Earliest Known Sources* (Leiden, 1995), 1: 222 (l. 13; night 71), 318–319 (night 133) [= H. Haddawy (trans.), *The Arabian Nights* (New York, 1990), 1: 153, 240–242].
98 Mahdi (ed.), *The Thousand and One Nights*, 1: 56 (l. 15) [= Haddawy (trans.), *The Arabian Nights*, 1: 3].
99 Mahdi (ed.), *The Thousand and One Nights*, 1: 490–491 (night 238) [= Haddawy (trans.), *The Arabian Nights*, 1: 391].
100 Mahdi (ed.), *The Thousand and One Nights*, 1: 280 (night 102) [= Haddawy (trans.), *The Arabian Nights*, 1: 206].
101 Ulrich Marzolph and Richard van Leeuwen, *The Arabian Nights Encyclopaedia* (Santa Barbara, 2004), 1: 341.

furthest end of China (*qajqār al-ṣīn*) and from the Islands, while she narrates of a beautiful prince from the interior island of China,[102] a place that in other versions is named the Khālidān Islands.[103]

Conclusion

Mamlūk communication with remote lands in Central Asia, sub-Saharan Africa and the Indian sub-continent was carried out by mediators who mastered a considerable volume of genuine and useful data, as is possible to deduce from Ibn Baṭūṭṭah's *Riḥlah.*[104] Bahrī-period geographers and encyclopaedists identified in them established religions, administrations and institutions. Commanders and clerks in Cairo and other urban centres of the Sultanate learned from these sources about neighbouring and distant lands. The Mamlūk audiences that consumed these literary sources had a global outlook that was not detached from the geo-strategic perceptions of the military and diplomacy machinery of the Sultanate. Although considerable parts of the remote zones that engaged the Mamlūk urban public were far beyond the immediate reach of the sultanate's army, navy and diplomacy, nevertheless they were presented on the mental map that the learned elites presumably "consulted." Using a rich figurative language, the sources supplied their audiences with information about remote locations which supplied the Sultanate with manpower and merchandise. This data was sufficient to fulfil the consumers' needs and its details were received as updated information. In the Bahrī-period texts, Eurasia, Central Asia, Islamic India and adjacent regions were depicted as belonging to the civilized world. These reports are in sharp contrast to the accounts of the islands of the oceans in writings from the Circassian period. This article has endeavoured to combine an inspection of three genres to outline the holistic worldview of the Circassian epoch, an era that experienced growing pressure from both internal discord and external threats

102 Mahdi (ed.), *The Thousand and One Nights*, 1: 540 (night 277) [= Haddawy (trans.), *The Arabian Nights*, 2: 170–172].

103 Edward William Lane (trans.), *The Arabian Nights' Entertainments* (London, 1840), 2: 78 (night 117), 116, 132, 217 (note 1 based upon de Sacy's remarks), 218 (note 3); Richard F. Burton (trans.), *The Book of the Thousand Nights and Night* (London, 1894), 3: 1.

104 H.A.R. Gibb (trans.), *The Travels of Ibn Battuta A.D. 1325–1354* (Cambridge, 1958; repr. London, 1969); Ross Dunn, *The Adventures of Ibn Battuta, a Muslim Traveller of the Fourteenth Century* (Berkeley, 2005); David Waines, *The Odyssey of Ibn Battuta: Uncommon Tales of a Medieval Adventurer* (Chicago, 2010). To the best of my knowledge, Ibn Battutah was not read in Mamlūk Cairo. Indeed, in the al-*Muqaddimah* Ibn Khaldūn mentions him, but in this case the historian narrates an event that he witnessed in his youth in North Africa. Walī al-Dīn ʿAbd al-Raḥmān Ibn Khaldūn al-Mālikī (732–808/1332–1406), *al-Muqaddimah* ed. ʿAbd al-Salām al-Shadādī (Rabat, 2005), 1: 310 [Rosenthal (trans.), 1: 369–371]; Waines, *The Odyssey of Ibn Battuta,* 6.

from advancing rivals. Its first section concentrated on the legal dimensions of the Mamlūks' world map. The division of the worlds into two opposing abodes did not lead contemporary jurists and army commanders to adopt a combatant mode. This position facilitated the use of an informative tone while dealing with lands beyond the Sultanate's frontiers.

The second section illuminated the multi-lingual/ethnic structure of 15th-century Cairene society, a society that accommodated considerable numbers of migrants and imported slaves who made up a rich human mosaic. The third section offered a reading on two descriptions of the Indian Ocean and the South China Sea. Together, these three parts illuminate the Mamlūk elite's prevailing *Weltanschauung.* The data scrutinized in this article reveals that in the last chapter of the Sultanate's history, its leading elite had only a vague knowledge of the lands that supplied Cairo with goods in high demand. There are no traces of inquiries made by the inhabitants of the Citadel during these years in pursuit of substantial information on regions, which they would soon lose. Since the Sultanate had no immediate interest in deploying naval forces in the Indian Ocean, it is no wonder that no demand for accurate geographical data was generated. The pseudo-information on mysterious islands and marvellous creatures provided them with sufficient data on wondrous lands. Indeed, already the Qur᾽ān tells of *jinn* who inhabit the invisible world. Moreover, as long as the details supplied by the literary sources responded to public expectations, the accuracy of the reports seems not to have troubled consumers. This also explains the insertion of accounts of mysterious creatures in geographical writings. Certainly, these texts confirmed the Islamic worldview. Accepted as sufficient to draw the *mappa mundi*, including depictions of lands and peoples, and to explain the global political order, these accounts seemed to have been consumed without restraint. The Sultanate's population perceived them as solid bricks for constructing its *Weltanschauung.*

Bibliography

Primary Sources

Anonymous. *Nūr al-maʿārif fī nuẓum wa-qawānīn wa-aʿrāf al-Yaman fī al-ʿahd al-Muẓaffarī al-wārif.* Ed. Muḥammad ʿAbd al-Raḥīm Jāzim. Sanaa, 2003–5.

ʿAbd al-Razzāq al-Samarqandī, Kamāl al-Dīn b. Iṣḥāq. *Maṭāliʿ-i saʿdaynva majmaʿ al-baḥrayn* [Kamaluddin Abdul-Razzaq Samarqandi's Mission to Calicut and Vijayanagara], in W.M. Thackston, (trans.) *A Century of Princes: Sources on Timurid History and Art.* Cambridge, MA, 1989.

al-Amshāṭī, Maḥmūd b. Aḥmad al-ʿAyntābī al-Ḥanafī. *Al-Qawl al-sadīd fī ikhtiyār al-imāʾ wal-ʿabīd: [risālah nādirah fī shará wa-taqlīb al-ʿabīd]*. Ed. Muḥammad ʿĪsá Ṣāliḥīyah. Beirut, 1996.

al-ʿAynī, Badr al-Dīn Maḥmūd b. Aḥmad al-Ḥanafī. *Al-Bināyah fī sharḥ al-hidāyah*. Beirut, 1411/1990.

al-ʿAynī, Badr al-Dīn Maḥmūd b. Aḥmad al-Ḥanafī. *Masāʾil al-Badrīyyah al-muntakhabah min al-fatāwá al-ẓahīrīyah*. Ed. Aḥmad al-Ghāmidī. Mecca, 1423/2012.

al-Buṣrawī, ʿAlā al-Dīn ʿAlī b. Yūsuf. *Taʾrīkh al-Buṣrawī*. Ed. Ḥasan al-ʿUlabī. Beirut, 1498/1988.

al-Dimashqī, Shams al-Dīn Abū ʿAbd Allāh Muḥammad al-Sūfī al-Anṣārī. *Al-Siyāsa fī ʿilm al-firāsah*. Beirut, 1426/2005.

al-Ḥujāwī, Sharaf al-Dīn Abū al-Najā Mūsá al-Maqdisī al-Ḥanbalī. *Al-Iqnāʿ li-ṭālib al-intifāʿ [fī fiqh al-imām al-mubajjal Abī ʿAbd Allāh Aḥmad Ibn Ḥanbal]*. Ed. ʿAbd Allāh Ibn ʿAbd al-Muḥsin al-Turkī. Al-Riyāḍ, 1419/1999.

Ibn al-Akfānī, Muḥammad b. Ibrāhim. *Kitāb Irshād al-qāṣid ilá asná al-maqāṣid*. Ed. ʿAbd al-Munʿim Muḥammad ʿUmar. Cairo, 1990.

Ibn al-Farrāʾ, Abū Yaʿlá Muḥammad b. al-Ḥusayn al-Ḥanbalī. *Kitāb al-Iʿtiqād*. Riyadh, 1423/2002.

Ibn al-Ḥimṣī, Shihāb al-Dīn Aḥmad b. Muḥammad. *Ḥawādith al-zamān wa-wafiyyāt al-shuyūkh wal-aqrān*. Ed. ʿAbd al-ʿAzīz Ḥarfush. Beirut, 1421/2000.

Ibn Faḍl Allāh al-ʿUmarī, Shihāb al-Dīn Aḥmad b. Yaḥyá. *Masālik al-abṣār fī mamālik al-amṣār*. Ed. K. Jabūrī. Beirut, 2010.

Ibn Ḥajar al-ʿAsqalānī, Shihāb al-Dīn Aḥmad b. ʿAlī al-Shāfiʿī. *[Risālah fī] al-Khiṣāl al-mukaffira lil-dhunūb al-mutaqaddimah wal-mutaʾakhirah*. Ed. A. A. Salīm Jeddah, 1422/2001.

Ibn Ḥajar al-Haytamī, Abū al-ʿAbbās Shihāb al-Dīn Aḥamd b. Muḥammad. *Al-Fatāwá al-kubrá al-fiqahiyyah*. Ed. ʿAbd al-Ḥamīd Aḥmad Ḥanafī. Cairo, 1357/1938.

Ibn Iyās, Muḥammad b. Aḥmad al-Ḥanafī. *Badāʾiʿ al-zuhūr fī waqāʾiʿ al-duhūr* [Die Chronik des Ibn Ijas]. Ed. M. Mustafa. Wiesbaden 1975; reprinted Cairo, 1429/2008.

Ibn Khaldūn, Walī al-Dīn ʿAbd al-Raḥmān al-Mālikī. *Al-Muqaddimah*. Ed. ʿAbd al-Salām al-Shadādī (Rabat, 2005) [Franz Rosenthal (trans.). *Al-Muqaddimah* (Princeton, 1967)].

Ibn al-Mallá al-Ḥaṣkafī, Aḥmad Ibn Muḥammad al-Ḥalabī al-Shāfiʿī. *Mutʿat al-adhhān min al-Tamattuʿ bil-iqrān bayna tarājim al-shuyūkh wal-aqrān*. Beirut, 1999.

Ibn Nafīs, ʿAlī b. Abī al-Ḥazm. *Al-Risāla al-Kāmila*. Ed. and trans. Max Meyerhof and Joseph Schacht. *The Theologus Autodidactus*. Oxford, 1968.

Ibn Taymiyya, Taqī al-Dīn Aḥmad b. ʿAbd al-Ḥalīm al-Ḥaranī. *Majmūʿ fatāwá*. Ed. ʿAbd al-Raḥmān b. Muḥammad b. Qāsim al-ʿĀṣimī al-Najdī al-Ḥanbalī. Al-Madīna, 1425/2004.

Ibn Ṭūlūn, Shams al-Dīn Muḥammad b. ʿAlī al-Ṣāliḥī. *Mufākahat al-khullān fī ḥawādith al-zamān*. Ed. Kh. al-Manṣūr. Beirut, 1998.

Ibn al-Wardī al-Maʿarrī, Zayn al-Dīn Abū Ḥafs ʿUmar b. al-Muẓaffar (691–749/1292–1349). *Tatimmat al-mukhtaṣar fī akhbār al-bashar [taʾrīkh Ibn al-Wardī]*. Cairo, 1285/1868.

Ibn al-Wardī, Sirāj al-Dīn al-Shāfiʿī. *Kharīdat al-ʿajāʾib wa-fariḍat al-gharāʾib*. Ed. M. Fākhūrī. Beirut, 1411/1991.

al-Ibshīhī, Abū al-Fatḥ Shihāb al-Dīn Muḥammad b. Aḥmad. *Al-Mustaṭraf fī kulli fanni mustaẓraf*. Ed. Ibrāhīm Ṣāliḥ. Beirut, 1419/1999.

al-Manūfī, Shihāb al-Dīn Aḥmad b. Muḥammad. "Les sources du Nil: Extrait d'un manuscrit arabe intitulé Kitāb al-Fayḍ al-Madīd fī Akhbār al-Nīl al-Sa'īd (le Livre du courant étendu, traitant de tout ce qui a rapport à l'heureux Nil)."Ed. and trans. Bargè." *Journal Asiatique.* 3rd ser., 3, (1837): 145–165.

al-Sakhāwī, Shams al-Dīn Muḥammad b. 'Abd al-Raḥmān (831–902/1424–1497). *Al-Dhayl al-tāmm 'alá duwal al-islām lil-dhahabī.* Ed. Ḥasan Ismā'īl Marwah and Maḥmūd al-Arnā'ūṭ. Beirut, 1992–1998.

Shaykh al-Rabwah, Shams al-Dīn Abū 'Abd Allāh Muḥammad al-Dimashqī (654–737/1256–1327). *Nukhbat al-dahr fī ajā'ib al-barr wal-baḥar.* Ed. A.F.M. von Mehern. St. Petersburg, 1865. Translated as Shems ed-Din Abou Abdallah Mohammed de Damas. *Manuel de la Cosmographie du Moyen Âge*, trans. M.A.F. Mehren. Saint-Pétersbourg, 1874.

Modern Studies

Abou El Fadl, Khaled. "Islamic Law and Muslim Minorities: The Juristic Discourse on Muslim Minorities." *Islamic Law and Society* 1 (1994): 141–187.

Aigle, Denise. "Les inscriptions de Baybars dans le Bilad al-Šam. Une expression de la légitimité du pouvoir." *Studia Islamica* 97 (2003): 73–77.

Alam, Muzaffar. *The Language of Political Islam in India c. 1200–1800.* New Delhi, 2010.

Amitai-Preiss, Reuven. *Mongols and Mamluks: The Mamluk-Ilkhanid War, 1260–1281.* Cambridge, 1995.

Apellániz, Francisco. "News on the Bulaq: a Mamluk-Venetian Memorandum on Asian Trade, AD 1503." European University Institute, Department of History and Civilization. *EUI Working Paper HEC* 2016/01.

Al-Azmeh, Aziz. "Barbarians in Arab Eyes." *Past & Present* 134 (1992): 3–18.

Bashir, Shahzad. *Fazlallah Astarabadi and the Hurufis.* Oxford, 2005.

Behrens-Abouseif, Doris. *Practising Diplomacy in the Mamluk Sultanate: Gifts and Material Culture in the Medieval Islamic World.* London, 2014.

Burton, Richard F., trans. *The Book of the Thousand Nights and Night.* London, 1894.

Doufikar-Aerts, Faustina C.W. "King Midas' Ears on Alexander's Head: In Search of the Afro-Asiatic Alexander Cycle." In Richard Stoneman, Kyle Erickson and Ian Netton, eds. *The Alexander Romance in Persia and the East.* Groningen, 2012, 61–80.

Dunn, Ross. *The Adventures of Ibn Battuta, a Muslim Traveller of the Fourteenth Century.* Berkeley, 2005.

Elder, Earl Edgar, trans. *Commentary on the Creed of Islam: Sa'd al-Din al-Taftazani on the Creed of Najm al-Din al-Nasafi.* New York, 1950.

Frenkel, Yehoshua. "Al-Biqā'ī's Naval War-Report." In Stephan Conermann, ed. *History and Society during the Mamlūk Period (1250–1517).* Bonn, 2014, 9–20.

Frenkel, Yehoshua. "Animals and Otherness in Mamluk Egypt and Syria." In Francisco de Asís García García, Mónica Ann Walker Vadillo and María Victoria Chico Picazabar, eds. *Animals and Otherness in the Middle Ages: Perspectives across Disciplines.* Oxford, 2013, 52–55.

Frenkel, Yehoshua. "Embassies and Ambassadors in Mamluk Cairo." In Frédéric Bauden (convener), *Mamluk Cairo: A Crossroad for Embassies* (Université de Liège, September 2012) (in preparation for publication).

Frenkel, Yehoshua. "Mamlūk Embassies and Diplomats in 15th-century Mediterranean – The Mamlūk Sultanate in the days of Qāʾit-Bāy and the *al-Ifranj*." Unpublished paper at the Second Conference of the School of Mamlūk Studies, Liége, June 2015.

Frenkel, Yehoshua. "The Mamluks among the Nations: A Medieval Sultanate in its Global Context." In Stephan Conermann, ed. *Everything is on the Move: The Mamluk Empire as a Node in (Trans-) Regional Networks.* Bonn, 2014, 61–79.

Frenkel, Yehoshua. "Volksroman under the Mamluks: The Case of Tamīm ad-Dārī Popular Sira." In Stephan Conermann, ed. *History and Society during the Mamlūk Period* (1250–1517). Bonn, 2014, 21–36.

Friedlaender, Israel. *Die Chadhirlegende und der Alexanderroman: Eine sagengeschichtliche und literarhistorische Untersuchung.* Leipzig, 1913.

Ghersetti, Antonella. "The Semiotic Paradigm: Physiognomy and Medicine in Islamic Culture." In Simon Swain, ed. *Seeing the Face, Seeing the Soul: Polemon's Physiognomy from Classical Antiquity to Medieval Islam.* Oxford, 2007, 281–308.

Gibb, H.A.R., trans. *The Travels of Ibn Battuta A.D. 1325–1354.* Cambridge, 1958; repr. London, 1969.

Harvey, Leonard Patrick. *Muslims in Spain, 1500 to 1614.* Chicago Press, 2005.

Hinds, Martin and H. Sakkout, H. "A Letter from the Governor of Egypt to the King of Nubia and Muqurra concerning Egyptian-Nubian Relations in 141/758." In Wadad al-Qadi, ed. *Studia Arabica et Islamica. Festschrift for Ihsan Abbas.* Beirut, 1981, 209–229.

Hirschler, Konrad. "Ibn Wāṣil: An Ayyūbid Perspective on Frankish Lordships and Crusades." In Alex Mallett, ed. *Medieval Muslim Historians and the Franks in the Levant.* Leiden, 2015, 136–160.

Holt, Malcolm Peter. *Early Mamluk Diplomacy, 1260–1290.* Leiden, 1995.

Ibn ʿAbd al-Khāliq al-Azharī, Ṣāliḥ b. Muḥammad. *Al-Fihris al-waṣfī lil-nusakh al-khaṭṭiyyah li-muʾalifāt Yūsuf b. ʿAbd al-Hādī Ibn al-Mibrad.* Kuwait, 1433/2012.

Klęczar, Aleksandra. "The Kingship of Alexander the Great and the Jewish Versions of the Alexander Narrative." In Richard Stoneman, Kyle Erickson and Ian Netton, eds. *The Alexander Romance in Persia and the East.* Groningen, 2012, 61–79.

Lambourn, Elizabeth. "India from Aden: *Khutba* and Muslim Urban Networks in Late Thirteenth-Century India." In Kenneth Hall, ed. *Secondary Cities and Urban Networking in the Indian Ocean Realm, c. 1400–1800.* Lanham, MD, 2008, 55–98.

Lane, Edward William, trans. *The Arabian Nights' Entertainments.* London, 1840.

Mahdi, Muhsin, ed. *The Thousand and One Nights (Alf Layla wa-Layla) from the Earliest Known Sources.* Leiden, 1995. Translation in H. Haddawy. *The Arabian Nights.* New York, 1990.

Mannheim, Karl. *Essays on the Sociology of Knowledge*, edited by Paul Kecskemeti. London, 1952.

Marzolph, Ulrich and Richard van Leeuwen. *The Arabian Nights Encyclopedia.* Santa Barbara, 2004.

Marzolph, Ulrich. "Medieval Knowledge in Modern Reading: A Fifteenth-Century Arabic Encyclopaedia of *Omni re Scibili.*" In Peter Binkley, ed. *Pre-Modern Encyclopaedic Texts*

Proceedings of the Second COMERS Congress (Groningen, 1–4 July 1996). Leiden, 1997, 407–419.

Mazor, Amir. *The Rise and Fall of a Muslim Regiment: The Mansuriyya in the First Mamluk Sultanates 678/1279–741/1341*. Bonn, 2015.

Müller, Hans. *Die Kunst des Sklavenkaufs*. Freiburg, 1980.

Reinaud, Joseph Toussaint. *Relation des voyages faits par les Arabes et les Persans dans l'Inde et à la Chine dans le IXe siècle de l'ère chrétienne*. Paris, 1845.

Ritter, Hellmut. "Ein arabisches Handbuch der Handelswissenschaft." *Der Islam* 7 (1916): 1–91.

Rubiés, Joan-Pau. *Travel and Ethnology in the Renaissance. South India through European Eyes, 1250–1625*. Cambridge, 2000.

El-Sayed, El-Bushra. "Perspectives on the Contribution of Arabs and Muslims to Geography." *GeoJournal* 26/2 (1992): 157–166.

de Slane, William McGuckin. *Catalogue des manuscrits arabes*. Paris, 1883–1895.

Spaulding, Jay. "Medieval Christian Nubia and the Islamic World: A Reconsideration of the Baqt Treaty." *The International Journal of African Historical Studies* 28/3 (1995): 577–594.

Toorawa, Shawkat M. "Waqwaq: Fabulous, Fabular, Indian Ocean (?) Island(s)." *Emergences* 10/2 (2000): 387–402.

Viladrich, Mercè. "Solving the 'Accursed Riddle' of the Diplomatic Relations between Catalonia and Egypt around 1430." *Al-Masaq* 14/1 (2002): 25–31.

Waines, David. *The Odyssey of Ibn Battuta: Uncommon Tales of a Medieval Adventurer*. Chicago, 2010.

Wansbrough, John. "A Mamluk Ambassador to Venice in 913/1507." *Bulletin of the School of Oriental and African Studies* 26 (1963): 503–530.

Wheeler, Brannon M. *Moses in the Qur'an and Islamic Exegesis*. London, 2002.

Wing, Patrick. "Indian Ocean Trade and Sultanic Authority: The nāẓir of Jeddah and the Mamluk Political Economy." *Journal of the Economic and Social History of the Orient* 57 (2014): 55–75.

Wolf, Mark J.P., ed. *The Routledge Companion to Imaginary Worlds*. New York: 2018.

Albrecht Fuess (Philipps University, Marburg)

How to Cope with the Scarcity of Commodities? The Mamluks' Quest for Metal

Introduction

For French Historian Fernand Braudel there is no history without geography. History, as he understands it, is not the sole result of human acts or social circumstances. The geographical settings are as well of outmost importance, as geography presents a tool to grasp long term developments in historic cycles and has the advantage of being less capricious and therefore very helpful in tracking down underlying structures. "La géographie, à ce jeu, cesse d'être un but en soi pour devenir un moyen. Elle aide à retrouver les plus lentes des réalités structurales, à organiser une mise en perspective selon la ligne de fuite de la plus longue durée."[1] The leading role of geography in French historical science is related to the fact that French pupils are taught the subject "Histoire – Geographie" in public schools. There is thus a high sensibility among French historians to place the history of mankind within its specific geographic milieu. In the Anglophone and German speaking scientific tradition this is less the case. Here both subjects are more separated. However due to the "spatial turn"[2] in cultural studies in the late Eighties the academic view on Geography, so much discredited, especially in Germany, by the "Lebensraum im Osten" concept of Nazi Germany, re-entered the academic debate. One proponent of this rediscovering Geography is thereby Karl Schlögel "Usually historiography follows time, its pattern is the chronicle, the timely sequence of events. This dominance of the temporal in the historical narrative and in philosophical thinking (…) has almost developed into common law and has been implicitly accepted and not been questioned any more", but he reminds us to recognize that this is not sufficient: "History does not occur solely in time, but in space as well". ("Ge-

1 Fernand Braudel, *La Méditerranée et Monde méditerranéen à l'époque de Philippe II.* (Paris: Armand Colin, [9]1990), vol. 1, 27.

2 See: Doris Bachmann-Medick: *Spatial Turn.* In: Doris Bachmann-Medick: *Cultural Turns. Neuorientierungen in den Kulturwissenschaften* . 3rd, revised ed. (Reinbek bei Hamburg: Rowohlt, 2009), 284–328.

schichte spielt nicht nur in der Zeit, sondern auch im Raum").[3] But despite a continuing presence of geographical approaches by French academia and a renewed interest by German and Anglophone academia, geographical settings as important aspect has not reached completely contemporary research in Oriental and Islamic studies. This can be explained by the strong philological approach of both fields since they have emerged very much from faculties of Theology and their interest in scriptural writings. There this might have lead to overemphasize textual evidence and unwittingly to neglect the space where history happens.

The following paper will therefore try to look at geography and especially the questions of resources within the geopolitical setting of the Mamluk Empire of the fifteenth and beginning of the sixteenth century. This will be done in order to compare it with its neighbours and add new sights on the history of the Middle East in the fifttheenth and sixteenth centuries. In this article the case of metal will be taken as an exemplary approach of the Mamluks towards resources. The Mamluk stance on the issue was thereby two-fold. On one hand they looked for resources within their own realm and on the other hand they relied on import. By comparing the Mamluk sultanate through a geopolitical lens with its strongest neighbours, i. e. the Ottoman Sultanate and the Safavid Empire the frame of their tripartite struggle might be further clarified. In their clashes they fought about political supremacy but as well over resources and fertile lands. For example the Ottoman – Mamluk war of 1485–1491 over Cilicia was in main parts a military quest for wood in times of a very ambitious Ottoman naval programme under Sultan Bayezid II.[4] However, in this example we already encounter an important caveat about geopolitical determinism. The Mamluks had the overlordship over Cilicia for long periods of time, but did not use it for a strong naval programme, as their main naval bases and arsenals on the Egyptian coast were quite too far away to transport the lumber over the dangerous Mediterranean, with its storms and pirates. The Mamluks were therefore less interested in lumber, but wanted control over the region in order to profit from its tributes and taxes. The same holds true for the Safavids, as their interest in naval activities was almost nil due to the specific geographical setting of its Empire. They wanted to control Eastern Anatolia as many of their followers from Qizilbash tribes lived there. Therefore "one" has to acknowledge that the same region might have very different functions even for neighbouring empires, depending on the specific hinterland and political constellations. Another point shall also be stressed here as well. It is not the aim of the paper to explain the downfall of the Mamluks solely as a direct

3 Karl Schlögel, *Im Raume Lesen wir die Zeit. Über Zivilisationsgeschichte und Geopolitik* (Frankfurt: Fischer, ^{3}2009), 9.

4 Hans Joachim *Kissling*, "Betrachtungen über die *Flottenpolitik* Sultan Bayezids II (1481–1512)," *Saeculum*, 20/1 (1969), 35–43.

consequence of resource scarceness and geopolitical settings. This kind of explanation would be too short sighted, but it shall be stressed that the resource situation was an important aspect for the history of the Near and Middle East in the premodern era.

Mamluks and Metal

Bullion. A vital resource for the Middle East is represented by bullion in order to be minted for coins as means of payment. Unfortunately, bullion is to be found only very seldom in the Middle East and West-Asia. Gold was very scarce in the Mamluk Empire and its import from Europe was well needed. Originally gold had come in Egypt from the Wādī al-ʿAlāqī region to the southeast of Aswan and often gold had been taken as well from Pharaonic graves. External gold arrived mainly from West Africa, the famous *bilād al-Takrūr.*[5] Unforgotten were in the Mamluk memory two legendary visits of rulers from *bilād al-Takrūr* in the thirteenth and fourteenth century on their way to Mecca. They apparently flooded the Market with such amounts of Gold that the *dīnār* lost considerable in value vis-à-vis the silver *dirham.* The ruler of Mali, Mansā al-Mūsā, is supposed to have given the sultan an *ḥiml* (camel load) of pure gold and apparently he carried with him even 100 *ḥiml* of gold which he generously distributed among the people during his pilgrimage.[6] Although the details of the story might be exaggerated it hints at two aspects. The Mamluks did not have own gold at hand and it usually came from sub-Saharan Africa. Unfortunately for the Mamluks, the Europeans interrupted of the trans-Saharan gold trade by redirecting it via the Maghreb to Europe in the fourteenth century. This then coincided in the 1370s with the collapse of Chinese and Middle Eastern silver production, so the whole bullion market was until the beginning of the fifteenth century in Central and Southern European hands.[7] African Gold reached the Mamluk Empire now through Italian sea faring nations, mainly Genoa and Venice. Venice played especially a leading role in this trade in the period from 1385 to 1412. The use of the Venetian gold ducat became widespread according to Ibn Taghrībirdī: "The use of this Euro-

5 Subhi Labib, *Handelsgeschichte Ägyptens im Spätmittelalter (1171–1517)* (Wiesbaden: Franz Steiner 1965), 261; ʿUmar al-Naqar, "Takrūr. The History of a Name," *The Journal of African History,* 10/3 (1969), 365–374.

6 Al-Maqrīzī, *Kitāb al-sulūk li-maʿrifa duwal al-mulūk,* ed. by Muḥammad Muṣṭafā Ziyāda, Cairo: Maṭbaʿa Lajnat al-Taʾlīf wa-Tarjam wa-Nashr 1956, II/1, 255; al-Qalqashandī, *Ṣubḥ al-Aʿshā fī Ṣinaʿat al-Inshā ʾ,* ed. Muḥammad Ḥusayn Shams al-Dīn, vol. 5 (Beirut: Dār al-kutub al-ʿilmīya), 278, 284; ʿUmar al-Naqar, "Takrūr," 370.

7 Ian Blanchard, *Mining, Metallurgy and Minting in the Middle Ages,* vol. 3: *Continuing Afro-European Supremacy, 1250–1450* (Stuttgart: Franz Steiner Verlag, 2005), 1309.

pean coinage ("ifrantī") had become frequent [since the beginning of the 800's/1397] in most of the cities of the world such as Cairo, Old Cairo, Syria, most of Asia Minor, the East, Hijaz and Yaman."[8]

As Jere Bacharach has shown in his ground breaking article "The dinar vs. the ducat" from 1973 Mamluk Sultans of the period tried to overcome the use of the Venetian ducat by minting own coins. However, it was only Sultan Barsbay (r. 1422–1438) who should succeed to abolish the use of the ducat in the Egyptian home market. Ibn Taghrībirdī depicts the following situation for the month of Ṣafar 829 (December 1425): "The sultan assembled the emirs, cadis and many merchants, and discussed with them the abolition of the use of the figured gold coin called the "ifrantī," a coinage of the Franks bearing the insignia of their infidelity, something which is not permitted by Islamic Law; he proposed that instead of it be struck a gold coinage with an Islamic stamp."[9] It seems that the gold for doing so might have been plundered in two subsequent raids on Cyprus in the years 1424 and 1425. A steady influx of gold then came a year later after the final conquest of Cyprus in 1426 and the ransom of 200,000 ducats the Cypriotes had to pay for King Janus who had been captured. The first payment of 50,000 ducats arrived in *Muḥarram* 831/*October* 1429 in Cairo. The sultan al-Ashraf Barsbāy (r. 1422–1438) immediately had the ducats re-minted as *ashrafī dīnār*s and this move helped to abandon the use of the Venetian ducat in the Mamluk empire.[10] In the following time period the annual tribute of 8000 ducats the kingdom of Cyprus had to pay to the Mamluks, ensured a steady source for re-minting.[11] Minting was done in Alexandria and Cairo. Cypriot gold was important as in the fifteenth century the gold of *bilād al-Takrūr* did not reach Egypt directly through the trans-Saharan trade any more. When the Portuguese then did install themselves at the cost of West Africa they took a firm grip on the African gold and brought it to Europe thereby avoiding the Maghrebi intermediaries.[12] The general gold scarcity later in that century in the Mamluk Empire let Sultan Qāyitbāy debase the *dīnār* and fix the weight at 3.37 grams instead of the 3.41 grams under Sultan Barsbay and Ibn Iyās tells us that the gold

8 Ibid., 1310; Ibn Taghrībirdī, *al-Nujūm al-Zāhira fī Mulūk Miṣr wa-al-Qāhira* ed. William Popper (Berkeley: University of California Press, 1936), VI, 596; William Popper, *History of Egypt 1382–1469 A.D.* (Berkeley: University of California Press, 1960), IV, 30.

9 Ibid.

10 Bacharach, Jere L. "The Dinar vs. the Ducat," *International Journal for Middle East Studies.* 4 (1973), 88.

11 See: Albrecht Fuess, "Was Cyprus a Mamluk Protectorate? Mamluk Influence on Cyprus between 1426 and 1517," *Journal of Cyprus Studies*, 11 (2005), [28/29], 22.

12 Labib, *Handelsgeschichte Ägyptens*, 272.

dīnārs under the last Mamluk sultan Qānṣawh al-Ghawrī represented a tremendous cheat for the people.[13]

The first descriptions of Ottoman gold coins are to be found in European sources from the 1420s onwards. Before that time the Ottomans relied on silver coins. In any case, the ducat's influence was clearly felt in the Ottoman Empire as well and the Ottoman authorities followed the Mamluk example and struck "ducat-like" gold coins in the 1470s after a fifteen years war with Venice had ended. The new gold coins were called *hasene* or *sulṭānī* and their weight (3.572 gr. to 3.51 gr.) and fineness was slightly higher than the Ashrafi and the Ducat. "Despite two small adjustments in the sixteenth century, the weight and the fineness of the *sulṭānī* remained basically unchanged until late in the seventeenth century."[14] The introduction of gold coins in the Ottoman Empire acknowledged the great role of gold coins in the Mediterranean trade, where the ducat had become the prime means of international trade settlements. Minting its own gold coins was a sign of showing the importance of the Ottoman Empire towards the Europeans and the Mamluks alike as the leading Muslim gold coin so far had been the Mamluk Ashrafi. The Ottoman gold derived mainly from Central and Eastern Europe in exchange for Oriental goods and some local gold was extracted in the Ottoman Balkans.[15] In contrast to the Ottomans and the Mamluks, the Safavids were not able to install a long lasting gold currency. The region of Iran always encountered problems acquiring gold. There was just not enough gold to struck gold coins on a regular basis. In the Ilkhanid period the traditional name for the Islamic gold coin *dīnār* was even used for silver coins as well.[16] At the beginning of the Safavid era there was therefore no appellation for gold coins. They were commonly just referred to as *tala*, i.e. gold pieces, but sometimes named *ashrafīs* using the name of the Mamluk gold coin.[17] Shāh Ismāʿīl (r. 1501–1524) did apparently struck these new gold coins copying the Mamluk and Ottoman monetary binary gold and silver system, but this should stay an exception.[18]

The silver *dirham* is the second classic Muslim coin. Traditionally a gold *dīnār* of one *mithqāl* (4.25 gr) corresponded to 20 to 25 *dirhams*. After the introduction of the gold Ashrafi of 3.41 gr. following the Venetian ducat the ratio changed. The

13 Ibn Iyās, *Badāʾiʿ al-Zuhūr fī Waqāʾiʿ al-Duhūr*, ed. Mohamed Mostafa, vol. IV (Wiesbaden: Franz Steiner, 1960, 153.

14 Şevket Pamuk, "Evolution of the Ottoman Monetary System", in *An Economic and Social History of the Ottoman Empire*, ed. Halil Inalcik, vol. 2: *1600–1914* (Cambridge: Cambridge University Press, 1994), 953–954.

15 Pamuk, "Evolution of the Ottoman Monetary System," 955.

16 Monika Gronke, *Derwische im Vorhof der Macht* (Stuttgart: Franz Steiner, 1993), 232.

17 Willem Floor, *Economy of Safavid Persia* (Wiesbaden: Reichert, 2000), 71.

18 Ibid., 76.

silver *dirhams* of the early fifteenth century were thinner, lighter, but of finer silver than their predecessors.[19] A main problem in the production of silver coins in the Mamluk Empire of the fifteenth century is that silver became very scarce for decades. As silver had to be generally imported from Europe this reflected the contemporary "silver famine" in Europe. Mines in central Europe had been emptied with the customary extraction methods and many of the precious metals had already left Central Europe in direction for the Levant in order to pay for spices and other goods and from there they had gone to India.[20] According to Peter Spufford, the African and Hungarian gold and the Serbian and Bosnian silver did not suffice to compensate for the outflow to the Middle East and the challenges of an international economy.[21] In contemporary Egypt, though, the Sultans were accused to have deliberately stopped minting silver coins.[22] There was even the claim that Mamluk silver had been exported to Europe for the benefit of Mamluk officials.[23] This, of course, did not correspond to the truth but there had to be an explanation for the disappearance of silver. However, when Martin Claus of Gotha solved the problem of water influx in the silver mines in the late fifties of the fifteenth centuries, mining resumed to pre-crisis level in Central Europe.[24] Moreover, new mines were discovered like the one at Schwats in Tirol in 1448 and later near the town of Joachimsthal in Bohemia, discovered in 1516.

Unfortunately, there were no silver ores in Mamluk Egypt to exploit. Because of the scarcity of silver, copper was increasingly used for coins in the fifteenth century. "As late as 1436 the Mamluke regime banned the use of silver for making vessels and utensils, and the people of Cairo were repeatedly instructed to deliver whatever silver they had to the mint."[25] A first Ottoman silver coin is said to be minted in 1326, during the reign of Sultan Orhan (r. 1324–1360). Its name was *akçe*, which has the connotation of "white". In the European West it was called an "asper." It weighted 1.15 grams in the beginning of the fourteenth century and although its weight did change during the following periods, its fineness was

19 Warren Schultz, "The Monetary History of Egypt, 642–1517," in *The Cambridge History of Egypt*, ed. by Carl Petry, Vol 1: *Islamic Egypt, 640–1517* (Cambridge: Cambridge University Press, 1998), 336.

20 Peter Spufford, *Money and its Use in Medieval Europe* (Cambridge: Cambridge University Press, 1989), 355.

21 Ibid., 356.

22 Maqrīzī, *Sulūk*, IV, 28–29.

23 Boaz Shoshan, "Exchange-Rate Policies in Fifteenth Century Egypt," in *Journal of the Economic and Social History of the Orient*, 29/1 (1986), 42.

24 M.M. Postan, *Medieval Trade and Finance* (Cambridge: Cambridge University Press, 2002), 171.

25 Shoshan, "Exchange-Rate Policies," 50; al-Maqrīzī, *Sulūk*, IV, 977. Ibn Iyās, *Badāʾiʿ*, II, 170.

upheld up to the end of the seventeenth century.[26] Mints were established in close connections to the silver mines on the Balkans. The *akçe* was the basic monetary unit of the Ottoman Empire in the fifteenth century. However, during the above mentioned "silver famine" the Ottomans prohibited the exportation of bullion. All bullion, be it local or imported, had to be transported to the Ottoman mints in order to produce coins.[27] Still, the Ottomans had the huge advantage compared to its Eastern neighbours to possess their own silver mines. Safavid silver coins had a very fine alloy and were smelted and purified before being coined as Persian currency.[28] Silver for the production of coins though had to be completely imported.[29] The term for the silver coins was *shāhī*. Besides, the denomination *dirham* was apparently used, but there was no actual coin with that name.[30] Paying with copper coins was limited for local business and trade and was usually not accepted by state officials when dealing with the state or paying taxes. Speaking of copper is repeating the same principal outline which was already mentioned for silver. The Ottoman Empire had its own abundant resources and the Mamluks and Safavids had to import them which made it more expensive for them.[31] Francesco Appelaniz has shown that starting with 1495 copper played an increasing role in Mamluk Venetian commerce, as Venice now paid for spices with copper instead of silver. The higher importation of the Venetians apparently reached the ears of the Ottomans as well who flooded the copper market of Alexandria.[32] The reason for switching from silver to copper is matter of debate and I will return to this issue later.

Metals for the Military Industry[33]

Other very important natural resources for the canon and firearms industry were also searched for in the Middle East of the fifteenth century. Saltpetre (Potassium Nitrate) was very important for the gunpowder production. There are large

26 Pamuk, "Evolution of the Ottoman Monetary System," 950.

27 Ibid., 951.

28 Floor, *Economy of Safavid Persia,* 73.

29 Willem Floor and Patrick Clawson, "Safavid Iran's Search for Silver and Gold," in *International Journal for Middle East Studies,* 32/3 (2000), 352.

30 Floor, *Economy of Safavid Persia,* 73.

31 Şevket Pamuk, *A Monetary History of the Ottoman Empire* (Cambridge: Cambridge Uniersity Press, 2000), 38.

32 Francisco Javier Appellániz Ruiz de Galarreta, *Pouvoir et Finance en Méditerranée pré-Moderne: Le deuxième état mamelouk et le commerce des épices (1382–1517)* (Barcelona: Consejo Superior de Investigaciones Científicas, 2009), 251–252.

33 For the issue of the development of Ottoman and Mamluk firearms, see: Albrecht Fuess, "Les Janissaires, les Mamlouks et les armes à feu. Une comparaison des systèmes militaires ottoman et mamlouk à partir de la moitié du quinzième siècle," *Turcica,* 41 (2009), 209–227.

natural deposits in India, Arabia and China, because they had suitable climatic conditions, i. e. hot climate and humidity. Most of Europe was deficient in this important ingredient of gunpowder, but Ottoman lands however possessed abundant saltpetre deposits.[34] For example, there were production centres in the *sancak* of Silistre and near Edirne in the Balkans. In Asia Minor there were several sites and by the seventeenth century thousands of families were making saltpetre for the gunpowder industries.[35] Sulphur could not be extracted from Ottoman soils in the same ample qualities than saltpetre. It was very hard work to extract the sulphur from the ore and in the Ottoman Empire only some of it could be found in the provinces of Van, Moldavia, on the Island of Melos and especially in Macedonia.[36] Because of the relative scarcity of sulphur it had to be transported from far for the production in the gunpowder mills. Necessary charcoal for melting processes was produced in Asia Minor, especially from oak.[37] Concerning ore deposits, Agoston states, "Unlike many of its rivals, the Ottoman Empire possessed rich ore deposits that were crucial in establishing domestic production capabilities."[38] Iron and copper could be found in large quantities, however the Empire lacked tin. This could constitute a problem as the majority of Ottoman cannons were cast of bronze, a copper-tin alloy. Tin had therefore quite often to be smuggled from Europe as the pope had banned the export of tin, copper and iron to the enemies of Christianity. But apparently there were enough European powers, like the French, in the century century who provided the Ottomans with the necessary tin in order that the Ottomans could fight the Habsburg Empire. Iron was found especially in present-day Bulgaria and Anatolia. Lead was extracted in the Empire's silver mines.[39] Copper was found in rich depositories in the Balkans and Anatolia, especially at the Black Sea near Trabzon.[40] With regard to natural resources to be used in military field, one can remark that from our modern day perspective Safavid Persia was potentially richly endowed with a variety of metals and minerals. However, most of the potential mining sites lay in very hostile natural surroundings and less populated areas. Transportation from these regions would have been very expensive. Therefore most mineral resources were imported, despite the fact that they could have been extracted in Iran itself.[41] Lead mines were found near Kerman and Yazd, but demand was apparently not

34 Gabor Agoston, *Guns for the Sultan. Military Power and the Weapons Industry in the Ottoman Empire* (Cambridge: Cambridge University Press, 2005), 97.
35 Ibid., 98.
36 Ibid., 100.
37 Ibid., 103.
38 Ibid., 165.
39 Ibid., 174.
40 Ibid., 171.
41 Floor, *Economy of Safavid Persia*, 303.

very high. However, iron was to be found at several places in Safavid Persia and there was no scarcity of this element. Apparently there was no shortage of copper, but the main purpose for which it was searched was coinage.[42]

The Mamluk Quest for Military Commodities and Metal

In contrast to the Ottomans and Safavids, the Mamluks lacked completely many of these important military resources. It seems that iron was very sparse in Mamluk times. In Syria only one iron mine near Beirut is mentioned by the Maghrebi traveller Ibn Baṭṭūṭa for the year 1326. From Beirut the iron was then exported to Egypt.[43] In general it seems that there was a shortage of metals and gunpowder ingredients in the Mamluk Empire, as the Mamluks had to ask the Ottomans for these materials when they wanted to fight the Portuguese in the Red Sea at the beginning of the sixteenth century.[44] In order to become self sufficient in the building of guns or casting of canons, the Mamluks looked actively for necessary ingredients such as copper within their realm. Apparently there were some ores for local minting use, but nothing compared to the Ottoman mines. In Ramaḍān 914/January 1509 the architect (*al-miʿmar*) Khayrbak, who had been ordered to ʿAqaba to erect towers and a *khān* send to sultan Qānṣawh al-Ghawrī stones in which he claimed to have found copper (*al-nuḥās al-aṣfar*). The sultan had the metal inside the stones cast and found out that there were apparently only negligible quantities of copper inside.[45] Copper, lead and tin were apparently very sparse. In Syria, the Ottomans would later on extract saltpetre in large quantities near Aleppo and sulphur besides the Dead Sea.[46] The Mamluks did not, so it seems, know at the beginning of the sixteenth century about these saltpetre deposits. Around 1510, an honest man came to Qānṣawh al-Ghawrī and told that he had found saltpetre near al-Karak. He cooked it and remarked that this was excellent saltpetre. The sultan rejoiced about this and bestowed upon the man 10 *dīnār*. He ordered to extract much more of the saltpetre.[47] However, even if saltpetre was now available in larger quantities, the lack of sulphur (*kibrīt*) was severely felt during preparations for an expedition against the Portuguese in 919/1514. The price soared but still little was found.[48]

42 Ibid., 66, 305.

43 Ibn Baṭṭūṭa, *Riḥlat Ibn Baṭṭūṭa* (Beirut: Dār Ṣādir, 1964), 62.

44 David Ayalon, *Gunpowder and Firearms in the Mamluk Kingdom: A Challenge to a Medieval Society* (London: Frank Cass, 1978), 130, note 258.

45 Ibn Iyās, *Badāʾiʿ*, IV, 144, Ayalon, *Gunpowder and Firearms*, 130, note 258.

46 Agoston, *Guns for the Sultan*, 99–100.

47 Ibn Iyās, *Badāʾiʿ*, IV, 204.

48 Ibid., 355.

Looking Elsewhere for Resources

Given the fact that Venice had been the main trading partner of Egypt and Syria at the end of the Mamluk era, it seems highly likely that the Mamluks would have turned for help in matters of natural resources towards the Venetians.[49] After the Venetians had taken over Cyprus through inheritance in 1489, they continued to pay the yearly tribute to the Mamluk sultan and had apparently even agreed that four Venetian ships would protect the Egyptian and Syrian shores against pirate incursions.[50] We know moreover that Italian military experts where present in the Mamluk Empire when the Great-Dawadar Āqbardī turned against Sultan al-Nāṣir Muḥammad II (r. 1496–1498) and besieged him in August of 1497 (Dhū al-ḥijja 902) in the citadel. He did so with the help of an Italian canon caster and troops with fire arms.[51] The outcome was unfortunate for this canon caster, Domenico, as he lost his head after the defeat of Āqbardī, which was later to be shown on a pike on Bāb al-Silsila.[52] The urge for valuable military resources and experts however increased even more after the Portuguese sailed round Africa and appeared in East Africa and the Red Sea. In these contexts, something really astonishing happened. For the first time in their history the Mamluk Sultan Qānṣawh al-Ghawrī (r. 1501–1516) sent an envoy to Venice, the apparently Spanish-born Dragoman Taghrībirdī, who was to stay ten months in Venice from the end of 1506 until mid-1507. During his stay, ambassadors went back and forth between Cairo and Venice asked the sultan for his consent before the final agreement was settled.[53] John Wansborough has argued that the main purpose of the visit were trade agreements. However, I would add to this matter the the request for military aid. The Mamluks had concluded trade agreements with Italian cities for centuries in Cairo, why should they now go abroad for the first time if they did not feel that it was essential for them? Recognizing European nations as equal by those envoys marked an unusual break with their established foreign policy.

There are two clues that allow me to speculate regarding the quest for military aid. In the first paragraph of the agreement of May 1507 it is written that the

49 For the discussion about the Venetian-Mamluk relations, see: Albrecht Fuess, "Why Venice, not Genoa? How Venice Emerged as the Mamluks' Favourite European Trading Partner after 1365," in *Union in Separation – Diasporic Groups and Identities in the Eastern Mediterranean (1100–1800)*, ed. Georg Christ et al. (Rome: Viella, 2015), 251–266.

50 Joseph Toussaint Reinaud, "Traités de commerce entre la république de Venise et les derniers sultans mameloucs d'Égypte, traduits de l'italien, et accompagnés d'éclaircissements par M. Reinaud," *Journal Asiatique, 2ème* serie, 4 (1829), 34–35; see also: Fuess, "Was Cyprus a Mamluk Protectorate?," 20.

51 Ibn Iyās, *Badāʾiʿ*, III, 366–376.

52 Ibn Iyās, *Badāʾiʿ*, III, 375.

53 See: John Wansbrough, "A Mamluk Ambassador to Venice in 913/1507," *Bulletin of the School of Oriental and African Studies*, 26/3 (1963), 503–530.

Venetians could pay taxes and debts in copper. While it has been argued that this constituted a sign of weakness from the part of the sultan, that he would now accept copper instead of silver, we can note that his army could make good use of it, as contemporary bronze canons consisted of more than 60% copper.[54] For example Sultan Qānṣawh al-Ghawrī ordered 200 canons to be send to Alexandria in February of 1516 to secure the port.[55] Where did the necessary copper come from? Some came from the Ottomans, but was this sufficient? The second clue concerns an episode of the year 1510 when the Venetian-Mamluk relationship was put under heavy strain after the Mamluks had captured Venetian envoys near Aleppo who had allegedly proposed to the Safavid Shah Ismāʿīl a military alliance. Sanuto recalls in his *Diarii* that at this point the former envoy, the drogoman Taghrībirdī, became very angry and complained heavily that besides this treason the Signoria had failed to send gifts and artillery, which Venice had promised to send to the Sultan during his stay in Italy.[56] However, the report of Thomà Contarini, the Venetian Consul in Alexandria, quoted by Sanuto outrightly denied the truth of these allegations, saying that Taghrībirdī had made this all up and had made it sound as if Venice had promised the Mamluk sultan "Maria et montes" ("the seas and mountains") but of course this was not true.[57] Apparently Taghrībirdī's had travelled as an envoy to the Ottomans before the mutual Mamluk-Ottoman naval expedition against the Portuguese had had more success.[58] In 916/1510–11 a Mamluk embassy had requested material help from the Ottomans and received 300 guns, 30,000 arrows, copper, iron, timber and large quantities (40 *qanṭar)* of good quality saltpetre (*bārud muṭayyab).*[59] Another sign for the quest for military help in times of war with the Ottomans is related by Ibn Iyās. He relates the story that Sultan Ṭūmān Bāy immediately after the defeat of Marj Dābiq at the beginning of 1517 had asked the Hospitallers of Rhodes for help, and that unconfirmed rumors stated that the Hospitallers had sent 40 military experts and artillery.[60]

These short collection of stories and anecdotes however seem to underline the fact that Mamluk Sultans were looking for natural resources for the military sector inside and outside of their realm. There was apparently not a steady influx of these goods from abroad, but more of an on-and-off trade depending upon the political circumstances. However, it was nothing that the European trading partners would have liked to be written down in an official agreement.

54 Wansbrough, "A Mamluk Ambassador," 525.
55 Ibn Iyās, *Badāʾiʿ*, IV, 471; V, 14.
56 Marino Sanuto, *I Diarii*, vol. XII (Venice: A spesi degli Editori,1886), 236.
57 Ibid.
58 Wansbrough, "A Mamluk Ambassador," 510.
59 Ibn Iyās, *Badāʾiʿ*, IV, 201.
60 Ibn Iyās, *Badāʾiʿ*, V, 139.

Conclusion

Which conclusion can be drawn from this discussion of resources? The Ottoman Empire possessed in abundance most resources that were needed for the context of the early sixteenth century. The Safavids are apparently second to the Ottomans in terms of resources, but they have just constituted their empire and are certainly still not aware of all its geographical potentials. The Mamluks were not favoured in the aspects depicted here compared to their neighbours. The Ottomans could therefore better cope with the resource challenge and also did not fall back behind their Central European neighbours. On the other hand, they could exploit the disadvantages in this sector of its Eastern neighbours. The Mamluks officials were well aware of their lack of commodities and tried to cope with it as best as they could. Numerous reforms of the fifteenth century, be it monetary, military or agricultural, are witness to these efforts as is their quest for metals. However, the costs of keeping up these levels seemed to have exhausted the Empire and the resource situation represented certainly a vital point where they could not match the Ottomans.

Table: Resource Situation around the Turn of the 16th Century in the Middle East

End of 15th Century	Ottoman Empire	Safavid Empire	Mamluk Empire
Saltpetre	Abundant	Potentially there (But not mined in the Early 16th century)	Shortage. In 1516 large quantities were found near al-Karak
Sulphur	Sufficient (Long transport ways)	Potentially there (Unclear if mined in 16th century)	Shortage at the beginning of the 16th century
Charcoal	Abundant	Enough, if needed	Could be obtained, but not an everyday good
Iron	Abundant	Abundant	Sparse. Only one mine near Beirut
Copper	Abundant	Sufficient.	Sparse
Tin	Not sufficient. Had to be imported	Very sparse	sparse
Lead	Abundant	Sufficient	Sparse
Gold	Gold mines available	Had to be imported.	Had to be imported or came as tribute from Cyprus
Silver	Abundant	Had to be imported	Had to be imported

Bibliography

Primary Sources

Ibn Baṭṭūṭa, *Riḥlat Ibn Baṭṭūṭa*. Beirut: Dār Ṣādir, 1964.

Ibn Iyās, *Badāʾiʿ al-Zuhūr fī Waqāʾiʿ al-Duhūr*, ed. Mohamed Mostafa. Wiesbaden: Franz Steiner, 1960–1975. 5 vols.

Ibn Taghrībirdī, *al-Nujūm al-Zāhira fī Mulūk Miṣr wal-Qāhira*, ed. William Popper. Berkeley: University of California Press, 1909–1960. 5 vols.; English Translation: William Popper, *History of Egypt 1382–1469 A.D.* Berkeley: University of California Press, 1954–1963. 9 vols.

al-Maqrīzī, *Kitāb al-sulūk li-maʿrifat duwal al-mulūk*, ed. by Muḥammad Muṣṭafā Ziyāda, Cairo: Maṭbaʿ at Lajnat al-Taʾlīf wal-Tarjam wal-Nashr, 1934–73. 4 vols., 12 parts.

al-Qalqashandī, *Ṣubḥ al-Aʿshā fī Ṣināʿat al-Inshāʾ*, ed. Muḥammad Ḥusayn Shams al-Dīn. Beirut: Dār al-Kutub al-ʿIlmīya 2000. 15 vols.

Sanuto, Marino. *I Diarii.* Venice: A spesidegli Editori, 1879–1902. 58 vols.

Secondary Sources

Agoston, Gabor. *Guns for the Sultan. Military Power and the Weapons Industry in the Ottoman* Empire. Cambridge: Cambridge University Press, 2005.

Appelláníz Ruiz de Galarreta, Francisco Javier. *Pouvoir et Finance en Méditerranée pré-Moderne: Le deuxième état mamelouk et le commerce des épices (1382–1517).* Barcelona: Consejo Superior de Investigaciones Científicas, 2009.

Ayalon, David. *Gunpowder and Firearms in the Mamluk Kingdom: A Challenge to a Medieval Society.* London: Frank Cass, 1978.

Bacharach, Jere L. "The Dinar vs. the Ducat." *International Journal for Middle East Studies.* 4 (1973), 77–96.

Bachmann-Medick, Doris. "Spatial Turn." In Doris Bachmann-Medick, ed. *Cultural Turns. Neuorientierungen in den Kulturwissenschaften.* 3rd, revised ed. Reinbek bei Hamburg: Rowohlt, 2009. 284–328.

Blanchard, Ian. *Mining, Metallurgy and Minting in the Middle Ages*, vol. 3: *Continuing Afro-European Supremacy*, 1250–1450. Stuttgart: Franz Steiner Verlag, 2005.

Braudel, Fernand. *La Méditerranée et le monde méditerranéen à l'époque de Philippe II.* 9Paris: Armand Colin 1990. 3 vols.

Floor, Willem. *Economy of Safavid Persia.* Wiesbaden: Reichert, 2000.

Floor, Willem and Patrick Clawson. "Safavid Iran's Search for Silver and Gold." *International Journal for Middle East Studies.* 32/3 (2000), 345–368.

Fuess, Albrecht. "Les Janissaires, les Mamlouks et les armes à feu. Une comparaison des systèmes militaires ottoman et mamlouk à partir de la moitié du quinzième siècle." *Turcica.* 41 (2009), 209–227.

–. "Was Cyprus a Mamluk Protectorate? Mamluk Influence on Cyprus between 1426 and 1517." *Journal of Cyprus Studies.* 11 (2005), [28/29], 11–28.

–. "Why Venice, not Genoa? How Venice Emerged as the Mamluks' Favourite European Trading Partner after 1365." In *Union in Separation – Diasporic Groups and Identities in the Eastern Mediterranean (1100–1800)*, ed. Georg Christ et al. Rome: Viella, 2015. 251–266.

Gronke, Monika. *Derwische im Vorhof der Macht.* Stuttgart: Franz Steiner, 1993.

Kissling, Hans Joachim. "Betrachtungen über die Flottenpolitik Sultan Bayezids II (1481–1512)." *Saeculum.* 20/1 (1969), 35–43.

Labib, Subhi. *Handelsgeschichte Ägyptens im Spätmittelalter (1171–1517).* Wiesbaden: Franz Steiner 1965.

al-Naqar, ʿUmar. "Takrūr. The History of a Name," *The Journal of African History*, 10/3 (1969), 365–374.

Pamuk, Şevket. *A Monetary History of the Ottoman* Empire. Cambridge: Cambridge University Press, 2000.

–. "Evolution of the Ottoman Monetary System", *An Economic and Social History of the Ottoman Empire*, ed. Halil Inalcik, vol. 2: *1600–1914.* Cambridge: Cambridge University Press, 1994. 947–985.

Postan, M.M. *Medieval Trade and Finance.* Cambridge University Press, 2002.

Spufford, Peter. *Money and its Use in Medieval Europe.* Cambridge: Cambridge University Press, 1989.

Reinaud, Joseph Toussaint."Traités de commerce entre la république de Venise et les derniers sultans mameloucs d'Égypte, traduits de l'italien, et accompagnés d'éclaircissements par M. Reinaud." *Journal Asiatique.* 2ème serie, 4 (1829), 22–50.

Schultz, Warren. "The Monetary History of Egypt, 642–1517." In *The Cambridge History of Egypt*, Vol 1: *Islamic Egypt, 640–1517.* Ed. Carl Petry. Cambridge: Cambridge University Press, 1998.

Shoshan, Boaz. "Exchange-Rate Policies in Fifteenth Century Egypt." *Journal of the Economic and Social History of the Orient.* 29/1 (1986), 28–51.

Schlögel, Karl. *Im Raume Lesen wir die Zeit. Über Zivilisationsgeschichte und Geopolitik.* [3]Frankfurt: Fischer 2009.

Wansbrough, John. "A Mamluk Ambassador to Venice in 913/1507." *Bulletin of the School of Oriental and African Studies.* 26/3 (1963), 503–530.

Jo Van Steenbergen (Ghent University)

Revisiting the Mamlūk Empire. Political Action, Relationships of Power, Entangled Networks, and the Sultanate of Cairo in Late Medieval Syro-Egypt[1]

In a most inspiring contribution to the *Cambridge History of Egypt*, published in 1998, Stephen Humphreys begins by sketching out one of the most glorious moments of Egypt's premodern Islamic history, "the half-century after 1300," in the following enthusiastic terms:

> The borders of its empire were secure, its armies were triumphant, its cities were bursting with new construction, it was the linchpin between two flourishing trade zones in the Indian Ocean and the Mediterranean, and its centrality in the intellectual and religious life of the Arabic-speaking Sunnī world was uncontested.[2]

In the same passage, he actually warns that it may be highly "misleading to identify one moment as normative and to judge all other periods against that one". Nevertheless, the preceding late thirteenth century period appears in the chapter in a manner that somehow announces the triumph of that "half-century after 1300":

> First, the Mamluk empire (in contrast to its Ayyūbid predecessor) was a highly centralized state; the empire rested on the fiscal resources of Egypt, and the exploitation of these resources was directed from the Cairo Citadel. [...] Second, the Mamlūk empire had two enemies, the Mongols of Ilkhānid Iran and the crusaders on the Syro-Palestinian littoral. [...] Third, the Mamlūks took power at an extremely turbulent moment in the political history of the Mediterranean basin. [...] In the face of all this, the early Mamlūk sultans (especially Baybars and Qalāwūn) constituted their empire as a fortress. In their judgment, their empire could not hope to pursue an expansionist policy with any prospects of success; indeed, unbridled expansionism would almost surely

1 This article has been finalised within the context of the project 'The Mamlukisation of the Mamluk Sultanate II: Historiography, Political Order and State Formation in Fifteenth-Century Egypt and Syria' (UGent, 2017–21); this project has received funding from the European Research Council (ERC) under the European Union's Horizon 2020 research and innovation programme (Consolidator Grant agreement No 681510).

2 R. Stephen Humphreys, "Egypt in the World System of the Later Middle Ages," *The Cambridge History of Egypt*. Volume I: *Islamic Egypt, 640–1517*, ed. C.F. Petry (Cambridge: Cambridge University Press, 1998), pp. 445–461, p. 445.

> lead to disaster. What they could do was to secure the borders of Egypt and Syria and convert these lands into a powerful citadel which the enemies of Islam could not penetrate. [...] Thus, the early Mamlūk empire derived exceptional prestige from the fact that it was the only major Muslim state between the Atlantic Ocean and the Hindu Kush which could hold its own against powerful non-Muslim enemies – the only one which could defend the cause of Islam in a desperate age.[3]

When eventually "in 1516 the Mamlūk empire confronted its last and final crisis," Humphreys explains that this was not so much a historical accident, but the outcome of a deeper, more structural transformation on a global scale for which these thirteenth and fourteenth century solutions and successes proved no longer valid:

> The crisis of 1516 was simply the culmination of world-wide processes that had been going on for more than 150 years. The Mamlūk empire had been constructed in and for the world of the thirteenth century, and its basic outlook and institutions had changed very little since that time.[4]

In many ways, Humphreys' approach to "the Mamlūk empire," its early and structurally defining successes, and its institutional sclerosis announcing its eventual downfall is itself the culmination of a long tradition of scholarship and of academic interest into the late medieval Sultanate of Egypt and Syria, into the centrality of its capital Cairo in late medieval Muslim life, and into the particular and widely interconnected nature of its political and other elites. In recent years, this more traditional scholarship, and especially the paradigms and assumptions with which it has been operating, have come under increasing scrutiny. Insights into the complexity of late medieval Muslim life in Syria, Egypt and beyond have been furthered and refined in important ways, and some of the traditional assumptions about the nature of political, social, cultural and economic action in the region continue to be revised. However, in this ongoing and endless dialectic process of the elaboration of a healthy and fruitful academic discourse on the time and region, one notion seems to linger on, often almost unconsciously, in ways that also emerge from Humphreys' chapter and from his insistent reference to this Sultanate of Cairo as "the Mamlūk empire". This concerns the idea that inside and outside this 'imperial' polity historical action was (and continued to be) defined and often even driven by the agency of one coherent and autonomous actor, the Sultanate. Above all, the autonomy and coherence of this historical actor today continue to be considered in many contexts as marked by the high level of political integration of its elites – or, as Humphreys phrased it, by the idea that "the Mamluk empire (in contrast to its Ayyūbid predecessor) was a highly

3 Ibid., pp. 452–4.
4 Ibid., p. 461.

centralized state [...] directed from the Cairo Citadel" – as well as by the integrity of its territory – Humphreys' "fortress" and "powerful citadel which the enemies of Islam could not penetrate."

It will be this chapter's aim to question the assumed link between these practices of integration and integrity on the one hand – which appear as empirical realities from many sources and studies – and the Sultanate as a dominant, autonomous and imperial historical actor on the other. It will problematise in particular the holistic nature of these assumptions, their merely descriptive value for understanding the region's history, and the potentially misleading consequences of their normative character. At the same time, this chapter will propose to reflect further on that powerful idea of the Sultanate as an empire. It will actually consider this notion of "empire" as a useful way out of this predicament, because it invites to engage with insights from other fields of historical research and to define valuable analytical tools to further and refine current assumptions about and understandings of late medieval Syro-Egyptian political action.

Whither the Mamlūk Empire?

The field of empire studies today is wide-ranging, having moved since many decades far beyond its historiographical and semantic origins in the study of the Roman *imperium* and its rich Euro-Mediterranean legacies. In this complex context of modern scholarship, the noun, the idea and the concept of "empire" appear as extremely rich and embodied with a variety of particular meanings that serve a similarly wide range of descriptive, analytical and ideological purposes. As a result, it has become extremely difficult to see the imperial forest for the trees; in fact, it may be said that various imperial forests (and even more obfuscating trees) have come to exist side by side, across that range of meanings and purposes, and that these are no longer necessarily interconnected in any meaningful way. As far as modern historical scholarship on pre-modern empires is concerned, one recent publication that usefully wraps up a lot of thinking and allows to see at least one imperial forest again, is Wolfgang Reinhard's introduction to the recent *History of the World* volume *Empires and Encounters. 1350–1750.* Amongst many things, Reinhard provides a most useful working definition for the notion of empire as a historical phenomenon: "Empire" is defined as "a political unit of large extent controlling a number of territories and peoples under a single sovereign authority," where the "extent" is relative and depends on how far advanced transport conditions and news dissemination are. The opposing concept is that of the "nation-state."[5] Working with and from this definition and its focus on the functionalist combination of territorial extent and centralising sovereignty, Reinhard explains that "in the period 1350–1750, there are only "empires" throughout the world."[6] Most historical empire studies, whether descriptive, analytical or both, indeed operate not only with some version of this definition, but also from the claim or assumption that this structural appearance of "empire" has been a dominant mode of pre-modern political organisation in the last 5,000 years of human history.[7]

The late medieval Sultanate of Egypt and Syria, however, is never included in any of these historical empire studies. Not even the *Empires and Encounters. 1350–1750* volume that Reinhard edited considered it relevant to refer to this political formation, even despite the fact that the Sultanate continued to appear between the thirteenth and early sixteenth centuries in a succession of dynastic and non-dynastic forms of state as one of the most powerful regional players between the eastern Mediterranean and the Indian Ocean.[8] Most empire studies simply tend to jump from the impressive medieval achievements of Chinggis Khan and his Mongol allies and successors, to the equally impressive early modern and modern achievements of the Ottoman dynasty, pushing the Syro-Egyptian Sultanate to the margins of these imperial enterprises and debates, at best. At the same time, it must also be admitted that the whole notion of "empire" has largely remained absent from any enterprises or debates within the Sultanate's own field of study. When "empire" is yet used – which seems to have been the case in only a handful of studies, including Humphreys' deliberate references in the aforementioned chapter – this appears never as a very conscious statement about the nature of the Sultanate's political organisation, but mainly only as a spatial device, a descriptive shortcut to situate one's research in a particular time

5 Wofgang Reinhard, "Introduction," in *Empires and Encounters. 1350–1750*, ed. W. Reinhard (Cambridge, MA: Harvard University Press, 2015), p. 12.

6 Reinhard, "Introduction," p. 15.

7 See Jack A. Goldstone and John F. Haldon, "Ancient States, Empires, and Exploitation. Problems and Perspectives," in *The Dynamics of Ancient Empires. State Power from Assyria to Byzantium*, eds. Ian Morris and Walter Scheidel (Oxford: Oxford University Press, 2008), pp. 1–29 ("'Empire' was thus arguably the normal or modal form of large political entity throughout Eurasia until quite recently," p. 18); Immanuel Wallerstein, *The Modern World-System I. Capitalist Agriculture and the Origins of the European World-Economy in the Sixteenth Century* (Berkeley: University of California Press, 2011; first edition 1974) ("Empires in this sense were a constant feature of the world scene for 5,000 years," p. 15).

8 On this succession of forms of state, see my "Appearances of Dawla and Political Order in Late Medieval Syro-Egypt. The State, Social Theory, and the Political History of the Cairo Sultanate," in *History and Society during the Mamluk Period (1250–1517). Studies of the Annemarie Schimmel Research College II*, ed. Stephan Conermann (Bonn: Bonn University Press, 2016), pp. 51–85.

and space.[9] Perhaps this chapter, therefore, should end it there, concluding that the history of the Sultanate and the concept of empire have never really matched well. It should perhaps then also be acknowledged that this may all well be for good reasons, since Reinhard's key characteristic of various "territories and peoples under a single sovereign authority" indeed seems to be contradicted by the fact that the Sultanate appears mostly in modern studies and research in non-imperial terms, as that "highly centralized state" and "fortress" of Humphreys' description: a relatively well integrated polity with little to no territorial and political ambitions beyond the natural frontiers of Egypt and Syria.

There are, however, also good reasons to try and think beyond such assumptions of the Sultanate's high levels of political integration and territorial integrity. One reason follows from a recent publication that adds a somewhat more analytical understanding of 'empire' to its approach to the Sultanate. This volume, *Everything is on the Move*, was therefore duly subtitled *The Mamluk*

9 A search in the Mamluk Bibliography for 'Mamluk empire' (and its variants [search term: mam%l%k%mpir%]) only retrieved 44 hits (www.mamluk.lib.uchicago.edu; consulted on March, 18, 2016), including Jean Sauvaget, *La poste aux chevaux dans l'empire des Mamelouks* (Paris: Adrien-Maisonneuve, 1941); Moshe Perlmann, "Notes on Anti-Christian Propaganda in the Mamlūk Empire,"*Bulletin of the School of Asian Studies*, 10 (1940–2): 843–61; Paul Balog, "History of the Dirhem in Egypt from the Fāṭimid Conquest until the Collapse of the Mamlūk Empire, 358–922 H./968–1517 A.D.," *Revue numismatique* (6th ser.), 3 (1961): 109–46; Jean-Claude Garcin, "La 'méditerranéisation' de l'empire mamelouk sous les sultans bahrides," *Rivista degli studi orientali*, 48 (1973–4): 109–16; Mounira Chapoutot-Remadi, "L'agriculture dans l'empire mamluk au Moyen Âge d'après al-Nuwayrî," *Les Cahiers de Tunisie*, 22 (1974): 23–45; Michael W. Dols, "The General Mortality of the Black Death in the Mamluk Empire," in *The Islamic Middle East, 700–1900*, ed. Avram L. Udovitch (Princeton: Darwin, 1981), pp. 397–428; Joseph H. Escovitz, "The Establishment of Four Chief Judgeships in the Mamlūk Empire," *Journal of the American Oriental Society*, 102 (1982): 529–31; R. Stephan Humphreys, "The Fiscal Administration of the Mamluk Empire," in *Islamic History: A Framework for Inquiry* (Princeton: Princeton UP, 1991), pp. 169–186 (Chap. 7); Andre Raymond, "Conflits maritimes, politique méditerranéenne et évolution de l'empire mamelouk égyptien au XVe siècle," *Les Cahiers de Tunisie*, 48 (1995): 165–76; Andre Clot, *L'Egypte des Mamelouks: l'empire des esclaves, 1250–1517* (Paris: Perrin, 1996); Jo Van Steenbergen, "The Political Role of Damascus in the Mamluk Empire: Three Events in the Period 741/1341–750/1349, Imperative for the Change of Power in Cairo," *Orientalia Lovaniensia Periodica*, 30 (1999): 113–28; Shaun E. Marmon, "Domestic Slavery in the Mamluk Empire: A Preliminary Sketch," in *Slavery in the Islamic Middle East*, ed. S.E. Marmon (Princeton: Markus Wiener Publishers, 1999), pp. 1–23; John Meloy, "Imperial Strategy and Political Exigency: The Red Sea Spice Trade and the Mamluk Sultanate in the Fifteenth Century," *Journal of the American Oriental Society*, 123/1 (2003): 1–19; Albrecht Fuess, "Sultans with Horns: The Political Significance of Headgear in the Mamluk Empire," *Mamlūk Studies Review*,12/2 (2008): 71–94; Roland-Pierre Gayraud, "Ceramics in the Mamluk Empire. An Overview," in *The Arts of the Mamluks in Egypt and Syria – Evolution and Impact*, ed. D. Behrens-Abouseif (Bonn: Bonn University Press, 2012), pp. 77–94; Stephen Conermann (ed.), *Everything is on the Move: The Mamluk Empire as a Node in (Trans-)Regional Networks* (Bonn: Bonn University Press, 2014).

Empire as a Node in (Trans-)Regional Networks. As its editor, Stephan Conermann, explained:

> In this volume, we try to understand the "Mamluk Empire," not as a confined space but as a region where several nodes of different networks existed side-by-side and at the same time.[10]

The latter clarification certainly hinges more on the default spatial descriptive use than on a more analytical network approach that is suggested in the volume's subtitle. Nevertheless, the latter suggestive subtitle simultaneously invites to further explore this idea of imperial nodes and networks. Perhaps, indeed, a lot may be gained from using the notion of "empire" to think of the Sultanate not as an integrated polity and as a confined territory, but as one of these nodes of networks that converged, became entangled and transformed in the regional metropolis of Cairo.

Another good reason for exploring these kinds of understandings emerges from the confrontation of particular empirical material, which challenges those assumptions of integration and integrity, with an interesting metaphor that has struck an analytical chord in quite a few empire studies. The latter concerns Viktor Liebermann's astronomical metaphor of the "solar polity." This metaphor reminds in highly insightful ways of Reinhard's particular qualities of "extent" and "sovereignty." But it also helps to better understand how those qualities were and remained interconnected by putting forward the equally interesting related metaphor of "gravitational pull." Lieberman explained this in the simplest of terms as follows:

> Each realm was a "solar polity"… in which provincial "planets" revolved around a sun whose "gravitational pull" diminished with distance. Insofar as each planet had its own satellite moons, its gravitational system replicated in decreasing scale the structure of the solar system as a whole.[11]

As for the former, empirical material, Patrick Wing's study of the dynamic relationship between the Aqquyunlu leader ʿUthmān Beg Qarā Yulūk (r. ca. 1400–35) in southeast Anatolia and the Sultanate problematises in highly suggestive ways any simple assumptions about that Sultanate's territorial integrity and about its politics of integration. Wing tellingly concludes that

> Evidence from the sources available suggests that we must accept that the limits of a sultan's authority were multivalent, that different varieties of frontier existed simultaneously, and changed according to historical circumstances. In fact, a frontier ideology

10 Stephan Conermann, "Networks and Nodes in Mamluk Times: Some Introductory Remarks," in *Everything is on the Move*, pp. 9–26, p. 9.

11 Vikor Lieberman, *Strange Parallels. Southeast Asia in Global Context, c. 800–1830.* Volume 1: *Integration on the Mainland* (Cambridge: Cambridge University Press, 2003), p. 33.

prevailed alongside the limits of the actual power held by the sultan in Anatolia. The ideological frontier was defined by the limits to which the symbolism and rhetoric of the Mamluk political order, including titles, ceremony, and deference to institutional hierarchies, were used to negotiate and consolidate political relationships. As we have seen, this ideological frontier did indeed extend beyond the Euphrates to Diyarbakr, and included the Aqquyunlu. However, the limits of the sultan's effective power, where his agents could compel a political actor like Qarā Yulūk to submit to his will, was a different matter. Sultan Barsbāy could not prevent Qarā Yulūk from pursuing his own political interests locally when they contradicted his own. Barsbāy could not remove Qarā Yulūk from power as he could under normal conditions in the Syrian provinces governed by his own *amirs*.[12]

John Meloy, in his detailed study of the political relationship throughout the long fifteenth century between the Sultanate and the Sharifian leadership of Mecca in the Hijaz, comes to parallel conclusions about the dynamic, multivalent and negotiated nature of that relationship.[13] These two cases illustrate above all how the Sultanate was connected with local elites beyond its natural frontiers and physical reach along multiple stages of more or less political integration. These and similar political relationships actually only acquire their full value and meaning, as more than mere outsiders to (or for that matter neighbours, buffer states, or any similar anachronisms from the modern interstate system, of) Cairo's political realities, when they are considered through the metaphorical lens of Lieberman's solar polity and its diminishing gravitational pull.

Similar, but more extreme examples of the high complexity of those politics of integration and of the wide range of that gravitational pull concern the following two cases, pertaining to two very different moments in the Sultanate's long history. In 1337 (737 AH), at the time of the disintegration of the Mongol Ilkhanate in Iran and the surrounding lands, one of the claimants to its legacy in

12 Patrick Wing, "Submission, Defiance, and the Rules of Politics on the Mamluk Sultanate's Anatolian Frontier," *Journal of the Royal Asiatic Society*, 25/3 (2015): 377–88, esp. pp. 387–8; a similar line of argument was also pursued in Veerle Adriaenssens and Jo Van Steenbergen, "Mamluk Authorities and Anatolian Realities: Jānibak al-Ṣūfī, Sultan al-Ashraf Barsbāy, and the Story of a Social Network in the Mamluk/Anatolian Frontier Zone, 1435–1438," *Journal of the Royal Asiatic Society*, 26/4 (2016): 591–630. For other, similar cases of the complex and dynamic political integration of the Anatolian frontier zone, see also Barbara Kellner-Heinkele, "The Turkomans and Bilād aš-Šām in the Mamluk Period," in *Land Tenure and Social Transformation in the Middle East*, ed. Tarif Khalidi (Beirut: American University, 1984), pp. 169–80; Shay Har-El, *Struggle for Domination of the Middle East: The Ottoman-Mamluk War, 1485–91* (Leiden: Brill, 1995).

13 John Meloy, *Imperial Power and Maritime Trade: Mecca and Cairo in the Later Middle Ages* (Chicago: Middle East Documentation Centre, 2010). For a similar story of multivalent overseas relationships of power and trade, see Nicholas Coureas, "Losing the War but Winning the Peace: Cyprus and Mamluk Egypt in the Fifteenth Century," in *Egypt and Syria in the Fatimid, Ayyubid and Mamluk Eras – VII*, eds. Urbain Vermeulen, Kristof D'hulster and Jo Van Steenbergen (Leuven: Peeters, 2013), pp. 351–61.

Iraq, ʿAlī Pādshāh, is reported to have sent an envoy to the sultan in Cairo requesting for the sultan's military support against his competitors and promising that "he would make [the sultan] ruler in Baghdad and that [ʿAlī Pādshāh] would act as his agent in the East and have the Friday sermon delivered in [the sultan's] name."[14] The enterprise came to naught, but is yet as indicative of the political relationships revolving around Cairo as another, more successful example. More than a century later, Qarā Yulūk's grandson Uzun Ḥasan led the Aqquyunlu leadership beyond its traditional eastern Anatolian grazing lands on a highly successful campaign of conquest and imperial formation (so that eventually the Friday sermon in Baghdad happened to be delivered in Ḥasan's name). Despite his regional successes, the political relationship with Cairo remained an issue of some relevance for Ḥasan, as it had been for his grandfather (at least until Ḥasan felt strong enough to claim his own sovereignty).[15] This is also suggested from the following report, recorded at Cairo's court:

> On 1 Rabīʿ al-Ākhir [863–5 February 1459], an envoy from Ḥasan Bak b. ʿAlī Bak b. Qarā Yuluk ascended the citadel. He kissed the ground and informed the sultan of the fact that Ḥasan Bak had acquired six citadels from the Georgians (*al-Karj*), and [that] he had sent the keys of one of them with [the envoy] to the sultan. … The sultan received him graciously, thanked him and bestowed a robe of honour upon him.[16]

This is of course but a highly selective set of empirical examples. They are not presented here, however, as conclusive evidence on the presence, absence or exact nature of any politics of integration into the Sultanate's gravitational pull. They are rather "symptomatic" – in a positive sense – of the complex reality of that pull, or at best of particular practices, discourses and relationships that it could (and occasionally certainly also did) generate across a substantial span of West-Asia. From the remote Caucasus region of Georgia Uzun Ḥasan thus presented himself symbolically – in more successful ways than ʿAlī Pādshāh had attempted to do more than a century before from Baghdad – as a "planet" that acknowledged the gravitational pull that was revolving around the sultan's person and court in Cairo. At least, it was considered important by contemporaries in Cairo to present and remember Uzun Ḥasan in the early 1460s and ʿAlī Pādshāh in the late 1330s from such a perspective.

---

14 Mūsā al-Yūsufī (d. 1358), *Nuzhat al-Nāẓir fī Sīrat al-Malik al-Nāṣir*, ed. A. Ḥuṭayṭ (Beirut: ʿĀlam al-Kutub, 1986), pp. 364–5. See also Patrick Wing, "The Decline of the Ilkhanate and the Mamluk Sultanate's Eastern Frontier," *Mamlūk Studies Review*, 11/2 (2007): 77–88.

15 See John Woods, *The Aqquyunlu. Clan, Confederation, Empire. Revised and Expanded Edition* (Salt Lake City: The University of Utah Press, 1999), pp. 87–123, esp. pp. 92, 100–2, 107–8.

16 Jamāl al-Dīn Yūsuf Ibn Taghrī Birdī (1411–70), *Ḥawādith al-duhūr fī madā al-ayyām wa-l-shuhūr*, ed. W. Popper, *Extracts from Abû 'l-Maḥâsin Ibn Taghrî Birdî's Chronicle, entitled Ḥawâdith ad-duhûr fî madâ 'l-ayyâm wash-shuhûr* (Berkeley: University of California Press, 1930–42), p. 321.

Just as these cases question any too one-dimensional approach to the politics of integration into the gravitational pull of the Cairo Sultanate, another selective set of examples and studies suggests that also any idea of the polity's territorial integrity should be refined if not redefined. One remarkable case, which appears as very meaningful in this context, concerns a short-lived enterprise of early fifteenth century local empowerment (framed in Cairo-centred sources as a rebellion) in southern Bilād al-Shām. One chronicle report summarises the enterprise as follows:

> In the month of Rabīʿ al-Awwal [816 – June 1413], there appeared a transgressor (*khārijī*) who made the claim that he was the Sufyānī. He was a man from ʿAjlūn whose name was ʿUthmān. He had been studying *fiqh* for a while in Damascus, and then he had come to ʿAjlūn where he had settled in the village of Ḥayḍūr (Jaydur). He delivered the Friday sermon in his own name, and some people submitted to his authority. He assigned *iqṭā*ʿs and announced that the harvests of the current year were to be free from taxes and that in the next year only the tithe would be collected from the farmers. Many people – Arabs, Turkmen and Turks – rallied around him, raising green banners. He sent his letters to the local districts. After the *basmala*, they read as follows: [from] the Sufyānī to the honourable X (*fulān*), join the knights of this *dawla* of the supreme Sufyānid sultan, king and *imām* … ; bring your horses and men to perform the *hijra* to Allāh and his Prophet and to fight on God's path, so that God's Word will prevail.[17]

This enterprise – which is also framed as having meant the end of "the rule of the Turks (*ḥukm al-Turk*), so that only the rule of the local leaders (?) (*ḥukm awlād al-nās*) remained"[18] – appears to have lasted for no longer than a few weeks. Before the end of the month another local leader (one further unknown Ghānim al-Ghazāwī) is reported to have intervened with his men, to have seized this al-Sufyānī and some of his supporters, to have transferred them to the regional center of Ṣafad, and – only then – to have informed the sultan of his actions.[19]

From the handful of available data, it appears that this al-Sufyānī and his supporters belonged to – or are at least presented as having belonged to – a local millenarian movement, constructed around ideas and actions of some form of Umayyad messianism (a combination not unfamiliar to local Syrian history since

17 Badr al-Dīn Maḥmūd al-ʿAynī (1361–1451), *ʿIqd al-Jumān fī tārīkh ahl al-zamān: ḥawādith wa-tarājim*, ed. ʿA. al-Ṭanṭāwī Qarmūṭ, 2 vols. (Cairo: al-Zahrā, 1989), 1: 183; this case is also reported with more detail in Aḥmad b. ʿAlī al-Maqrīzī (1363–1442), *Kitāb al-Sulūk li-Maʿrifat Duwal al-Mulūk*, ed. S. ʿA. ʿĀshūr, vols. 3–4 (Cairo: Maṭbaʿat Dār al-Kutub, 1972), 4: 262–3 (al-Maqrīzī mentions al-Sufyānī's full name as "ʿUthmān b. Aḥmad b. ʿUthmān b. Maḥmūd b. Muḥammad b. ʿAlī b. Faḍl b. Rabīʿa, also known as Ibn Thaqqāla, one of the *faqīh*s of Damascus"; he also claims that "he said: 'I am sultan al-Malik al-Aʿẓam al-Sufyānī'").

18 Al-Maqrīzī, *Sulūk*, p. 263.

19 Ibid.

Abbasid times).[20] The point of referring to this case in this detail in the context of the current chapter, however, is not this particular form of millenarian political activism and local state formation. It is rather the remarkable fact that al-Sufyānī and his supporters in southern Bilād al-Shām did not acknowledge – and are not portrayed otherwise in any report – any gravitational pull as emanating from Cairo; they rather appear as turning the Sultanate's institutional forms and meaning to their own ends, to proclaim their own "solar polity" – or, according to contemporary observers, their own *dawla* – in the local context of southern Bilād al-Shām. The point is furthermore that this millenarian Sufyanid endeavour appears as unsuccessful and short-lived due to very *ad hoc* reactions among other local leaderships, and not as a result of any institutional action from the Sultanate and its agents; these seem only to have been informed, and their gravitational pull only appears to have been invoked, after the events, as though to formalise the local settlement and confirm the local outcome. What this Sufyanid case and the Sultanate's total absence from it then suggest more in general appears above all from how it contrasts in remarkable and quite unexpected ways with the above cases involving Uzun Ḥasan in Georgia or for that matter ʿAlī Pādshāh in Baghdad. Despite the closeness to Cairo of the movement in ʿAjlūn in 1413 and its positioning deep inside the territories that were claimed for the Sultanate, it appears here at the same time as much further removed from Cairo's gravitational pull than Uzun Ḥasan presented himself to be in his expanding Aqquyunlu territories (at least until the mid-1460s) and than ʿAlī Pādshāh attempted to be from Iraq.

This case, that thus questions any assumption about the actual territorial integrity of the Sultanate, brings to mind other, similar cases, that similarly appear as much further removed from Cairo's gravitational pull than their placements within the Sultanate's territories suggest. These involve events and dynamics surrounding bedouin groups and other "marauding nomads" in Egypt or Syria. They also concern other religious movements, sectarian communities and marginal social groups operating in rural as well as urban contexts, that very often tend to escape from our sources' radars in ways that are again symptomatic of their irrelevance or successful resistance to the Sultanate's gravitational pull. These "subaltern" cases finally certainly also concern competitors and former partners of that gravitational pull, and their resistance to it, their escape into its margins, or their attempts to subvert it.[21]

20 See Paul M. Cobb, *White Banners. Contention in ʿAbbasid Syria, 750–880* (Albany: SUNY Press, 2001).

21 See Adriaenssens and Van Steenbergen, "Mamluk Authorities and Anatolian Realities"; Shaun Marmon, "Black Slaves in Mamlūk Narratives: Representations of Transgression," *Al-Qanṭara*, 28/2 (2007): 435–64; William M. Brinner, "The Significance of the Ḥarāfīsh and Their Sultan," *Journal of the Economic and Social History of the Orient*, 6 (1963): 190–215;

All this then finally suggests that in terms of not just political integration but also of territorial integrity the Sultanate was much more complex a political phenomenon than tends to be acknowledged or assumed. In 1413 in southern Bilād al-Shām (and in any similar case and moment) the Sultanate appears furthermore as not much of an empire either, at least not simply in the way suggested by Reinhard's combined qualities of extent and sovereignty. The gravitational paradox that emerges from Uzun Ḥasan's case in Georgia and from al-Sufyānī's in southern Bilād al-Shām makes moreover clear that Lieberman's image of the solar polity and its diminishing pull is of no analytical help either. Any impressions of the importance of physical distance and any assumptions about territorial integrity that are implied by these metaphors appear as problematic. They appear as insufficiently fit to fully account for the nature of political relations involved in both cases, and in so many others like them, beyond any *ad hoc* descriptions of the ups and downs of the Sultanate's political integration and territorial integrity.

Towards a Theory of Pre-modern West-Asian Empire

It will be argued here that things will only become of real analytical interest once questions can be asked that allow to think beyond holistic ideas about the Sultanate's political elites and territories. Perhaps there is much more that can be learned beyond any description of al-Sufyānī's case as a moment of crisis in the Sultanate's historical trajectory of political integration and territorial integrity, and Uzun Ḥasan's as one of success. Since this particular empirical material may also be read as symptomatic of an even more complex political reality than generally tends to be acknowledged, this chapter operates from the assumption that the analytical tools that have so far been employed may simply be insufficiently refined. Reinhard's combined imperial qualities of extent and sovereignty, and Lieberman's connecting metaphors of the solar polity and its gravitational pull, will therefore be embedded here in a wider reflection on empire as a category of historical analysis, and on its construction as a useful ideal type of political action for furthering understandings of the Syro-Egyptian

---

Sarah Büssow-Schmitz, "Rules of Communication and Politics between Bedouin and Mamluk Elites in Egypt: The Case of the al-Aḥdab Revolt, c. 1353," *Eurasian Studies*, 9/1–2 (2011): 67–104; Jean-Claude Garcin, "Note sur les rapports entre bédouins et fallahs à l'époque mamluke," *Annales Islamologiques*, 14 (1978): 147–63; Yosef Rapoport, "Invisible Peasants, Marauding Nomads: Taxation, Tribalism, and Rebellion in Mamluk Egypt," *Mamlūk Studies Review*, 8/2 (2004): 1–22; Patrick Lantscher, "Fragmented Cities in the Later Middle Ages: Italy and the Near East Compared," *English Historical Review*, 130 (2015): 546–82.

Sultanate, as an important stakeholder in the pre-modern history of Muslim West Asia.

Most applications of any notion of "empire" in research that pertains to the field of the pre-modern history of Muslim West Asia continue to draw inspiration for their analyses from the Weberian ideal types of charismatic and traditional authority. These theoretical types of legitimate authority were successfully adopted for and adapted to empire studies in the 1960s by the renowned Israeli sociologist Shmuel N. Eisenstadt (1923–2010). Eisenstadt's structural-functionalist definition actually endowed the notion of "empire" in impactful ways with a wider validity as a powerful analytical tool for research:

> The term "empire" has normally been used to designate a political system encompassing wide, relatively high centralized territories, in which the center, as embodied both in the person of the emperor and in the central political institutions, constituted an autonomous entity. Further, although empires have usually been based on traditional legitimation, they have often embraced some wider, potentially universal political and cultural orientation that went beyond that of any of their component parts.[22]

Different components of this definition – which reverberates in its own functionalist ways in Reinhard's qualities of extent and sovereignty – have certainly made their re-appearance, in more or less consciously constructed direct and indirect genealogies, in the field of the pre-modern history of Muslim West Asia. This crossover is most explicitly effected and exemplified in Stephen Blake's "the patrimonial-bureaucratic empire of the Mughals" (which acknowledges indeed that it drew "heavily on Max Weber's work on the patrimonial state").[23] By and large all studies of imperial forms in pre-modern Muslim West Asia indeed tend to think – as Blake did for the Mughal empire in India – from the top-down perspective of the imperial household and bureaucracy, identified by Eisenstadt as some socially transcendent "autonomous entity" of "the center, as embodied

22 See Shmuel N. Eisenstadt, "Empires," *International Encyclopaedia of the Social Sciences* (1968), 5: 41; see also S.M. Eisenstadt, *The Political Systems of Empires* (New Brunswick: Transaction Publishers, 1993; first edition 1963). Eisenstadt's work on empires has had, for instance, an important impact on the formulation of Immanuel Wallerstein's modern world-system theory (see I. Wallerstein, *The Modern World-System I. Capitalist Agriculture and the Origins of the European World-Economy in the Sixteenth Century* [Berkeley: University of California Press, 2011; first edition 1974]).

23 Stephen P. Blake, "The Patrimonial-Bureaucratic Empire of the Mughals," *The Journal of Asian Studies*, 39/1 (1979): 77–94 (p. 79); see also more recently his "Returning the Household to the Patrimonial-Bureaucratic Empire: Gender, Succession, and Ritual in the Mughal, Safavid and Ottoman Empires," in *Tributary Empires in Global History*, eds. Peter F. Bang and Christopher A. Bayly (New York: Palgrave Macmillan, 2011), pp. 214–26. See also Marie E. Subtelny, *Timurids in Transition. Turko-Persian Politics and Acculturation in Medieval Iran* (Leiden: Brill, 2007), for another explicit engagement with Weberian ideal types along similar analytical lines.

both in the person of the emperor and in the central political institutions". Many of these studies also tend to think from the perspective of Eisenstadt's "traditional legitimation," along the patriarchal and patrimonial ties that connected the central household and bureaucracy to society. Finally, many also tend to think from the perspective of some "wider, potentially universal orientation," engendered by a ruler endowed with a natural charisma, or empowering the ruler with such a powerful charisma of universal authority. For all its usefulness and relevance, this paradigmatic vision in modern academic discourses on pre-modern Muslim West Asia does appear to have certain analytical shortcomings.[24] Most relevant for the purpose of this chapter is the problem that this Weberian model reduces elites and other social groups to the status of passive or, at best, reactive agents of history, seeing them merely as subjects of one central actor and his structuring agency: the ruler, his patrimonial authority, and the one-directional gravitational pull emanating from that authority.

Since the 1960s and Eisenstadt's pioneering work there certainly have been developed more complex analytical models of empire that leave room for the imagination of more complex types of historical action. They also deserve to be considered here, not in the least because some of them have also been applied to pre-modern Muslim West Asian contexts. As it happens, in a recent publication classicist and world historian Walter Scheidel presented a detailed survey of many of these "recent definitions of imperial states."[25] Portraying empire most pertinently as a particular historical form of state, this survey was embedded in an extremely thorough and intelligent assessment of the historical sociology of the state. There is therefore no need to repeat here Scheidel's detailed discussion and comparison of seminal empire scholarship by Shmuel Eisenstadt, Michael Doyle, Susan Reynolds, Michael Mann, Stephen Howe and, more recently, Jane Burbank and Frederick Cooper, or Jack Goldstone and John Haldon.[26] More relevant to pursue here further are two issues that are foregrounded by Scheidel on the basis of his consideration of that scholarship. The first issue concerns the suggestion that understanding empire is about understanding elites and their relationships first and foremost. As Scheidel phrased this, "it was the relationship between

24 See Michael Curtis, *Orientalism and Islam: European Thinkers on Oriental Despotism in the Middle East and India* (Cambridge: Cambridge University Press 2009).

25 Walter Scheidel, "Studying the State," in *The Oxford Handbook of the State in the Ancient Near East and Mediterranean*, eds. Peter F. Bang and Walter Scheidel (Oxford: Oxford UP, 2013), pp. 5–57, esp. pp. 27–30 ('Empires').

26 Eisenstadt, *Political Systems of Empires*; Michael Doyle, *Empires* (Ithaca: Cornell UP, 1986); Stephan Howe, *Empire. A Very Short Introduction* (Oxford: Oxford UP, 2002); Susan Reynolds, "Empires: a Problem of Comparative History," *Historical Research* 79 (2006): 151–65; Jane Burbank and Frederick Cooper, *Empires in World History. Power and the Politics of Difference* (Princeton: Princeton UP, 2010); Goldstone and Haldon, "Ancient States, Empires, and Exploitation."

central and peripheral *elites* (sic) that was crucial."[27] The second issue, which further qualifies this relational prioritisation, is that the success of empire depended not so much on the simple coercive subordination of the peripheries by the center, but rather on the harmonising of interests between central and peripheral elites. In this context, Scheidel explains how the whole of the unequal elite relationships of empire can be usefully represented through a metaphor that was first suggested by Alexander Motyl.

> Alexander Motyl emphasizes the fragmentation of the imperial periphery and the central position of the imperial core, envisioning empire a "hierarchically organized system with a hublike structure – a rimless wheel – within which a core elite and state dominate peripheral elites and societies by serving as intermediaries for their significant interactions and by channeling resource flows from the periphery to the core and back to the periphery."[28]

This metaphor of the "rimless wheel," also known as the rimless "hub-and-spoke-structure," helps to envisage in remarkably powerful ways that the point of "imperial" relationships was, by necessity, to promote the vertical integration of peripheral elites and, at the same time, those elites' horizontal segmentation. Those relationships between central and peripheral elites were therefore defined by the need not just to harmonise diverse central and peripheral interests, but also to prevent the horizontal integration of peripheral elites in ways that might endanger the harmony of that vertical integration.

> In Motyl's simile, empires have no "rim" because the periphery is not integrated and significant interactions between peripheries cannot occur without the intermediation of the core. "The result is a conceptually distinct core that dominates conceptually distinct peripheries bound minimally to one another." The rimless spoke system worked well because it meant that peripheries could not easily band together against the center; they were structurally competitors and not cooperators because all of them were contributors and recipients of imperial resources; and their elites benefited from status being promoted by a distant center.[29]

Motyl's idea of imperial relationships joining forces as though in a rimless wheel structure with imperial effects was further developed and adapted to pre-modern Muslim West Asian contexts in a monograph on the Ottoman empire, published in 2008 by Karen Barkey.[30] In this analytical pursuance of the question of the remarkable longevity of the Ottoman imperial enterprise between the fourteenth

---

27 Scheidel, "Studying the State", p. 28.
28 Scheidel, "Studying the State," p. 27; referring to Alexander J. Motyl, *Imperial Ends: The Decay, Collapse, and Revival of Empires* (New York: Columbia University Press, 2001), p. 4.
29 Scheidel, "Studying the State," 28, referring to Motyl, *Imperial Ends*, p. 7.
30 Karen Barkey, *Empire of Difference. The Ottomans in Comparative Perspective* (Cambridge: Cambridge University Press, 2008).

and twentieth centuries, Barkey infuses Motyl's analytical model most effectively with a social network perspective. Barkey thinks of the rimless wheel structure as "a hub-and-spoke network pattern, where each spoke was attached to the center but was less directly related to the others".[31] The key point for her understanding of Ottoman imperial longevity re-appears then as an understanding of the ability of the Ottoman central elites to continuously re-invent themselves as "brokers across structural holes." The latter concept is Barkey's social network way of asking how these elites managed to remain the main intermediaries between peripheral groups, interests and institutions across large parts of Eurasia and North-Africa for such a long time. The answers that she produces focus on the dynamic construction in an Ottoman imperial – hub-and-spoke structural – context of particular types of cultural, political and economic relationships between Ottoman and peripheral elites. Barkey usefully summarises this general point by explaining that she "argued that to maintain this structure and remain dominant and flexible, an empire needed to maintain legitimacy, diversity, and the flow of resources and manpower through a stable relationship with the intermediary elites."[32] Key concepts defining, ensuring and explaining imperial relationships in the Ottoman imperial context appear as the classic notions of legitimation (reminding of Reinhard's sovereignty) and of patrimony (reminding of Blake's patrimonial-bureaucratic system). The former indeed includes for Barkey the acceptance by peripheral elites of Ottoman claims to universal authority, of a political order of global imagination topped by the Ottoman sultan. The latter notion focuses on the creation and creative maintenance of particular resource flows from the peripheries to the center, and back again, especially in the changing forms of booty, tribute, taxation, tax farming, salaries, military service and forced labour, and with the purpose of creating or pursuing imperial stability.

The third feature that is identified by Barkey as crucial for her argument is the more complex and fluid concept of diversity. Reminding in more subtle ways of Reinhard's reference to various "territories and peoples under a single sovereign authority" (which radically opposes the concept of empire to that of the homogenising nation-state),[33] the cultivation of diversity appears indeed as the most typical of all imperial features. This abstract feature of diversity (to be understood as the management of difference in every social practice) is further defined by Barkey when she explains that "divide and rule, 'brokerage', segmentation, and integration become the basis structural components of

31 Barkey, *Empire of Difference*, p. 10.
32 Barkey, *Empire of Difference*, p. 193.
33 See also Burbank and Cooper's similar notion of the "politics of difference"; Burbank and Cooper, *Empires in World History*, pp. 11–3.

empire."[34] These components are pursued especially, according to Barkey, through the construction of boundaries that separate groups, communities and individuals and that thus maintain horizontal segmentation, and therefore also the imperial rimless wheel structure. In this manner these imperial boundaries served above all to separate the empire and its local intermediaries (marked by office, income, kinship, gifts and similar trappings of social distinction and integration) from other local elites, groups and relationships, or – otherwise put – they served to separate the "imperial state" from a diverse imperial society. However, these boundaries and their political meanings are not natural and self-evident. They are not simply imposed top-down by central elites on others either. As Barkey surmised, "… the boundary marking itself happens in the messy intermediate space in which state makers meet different groups and negotiate the terms of separation, difference, similarity, and cooperation."[35] Boundaries are always constructed and negotiated in the diverse relationships between elites, who pursued the maintenance of the Ottoman rimless-wheel structure as well as the harmonising of diverse interests. The appearances of difference that emerged from them should therefore never simply be considered as natural and self-evident, nor as originating from any coherent form of state policy. These continuously renegotiated boundaries actually contributed themselves to the appearance of a bipolar imperial system of central state versus diverse society, an appearance that should therefore be looked at more as a consequence than as a cause of their construction through practices of vertical integration and horizontal segmentation.

The full, and more complex, imperial picture that emerges from all this, is therefore that Reinhard's combined imperial qualities of territorial extent and centralising sovereignty, and Lieberman's connecting metaphors of the solar polity and its gravitational pull, may be further refined by bringing into the analysis Scheidel's relational emphasis, Barkey's practical emphasis on negotiated diversity, boundary marking and brokerage across structural holes, and Motyl's structural emphasis on the rimless wheel metaphor as an ideal type of imperial state formation. Each of these distinct analytical features of imperial political action is not just grounded in modern imperial theory, but also intricately interconnected with (and analytically meaningful from the perspective of) Barkey's call for a social network approach. However, the purpose for their formulation in the present context will not be to push and mould them all into yet another grand model of empire as a particular type, node or entanglement of social networking. These additional perspectives should rather be considered as helpful components of a rich, eclectic and refined toolbox for the imperial

34 Barkey, *Empire of Difference*, p. 10.
35 Barkey, *Empire of Difference*, p. 13.

analysis of historical political action. Their application and further problematisation in the context of the particularity of the Syro-Egyptian Sultanate, and of the analytical question of its imperial qualities, is therefore what will matter here.

Practices and Structural Appearances of Imperial State Formation in the Sultanate of Cairo

It is, as always, important not to simply impose onto the realities and appearances of the Syro-Egyptian Sultanate an analytical grid that may have served its purpose elsewhere. This is certainly also a valid observation for any analysis of that Sultanate through the imperial prism of territorial extent and centralising gravitational pull; of imperial relationships between central and peripheral elites pursuing sovereignty, the flow of resources, and the management of difference; and of the mediation and brokerage across structural holes of imperial networks. Nevertheless, as long as the particularity of the Syro-Egyptian Sultanate as a specific time and space of historical political action within the wider context of pre-modern Muslim West Asia is acknowledged, such a prism may actually enable a much better understanding of that distinct particularity. It may even help to further current understandings of that afore-mentioned analytical paradox that appeared from the contrasting cases of al-Sufyānī in nearby southern Bilād al-Shām and of Uzun Ḥasan in remote Georgia.

The last part of this chapter will try to clarify this assertion and provide some further food for thought through a brief presentation of two cases that are more internal to the imperial workings of the Sultanate. The one pertains to the first half of the fourteenth century, the other to the second half of the fifteenth. Analytically, they provide most suggestive complementary insights into the practical and structural nature of the relationships that appeared to be emanating from the Sultanate's imperial center in Cairo.

The story of the amir Sayf al-Dīn Tankiz al-Ḥusāmī al-Nāṣirī (d. 740/1340) is quite well-known today thanks to the work of Ḥayāt Nāṣir al-Ḥajjī, Ellen Kenney and Stephan Conermann.[36] It is one of those stories of high social mobility and empowerment that tend to be considered as typical for the political elites of the Sultanate. Enslavement brought Tankiz to Egypt as a young boy, membership of the royal bodyguard in the 1290s introduced him into Egypt's political elites, and

36 Ḥayāt Nāṣir al-Ḥajjī, *Al-Amīr Tankiz al-Ḥusāmī, nāʾib al-Shām fī l-fatra 712–741 h./1312–1340 M* (Kuwait: Jāmiʿat al-Kuwayt, 1980); Ellen Kenney, *Power and Patronage in Medieval Syria. The Architecture and Urban Works of Tankiz al-Nāṣirī* (Chicago: MEDOC, 2009); Stephan Conermann, "Tankiz ibn ʿAbd Allāh al-Ḥusāmī (d. 740/1340) as Seen by His Contemporary al-Ṣafadī (d. 764/1363)," *Mamlūk Studies Review*, 12/2 (2008): 1–24.

service as an amir at the court of al-Nāṣir Muḥammad b. Qalāwūn (r. 1293–4; 1299–1309; 1310–41) transformed him into a leader in his own right. Sent to Damascus in 1312 to serve as al-Nāṣir Muḥammad's *nāʾib al-Shām*, Tankiz was eventually promoted by his sovereign to the new regional status of Syrian viceroy, to whom all the sultan's governors and other officials in the Syrian regions were subordinated; in 1340, however, after many years of successful Syrian service in this capacity, Tankiz fell from favour, an army was sent from Egypt, he was seized and eventually he was killed as the sultan's prisoner in Alexandria.

Tankiz' long and eventful career in the Syrian limelight of sultan al-Nāṣir Muḥammad's authority may also be usefully reconstructed as a powerful illustration of the analytical value and validity of that network prism of imperial relations, practices and structural appearances. Seen from this perspective, Tankiz originated as an important participant in al-Nāṣir Muḥummad's political network, sent out in 1312 as its intermediary to connect with and mediate between local power elites and social groups, first in Damascus and eventually also in the rest of Syria. Throughout his long career of twenty-eight years, contemporary narrative source reports, extant monuments, and remaining artefacts attest not just to Tankiz' regional Syrian empowerment and enrichment, but also to al-Nāṣir Muḥammad's pursuance of all kinds of practices of vertical integration vis-à-vis his main Syrian agent. These materialised in the format of long lists of gifts that were exchanged between both leaders, in mutual marriage relations that were concluded or promised, and in honours, offices and regular income that were awarded to him and to members of his family and entourage. One of his biographers, the contemporary Syrian scribe and litterateur Khalīl b. Aybak al-Ṣafadī (d. 1363) summarised this ongoing process of Tankiz' integration into the sultan's sphere of power and influence as follows:

> [Tankiz] constantly rose in rank which doubled his *iqṭāʿ*, his presents, and his income in horses, fabric, birds, and birds of prey, so that he was given the title of *Aʿazz Allāh Anṣār al-Maqarr al-Karīm al-ʿĀlī al-Amīrī*, and among his courtesy titles was *al-Atābakī al-Zāhidī al-ʿĀbidī.* He was called *Muʿizz al-Islām wa-l-Muslimīn, Sayyid al-Umarāʾ fī al-ʿĀlamīn.* And it was not known to us that letters of a sultan can also be written by a governor or by someone who is not a governor but has a different function or position. The sultan hardly took any steps without sending for and consulting with him. […] Sharaf al-Dīn al-Nashw told me: 'What was given as a present by the sultan in the year 733 [1332–33] added up to 1,050,000 dirhams in addition to the horses and saddles which he was [also] given, the money in cash, the yield of the crops, and the small livestock which he owned in Syria. […] After that he betook himself [to the sultan] four times, I think, and every time the presents he received were doubled. His power and his reputation increased until the Egyptian amirs who were the [sultan's] bodyguards dreaded him.[37]

37 Translated by Conermann, "Tankiz," p. 9; citing Khalīl b. Aybak al-Ṣafadī (1297–1363), *Kitāb*

At the same time however, al-Nāṣir Muḥammad matched this policy of Tankiz' vertical integration with the deployment of practices of horizontal segmentation in Syria. The remarkable invention of the Ayyūbid sultanate of Ḥamā in 1320 and the long-aspired subordination of the *amīr al-ʿArab* Muhannā in 1334 indeed should not just be seen as integrating the Syrian bedouin leadership and the elites of Ḥamā into the sultan's power network. Through these actions the sultan also kept these groups and communities locally divided in parallel and perhaps even competitive relationships. Among these relationships political and socio-economic priority was thus generated for those ties that bound them to Cairo. The outcome of these practices, of which the cases of Ḥamā and Muhannā may well only represent the tip of an iceberg, imposed furthermore important political boundaries on Tankiz' expanding Syrian authority.[38]

The latter longstanding and continuously expanding authority appears in fact as increasingly locally integrated. The success of this local integration, as a set of relationships distinct to those integrating Tankiz simultaneously into the sultan's network, is not in the least also suggested by the impressive architectural legacy that Tankiz left behind, which was studied in much detail by Ellen Kenney and which attests to the active participation of Tankiz and his own agents in various local socio-economic and cultural flows and circulations of people, ideas and resources. In the course of his career of twenty-eight years in Syria Tankiz' role thus also changed substantially. From an intermediary and negotiator for al-Nāṣir Muḥammad's power he gradually transformed into a power broker in his own right. Participating in, and also initiating, practices of integration and segmentation in the local contexts of his Syrian claims to authority, Tankiz connected Syrian leaderships to his own gravitational pull, as that was emanating from his headquarters in Damascus. Amid the contingent effects (and – over time – the increasingly structural appearances) of this process and its continuous focus on Tankiz' court in Damascus, and despite al-Nāṣir Muḥammad's relentless efforts at Syrian segmentation, the sultan's pull from Cairo came to appear increasingly distant and abstract, if not almost redundant, for many Syrian elites, including even for Tankiz himself. In many ways therefore Tankiz gradually

---

Wāfī bi-l-Wafayāt, eds. S. Dedering *et al.*, *Das biographische Lexikon des Ṣalaḥaddīn Ḫalīl Ibn Aibak aṣ-Ṣafadī*, 30 vols (Beirut: Orient-Institut der DMG, 2008–10), 10: 420–43.

38 See Peter M. Holt, *The Memoirs of a Syrian Prince, Abu 'l-Fidā', Sultan of Ḥamāh (672–732/1273–1331)* (Wiesbaden: Franz Steiner Verlag, 1983); M.A. Hiyari, "The Origins and Development of the Amīrate of the Arabs during the Seventh/Thirteenth and Eighth/Fourteenth Centuries," *Bulletin of the School of Oriental and African Studies*, 38 (1975): 509–24. See also Kamil S. Salibi, "The Buḥturids of the Ġarb: Mediaeval Lords of Beirut and of Southern Lebanon", *Arabica* 8 (1961): 74–97; Kellner-Heinkele, "Turkomans." See especially also relevant chapters in A. Troadec, "Les Mamelouks dans l'espace syrien: stratégies de domination et résistances (658/1260–741/1341)," Ph.D. Dissertation, Ecole Pratique des Hautes Etudes (Paris, 2014).

moved from the imperial center of the Sultanate under al-Nāṣir Muḥammad to its periphery, eventually even establishing a rival imperial center. When this happened – or at least when Tankiz' actions were thus explained at al-Nāṣir Muḥammad's court in Cairo – the sultan's pull, the centrality of his sovereignty, and concomitant political and economic relationships had to be restored through violence and military action. An army was therefore sent, Tankiz was seized and eventually killed, and the remnants of his local networks were subdued and appropriated by a new agent of the sultan.

This almost structural appearance of the widening of the political distance that separated an agent such as Tankiz from the imperial center in Cairo, and that transformed his role from intermediary to broker in his own right may actually be identified as a recurrent phenomenon in the Sultanate's long history. More tangible illustrations of this constant reconfiguration of center and periphery in the Sultanate's political relationships emerge from various other famous (and infamous) historical cases. These include the so-called "rebellions" in Syria of the amirs Sunqur al-Ashqar (d. 1293) and Baybughā Rūs (d. 1353), in 1279 and 1352 respectively; both eventually decided to cut all ties with Cairo, culminating in both cases in the highly symbolic act of proclaiming themselves sultan in Damascus, with the respective royal titles of al-Malik al-Kāmil and al-Malik al-ʿĀdil.[39] The same course of historical action was pursued by the *nāʾib al-Shām* Shaykh al-Maḥmūdi (d. 1421) in 1412; culminating in the public execution of sultan al-Nāṣir Faraj and the enthronement of the caliph al-Mustaʿīn as sultan, Shaykh's actions appear *in hindsight* as much more successful than those of his predecessors Sunqur and Baybughā. Whereas in the latter two cases their Syrian actions came to naught, Shaykh eventually managed to occupy the court in Cairo, to proclaim himself sultan with the title of al-Malik al-Muʾayyad, and to transform his erstwhile Syrian network through continued military and political action into the nucleus of a new imperial political order that was emanating from Cairo.[40] Other relevant cases concern the so-called "desertions" of the senior amirs Sayf al-Dīn Qipchaq and Qarāsunqur al-Manṣūrī (d. 1327), in 1298 and 1312 respectively; in both cases, it may be argued that they were actually drawn to a competing gravitational pull that was emanating at the time from the Ilkhanid

39 See Linda S. Northrup, *From Slave to Sultan. The Career of al-Manṣūr Qalāwūn and the Consolidation of Mamluk Rule in Egypt and Syria (678–689 A.H./1279–1290 A.D.)* (Stuttgart: Franz Steiner Verlag, 1998), pp. 90–7; Jo Van Steenbergen, *Order Out of Chaos. Patronage, Conflict and Mamluk Socio-Political Culture, 1341–1382* (Leiden: Brill, 2006), pp. 136, 156, 192.

40 See Julien Loiseau, *Reconstruire la maison du sultan. 1350–1450. Ruine et Recomposition de l'ordre urbain au Caire*, 2 vols. (Le Caire: IFAO, 2010); Clément Onimus, "Les émirs dans le sultanat mamelouk sous les sultans Barqūq et Farağ (1382–1412)," Ph.D. Dissertation, Ecole Pratique des Hautes Etudes (Paris) and Ghent University, 2013.

Mongol court in Azerbaijan.[41] This process of the constant reconfiguration and renegotiation of the categories of center and periphery emerges in similar ways from the stories of the *nā'ib al-Shām* Jānim al-Ashrafī (d. 1462) and of the *nā'ib Ḥalab* Khāyirbak al-Jārkasī (d. 1522). In 1462 Jānim appealed to the regional brokerage of the aforementioned Aqqoyunlu ruler Uzun Ḥasan when sultan al-Ẓāhir Khushqadam (r. 1461–7) in Cairo pushed him out of the Sultanate's imperial network.[42] A parallel movement may be recorded for Khāyirbak, who in 1516 moved quite organically and successfully from Cairo's periphery to that of Ottoman Constantinople by re-orienting his imperial relationships from sultan Qāniṣawh (r. 1501–16) to sultan Selim (r. 1512–20).[43] In more symbolic and less impactful ways, the same reconfiguration of imperial relationships of center and periphery may finally also help to better imagine what it meant for Uzun Ḥasan to proclaim, in the later 1460s in the wake of his conquests in the East, his full and absolute sovereignty, ending any impression of the pursuance of integration, however symbolically, into the Sultanate's political networks.[44]

What these illustrious and multivalent cases, from Tankiz to Khāyirbak and from al-Mu'ayyad Shaykh to Uzun Ḥasan, have in common is above all indeed their centrifugal dynamics, culminating more often than not in violent dissolutions, in the dislocation of relationships, and in the emergence of rival power centers. These dynamics and their centrifugal patterns appear furthermore as the structural outcome of the constant struggle in social practice over the gravitational pull that was emanating from Cairo, and therefore over the very categories of the Sultanate's periphery and center. The case of Tankiz represents therefore first and foremost (as do those of so many others like him) an example of how these centrifugal dynamics never ceased to structure (and restructure) the Sultanate and its continuously shifting imperial boundaries.

What also emerges from considering all these cases together is that this endless negotiation of boundaries between periphery and center happened in a way that may be considered quite particular for the Syro-Egyptian Sultanate.

41 Reuven Amitai, "The Mongol Occupation of Damascus in 1300: A Study of Mamluk Loyalties", in *The Mamluks in Egyptian and Syrian Politics and Society*, eds. Amalia Levanoni and Michael Winter (Leiden: Brill, 2004), pp. 21–41; Peter M. Holt, *The Age of the Crusades. The Near East from the Eleventh Century to 1517* (London: Longman, 1986), p. 113; Amir Mazor, *The Rise and Fall of a Muslim Regiment. The Manṣūriyya and the First Mamluk Sultanate, 678/1279–741/1341* (Bonn: Bonn UP, 2015), pp. 103–5, 200–1.

42 Woods, *The Aqquyunlu*, p. 92.

43 Carl F. Petry, *Twilight of Majesty. The Reign of the Mamlūk Sultans al-Ashraf Qāytbāy and Qānṣūh al-Ghawrī in Egypt* (Seattle: University of Washington Press, 1993),pp. 199–228; Michael Winter, "The Ottoman Occupation," in *Cambridge History of Egypt*, pp. 504–10; Robert Irwin, "Gunpowder and Firearms in the Mamluk Sultanate Reconsidered," in *The Mamluks in Egyptian and Syrian Politics and Society*, pp. 117–139.

44 Woods, *The Aqquyunlu*, pp. 107–8.

"The boundary marking itself," to paraphrase Barkey's assertion for the Ottoman imperial context, did not just "happen in the messy intermediate space in which state makers meet different groups and negotiate the terms of separation, difference, similarity, and cooperation."[45] It also happened, over and over again, in the messy spaces in which those "state makers" continued to meet each other, where they continued to redefine what appeared to themselves and to their supporters as the Sultanate's imperial center. This center therefore was as much a variable in the history of the Sultanate's political action, as its many peripheries were. Of course, the region-wide sovereign appearance of the court at the regional metropolis of Cairo, and its longstanding memory as a space of power and glory, qualifies this statement. However, the example of Shaykh al-Maḥmūdī's successful movement to Cairo from the Syrian periphery, and of his total displacement of the former sultan's political relationships, reminds one at the same time that this symbolic appearance of centrality and harmonious political order went hand in hand with a far more volatile social reality of central elites and relationships.

From the Sultanate's history during the second half of the fifteenth century another remarkable case of empowerment and negotiation has been preserved that presents itself as equally insightful, in complementary "symptomatic" ways to the centrifugal one of Tankiz, into this particularity of the volatility of not just the Sultanate's peripheries, but also its center. This concerns a centripetal movement that appears here as an example of yet another type of process that contributed to this endless (re)structuring of the Sultanate and its boundaries. This centripetal movement actually revolves around the somewhat surprisingly gendered life and times of the Banū Khāṣṣ Bak.

This appears indeed as a gendered story of two powerful women, the wives of the sultans Īnāl (r. 1453–61) and Qāytbāy (r. 1467–96): Zaynab bint Ḥasan b. Khāṣṣ Bak (d. 1479) and Fāṭima bint ʿAlī b. Khāṣṣ Bak (d. 1504). Their's is a story that is best known from the detailed studies of these sultans' reigns by Lucian Reinfandt and Carl Petry respectively.[46] The genealogical origins of these women

45 Barkey, *Empire of Difference*, p. 13.

46 Lucian Reinfandt, *Mamlukische Sultansstiftungen des 9./15. Jahrhunderts: nach den Urkunden der Stifter al-Ašraf Īnāl und al-Muʾayyad Aḥmad ibn Īnāl* (Berlin, 2003); idem, "Was geschah in der Zeit zwischen Barsbāy und Qāytbāy? Überlegungen zu einer Neubewertung des späten Mamlukensultanats," in *Norm und Abweichung, Akten des 27. Deutschen Orientalistentages*, eds. Stefan Wild and Hartmut Schild (Würzburg, 2001), pp. 269–278; idem, "Religious Endowments and Succession to Rule: The Career of a Sultan's Son in the Fifteenth Century," *Mamlūk Studies Review*, 6 (2002): 51–62. Carl F. Petry, "Class Solidarity versus Gender Gain: Women as Custodians of Property in Late Medieval Egypt," in *Women in Middle Eastern History*, ed. N. Keddie and B. Baron (New Haven: Yale University Press, 1991), pp. 122–42; idem, *Twilight of Majesty*, pp. 32–3, 165; idem, *Protectors or Praetorians. The Last Mamlūk Sultans and Egypt's Waning as a Great Power* (Albany: SUNY Press, 1994), pp. 200–2;

and their family lay with an amir of some social status in the first half of the fourteenth century. This amir Khāṣṣ Bak, or Khāṣṣ Turk, appears from the historical record as a royal favourite and high-ranking amir for many years at the court of sultan al-Nāṣir Muḥammad in Cairo, who sent him as an amir to Damascus shortly before 1330; nothing much else is known about him, apart from the fact that he died in Damascus in 1333, and that his son Ṣalāḥ al-Dīn Khalīl (d. 1363) served in the entourage of the *nāʾib al-Shām* Tankiz first, and then remained as a low-ranking amir in Damascus until his own death thirty years later.[47] The descendants of these two amirs then entirely disappear from the historiographical radar until the mid-fifteenth century, except for one Badr al-Dīn al-Ḥasan b. Khāṣṣ Bak (d. 1410), the father of Zaynab. This Ḥasan is identified in contemporary texts as combining a career as a leading Ḥanafī scholar, as a *jundī* (which probably refers above all to his entitlement to some kind of military income), and as a *muqaddam al-mamālīk al-sulṭāniyya* (which probably refers to his involvement, as a Ḥanafī scholar, in the education of the sultan's mamluks). The court historian Ibn Taghrī Birdī even claims that Ḥasan "enjoyed the respect of the *akābir al-dawla*, amirs and others." He furthermore suggests that his teacher al-Maqrīzī would have attended Ḥasan's reciting of the two main Ḥadīth collections of Sunni scholarship, the *Ṣaḥīḥ*s of al-Bukhārī and Muslim, in Mecca in the year 1381.[48]

This Ḥasan b. Khāṣṣ Bak thus clearly belonged to the cultural elite of Ḥanafī scholars at the courts of sultan al-Ẓāhir Barqūq (r. 1382–9, 1390–9) and, probably also, of his son al-Nāṣir Faraj. His daughter Zaynab eventually married the amir Īnāl al-Ajrūd (d. 1461) before 1432, when Īnāl was *nāʾib* in Gaza. She remained Īnāl's sole consort, also when he became sultan in 1453. Zaynab's niece Fāṭima, whose father ʿAlī remains unknown, married the amir Qāytbāy at some unknown date after 1458, during Īnāl's reign. Like Zaynab before her, Fāṭima also remained the sultan's sole wife. She retained a leading position in her husband's harem throughout his long reign, and continued to enjoy high status and respect at the

idem, "The Estate of al-Khuwand Fāṭima al-Khāṣṣbakiyya: Royal Spouse, Autonomous Investor," in *The Mamluks in Egyptian and Syrian Politics and History*, pp. 277–94. See more recently also Albrecht Fuess, "How to Marry Right. Searching for a royal spouse at the Mamluk court of Cairo in the fifteenth century," *DYNTRAN Working Paper* 21 (February 2017).

47 Al-Ṣafadī, *Aʿyān al-ʿAṣr wa-Aʿwān al-Naṣr*, ed. ʿA. Abū Zayd *et al.*, 6 vols. (Damascus and Beirut: Dār al-Fikr, 1998), 2: 306–7 ("Khāṣṣ Turk, al-Amīr Sayf al-Dīn al-Nāṣirī"); al-Ṣafadī, *al-Wāfī*, 13: 245; Ibn Taghrī Birdī, *al-Manhal al-Ṣāfī wal-Mustawfī baʿda al-Wāfī*, eds. M.M. Amīn, N.M. ʿAbd al-ʿAzīz *et al.*, 7 vols. (Cairo: al-Hayʾa al-Miṣriyya al-ʿĀmma lil-kitāb, 1984–1993), 5: 197–8 ("Khāṣṣ Bak b. ʿAbd Allāh al-Nāṣirī, al-Amīr Sayf al-Dīn"); Ibn Taghrī Birdī tellingly adds: "I think that he is the patriarch of the well-known Banū Khāṣṣ Bak group (*wālid al-jamāʿa Banī Khāṣṣ Bak al-mashhūrīn*)."

48 Ibn Taghrī Birdī, *Manhal*, 5: 73–4.

court of his successors until her own death in 1504.[49] Zaynab's firstborn son Aḥmad b. Īnāl (d. 1488) briefly reigned as sultan al-Muʾayyad Aḥmad in 1461. Despite his mature age at the time of his accession – unusual for sultans' sons in the fifteenth century – and despite his political experience after many years of service at his father's court, Aḥmad soon lost the sultanate to his father's right-hand amir Khushqadam. The entire family was then removed from the Sultanate's center in Cairo to Alexandria, where they were made to stay in some form of exile during the six years of Khushqadam's reign. When Qāytbāy acceded to the sultanate in 1467, however, Zaynab is reported to having returned to the court in Cairo, where she joined her niece Fāṭima and her royal husband; Zaynab's granddaughter is furthermore said to have married one of the most important members of Qāytbāy's entourage, the powerful amir Yashbak min Mahdī (who was killed in 1480 in a campaign against supporters of the Aqquyunlu leader Yaʿqūb, the son and successor of Uzun Ḥasan).[50] Beyond the remarkably high-profile intricacies of the Banū Khāṣṣ Bak's family life and political relationships, the studies of Lucian Reinfandt and Carl Petry have above all demonstrated that throughout the second half of the fifteenth century both women were not just powerful members of the courts of sultans Īnāl and Qāytbāy, but also successful economic entrepreneurs, who left an unusual amount of documentary traces. From this variety of documentary evidence it appears that Zaynab and Fāṭima actually controlled and managed, as the active supervising managers of various religious endowments, substantial wealth and real estate in Egypt and Syria, during as well as after their marriages. In fact, these rich family estates that they controlled may well have been an important factor in the success of their husbands to obtain and secure the Sultanate's throne in Cairo, in 1453 and in 1467 respectively.[51]

What is most relevant to retain from all this in the context of this chapter is that these stories and data provide haphazard insights into a remarkable, long-standing, and stable network of family, wealth, office, scholarship, and status, that appears as regularly moving in and out of the imperial limelight of Cairo's court, from the days of al-Nāṣir Muḥammad in the early 1300s to those of sultan Qāniṣawh in the early 1500s. Otherwise put, insights are thus provided in what presents itself as the long and winding history of the endless negotiations of this particular family network's members, in Cairo, in Damascus, in Alexandria, and even in Mecca, of Barkey's "terms of their separation, difference, similarity, and

49 See Reinfandt, *Mamlukische Sultansstiftungen*, pp. 46–7; Reinfandt, "Religious Endowments and Succession to Rule"; Petry, "The Estate of al-Khuwand Fāṭima al-Khāṣṣbakiyya."

50 Reinfandt, *Mamlukische Sultansstiftungen*, pp. 46–50; Reinfandt, "Religious Endowments and Succession to Rule," pp. 60–1; Woods, *The Aqquyunlu*, p. 130.

51 Reinfandt, *Mamlukische Sultansstiftungen*, pp. 46, 58; Reinfandt, "Religious Endowments and Succession to Rule," p. 59; Petry, "The Estate of al-Khuwand Fāṭima al-Khāṣṣbakiyya."

cooperation." The story of the Banū Khāṣṣ Bak therefore illustrates that there is not just a lot of movement in and out of the Sultanate's imperial formation at the peripheries, but also in the center, among elite networks who were constantly negotiating their stakes in that center. In many ways this reminds of the networking and factionalism that has been discussed for the first half of the fifteenth century by Henning Sievert, Amalia Levanoni, and Robert Irwin.[52] But it appears here in even more complex ways than imagined by Irwin, Levanoni or – most recently – Sievert. In this case, the Banū Khāṣṣ Bak does not appear as a short-lived political faction, but rather as an extremely successful, coherent and flexible imperial network, with various members and "state makers" who managed to broker power relationships across a variety of central structural holes for most of the second half of the fifteenth century.

What is furthermore illustrated by this story of the ongoing brokerage of a successful network's active participation in (and reconfiguration of) what was made to appear as the Sultanate's imperial center is the high complexity of this particular network's composition and activities. It was, most importantly, not just made up of *mamlūk*s and amirs, and it did not just engage in imperial politics. It was also deeply involved in parallel socio-economic and cultural (and political) realities that could even remain oblivious to the realities of the Sultanate's imperial center and periphery, and to the relationships and practices that connected and bound them.[53] In the case of the Banū Khāṣṣ Bak family, that internal segmentation of this network's historical action appeared not just from Zaynab's and Fāṭima's socio-economic entrepreneurship. It was actually suggested most forcefully when, in 1482, the family's leading agent in Alexandria, the former sultan al-Muʾayyad Aḥmad b. Īnāl, was elected *shaykh* of the local branch of the Shādhiliyya Sufi order.[54] Aḥmad thus managed to restore, in a certain way, boundaries that had similarly marked out his leadership before, but he now did

52 Henning Sievert, "Family, Friend or Foe? Factions, Households and Interpersonal Relations in Mamluk Egypt and Syria," in *Everything is on the Move*, pp. 84–125; Amalia Levanoni, "The Sultan's Laqab – A Sign of a New Order in Mamluk Factionalism?", in *The Mamluks in Egyptian and Syrian Politics and Society*, 79–115; Robert Irwin, "Factions in Medieval Egypt," *Journal of the Royal Asiatic Society*, 118/2 (1986): 228–46.

53 For interesting parallels from the politics of commercial relationships, which similarly remind one of a type of segmentation of historical action within particular bundels and entanglements of networks, see Francisco Javier Apellaniz Ruiz de Galarreta, "Banquiers, diplomates et pouvoir sultanien: une affaire d'épices sous les Mamelouks circassiens," *Annales Islamogolgiques*, 38/2 (2004): 285–304; idem, *Pouvoir et finance en Méditerranée pré-moderne: le deuxième Etat mamelouk et le commerce des épices* (Madrid: Consejo Superior de Investigaciones Cientificas, 2009); Georg Christ, "The Venetian Consul and the Cosmopolitan Mercantile Community of Alexandria at the Beginning of the Ninth/Fifteenth Century," *al-Masāq*, 26/1 (2014): 62–77; idem, "Beyond the Network – Connectors of Networks: Venetian Agents in Cairo and Venetian News Management," in *Everything is on the Move*, pp. 27–60.

54 Reinfandt, "Religious Endowments and Succession to Rule," p. 53.

so by tapping into a trans-regional bundle of networks that was quite distinct from that of the Sultanate's.

Conclusions

From the above discussions of the Sultanate's imperial appearances in theory and practice it becomes clear that any application of the particular imperial prism of practices and structural appearances that was advocated here actually enables one to look at the Sultanate's long history of political action in Egypt, Syria and beyond as though through an imperial microscope. It presents itself as a prism that offers the opportunity to magnify relationships of power and to expose their full complexity, in the Sultanate's center – the sultan's court in Cairo – as well as in the Sultanate's many peripheries. It even makes it possible to resolve, in analytical rather than descriptive terms, apparent paradoxes, such as the one that emerged from the cases of al-Sufyānī in southern Bilād al-Shām in 1413 and of Uzun Ḥasan in Georgia in 1459.

Applying this particular prism means understanding the Syro-Egyptian Sultanate as a bundle of diverse but entangled networks, that appear to operate – or present themselves as operating – on a trans-local canvas of connectivity, making wide (even universalising) claims to sovereignty. This hegemonic political discourse of the Sultanate's sovereignty that was emanating from Cairo appears to have retained a powerful transformative effect on all kinds of practices of political integration and segmentation throughout much of Muslim West Asia. Thus, it continued to draw local leaders such as ʿAlī Pādshāh, Uzun Ḥasan and many others like them into Cairo's gravitational pull for a long time between the thirteenth and early sixteenth centuries.

Applying this particular prism, however, also means acknowledging that these hegemonic appearances that separated center from periphery were not just very meaningful and did not just have substantial impact throughout the region. They were always also locally negotiated, and as such they could also always be contested, and perhaps even ignored, as happened in the case of al-Sufyānī's millenarian movement in southern Bilād al-Shām. These imperial appearances of the Syro-Egyptian Sultanate were always constructed in the micro-history of people and their negotiation of particular cultural, socio-economic and political relationships (a negotiation that was always defined simultaneously by the harmonising of multivalent interests and by particular forms of physical, symbolic and perhaps even economic violence).

As a consequence, it were first and foremost particular relationships between people that were thus structured into the bundle of diverse but entangled social networks that marked out the Sultanate of Cairo and its political action. In turn, these political relationships were themselves also always structured, whether in the Sultanate's center or in its many and diverse urban and rural peripheries in Egypt, Syria and beyond, in three interconnecting and overlapping practical ways that equally contributed to that marking out of the Sultanate and its political action. Firstly, these relationships always appeared as extremely fluid and multivalent, because they were defined and staked out by all kinds of boundaries that were continuously disputed and reconfigured, not just in the various peripheries, but also in what was constructed, disputed and continuously reconfigured as the Sultanate's imperial center. Secondly, they always appeared as pulsating in irregular fashion (rather than as emanating smoothly) from the gravitational pull of one or another sultan's court in Cairo, leaving many holes in between them. Thirdly, they always appeared as permeable and as crisscrossed by many other, equally fluid, relational realities that appeared to be pulsating from other local or trans-local centers of social, economic, cultural or even political action. It is this fluid, pulsating and permeable micro-history of all kinds of particular relationships and their structural (and structuring) appearances that begs for much deeper and finer analyses through the imperial microscope. Only then some of these many micro-histories' highly impactful imperial, "solar," appearances throughout Egypt, Syria and wider Muslim West-Asia, as the long-standing sovereign Sultanate of Cairo, may reveal more of the multiple subtleties of their actual, sometimes even paradoxical, historical meanings.

Bibliography

Adriaenssens, V., and J. Van Steenbergen, "Mamluk Authorities and Anatolian Realities: Jānibak al-Ṣūfī, sultan al-Ashraf Barsbāy, and the story of a social network in the Mamluk/Anatolian frontier zone, 1435–1438", *Journal of the Royal Asiatic Society* 26/4 (2016): 591–630.

Amitai, R., "The Mongol Occupation of Damascus in 1300: A Study of Mamluk Loyalties", in *The Mamluks in Egyptian and Syrian Politics and Society*, eds. A. Levanoni and M. Winter (Leiden: Brill, 2004), pp. 21–41.

Apellaniz Ruiz de Galarreta, F.J., "Banquiers, diplomates et pouvoir sultanien: une affaire d'épices sous les Mamelouks circassiens", *Annales Islamologiques* 38/2 (2004): 285–304.

–, *Pouvoir et finance en Méditerranée pré-moderne: le deuxième Etat mamelouk et le commerce des épices* (Madrid: Consejo Superior de Investigaciones Cientificas, 2009).

al-ʿAynī, Badr al-Dīn Maḥmūd (1361–1451), *ʿIqd al-Jumān fī tārīkh ahl al-zamān: ḥawādith wa-tarājim*, ed. ʿA. al-Ṭanṭāwī Qarmūṭ, 2 vols. (Cairo: al-Zahrā, 1989).

Balog, P., "History of the Dirhem in Egypt from the Fātimid Conquest until the Collapse of the Mamlūk Empire, 358–922 H./968–1517 A.D.", *Revue numismatique* (6th ser.) 3 (1961): 109–46.

Barkey, K., *Empire of Difference. The Ottomans in Comparative Perspective* (Cambridge: Cambridge UP, 2008).

Blake, S.P., "The Patrimonial-Bureaucratic Empire of the Mughals", *The Journal of Asian Studies* 39/1 (1979): 77–94.

–, "Returning the Household to the Patrimonial-Bureaucratic Empire: Gender, Succession, and Ritual in the Mughal, Safavid and Ottoman Empires", in *Tributary Empires in Global History*, eds. P.F. Bang & C.A. Bayly (New York: Palgrave Macmillan, 2011), pp. 214–26.

Brinner, W.M., "The Significance of the Ḥarāfīsh and Their Sultan", *Journal of the Economoc and Social History of the Orient* 6 (1963): 190–215.

Burbank, J., & F. Cooper, *Empires in World History. Power and the Politics of Difference* (Princeton: Princeton UP, 2010).

Büssow-Schmitz, S, "Rules of Communication and Politics between bedouin and Mamluk elites in Egypt: the case of the al-Aḥdab revolt, c. 1353", *Eurasian Studies* 9/1–2 (2011): 67–104.

Chapoutot-Remadi, M., "L'agriculture dans l'empire mamluk au Moyen Âge d'après al-Nuwayrī", *Les Cahiers de Tunisie* 22 (1974): 23–45.

Clot, A., *L'Egypte des Mamelouks: l'empire des esclaves, 1250–1517* (Paris: Perrin, 1996).

Cobb, P.M., *White Banners. Contention in 'Abbasid Syria, 750–880* (Albany: SUNY Press, 2001).

Conermann, St., "Tankiz ibn ʿAbd Allāh al-Ḥusāmī (d. 740/1340) as Seen by His Contemporary al-Ṣafadī (d. 764/1363)", *Mamlūk Studies Review* 12/2 (2008): 1–24.

–, (ed.), *Everything is on the Move: The Mamluk Empire as a Node in (Trans-)Regional Networks* (Bonn: Bonn UP, 2014).

–, "Networks and Nodes in Mamluk Times: some introductory remarks", *Everything is on the Move: The Mamluk Empire as a Node in (Trans-)Regional Networks*, ed. Stephan Conermann (Bonn: Bonn UP, 2014), pp. 9–26.

Coureas, N., "Losing the War but Winning the Peace: Cyprus and Mamluk Egypt in the Fifteenth Century", in *Egypt and Syria in the Fatimid, Ayyubid and Mamluk Eras* – VII, eds. U. Vermeulen, K. D'hulster & J. Van Steenbergen (Leuven: Peeters, 2013), pp. 351–61.

Christ, G., "The Venetian Consul and the Cosmopolitan Mercantile Community of Alexandria at the Beginning of the Ninth/Fifteenth Century", *al-Masāq* 26/1 (2014): 62–77.

–, "Beyond the Network – Connectors of Networks: Venetian Agents in Cairo and Venetian News Management", in *Everything is on the Move: The Mamluk Empire as a Node in (Trans-)Regional Networks*, ed. Stephan Conermann (Bonn: Bonn UP, 2014), pp. 27–60.

Curtis, M., *Orientalism and Islam: European thinkers on Oriental Despotism in the Middle East and India* (Cambridge: Cambridge UP, 2009).

Dols, M.W., "The General Mortality of the Black Death in the Mamluk Empire", in *The Islamic Middle East, 700–1900*, ed. A.L. Udovitch (Princeton: Darwin, 1981), pp. 397–428.

Doyle, M., *Empires* (Ithaca: Cornell UP, 1986).

Eisenstadt, S.M., *The Political Systems of Empires* (New Brunswick: Transaction Publishers, 1993; first edition 1963).

Escovitz, J.H., "The Establishment of Four Chief Judgeships in the Mamlūk Empire", *Journal of the American Oriental Society* 102 (1982): 529–31.

Fuess, A., "Sultans with Horns: The Political Significance of Headgear in the Mamluk Empire", *Mamlūk Studies Review* 12/2 (2008): 71–94.

Garcin, J.-Cl., "La 'méditerranéisation' de l'empire mamelouk sous les sultans bahrides", *Rivista degli studi orientali* 48 (1973–4): 109–16.

–, "Note sur les rapports entre bédouins et fallahs à l'époque mamluke", *Annales Islamologiques* 14 (1978): 147–63.

Gayraud, R.-P., "Ceramics in the Mamluk Empire. An Overview", in *The Arts of the Mamluks in Egypt and Syria – Evolution and Impact*, ed. D. Behrens-Abouseif (Bonn: Bonn UP, 2012), pp. 77–94.

Goldstone, J.A., and J.F. Haldon, "Ancient States, Empires, and Exploitation. Problems and Perspectives", in *The Dynamics of Ancient Empires. State Power from Assyria to Byzantium*, eds. I. Morris and W. Scheidel (Oxford: Oxford UP, 2008), pp. 1–29.

al-Ḥajjī, Ḥ.N., *Al-Amīr Tankiz al-Ḥusāmī, nāʾib al-Shām fī l-fatra 712–741 h./1312–1340 M* (Kuwait: Jāmiʿat al-Kuwayt, 1980).

Har-El, Sh., *Struggle for Domination of the Middle East: The Ottoman-Mamluk War, 1485–91* (Leiden: Brill, 1995).

Hiyari, M.A., "The Origins and Development of the Amīrate of the Arabs during the Seventh/Thirteenth and Eighth/Fourteenth Centuries", *Bulletin of the School of Oriental and Asian Studies* 38 (1975): 509–24.

Holt, P.M., *The Memoirs of a Syrian Prince, Abu 'l-Fidā', Sultan of Ḥamāh (672–732/1273–1331)* (Wiesbaden: Franz Steiner Verlag, 1983).

–, *The Age of the Crusades. The Near East from the Eleventh Century to 1517* (London: Longman, 1986).

Howe, S., *Empire. A Very Short Introduction* (Oxford: Oxford UP, 2002).

Humphreys, R.St., "Egypt in the World System of the Later Middle Ages", *The Cambridge History of Egypt. Volume I. Islamic Egypt, 640–1517*, ed. C.F. Petry (Cambridge: Cambridge UP, 1998), pp. 445–461.

–, "The Fiscal Administration of the Mamluk Empire", in *Islamic History: A Framework for Inquiry* (Princeton: Princeton UP, 1991), pp. 169–186 (Chap. 7).

Ibn Taghrī Birdī, Jamāl al-Dīn Yūsuf (1411–70), *Ḥawādith al-Duhūr fī madā l-ayyām wa-l-shuhūr*, ed. W. Popper, *Extracts from Abû 'l-Maḥâsin Ibn Taghrî Birdî's Chronicle, entitled Ḥawâdith ad-duhûr fî madâ 'l-ayyâm wash-shuhûr* (Berkeley: University of California Press, 1930–42).

–, *al-Manhal al-Ṣāfī wa-l-Mustawfī baʿda l-Wāfī*, eds. M.M. Amīn, N.M. ʿAbd al-ʿAzīz *et al*, 7 vols. (Cairo: al-Hayʾa al-Miṣriyya al-ʿĀmma li-l-kitāb, 1984–1993).

Irwin, R., "Factions in Medieval Egypt", *Journal of the Royal Asiatic Society* 118/2 (1986): 228–46.

–, "Gunpowder and Firearms in the Mamluk Sultanate Reconsidered", in *The Mamluks in Egyptian and Syrian Politics and Society*, pp. 117–139.

Kellner-Heinkele, B., "The Turkomans and Bilād aš-Šām in the Mamluk Period", in *Land Tenure and Social Transformation in the Middle East*, ed. T. Khalidi (Beirut: American University, 1984), pp. 169–80.

Kenney, E., *Power and Patronage in Medieval Syria. The Architecture and Urban Works of Tankiz al-Nāṣirī* (Chicago: MEDOC, 2009).

Lantscher, P., "Fragmented Cities in the Later Middle Ages: Italy and the Near East Compared", *English Historical Review* 130 (2015): 546–82.

Levanoni, A., "The Sultan's Laqab - A Sign of a New Order in Mamluk Factionalism?", in *The Mamluks in Egyptian and Syrian Politics and Society*, 79–115.

Lieberman, V., *Strange Parallels. Southeast Asia in Global Context, c. 800–1830. Volume 1: Integration on the Mainland* (Cambridge: Cambridge UP, 2003).

Loiseau, J., *Reconstruire la maison du sultan. 1350–1450. Ruine et Recomposition de l'ordre urbain au Caire*, 2 vols. (Le Caire: IFAO, 2010).

al-Maqrīzī, Aḥmad b. ʿAlī (1363–1442), *Kitāb al-Sulūk li-Maʿrifat Duwal al-Mulūk*, ed. S. ʿA. ʿĀshūr, vols. 3–4 (Cairo: Maṭbaʿat Dār al-Kutub, 1972).

Marmon, S.E., "Domestic Slavery in the Mamluk Empire: a preliminary sketch", in *Slavery in the Islamic Middle East*, ed. S.E. Marmon (Princeton: Markus Wiener Publishers, 1999), pp. 1–23.

–, "Black Slaves in Mamlūk Narratives: Representations of Transgression,"*Al-Qanṭara* 28/ 2 (2007): 435–64.

Mazor, A., *The Rise and Fall of a Muslim Regiment. The Manṣūriyya and the First Mamluk Sultanate, 678/1279–741/1341* (Bonn: Bonn UP, 2015).

Meloy, J., "Imperial Strategy and Political Exigency: The Red Sea Spice Trade and the Mamluk Sultanate in the Fifteenth Century", *Journal of the American Oriental Society* 123/1 (2003): 1–19.

–, *Imperial Power and Maritime Trade: Mecca and Cairo in the later Middle Ages* (Chicago: MEDOC, 2010).

Motyl, A.J., *Imperial Ends: The Decay, Collapse, and Revival of Empires* (New York: Columbia UP, 2001).

Northrup, L.S., *From Slave to Sultan. The Career of al-Manṣūr Qalāwūn and the Consolidation of Mamluk Rule in Egypt and Syria (678–689 A.H./1279–1290 A.D.)* (Stuttgart: Franz Steiner Verlag, 1998).

Onimus, C., "Les émirs dans le sultanat mamelouk sous les sultans Barqūq et Farağ (1382–1412)", PhD Dissertation, Ecole Pratique des Hautes Etudes (Paris) & Ghent University, 2013.

Perlmann,M., "Notes on Anti-Christian Propaganda in the Mamlūk Empire", *Bulletin of the School of Oriental and Asian Studies* 10 (1940–2): 843–61.

Petry, C.F., "Class Solidarity versus Gender Gain: Women as Custodians of Property in Late Medieval Egypt", in *Women in Middle Eastern History*, ed. N. Keddie & B. Baron (New Haven: Yale UP, 1991), pp. 122–42.

–, *Twilight of Majesty. The Reign of the Mamlūk Sultans al-Ashraf Qāytbāy and Qānṣūh al-Ghawrī in Egypt* (Seattle: University of Washington Press, 1993).

–, *Protectors or Praetorians. The Last Mamlūk Sultans and Egypt's Waning as a Great Power* (Albany: SUNY Press, 1994), pp. 200–2.

–, "The Estate of al-Khuwand Fāṭima al-Khāṣṣbakiyya: Royal Spouse, Autonomous Investor", in *The Mamluks in Egyptian and Syrian Politics and History*, pp. 277–94.

Rapoport, Y., "Invisible Peasants, Marauding Nomads: Taxation, Tribalism, and Rebellion in Mamluk Egypt", *Mamlūk Studies Review* 8/2 (2004): 1–22.

Raymond, A., "Conflits maritimes, politique méditerranéenne et évolution de l'empire mamelouk égyptien au XVe siècle", *Les Cahiers de Tunisie* 48 (1995): 165–76.

Reinfandt, L., "Was geschah in der Zeit zwischen Barsbāy und Qāytbāy? Überlegungen zu einer Neubewertung des späten Mamlukensultanats", in *Norm und Abweichung, Akten des 27. Deutschen Orientalistentages*, eds. Stefan Wild and HartmutSchild (Würzburg, 2001), pp. 269–278.

–, "Religious Endowments and Succession to Rule: The Career of a Sultan's Son in the Fifteenth Century", *Mamlūk Studies Review* 6 (2002): 51–62.

–, *Mamlukische Sultansstiftungen des 9./15. Jahrhunderts: nach den Urkunden der Stifter al-Ašraf Īnāl und al-Mu'ayyad Aḥmad ibn Īnāl* (Berlin, 2003).

Reinhard, W., ed., *Empires and Encounters. 1350–1750* (Cambridge, Mss: Harvard UP, 2015).

Reynolds, S., "Empires: a problem of comparative history", *Historical Research* 79 (2006): 151–65.

al-Ṣafadī, Khalīl b. Aybak (1297–1363), *Kitāb Wāfī bi-l-Wafayāt*, eds. S. Dedering *et al*, *Das biographische Lexikon des Ṣalaḥaddīn Ḫalīl Ibn Aibak aṣ-Ṣafadī*, 30 vols (Beirut: Orient-Institut der DMG, 2008–10).

–, *A'yān al-'Aṣr wa-A'wān al-Naṣr*, ed. 'A. Abū Zayd *et al*, 6 vols. (Damascus and Beirut: Dār al-Fikr, 1998).

Salibi, K.S., "The Buḥturids of the Ġarb: Mediaeval Lords of Beirut and of Southern Lebanon", *Arabica* 8 (1961): 74–97.

Sauvaget, J., *La poste aux chevaux dans l'empire des Mamelouks* (Paris: Adrien-Maisonneuve, 1941).

Scheidel, W., "Studying the State", in *The Oxford Handbook of the State in the Ancient Near East and Mediterranean*, eds. P.F. Bang & W. Scheidel (Oxford: Oxford UP, 2013), pp. 5–57.

Sievert, H., "Family, friend or foe? Factions, households and interpersonal relations in Mamluk Egypt and Syria", in *Everything is on the Move: The Mamluk Empire as a Node in (Trans-)Regional Networks*, ed. Stephan Conermann (Bonn: Bonn UP, 2014), pp. 84–125.

Subtelny, M.E., *Timurids in Transition. Turko-Persian Politics and Acculturation in Medieval Iran* (Leiden: Brill, 2007).

Troadec, A., "Les Mamelouks dans l'espace syrien: stratégies de domination et résistances (658/1260–741/1341)", PhD Dissertation, Ecole Pratique des Hautes Etudes (Paris, 2014).

Van Steenbergen, Jo, "The Political Role of Damascus in the Mamluk Empire: Three Events in the Period 741/1341–750/1349, Imperative for the Change of Power in Cairo." *Orientalia Lovaniensia Periodica* 30 (1999): 113–28.

–, *Order Out of Chaos. Patronage, Conflict and Mamluk Socio-Political Culture, 1341–1382* (Leiden: Brill, 2006).

–, "Appearances of Dawla and Political Order in Late Medieval Syro-Egypt. The State, Social Theory, and the Political History of the Cairo Sultanate (thirteenth-sixteenth Centuries)." *History and Society During the Mamluk Period (1250–1517): Studies of the Annemarie Schimmel Research College II*, ed. Stephan Conermann (Göttingen: Bonn UP, 2016), pp. 53–88.

Wallerstein, I., *The Modern World-System I. Capitalist Agriculture and the Origins of the European World-Economy in the Sixteenth Century* [Berkeley: University of California Press, 2011; first edition 1974).

Wing, P., "The Decline of the Ilkhanate and the Mamluk Sultanate's Eastern Frontier", *Mamlūk Studies Review* 11/2 (2007): 77–88.

–, “Submission, Defiance, and the Rules of Politics on the Mamluk Sultanate’s Anatolian Frontier”, *Journal of the Royal Asiatic Society* 25/3 (2015): 377–88.

Woods, J., *The Aqquyunlu. Clan, Confederation, Empire. Revised and Expanded Edition* (Salt Lake City: The University of Utah Press, 1999).

al-Yūsufī, Mūsā (d. 1358), *Nuzhat al-Nāẓir fī Sīrat al-Malik al-Nāṣir*, ed. A. Ḥuṭayṭ (Beirut: ʿĀlam al-Kutub, 1986).

II. Local Concerns with Wider Implications

Robert Irwin (London)

How Circassian Were the Circassian Mamluks?

The rule of the Circassian Mamluks came to an end in 1517, but it may be helpful to start by looking at a feature of North African regimes in the two centuries that followed the Ottoman conquest of Egypt. In that period, as is well known, it was common for "professional Turks," European apostates from Christianity, to command Muslim fleets and armies. The famous names include Hassan Veneziano, Uj Ali and Murad Rais. Most of the "professional Turks" converted to Islam after being taken captive by Muslim pirates or soldiers.[1] However, it also seems to be case that some men chose to travel voluntarily to the Islamic lands and converted there in order to further their careers. Conversion then could be seen as a good career move, for Muslim society, in Istanbul or in Algiers, was relatively free from class distinctions, and the highest positions were open to the talented and the hardworking. Quite a few ex-Christians rose to become viziers, admirals or generals. Nabil Matar has drawn attention to the considerable numbers of Englishmen (thousands of them) who, attracted by good pay or possibly the prospect of exciting careers, enlisted in Muslim armies or fleets.[2] Linda Colley has estimated that between the beginning of the seventeenth century and the middle of the eighteenth at least 20,000 British and Irish were taken captive and enslaved in Barbary.[3] European gunners were especially welcomed by Muslim commanders. In this sort of context, ipsimission (the selling of oneself into slavery) was quite common.[4]

1 On the Barbary Corsairs and renegades, see: John B. Wolf, *The Barbary Coast: Algeria Under the Turks*, (New York: W.W. Norton, 1979); Stephen Clissold, *The Barbary Slaves*, (London: Paul Elek, 1977); Seton Dearden, *A Nest of Corsairs: The Fighting Karamanlis of the Barbary Coast*, (London: John Murray, 1976); Bartolomé Bennassar and Lucie Bennassar, *Les Chrétiens d'Allah: L'histoire extraordinaire des renégats XVIe-XIIe siècles*, (Paris: Perrin, 1989).

2 Nabil Matar, *Turks, Moors and Englishmen in the Age of Discovery*, (New York: Columbia University Press, 1998), 43–63; cf. Linda Colley, *Captives: Britain, Empire and the World, 1600–1850*, (London: Cape, 2002), 43–134.

3 Colley, *Captives:* 56.

4 On ipsimission, see Daniel Pipes, *Slave Soldiers and Islam: The Genesis of a Military System*, (New Haven and London: Yale University Press, 1981): 18–23.

If that was the case in the sixteenth and seventeenth centuries, why should it have been so very different in the fifteenth century? The reason we have thought it was otherwise is that the Arabic sources of the period rarely mention European mamluks. This kind of European was all but invisible in Mamluk Egypt and Syria. But consider that we do know of Europeans working in Yuan and Ming China and in the Mongol Ilkhanate, but we only know of them from European sources. Chinese and Persian sources from the Mongol period sources do not mention the alien presence. It seems likely that the same sort of thing was going on in Mamluk Egypt and Syria, where the Arab chroniclers preferred not to mention European mamluks and other prominent European residents. In Egypt and Syria there are occasional mentions in the Arabic sources of European mamluks – for example, the fifteenth-century sultan, Khushqadam, was identified as being of Greek origin.[5] But such indications are rare.

The case of Emmanuel Piloti is instructive. Piloti (b. 1371), a Venetian of Cretan origin, lived for several decades in Cairo. He enjoyed high favour at the court of the Sultan Faraj and was employed by the Sultan on a diplomatic mission to the Duke of Naxos. In 1411 he used his influence to protect Jews and Christians from expulsion from Egypt.[6] No Arabic source mentions the existence of this man. Again take the case of Bertrando de Mignanelli. Born in Siena in 1370, he settled in Damascus and prospered as a merchant there. He was a friend of the Sultan Barqūq and did some translation work for him. He was also a friend of Barqūq's great enemy and protagonist in the civil war of the 1390s, Nuʿayr the paramount chief of the Banū Faḍl Arabs in Syria.[7] No Arabic source mentions the presence of Mignanelli in Syria.

The Irishman Simon Semeonis who was in Palestine in 1323 reported that though the governor of Qaṭyā was reportedly a renegade, that is to say a convert to Islam, he was actually an Armenian Christian.[8] Mignanelli stated that Tamurtāsh, the Mamluk governor of Aleppo, who faced down Timur in 1401 was a Greek from Salonika.[9] According to Pero Tafur, who travelled in the East in the 1430s, mamluks were recruited from the Russians, Mingrelians, Caucasians, Circassians, Bulgarians and Armenians. He was looked after by the chief *Tarjuman*, or

5 Ibn Taghrībirdī, *Al-Nujūm al-Zāhirah fī Mulūk Miṣr wal-Qāhirah*, 12 volumes, (Cairo, 1929–56), 7: 685.

6 Emmanuele Piloti, *L'Égypte au commencement du quinzième siècle d'aprés le traité d'Emmanuel Piloti de Crète, incipit 1420*, ed. P.H. Dopp, (Louvain and Paris: Nauwelaerts, 1958).

7 Walter J. Fischel, "'Ascensus Baroch.' A Latin Biography of the Mamluk Sultan Barquq of Egypt," *Arabica*, 6 (1959), 57–74, 152–172; idem, "'Vita Tamerlani.' A New Latin Source on Tamerlane's Conquest of Damascus (1400–1401) by B. de Mignanelli, translated into English with an introduction and commentary," *Oriens*, 9 (1956), 201–233.

8 Simon Semeonis, *Itinerarium ab Hybernia ad Terram Sanctam*, tr. Maria Esposito (Dublin: Dublin Institute for Advanced Studies, 1960), 18, 102–3.

9 Fischel, "Vita Tamerlani," 20 and n.

Interpreter, who was at that time a Jewish renegade from Spain. Pero Tafur met a Portuguese mamluk in Jerusalem. According to Tafur, the Castilian pirate, Pedro de Laranda, was commander of al-Muʾayyad Shaykh's fleet, though he was later to be executed for his refusal to abjure Christianity.[10] At the beginning of the fifteenth century the Bavarian Johannes Schiltberger implied that he had been in the service of the Mamluk Sultan Barsbāy.[11] (But Schiltberger is admittedly a confusing and sometimes unreliable source.) Piloti reported how Faraj was betrayed by two of his commanders, respectively from Salonica and Sclavonia.[12] Ghillelbert de Lannoy in the 1420s listed among the mamluks Tatars, Turks, Bulgarians, Hungarians, Sclavonians, Wallachians, Russians and Greeks.[13] In the 1430s the Burgundian, Bertrandon de la Brocquière, got some of his information from a renegade Bulgarian.[14] A few years later Ludolph von Suchem in Hebron met three Germans from Minden who had converted to Islam because they thought that they had found a wealthy patron. (They were disappointed in their hopes).[15]

According to Anselm Adorno (who was in Egypt in 1470), among the mamluks were numerous Greeks, Italians, Albanians, Slavs, Russians and other renegades and apostates.[16] Bernhard von Breydenbach, in Egypt in 1483, met a mamluk from Basel, and lots of Hungarian mamluks – who had remained secret Christians and they came together for prayer in a secret crypt. According to Bernhard von Breydenbach, Qāytbāy's fortress in Alexandria was built by a German mamluk from Oppenheim.[17] In the early 1480s Felix Fabri, who travelled for part of the time with Breydenbach, also mentions the mamluk from Basel and various German mamluks[18] Moreover, the army that Fabri encountered at Gaza included

10 Pero Tafur, *Travels and Adventures 1435–1439*, tr. and ed. Malcolm Letts, (London: Routledge, 1926), 72, 97, 137.

11 Johann Schiltberger, *The Bondage and Travels of Johann Schiltberger, a native of Bavaria , in Europe, Asia and Africa, 1396–1427*, tr. J. Buchan Telfer, (London: Hakluyt Society, 1879), 51–2.

12 Piloti, *L'Egypte*, 35.

13 Lannoy, *Oeuvres de Ghilelbert de Lannoy, voyageur, diplomate et moraliste*, ed. C. Potvin (Louvain: Académie Royal des Sciences, des Lettres et des Beaux-Arts de Belgique, 1878), 118.

14 De la Brocquiere, "The Travels of Bertrandon de la Brocquiere. A.D. 1432, 1433," in Thomas Wright (ed. and tr.), *Early Travels in Palestine* (London: Bohn, London, 1848), 301–2.

15 Ludolph von Suchem, "'Description of the Holy Land' (1350 A.D.)," tr. A. Stewart, in *Palestine Pilgrim Text Society Library*, 12 (London, 1895–6), 91–2.

16 Anselm Adorno, *Itinéraire d'Anselme Adeorno en Terre Sainte (1470–1471)*, ed. and tr. Jacques Heers and Georgette de Groer (Paris: Centre National de la Recherche Scientififique, 1978), 199.

17 Bernhard von Breydenbach, *Les saintes peregrinations de Bernard de Breydenbach, 1483*, ed. and tr. F. Larrivaz (Cairo, 1904), 77.

18 Felix Fabri, *Le voyage en Égypte de Felix Fabri*, 1483, 3 vols, ed. and tr. Jacques Masson (Cairo: L'Institut français d'archéologie orientale du Caire, 1975), 3:913–5.

Hungarians, Sicilians and Catalans.[19] Joos van Ghistele who was in Egypt in the years 1482–3, claimed that the Sultan's great treasurer was a mamluk from Danzig called Nasr al-Din. Van Ghistele referred to Greek, Albanian, Italian and Vlach mamluks.[20] In 1484 Lionardo Frescobaldi's Grand *Tarjuman* was a renegade Venetian.[21] Arnold von Harff, who was in the Cairo in 1496, also met a mamluk from Basel and another from Denmark. Von Harff lodged in house of chief Dragoman (i.e., *Tarjuman*) who was of Genoese origin. He reported that mamluks were acquired from Slavonia, Greece, Albania, Circassia, Hungary and Italy, though only rarely from Germany.[22] Thenaud, in the last decade of the Mamluk Sultanate met a Mamluk from Languedoc.[23] But, of course, as Ulrich Haarmann pointed out, it was natural to for Western pilgrims to emphasise and overemphasise their encounters with mamluks of European and they were perhaps too careless in assuming that the mamluks they met were often renegades.[24]

Even so, one gets the impression that quite a few Europeans had entered into service as mamluks not after being captured and enslaved, but after voluntarily embracing the status of renegade. Most of the accounts I have drawn on here were produced in the fifteenth century, the heyday of the Circassian mamluks. But, if we did not have the merchant, Emmanuele Piloti's testimony, one would not necessarily have guessed that, well into the Circassian era, until at least as late as the reign of al-Ashraf Barsbāy, Turkish or Tatar white slaves cost more to buy than did Circassians.[25] Apart from the traditional Black Sea sources, Egypt must have received much of its supply of white slaves from the Ottoman Sultanate. According to Piloti, after the Crusaders' defeat at Nicopolis in 1396 the Ottomans sold two hundred Italian and French prisoners of war to Egypt.[26] Then Ottoman victories over the Hungarians in the 1440s and later in the fifteenth century, the

19 Fabri, *Voyage*, 1:31–3.

20 Joos van Ghistele, *Le voyage en Égypte de Joos van Ghistele 1482–3*, ed. and tr. Renée Bauwens Préaux (Cairo: L'Institut français d'archéologie orientale du Caire, Cairo, 1976), 30–31, 33–34, 36–37, 80.

21 *A Visit to the Holy Places of Egypt, Sinai, Palestine and Syria in 1384 by Frescobaldi, Gucci & Sigoli*, ed. and tr. Theophilus Bellorini and Eugene Hoade (Jerusalem: Studium Biblicum Franciscanum, Jerusalem, 1948), 45.

22 Von Harff, *The Pilgrimage of Arnold Von Harff*, ed. and tr. Malcolm Letts (London: Hakluyt Society, London, 1946), 102–3, 120.

23 Jean Thenaud, *Le voyage d'Outremer (Égypte, Mont Sinay, Palestine)*, ed. Charles Schefer (Paris: Recueil de voyages et de documents pour server à l'histoire de la géographie, 1884), 64.

24 For more on Europeans in the service of the Mamluk Sultans as mamluks, interpreters, technical advisers or artisans, see Ulrich Haarmann, "The Mamluk System of Rule in the Eyes of Western Travellers," *Mamlūk Studies Review*, 5 (2001), 6–16; idem, "Joseph's law – the Careers and Activities of Mamluk Descendants before the Ottoman Conquest of Egypt," in Thomas Philipp and Ulrich Haarmann (eds.), *The Mamluks in Egyptian Politics and Society*, (Cambridge, 1998), 55–6, 59–60.

25 Piloti, *Traité*, 53.

26 Ibid: 229.

conquest of Serbia, Wallachia and Albania and the capture of Constantinople, and the subsequent occupation of Morea and Trebizond provided a lot of human booty for the Turks to sell on to Egypt. Doubtless corsairs also played a role in supplying the slave markets and some European renegades may have joined the ranks of the mamluks as volunteers. It is even possible that conversion was not always insisted upon. In 1503 the adventurous Italian Lodovico Varthema, in Damascus and wanting to visit Mecca, "formed a great friendship with captain of the Mamelukes of the caravan, who was a Christian renegade, so that he clothed me like a Mameluke and gave me a good horse, and placed me in company with the other Mamelukes."[27]

Wherever the mamluks came from, whether from Circassia or from other parts of Europe, they almost invariably were given Turkish names when they became mamluks. In Sauvaget's *Noms et surnoms de Mamelouks*, most *isms* listed are Turkish, a few are Mongol and there is at least one Persian name. There are no obviously Circassian names – nor does one find anything like Hermann al-Ashrafi, Sandor al-Bashmaqdar, or Giovanni al-Shamsi. Instead the Circassian, European and Turkish mamluks regularly bore Turkish names like Aqqūsh, Alṭūnbughā, Aytamish, Alṭūnbāy, Barsbāy and so on.[28]

But enough about western European mamluks. What about the Circassians? What was the ethnic composition and culture of Circassia? How much Circassian culture travelled south to Egypt with the Circassians? Was Circassian the language of the court and the army? Did the young Circassians bring Christianity or Caucasian paganism with them in their slave's baggage? What if anything changed when the Mamluk recruiting grounds changed?

First, one should note that the switch from the purchase of Qipchaq Turks did not reflect a decline in the prestige of the Qipchaqs. The prices that Emmanuel Piloti, writing in the early fifteenth century, quoted for young mamluks indicates that Turks continued to fetch higher prices than did the Circassians or any of the other enslavable races. (The Tatar, by which Piloti meant Turk or Mongol, commonly fetched between 130 and 140 ducats, while the Circassian slave was likely to sell for only 110–120 ducats.)[29] Pero Tafur (also early fifteenth century) confirms that Turks still sold for a third more than any other race. Caffa's slave market sold Russians, Mingrelians, Caucasians, Circassians, Bulgarians, Armenians and others. It is perhaps noteworthy that Tafur placed no special emphasis

27 *Travellers in Disguise: Narratives of Eastern Travel by Poggio Bracciolini and Ludovico di Varthema*, tr. John Winter Jones and ed. Lincoln Davis Hammond, (Department of Romance Languages and Literatures, Harvard University, Harvard, Mass., 1963), 63.

28 Jean Sauvaget, "Noms et surnoms des Mamelouks," *Journal Asiatique*, 238 (1950), 31–58; cf. David Ayalon, "Names, Titles and 'Nisbas' of the Mamluks," *Israel Oriental Studies*, 5 (1975), 196–7.

29 Piloti, *Traité*, 53.

on the Circassians.[30] Nevertheless, it is clear that in fourteenth and fifteenth century Egypt, mamluks who were of Circassian origin, or at least believed themselves to be such took great pride in this and took pains to bring Circassian relatives to Egypt.[31]

Though Qipchaq slaves remained highly desirable, from the late fourteenth century onwards they were in relatively short supply because of the ravages of the plague and because so many Turks in southern Russia and the Caucasus had converted to Islam and were therefore, technically at least not enslavable. It is also interesting to note that references in European sources to Circassian slaves become very rare after the mid-fifteenth century.[32] The trade in Circassian slaves was managed by the Genoese in the Crimean port of Caffa, and by Venetians in Tana. The capture of these ports by Timur in 1395 seems to have brought only temporary disruption to the slave trade.

Genoese records of their commerce in the Black Sea in the early fifteenth century indicate that they were buying Circassians, Abkhazes, Mingrelians and Georgians. Abkhazes feature particularly frequently.[33] After 1453 the Black Sea was formally closed to Christian shipping. But the Genoese based in Chios were still managing to trade in slaves – Russians, Circassians, Abkhazes and Mingrelians, as well as captives taken by the Ottomans in their Balkan wars and human booty acquired in piratical raiding on the coast of Asia Minor. But the Genoese trade in slaves seems to have shrunk in this period.[34] Moreover references to Russian and Circassian slaves become rare. But in 1475 Gedik Ahmed Pasha, Mehmed II's grand vizier, annexed Caffa.[35] It is probable that this had an adverse effect on the trade in Circassian slaves and the Mamluk-Ottoman war of 1485–91 must have brought further disruption to that trade.

Even after the switch from southern Russian recruiting grounds to the Caucasus which took place some time in the second half of the fourteenth century, Arab chroniclers do not seem to have regarded the change as being of vast importance and they referred to the Circassians indifferently as "Turks" – just as

30 Tafur, *Travels*, 133.

31 Koby Yosef, "*Dawlat al-atrāk* or *dawlat al-mamālik?* Ethnic Origin or Slave Origin as the Defining Characteristic of the Ruling Elite in the Mamluk Sultanate," *Jerusalem Studies in Arabic and Islam*, 39 (2012), 387–410. On the identity and language of the Circassian mamluks, see now Julien Loiseau, *Les Mamelouks XIIIe–XVI siècle* (Paris: Éditions du Seuil, 2014), 174–205.

32 Charles Verlinden, *L'Esclavage dans l'Europe Médiévale*, 2 vols, (Ghent: Rijksuniversiteit, 1977) 2:342.

33 Jacques Heers, *Gênes au XV*^e^ *Siècle, activité économique et problèmes sociaux* (Paris: S.E.V.P.E.N., Paris, 1961), 365–371.

34 Ibid., 402–4.

35 Caroline Finkel, *Osman's Dream: The Story of the Ottoman Empire 1300–1923* (London: John Murray, 2005), 68.

earlier in the thirteenth century they had referred to the Ayyubid Kurds as "Turks." Ethnography was not the strong suit of the medieval Arab chronicler. Al-Maqrīzī referred to the Ayyubid dynasty as "Dawlat al-Atrāk". Al-ʿAynī in *Al-Sayf al-muhannad*, an accession manual written for al-Muʾayyad Shaykh, wrote about the ethnographic history of the Circassian Turks (*sic*) and claimed that there were originally four Turkish tribes of Circassians (*min al-tāʾifa al-turkiyya*): the Jarkas, the Arkas, the As and the Kasa. All descended from Noah's second son, Japeth – as did all the other Turkish peoples including the Ghuzz, the Qipchaqs, the Khitai and so forth. To return to the Circassians, the four big tribes broke down into many sub-tribes, some of which were also listed by al-ʿAynī. Particularly noteworthy were, first, the Basna, one of the largest groups and one that was related to the Mongols, and secondly, the Karmuk. It was from the noble lineage of Karmuk that the Sultan al-Muʾayyad descended. To al-ʿAynī's way of thinking, the Circassian Karmuk were not only Turks, but also Arabs, by virtue of their (legendary) intermarriage with the pre-Islamic Ghassanid Arabs who had fled to Circassia.[36] Previously, Ibn Khaldūn had similarly presented the Circassians as Turco-Arabs, stating in the *Kitāb al-ʿIbar* that the Jarkas *qabīla* (tribe) is from the Turks and this is known to the genealogists, and that the Jarkas had intermarried with the Ghassanid Arabs.[37] Even though al-ʿAynī regarded the Circassians as a sub-grouping of the Turks, he seems to have been aware of a distinction between the two, as he tells us that he used to think that Muʾayyad's mother was a Turk before being corrected on this matter by the Sultan himself: she was a Circassian.[38] (Incidentally, though Muʾayyad was a Circassian, he favoured Turks over Circassians when it came to recruiting and promoting.)

In a second legitimation manual, prepared for the Circassian Sultan Tatar and entitled *Al-Rawḍ al-zāhir fī sīrat al-Malik Ẓāhir*, al-ʿAynī covered essentially the same ethnographic ground more briefly, but a new and bizarre feature in the *Rawḍ* was al-ʿAynī's contention that that Baybars I was "the first Sultan who was Circassian in speech and his speech was of the As."[39]

The Circassian Sultan Qānṣawh al-Ghawrī was, like al-ʿAynī a believer in the Ghassanid contribution to the Circassian bloodstock. In the *Kitāb Nafāʾis majālis al-sulṭāniyya*, (a record made by Ḥusayn ibn Muḥammad al-Ḥusaynī of a series of sessions of talk between the Sultan and certain favoured courtiers and scholars in 1505), the Sultan was asked "What is the meaning of al-Jarkas?". The Sultan replied "The origin of Jarkas is Sarkas," and he went on to tell the story of the

36 Badr al-Dīn al-ʿAynī, *Sayf al-muhannad fī sīrat al-malik al-muʾayyad*, ed. Fahīm Muḥammad Shaltūt (Cairo: Dār al-Kitāb al-ʿArabī, 1967), 26–29.

37 Ibn Khaldūn, *Kitāb al-ʿIbar*, 7 vols. (Beirut: Dār al-Kutub al-Lubnānī, 1956–61), 5: 372.

38 Al-ʿAynī, *Sayf*, 30.

39 Al-ʿAyni, *Al-Rawḍ al-zāhir fī sīrat al-Malik Ẓāhir*, ed. Hans Ernst (Cairo: Dār Iḥyāʾ al-Kutub al-ʿArabiyya, 1962), 5–6.

flight of a Ghassanid, wanted for murder, to the court of the Byzantine Emperor Heraclius and how the latter settled the Ghassanid and his followers in the *Bilād al-Dasht* (or steppe land). In a later session, in the context of a discussion of the qualifications needed by a leader of the Islamic community, Qānṣawh al-Ghawrī insisted that the Circassians descended from Isḥāq (the Biblical Isaac).[40]

Despite Qānṣawh's actual Circassian origin and his belief that he was ultimately of Semitic descent, the culture he embraced and promoted was essentially a Turkish culture – and that is broadly speaking true of all his Circassian predecessors. In yet another session recorded in the *Nafāʾis*, Qānṣawh boasted of being fluent in Arabic, Persian, Turkish, Kurdish, Armenian, Circassian (Jarkasi), as well as Abkhaz and As (Ossetish).[41] However, while Qānṣawh remembered his original tongue and while he could reminisce about his childhood in Circassia, the adult Sultan had become a naturalised Turk. He wrote poetry in Turkish and he interested himself in the history of such Turkish figures as Maḥmūd of Ghazna and Baybars I. There is no evidence that he had any interest in Circassian history or culture. Qānṣawh's sponsorship of a translation of Firdawsī's *Shāhnāma* into Turkish is particularly noteworthy. Although Qānṣawh had commissioned this translation, it was not, he claimed, for his own benefit, for he was, of course, fluent in Persian. Rather, according to the translator, al-Ḥusaynī, the Sultan wanted the translation done so that his Turkish-speaking emirs might benefit from it. (I should here note that translating it into Circassian was not an option as Circassian was not at that time a written language.) Other Turkish works were similarly translated or copied under the patronage of the Circassian Sultan, for example a Ḥanbalī devotional manual by Ibn al-Layth in Qipchaq Turkish was copied for Qānṣawh's library. It is indeed one of the most curious features of the Circassian period that, on the evidence of what has survived, more works were then translated from Arabic or Persian into Qipchaq, or one of the other Turkish dialects, than in the preceding Qipchaq Mamluk period.[42]

Qānṣawh was unusual in the depth of his culture, but he was not unusual in the language of his culture. Al-Ashraf Qaytbāy, also of Circassian origin, wrote poetry in Turkish and so did the Circassian Emir Yashbak min Mahdī. We know from the researches of Ulrich Haarmann and Donald Little that a number of

40 Ḥusayn ibn Muḥammad al-Ḥusaynī, "*Kitāb Nafāʾis majālis al-sulṭāniyya*," separately paginated in *Majālis al-Sulṭān al-Ghawrī: Ṣafaḥāt min Taʾrīkh Miṣr fī al-Qarn al-ʿĀshir al-Hijrī* (Cairo: Maṭbaʿat Lajnat al-Taʾlīf wal-Tarjama wal-Nashr, 1946), 85, 107–8.

41 Ibid., 132–3.

42 On the Turko-Persian culture of Qānṣawh's court, see Mohammed Awad, "Sultan al-Ghawri. His Place in Literature and Learning (three Books Written Under His Patronage)," *Actes du XXe Congrès des Orientalistes, Bruxelles, 1938* (Louvain, 1940), 321–322; Barbara Flemming, "Aus den Nachtgesprächen Sultan Ġauris," in *Folia Rara, Festschrift für Wolfgang Voigt*, eds. H. Franke, W. Heissig and W. Treue, (Wiesbaden: Steiner, Wiesbaden, 1967), 22–8; idem, "Šerif, Sulttan Ġavri und die 'Perser'," *Der Islam*, 45 (1969), 71–94.

Turkish and Mongol officers interested themselves in Turkish and Mongol folklore.[43] Now the Circassian Nart cycle is full of marvellous and fascinating material – the golden tree and its guardian lady, the undersea kingdom, the ferryman who guards the souls of the Narts, the Nart Prometheus, the labyrinth city of Ghud-Ghud, the child who is conceived and reared in the grave, the souls of the sleeping travelling the world as flies, and the Lady Tree which was "a tree but not a tree, a person and not a person."[44] Why do we hear nothing about the Circassian Nart Saga in Circassian Mamluk Egypt?

That the culture of the Circassian court and army should turn out to be Turkish is at first sight curious. But there are several factors to be born in mind. First, medieval Circassia seems to have had no written literary culture of its own. Robbery was an honourable profession in Circassia. This is Schiltberger on Circassia:

> Item, a country called Starchas, which also lies by the Black Sea, where the people are of Greek faith; but they are a wicked people, because they sell their own children to the Infidels, and steal the children of other people and sell them; they are also highway robbers, and have a peculiar language. It is also their custom, that when one of their number is killed by lightning, they lay him in a box and put it on a high tree …[45]

Secondly, it is unlikely that all the slaves who were recruited in Circassia really were Circassian in any strict sense. The Caucasus was an ethnographic and linguistic patchwork of considerable complexity. As George Steiner has noted:

> Despite decades of comparative philological study and taxonomy, no linguist is certain of the language atlas of the Caucasus, stretching from Bzedux in the north-west to Rut'ul and Kuri in the Tatar regions of Azerbeidjan. Dido, Xwarsi, and Qapuci, three languages spoken between the Andi and Koissou rivers, have been tentatively identified and distinguished, but are scarcely known to any but native users. Arci, a language with a distinctive phonetic and morphological structure, is spoken by one village of 850 inhabitants. Oubykh, once a flourishing tongue on the shores of the Black Sea, survives today in a handful Turkish localities near Ada Pazar.[46]

43 Ulrich Haarmann, "Arabic in Speech, Turkish in Lineage: Mamluks and Their Sons in the Intellectual Life of Fourteenth-Century Egypt and Syria," *Journal of Semitic Studies*, 33 (1988), 81–114; idem, "*Der Schatz im Haupt des Götzen*," in Haarmann and Peter Bachmann (ed.), *Die Islamische Welt zwischen Mittelalter und Neuzeit: Festschrift für Hans Robert Roemer zum 65. Geburstag* (Wiesbaden: Franz Steiner, 1979), 198–229; Donald P. Little, "Notes on Aitamiš, a Mongol Mamluk," in ibid., 387–401.

44 On the Nart saga, see John Colarusso, *Nart Sagas from the Caucasus: Myths and Legends from the Circassians, Abazas, Abkhaz and Ubykhs* (Princeton: Princeton University Press, 2002).

45 Schiltberger, *Bondage*, 50.

46 George Steiner, *After Babel: Aspects of Language and Translation* (London: Oxford University Press, 1975), 43.

According to Julius von Klaproth, apart from languages properly speaking, the Circassians also had a secret raiders' and hunters' language. In addition, young Circassian princes had to learn a special language as part of an initiatory *rite de passage.* Klaproth, who travelled through Circassia in the early nineteenth century, compared the region to the patchwork of principalities in Germany before the Napoleonic wars. And he noted that the Circassians rarely sold their own people to the Turks. Rather, they sold slaves made captive from neighbouring Imerethi and Mingrelia.[47] It seems unlikely then that mostly Circassians *de pur sang* were acquired by ethnographically discriminating slavers. Rather the Caucasus supplied Mamluk Egypt and Syria with Mingrelians, Ubykhs, Ossetes, Abkhaz, Alans and Georgians – and Circassians. But it is even possible that some of the "Circassians" were actually Qipchaq Turks. From the eleventh century onwards both Qipchaq and Ghuzz Turks had settled in parts of the Caucasus. King David and Queen Tamar of Georgia had encouraged large numbers of Qipchaqs to move south through the Caucasus and had employed them in their armies.[48]

A final problem remains, that is difficult to solve. In fifteenth century Tuscany the white slaves – Russians, Circassians and Tatars – evolved a special slaves' jargon and a few bawdy poems survive as evidence of this.[49] There is no evidence of any such jargon in fifteenth-century Egypt or Syria. It is possible that newly imported non-Turkish mamluks received instruction in Turkish as part of their training in Egypt. However, although both al-Maqrīzī and Piloti tell us about teachers who used to visit the Cairo Citadel to instruct young mamluks in Arabic, we know nothing about how and from whom those mamluks learned Turkish.[50] Even so, according to Leo Africanus, writing in the early sixteenth century, the mamluks brought to Egypt were taught Turkish, as well as Arabic writing.[51] It is possible that, given the extraordinary linguistic diversity of the Caucasus where hundreds of languages were and are spoken and in which some languages were confined to a single village, then perhaps a form of Turkish functioned as a lingua franca in the medieval Caucasus. Ayalon suggested as much.[52] That this was indeed the case is confirmed by John of Sulṭāniyya's report on the region, the

47 Julius von Klaproth, *Travels in the Caucasus and Georgia Performed in the Years 1807 and 1808* (London, 1814), 34, 319.

48 W.E.D. Allen, *A History of the Georgian People from the Beginning Down to the Russian Conquest in the Nineteenth Century* (London: Routledge and Kegan Paul, London, 1932), 99, 106, 111–112.

49 Iris Origo, "The Domestic Enemy: The Eastern Slaves in Tuscany in the Fourteenth and Fifteenth Centuries," *Speculum*, 30/3 (July 1955), 338–339.

50 Piloti, *L'Egypte*, 54–55.

51 Natalie Zemon Davis, *Trickster Travels: A Sixteenth-century Muslim between Two Worlds*, (London: Faber, 2007), 148.

52 Ayalon, "Names, Titles and 'Nisbas'," 198–199n.

Libellus de notitia orbis (1404) in which he lists some of the Christian races in the Caucasus – Greeks, Armenians, Ziks, Goths, That's, Volaks, Russians, Circassians, Leks, Yass, Alans Avars, Kazikumyks – and he adds that almost all of them speak the Tatar language (by which he almost certainly meant Turkish).[53] In such circumstances, Turkish might serve as the lingua franca that was to be for many Circassians, Ubykhs, Alans and the rest of them a passport to promotion in Mamluk Egypt. In any case, it is clear that during what is known as the Circassian Mamluk period Turkish was the language used by the mamluks in Egypt and Syria.

Bibliography

Primary Sources

Adorno, Anselm. *Itinéraire d'Anselme Anselme Adeornoen Terre Sainte (1470–1471).* Ed. and tr. Jacques Heers and Georgette de Groer. Paris: Centre National de la Recherche Scientifique, 1978.
al-ʿAyni, Badr al-Dīn. *Al-Rawḍ al-zāhir fī sīrat al-Malik Ẓāhir*, ed. Hans Ernst. Cairo: Dār Iḥyāʾ al-Kutub al-ʿArabiyya, 1962.
al-ʿAynī, Badr al-Dīn. *Al-Sayf al-muhannad fī sīrat al-malik al-muʾayyad*, ed. Fahīm Muḥammad Shaltūt. Cairo: Dār al-Kitāb al-ʿArabī, 1967.
Bellorini, Theophilus and Eugene Hoade, ed. and tr. *A Visit to the Holy Places of Egypt, Sinai, Palestine and Syria in 1384 by Frescobaldi, Gucci & Sigoli.* Jerusalem: Studium Biblicum Franciscanum, Jerusalem, 1948.
von Breydenbach, Bernhard. *Les saintes peregrinations de Bernard de Breydenbach, 1483.* Ed. and tr. F. Larrivaz. Cairo, 1904.
de la Brocquiere, Bertrandon. "The Travels of Bertrandon de la Brocquiere. A.D. 1432, 1433." In Thomas Wright, ed. and tr. *Early Travels in Palestine.* London: Bohn, 1848.
Fabri, Felix. *Le voyage en Égypte de Felix Fabri, 1483.* Ed. and tr. Jacques Masson. Cairo: L'Institut français d'archéologie orientale du Caire, 1975. 3 vols.
van Ghistele, Joos. *Le voyage en Égypte de Joos van Ghistele 1482–3.* Ed. and tr. Renée Bauwens Préaux. Cairo: L'Institut français d'archéologie orientale du Caire 1976.
Von Harff, Arnold. *The Pilgrimage of Arnold Von Harff.* Ed. and tr. Malcolm Letts London: Hakluyt Society, London, 1946.
al-Ḥusaynī. Ḥusayn ibn Muḥammad. "Kitāb Nafāʾis majālis al-sulṭāniyya," separately paginated in *Majālis al-Sulṭān al-Ghawrī: Ṣafaḥāt min Taʾrīkh Miṣr fī al-Qarn al-ʿĀshir al-Hijrī.* Cairo: Maṭbaʿat Lajnat al-Taʿlīf wal-Tarjama wal-Nashr, 1946.
Ibn Khaldūn, Walī al-Dīn ʿAbd al-Raḥmān ibn Muḥammad. *Kitāb al-ʿibar wa-diwān al-mubtadaʾ waʾl-khabar fī ayyām al-ʿarab waʾl-ʿajam waʾl-barbar wa-man ʿaṣarahum min dhawī al-sulṭān al-akbar.* Beirut: Dār al-Kutub al-Lubnānī, 1956–61. 7 vols.

53 Lajos Tardy, "The Caucasian people and their neighbours in 1404," *Acta Orientalia scientarium Hungarica*, 32 (1978), 90.

Ibn Taghrībirdī, Jamāl al-Dīn Abū al-Maḥāsin Yūsuf. *Al-Nujūm al-zāhira fī mulūk Miṣr wal-Qāhira.* Cairo: Dār al-Kutub al-Miṣriyya, 1929–56. 12 vols.

de Lannoy, *Ghilelbert. Oeuvres de Ghilelbert de Lannoy, voyageur, diplomate et moraliste.* Ed. C. Potvin. Louvain: Académie royal des Sciences, des Lettres et des Beaux-Arts de Belgique, 1878.

Piloti, Emmanuele Piloti. *L'Égypte au commencement du quinzième siècle d'aprés le traité d'Emmanuel Piloti de Crète, incipit 1420.* Ed. P.H. Dopp. Louvain and Paris: Nauwelaerts, 1958.

Schiltberger, Johann. *The Bondage and Travels of Johann Schiltberger, a native of Bavaria, in Europe, Asia and Africa, 1396–1427.* Tr. J. Buchan Telfer. London: Hakluyt Society, 1879.

Semeonis, Simon. *Itinerarium ab Hybernia ad Terram Sanctam.* Tr. Maria Esposito. Dublin: Dublin Institute for Advanced Studies, 1960.

von Suchem, Ludolph. "'Description of the Holy Land' (1350 A.D.)." Tr. A. Stewart. In *Palestine Pilgrim Text Society Library* (London), 12 (1895–6).

Thenaud, Jean. *Le voyage d'Outremer (Égypte, Mont Sinay, Palestine).* Ed. Charles Schefer. Paris: Recueil de voyages et de documents pour server à l'histoire de la géographie, 1884.

Modern Studies

Allen, W.E.D. *A History of the Georgian People from the Beginning Down to the Russian Conquest in the Nineteenth Century.* London: Routledge and Kegan Paul, London, 1932.

Awad, Mohammed. "Sultan al-Ghawri. His Place in Literature and Learning (three Books Written under His Patronage." *Actes du XXeCongrès des Orientalistes, Bruxelles, 1938.* Louvain, 1940. 321–322.

Ayalon, David. "The Circassians in the Mamlūk Kingdom." *Journal of the American Oriental Society.* 69 (1949), 135–147. Reprinted in D. Ayalon, *Studies on the Mamlūks of Egypt.* London: Variorum, 1979.

Ayalon, David. "Names, Titles and 'Nisbas' of the Mamluks." *Israel Oriental Studies.* 5 (1975), 189–232. Reprinted in D. Ayalon, *The Mamlūk Military Society.* London: Variorum, 1977.

Bennassar, Bartolomé and Lucie Bennassar., *Les Chrétiens d'Allah: L'histoire extraordinaire des renégats XVIe-XIIe siècles.* Paris: Perrin, 1989.

Clissold, Stephen. *The Barbary Slaves.* London: Paul Elek, 1977.

Colarusso, John. *Nart Sagas from the Caucasus: Myths and Legends from the Circassians, Abazas, Abkhaz and Ubykhs.* Princeton: Princeton University Press, 2002.

Davis, Natalie Zemon. *Trickster Travels: A Sixteenth-century Muslim between Two Worlds.* London: Faber, 2007.

Dearden, Seton. *A Nest of Corsairs: The Fighting Karamanlis of the Barbary Coast.* London: John Murray, 1976.

Finkel, Caroline. *Osman's Dream: The Story of the Ottoman Empire 1300–1923.* London: John Murray, 2005.

Fischel, Walter J. "'Ascensus Baroch.' A Latin Biography of the Mamluk Sultan Barquq of Egypt." *Arabica.* 6 (1959), 57–74, 152–172.

Fischel, Walter. "'Vita Tamerlani.' A New Latin Source on Tamerlane's Conquest of Damascus (1400–1401) by B. de Mignanelli, Translated into English with an Introduction and Commentary." *Oriens*, 9 (1956). 201–233.

Flemming, Barbara. "Aus den Nachtgesprächen Sultan Ġauris." In H. Franke, W. Heissig and W. Treue, eds. *Folia Rara, Festschrift für Wolfgang Voigt.* Wiesbaden: Franz Steiner, 1967, 22–8.

Flemming, Barbara. "Šerif, Sultan Ġavri und die 'Perser'." *Der Islam*, 45 (1969), 71–94.

Heers, Jacques. *Gênes au XVe Siècle, activité économique et problems sociaux.* Paris: S.E.V.P.E.N., 1961.

Haarmann, Ulrich. "Arabic in Speech, Turkish in Lineage: Mamluks and Their Sons in the Intellectual Life of Fourteenth-Century Egypt and Syria." *Journal of Semitic Studies* 33 (1988), 81–114.

Haarmann, Ulrich. "Der Schatz im Haupt des Götzen." In Ulrich Haarmann and Peter Bachmann, eds. *Die Islamische Welt zwischen Mittelalter und Neuzeit: Festschrift für Hans Robert Roemer zum 65. Geburstag.* Wiesbaden: Franz Steiner, 1979, 198–229.

Haarmann, Ulrich. "Joseph's Law – the Careers and Activities of Mamluk Descendants before the Ottoman Conquest of Egypt." In Thomas Philipp and Ulrich Haarmann, eds. *The Mamluks in Egyptian Politics and Society.* Cambridge: Cambridge University Press, 1998. 55–87.

Haarmann, Ulrich. "The Mamluk System of Rule in the Eyes of Western Travellers," *Mamlūk Studies Review*, 5 (2001), 1–24.

Jones, John Winter, tr., and Lincoln Davis Hammond, ed. *Travellers in Disguise: Narratives of Eastern Travel by Poggio Bracciolini and Ludovico di Varthema.* Cambridge, MA: Harvard University, Department of Romance Languages and Literatures, 1963.

von Klaproth, Julius. *Travels in the Caucasus and Georgia Performed in the Years 1807 and 1808.* London, 1814.

Little, Donald P. "Notes on Aitamiš, a Mongol Mamluk." In Ulrich Haarmann and Peter Bachmann, eds. *Die Islamische Welt zwischen Mittelalter und Neuzeit: Festschrift für Hans Robert Roemer zum 65 Geburstag.* Wiesbaden: Franz Steiner, 1979. 387–401. Reprinted in D.P. Little, *History and Historiography of the Mamlūks.* London: Variorum Reprints, 1986.

Loiseau, Julien. *Les Mamelouks XIIIe–XVI siècle.* Paris: Éditions du Seuil, 2014.

Matar, Nabil. *Turks, Moors and Englishmen in the Age of Discovery.* New York: Columbia University Press, 1998.

Origo, Iris. "The Domestic Enemy: The Eastern Slaves in Tuscany in the Fourteenth and Fifteenth Centuries." *Speculum*, 30/3 (July 1955), 321–366.

Pipes, Daniel. *Slave Soldiers and Islam: The Genesis of a Military System.* New Haven and London: Yale University Press, 1981.

Sauvaget, Jean. "Noms et surnoms des Mamelouks." *Journal Asiatique.* 238 (1950), 31–58.

Steiner, George. *After Babel: Aspects of Language and Translation.* London: Oxford University Press, 1975.

Tardy, Lajos. "The Caucasian People and Their Neighbours in 1404." *Acta Orientalia scientarium Hungarica.* 32 (1978), 83–111.

Verlinden, Charles. *L'Esclavage dans l'Europe Médiévale.* Ghent: Rijksuniversiteit: Ghent, 1977. 2 vols.

Wolf, John B. *The Barbary Coast: Algeria under the Turks.* New York: W.W. Norton, 1979.

Yosef, Koby. "Dawlat al-atrāk or dawlat al-mamālik? Ethnic Origin or Slave Origin as the Defining Characteristic of the Ruling Elite in the Mamluk Sultanate." *Jerusalem Studies in Arabic and Islam*, 39 (2012), 387–410.

Nimrod Luz (Kinneret College on the Sea of Galilee)

Reconstructing the Urban Landscape of Mamluk Jerusalem: Spatial and Socio-political Implications

Introduction

In this chapter I forge links between the study of material culture (the built environment writ large) and a reading of socio-political issues in cities as a way of contributing to the study of the Mamluk period in the wider region. My point of departure and main case study is the city of Jerusalem during the Mamluk period. To begin with I discuss the theoretical and empirical implications of looking at the city as a cultural process and as a landscape. Following I present the outcomes of a survey of the built environment of Jerusalem focusing on the Mamluk era with the objective of shedding light on the particular morphology of the city during this period. Based on this extensive survey I established a set of benchmarks which enabled me to unearth and understand the hitherto unexplored vernacular architecture of the city. This in-depth look at the materiality of the urban landscape is taken in this chapter further to suggest that the construction of a more nuanced lexicon of the building language, the materiality of cities, of the Mamluk period may be used to understand better a complex of urban phenomena and developments elsewhere in the Middle East. Thus, following a discussion of the vernacular building language in Mamluk Jerusalem, I examine various intricate urban issues in the region. These case studies will help clarify how the reading of the tangible city constitutes a crucial and highly helpful medium through which we can read better not just the physical layout of the city but also the socio-political and cultural dimension of urbanism.

Urban Landscape and the City as a Cultural Process

Against the dominance of the quantitative (and technical) approach that prevailed in the field of urban studies during the 1960s to1980s, Agnew, Mercerand Sopher suggested that the city should be examined "in cultural context":

> The study of the city in cultural context implies two things. First network of practices and ideas exist that are drawn from the shared experiences and histories of social groups. Secondly, these practices and ideas can be invoked to account for specific patterns of urban growth and urban form.[1]

Put differently, the city should be understood and explored as a cultural product and process. This sort of study may be conducted via the urban form – the city's built environment. But how do we move from a theoretical awareness to the cultural aspects of cities to sound explorations into the urban form?

Culture is an ever-changing concept. Therefore, it is but a temporary representation of a given society's norms and ideals. Once the conflicts and struggles over these norms have been settled, they are considered the cultural pillars of that society. However, these norms are constantly in flux or under pressure to be altered. In consequence, the spatial outcomes of these ideals are also inherently transient, as they are the ramifications of the social and political changes within any society. According to this perspective, the study of the city in a cultural context need not be understood as researching culture through the mediation of the city, but rather a theoretical awareness of the dynamic quality of culture and, above all, its political implications. Therefore, it is imperative to realize that the very classification or omission of a phenomenon under the heading of culture constitutes a political act, which is usually the sole prerogative of those in power. For example, the Romans deemed outsiders to be a-cultural (barbaric), while Mamluk officers shaped the urban milieu as they saw fit, in accordance with their political needs, religious norms and aesthetic tastes. By grasping culture as an idea, rather than an entity, the study of cities may well avoid the fixation over arriving at a clear-cut, complete, and overly rigorous definition of what constitutes a city in the Islamic world. Moreover, we are less likely to view the city as frozen in time. Instead, it offers the possibility of dynamic means for examining historical and geographical processes in their societies and appreciating that they were and remain vibrant entities that are in a constant state of flux. That said, to study the city in cultural context may well be an inspiring idea but it is simply too vague. Therefore, it seems essential at this juncture to address more directly the way I navigate between the above understanding of culture and the exploration of Mamluk period. The mediating term and context for the study of cities is by and large, landscape. In what follows I will contextualize it from an historical and cultural geographical point of view.

Landscape is surly one of the more vexing and therefore fascinating human creations. It is anything but self-explanatory, simple or innocent. Certainly, it is not a neutral arena in which social relations matter-of-factly or accidently unfold.

1 John A. Agnew, John Mercer and David E. Sopher, eds, *The City in Cultural Context* (Boston, London, Sydney: Routledge, 1984), p. 1.

Landscape, as the argument goes, is not just simply out there to be studied as a natural phenomenon. It is certainly not "nature."[2] In this context, landscape is "culture" before it is "nature."[3] The very word landscape in its cultural meaning entails the existence and work of human agents.[4] Hence, landscapes simply do not exist without human agents. Landscape is society's unwitting mirror in which and through which ideas, codes of practice, religious norms and cultural standards take physical form. Therefore, landscape consists of physical phenomena but is not confined to the physical manifestations of objects. This is, perhaps, the most comprehensive medium through which societies and individuals have expressed their uniqueness, aspirations and status, among many other socio-political needs. Therefore, landscape is essentially a cultural praxis, as it is the outcome of a society's ideals, images and at times code of practice in a given time and particular geography. As such, cultural landscape is a highly politicized construction, sphere or process.[5] And (to state the obvious) it is certainly the product of human labor. Hence, landscape is a beguiling phenomenon: though manmade and perceived as a natural outcome of human labor, it is anything but natural. The formation of landscape is inexorably linked to politics, power structures and surely struggles over meanings and ownership. The creation or rather the construction of landscape is all about power, and thus entails disputes and the use of force. Therefore, the construction of landscape is a continuous dialogue and indeed struggle between different forces. Along the way, power is used, implemented and contested, for there are no power relations without resistance.[6]

The use of power in the construction of landscape is unavoidably linked with ideology or put simply the way people want to represent themselves.[7] Landscapes are ideological also because they can be used to endorse, legitimize, and/or challenge social and political control.[8] Thus, landscapes carry signs and symbols which represent social norms, identity, memory, cultural codes, and surely the

2 Yi-Fu. Tuan, "Thought and Landscape," in *Interpretations of Ordinary Landscapes: Geographic Essays*, ed. Donald W. Meinig (New York: Oxford University Press, 1979), pp. 89–102.

3 Simon Schama, *Landscape and Memory* (New York: Vintage, 1996), p. 5.

4 Ken Olwig, "Sexual Cosmology: Nation and Landscape at the Conceptual Interstices of Nature and Culture, or: What does Landscape Really Mean?" *Landscape: Politics and Perspectives*, ed. B. Bender (Oxford: Berg, 1993), pp. 307–308.

5 Denis E. Cosgrove, *Social Formation and Symbolic Landscape* (London: University of Wisconsin Press, 1984); James S. Duncan, *The City as Text: The Politics of Landscape Interpretation in the Kandyan Kingdom* (Cambridge: Cambridge University Press, 1990).

6 Michel Foucault, *Power/Knowledge: Selected Interviews and Other Writings 1972–1977*, ed. Colin Gordon, (London: Pantheon Books, 1980).

7 Allan, H. Baker and Gideon Bigger, eds., *Ideology and Landscape in Historical Perspective*, (Cambridge: Cambridge University Press, 1992), pp. 1–12.

8 Lily Kong, "Ideological Hegemony and the Political Symbolism of Religious Buildings in Singapore," *Environment and Planning D: Society and Space* 11 (1993): 25.

ways these were, and still are, fought and debated among different forces. Landscape is one of the most complex and intriguing signifying systems saturated with signs, symbols and meanings.[9] In what follows I offer a reading of a few landscape formations in Mamluk Jerusalem. Against what I have described hitherto I trust the connections among the built environment and the less tangible aspects of the city will be better understood.

Unearthing the Vernacular Architecture of Mamluk Jerusalem

I think the question of vernacular architecture is not only fascinating but crucial for the exploration of one particular period in multi-layered and multi-historical cities such as Mamluk Jerusalem. In order to understand better the nature of the Mamluk Jerusalem's built environment and to overcome this problematic situation in which layers of different periods might co-exist one has to; metaphorically, take out one drawer from a multi-storied cupboard. This demanded the construction of a new methodology and ways to survey the city. Therefore, in what follows I outline this methodology and the survey outcomes as a way to make better sense of the city. To begin with, the first issue to be remedied is the oft-repeated understanding of Mamluk Architecture as being confined to the public cum monumental parts of the city.[10] To put it bluntly, the built environment of the city encompasses more private and less ostentatious buildings then monumental ones although they are usually neglected in urban surveys. A city's constructed environment is divided into two main architectural orders or spheres: the higher order, which is comprised of public infrastructure, institutions, and other buildings; and the lower order, which encompasses all the buildings in the private domain, hereafter, vernacular architecture.[11]

Despite the obvious significance of vernacular architecture, art historians and architects, among others, generally focus on public and monumental architecture. Accordingly, works on Mamluk architecture are, by and large, devoted to monumental and public buildings.[12] These public buildings, compounds and

9 James S. Duncan, and Nancy G. Duncan, "Re(reading) the Landscape," *Environment and Planning D: Society and Space* 6 (1998): 117–126.

10 This is readily apparent in the work of Burgoyne on the architecture of Jerusalem during the Mamluk period in which he addresses only monumental buildings. Michael H. Burgoyne, with the contribution of Donald. S. Richard, *Mamluk Jerusalem, an Architectural Survey.* (London: British School of Archaeology Jerusalem, 1987).

11 For a discussion on order and hierarchy in urban landscapes, see Amos Rapoport, "Culture and the Urban Order," in *The City in Cultural Context*, ed. John A. Agnew, John Mercer and David E. Sopher (Boston, London, Sydney: Routledge, 1984), pp. 50–72.

12 See, e.g., Robert Hillenbrand, *Islamic Architecture: Form, Function and Meaning*, (New York, 1994). And see various surveys on architecture in the region; Martin S. Briggs, *Muhammadan*

infrastructures, which are somehow connected either with the Mamluks or the upper echelons of the urban society, comprise an important part of the city. But the city is so much more than just magnanimous buildings. Like any other city, Jerusalem also has more mundane and humble architecture than public parts. This type of architecture which surely consist the majority of the city's built environment is called Vernacular Architecture. This concept refers to structures that are built by non-architects and generally without architects.[13] This type of architecture is driven by practical needs, typically eschews theoretical principles and is usually lacking in aesthetic qualities. As I will demonstrate in what follows, it was inspired also by the prevailing Mamluk's public architecture. In order to unearth and understand these essential parts of the city I conducted a survey which followed a few basic components: 1. A study of urban landscapes of the pre-Mamluk periods. 2. A study of Mamluk public architecture, with a special emphasis on external features. 3. The demarcation of an area of approximately 60–80 m wide adjacent to the western and northern walls Haram al-Sharīf ("The Noble Sanctuary"). This area was largely empty before the Mamluks assumed control of Jerusalem and was built up during the Mamluk period. My point of departure is that any element which surfaced in this area and could be established as pre-modern architecture was in all likelihood from the Mamluk period. Consequently, this expanse constituted the Archimedean point of the entire survey. 4. In the absence of a clear marker of Mamluk architecture, an examination of the stratigraphic relations between the various parts of an area, once the accurate date of origin of at least one structure had been determined. 5. Methodology of the actual survey: The first phase of the survey consisted of an exhaustive study of the documented Mamluk compounds' external characteristics. Thereafter, the survey was extended to adjacent unidentified buildings in an effort to establish their dating in comparison with the documented buildings. The analysis of the "Mamluk area" yielded a set of indicators of vernacular architecture, which were subsequently utilized throughout the Old City of Jerusalem. Over the course of the entire survey, I never identified an area or site as Mamluk

Architecture in Egypt and Palestine (Oxford: Da Capo Press Series in Architecture and Decorative Art, 1924); Keppel A. C. Creswell, *The Muslim Architecture of Egypt, Ayyubid and Early Bahri Period* (Oxford, The Clarendon Press, 1959); Derek Hill and Oleg Grabar, *Islamic Architecture and its Decoration, A.-D. 800–1500* (London: Faber, 1964); Julian Raby (ed.), *The Art of Syria and the Jazira 1100–1250, Oxford Studies in Islamic Art*, vol. I (Oxford, Oxford University Press, 1985).

13 See Amos Rapoport, *House Form and Culture*, (Englewood Cliffs, NJ: Prentice Hall, 1969); idem, "Vernacular Architecture and the Cultural Determinants of Form," in *Buildings and Society: Essays on the Social Development of the Built Environment*, ed. Anthony, D. King (London: Taylor and Francis, 1980), 283–304; Hassan Fathy, *Natural Energy, Vernacular Architecture. Principles and Examples with Reference to Hot Arid Climates* (Chicago: United Nations University Press, 1986), pp. 64ff.

solely on the basis of a few indicators. Instead, the immediate vicinity was always examined for identified buildings or established dating that could serve as anchors for the establishment of precise dating of vernacular constructions.

Elements of Mamluk Vernacular Architecture

Over the course of the survey, I discovered that the following elements were recurring themes in Mamluk vernacular architecture:

1. **Vaults.** The field survey identified two principal types of vaults:
   a. **Decorated or public vault:** Two main types of endings were identified on the decorated vault:
      1. **The decorated round spring stone**
      2. **The right-angle spring stone** turns up in both monumental and vernacular buildings.
   b. **The "private" double-arched vault** was the most prevalent of its kind in the streets and alleys of Mamluk Jerusalem. The two principal types are distinguished by their conjoining point with the underlying wall:
      1. **Right-angled spring stones**, which resemble those found in decorated public vaults.
      2. **Smooth vaults without cantilevers.** The point of contact between this sort and the wall is merely a subtle unimpeded line.
2. **Double Relieving Arch.** This essential element reinforces various structures, such as doorways, vaults and windows. The double relieving arch turns up in monumental Mamluk architecture and is also commonplace in vernacular buildings. In numerous instances, the relieving arch offered the first hint that I had come across an example of Mamluk vernacular architecture.
3. **Windows.** Several types of windows were discovered over the course of my fieldwork. The survey yielded two main types of vernacular windows:
   a. **The single, twin or triple rectangular window**
   b. **The simple square or rectangular window:** There are many versions of this unadorned opening, but we can point to two dominant styles:
      1. **Square or rectangular window.**
      2. **Narrow elongated window.**
4. **Air Vents.** Positioned above the window frames are a recurring theme in Jerusalem Mamluk architecture. There are three types:
   a. **Rosette shaped vent** – a decorated vent 15 to 20 cm in diameter.
   b. **Round air vent** – closely resembles the rosette style, but is less refined.
   c. **Simple air vent** – an unadorned vent that is usually square.
5. **Arches over Windows.** Three predominant types of relieving arches (also known as discharging arches) were used to reinforce windows:

   a. **The elaborately decorated relieving arch**, in which the functional arch is upgraded into a decorative element.
   b. **Decorated relieving arch** – a crude version of the first.
   c. **The simple relieving arch** practically takes the shape of a linear line, not more than 2 cm wide.
6. **Doorways.** There exist three main types:
   a. **Doorways incorporating Mamluk stylistic motifs** are relatively more ornate than the original model.
   b. **The Arched doorway with arched canopy.**
   c. **Amorphous doorway**
7. **Chamfer (*Shath*).** The *shath* or chamfer is a decorative element that is formed by cutting a sharp angle (usually 45°) between two conjoining walls.
8. **External Components and Accessories.**
   a. **Porches.** Residential porches are informed by a series of two to four cantilevers supporting a stone platform over six feet long.
   b. **External lattice.** Known regionally as *mashrabiyya* or *kishk*, this window screen also appears monumental Mamluk architecture.
   c. **Round stone cantilever.**
9. **Imitation of Monumental Mamluk Motifs.** As noted, public Mamluk architecture served as a frame of reference for and a paradigm of styles, motifs and techniques for private and/or vernacular architecture.
   a. **Facade and doorway.** The expansive Mamluk façade, in which the actual door is appreciably smaller than the entrance area, has been found in private houses throughout the Old City,
   b. **Ablaq** is a term referred to an architectural style involving alternating or fluctuating rows of light and dark stone, usually a combination of white, red and black. This is a rather distinctive Mamluk style usually to be found in monumental cum public compounds which adorns several luxurious private homes in Jerusalem.
   c. **Ornamentation.** As noted, Jerusalem's vernacular builders were inclined to absorb and borrow motifs from monumental Mamluk architecture.

Conclusions of the Field Survey

The data collected in this survey suggests that it is indeed possible to examine multi-layered historical cities on the micro-level. In the case at hand, I managed to collect a large number of architectural and stylistic indicators that *in toto*, enabled me to attain the following results: to reveal and decipher an inclusive urban vernacular language; and to leverage these elements into a better understanding of the built environment of Jerusalem during the Mamluk era. Following my survey and against several reservations that still need to be considered, I have drawn up a map of Mamluk Jerusalem that marks the location of the city's vernacular and public architecture. In addition, the map highlights parts of the Old City where elements of Mamluk architecture can still be found.[14]

In what follows I set out to demonstrate the importance of a better understanding of the built environment for a plethora of socio-cultural and political urban themes of the Mamluk period. Thus, I will portray houses and residential units, discuss the social aspects of the neighbourhood and engage in a re-evaluation of the role of religious endowments to the urban development of Mamluk Jerusalem.

Houses and Residential Units: Are They All Courtyard Houses?

Like any other product of human endeavour, the house is a cultural and social artefact. As such, it may be considered a non-verbal document that sheds light on the agents and agencies responsible for their construction.[15] Arguably, the first scholar in Islamic studies to broach this topic was arguably George Marçais, who avers that the traditional courtyard house, particularly its introverted style, exemplifies Islamic moral values and needs: It is well adapted to the patriarchal view of the family and creates for it an enclosed sphere; it conforms easily with the element of secrecy dear to the private life of the Muslim; and this idea is reflected in the architectural arrangement both in elevation and in plan.[16] In the face of such extensive generalization, it is worth remembering that the advent of the courtyard house predates the advent of Islam by a few thousand years.[17] Remains of courtyard houses dating from as far back as three thousand BCE have been excavated throughout the Middle East and along the entire Mediterranean basin.[18] These ancient communities availed themselves of this style in order to cope with weather conditions and meet the cultural demands that existed in the region well before the

14 These issues are discussed at length at Nimrod Luz, *The Mamluk City of the Middle East. History, Culture and the Urban Landscape* (Cambridge: Cambridge University Press, 2014) 49ff.

15 Geraldine Pratt, "The House as an Expression of the Social World," in *Housing and Identity* ed. James S. Duncan, (New York: Holmes and Meier, 1982), pp. 135–180.

16 George Marçais, "Dār," *Encyclopedia of Islam* (second edition), 2: 113–115.

17 Andre Raymond, *Grande villes arabes à l'époque ottoman*, (Paris: Sindbad, 1985), pp. 58ff.

18 The earliest courtyard model was discovered during an excavation at Çatalhöyük. Radiocarbon dating has established that some of the courtyard houses were constructed as far back as 5600 BCE; see James Mellaarat, *Çatal Hüyük: A Neolitic Town in Anatolia* (London: McGraw-Hill, 1967). For a similar ground plan, see Leonard Woolley, *Ur of Chaldes*, revised and updated edition by Paul R. S. Mooery (Ithaca: Inexile, 1982). Pauty discusses the courtyard house in Egypt and Syria from the third millennium BCE to the seventh century CE; Edmund Pauty, *Les palais et les maisons d'époque Musulmane, au Caire*, (Le Caire: Institut français d'archéologie orientale, 1932), pp. 13–25.

Mamluk Jerusalem - Layout of Monumental-Public buildings and vernacular components

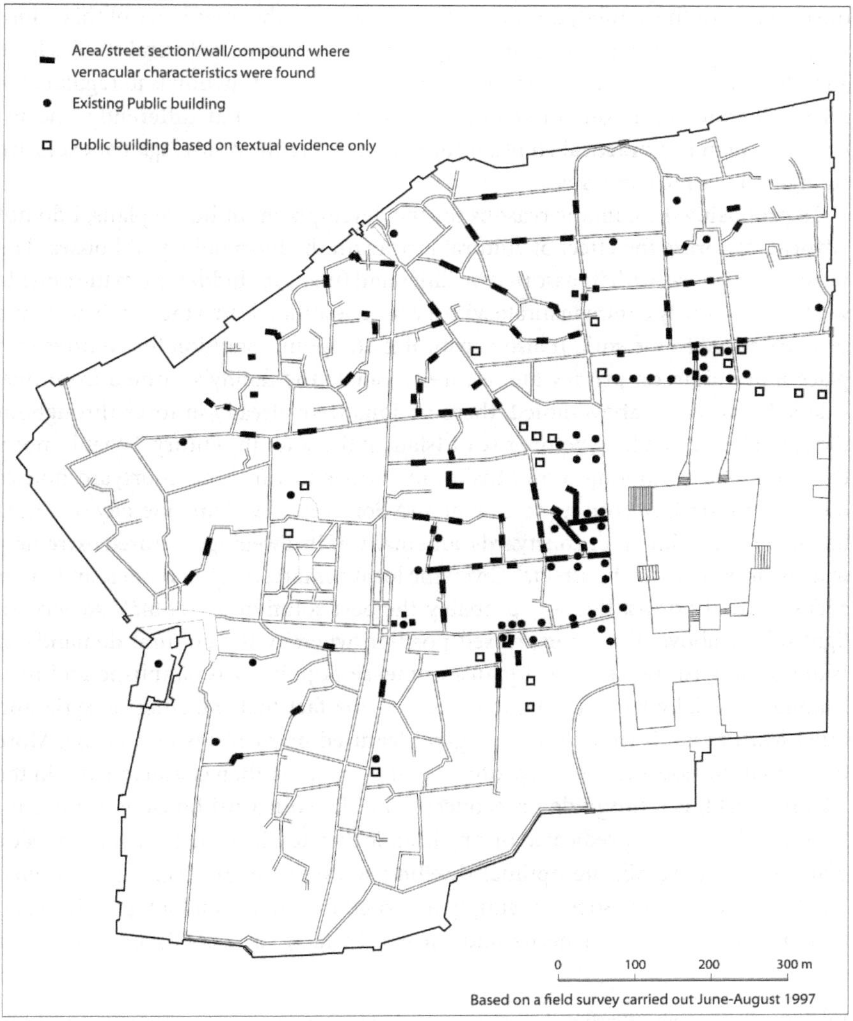

Map 1

revelation of the Quran. Furthermore, it is difficult to believe that this was the only available house form in the pre-modern Middle East for the simple reason that not all city dwellers could have afforded this type of residence. Last but not least, other types of housing have indeed been found. The ancient roots of the courtyard house do not rule out the possibility that religious norms played a vital role in the personal choice of a house type, but it does indicate that the reasons go well beyond the mere desire to abide by Islamic law. While the courtyard style dovetailed smoothly with the urban socio-cultural needs of Mamluk Syria (such as privacy or the intimacy of the family), this in itself cannot explain the prevalence of this house form or the fact that it precedes the rise of Islamic civilization. Several studies have already demonstrated that the inner courtyard's primary function is to regulate the micro-climatic conditions in semi-arid environments.[19] Put differently, the introverted plan is a practical solution for safeguarding the house against excessive sunlight, hot winds and dust.

In proposing the climatic reasons for the development of house plans, I do not advocate ignoring the effect of cultural factors on the morphology of houses. The introverted house, with its assorted facilities and functions hidden from the outside world, is obviously commensurate with a worldview that deems the family to be the primary social framework. It also constitutes an optimal solution for cultures that place a premium on privacy and aspire to isolate the family's women from outsiders. However, as above-noted, these notions were already in force throughout the extended region long before rise of Islam in the seventh century. What is more, there are cities with long-term Muslim majorities in which no courtyard houses have been found. According to Golvin and Formont, the Yemenite city of Thulā had no houses with inner courtyards, and many of its dwellings featured extremely wide windows facing the street.[20] Given the local climate, religious codes, and other socio-cultural norms, this was probably the best solution for Thulā's society. In light of the above, the oft-expressed position whereby the cultural demands of Islam undergird the courtyard plan's immense popularity is simplistic and misleading, especially when taking into account the fact that the cities of Syria and other Muslim lands (most notably Egypt) featured many forms of housing. More than anything else, this view, like others that pertain to urban characteristics in the Islamic world, is a misguided preconception. The courtyard house is neither inherently Muslim nor predicated on any Islamic dictates. Instead, the inside-outside plan offers, above all, the optimal dwelling solution for the region's somewhat harsh climate. Islamic societies simply inherited this model and adapted it to suit their members' personal needs and means. In fact, stressing Islam's role as a

19 Youssef Belkacem, "Bioclimatic Patterns and Human Aspects of Urban Form in the Islamic Cities," in *The Arab City, Its Character and Islamic Cultural Heritage*, ed. Ismail Seragldin and Samer El-Sadeq (Riyadh: The Arab Urban Development Institute, 1982), pp. 2–12; Baruch Givoni, *Climate Consideration in Building and Urban Design* (New York: Wiley 1998), pp. 343–351; Guy T. Petherbridge, "Vernacular Architecture: The House and Society," in *Architecture of the Islamic World*, ed. George Michell, (London: Thames and Hudson, 1987), pp. 176–208, esp. 199–201; Jamal Akbar, "Courtyard Houses: A Case Study from Riyadh, Saudi Arabia," in *The Arab City, Its Character and Islamic Cultural Heritage*, ed. Ismail Seragldin and Samer El-Sadeq (Riyadh: The Arab Urban Development Institute, 1982), pp. 162–176.

20 Lucien Golvin et Marie-Christine Formont, *Thula, architecture et urbanisme d'une cite de haute montagne en République Arabe du Yémen*, Mémoire no. 30 (Paris: Editions Recherche sur les civilisations, 1984).

cultural factor is misleading because, under the vague heading of culture, Islamic societies also possess traits that have nothing to do with religion. Like any analysis of material findings, we are confined to the evidence at hand. In researching houses, it is imperative to recognize the fact that lower-class buildings are more susceptible to contingency and thus much less likely to survive the march of time than those of the upper class. Moreover, we can assume that modest residences are under-represented in written records and literary accounts. As a result, most of the researchable dwellings belong to wealthier strata of society. Raymond encountered this same problem during his fieldwork in Ottoman cities[21] and stresses the inherent bias that informs these sorts of surveys. Moreover (and once again), this inclination is all the more glaring in the vast disproportion between the myriad studies on public and monumental buildings, on the one hand, and the meagre amount of research on vernacular architecture and common residential dwellings, on the other.[22] Needless to say, our knowledge about private houses in general and the abodes of the less fortunate in particular is inferior to the substantial documentation of palaces and mansions. Given the dearth of evidence, we can only speculate as to the number of, say, mud and straw-brick domiciles or wooden huts in fourteenth-century Tripoli or fifteenth-century Safad. What we do know is that, as opposed to wood, materials like mud, straw, and stone were widely available in Syria, so that there may very well have been a considerable number of modest dwellings during the Mamluk period that have vanished from the urban landscape. Furthermore, Mamluk-era buildings have probably endured more change and elimination than those from the Ottoman-era simply because they are older. Against this backdrop, it is incumbent upon any researcher of the Mamluk landscape to acknowledge the unsurpassable obstacles that stand in the way of firm and definitive conclusions. With this in mind in, let us embark on a survey of the various types of residences and domestic solutions during the Mamluk period.

Ordinary Private Houses

The Syrian city featured but a small handful of individual or private house types during the Mamluk era. As reflected in various sources from this period, the common term for the house was *dār*, which usually referred to a structure consisting of several parts: residential units or rooms; courtyards; and necessary

21 André Raymond, *The Great Arab Cities in the 16th–18th Centuries: An Introduction.* Hagop Kevorkian Series on Near Eastern Art and Civilization (New York and London: New York University Press, 1984), pp. 70–71.

22 A case in point is the voluminous research on houses in Mamluk Cairo by Jean-Claude Garcin et al., eds., *Palais et maisons du Caire I: époque Mamelouke (XIIIe–XVIe siècles)* (Paris: Editions du Centre National de la Recherche Scientifique, 1982).

amenities, like cisterns, ovens, storage chambers (*makhzān*) and toilets. Private houses were built of local stone, mainly limestone. Most ornaments, which were primarily found in luxurious residences, were made of marble (either imported or in secondary use), but there are also rare cases in which basalt was used.[23] Over the course of the field survey, I identified the following primary morphological and architectural traits of the private Mamluk house:

The façade: the part of the house facing the street, included a single-entry gate, which was usually lower than the average person's height and no more than a meter thick. The entrance itself was a massive door (either wood or metal), which stressed the transition from the public (or semi-public) street into the private domain. Most of the houses surveyed were no more than two stories high. In those buildings with a third floor, there are usually architectural indications of post-Mamluk construction. The most obvious one is the sharp contrast between the stones used by early and later (especially Ottoman) builders. The paucity of extant three-storey edifices does not necessarily mean that houses in Jerusalem were limited to two floors, as were their counterparts in Cairo; due to the greater exposure to the elements, the top floor was more susceptible to erosion and thus demanded renovations and other changes over the years. **Windows and porches:** The front windows of domestic spaces were relatively small, and few variations of this element turned up in the survey. For the most part, there were no windows on the street level and the exceptions were ordinarily very small and shaded or covered with a grille. Porches were uncommon in modest private homes. The dimensions of those few that were put up were diminutive compared to the *kishk*, a popular type of balcony in Mamluk-era public buildings. **Roofs:** Similar to the area's rural building tradition, the roofwas built in the shape of a masonry dome. **Courtyards:** In some of the private houses, a corridor led from the gate into a private courtyard. The corridor was usually angular and included a few twists and turns. The size of the courtyards varied considerably. The residential units (*bayt*, pl. *buyūt*) were built on the perimeter of the lot and their entrances faced the courtyard. In multiple-storey houses, the flight of stairs was ordinarily at the side of the courtyard. A small share of these buildings featured a central courtyard, namely an inner expanse that was surrounded on all sides by the compound's structures. However, many other courtyard houses were aligned according to completely different models.

The survey established the fact that the original features of the buildings' exterior were, by and large, preserved. Conversely, the internal parts stood a much greater

23 It is worth noting that marble is not native in Syria and was thus always imported. The supply of basalt in Jerusalem was limited, so that its very use indicates a heavy financial investment.

chance of being altered due to recurrent renovations, transfer of ownership or a change in the economic fortunes of the residents. Unfortunately, in order to enter the threshold of the residential unit and gain an understanding of the interior parts, I was compelled to rely almost entirely on written documentation.

Examples of Courtyard Houses

1. On 4 Rabīʿ II 778/21 August 1376, a house was purchased in the Christian neighbourhood (Ḥarāt al-Nasārā) of Jerusalem.[24] The property, known as Dār ibn al-Lawnayn, consisted of three vaulted units (*buyūt*), a kitchen and toilet facilities. The residential units surrounded a courtyard with two cisterns and fruit-bearing trees. Another vaulted room, which functioned as a storage chamber, was constructed below the courtyard. The building's entrance opened onto an alley to the east of the compound. Several courtyard houses of this type were found during the survey. 2. The house of one Shaykh Burhān al-Dīn was constructed on the basis of a different plan. The shaykh purchased his house on 21 Dhū al-Qaʿda 780 (12 March 1379) for 825 dirhams.[25] Aside for the building's vaulted upper and lower levels, the deed of transaction notes that the property also included a courtyard and an external toilet unit. In this particular case, the courtyard was adjacent to the building. However, few of the houses that turned up in the field survey were arranged in this fashion.

As already noted, the term *dār* did not refer exclusively to houses that adhered to the central courtyard plan. In fact, some houses (*diyār*) had no courtyard whatsoever and opened directly into the street or alley along which they were built. This term comes up in hundreds of Mamluk-era documents that were found at the Ḥaram al-Sharīf in Jerusalem. Few are the instances in which a courtyard is mentioned; and even then, it is uncertain if the record is referring to the central variety. Furthermore, the early Ottoman *sijill* documents no less than 228 houses in Jerusalem, only 42 of which had a courtyard (either enclosed or adjacent).[26] The urban reality that emerges from the *sijill* not only sheds light on the formative years of the Ottoman period, but on the final decades of the Mamluk era, if not more. Therefore, we may conclude that most private houses in

24 Donald P. Little, *A Catalogue of the Islamic Documents from the Ḥaram al-Sharīf in Jerusalem* (Beirut and Wiesbaden: Franz Steiner Verlag, 1984), 255, no. 35. I am indebted to Mr. Khader Salameh for enabling me to examine the original documents of the Mamluk archive at the Ḥaram al-Sharīf's library.

25 Little, *Catalogue*, 278, no. 39.

26 Khader Salāmeh, "Aspects of the Sijils of the Shariʿa Court in Jerusalem," in *Ottoman Jerusalem: The Living City 1517–1917*, eds. Sylvia Auld and Robert Hillenbrand (London: Al-Tajir, 2000), vol. 1: 128–132.

Jerusalem did not have courtyards, but were what Raymond humorously referred to as "atypical houses."[27]

Luxurious Houses

A number of private houses whose proportions, plans and lavishness far exceed those of the average domiciles in the city were discovered over the course of my fieldwork in Jerusalem. These residences were characterized by top-grade construction material, external ornamentation and grandiose plans. In addition, they borrowed elements and styles from monumental Mamluk architecture. For example, a palatial house with Ablaq-style outer walls and broad windows turned up above Ṭarīq al-Wād (the site of the minor cardo of Roman Jerusalem). Another house of this calibre turned up along one of the city's main streets (Ṭariīq al-Aqaba), opposite Dār al-Sitt Tunshuq. To begin with, the building boasts a monumental façade and entrance. Unlike the city's less ostentatious domestic spaces where the entrance is through a corridor, this two-storey house is surrounded by a towering, single-entry gate structure that opens to a small inner court and an imposing entrance to the house itself. The upper floor is graced by sizable windows and an exquisitely decorated porch. A common feature of all the houses in this category was their accessibility, as they were either close to or overlooked the Mamluk city's main thoroughfares. This shared trait implies that there was a connection between economic status, personal preference and house location. Apparently, the city's affluent chose to reside in highly convenient places. Economic status was certainly a key factor in housing-related decisions, as the rich were able to choose a location that better suited their needs. Although such a conclusion is based on a qualitative analysis (rather than a quantitative one), it seems as though prosperity was indeed an important factor when selecting the location of one's home. While this observation might appear to be self-evident, it need not be taken lightly on account of the literature near fixation with religious or ethnic motivations for housing choices in Middle Eastern cities. The connection between wealth and location is supported by Jean-Claude David, who identified and classified typical house types in early Ottoman Aleppo.[28] By virtue of a comprehensive survey, David revealed a concentric hierarchy of houses around the city's centre.[29] In Jerusalem too, the closer the lot was to the centre, the steeper the price. Raymond detected similar concentric rings in other Middle

27 Raymond, *The Great Arab Cities*, p. 87.
28 Jean-Claude David, "Alep, déradation et tentatives actuelles de rédaptation des structures urbaines traditionnelles," *Bulletin d'Étude Orientale*, 28 (1978): 19–50.
29 Ibid., map no. 12.

Eastern cities during the Ottoman period.[30] Therefore, we may infer that this phenomenon was prevalent throughout the entire region.

This short analysis of houses and domestic spaces has clearly demonstrated the importance of an intimate acquaintance of the built environment to understand better various urban infrastructures and themes. Attaining a set of indicators of the vernacular building language of the period has enabled me to get closer to and identify housing of the Mamluk period. My inquiry revealed that the term *dār* for a house is an umbrella term for a variety of house plans. Moreover, I could demonstrate that the courtyard house which is considered a recurrent fashion was not the common solution nor has it little to do with Islamic norms. While the house plan is undoubtedly a morphological expression of culture and influenced by social forces, the contours and attributes of a house, like culture itself, should not be attributed to any single factor. A house's space, layout and usage are malleable and ever-changing elements, for within any society there are numerous variables that come into play when constructing a residence. What is more, every individual brings his or her own needs into the final equation. I was able to show that economic status had direct bearing on location and style of houses as the following picture of a luxurious house located on one of the main thoroughfares of Mamluk Jerusalem indicates.

30 Raymond, *The Great Arab Cities*, pp. 58ff.

Neighbourhoods as Social Entities

The neighbourhood has apparently been a fixture on the urban landscape since the city first emerged on the world stage. Lewis Mumford, a fervent advocate of the virtues of the historical city, deems the neighbourhood to be an integral part of the urban sphere and a natural outcome of people and communities clustering together: Neighbourhoods, in some primitive, inchoate fashion exist wherever human beings congregate, in permanent family dwellings; and many of the functions of the city tend to be distributed naturally – that is, without any theoretical preoccupation or political direction – into neighbourhoods.[31] Mumford sees the neighbourhood as a "fact of nature" – a spontaneous outcome of people bonding together simply due to the proximity of their dwellings. Like the house, the street or the market, the neighbourhood is an indispensable component of the city, for it provides its residents, among other things, with a sense of security and belonging. Thus, it is a fixture of the urban landscape of both historical and present cities worldwide. Arguably, the most comprehensive account of neighbourhoods in Mamluk Jerusalem is to be found at the city's native son Mujīr al-Dīn ʿAbd al-Raḥmān ibn Muḥammad al-ʿUlaymī al-ʿUmarī al-Maqdisī al-Ḥanbalī book dedicated to unravel its history, glory and important persona; *al-Uns al-Jalīl bi-Taʾrīkh al-Quds wal-Khalīl* (ca. 1495). As a descent of a noble family whose members served also as Ḥanbalī judges in Jerusalem as well as other places, Mujīr al-Dīn received a comprehensive and elite education which landed him not only the prestigious role as a judge but also made him privy to the city's history and archives as the case may be.[32] Based on Mujīr al-Dīn's comprehensive account, which is supplemented by documents from the Ḥaram al-Sharīf it would seem that Jerusalem had some fifty (!) neighbourhoods. The following passage from Mujīr al-Dīn's text bear witness to the dynamism of Jerusalem neighbourhoods in all that concerns their names, boundaries and demographics:

> These are the famous residential neighbourhoods of Jerusalem: among them al-Maghāriba located near the wall of the mosque due west and it belongs to people from the Maghrib, as it was endowed to them and because they reside therein. Al-Sharaf neighborhood is found due west of it and it is named after one of the eminent residents of the city, Sharaf al-Dīn Mūsā who had many famous descendants called the Banū al-Sharaf. It was formerly known as the Neighbourhood of the Kurds. Al-ʿAlam neighbourhood is called after a man named ʿAlam al-Dīn Sulaymān… [He] died circa 770 H

31 Lewis Mumford, "The Neighbourhood and the Neighbourhood Unit," *Town Planning Review*, 24 (1954): 256–270.

32 In addition to the data presented to us in the book itself on its author see also, Donald P. Little, "Mujīr al-Dīn's al-ʿUlaymī's Vision of Jerusalem in the Ninth-Fifteenth Century" *Journal of the American Oriental Society*, 115/2 (1995): 237–247

> [1369]...[and] had many famous descendants, among them his son ʿUmar who served as the inspector of endowments in Jerusalem and Hebron and his brother Sharaf al-Dīn Mūsā, who is buried in the above mentioned neighbourhood which is located north of al-Sharaf neighbourhood. And within that neighborhood lies the al-Khāyadra neighbourhood, so named after a *zāwiya* located therein that belongs to a Sufi order by that name. And the neighbourhood of al-Saltayn in the proximity of al-Sharaf neighbourhood to the south-west. And the Jewish neighbourhood is to be found west of al-Saltayn and within it lays the neighbourhood of al-Rīsha.[33]

According to Mujīr al-Dīn, there are manifold reasons behind the names of Jerusalem's residential areas. Some of them give expression to the common ethnic origin of or kinship between some of the area's residents. Another prominent reason is the shared religion or denomination of (probably) most of the neighbours. Moreover, an area may draw its appellation from a unique institution, such as a Sufi lodge, within its boundaries. Mujīr al-Dīn's historical survey of what was first called the neighbourhood of the Kurds and then al-Sharaf attests to the flexibility of these labels. This area was apparently populated by people of Kurdish descent.[34] During the fourteenth century, one Sharaf al-Dīn Mūsā built his house on that very neighbourhood and was buried there as well. Due to Mūsā's public standing, this neighbourhood began to be associated with him, instead of the Kurds. His descendants remained in the area and formed a new distinctive social group within the city. The new toponym supplanted the old one, so that the distinguished *qāḍī* had to specifically remind his readers of its past history. It is safe to assume that both Kurds and Sharaf al-Dīn Mūsā's kin lived side by side during the 1300s. In 796/1394, a will was drawn up for Umayma bint Mūsā bint Isḥāq al-Dimashqiyya, a female resident of "the Kurdish neighbourhood," who lived in the house of Ḥamīs ibn al-Sharaf.[35] Umayma was probably not of Kurdish descent, for this sort of information would have been included in her will, as we find in other wills. She may have been a member of the Sharaf family, but this cannot be confirmed. As we can see, Mujīr al-Dīn goes to great lengths to explain the social provenance of a neighbourhood's name, but is far less concerned with its exact location or borders. The importance of this text lies in the fact that it documents the malleability of Jerusalem's neighbourhoods and the mobility of its populace during the Mamluk era. Furthermore, it demonstrates that social affiliations defined the spatial boundaries of neighbourhoods and not the other way around. We may thus conclude that the most

33 Mujīr al-Dīn, ʿAbd al-Raḥmān, b. Muḥammad al-Ḥanbalī al-ʿUlaymī, *al-Uns al-Jalīl bi-Taʾrīkh al-Quds wal-Khalīl* (Baghdad: Maktabat al-Nahda, 1990), vol. 2: 52.

34 Jerusalem was not the only place in which the Mamluk authorities resettled Kurds and other tribal groups. See David Ayalon, "The Wafidiyya in the Mamluk Kingdom," *Islamic Culture*, 25 (1951): 89–104.

35 Little, *Catalogue*, p. 143, no. 558.

important determinant of a neighbourhood's toponym was usually its social-cultural attributes.

Dale Eickelman's study on present-day socio-spatial relationships in Boujad – a city in contemporary Morocco some two-hundred kilometres southeast of Casablanca – strengthens my analysis of fifteenth-century Jerusalem. Boujad was founded in the sixteenth century as a religious lodge.[36] In his rich ethnographic survey, Eickelman demonstrates how the city's inhabitants interact with and comprehend their urban landscape. Boujad consists of anywhere between 30 and 43 *darbs* (quarters).[37] This imprecise figure stems from differences between how his various informants remember the city's social history and experience the urban area. Each *darb* is comprised of households that are bound together by various social and personal ties. The locals refer to these intricate relations as *qaraba*, a key concept that literally means closeness, but possesses several contextual senses: forms of kinships (real or imagined); ties of patronage; ad-hoc alliances; and occasionally bonds that developed over time due to regular encounters. The *darb* is essentially the dispersal of *qaraba* over a contiguous physical space. Therefore, the dimensions of Boujad's neighbourhoods are, by and large, the product of the informant's knowledge and perception of *qaraba*. In other words, it is a person's social standing, relationships, economic needs and other related factors that dictate his or her view of the urban expanse, not its physical contours. Eickelman clearly shows that all urbanites carve out their own logical space of the city primarily on the basis of cognitive, rather than spatial, knowledge. Put differently, on the social awareness and the social ties and networks of city dwellers. In consequence, neighbourhood boundaries stem from personal experience. Remote as Boujad may seem, Eickelman indeed sheds light on our analysis of Mamluk-era neighbourhoods. For the most part, people relate to their neighbourhood in a highly personal and thus quite subjective manner. From a morphological standpoint Mujīr al-Dīn's above-noted account of the changing boundaries of neighbourhoods demonstrates that urban neighbourhoods are anything but frozen or inert physical entities, as their residents and other stakeholders – not least the government – constantly reconfigure the spatial expanse by means of their social capital, drive and imagination. The changing names of neighbourhoods and the construction of new ones within relatively short time spans are indeed indicative of the population flows within the city. Put differently, physical obstacles were fleeting, so that the neighbourhood's social makeup and territorial dimensions were conducive to change. Along with the physical modifications and population flow, the residents con-

36 Dale F. Eickelman, "Is there an Islamic City? The Making of a Quarter in a Moroccan Town," *International Journal of Middle East Studies*, 5 (1974): 274–294.

37 Ibid., p. 283.

tinually transformed the neighbourhood's intangible character. Correspondingly, they also altered its morphological configuration, albeit at a slower pace. By means of their shifting socio-cultural cognition and experience, the inhabitants of the Boujad *darb* and the Jerusalem's *ḥāra* constantly revamped their urban space.

Endowments as Catalysts for Urban Development

My final case study which aims to demonstrate the connections among architecture and ways of deciphering the urban landscape numerous implications revolves around one of the main urban institutions of the Mamluk period; religious endowments. Following Saladin's decisive victory at the Horns of Ḥaṭṭīn and the subsequent return of Islamic rule to Jerusalem, the city was swept up in a building frenzy. Endowments were the primary means that Saladin employed to convey the message that Islam had reasserted its hegemony over the sacred city and to engrave his personal insignia on the urban landscape. Besides the projects he initiated within the Ḥaram al-Sharīf, he confiscated two Christian compounds and converted one of them into a *khānqāh* (Sufi lodge) and another into *madrasa*, respectively.[38] These buildings are the first documented act of Muslim encroachment on Christian religious institutions in Jerusalem. This pair of twelfth-century appropriations notwithstanding, from the onset of the Islamic conquest of Jerusalem in the seventh century, the city's Christian sites were protected and administered by Christians, as per the laws set forth in the so-called Pact of ʿUmar.[39] Saladin launched these foundation projects to suppress the city's previous position as the capital of the Frankish kingdom and to buttress the dominant status of Islam therein. The Mamluks carried out this policy with even greater zeal than the Ayyubids, as they also made heavy use of charitable trusts in order to develop new areas within the empire's cities. An analysis of Mamluk urban layouts shows that besides founding endowments in established locales, the elite repeatedly set up new ones in underdeveloped areas and/or those free of ownership constraints. In other words, the Mamluk aristocracy had a

38 Yehoshua Frenkel, "Political and Social Aspects of Islamic Religious Endowments (awqāf): Saladin in Cairo (1169–73) and Jerusalem (1187–93)," *Bulletin of the School of Oriental and African Studies*, 62/1 (1999): 1–20. Also see Heinz Halm, "The Re-Establishment of Sunni Fiqh in Jerusalem under the Ayyubid Rule," in *The Third International Conference on Bilād al-Sham: Palestine*, vol. I: *Jerusalem* (Amman: University of Jordan 1983), pp. 111–112.

39 See Muḥammad Ibn Jarīr Abū Jaʿfar al-Ṭabarī, *Taʾrīkh al-Rusul wal-Mulūk*, new edition (Leiden: Brill, 1964), pp. 2405–2406. An analysis of the pact and its ramifications on Islamic jurisprudence and political conduct towards non-Muslim see, Milka Levy-Rubin, *Non-Muslims in the Early Islamic Empire: from Surrender to Coexistence.* (Cambridge, Cambridge University Press, 2011), pp. 58–87.

propensity for building in hitherto empty areas. In so doing, they dictated new urban directions, as these projects would lure further development to the immediate vicinity. The iterations of this sort of activity throughout the empire indeed constitute a veritable policy or at least a shared and common understanding of what constitutes public cum monumental compounds.

In Jerusalem, this policy was executed mostly in the area surrounding the Ḥaram al-Sharīf, the Muslim religious centre of the city since the Islamic conquest in 638. During the Mamluk period, numerous endowments were constructed on barren lots in relatively close proximity to the holy precinct. In fact, this building spree engendered a new urban reality. The evidence seems to point to the fact that, until the Mamluks, there was quite a bit of empty space between the Ḥaram's western wall and the rest of the built-up area in the city. More specifically, it appears as though there was an open urban zone, ranging between thirty and sixty meters wide, from the Gate of the Chain – due north of the compound – to the north-western corner of the sanctuary. For this reason, the religious centre was perceived as being external to the city.[40] It also bears noting that, on the eve of the Ayyubid conquest, the Ḥaram's western wall had only two gates facing the city;[41] however, by the end of the Mamluk period, it boasted at least eight. The reason for these new entrances was that the hitherto undeveloped land had become a prime location for foundation projects. Residential houses soon followed, thereby requiring even more passageways to the religious centre.

The British School of Archaeology conducted a survey of Ṭarīq Bāb al-Ḥadīd (Iron Gate Street), a small alley connecting one of the main thoroughfares of the city to the Ḥaram.[42] The survey, headed by Michael Burgoyne, tells the story of the urban development that was spurred on by a series of *waqf* (endowment) initiatives. At least half a dozen large-scale religious compounds were built along that small alley between 1294 and 1481. All of them were founded by high-ranking amirs, who strutted their wealth on this small stretch of land. The intense construction in this area led *inter alia* to the opening of a new gate (the aforementioned Iron Gate) sometime during the early fourteenth century.[43] Moreover, the particular location of this activity was yet another indication of the Ḥaram al-Sharīf's importance to the city's Muslims.

40 Dan Bahat, *The Topography and Toponomy of Crusader Jerusalem*, PhD dissertation, the Hebrew University (Jerusalem, 1990), pp. 54, 66 and 139 [Hebrew].

41 Ibid., p. 139.

42 Michael H. Burgoyne, "Ṭarīq Bāb al-Ḥadīd – A Mamlūk Street in the Old City of Jerusalem," *Levant*, 5 (1973): 12–35.

43 In contrast, Oleg Graber dates this gate to the late Ayyubid period, but does not support his claim with specific data; idem, "A New Inscription from the Ḥaram al-Sharīf in Jerusalem" in *Studies in Islamic Art and Architecture in Honor of K. A. C. Creswell* (Cairo: American University in Cairo Press, 1965), p. 82.

Layout of Pious Buildings in Jerusalem

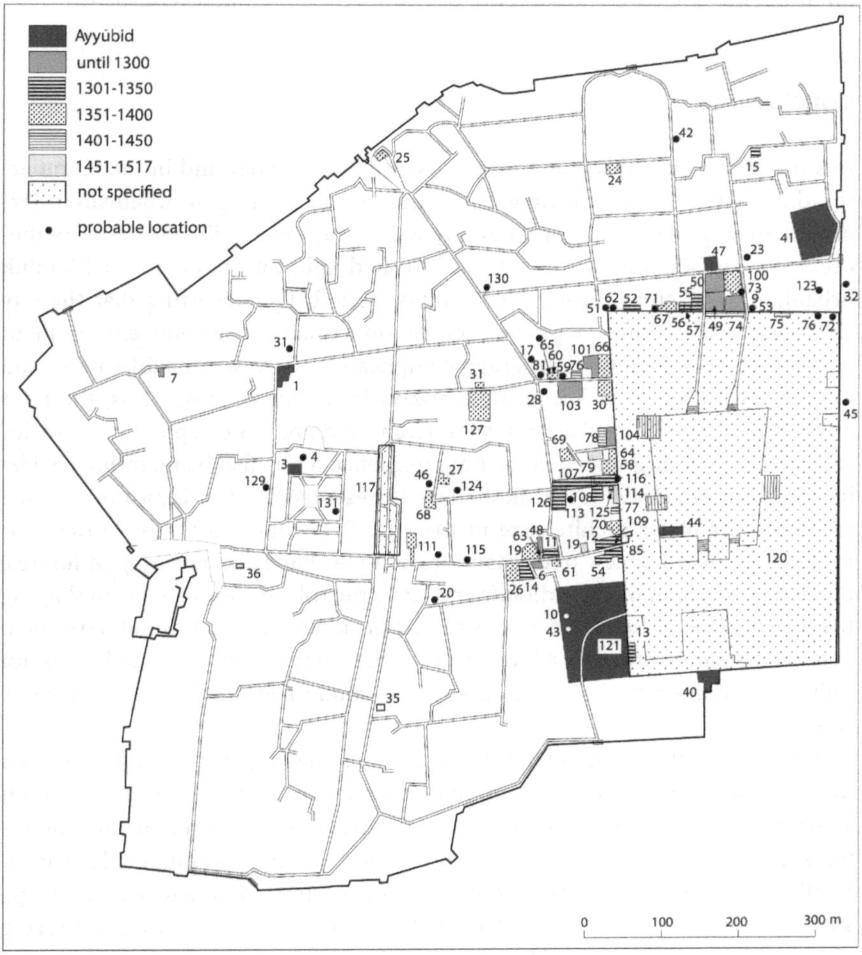

Map 2

My analysis of the spatial layout of endowed buildings throughout Jerusalem thus reveals that *waqfs* served as a major catalyst for change. Many of these institutions became the focal point of new urban centres or new development areas and played a substantial role in its morphological realignment. My study of endowments and the urban layout suggest that *waqfs* became indeed a major urban infrastructure and a way to circumnavigate some of the obstacles of the lacunas of urban codes and institutions. The mechanisms employed were a direct result of the prevailing sociocultural norms under the Mamluks. Further, endowments became a central factor and institution and had an enormous impact on urban life and surely urban built environment in Mamluk Jerusalem.

Conclusions

In sum, throughout this paper I demonstrate how a better and intimate understanding of the built environment is crucial to our reading of urbanism in Jerusalem during the Mamluk period. My main goal was to allow for a more theoretical understanding of the city and to shed light on the nature of Mamluk urbanism or of cities during the Mamluk period. By suggesting that the city should be read as a cultural process and by contextualizing the built environment as landscape (in its cultural geographic implications) my work enables us to read the city as a process and indeed as always in a state of flux. Thus, the built environment may be read as both an outcome and process of a plethora of socio-cultural and political issues which both influence it but also being influenced by its construction. Drawing on these ideas I presented a set of indicators for the study of vernacular architecture in the city. Following I have made the connections among this new understanding and the shape and meaning of houses, the nature of urban neighborhoods and lastly the role of endowments in shaping the urban milieu. The ramifications of this work far exceeds Mamluk Jerusalem and need be understood as a blue print for the study of urbanism and cities not only of the Mamluk period but indeed the pre-modern Middle East under Islamic rule.

My overarching argument in this paper is that the ongoing attempts to draw a direct corollary between Islamic imperative and urban architecture and the built environment also inform not only the literature on residential neighbourhoods but surely the (mis)conception on their various tangible and intangible aspects. In all likelihood, the neighbourhood has been a fixture on the urban landscape since the dawn of the city. More than anything else, it fulfils mankind's enduring need for a sense of place and belonging. This urge "to feel at home" is indeed a common human trait that transcends social, religious or cultural boundaries. My analysis of the residential units of Jerusalem follows my argument in favour of a more general approach to the historical city of the Middle East. Instead of merely viewing it as the tangible product of a specifically religious ideal of urbanism, the so-called "Islamic city" should be seen as an urban entity that informs many cultures. Accordingly, my disquisition on the Mamluk city draws heavily from Mumford's argument theory that the neighbourhood is practically a "fact of nature."[44] In other words, it is an "organic" factor that inheres all urban societies

44 Mumford, "The Neighbourhood and the Neighbourhood Unit."

past and present, regardless of race or creed. The present study also found the Mamluk neighbourhood to be a socially-oriented framework that covers a certain expanse, and not the other way around. Put differently, the neighbourhood is primarily defined by the socio-cultural needs and ties of its inhabitants. As a result, its spatial borders and physical characteristics are quite flexible. One problem encountered by scholars of pre-modern urban neighbourhoods is the confusion between etymology and nomenclature in the source material. More specifically, the names and terms for neighbourhoods that surface in literary descriptions and, on occasion, even in legal documents tend to fall under the heading of the era's local nomenclature, rather than its administrative or official terminology. In addition, it is difficult to establish the precise municipal or administrative function of the "typical" residential neighbourhood in the pre-modern Middle East. Therefore, any attempt to characterize an urban neighbourhood must focus on the social realm, not its spatial configuration. With this in mind, I intend to further pursue this study as a way to understand better the nature of the residential units in Mamluk Jerusalem and throughout al-Shām and surely the entire landscape of the Mamluk city therein.

Bibliography

Agnew, John, John Mercer and David Sopher, eds. *The City in Cultural Context.* Boston, London, Sydney: Routledge, 1984.

Akbar, Jamal. "Courtyard Houses: A Case Study from Riyadh, Saudi Arabia." In *The Arab City, Its Character and Islamic Cultural Heritage.* Ed. Ismail Seragldin and Samer El-Sadeq. Riyadh, 1982, 162–176.

Ayalon, David. "The Wafidiyya in the Mamluk Kingdom," *Islamic Culture*, 25 (1951): 89–104.

Bahat, Dan. *The Topography and Toponomy of Crusader Jerusalem*, PhD dissertation, the Hebrew University of Jerusalem, 1990. [Hebrew]

Baker, H. Allan and Gideon Bigger, eds. *Ideology and Landscape in Historical Perspective.* Cambridge, 1992, 1–12.

Belkacem, Youssef. "Bioclimatic Patterns and Human Aspects of Urban Form in the Islamic Cities." In *The Arab City, Its Character and Islamic Cultural Heritage.* Ed. Ismail Seragldin and Samer El-Sadeq. Riyadh, 1982: 2–12.

Briggs, S. Martin. *Muhammadan Architecture in Egypt and Palestine.* Oxford, 1924.

Burgoyne, Michael. "Ṭarīq Bāb al-Ḥadīd – A Mamlūk Street in the Old City of Jerusalem." *Levant*, 5 (1973): 12–35.

–. *Mamluk Jerusalem, an Architectural Survey.* London, 1987.

Cosgrove, E. Denis. *Social Formation and Symbolic Landscape.* London, 1984.

Creswell, A.C. Keppel. *The Muslim Architecture of Egypt, Ayyubid and Early Bahri Period.* Oxford, 1959.

David, Jean-Claude. "Alep, déradation et tentatives actuelles de rédaptation des structures urbaines traditionnelles." *Bulletin d'Étude Orientale* 28 (1978): 19–50.

Mumford, Lewis. "The Neighbourhood and the Neighbourhood Unit." *Town Planning Review* 24 (1954): 256–270.

Duncan, James. *The City as Text: The Politics of Landscape Interpretation in the Kandyan Kingdom.* Cambridge, 1990.

Duncan, James S. and Nancy G. Duncan. "Re(reading) the Landscape." *Environment and Planning D: Society and Space* 6 (1998): 117–126.

Eickelman, Dale F. "Is there an Islamic City? The Making of a Quarter in a Moroccan Town." *International Journal of Middle East Studies* 5 (1974): 274–294.

Fathy, Hassan. *Natural Energy, Vernacular Architecture. Principles and Examples with Reference to Hot Arid Climates.* Chicago, 1986.

Foucault, Michel. *Power/Knowledge: Selected Interviews and Other Writings 1972–1977.* Ed. Colin Gordon. London, 1980.

Frenkel, Yehoshua. "Political and Social Aspects of Islamic Religious Endowments (awqāf): Saladin in Cairo (1169–73) and Jerusalem (1187–93)." *Bulletin of the School of Oriental and African Studies* 62/1 (1999): 1–20.

Garcin, Jean-Claude, Bernard Maury, Jacques Revault and Mona Zakariya, eds., *Palais et maisons du Caire I: époque Mamelouke (XIIIe-XVIe siècles).* Paris, 1982.

Givoni, Baruch. *Climate Consideration in Building and Urban Design.* New York, 1998.

Golvin, Lucien et, Marie-Christine Formont. *Thula, architecture et urbanisme d'une cite de haute montagne en République Arabe du Yémen.* Paris, 1984.

Grabar, Oleg. "A New Inscription from the Ḥaram al-Sharīf in Jerusalem." In *Studies in Islamic Art and Architecture in Honour of K. A. C. Creswell.* Cairo, 1965, 72–83.

Halm, Heinz. "The Re-Establishment of Sunni Fiqh in Jerusalem under the Ayyubid Rule." In *The Third International Conference on Bilād al-Sham: Palestine*, vol. I: *Jerusalem.* Amman, 1983, 111–112.

Hill, Derek, and Oleg Grabar. *Islamic Architecture and its Decoration, A. D. 800–1500.* London, 1964.

Hillenbrand, Robert. *Islamic Architecture: Form, Function and Meaning.* New York, 1994.

Kong, Lily. "Ideological Hegemony and the Political Symbolism of Religious Buildings in Singapore." *Environment and Planning D: Society and Space* 11 (1993): 23–45.

Levy-Rubin, Milka. *Non-Muslims in the Early Islamic Empire: from Surrender to Coexistence.* Cambridge, 2011.

Little, Donald P. *A Catalogue of the Islamic Documents from the Ḥaram al-Sharīf in Jerusalem.* Beirut and Wiesbaden, 1984.

–. "Mujīr al-Dīn's al-ʿUlaymī's Vision of Jerusalem in the Ninth-Fifteenth Century." *Journal of the American Oriental Society* 115/2 (1995): 237–247.

Luz, Nimrod. *The Mamluk City of the Middle East. History, Culture and the Urban Landscape.* Cambridge, 2014.

Marçais, George. "Dār." *Encyclopedia of Islam*, 2nd edition. 2: 113–115.

Mellaarat, James. *Çatal Hüyük: A Neolitic Town in Anatolia.* London, 1967.

Olwig, Ken "Sexual Cosmology: Nation and Landscape at the Conceptual Interstices of Nature and Culture, or: What does Landscape Really Mean?" *Landscape: Politics and Perspectives.* Ed.B. Bender. Oxford, 1993: 307–43.

Pauty, Edmund. *Les palais et les maisons d'époque Musulmane, au Caire*. Le Caire: Institut français d'archéologie orientale, 1932.

Petherbridge, Guy. "Vernacular Architecture: The House and Society." In *Architecture of the Islamic World*. Ed. George Michell. London, 1987, 176–208.

Pratt, Geraldine. "The House as an Expression of the Social World." In *Housing and Identity*. Ed. James S. Duncan. New York, 1982, 135–180.

Raby, Julian, ed. *The Art of Syria and the Jazira 1100–1250*, published in *Oxford Studies in Islamic Art*. Oxford, 1985.

Rapoport, Amos. *House Form and Culture*. Englewood Cliffs, NJ, 1969.

–. "Vernacular Architecture and the Cultural Determinants of Form." In *Buildings and Society: Essays on the Social Development of the Built Environment*. Ed. Anthony D. King. London, 1980, 283–304.

–. "Culture and the Urban Order." In *The City in Cultural Context*. Ed. John A. Agnew, John Mercer and David E. Sopher. Boston and London, 1984, 50–72.

Raymond, Andre. *Grande villes arabes à l'époque ottoman*. Paris, 1985.

Salāmeh, Khader. "Aspects of the Sijils of the Shariʿa Court in Jerusalem." In *Ottoman Jerusalem: The Living City 1517–1917*. Eds. Sylvia Auld and Robert Hillenbrand. London, 2000, 1: 128–132.

Schama, Simon. *Landscape and Memory*. New York, 1996.

al-Ṭabarī, Muḥammad Ibn Jarīr Abū Jaʿfar. *Taʾrīkh al-Rusul wal-Mulūk*. New edition. Leiden, 1964.

Tuan, Yi-Fu. "Thought and Landscape." In *Interpretations of Ordinary Landscapes: Geographic Essays*. Ed. Donald W. Meinig. New York, 1979, 89–102.

al-ʿUlaymī, Mujīr al-Dīn, ʿAbd al-Raḥmān, b. Muḥammad al-Ḥanbalī. *Al-Uns al-Jalīl bi-Taʾrīkh al-Quds wal-Khalīl*. Baghdad, 1990. 2 vols.

Woolley, Leonard. *Ur of Chaldes*. Revised and updated edition by Paul R. S. Mooery. Ithaca, 1982.

Koby Yosef (Bar-Ilan University, Ramat Gan)

Cross-Boundary Hatred: (Changing) Attitudes towards Mongol and "Christian" *mamlūks* in the Mamluk Sultanate

Introduction

The Mamluk Sultanate of Egypt and Syria (1250–1517) was not an isolated island. Its internal social relationships, policies, attitudes and ideologies were affected by external circumstances. It is not possible to fully understand the former without taking the Sultanate's dynamic relationships with the surrounding states and political entities into consideration.[1] Changes in external circumstances brought about changes within the Sultanate and vice versa. By examining (changing) attitudes towards Mongol and non-Turkish *mamlūk*s during the Mamluk Sultanate as reflected mainly in Mamluk chronicles and biographical dictionaries, it will be demonstrated how external political and social circumstances affected Mamluk society and perceptions of ethnic identity within that society. Until the further strengthening of the Ilkhan's (1259–1335) conversion to Sunnī Islam

Prelimary note: A draft of this article was written during a six months stay in the Annemarie Schimmel Kolleg for "History and Society during the Mamluk Era, 1250–1517" in the University of Bonn (March 2012-September 2012), and first presented at the conference "Everything is on the Move: The 'Mamluk Empire' as a Node in (Trans-) Regional Networks" held in Bonn between 6–9/12/2012 under the auspices of the Annemarie Schimmel Kolleg. I would like to thank Professor Stephan Conermann, then the sole director of the Kolleg, for inviting me to Bonn as a fellow in the Kolleg, and for the conference. A more elaborated version was presented at the Minerva-Gentner Israeli-German Symposium "The Mamluk Sultanate from the Perspective of Regional and World History: Economic, Social and Cultural Development in an Era of Increasing International Interaction and Competition" held in the Hebrew University of Jerusalem between 11–16/06/2014, under the auspices of the Annemarie Schimmel Kolleg and the Nehemia Levtzion Center for Islamic Sudies in the Hebrew University of Jerusalem. I would like to thank the Minerva Fund, the Annemarie Schimmel Kolleg, the Nehemia Levtzion Center for Islamic Studies, and the organizers of the conference, Professor Stephan Conermann and Professor Reuven Amitai.

1 See for example Reuven Amitai, *Mongols and Mamluks: The Mamluk-Īlkhānid War, 1260–1281* (Cambridge: Cambridge University Press, 1995), 1–2; Stephen R. Humphreys, "Ayyubids, Mamluks, and the Latin East in the Thirteenth Century," *Mamlūk Studies Review* 2 (1998): 1–17 (especially 5).

during the reign of Abū Saʿīd (1316–1335),[2] and the end of the war with the Ilkhanate in 1323, Mongols in general, and specifically Mongol *mamlūks* who were war captives, were generally perceived in a negative manner within the Mamluk Sultanate. In that period, a separation between the Turkish and Mongol ethnic groups can be identified, both perceived as being even remoter from the group of non-Turkish *mamlūks* of "Christian" background (Europeans and Caucasian peoples) reminiscent of the Sultanate's other eminent enemy – the Crusaders. The peace agreement with the Ilkhans and demographic changes in the so-called Golden Horde (*Bilād al-Qifjaq*) during al-Nāṣir Muḥammad ibn Qalāwūn's third reign (1310–1341) resulted in a change in perceptions of ethnic identities within the Sultanate, the annulment of the differentiation between Turks and Mongols, and in a construction of a new united Turco-Mongol ethnic identity. The non-Turkish *mamlūks* continued to be perceived as the "other" and were subject to discrimination, which affected the patterns of their social ties, and perhaps eventually contributed to a transformation of Mamluk society.

1. Attitudes towards Mongols

1.1. The Mamluk Sultanate's Interaction with the Surrounding Mongol Khanates until al-Nāṣir Muḥammad's Third Reign and Its Attitude towards Them

From the earliest stages of its existence, the Mamluk Sultanate faced two eminent enemies – the Mongols and the Crusaders.[3] Its relationship with its Mongol neighbors was quite complicated and the feelings towards them were a mixture of respect, admiration, an inferiority complex, fear and hate.[4] The Mongols were considered to be ethnically related to the Turks,[5] and the Mamluks admired their

2 Bertold Spuler, "Ilkhāns," *The Encyclopaedia of Islam*, 2nd Edition (Leiden: Brill, 1971), 3: 1120–3.

3 See for example Humphreys, "Ayyubids, Mamluks," 5, 11; David Ayalon, "The Great Yāsa of Chingiz Khān: A Re-examination (C1)," *Studia Islamica* 36 (1972): 117.

4 See for example Anne F. Broadbridge, "Mamluk Legitimacy and the Mongols: The Reigns of Baybars and Qalāwūn," *Mamlūk Studies Review* 5 (2001): 105; Ayalon, "The Great Yāsa (C1)," 128; Charles J. Halperin, "The Kipchak Connection: The Ilkhans, the Mamluks and Ayn Jalut," *Bulletin of the School of Oriental and African Studies* 63/2 (2000): 239.

5 See for example Ayalon, "The Great Yāsa (C1)," 117, 121, 126; Reuven Amitai, "Northern Syria between the Mongols and Mamluks: Political Boundary, Military Frontier, and Ethnic Affinities," in *Frontiers in Question: Eurasian Borderlands c. 700–1700*, ed. Daniel Power and Naomi Standen (London: Macmillan, 1999), 131, 146. Muslim writers tended to see the Mongols as part of the Turkish peoples, see for example Amitai, *Mongols and Mamluks*, 220 (note 32); Josephine van den Bent, "'None of the Kings on Earth is Their Equal in *ʿAṣabiyya*': The Mongols in Ibn Khaldūn's Works," *Al-Masāq* 28/2 (2016): 178 (especially note 34). There is evidence (at

military prowess and military organization.[6] Because of this perceived ethnic relatedness, a person described as "Turk" (*al-turkī*) in Mamluk sources may be of Turkish or Mongol origin.[7] At the same time, however, some of the Mongols were bitter and hated enemies. Whereas the Sultanate was in a state of peace with the Muslim khans of the northern Golden Horde, on which it was dependant for the supply of Qipchaq *mamlūks*,[8] the non-Muslim Mongol Ilkhans based in Persia kept on attacking the Sultanate from the east[9] and scorned its rulers because they were of servile origins and lacked a respected genealogy.[10] The reaction of the

least from the early thirteenth century) that the belief that the Turks and Mongols belonged to the same stock was not confined to Muslim writers but was shared by those people themselves, see David Ayalon, "The Great Yāsa of Chingiz Khān: A Re-examination (C2). Al-Maqrīzī's Passage on the *Yāsa* under the Mamluks," *Studia Islamica* 38 (1973): 148–51.

6 See for example David Ayalon, "The Wafidiya in the Mamluk Kingdom," *Islamic Culture* 25 (1951): 98; idem, "The Great Yāsa (C1)," 127–8.

7 It has been often emphasized that the term "Turks" in plural (*atrāk/turk*) lost its ethnic specificity during the Mamluk Sultanate, and thus may refer to all members of the Mamluk ruling elite without consideration of their ethnic origin; see for example David Ayalon, "Names, Titles, and 'Nisbas' of the Mamluks," *Israel Oriental Studies* 5 (1975): 197–8; William Popper, *Egypt and Syria under the Circassian Sultans 1382–1468 A.D.: Systematic Notes to Ibn Taghrī Birdī's Chronicles of Egypt* (Berkeley, 1955), 2, 7; however, it is sometimes wrongly assumed that the *nisba* "*al-turkī*" also lost its ethnic specificity; see Ayalon, "Names," 219–23. In fact the *nisba* "*al-turkī*" during the Mamluk Sultanate refers almost only to Turks and Mongols (including Oirats), and sometimes to Alans (*āṣ*) and Russians (*rūs*) that during the early Mamluk period were perceived as "Tatars"; see Koby Yosef, "Ethnic Groups, Social Relationships and Dynasty in the Mamluk Sultanate (1250–1517)," PhD dissertation (University of Tel-Aviv, 2011) [in Hebrew]: 1: 139–41, 130–1; and see also idem, "The Names of the *Mamlūks* – Ethnic Groups and Ethnic Solidarity in the Mamluk Sultanate (1250–1517)," in *Egypt and Syria under Mamluk Rule: Political, Social and Cultural Aspects*, ed. Amalia Levanoni (forthcoming). For Mongol *mamlūks* referred to as "*al-turkī*," see Yosef, "Ethnic Groups," 2: 3–5; Amir Mazor, *The Rise and Fall of a Muslim Regiment. The Manṣūriyya in the First Mamluk Sultanate 678/1279–710/1341* (Bonn: Bonn University Press, 2015), 36.

8 See for example "The Great Yāsa (C1)," 117, 129.

9 See for example Reuven Amitai, "The Resolution of the Mongol-Mamluk War," in *Mongols, Turks, and Others: Eurasian Nomads and the Sedentary World*, ed. Reuven Amitai and Michal Biran (Leiden: Brill, 2005), 359–61; idem, "Mongol Imperial Ideology and the Ilkhanid War against the Mamluks," in *The Mongol Empire and its Legacy*, ed. Reuven Amitai-Preiss and David Morgan (Leiden: Brill, 1999), 57; idem, *Mongols and Mamluks*, 1–2; idem, "Mamluks of Mongol Origin and Their Role in Early Mamluk Political Life," *Mamlūk Studies Review* 12/1 (2008): 119; Denise Aigle, "The Mongol Invasions of Bilād al-Shām by Ghāzān Khān and Ibn Taymīyah's Three 'Anti-Mongol' Fatwas," *Mamlūk Studies Review* 11/2 (2007): 89.

10 See for example Taqī al-Dīn Aḥmad ibn ʿAlī al-Maqrīzī, *Kitāb al-Sulūk li-Maʿrifat Duwal al-Mulūk*, ed. Muḥammad Muṣṭafá Ziyāda and Saʿīd ʿAbd al-Fattāḥ ʿĀshūr (Cairo: Dār al-Kutub al-Miṣriyya, 1934–1973), 1: 427; Ṣārim al-Dīn Ibrāhīm ibn Muḥammad ibn Aydamur Ibn Duqmāq, *Nuzhat al-Anām fī Taʾrīkh al-Islām*, ed. Samīr Ṭabbāra (Beirut: Al-Maktaba al-ʿAṣriyya, 1999), 261; Anne F. Broadbridge, *Kingship and Ideology in the Islamic and Mongol Worlds* (Cambridge: Cambridge University Press, 2008), 13, 29, 33–4; idem, "Mamluk Legitimacy and the Mongols," 92–5, 117; Denise Aigle, *The Mongol Empire between Myth and Reality: Studies in Anthropological History* (Leiden: Brill, 2014), 223; idem, "The Mongol

Mamluks was twofold – offensive and defensive. On the one hand, they scorned the Ilkhans for not being Muslims and depicted them in negative terms.[11] On the other, they tried to suppress their servile origins and attach themselves to established dynasties or respected Mongol families.[12] Al-Ẓāhir Baybars (d. 1277), who was called a slave by the Ilkhans, tried to forge a Genghisid genealogy[13] and established marital ties with the family of the last Ayyūbid ruler in Egypt al-Ṣāliḥ Ayyūb (d. 1249), and with families of senior Mongol immigrants (*wāfidiyya*).[14] Al-Manṣūr Qalāwūn (d. 1290), who like al-Ẓāhir Baybars before him was criticized by the Ilkhans because of his humble origins, married daughters of Mongol immigrants,[15] among them Ashlūn bint Sukatāy who is sometimes said to have been a descendant of Genghis Khān (*al-ʿaẓm al-qānī*).[16] Almost all the Mamluk sultans until the days of al-Nāṣir Muḥammad ibn Qalāwūn (d. 1341) married Mongol women, and sons of al-Ẓāhir Baybars and al-Manṣūr Qalāwūn, who became sultans, were half Mongols and were probably exposed to Mongol in-

---

Invasions of Bilād al-Shām," 104; Amitai, *Mongols and Mamluks*, 36; idem, "Mongol Imperial Ideology," 4; Halperin, "The Kipchak Connection," 231.

11 Broadbridge, *Kingship and Ideology*, 12–13, 27–8, 38–42, 65, 74; Aigle, "The Mongol Invasions of Bilād al-Shām," 97, 112; and see Badr al-Dīn Maḥmūd al-ʿAynī, *ʿIqd al-Jumān fī Taʾrīkh Ahl al-Zamān*, ed. Muḥammad Muḥammad Amīn (Cairo: Dār al-Kutub wal-Wathāʾiq al-Qawmiyya, 2009–2010), 1: 216; Abū al-Fidāʾ Ismāʿīl ibn ʿUmar Ibn Kathīr, *al-Bidāya wal-Nihāya fī al-Taʾrīkh* (Beirut: Dār al-Maʿārif, 1966), 13: 215, 248; Yūsuf Ibn Taghrībirdī, *Kitāb al-Nujūm al-Zāhira fī Mulūk Miṣr wal-Qāhira*, ed. Fahīm Muḥammad Shaltūt et al. (Cairo: Dār al-Kutub al-Miṣriyya, 1963–1972), 8: 53; Shams al-Dīn Muḥammad ibn Aḥmad al-Dhahabī, *Taʾrīkh al-Islām wa-Wafayāt al-Mashāhīr wal-Aʿlām*, ed. ʿUmar ʿAbd al-Salām Tadmurī (Beirut: Dār al-Kitāb al-ʿArabī, 1989–2004), 50: 182; 51: 346; Quṭb al-Dīn Mūsá ibn Muḥammad ibn Aḥmad al-Yūnīnī, *Dhayl Mirʾāt al-Zamān* (Hyderabad: Dāʾirat al-Maʿārif al-ʿUthmāniyya, 1954–1961), 4: 177–8.

12 Koby Yosef, "The Term *Mamlūk* and Slave Status during the Mamluk Sultanate," *al-Qantara* 19/1 (2013): 14–17; and see also Aigle, *The Mongol Empire*, 226; Anne Troadec, "Baybars and the Cultural Memory of Bilād al-Shām: The Construction of Legitimacy," *Mamlūk Studies Review* 18 (2014–2015): 113–48 (especially 113, 118–19).

13 Khalīl ibn Aybak al-Ṣafadī, *al-Wāfī bil-Wafayāt*, ed. Helmut Ritter et al. (Wiesbaden: Franz Steiner Verlag, 1962–2004), 7: 311.

14 Ibn Duqmāq, *Nuzhat al-Anām*, 171; Nāṣir al-Dīn Muḥammad Ibn al-Furāt, *Taʾrīkh al-Duwal wal-Mulūk*, ed. Q. Zurayk and N. ʿIzz al-Dīn (Beirut: Al-Maṭbaʿa al-Amrīkāniyya, 1936–1942), 7: 90; Shihāb al-Dīn Aḥmad ibn ʿAbd al-Wahhāb al-Nuwayrī, *Nihāyat al-Arab fī Funūn al-Adab*, ed. Fahīm Muḥammad Shaltūt et al. (Cairo: Al-Muʾassasa al-Miṣriyya al-ʿĀmma lil-Taʾlīf wal-Nashr, 1964–1998), 30: 368; al-Maqrīzī, *al-Sulūk*, 1: 640; 2: 337; Muḥammad ibn ʿAlī ibn Ibrāhīm Ibn Shaddād, *Taʾrīkh al-Malik al-Ẓāhir*, ed. Aḥmad Ḥuṭayṭ (Wiesbaden: Franz Steiner Verlag, 1983), 144.

15 P. M. Holt, "An-Nāṣir Muḥammad b. Qalāwūn (684–741/1285–1341): His Ancestry, Kindred, and Affinity," in *Egypt and Syria in the Fatimid, Ayyubid and Mamluk Eras, Proceedings of the 1st, 2nd, and 3rd International Colloquium*, ed. Urbain Vermeulen and Daniel De Smet (Leuven: Uitgeverij Peeters, 1995), 314.

16 Muḥyī al-Dīn ʿAbd Allāh Ibn ʿAbd al-Ẓāhir, *Tashrīf al-Ayyām wal-ʿUṣūr fī Sīrat al-Malik al-Manṣūr*, ed. Murād Kāmil (Cairo: Al-Sharika al-ʿArabiyya lil-Ṭibāʿa wal-Nashr, 1961), 110.

fluence in the Mamluk court and the sultan's household.[17] Mongol wives and Mongol emissaries were potential agents of cultural influence.[18]

External political factors also affected the composition of the Mamluk army and ruling elite. Because of internal disputes within the Ilkhanate, starting from the days of al-Ẓāhir Baybars (1260–1277), Mongol immigrants or refugees (*wāfidiyya*) came to the Sultanate from the Ilkhanate.[19] In addition, many Mongols became war captives and slaves in the course of the struggle between the Sultanate and the Ilkhans. It is known that al-Manṣūr Qalāwūn owned large numbers of Mongol *mamlūks*,[20] and there is evidence that many of them were war captives.[21] These Mongol *mamlūks* constituted a significant part of the Mamluk elite until al-Nāṣir Muḥammad's third reign.[22] The Mongol *wāfidiyya* and *mamlūks* were other potential agents of cultural influence.[23]

17 Nobutaka Nakamachi, "The Rank and Status of Military Refugees in the Mamluk Army: A Reconsideration of the *Wāfidīyah*," *Mamlūk Studies Review* 10/1 (2006): 73 (and see also 74–5); Holt, "An-Nāṣir Muḥammad b. Qalāwūn," 313–15; Amitai, "Mamluks of Mongol Origin," 134–5; and see idem, "Northern Syria," 146; and see also Ayalon, "The Wafidiya," 90, 100.

18 Donald P. Little, "Diplomatic Missions and Gifts Exchanged by Mamluks and Ilkhans," in *Beyond the Legacy of Genghis Khan*, ed. Kinda Komoroff (Leiden: Brill, 2006), 42; and see also idem, "Notes on Aitamiš, a Mongol Mamlūk," in *Die islamische Welt zwischen Mittelalter und Neuzeit: Festschrift für Hans Robert Roemer zum 65. Geburtstag*, ed. Ulrich Haarmann and Peter Bachmann (Beirut: Orient-Institut der Deutschen Morganlandischen Gesellschaft/ Wiesbaden: Franz Steiner, 1979), 400.

19 Ayalon, "The Wafidiya," 89; Nakamachi, "The Rank and Status," 55–6.

20 Ayalon, "The Great Yāsa (C1)," 124; Amitai, "Mamluks of Mongol Origin," 120.

21 See for example Reuven Amitai, "The Mongol Occupation of Damascus in 1300: A Study of Mamluk Loyalties," in *The Mamluks in Egyptian and Syrian Politics and Society*, ed. Amalia Levanoni and Michael Winter (Leiden: Brill, 2004), 24–5; idem, "Mamluks of Mongol Origin," 120; and see also Aḥmad ibn ʿAlī Ibn Ḥajar al-ʿAsqalānī, *al-Durar al-Kāmina fī Aʿyān al-Miʾa al-Thāmina*, ed. ʿAbd al-Wārith Muḥammad ʿAlī (Beirut: Dār al-Kutub al-ʿIlmiyya, 1997), 1: 280, 295–6; Taqī al-Dīn Aḥmad ibn ʿAlī al-Maqrīzī, *Kitāb al-Muqaffá al-Kabīr*, ed. Muḥammad al-Yaʿlāwī (Beirut: Dār al-Gharb al-Islāmī, 1991), 2: 562; Baybars al-Manṣūrī al-Dawādār, *al-Tuḥfa al-Mulūkiyya fī al-Dawla al-Turkiyya*, ed. ʿAbd al-Ḥamīd Ṣāliḥ Ḥamdān (Beirut: Al-Dār al-Miṣriyya al-Lubnāniyya, 1987), 84; al-ʿAynī, *ʿIqd al-Jumān*, 2: 159.

22 Yosef, "Ethnic Groups," 1: 52–3.

23 Ayalon, "The Great Yāsa (C1)," 134; Little, "Diplomatic Missions," 42; for potential Mongol cultural influences on the Mamluks, see Ayalon, "The Great Yāsa (C1)," 130–1; Halperin, "The Kipchak Connection," 241–2.

1.2. Turkish-period Mamluk Historians and the Attitudes and Perceptions that They Reflect

Before moving on to discuss perceptions of Mongol *mamlūks* and *wāfidiyya*, and attitudes towards them during the Turkish period of the Sultanate (1250–1382) as reflected in Mamluk history books, a word on the nature of our sources is in order. As noted by Donald Little, during the Turkish period of the Sultanate historians, almost with no exceptions, "took a decidedly favorable attitude towards the ruling elite. This is particularly true of the historians who held official positions in the bureaucracy or the army, both in Egypt and Syria."[24] Most history books from that period were written by court-affiliated Arab bureaucrats with a background of conventional religious education, or by Arab Syrian religious scholars affiliated with the religious establishment. Notwithstanding this, some history books were written by historians closely associated with the Mamluk military institution either as *mamlūks* or as descendants of *mamlūks*.[25] The writings of historians of *mamlūk* origin show a clear pro-Qalāwūnid bias. Baybars al-Manṣūrī (d. 1325), a *mamlūk* of al-Manṣūr Qalāwūn, "wrote as a partisan of the Qalāwūnid house and most specifically as the encomiast of his master, al-Nāṣir Muḥammad ibn Qalāwūn."[26] Qaraṭāy al-ʿIzzī al-Khāzindārī's (died after 1308) history book shows similar tendencies.[27] As for historians who were Arabized descendants of *mamlūks*, Ibn al-Dawādārī (flourished in the days of al-Nāṣir Muḥammad) wrote a history book that was dedicated to al-Nāṣir Muḥammad ibn Qalāwūn, which shows a clear pro-Qalāwūnid bias.[28] Al-Ṣafadī (d. 1363), the other notable Turkish-period historian who was a *mamlūk*'s descendant, owed his position to Qalāwūnid sultans. During the Turkish period, the historians who were *mamlūks* or descendants of *mamlūks* were all of some "Turkish" background, and none of them was of European or Caucasian background.

---

24 Donald P. Little, "Historiography of the Ayyūbid and Mamlūk Epochs," in *The Cambridge History of Egypt*. Vol. 1: *Islamic Egypt, 640–1517*, ed. Carl F. Petry (Cambridge: Cambridge University Press, 1998), 420.

25 Little, "Historiography," 420; and see also ibid., 413.

26 Robert Irwin, "Mamluk History and Historians," in *Arabic Literature in the Post-Classical Period*, ed. Allen Richards (Cambridge: Cambridge University Press, 2006), 163; and see also P. M. Holt, "Literary Offerings: A Genre of Courtly Literature," in *The Mamluks in Egyptian Politics and Society*, ed. Thomas Philipp and Ulrich Haarmann (Cambridge: Cambridge University Press, 1998), 4.

27 See for example Qaraṭāy al-ʿIzzī al-Khāzindārī, *Taʾrīkh Majmūʿ al-Nawādir mimmā Jará lil-Awāʾil wal-Awākhir*, ed. ʿUmar ʿAbd al-Salām Tadmurī (Ṣaydā and Beirut: al-Maktaba al-ʿAṣriyya, 2005), 265–8.

28 Koby Yosef, "*Dawlat al-Atrāk* or *Dawlat al-Mamālīk?* Ethnic Origin or Slave Origin as the Defining Characteristic of the Ruling Elite in the Mamluk Sultanate," *Jerusalem Studies in Arabic and Islam* 39 (2012): 395.

Court-affiliated bureaucrat Arab historians such as Ibn ʿAbd al-Ẓāhir (d. 1292), Shāfiʿ ibn ʿAlī (d. 1330), and Ibn Shaddād al-Ḥalabī (d. 1285), wrote "official" royal biographies of Qipchaq sultans under royal patronage and supervision.[29] The Syrian Arab historians who were religious scholars wrote mainly universal chronicles. Their distance from the court and the fact that they did not hold official positions should account for the fact that they show a more sober attitude towards Mamluk sultans. Notwithstanding this, as noted, they generally show favorable attitude towards the ruling elite. Even those of them who do not seem to be too enthusiastic about Mamluk rulers,[30] do not criticize them as vehemently as Circassian-period historians of religious background criticize contemporary Mamluk rulers.

The fact that in contrast to the Circassian period (1382–1517) in which almost all effective rulers were *mamlūks*, most of the Turkish-period rulers were Arabized descendants of *mamlūks* (the Qalāwūnids) must have contributed to the relatively positive attitudes of Arab historians towards Mamluk rule during the Turkish period. There is evidence that while the local population was not too enthusiastic about *mamlūk* rule, they did support the Qalāwūnids.[31] In addition, the Qalāwūnids were not only Arabized but also adhered to, or at least showed inclination towards, the Shāfiʿī school of law,[32] the dominant school of law in Egypt, to which adhered also many of the Turkish-period historians (al-Nuwayrī, al-Dhahabī, Ibn al-Wardī, Ibn Faḍl Allāh al-ʿUmarī, al-Ṣafadī, Ibn Ḥabīb, and Ibn Kathīr). Moreover, as we will see below in section 1.3.5, there is evidence that in contrast to other ethnic groups, Qipchaqs did tend to know the Arabic language, which must have also contributed to feelings of closeness between the Arab population, Arab historians among them, and the Qipchaq amirs. The sources we have, therefore, reflect in sum the collective attitudes and perceptions of the Qipchaq sultans, especially the Qalāwūnids, and by extension those of the Qipchaq ethnic group,[33] on the one hand, and those of the Arab local civilian elite, especially the Shāfiʿīs, on the other hand. Since historical writing during the Circassian period (1382–1517) was dominated by Arab Shāfiʿī historians these attitudes and perceptions were preserved and reflected also in their writing (for

29 Little, "Historiography," 420–3; Irwin, "Mamluk History and Historians," 162–3.

30 See for example Irwin, "Mamluk History and Historians," 161; but see Konrad Hirschler, "Studying Mamluk Historiography. From Source-Criticism to the Cultural Turn," in *Ubi Sumus? Quo Vademus? Mamluk Studies – State of the Art*, ed. Stephan Conermann (Göttingen: Bonn University Press, 2013), 178–9.

31 Boaz Shoshan, *Popular Culture in Medieval Cairo* (Cambridge: Cambridge University Press, 2002), 52–6; Yosef, "The Term *Mamlūk*," 14–15.

32 I cannot elaborate on this in the scope of this article.

33 See more on that in Yosef, "*Dawlat al-Atrāk* or *Dawlat al-Mamālīk?*," 394–7, 399–400.

a more detailed discussion on Circassian-period historians see section 3.4.3 below).

1.3. Attitudes towards Mongol *mamlūk*s and Mongol *wāfidiyya* until al-Nāṣir Muḥammad's Third Reign

1.3.1. The Terms *Tatar* and *Mughul*

In Mamluk sources Mongols are referred to either as *Mughul/Mughūl* (sing. *Mughulī/Mughūlī*) or *Tatar/Tatār/Ṭaṭar* (sing. *Tatarī/Tatārī/Ṭaṭarī*). The exact meaning of the terms "Mongol" and "Tatar" has been a matter of some debate. Some scholars have emphasized the interchangeability of the two names. According to István Vásáry, "by the middle of the thirteenth century the ethnonyms *Mongol* and *Tatar* has become totally synonymous," but *Tatar* was used more commonly.[34] Vásáry noted however that these ethnonyms were primarily political names referring to the leading tribe of the confederacy or state, and can be utilized in ethnic history only in a limited way.[35] According to Peter Jackson, during the eighth and ninth centuries the Tatars played a prominent role in Inner-Asian affairs and it seems that for Chinese and Islamic writers their name became synonymous with non-Turkish steppe people including the Mongols.[36] The Mongol conquerors became known in the Islamic world and Europe as "Tatars." Politically, the term seems to have embraced also client rulers and their subject, who by being designated "Tatar" ("you are now a Tatar like us") were subjugated to the Mongols.[37] Other scholars suggested that the two terms were somewhat different. David Morgan suggested on philological grounds that in the context of the Mongol Empire, "Mongol" referred to ethnically Mongol people and "Tatar" "carried the implication of people who have become (politically) Mongol."[38] Working with Mamluk Arabic sources, Reuven Amitai was under the impression that this distinction is confirmed and that "[t]he use of *mughul* instead of the generally found *tatar* would seem to indicate… 'true' Mongols, and not Turks or other soldiers who served the Mongols, all of whom seem to be lumped under the rubric *tatar*."[39] Josephine van den Bent found that Ibn Khaldūn

34 István Vásáry, *Cumans and Tatars. Oriental Military in the Pre-Ottoman Balkans, 1185–1365* (Cambridge: Cambridge University Press, 2005), 9.
35 Ibid.
36 Peter Jackson, *The Mongols and the West, 1221–1410* (London and New York: Routledge, 2014), 36.
37 Ibid., 41.
38 David Morgan, *The Mongols* (Oxford: Basil Blackwell, 1986), 57.
39 Amitai, *Mongols and Mamluks*, 108; and see also ibid., 113 (note 30). And see also Jürgen Paul, "Mongols Aristocrats and Beyliks in Anatolia. A Study of Astarādī's *Bazm va Razm*," *Eur-*

(d. 1406) "appears to see *mughul* and *tatar* as existing alongside one another" and refers to Hülegü (d. 1265) as belonging to "the great *mughul* in his lineage." However, the terms are not consistently used throughout Ibn Khaldūn's works.[40]

In *Taqwīm al-Buldān* written between 1316 and 1321, Abū al-Fidā᾽ (d. 1331) quotes the geographer Ibn Saʿīd al-Maghribī (d. 1286) and says that in the area of Qarāqurūm (the capital of the Mongol Empire) lies "the Land of the Mongols" (*Bilād al-Mughul*) who are the "pure Tatars" (*khāliṣat al-tatar*), from them come the Great Khāns.[41] In his chronicle, Abū al-Fidā᾽ reports that in the Battle of Abulustayn (Elbistan) in 1277 the Mamluks faced "Tatar" troops (*jamʿ min al-tatar*) who were "pure Mongols" (*naqāwat al-mughul*).[42] The term "the Land of the Mongols" (*Bilād al-Mughul/Bilād al-Mughūl*) is only rarely used in Mamluk sources, but when it appears it almost always refers to the Mongol's homeland or the Land of the Great Khāns in the East.[43] In extremely rare cases, however, it refers to the Ilkhanate.[44] Normally, and quite often, the Ilkhanate is referred to as "the Land of the Tatars" (*Bilād al-Tatar/Bilād al-Tatār/Bilād al-Ṭaṭar*).[45] In fact, as far as I know, the term "the Land of the Tatars" is never used in reference to the Mongols' homeland or the Land of the Great Khāns in the East, and at least until the late Turkish period it also never refers to the Golden Horde which is normally

---

asian Studies 9/1–2 (2011): 115 (note 35) – "*tatar* was one of the catch-all terms used to refer to all those who came during and after the Mongol, or Tatar, invasion."

40 Josephine van den Bent, "None of the Kings on Earth," 173 (note 8).

41 ʿImād al-Dīn Ismāʿīl ibn ʿAlī Abū al-Fidā᾽, *Kitāb Taqwīm al-Buldān*, ed. Raynūd and al-Barūn Māk Kūkīn Dīslān (Paris: Dār al-Ṭibāʿa al-Sulṭāniyya, 1840), 505; and see also Shihāb al-Dīn Aḥmad ibn ʿAlī al-Qalqashandī, *Ṣubḥ al-Aʿshá fī Ṣināʿat al-Inshā᾽* (Cairo: al-Maṭbaʿa al-Amīriyya, 1913–1919), 4: 480.

42 ʿImād al-Dīn Ismāʿīl ibn ʿAlī Abū al-Fidā᾽, *al-Mukhtaṣar fī Akhbār al-Bashar* (Cairo: Al-Maṭbaʿa al-Ḥusayniyya al-Miṣriyya, 1907), 4: 9.

43 Except for the above-mentioned references, see Ibn Faḍl Allāh al-ʿUmarī, *Kitāb Masālik al-Abṣār wa-Mamālik al-Amṣār*, ed. ʿAbd Allāh ibn Yaḥyá al-Sarīḥī et al. (Abu Dhabi: al-Majmaʿ al-Thaqāfī, 2001–2004), 3: 8; Shihāb al-Dīn Aḥmad ibn Muḥammad Ibn ʿArabshāh, *Kitāb ʿAjā᾽ib al-Maqdūr fī Akhbār Tīmūr*, ed. Aḥmad ibn Muḥammad ibn ʿAlī al-Anṣārī al-Yamanī al-Shirwānī (Calcutta: [s.n.], 1232 [1817]), 286; al-ʿAynī, *ʿIqd al-Jumān*, 1: 365; Yūsuf Ibn Taghrībirdī, *al-Manhal al-Ṣāfī wal-Mustawfá baʿda al-Wāfī*, ed. Muḥammad Muḥammad Amīn (Cairo: Al-Hay᾽a al-Miṣriyya al-ʿĀmma lil-Kitāb, 1984–2006), 2: 141; Muḥammad ibn ʿAbd al-Raḥmān al-Sakhāwī, *al-Ḍaw᾽ al-Lāmiʿ li-Ahl al-Qarn al-Tāsiʿ* (Beirut: Dār al-Jīl, 1992), 2: 127.

44 Abū Bakr ibn ʿAbd Allāh Ibn al-Dawādārī, *Kanz al-Durar wa-Jāmiʿ al-Ghurar*, ed. H. R. Roemer (Cairo: Qism al-Dirāsāt al-Islāmiyya bil-Maʿhad al-Almānī lil-Āthār, 1960–1982), 9: 268; al-Maqrīzī, *al-Sulūk*, 1: 873; al-ʿAynī, *ʿIqd al-Jumān*, 1: 454. Al-ʿAynī is quoting al-Yūsufī, and al-Maqrīzī is known to have relied heavily on al-Yūsufī without mentioning his name, so it is quite possible that almost all usages of the term *Bilād al-Mughul/Bilād al-Mughūl* in reference to the Ilkhanate stem from al-Yūsufī.

45 Just for example, see Khalīl ibn Aybak al-Ṣafadī, *Aʿyān al-ʿAṣr wa-Aʿwān al-Naṣr*, ed. ʿAlī Abū Zayd (Beirut: Dār al-Fikr al-Muʿāṣir, 1998), 1: 523, 615, 656, 707; and see Anne F. Broadbridge, "Sending Home for Mom and Dad: The Extended Family Impulse in Mamluk Politics," *Mamlūk Studies Review* 15 (2011): 16.

named after its ruler (*Bilād Barka/Bilād Uzbak*),[46] or after its Qipchaq inhabitants (*Bilād al-Qifjāq*, or simply *al-Bilād*,[47] and more rarely *Dasht al-Qibjāq*).[48]

All this would seem to suggest that Mamluk scholars, especially geographers perhaps, differentiated to a certain degree between *mughul* (Mongols) and *tatar* (Mongols, especially the Ilkhans, and people annexed to them). As far as I know, Turkish-period historians always refer to Ghengisid rulers by the *nisba* "*al-mughulī*" and not by the *nisba* "*al-tatarī*," which also testifies to this fact. Abū al-Fidāʾ who, as we have seen, shows some awareness to this differentiation also reports that among the "Tatar" troops of Hülegü there was a commander (*rajul min al-tatar*) that originally was a respected Qipchaq (*min akābir al-qibjāq*) who ran away from the "Tatars" (*al-tatar*) when they defeated the Qipchaqs (*al-qibjāq*) and arrived in Ayyūbid Aleppo. Eventually however, he decided to return to the "Tatars."[49] In this case, it is clear that conquered people could become "Tatar" politically;[50] it is noteworthy however that at least for some time they kept their ethnic identity and could be recognized by Mamluk scholars as belonging to non-Mongol ethnic groups.

On the one hand, it is not clear if we can infer from all this that Mamluk scholars used the term *mughul* in a consistent manner. The term *mughul* appears quite often in Mamluk history books and it is reasonable that at least at times it was used quite loosely. This however is a matter for further research. On the other hand, it is clear that in Mamluk context during the period under discussion *tatar* is not simply a political term, but rather also an ethnic term. Had it been the case we would have expected that Qipchaqs subjugated to the Mongol rulers of the

46 See for example Mūsá ibn Muḥammad ibn Yaḥyá al-Yūsufī, *Nuzhat al-Nāẓir fī Sīrat al-Malik al-Nāṣir*, ed. Aḥmad Ḥuṭayṭ (Beirut: ʿĀlam al-Kutub, 1986), 212; Shams al-Dīn al-Shujāʿī, *Taʾrikh al-Malik al-Nāṣir Muḥammad b. Qalāwūn al-Ṣāliḥī wa-Awlādihi*, ed. Barbara Schäfer, published as *Die Chronik aš-Šujāʿīs* (Wiesbaden: Franz Steiner Verlag, 1977), 33; and see also Abū Bakr ibn Aḥmad Ibn Qāḍī Shuhba, *Taʾrīkh Ibn Qāḍī Shuhba*, ed. ʿAdnān Darwīsh (Damascus: Institut français de Damas, 1977–1997), 2: 264, 278. Later on it was also referred to as *Dasht Barka*, see for example Taqī al-Dīn Aḥmad ibn ʿAlī al-Maqrīzī, *Durar al-ʿUqūd al-Farīda fī Tarājim al-Aʿyān al-Mufīda*, ed. Maḥmūd al-Jalīlī (Beirut: Dār al-Gharb al-Islāmī, 2002), 1: 433–4.

47 Al-ʿUmarī, *Masālik al-Abṣār*, 3: 27; al-Yūsufī, *Nuzhat al-Nāẓir*, 213; al-Ṣafadī, *al-Wāfī bil-Wafayāt*, 10: 143; idem, *Aʿyān al-ʿAṣr*, 4: 138; Ibn Qāḍī Shuhba, *Taʾrīkh Ibn Qāḍī Shuhba*, 2: 158, 279.

48 Al-ʿUmarī, *Masālik al-Abṣār*, 3: 190; Later on it was more often referred to as *Dasht (al-) Qibjāq*, see for example al-Maqrīzī, *Durar al-ʿUqūd*, 1: 433–4; Ibn Taghrībirdī, *al-Manhal al-Ṣāfī*, 4: 113; al-Sakhāwī, *al-Ḍawʾ al-Lāmiʿ*, 5: 97; or simply as *Bilād al-Dasht*, see Ibn Taghrībirdī, *al-Manhal al-Ṣāfī*, 2: 141; al-Sakhāwī, *al-Ḍawʾ al-Lāmiʿ*, 2: 127.

49 Abū al-Fidāʾ, *al-Mukhtaṣar fī Akhbār al-Bashar*, 3: 202.

50 For another example of a person who "became Tatar" (*ṣāra tatariyyan*), see Shams al-Dīn Muḥammad ibn Aḥmad al-Dhahabī, *Siyar Aʿlām al-Nubalāʾ*, ed. Muḥammad Ayman (Cairo: Dār al-Ḥadīth, 2006), 16: 398.

Golden Horde will be referred to as "Tatars," but during the period under discussion this is not the case. As mentioned, during the period under discussion the Golden Horde is never referred to as the "Land of the Tatars."

We turn now to *mamlūks* designated as "Tatar" and "Mongol," an issue that is more relevant to the matter at hand.[51] Some of the *mamlūks* are referred to in Mamluk sources only as "Mongol" and not as "Tatar": Baydarā al-Manṣūrī (d. 1293),[52] Kurjī al-Ashrafī (d. 1299), Ṭughjī al-Ashrafī (d. 1299),[53] Kitbughā al-Manṣūrī (d. 1302),[54] and Qibjaq al-Manṣūrī (d. 1310).[55] It is noteworthy that Abū al-Fidāʾ implies that Qibjaq was a "pure Mongol" (*naqāwat al-mughul*),[56] and according to al-Ṣafadī, "He spoke and wrote excellent Mongolian,"[57] and that Kitbughā is known to have been an Oirat.[58] It suggests that perhaps these *mamlūks* were not designated "Mongol" by chance.

Other *mamlūks* are referred to both as "Mongol" and "Tatar." Jarmak al-Nāṣirī (d. 1292) is described as "a Tatar who was one of the senior Mongol amirs" (*ṭaṭarī al-jins min kibār al-mughūl*).[59] Salār al-Manṣūrī (d. 1310) is referred to as "Mongol," "Tatar" and "Oirat."[60] Ṭughluq al-Ashrafī (d. 1325) is referred to as "Mongol" (*min jins al-mughūl*)[61] and "Tatar" (*al-tatarī*).[62] Aytamush al-Ashrafī (d. 1336) is referred to as a "pure Mongol" (*min khāliṣ jins al-mughul*) of noble origin (*aṣīl*) who spoke and wrote Mongolian, and knew the customs of the Mongols, but also as a "Tatar" (*ṭaṭarī al-jins*).[63] The fact that Salār is described as an Oirat and Aytamush as noble and "pure Mongol" strongly suggests that also in this case the *mamlūks* were not designated as "Mongols" by mere chance. On the other hand, it confirms that "Tatar" was used mostly as an ethnic label. Indeed, Little who examined Aytamush al-Ashrafī's biography in a careful manner was under the impression that "the two terms *Mughul* and *Tatar* are

51 Only *mamlūks* who have biographical entries will be discussed.
52 Al-ʿAynī, *ʿIqd al-Jumān*, 3: 216.
53 Ibid., 3: 242.
54 Mazor, *The Manṣūriyya*, 38.
55 Al-ʿAynī, *ʿIqd al-Jumān*, 3: 242; Ibn Ḥajar al-ʿAsqalānī, *al-Durar*, 3: 145; Abū al-Fidāʾ, *al-Mukhtaṣar fī Akhbār al-Bashar*, 4: 9.
56 Ibid.
57 Amitai, "Mamluks of Mongol Origin," 124; Mazor, *The Manṣūriyya*, 38.
58 Ibid.
59 Al-Maqrīzī, *Kitāb al-Muqaffá*, 3: 23.
60 Al-Ṣafadī, *Aʿyān al-ʿAṣr*, 2: 489; 3: 491; Shams al-Dīn Muḥammad ibn Aḥmad al-Dhahabī, *al-ʿIbar fī Khabar man Ghabar*, ed. Abū Hājar Muḥammad al-Saʿīd ibn Basyūnī Zaghlūl (Beirut: Dār al-Kutub al-ʿIlmiyya, 1985), 4: 24; and see also Amitai, "Mamluks of Mongol Origin," 123; Mazor, *The Manṣūriyya*, 38.
61 Al-Yūsufī, *Nuzhat al-Nāẓir*, 277.
62 Ibn Taghrībirdī, *al-Nujūm*, 9: 109.
63 Little, "Notes on Aitamiš," 391; Amitai, "Mamluks of Mongol Origin," 124.

interchangeable."[64] According to al-Ṣafadī, Aytamush and his brother Ariqṭāy spoke Turkish and Qipchaqi fluently (*wa-humā fī lisān al-turk wal-qibjāqī faṣīḥān*), which seems to refer to the language of the Golden Horde.[65] This piece of information is important. Aytamush is the only *mamlūk* labeled "Tatar" (or "Mongol") during the period under discussion that seems to have originated from the Golden Horde. The others originated (or seem to have originated) from the Ilkhanate. If, as we tend to assume, during that period many Qipchaqs arrived from the Golden Horde,[66] and still the only *mamlūk* that originated from there who is labeled "Tatar" seems to have been a "pure Mongol," it gives extra credence to the opinion that in Mamluk context the term "Tatar" had an ethnic connotation. Without this piece of information, it could have been claimed that during that period "Tatar" *mamlūks* were only *mamlūks* that arrived from the Ilkhanate, and *mamlūks* arriving from the Golden Horde, whether Qipchaq or Mongol, were never labeled as "Tatar."

Other *mamlūks* are referred to only as "Tatar": Kuvendik al-Sāqī (d. 1281),[67] Sunqur al-Ashqar (d. 1291),[68] Karatāy (d. 1299),[69] Quṭlūbak al-Manṣūrī (d. 1310),[70] Balabān al-Manṣūrī (d. 1325),[71] Ṭaynāl al-Ashrafī (d. 1343),[72] Qumārī Amīr Shikār (d. 1343),[73] and Ṭuqṣubā al-Ẓāhirī (d. 1345–6).[74] While not referred to as "Mongols," most of them are connected to political activity based on ethnic solidarity,[75] to Mongol culture and Mongol circles,[76] and/or described negatively[77] or as having Mongol stereotypical attributes. All this strongly suggests that the description of these *mamlūks* as "Tatar" labels them as ethnic Mongols or at least as culturally Mongol. The label "Tatar" in *mamlūk* context during the period under discussion, is not much different than the label "Mongol," and aims at constructing the image of the labeled as the "other."

64 Little, "Notes on Aitamiš," 391.

65 Amitai, "Mamluks of Mongol Origin," 125. Only in Circassian-period sources Ariqṭāy is referred to as "*al-Qifjaqī*"; see Ibn Ḥajar al-ʿAsqalānī, *al-Durar*, 1: 206. In all likelihood, Ibn Ḥajar deduced this *nisba* from al-Ṣafadī's information.

66 See also al-ʿUmarī, *Masālik al-Abṣār*, 3: 179.

67 Ibn al-Dawādārī, *Kanz al-Durar*, 8: 227.

68 Shāfiʿ ibn ʿAlī, *al-Faḍl al-Maʾthūr min Sīrat al-Sulṭān al-Malik al-Manṣūr*, ed. ʿUmar ʿAbd al-Salām Tadmurī (Beirut: Al-Maktaba al-ʿAṣriyya, 1998), 41.

69 Al-ʿAynī, *ʿIqd al-Jumān*, 3: 486; al-Maqrīzī, *Kitāb al-Muqaffá*, 4: 31; idem, *al-Sulūk*, 2: 881.

70 Ibn al-Dawādārī, *Kanz al-Durar*, 9: 113; Mazor, *The Manṣūriyya*, 38.

71 Al-Ṣafadī, *Aʿyān al-ʿAṣr*, 2: 47.

72 Al-Shujāʿī, *Taʾrikh al-Malik al-Nāṣir Muḥammad*, 250.

73 Ibn Qāḍī Shuhba, *Taʾrīkh Ibn Qāḍī Shuhba*, 2: 341.

74 Al-Maqrīzī, *Kitāb al-Muqaffá*, 4: 30.

75 On Ṭuqṣubā al-Ẓāhirī and Karatāy see ibid., 4: 30–1; on Sunqur al-Ashqar and Kuvendik al-Sāqī see below in section 1.3.2.

76 Al-Ṣafadī, *Aʿyān al-ʿAṣr*, 4: 122, 124.

77 On the description of Qumārī Amīr Shikār as arrogant and stupid, see al-Shujāʿī, *Taʾrikh al-Malik al-Nāṣir Muḥammad*, 250.

1.3.2. Mongol *wāfidiyya* and Mongol War Captives as Treacherous, Disloyal and Untrustworthy Elements in Mamluk Society

Due to the fact that the Mongol *wāfidiyya* and some *mamlūks* who were war captives were not fully socialized in Mamluk society, and because the Sultanate was at war with their state of origin, they were seen in a negative light and were sometimes criticized for not being (true) Muslims. They were accused of being a treacherous, disloyal and untrustworthy element in Mamluk society, of conspiring against Qipchaq sultans, of collaborating with the Mongol Ilkhans, or of trying to escape to the Ilkhan's territories.[78] Contemporary sources mention quite a few instances of Mongol political action motivated by ethnic solidarity (*jinsiyya*).[79] For example, Ibn Shaddād writes that in the year 1273 al-Ẓāhir Baybars arrested a group of 13 "Tatars" who corresponded with the Ilkhans and promised them to collaborate with them against the Muslims if they will try to take over Syria.[80] They were most probably *wāfidiyya*, because Ibn Shaddād mentions them only by name and does not provide a master's *nisba*, because most of their names are not attested as names of *mamlūks* in that period, and because there is no evidence that in al-Ẓāhir Baybars' days Mongol *mamlūks* were bought in large numbers; most of the supporters of the amir Kuvendik al-Sāqī (d. 1281), who revolted against al-Manṣūr Qalāwūn in the year 1281 and tried to assassinate him, were Mongol *wāfidiyya*, and he seems to have been a Mongol himself.[81] After his failed attempt he joined the Mongol amir Sunqur al-Ashqar (d. 1291) who also revolted against al-Manṣūr Qalāwūn and corresponded with the Ilkhans suggesting that they take control of Syria and Egypt;[82] when al-ʿĀdil

78 See for example al-Ṣafadī, *al-Wāfī*, 25: 178–9; al-Maqrīzī, *al-Sulūk*, 2: 76, 87; and see also Yosef, "*Dawlat al-Atrāk* or *Dawlat al-Mamālīk?*," 396–7; idem, "The Term *Mamlūk*," 13–14; and see Nasser O. Rabbat, "The Changing Concept of *Mamlūk* in the Mamlūk Sultanate in Egypt and Syria," in *Slave Elites in the Middle East and Africa: A Comparative Study*, ed. Toru Miura and John Edward Philips (London and New York: Kegan Paul International, 2000), 92–3.

79 See for example al-ʿAynī, *ʿIqd al-Jumān*, 3: 242–3; Ibn Taghrībirdī, *al-Nujūm*, 8: 42; and see also Little, "Notes on Aitamiš," 398.

80 Ibn Shaddād, *Taʾrīkh al-Malik al-Ẓāhir*, 104–5; Ibn Kathīr, *al-Bidāya wal-Nihāya*, 13: 268.

81 Amitai, relying on al-Maqrīzī, suggests that the role of the Mongol *wāfidiyya* in this event was marginal; see Amitai, "Mamluks of Mongol Origin," 126–7; however, Turkish-period authors explicitly mention that most of Kuvendik al-Sāqī's supporters were Mongol, see for example Shams al-Dīn Muḥammad ibn Aḥmad al-Dhahabī, *al-Mukhtār min Taʾrīkh Ibn al-Jazarī*, ed. Khuḍayr ʿAbbās Muḥammad Khalīfa al-Munshadāwī (Beirut: Dār al-Kitāb al-ʿArabī, 1988), 305 (*kāna ḥalafa li-Kuwindik naḥw 3000 min al-jaysh wa-akthar man ḥalafa tatar*); for Kuvendik al-Sāqī's ethnic origin, see Ibn al-Dawādārī, *Kanz al-Durar*, 8: 227 (*fa-rakiba Kuwindik fī jamāʿa min jinsihi al-tatār* – Kuvendik led to battle a group of his Mongol kinsmen). Amitai "felt" that Kuvendik al-Sāqī was a Mongol, but mentioned that although some scholars have attributed to him a Mongol origin he could not find a clear evidence for that, see Amitai, "Mamluks of Mongol Origin," 126–7. The above-mentioned reference from *Kanz al-Durar* suggests that in all likelihood he was indeed a Mongol.

82 Al-Maqrīzī, *al-Sulūk*, 1: 686; (pseudo-) Ibn al-Fuwaṭī, *Kitāb al-Ḥawādith li-Muʾallif min al-*

Kitbughā (d. 1302, r. 1294–1296), the Oirat war captive, became sultan, he was accused of promoting the Oirat *wāfidiyya*,[83] who were accused on their part of not being Muslims.[84] His period of rule was deemed by contemporaries as a "Mongol State" (*Dawlat al-Mughul*), and a link was explicitly made between his Mongol origin and disasters that happened during his reign;[85] when al-Nāṣir Muḥammad ibn Qalāwūn returned to power in the year 1310 he wanted to promote Oirat immigrants, who had served the amirs before abandoning them and becoming his servants. However, his royal mamluks (*mamālīk al-sultān*) protested and made him change his mind: "They harshly criticized and condoned them for betraying their masters, and said that they are no good" (*aktharū min dhammihim wal-ʿayb ʿalayhim bi-kawnihim khāmarū ʿalá ustādhīhim* [!] *wa-annahum lā khayr fī-him*);[86] shortly afterwards al-Nāṣir Muḥammad arrested a large number of Mongols, many of them *wāfidiyya*, because "he was afraid of their evil deeds and their tendency to cause trouble" (*khawfan min sharrihim wa-iqāmatihim al-fitan*).[87]

As for war captives, al-Ḥājj Bahādur al-Manṣūrī (d. 1310), for example, was said to have been an evil and cruel man (*la yaḥẓá bil-surūr illā idhā ajrá qanāt al-shurūr*) who liked to instigate conflict (*muḥibb lil-fitan*), and was also accused of

Qarn al-Thāmin al-Hijrī wa-Huwa al-Kitāb al-Musammá Wahman bil-Ḥawādith al-Jāmiʿa wal-Tajārib al-Nāfiʿa wal-Mansūb li-Ibn al-Fuwaṭī, ed. Mahdī al-Najm (Beirut: Dār al-Kutub al-ʿIlmiyya, 1997), 452; for Sunqur al-Ashqar's Mongol origin, so far gone unnoticed by Mamlukists, see Shāfiʿ ibn ʿAlī, *al-Faḍl al-Maʾthūr*, 41.

83 On the Oirats, see Agnes Birtalan, "An Oirat Ethnogenetic Myth in Written and Oral Traditions," *Acta Orientalia Academiae Scientiarum Hung.* 55/1–3 (2002): 70; Patrick Wing, "The Decline of the Ilkhanate and the Mamluk Sultanate's Eastern Frontier," *Mamlūk Studies Review* 11/2 (2007): 78–9; and see now also Ishayahu Landa, "Oirats in the Ilkhanate and the Mamluk Sultanate in the Thirteenth to the Early Fifteenth Centuries: Two Cases of Assimilation into the Muslim Environment," *Mamlūk Studies Review* 19 (2016): 149–191.

84 Ibn Ḥajar al-ʿAsqalānī, *al-Durar*, 4: 159; al-ʿAynī, *ʿIqd al-Jumān*, 3: 463; and see also Landa, "Oirats," 161.

85 Yosef, "*Dawlat al-Atrāk* or *Dawlat al-Mamālīk?*," 395; Ibn Ḥajar al-ʿAsqalānī, *al-Durar*, 4: 159; and see also Holt, "Literary Offerings," 5–6. According to John Mandeville, the Qipchaqs (*Comanians*) deposed the Mongol (*Tartar*) usurper Kitbughā because they wanted a ruler of their own kind; see John Mandeville, "The Book of Sir John Maundeville. A.D. 1322–1356," in *Early Travels in Palestine, Comprising the Narratives of Arculf, Willibald, Bernard, Säwulf, Sigurd, Benjamin of Tudela, Sir John Maundeville, De la Brocquière, and Maundrell*, ed. Thomas Wright (London: Henry G. Bohn, 1848), 146.

86 Al-Maqrīzī, *al-Sulūk*, 2: 83. Interestingly, Mamluk refugees to the Ilkhanate were also perceived by Ilkhanid amirs as traitors that should not be trusted, see al-ʿAynī, *ʿIqd al-Jumān*, 5: 342.

87 Al-Maqrīzī, *al-Sulūk*, 2: 83. He arrested the four brothers of the Mongol war captive Salār al-Manṣūrī, the Mongol Binajār, the Mongol immigrant Ṣalaghāy and his sons Mūsá and Ghāzī (see al-Maqrīzī, *al-Sulūk*, 1: 501), the Mongol immigrants ʿAlī and Alāqūsh (see al-Maqrīzī, *al-Sulūk*, 1: 708–9), and the Mongol ʿAbd Allāh al-Silāḥdār (see al-ʿAynī, *ʿIqd al-Jumān*, 3: 242).

being in the un-Islamic habit of drinking wine, even in public;[88] in the biographical entry of the Mongol Qibjaq al-Manṣūrī (d. 1310), al-Ṣafadī mentions that although he was one of the senior *mamlūks* of his master the sultan al-Manṣūr Qalāwūn, the latter did not trust him (*wa-maʿa hādhā ustādhuhu lā yathiqu bi-hi wa-lā yaskunu ʿalayhi*) and did not want to take him to Syria because he was afraid that he would run away, join the Ilkhans, and cause trouble (*fitna*).[89] Indeed, in 1298 Qibjaq escaped to Ilkhanid territories where he was well received.[90] Some Mamluk historians accuse him of encouraging the Ilkhans to launch a campaign into Syria,[91] and of being a false Muslim and a hypocrite (*munāfiq*), and traitor to the Muslims who has surrendered Damascus to the Mongol enemy.[92] What is most important for the matter at hand is that al-Ṣafadī mentions right in the beginning of the biographical entry that Qibjaq al-Manṣūrī was captured in war and was not bought from a slave dealer (*aṣluhu muktasab lā bil-shirāʾ*).[93] Moreover, he makes it clear that al-Manṣūr Qalāwūn's reservations regarding Qibjaq al-Manṣūrī were related to the fact that he was a war captive, when he mentions that al-Manṣūr Qalāwūn had the same reservations with respect to ʿAbd Allāh, another *mamlūk* of him who was also a war captive (*muktasab*).[94] Even if this story is apocryphal, as Amitai suggests, it represents attitudes towards Mongol war captives;[95] when Salār al-Manṣūrī (d. 1310), an Oirat war captive who was a slave of al-Manṣūr Qalāwūn (*iktasabahu… min al-tatar*),[96] went to the Battle of Shaqḥab with the Mongols in 1303, he is reported to have said that the people suspect him because "they think that I am affiliated with the Mongols, because I am one of their kind" (*nasabūnī ilá al-tatār li-kawnī min jinsihim*);[97] the historian Abū al-Fidāʾ mentions that a Mongol by the name of Mandū who used to harm the Muslims was captured in the year 1315 "and when he was captured he was given to the amir Qilī who gave him in his turn to one of his Mongol *mamlūks*. Mandu escaped together with this *mamlūk* who was in

88 Al-Ṣafadī, *Aʿyān al-ʿAṣr*, 2: 55.
89 Idem, *al-Wāfī*, 24: 178–9.
90 Amitai, "The Mongol Occupation of Damascus," 22–4.
91 Ibid., 24.
92 Ibid., 36.
93 Al-Ṣafadī, *al-Wāfī*, 24: 178.
94 Al-Ṣafadī writes that al-Manṣūr Qalāwūn was of the opinion that "this boy Qibjaq and this boy ʿAbd Allāh, another *mamlūk* of him who was also a war captive (*mamlūk ākhar kāna ʿindahu min al-muktasabīn ayḍan*), should not be taken to Syria, because when they will arrive in Syria they will run away and cause trouble," al-Ṣafadī, *al-Wāfī*, 24: 179.
95 Amitai, "Mamluks of Mongol Origin," 133. Amitai relies here on Ibn al-Furāt, a much later source, who is not emphasizing the fact that al-Manṣūr Qalāwūn's reservations were related to the fact that Qibjaq al-Manṣūrī was a war captive; and see also Amitai, "The Mongol Occupation of Damascus," 25.
96 Al-ʿAynī, *ʿIqd al-Jumān*, 5: 236.
97 Ibid., 4: 234.

charge of him" (*wa-lammā umsika sullima ilá al-amīr Qilī wa-sallamahu al-madhkūr ilá baʿḍ mamālīkihi al-tatar fa-haraba Mandū al-madhkūr wa-haraba maʿahu al-mamlūk alladhī kāna murassam ʿalayhi*).[98] The message of this anecdote is clear. One should not leave two Mongols alone together, especially if they are war captives, because they might conspire or run away.

At least two of the Mongol war captives hailed from respected families (Qibjaq al-Manṣūrī and Salār al-Manṣūrī),[99] and we may assume that this was also the case with other Mongol war captives who became amirs in the Mamluk Sultanate. Abū al-Fidāʾ mentions that in the Battle of Abulustayn in 1277, the Mamluks killed most of the senior Mongol amirs (*ghālib kubarāʾihim*) and captured others, some of whom became later on amirs in the Mamluk Sultanate, among them Qibjaq and Arsalān (this should be probably Salār).[100] It is reported that in 1303, Sultan al-Nāṣir Muḥammad picked from the Mongol prisoners a few amirs and all the rest were executed.[101] The fate of low-ranking Mongol war captives who were not executed is only rarely mentioned in Mamluk sources. Qaraṭāy al-ʿIzzī al-Khāzindārī, however, reports that before the Battle of Ḥimṣ in 1281 al-Manṣūr Qalāwūn made an oath before God that if the Muslims will win the battle against the accursed Mongols (*malāʿīn*) he will build a *madrasa* and a hospital.[102] According to Qaraṭāy, the Manṣūrī complex was indeed built "on the shoulders of the Mongols" (*ʿalá aktāf al-tatar*), and more specifically Mongol (*tatar*) war captives (*asrá*), in all likelihood from the Battle of Ḥimṣ.[103] Seeing the suffering of the Mongol workers and hearing their crying, Sanjar al-Shujāʿī (d. 1294) the amir in charge of the works promised them that after the works will be done he will manumit them and give them land allocations (*iqṭāʿāt*) in the *Ḥalqa* formation.[104] When the complex was ready in 1285, Sanjar al-Shujāʿī told al-Manṣūr Qalāwūn what he had promised the Mongols in his name. Al-Manṣūr Qalāwūn is reported to have said to Sanjar that he had made a mistake: "Don't you know that these Mongols are our enemies and have come to fight and kill us? They all have wives, property, occupation, and servants (*kataba*) back in the east (*al-sharq*). If we will

98 Abū al-Fidāʾ, *al-Mukhtaṣar*, 4: 75.

99 Koby Yosef, "Mamluks and Their Relatives in the Period of the Mamluk Sultanate (1250–1517)," *Mamlūk Studies Review* 16 (2012): 57; Amitai, "Mamluks of Mongol Origin," 123–4.

100 Abū al-Fidāʾ, *al-Mukhtaṣar*, 4: 9.

101 Quṭb al-Dīn Mūsá ibn Muḥammad ibn Aḥmad al-Yūnīnī, *Dhayl Mirʾāt al-Zamān: Taʾrīkh al-Sanawāt 697–711 H/1297–1312 M*, ed. Ḥamza Aḥmad ʿAbbās (Abū Ẓabī: Hayʾat Abū Ẓabī lil-Thaqāfa wal-Turāth, al-Majmaʿ al-Thaqāfī, 2007), 2: 705.

102 Qaraṭāy al-ʿIzzī al-Khāzindārī, *Taʾrīkh Majmūʿ al-Nawādir*, 293; and see Linda S. Northrup, *From Slave to Sultan: The Career of al-Manṣūr Qalāwūn and the Consolidation of Mamluk Rule in Egypt and Syria (678–689 A.H./1279–1290 A.D.)* (Stuttgart: Franz Steiner Verlag, 1998), 122.

103 Qaraṭāy al-ʿIzzī al-Khāzindārī, *Taʾrīkh Majmūʿ al-Nawādir*, 294; and see Julien Loiseau, "Frankish Captives in Mamlūk Cairo," *Al-Masāq* 23/1 (2011): 39.

104 Qaraṭāy al-ʿIzzī al-Khāzindārī, *Taʾrīkh Majmūʿ al-Nawādir*, 294–5.

put them in the *Ḥalqa* formation they will become our servants (*aṣḥāb*) but will still remain our enemies (*wa-hum aʿdāʾ*).... If they will know that we are planning to harm [the Mongols] they will tell them (*in raʾaw sharr naqalūhu*). If one of them will have an opportunity he will run away to his homeland (*bilādihi*)."[105] In order not to break Sanjar al-Shujāʿī's promise, the Mongol war captives were eventually manumitted and sent to Qūs to function as a barrier (*sadd*) between the Mamluk Sultanate (*al-muslimīn*) and Sudān.[106] Even if not historically accurate,[107] it reflects in a most vivid manner the perception of Mongol war captives as potential traitors that cannot be trusted who might escape or collaborate with the Sultanate's enemies.

1.3.3. Mongol Identity – Names and Career Paths

The fact that Mongols and Qipchaqs many times had different names, or were given different names by Qipchaq sultans, was used, or meant, to construct a distinct Turkish ethnic identity, separated from that of the Mongols, and most certainly contributed to broaden the rift between these two ethnic groups.[108] Some Mongols were members of the *Burjiyya* unit comprised mainly of non-Turks, and filled in court posts reserved mainly for members of this unit. Qipchaqs were never members of the *Burjiyya* and did not fill these posts at least until al-Nāṣir Muḥammad's third reign. The Qipchaqs had their own barracks in which they were trained to fill other posts. Qipchaqs and Mongols were thus at least partially separated in their trainings and career paths.[109]

1.3.4. Mongol Identity – Physical Appearance and Stereotypical Attributes

Mongols had a distinct physical appearance. It is said, for example, that Aytamush al-Ashrafī's features betrayed his Mongol origin (these features, however, are not specified).[110] This was another factor that was used in the con-

105 Ibid., 296.

106 Ibid.

107 Qaraṭāy is known to have reported anecdotes that no other historian reports, some were perhaps invented; see Robert Irwin, "Mamluk History and Historians," 164. The sending of Mongols to Qūs can be corroborated, but this is not the place to elaborate on it.

108 Yosef, "The Names of the *Mamlūks*"; idem, "Ethnic Groups," 1: 30–53.

109 Idem, "The Names of the *Mamlūks*"; idem, "Ethnic Groups," 1: 36–42.

110 Little, "Notes on Aitamiš," 391; according to European travelers, the Mongols had small (narrow) eyes, little (sparse) beards and a paucity of hair. They are normally also depicted as treacherous, see for example John Mandeville, "The Book of Sir John Maundeville," 254; and see also Angus Stewart, "If the Cap Fits: Going Mongol in Thirteenth Century Syria," *Journal of the Royal Asiatic Society* 26/1–2 (2016): 137–8. Some of the physical features attributed to Mongols are of course Central Asian in general and not specifically Mongol; see Hannah

struction of a separate Mongol ethnic identity perceived in a negative manner. According to medieval perceptions, each ethnic group had its own typical physical features. Mamluk historians often mention the physical attributes of a *mamlūk* right after his ethnic origin, or vice versa,[111] thus exemplifying how physical attributes were considered identity markers and were closely related to construction of perceptions regarding ethnic identity. Moreover, physical attributes were considered indicators of character.[112] In books of advice for those interested in buying slaves, one can find stereotypical physical descriptions of *mamlūks* of various ethnic origins alongside their stereotypical attributes.[113] Physically, a stereotypic Mongol in the Mamluk Sultanate[114] was perceived as

Barker, "Egyptian and Italian Merchants in the Black Sea Slave Trade, 1260–1500," PhD dissertation (Columbia University, 2014), 80; Doris Behrens-Abouseif, "The Baptistère de Saint Louis: A Reinterpretation," *Islamic Art* 3 (1988–1989): 8 (note 7); David Storm Rice, *Le Baptistère de Saint Louis: A Masterpiece of Islamic Metal Work* (Paris: Éditions du Chêne, 1951), 13. Notwithstanding this, as mentioned, Aytamush al-Ashrafī's features were considered specifically Mongol and not Central Asian in general. Moreover, some art historians believe that the Baptistère de Saint Louis should be dated to the days of al-Ẓāhir Baybars, and that it represents figures divided along ethnic lines into the Turks and the Mongols who formed the two dominant groups in al-Ẓāhir Baybars' court; see Behrens-Abouseif, "The Baptistère de Saint Louis," 7 (Abouseif dated the Baptistère to al-Ẓāhir Baybars' days, and argued that it represents two distinct ethnic groups one of whom is "Mongol-looking," but she did not explicitly identify the other group as Turks); Nasser Rabbat, "In Search of a Triumphant Image: The Experimental Quality of Early Mamluk Art," in *The Arts of the Mamluks in Egypt and Syria: Evolution and Impact*, ed. Doris Behrens-Abouseif (Bonn: Bonn University Press, 2012), 26 (Rabbat accepted Abouseif's dating and made a further logical step in identifying the two groups as Mongols and Turks, because these were the only dominant ethnic groups during the days of al-Ẓāhir Baybars); and see also David Storm Rice, "The Blazons of the 'Baptistere de Saint Louis'," *Bulletin of the School of Oriental and African Studies* 13/2 (1950): 369–70; idem, *Le Baptistère de Saint Louis*, 11–17. Even more importantly, in Mamluk sources some physical attributes that are shared by Central Asian people are attributed until al-Nāṣir Muḥammad's third reign mainly to Mongols in a stereotypic manner, and are presented many times alongside other characteristics attributed mainly to Mongols (see below). In Mamluk context they thus become markers of Mongol identity, and are used to construct the image of the Mongols as "others."

111 See for example al-Ṣafadī, *A'yān al-'Aṣr*, 2: 491; Shams al-Dīn Muḥammad ibn Aḥmad al-Dhahabī, *Kitāb Duwal al-Islām*, ed. Fahīm Muḥammad Shaltūt (Egypt: Al-Hay'a al-Miṣriyya al-'Āmma lil-Kitāb, 1974), 2: 197, 202.

112 Barker, "Egyptian and Italian Merchants," 63.

113 See for example Hans Müller, *Die Kunst des Sklavenkaufs nach arabischen, persischen and türkischen Ratgebern vom 10. bis zum 18. Jahrhundert* (Freiburg-im-Breisgau: Klaus Schwarz Verlag, 1980), 65–71; and see also Robert Irwin, "The Image of the Byzantine and the Frank in Arab Popular Literature of the Late Middle Ages," in *Latins and Greeks in the Eastern Mediterranean after 1204*, ed. Benjamin Arbel, Bernard Hamilton, and David Jacoby (London: Frank Cass and Company Limited, 1989), 228–9.

114 The full analysis regarding the stereotypical characteristics which is based on a large database cannot be given in the scope of this article. For the full data, see Yosef, "Ethnic Groups," 1: 146–70.

blackish (*asmar*),[115] with sparse beard (*khafif al-liḥya/liḥyatuhu fī ḥanakihi*).[116] Blackish color was sometimes linked to evilness.[117] Some Mongols became the awe-inspiring *ṣilāḥdāriyya* (arms-bearers) who surrounded the sultan during ceremonies.[118] This probably enhanced their image as cruel and fearsome.[119] Other stereotypical characteristics attributed to the Mongols in the Mamluk Sultanate were naivety (*salāmat bāṭin/sadhāja*),[120] or in other words, lack of sophistication, ignorance, and uncouthness, and a sexual affinity for young men (*mayl lil-aḥdāth*).[121] Accusations of sexual immorality are sometimes accompanied with accusations of wine drinking and treachery and all are meant to label the accused as an enemy and "barbarian," an "other" who is not a (true) Muslim.[122]

115 Thus, for example, al-ʿĀdil Kitbughā is said to have been "a blackish Mongol" (*wa-kāna asmar mughulī*), al-Dhahabī, *Duwal al-Islām*, 2: 197; and one of Salār al-Manṣūrī's physical traits attached to his ethnic origin was blackish skin, see al-Ṣafadī, *Aʿyān al-ʿAṣr*, 2: 491. At least with respect to persons related to the Mamluk military institution, until al-Nāṣir Muḥammad's third reign, this attribute was connected almost exclusively to Mongols, see Yosef, "Ethnic Groups," 1: 151–4.

116 According to Ibn Iyās, Salār al-Manṣūrī had a sparse beard because he was a Mongol (*fī ḥanakihi baʿḍ shaʿarāt li-annahu kāna min al-tatar*), Muḥammad ibn Aḥmad Ibn Iyās, *Badāʾiʿ al-Zuhūr fī Waqāʾiʿ al-Duhūr* (Cairo: Maṭābiʿ al-Shaʿb, 1960), 1: 127. On Salār al-Manṣūrī's physical features see also Rice, *Le Baptistère de Saint Louis*, 16–17. I would like to thank Professor Hana Taragan for this reference and for her help in all that has to do with the Baptistère. Salār al-Manṣūrī was mocked by the people of Cairo for being beardless and a link was made between his physical appearance (i.e. ethnic origin) and his incompetence as Vice-Sultan, see for example al-Maqrīzī, *Durar al-ʿUqūd*, 1: 103; and see Shoshan, *Popular Culture*, 53. Until al-Nāṣir Muḥammad's third reign, this physical feature was attributed almost exclusively to Mongols, see Yosef, "Ethnic Groups," 1: 146–50.

117 See for example Ibn Taghrībirdī, *al-Nujūm*, 7: 95.

118 We know that during the days of al-Manṣūr Qalāwūn (1279–1290) Mongols were given this post which was mainly reserved for members of the *Burjiyya* unit, see Yosef, "The Names of the *Mamlūks*"; idem, "Ethnic Groups," 1: 36–42. Al-Ẓāhir Baybars is said to have given this post to Mongol *wāfidiyya*, see Ibn Shaddād, *Taʾrīkh al-Malik al-Ẓāhir*, 337–8.

119 Al-Nāṣir Muḥammad appointed to these posts *mamlūks* who had a fearsome appearance (*akhadha jamāʿa min mamālīkihi ʿamilahum silāḥdāriyya li-ashkālihim al-hāʾila*): see al-Ṣafadī, *Aʿyān al-ʿAṣr*, 2: 56.

120 Until al-Nāṣir Muḥammad's third reign, this characteristic was attributed mainly to Mongols, see Yosef, "Ethnic Groups," 1: 150–1; and see note 167 below.

121 This habit was attributed to the Ilkhans, see for example al-Maqrīzī, *al-Sulūk*, 1: 775; the habit was said to have been connected to a Mongol immigrant, Ibn al-Dawādārī, *Kanz al-Durar*, 9: 74–5. Within the Mamluk Sultanate and until al-Nāṣir Muḥammad's third reign, this habit was attributed almost exclusively to Mongols, see Yosef, "Ethnic Groups," 1: 157.

122 The Mongols who occupied Damascus in 1300 are said to have taken the mosque as their residence, in which they preformed illicit sex with women and young men and drunk wine (*yaznūna wa-yalūṭūna wa-yashrabūna al-khamr*), see al-Maqrīzī, *al-Sulūk*, 1: 893; the Il-khanid ruler Öljeitü (d. 1316) is said to have been a Shīʿī who used to drink wine, ibid., 2: 159; the judge Taqī al-Dīn Ibn Bint al-Aʿazz (d. 1295) was accused of adultery, sodomy, wine drinking, cavorting with Christians, and even of being a crypto-Christian, see Nathan Hofer, "The Origins and Development of the Office of the 'Chief Sufi' in Egypt, 1173–1325," *Journal*

1.3.5. Mongol Identity – Lack of Knowledge of the Arabic Language

Another factor that most probably contributed to the negative attitudes towards Mongols in the Mamluk Sultanate was the fact that, in contrast to the Qipchaqs, they tended not to know Arabic, or at least refrained from speaking it. It is said that Bashtāk al-Nāṣirī (d. 1341), who was probably a Mongol,[123] knew Arabic but did not speak it (refrained from speaking it?).[124] Like him, Ulmās al-Ḥājib al-Nāṣirī (d. 1333), who most probably was also a Mongol,[125] did not know Arabic (or refrained from speaking it). According to the historian Ibn Taghrībirdī (d. 1470), Ulmās "did not understand Arabic, and he did that on purpose in order to maintain respect" (*lā yafhamu bil-ʿarabiyya yafʿalu dhālika ʿāmidan li-iqāmat al-ḥurma*).[126] According to al-Ṣafadī, the Ilkhanid ruler Ghāzān (d. 1304) "understood most of what was spoken in front of him in the Arabic language, however, he did not show that he understood it out of respect for the pure Yāsa of Genghis Khān" (*yafhamu akthar mā yuqālu quddāmahu bil-ʿarabī wa-la yuẓhiru annahu yafhamu taʿāẓuman li-ajli yāsā Jinkizkhān al-khāliṣa*).[127] It thus seems that some Mongol *mamlūks* did not want to learn Arabic, or at least refrained from speaking it, for cultural or even ideological reasons, that is, out of respect for Genghis Khān's ordinances.

---

of Sufi Studies 3/1 (2014): 28 (note 107); for a Christian clerk in the Circassian period accused of sodomy, wine drinking, and having sex with young Muslims, see ʿAbd al-Bāsiṭ ibn Khalīl ibn Shāhīn al-Ẓāhirī al-Malaṭī, *Nayl al-Amal fī Dhayl al-Duwal*, ed. ʿUmar ʿAbd al-Salām Tadmurī (Beirut and Ṣaydā: Al-Maktaba al-ʿAṣriyya, 2002), 4: 232; for perception of the Byzantines as sexually immoral and treacherous, see Nadia Maria El-Cheikh, "Byzantium through the Islamic Prism from the Twelfth to the Thirteenth Century," in *The Crusades from the Perspective of Byzantium and the Muslim World*, ed. Angeliki E. Laiou and Roy Parviz Mottahedeh (Washington: Dumbarton Oaks Research Library and Collection, 2001), 58; for perception of the Franks as treacherous and "barbarian" enemy lacking in sexual morality, and defined as a non-Muslim "other," see Carole Hillenbrand, *The Crusades: Islamic Perspectives* (New York: Routledge, 2000), 270, 273–4, 282, 303; on Franks and Byzantines see more in section 3.2 below.

123 Amitai, "Mamluks of Mongol Origin," 137.

124 Al-Ṣafadī, *Aʿyān al-ʿAṣr*, 1: 690 (*kāna yaʿrifu bil-ʿarabī wa-lā yatakallamu bi-hi*).

125 He is said to have had almost every stereotypical attribute of Mongols – he was blackish, naïve, with sexual affinity for young men, see al-Ṣafadī, *Aʿyān al-ʿAṣr*, 1: 618; idem, *al-Wāfī*, 9: 371; Ibn Taghrībirdī, *al-Manhal al-Ṣāfī*, 3: 91; al-Maqrīzī, *Kitāb al-Muqaffá*, 2: 293; idem, *al-Sulūk*, 2: 366; moreover, he associated with the Oirat *wāfidiyya*, and a Mongol immigrant knew him from the days before his arrival to the territories of the Sultanate, see Ibn Taghrībirdī, *al-Manhal al-Ṣāfī*, 4: 14; al-Maqrīzī, *al-Sulūk*, 2: 366; finally, he was a relative of Yalbughā al-Yaḥyāwī (d. 1347), whose father arrived in the Sultanate from "the Land of the Tatars" (*Bilād al-Tatar*), see al-Ṣafadī, *Aʿyān al-ʿAṣr*, 2: 520; Ibn Taghrībirdī, *al-Manhal al-Ṣāfī*, 6: 358.

126 Idem, *al-Nujūm*, 9: 108.

127 Al-Ṣafadī, *Aʿyān al-ʿAṣr*, 4: 9. For a discussion on this text, Ghāzān, and the Yāsa, see Reuven Amitai, "Ghazan, Islam and Mongol Tradition: A View from the Mamlūk Sultanate," *Bulletin of the School of Oriental and African Studies* 59/1 (1996): 3–4 (especially note 22).

Additional evidence that Mongols tended not to know Arabic comes from the following. We are informed that in the year 1279, during the reign of al-Saʿīd Muḥammad ibn al-Ẓāhir Baybars (d. 1279, r. 1277–1279), two factions formed – one consisting of Arabized (*mustaʿraba*)[128] people and the other of "Tatars."[129] The "Tatars" (among them *wāfidiyya*) wanted to dethrone the sultan al-Saʿīd Muḥammad, while the Arabized faction supported him. This is yet another example of Mongols (among them *wāfidiyya*) conspiring against Qipchaq sultans; however, importantly, it also teaches us that Mongols tended not to know Arabic. Moreover, the Arabized faction could have only been comprised of Qipchaqs, since at that time there existed no other significant ethnic group in the Sultanate.[130] Therefore, it seems that, in contrast to the commonly held view by modern scholars, the Qipchaqs did tend to know Arabic.[131] It should not be so surprising that Qipchaqs were more familiar with the Arabic language than were the Mongols (and non-Turks in general as we will see below in section 3.4.3),[132] because the Qipchaqs did not have to learn the Turkish *lingua franca* of the ruling elite and *mamlūks*, and, therefore could use their mental resources to learn Arabic. The fact that Qipchaqs tended to know Arabic must have enabled them to communicate with the local religious elite,[133] and this, in its turn, probably contributed to the fact that Mamluk history books show positive attitudes towards them, and reflect their (negative) perceptions of other ethnic groups. After

---

128 For the connection between the expression *mustaʿrab* and fluency in the Arabic language, see for example al-Malaṭī, *Nayl al-Amal*, 8: 68; Ulrich Haarmann, "Arabic in Speech, Turkish in Lineage: Mamluks and Their Sons in the Intellectual Life of Fourteenth-Century Egypt and Syria," *Journal of Semitic Studies* 33/1 (1988): 96.

129 Shāfiʿ ibn ʿAlī, *al-Faḍl al-Maʾthūr*, 41.

130 See note 110 above.

131 For the view that almost all *mamlūks* did not know Arabic (no matter what their ethnic origin was), see for example David Ayalon, "Mamlūk: Military Slavery in Egypt and Syria," in D. Ayalon, *Islam and the Abode of War* (Aldershot: Variorum, 1994), article II, 17; Mazor, *The Manṣūriyya*, 42–5; Nasser O. Rabbat, "Representing the Mamluks in Mamluk Historical Writing," in *The Historiography of Islamic Egypt (c. 950–1800)*, ed. Hugh Kennedy (Leiden: Brill, 2001), 70–1; On the other hand, according to Haarmann, most *mamlūks* must have been able to communicate in Arabic, Haarmann, "Arabic in Speech," 92–3; however, he does not differentiate between ethnic groups in this regard.

132 For the full analysis based on a large database, see Yosef, "Ethnic Groups," 1: 154–6. Until al-Nāṣir Muḥammad's third reign, lack of knowledge of the Arabic language seems to have been connected almost exclusively to Mongols and non-Turks. Al-Manṣūr Qalāwūn, possibly the only Qipchaq who is said to have barely spoken Arabic (see for example Rabbat, "Representing the Mamluks," 70), is also the only *mamlūk* that is being provided an "excuse" for that, namely, that he arrived to the Sultanate at a relatively late age, see for example Ibn Taghrībirdī, *al-Manhal al-Ṣāfī*, 9: 95. It implies that Qipchaqs normally tended to know Arabic.

133 Rabbat suggests that the "language barrier must have caused communication problems between the mamluks and the literati"; Rabbat, "Representing the Mamluks," 70. Again, a differentiation must be made in this respect between different ethnic groups.

all, most of the Mamluk-period history books that we have were written by Arab religious scholars/bureaucrats or Arabized sons of *mamlūks*.

As noted by Hannah Barker, "[l]anguage was strongly associated with religion and slavery in both Christian and Muslim cultures,"[134] and "Muslims might not be recognized if they could not communicate in Arabic, and under the wrong conditions this could lead to their enslavement."[135] Abū Ḥāmid al-Maqdisī (d. 1483) reports that al-Ashraf Barsbāy's (d. 1438) recently bought slaves (*julbān*) did not know Arabic (*ghutm*, *ʿujm*) and had no connection to Islam.[136] Accusations of insufficient knowledge of Arabic are accompanied at times with accusations of sexual immorality and un-Islamic behavior,[137] treachery and collaboration with the enemy.[138] In short, depicting a Mongol as not knowing Arabic was a main instrument in labeling him as an enemy and "barbarian," and an "other" who is not a (true) Muslim. For example, Ulmās al-Ḥājib al-Nāṣirī, who as mentioned was in all likelihood a Mongol who did not know Arabic, is portrayed as "disreputable and altogether despicable amir."[139] Ulmās and his brother are depicted as cruel and exploitative persons (*ẓulm*, *ʿasf*), and specifically his brother is said to have used to drink wine.[140] Ulmās is said to have had a sexual inclination towards young men. He even opened a secret door next to the wall indicating the direction of prayer (*qibla*) in a mosque in the vicinity of his residence through which he brought young men to his home and had sex with them. Sometimes before having sex he was using drugs.[141] He is also said to have had pigs in his stables and to have bred pigs in several villages of his landed

134 Barker, "Egyptian and Italian Merchants," 51.

135 Ibid., 52; for the link between language and religion see also Eliyahu Ashtor, *Toldot ha-Yehudim bi-Mitsrayim ve-Suriya taḥat Shilton ha-Mamlukim* [The History of the Jews in Egypt and Syria und the Rule of the Mamluks] (Jerusalem: Mosad ha-Rav Quq she-ʿal Yad ha-Mazraḥi ha-ʿOlami, 1944, 1951 and 1970), 1: 345–6; and see also Jonathan P. Berkey, "The Mamluks as Muslims: The Military Elite and the Construction of Islam in Medieval Egypt," in *The Mamluks in Egyptian Politics and Society*, ed. Thomas Philipp and Ulrich Haarmann (Cambridge: Cambridge University Press, 1998), 163, 166; idem, "Mamluks and the World of Higher Islamic Education in Medieval Cairo, 1250–1517," in *Modes de transmission de la culture religieuse en Islam*, ed. Hassan Elboudrari (Cairo: Institut français d'archéologie orientale, 1993), 94, 96.

136 Abū Ḥāmid Muḥibb al-Dīn Muḥammad ibn Khalīl al-Maqdisī, *Kitāb Duwal al-Islām al-Sharīfa al-Bahiyya wa-Dhikr mā Ẓahara lī min Ḥikam Allāh al-Khafiyya fī Jalb Ṭāʾifat al-Atrāk ilá al-Diyār al-Miṣriyya*, ed. Ṣubḥī Labīb and Ulrich Haarmann (Beirut: Orient-Institut der Deutschen Morgenländischen Gesellschaft, 1997), 125.

137 See for example ʿAbd al-Bāsiṭ ibn Khalīl ibn Shāhīn al-Ẓāhirī al-Malaṭī, *al-Majmaʿ al-Mufannan bil-Muʿjam al-Muʿanwan*, ed. ʿAbd Allāh Muḥammad al-Kundarī (Kuwait: Dār al-Nashr al-Islāmiyya, 2011), 631–2.

138 See for example Ashtor, *Toldot ha-Yehudim*, 1: 346; and see also al-Maqrīzī, *al-Sulūk*, 2: 495.

139 Rabbat, "Representing the Mamluks," 71.

140 Al-Yūsufī, *Nuzhat al-Nāẓir*, 169; Ibn al-Dawādārī, *Kanz al-Durar*, 9: 374.

141 Al-Yūsufī, *Nuzhat al-Nāẓir*, 168–9.

estates, which were sold to Frankish merchants.[142] Ibn al-Dawādārī concludes that he was not a true Muslim (*kāna ẓāhiruhu musliman wa-bāṭinuhu bi-khilāf dhālika*).[143]

1.4. The Construction of Turco-Mongol Identity during al-Nāṣir Muḥammad's Third Reign (1310–1341)

After al-Nāṣir Muḥammad took back the reins of power in the year 1310 we hear of extensive purges of Mongols.[144] However, during al-Nāṣir Muḥammad's third reign the Mongol Ilkhans converted to Sunnī Islam and the war with them came to an end in the year 1323.[145] Contemporary sources have al-Nāṣir Muḥammad say that because of that Mongols and Turks are now "one people" (*jins wāḥid*)[146] and the Ilkhans were no longer depicted in a negative manner. At the same time the Qalāwūnid dynasty consolidated its prestige,[147] and, as a result, al-Nāṣir Muḥammad no longer felt the need to attach himself to Mongol families. He divorced his Mongol wives and started creating marital ties with the families of his amirs.[148] During his third reign, al-Nāṣir Muḥammad bought large numbers of *mamlūks* from the Golden Horde (*Bilād al-Qifjaq*).[149] By the time of al-Nāṣir Muḥammad's third reign the Mongols had already intermingled with the Qipchaqs in *Bilād al-Qifjaq*, and the population of that area became a mixture of Qipchaqs and Mongols (Turco-Mongols) which is referred to as "one people" (*jins wāḥid*).[150] The ending of the war with the Ilkhans also put a stop to the influx of Mongol immigrants[151] and war captives[152] from the Ilkhanate into the Sulta-

142 Julien Loiseau, "Frankish Captives," 44; and see also al-Yūsufī, *Nuzhat al-Nāẓir*, 168.

143 Ibn al-Dawādārī, *Kanz al-Durar*, 9: 374.

144 See for example al-Maqrīzī, *al-Sulūk*, 2: 87; and see also Reuven Amitai, "The Remaking of the Military Elite of Mamlūk Egypt by al-Nāṣir Muḥammad b. Qalāwūn," *Studia Islamica* 72 (1990): 145–6.

145 See for example idem, "The Resolution of the Mongol-Mamluk War," 379–84.

146 Ayalon, "The Great Yāsa (C1)," 122.

147 Broadbridge, *Kingship and Ideology*, 99–167; and see also Jo Van Steenbergen, *Order out of Chaos. Patronage, Conflict and Mamluk Socio-Political Culture. 1341–1382* (Leiden: Brill, 2006), 22–6; idem, "Is Anyone my Guardian…? Mamlūk Under-age Rule and the Later Qalāwūnids," *Al-Masāq* 19/1 (2007): 61–2.

148 Holt, "An-Nāṣir Muḥammad b. Qalāwūn," 315–23 (especially 315–16); Yosef, "Ethnic Groups," 1: 289–304.

149 Al-Maqrīzī, *al-Sulūk*, 2: 524–5; and see also al-ʿUmarī, *Masālik al-Abṣār*, 3: 179 (during his days *mamlūks* from *Bilād al-Qifjaq* constituted the majority of the army).

150 Ayalon, "The Great Yāsa (C1)," 121, 127; and see also Halperin, "The Kipchak Connection," 238–9. By that time in the territories of the Sultanate the Mongol immigrants that had arrived to the Sultanate before al-Nāṣir Muḥammad's third reign have also intermingled with the Turks, see al-ʿAynī, *ʿIqd al-Jumān*, 3: 356; and see also Landa, "Oirats," 183–6, 191.

151 Ayalon, "The Wafidiya," 102. During the 1320s, shortly after the peace agreement, few

nate. The changes in the social and political circumstances in the surrounding states resulted in a change in perceptions of ethnic identities, the annulment of the differentiation between Turks and Mongols within the Sultanate, and in a construction of a new united Turco-Mongol ethnic identity.[153] *Mamlūks* who arrived in the Sultanate starting from the 1320s are no longer labeled "Mongol" or "Tatar" by Turkish-period Mamluk historians.[154] Even if some "pure" Mongols did enter the Sultanate they no longer came from a non-Muslim enemy state but rather from a friendly Muslim one alongside with Turks and Turco-Mongols all simply referred to now as "Turks" (*turk/atrāk*),[155] and they were no longer war captives but rather sold by their families.[156] With the disappearance of the labels "Mongol" and "Tatar," stereotypical characteristics of Mongols, such as blackish skin, sparse beard, naivety, sexual affinity for young men, and lack of knowledge of the Arabic language, also stop being used in connection with *mamlūks* until the late Turkish period or even the days of al-Ẓāhir Barqūq (1382–1399).[157] During al-Nāṣir Muḥammad's third reign, court chroniclers seem to celebrate the consolidation of a "Turkish State" by incorporating the expression *al-Dawla al-Turkiyya* in the title of treatises dedicated to al-Nāṣir Muḥammad.[158]

maternal relatives of al-Nāṣir Muḥammad immigrated to Cairo. In 1328, six hundred followers of Tamurtāsh ibn Jūbān (d. 1328) the governor of al-Rūm in Ilkhanid territory arrived at Egypt, Nakamachi, "The Rank and Status," 59–61, 80.

152 There is no evidence for Mongol war captives after the year 1316. Until that year, and during al-Nāṣir Muḥammad's third reign, the sources report on few Mongol war captives, see for example al-Maqrīzī, *al-Sulūk*, 2: 105–6, 148, 162.

153 See Yosef, "The Names of the *Mamlūks*"; idem, "Ethnic Groups," 1: 62–7, 75–6; and see also Ayalon, "The Great Yāsa (C1)," 127.

154 *Mamlūks* who arrived in the Sultanate starting from the 1320s are never labeled as "Mongol" (*mughul*) also by Circassian-period historians. Already Ayalon noted that "Mongol" *mamlūks* (*mughul*) are mentioned only in the Turkish period, see Ayalon, "Mamlūk: Military Slavery," 8. On *mamlūks* labeled by Circassian-period historians "Tatar" who arrived in the Sultanate starting from the late Turkish period, but especially starting from the days of al-Ẓāhir Barqūq (1382–1399), see section 1.5 below. The fact that the term *mughul* disappeared all-together but the term *tatar* continued to be in use is another indication that the term *mughul* was used in the early Turkish period mostly as an ethnic label.

155 See for example al-ʿUmarī, *Masālik al-Abṣār*, 3: 429 (the army of Egypt is comprised of Turks [*atrāk*], Circassians, Rūmīs, Kurds, and Turkmen); In *Ṣubḥ al-Aʿshá* completed in 1412, after referring to al-ʿUmarī's saying that the Turks (*turk*) of *Bilād al-Qibjaq* are the majority in the army, al-Qalqashandī (d. 1418) says that in his days the number of Turkish *mamlūks* (*al-mamālīk al-turk*) decreased significantly; see al-Qalqashandī, *Ṣubḥ al-Aʿshá*, 4: 458.

156 See for example al-ʿUmarī, *Masālik al-Abṣār*, 3: 179; al-Maqrīzī, *al-Sulūk*, 2: 525.

157 See Yosef, "Ethnic Groups," 1: 147, 151, 156–7; 2: 174–6.

158 Idem, "*Dawlat al-Atrāk* or *Dawlat al-Mamālīk?*," 395.

1.5. "Tatars" and "Turks" during the Late Turkish Period and the Circassian Period (1382–1517)

Circassian-period historians refer occasionally to *mamlūks* who arrived in the Sultanate during the late Turkish period as "Tatar" (*tatar*). They use this label much more commonly, however, with reference to *mamlūks* who arrived in the Sultanate starting from the days of al-Ẓāhir Barqūq (1382–1399). How should we understand this term? As will be argued below, a general and broad distinction should be made between *mamlūks* who arrived in the Sultanate during the Timurid westward expansion (roughly 1370–1400) and those who arrived circa 1400 and afterwards. The Timurid expansion seems to have made latent ethnic and political animosities resurface. After the 1320s only rarely do Mamluk historians refer to their eastern neighbors as "Tatars," and to their land as the "Land of the Tatars," and more generally they dedicate to them much less space in their writing. This however changes with the conquests of Tīmūr (d. 1405). For example, in *al-Nujūm al-Zāhira*, after Ibn Taghrībirdī refers to the land of the Sultanate's eastern neighbors as "the Land of the Tatars" (*Bilād al-Tatar*) when he describes the escape of two Mamluk amirs to the Ilkhanate in 1312, he does not refer to it so until he describes the escape of a Turkish amir to Timurid territories when the Circassian al-Ẓāhir Barqūq ascended the throne in 1382.[159] In addition, after hardly referring to his eastern neighbors as "Tatars" from about the 1320s, during the Timurid conquest of Syria in 1400 such references abound. The "Tatars" are of course depicted in a very negative manner. Just for example, during the conquest of Aleppo the "Tatars" are said to have killed all the children and raped the women. Ibn Taghrībirdī says that the "Tatars" used to take women to the mosque and rape them in groups in front of their fathers and brothers.[160]

Table A below surveys *mamlūks* labeled "Tatar" who arrived in the Sultanate after the 1320s and have a biographical entry in Mamluk sources. Most of the information regarding "Tatars" appears in the history books of two historians, ʿAbd al-Bāsiṭ ibn Khalīl ibn Shāhīn al-Ẓāhirī al-Malaṭī (d. 1514) and Ibn Taghrībirdī (d. 1470), so it will be easier to focus on them. As can be seen from the Table, as we progress in time the term "Tatar" becomes more common. Moreover, Ibn Taghrībirdī almost never labels *mamlūks* as "Tatars" in their biographical entries where they are labeled "Turks," but rather in the historical narrative when referring to past events. According to their ages, years of death, and masters, the six *mamlūks* who are not labeled "Tatar" in their biographical entries (nos. 1, 3–7) seem to have arrived mainly during the early days of al-Ẓāhir Barqūq, and Qujqār al-Qardumī (no. 1) probably arrived a little bit earlier. Two out of the six are

159 Ibn Taghrībirdī, *al-Nujūm*, 9: 33, 276; 11: 229.
160 Ibid., 12: 223–4.

known to have originated from the east (nos. 6–7). Three out of the six are described in a negative manner (see the rubric "Bad" in Table A) and/or attributed characteristics that were attributed to Mongols until al-Nāṣir Muḥammad's third reign but disappeared from the sources for some decades: Qujqār al-Qardumī (no. 1) is said to have been ignorant and naïve who drunk wine excessively; Baybughā al-Muẓaffarī (no. 2) is said to have been a bad person who respected Ghengis Khān as a prophet; and Dawlāt Khujā al-Ẓāhirī (no. 6) who was captured from Tīmūr's army in 1393 is said to have been an evil doer, and a sinner who was not a true Muslim, whose death made the people very happy. These *mamlūks* are referred to as "Tatar" in the course of narratives that refer to events which took place in 1393, 1400, 1414, and 1421. In their biographical entries, however, Ibn Taghrībirdī refers to all as "Turks." All this suggests that we are dealing here with two layers of reference. One layer (the historical narrative) reflects older usages, and the other (biographical entries written in part retrospectively) reflects the usages of Ibn Taghrībirdī's days that became common after these *mamlūks* have died.

I will give two examples. Dawlāt Khujā al-Ẓāhirī (d. 1438) [no. 6] is referred to in the course of the historical narrative of the year 1393 as "a Tatar man" (*rajul tatarī*) who was a war captive. He was one of Tīmūr's commanders (*aṣḥāb*) brought in chains to Cairo. He was investigated by al-Ẓāhir Barqūq and revealed the presence of 7 "Persian" (*ʿajam*) spies in Cairo.[161] In his biographical entry, however, Ibn Taghrībirdī labels him "Turk" (*turkī al-jins*). In the biographical entry of Asanbāy al-Zardakāsh al-Ẓāhirī (d. 1448) [no. 7], Ibn Taghrībirdī mentions that he was bought by al-Ẓāhir Barqūq circa 1380 and captured by Tīmūr in Damascus in 1400. Then, he reports in first person what Asanbāy had told him in his own words (*ḥaddathanī Asanbāy… min lafẓihi… qāla*). Asanbāy related that when he was captured and brought to Tīmūr the latter asked him about his origin (*sa'alanī ʿan jinsī*) and Asanbāy replied to him that he was a "Tatar" (*fa-qultu la-hu tatarī*).[162] Then, Ibn Taghrībirdī returns to his account of Asanbāy's biography (*intahá kalām Asanbāy qultu…*), and says that in 1405 Asanbāy left the "Land of the Persians" (*kharaja min al-ʿAjam*) and returned to Egypt. In the end of the biographical entry, when Ibn Taghrībirdī himself relates to Asanbāy's origin he says that he was a "Turk" (*turkī al-jins*).[163] Then he adds that during the days of al-Ashraf Barsbāy (1422–1438) it was said that Asanbāy was one of the noble Turks of Baghdad (*min atrāk Baghdād al-ashrāf*).[164]

161 Al-Maqrīzī, *al-Sulūk*, 3: 802.
162 Ibn Taghrībirdī, *al-Manhal al-Ṣāfī*, 2: 433.
163 Ibid., 2: 434.
164 Ibid.

Table A: *Mamlūks* Labeled "Tatar" who Arrived in the Sultanate after the 1320s[165]

Name (Year of Death)	Master, Age	Bad	Origin	Reference
1. Qujqār al-Qardumī (d. 1421)	Qardum al-Ḥasanī (d. 1397)	+	Turk	Ibn Tagh./ biography[166]
			In a Tatar group	1421[167]
EXCEPTION	******************	****	************	***********
2. Shāhīn al-Ẓāhirī (d. 1430)	Shaykh al-Ṣafawī (d. 1398)— al-Ẓāhir Barqūq (d. 1399), 80~		<u>Tatar</u> **Muslim from Sarāy**	Malaṭī/ biography[168]
***********************	******************	****	************	***********
3. Tumāntamur al-Yūsufī al-Ẓāhirī (d. 1415)	al-Ẓāhir Barqūq		Turk	Ibn Tagh./ biography[169]
			In a Tatar group	1414[170]

165 Under the rubric "Bad" it is indicated if the *mamlūk* is negatively described. The table does not include *mamlūks* that do not have a biographical entry, but as far as I know, no *mamlūk* was labeled "Tatar" before the first *mamlūks* that appear in the Table. The Table does not include *mamlūks* who are not referred to as "Tatar" explicitly. According to al-Maqrīzī, Arghūn ibn Amīr Shāh (d. 1372) who grew up in al-Nāṣir Ḥasan's household, was known as Arghūn Tatar, see al-Maqrīzī, *Kitāb al-Muqaffá*, 2: 24. According to Īmān 'Umar Shukrī's reading of *Iqd al-Jumān*'s manuscript, Qarā Bulāṭ al-Aḥmadī al-Yalbughāwī (d. 1385), the *mamlūk* of Yalbughā al-'Umarī was a "Tatar man" (*rajul tatarī*) who commanded right and forbade wrong, see Badr al-Dīn Maḥmūd al-ʿAynī, *Al-Sulṭān Barqūq Muʾassis Dawlat al-Mamālīk al-Jarākisa 1382–1398 Mīlādī/784–801 Hijrī: min khilāl Makhṭūṭ 'Iqd al-Jumān fī Taʾrīkh Ahl al-Zamān li-Badr al-Dīn al-ʿAynī*, ed. Īmān ʿUmar Shukrī (Cairo: Maktabat Madbūlī, 2002), 180. More reasonably, however, he was described as a "good man" (*rajul jayyid*) who commanded right and forbade wrong, see Ibn Qāḍī Shuhba, *Taʾrīkh Ibn Qāḍī Shuhba*, 1: 175.

166 Ibn Taghrībirdī, *al-Manhal al-Ṣāfī*, 9: 33 (*turkī al-jins*, sparse beard [*fī ḥanakihi baʿḍ shaʿarāt*], drinking wine in an excessive manner); idem, *al-Nujūm*, 14: 240.

167 Ibid., 14: 108 (part of a group that is said to have been comprised of "Tatars" [*firqa… min jins al-tatar*], and also "naïve like Tatar people usually are" [*salāmat bāṭin ka-mā hiya 'ādat jins al-tatar*], ignorant [*jahl*]).

168 ʿAbd al-Bāsiṭ ibn Khalīl ibn Shāhīn al-Ẓāhirī al-Malaṭī, *al-Rawḍ al-Bāsim fī Ḥawādith al-ʿUmur wal-Tarājim*, ed. ʿUmar ʿAbd al-Salām Tadmurī (Beirut: Al-Maktaba al-ʿAṣriyya, 2014), 4: 120 (it was said that he was *tatarī al-aṣl muslim min Sarāy*); idem, *Nayl al-Amal*, 4: 296.

169 Ibn Taghrībirdī, *al-Nujūm*, 14: 136.

170 Ibid., 14: 23 (in 1414 he and two other *mamlūks* are said to have been Tatar [*jinsuhum tatar*]).

(Continued)

Name (Year of Death)	Master, Age	Bad	Origin	Reference
4. Qujuq al-Shaʿbānī al-Ẓāhirī (d. 1426)	al-Ẓāhir Barqūq		Turk	Ibn Tagh./ biography[171]
			In a Tatar group	1414[172]
5. Baybughā al-Muẓaffarī al-Ẓāhirī (d. 1430)	al-Ẓāhir Barqūq, 60~	+	Turk	Ibn Tagh./ biography[173]
			In a Tatar group	1414[174]
6. Dawlāt Khujā al-Ẓāhirī (d. 1438)	al-Ẓāhir Barqūq, almost 70	+	Turk[175]	Ibn Tagh./ biography
	war captive in 1393		Tatar[176]	1393 (Tīmūr)
7. Asanbāy al-Zardakāsh al-Ẓāhirī (d. 1448)	al-Ẓāhir Barqūq, 80+ or 90 (bought in 1380~)		Turk	Ibn Tagh./[177] biography
			Turks of Baghdād	1422–1438[178]
			Tatar	1400 (Tīmūr)[179]
**********************	******************	****	************	***********
**********************	******************	****	************	***********

171 Idem, *al-Manhal al-Ṣāfī*, 9: 35 (*turkī al-jins*).

172 Idem, *al-Nujūm*, 14: 23 (in 1414 he and two other *mamlūks* are said to have been Tatar [*jinsuhum tatar*]).

173 Idem, *al-Manhal al-Ṣāfī*, 3: 492 (*turkī al-jins*, respecting Ghengis Khān as a prophet, a bad person [*sayyiʾ al-akhlāq*]); and see al-Sakhāwī, *al-Ḍawʾ al-Lāmiʿ*, 3: 22 (*al-turkī*).

174 Ibn Taghrībirdī, *al-Nujūm*, 14: 23 (in 1414 he and two other *mamlūks* are said to have been Tatar [*jinsuhum tatar*]).

175 Ibid., 15: 218 (*turkī al-jins*, an evil doer and unreligious person [*ẓālim, fājir, fāsiq, ghashūm, jāhil, ḍāll, khabīth*]); idem, *al-Manhal al-Ṣāfī*, 5: 330–1 (*turkī*); and see also idem, *al-Nujūm*, 15: 104 (the people were happy when he died), 14: 360 (*turkī al-jins*, evil doer [*kathīr al-sharr*]); al-Maqrīzī, *al-Sulūk*, 4: 1061 (not a true Muslim [*laysa bi-muslim*]); al-Sakhāwī, *al-Ḍawʾ al-Lāmiʿ*, 3: 21; al-Malaṭī, *Nayl al-Amal*, 5: 34.

176 Al-Maqrīzī, *al-Sulūk*, 3: 802 (a Tatar man [*rajul tatarī*]) who was a war captive. One of Tīmūr's commanders [*aṣḥāb*]).

177 Ibn Taghrībirdī, *al-Manhal al-Ṣāfī*, 2: 434 (*turkī al-jins*).

178 Ibid. (*min atrāk Baghdād al-ashrāf*); and see also idem, *al-Nujūm*, 15: 527 (*sayyid sharīf min ashrāf Baghdād al-atrāk*); and see al-Malaṭī, *Nayl al-Amal*, 5: 249; idem, *al-Majmaʿ al-Mufannan*, 553–4 (captured in wars in Baghdād).

179 Ibn Taghrībirdī, *al-Manhal al-Ṣāfī*, 2: 433 (*tatarī*).

(Continued)

Name (Year of Death)	Master, Age	Bad	Origin	Reference
8. Kūkāy min Ḥamza al-Ẓāhirī (d. 1465)	al-Ẓāhir Barqūq, 70 or 70+		Tatar Turk	Malaṭī/ biography[180]
9. Aranbughā al-Yūnusī al-Nāṣirī (d. 1453)	al-Nāṣir Faraj (d. 1412), 70+		Tatar Turk	Malaṭī/ biography[181]
			Tatar/Turk	Ibn Tagh./ biography[182]
10. Tamurbāy min Ḥamza Ṭaṭar al-Nāṣirī (d. 1462)	al-Nāṣir Faraj, 80 or 80+		Tatar/Turk	Malaṭī/ biography[183]
11. Asanbughā al-Yashbakī al-Nāṣirī (d. 1471)	Yashbak al-Aʿraj—al-Nāṣir Faraj, 70+		Tatar Turk	Malaṭī/ biography[184]
12. Īnāl Bāy al-Nawrūzī (d. 1457)	Nawrūz al-Ḥāfiẓī (d. 1414)		Tatar	Malaṭī/ biography[185]
13. Asanbughā min Ṣafar Khujā (d. 1468)	al-Muʾayyad Shaykh (d. 1421), 80~	+	Tatar Turk/ Tatar	Malaṭī/ biography[186]
14. Baktamur al-Abūbakrī al-Ashrafī (d. 1465)	al-Ashraf Barsbāy (d. 1438)		Tatar Turk	Malaṭī/ biography[187]
15. Taghrībirdī al-Shamsī Ṭaṭar al-Ẓāhirī (d. 1489)	al-Ẓāhir Jaqmaq (d. 1453), almost 60		**Muslim** Turk/ Tatar	Malaṭī/ biography[188]
16. Aqbirdī Ṭaṭar al-Ẓāhirī (d. 1490)	al-Ẓāhir Jaqmaq		Tatar	Malaṭī/ biography[189]
17. Aqbirdī al-Ẓāhirī al-Khāṣṣakī (after 1485~)	al-Ẓāhir Jaqmaq		Tatar	Malaṭī/ biography[190]
18. Alṭun Khujā al-Ibrāhīmī al-Ẓāhirī (after 1485~)	al-Ẓāhir Jaqmaq, almost 70 in 1485~		Tatar	Malaṭī/ biography[191]

180 Al-Malaṭī, *al-Rawḍ al-Bāsim*, 3: 173 (*turkī tatarī al-jins*, naïve [*salīm al-bāṭin wal-fiṭra*]), idem, *Nayl al-Amal*, 6: 231 (*tatarī al-jins… salīm al-fiṭra*).

181 Idem, *al-Majmaʿ al-Mufannan*, 506–7 (*turkī al-jins tatarī*).

182 Ibn Taghrībirdī, *al-Nujūm*, 16: 163 (*tatarī al-jins*); idem, *Ḥawādith al-Duhūr fī Madá al-Ayyām wal-Shuhūr*, ed. Muḥammad Kamāl al-Dīn ʻIzz al-Dīn (Beirut: ʿĀlam al-Kutub, 1990), 2: 466 (*kānā aṣl Aranbughā hādhā turkī*).

183 Al-Malaṭī, *al-Rawḍ al-Bāsim*, 2: 179 (*kāna tatarī al-jins fa-li-hādhā qīla la-hu tatar*); idem, *al-Majmaʿ al-Mufannan*, 780 (*wa-kāna turkī al-jins sādhaj salīm al-fiṭra*).

184 Ibid., 558 (*turkī tatarī al-jins*).

185 Ibid., 617 (*kāna tatariyyan*).

186 Ibid., 555–6 (*tatarī al-jins*, "evil man" [*sharāsat akhlāq, ghayr maḥmūd al-sīra, jabbār, ʿanīd, shayṭān*]; idem, *al-Rawḍ al-Bāsim*, 3: 432 (*turkī tatarī al-jins*).

187 Ibid., 3: 69 (*turkī tatarī al-jins*).

188 Idem, *al-Majmaʿ al-Mufannan*, 740–1 (*turkī al-jins muslim al-aṣl*); idem *al-Rawḍ al-Bāsim*, 2: 235–6 (*al-maʿrūf bi-ṭaṭar li-kawnihi tatarī al-jins… wa-huwā turkī ka-mā qultu muslim al-aṣl*).

189 Idem, *al-Majmaʿ al-Mufannan*, 571 (*tatarī al-jins*); and see also idem, *Nayl al-Amal*, 8: 208.

190 Idem, *al-Majmaʿ al-Mufannan*, 571 (*tatarī al-jins*).

191 Ibid., 586 (*tatarī al-jins*).

To sum it up so far, the "Tatar" discussed above originated in all likelihood from territories under the control of Tīmūr and were labeled so because they were ethnically, or politically and culturally "Mongol." Mamluk sources report of few other *mamlūks* that are said to have originated from the east in that period but without labeling them as "Tatar" (see Table B below). At least two of them came from Timurid lands during the Timurid expansion. One was a Samarkandi (no. 2 in Table B) that was captured (by the Timurids?), and the other is explicitly said to have originated from Timurid territories (no. 3). Two are labeled as "Turks" and one is said to have been a Chagatai (no. 3). None is being characterized in a negative manner or attributed characteristics that are typical of Mongols. This possibly suggests that Mamluks historians could differentiate to a certain degree between the Timurids and their subjugated people. In any case, and more importantly, at some point the label "Tatar" in reference to *mamlūks* who originated from Timurid territories came out of use. Judging by references to "Tatar" *mamlūks* in the historical narrative by Ibn Taghrībirdī, it happened circa 1420. But why exactly did that happen?

Table B: *Mamlūks* Originating from the East after the 1320s[192]

Name (Year of Death)	Master, Age	Place	Origin
1. Jaraktamur al-Ashrafī (d. 1377)	al-Ashraf Shaʿbān (d. 1377), 20~	The East (*Bilād al-Sharq*)	*Al-Turkī*[193]
2. Yalbughā al-Sālimī al-Ẓāhirī (d. 1409)	al-Ẓāhir Barqūq, 30+	Samarkand	Turk (*min atrāk*)/[194] Muslim (*ḥūrr al-aṣl*)/ captured (*subiya, suriqa*)
3. Qujqār al-Baktamurī (d. 1428)	Baktamur Jilliq (d. 1412), 60–70~	Bilād Tīmūr Lank	Chagatai[195] (*Shaqaṭāy/Jaghaṭāy*)

The Timurid dynasty gradually continued to undergo a process of Persianization; after the death of Tīmūr and during the reign of his son Shāh Rūkh (1407–1447), they became known as the "kings of the Persians" (*mulūk al-ʿajam/aʿjām*), and not

192 Table B includes only *mamlūks* who have a biographical entry in Mamluk sources. It does not include *mamlūks* that came from the east and are labeled "Tatar" (on them, see nos. 6–7 in Table A above).

193 Ibn al-Furāt, *Taʾrīkh al-Duwal wal-Mulūk*, 9: 422; Ibn Qāḍī Shuhba, *Taʾrīkh Ibn Qāḍī Shuhba*, 3: 522.

194 Aḥmad ibn ʿAlī Ibn Ḥajar al-ʿAsqalānī, *Dhayl al-Durar al-Kāmina fī Aʿyān al-Miʾa al-Thāmina*, ed. Aḥmad Farīd al-Mazīdī (Beirut: Dār al-Kutub al-ʿIlmiyya, 1998), 139; Ibn Taghrībirdī, *al-Manhal al-Ṣāfī*, 12: 174; al-Sakhāwī, *al-Ḍawʾ al-Lāmiʿ*, 10: 289.

195 Ibn Taghrībirdī, *al-Manhal al-Ṣāfī*, 9: 34; Badr al-Dīn Maḥmūd al-ʿAynī, *ʿIqd al-Jumān fī Taʾrīkh Ahl al-Zamān*, ed. ʿAbd al-Razzāq al-Ṭanṭāwī al-Qarmūṭ (Cairo: Al-Zahrāʾ lil-Iʿlām al-ʿArabī, 1989), 348.

as "Tatars."[196] It is not rare to find *mamlūks* that have arrived in Egypt during the days of al-Ẓāhir Barqūq said to have known Persian, or to have been known as "Persians," some of them functioned as envoys to the Timurids (see Table C below). Some of them are labeled as "Turks" in their biographical entries and none is labeled as "Tatar." Still, almost all are described in a negative manner (see the rubric "Bad" in the Table). Three of them are characterized as having sparse beards, a typical attribute of Mongols (nos. 3–5 in Table C). One is said to have known the Mongol language (no. 1 in Table C). Asanbughā al-Dawādār (d. 1400) [no. 2 in Table C] was accused of cooperating with the "Tatars" during the conquest of Damscus in 1400 because he was "Persian/Persianized" (*aʿjamī*).[197] It is quite clear that these *mamlūks* originated from the east. Ethnically speaking, some of them were as "Tatar" as the afore-mentioned *mamlūks* labeled as "Tatar" (especially the ones with the sparse beards and the one who knew the Mongol language). The label "Persian" was used to characterize *mamlūks* originating from Timurid territories as an "other" instead of the label "Tatar."

Table C: "Persian" (*ʿAjam*) *Mamlūks* and Envoys to the Timurids[198]

Name (Year of Death)	Master, Age	Connection to Persian and/or the Timurids	Bad	Description
1. Manklībughā al-Ṣalāḥī (d. 1432)	al-Ẓāhir Barqūq, old	known as *al-ʿAjamī*/ spoke Persian/ knew the Mongol language (*al-mughulī*)/ an envoy to Tīmūr	+[199]	
2. Asanbughā al-Dawādār (d. 1400)	al-Ẓāhir Barqūq	Persian (*Aʿjamī*)	+[200]	Sparse beard

196 For the representation of the Ilkhans in the popular *Sirat Baybars*, not as "Tatars," but as Persian Zoroastrian Shīʿīs, which reflects later realities, see Thomas Herzog, "La mémoire des invasions mongoles dans la Sīrat Baybars. Persistances et transformations dans l'imaginaire populaire arabe," in *Le Bilād al-Šām face aux Mondes Extérieurs: La perception de l'Autre et la représentation du Souverain*, ed. Denise Aigle (Damascus-Beirut: Presses de l'ifpo, 2012), 346–50. For representation of Tīmūr's supporters as "Tatars" and Zoroastrians (*majūs*) in the conventional history books, see Ibn al-Furāt, *Taʾrīkh al-Duwal wal-Mulūk*, 9: 10. Note that in the above-mentioned biography of Asanbāy al-Zardakāsh al-Ẓāhirī that was captured and brought to Tīmūr, when Ibn Taghrībirdī returns to his own account he says that Asanbāy left the "Land of the Persians" (*kharaja min al-ʿAjam*), see above at note 163.

197 Ibn Qāḍī Shuhba, *Taʾrīkh Ibn Qāḍī Shuhba*, 4: 210. As mentioned, Dawlāt Khujā the "Tatar" commander of Tīmūr who was captured, revealed the presence of "Persian" (*ʿajam*) spies in Cairo, see above at note 161.

198 Table C includes only *mamlūks* who have a biographical entry in Mamluk sources.

199 Al-ʿAynī, *ʿIqd al-Jumān* (ed. al-Qarmūṭ), 438 (*ghayr mashkūr*); Ibn Taghrībirdī, *al-Manhal al-Ṣāfī*, 11: 286; al-Sakhāwī, *al-Ḍawʾ al-Lāmiʿ*, 10: 173; Ibn al-Furāt, *Taʾrīkh al-Duwal wal-Mulūk*, 9: 453 (he knew the Mongol language [*al-mughulī*]).

200 Ibn Qāḍī Shuhba, *Taʾrīkh Ibn Qāḍī Shuhba*, 4: 210.

(*Continued*)

Name (Year of Death)	Master, Age	Connection to Persian and/or the Timurids	Bad	Description
3. Arghūn Shāh al-Baydamurī al-Ẓāhirī (d. 1400)	al-Ẓāhir Barqūq, 30+	knew Persian/ Turk (*Turkī al-jins*)	[201]	Sparse beard
4. Kuzul al-Muḥammadī al-Ẓāhirī (d. 1445)	al-Ẓāhir Barqūq, 80+	*Al-ʿAjamī*/ Turk (*Turkī al-jins*)	+[202]	Sparse beard
5. Aqṭuwah al-Mūsāwī al-Ẓāhirī (d. 1448)	al-Ẓāhir Barqūq, 70+	envoy to Timurids/ Turk (*Turkī al-jins*)/ *Muslim al-Aṣl*	+[203]	Sparse beard

More importantly, at about the same time the label "Tatar" acquired a different meaning. Let us return now to Table A. As mentioned, Ibn Taghrībirdī almost never labels *mamlūks* as "Tatar" in their biographical entries where they are labeled "Turks," but rather in the historical narrative when referring to past events. The only exception is Aranbughā al-Yūnusī al-Nāṣirī (d. 1453) [no. 9 in Table A], which was a *mamlūk* of al-Nāṣir Faraj who probably arrived in Egypt circa 1400, later than the other *mamlūks* labeled "Tatar" by Ibn Taghrībirdī in the historical narrative. It is significant that he is not characterized in a negative manner or attributed characteristics typical of Mongols. It is also the point where the labeling of Ibn Taghrībirdī converges with that of al-Malaṭī. Putting aside Shāhīn al-Ẓāhirī (d. 1430) [no. 2 in Table A] who probably arrived in Egypt in the 1360s or 1370s and is receiving "a special treatment" from al-Malaṭī only because he was his grandfather, all the other *mamlūks* labeled as "Tatar" by al-Malaṭī arrived in Egypt circa 1400 or later (nos. 8–18 in Table A). Usually al-Malaṭī refers to these *mamlūks* as "Tatar Turks" (nos. 8–9, 11, 13–14).[204] To whom is he referring?

Shāhīn al-Ẓāhirī (no. 2 in Table A) is said to have originated from Sarāy in the Golden Horde. Asandamur al-Sharābī (d. 1469) that is labeled by al-Malaṭī "Tatar" (*al-tatarī*) is said to have been taken captive in the Crimea and to have seen most of the *Dasht*.[205] Al-Malaṭī refers to the ruler of the Golden Horde as "the king of the Tatars in the Land of the Qipchaqs" (*malik al-tatār bi-Dasht Qibjaq*).[206] Most significantly, he reports on a prisoner of the Franks sold to

201 Al-Sakhāwī, *al-Ḍawʾ al-Lāmiʿ*, 2: 267 (he was somewhat frivoulous [*nawʿ khiffa*]); Ibn Taghrībirdī, *al-Manhal al-Ṣāfī*, 2: 304.
202 Ibid., 9: 130–1 (*ghayr mashkūr*).
203 Al-Sakhāwī, *al-Ḍawʾ al-Lāmiʿ*, 2: 318–19 (*lam yakun mashkūr al-sīra*); Ibn Taghrībirdī, *al-Manhal al-Ṣāfī*, 3: 9; al-Malaṭī, *Nayl al-Amal*, 5: 249–50.
204 And see idem, *al-Majmaʿ al-Mufannan*, 112 (*baʿḍ aṣḥābī min al-turk al-tatār*).
205 Ibid., 559.
206 Idem, *Nayl al-Amal*, 2: 332.

slavery who was a "Turk" (*turkī al-jins*) from the "Land of the Tatar Qipchaqs" (*Dast Qibjāq al-Tatar*). Then he relates that after this person told him that he was one of the Muslim prisoners, he told the slave dealer that he was "a Turk, and a good Muslim" (*turkī al-jins min khiyar al-muslimīn*). This person used to tell al-Malaṭī all sorts of stories on "the Land of the Tatars" (*Bilād al-Tatar*). Al-Malaṭī concludes by saying that he was a good and religious man who was pure at heart (*salīm al-bāṭin wal-fiṭra*).[207] It is clear that for him the "Tatar Turks" are the inhabitants of the Golden Horde, referred to in earlier period as Turks or Qipchaqs. It is noteworthy that among the 12 *mamlūks* labled "Tatar" by al-Malaṭī only one is described in a negative manner (no. 13 in Table A), and none is attributed physical features that in earlier periods were connected to Mongols (blackish skin and sparse beard). While two of the "Tatars" are said to have been *salīm al-bāṭin/al-fiṭra* (nos. 8, 10) it is clearly not meant anymore to depict them as unsophisticated, ignorant, and uncouth, but rather as pure at heart. In general, there is almost nothing negative about the "Tatars" anymore, simply because they are the heirs of the Qipchaq Turks of the Turkish period.

The "Tatar Turks" of the Golden Horde are reffered to as "Turks" because they were culturally Turks and spoke a Turkish language. But why were they reffered to suddenly as "Tatars"? It has been noted by turkologists that Qipchaq-speaking groups laid the foundations for the Khanate of the "Crimean Tatars" who were an amalgam of Turkicized Mongols, Qipchaqs, and the Turkicized population of the Crimea.[208] Following the conversion of Uzbek (1312–1341), Islam provided a source of identity for the inhabitants of the Golden Horde,[209] and the Mongols have gradually transformed during the fourteenth century into "Turkic-speaking Muslim Tatars."[210] The Turkish peoples today called Tatar "framed their Islamization… as a key to their communal formation."[211] It has also been suggested that the fact that Rus' sources refer to the successor states of the Golden Horde in the fifteenth century as "Tatar" reflects the new identity of these states which became Muslim and Turkicized.[212] It seems that in Mamluk sources (and later

207 Idem, *al-Rawḍ al-Bāsim*, 2: 174–5.

208 Peter B. Golden, "Migration, Ethnogenesis," in *The Cambridge History of Inner Asia. The Chinggisid Age*, ed. Nicola Di Cosmo, Allen J. Frank, and Peter B. Golden (Cambridge: Cambridge University Press, 2009), 115.

209 Ibid.

210 Arsenio Peter Martinez, "Institutional Development, Revenues and Trade," in *The Cambridge History of Inner Asia. The Chinggisid Age*, ed. Nicola Di Cosmo, Allen J. Frank, and Peter B. Golden (Cambridge: Cambridge University Press, 2009), 92.

211 Devin DeWeese, "Islamization in the Mongol Empire," in *The Cambridge History of Inner Asia. The Chinggisid Age*, ed. Nicola Di Cosmo, Allen J. Frank, and Peter B. Golden (Cambridge: Cambridge University Press, 2009), 125.

212 Timothy May, "Tatars," in *The Mongol Empire: A Historical Encyclopedia*, ed. Timothy May (Santa Barabara, California: ABC-CLIO, 2017), 1: 250.

Arabic sources) the label "Tatar" is more related to Islam than to Turkification.[213] According to al-Malaṭī, Shāhīn al-Ẓāhirī (no. 2 in Table A) was said to have been "a Tatar Muslim from Sarāy" (*tatarī al-aṣl muslim min Sarāy*).[214] As mentioned, al-Malaṭī also reports on a prisoner of the Franks who was a "Turk" (*turkī al-jins*) from the "Land of the Tatar Qipchaqs" (*Dast Qibjāq al-Tatar*), and then labels him as "a Turk, and a good Muslim" (*turkī al-jins min khiyar al-muslimīn*).[215] In this case, it seems that a "Muslim Turk" is synonymous with "Tatar Turk." It becomes even clearer from al-Malaṭī's description of Taghrībirdī al-Shamsī Ṭaṭar al-Ẓāhirī (d. 1489) [no. 15 in Table A]. In *al-Majmaʿ al-Mufannan*, al-Malaṭī says that he was a "Muslim Turk" (*turkī al-jins muslim al-aṣl*).[216] In *al-Rawḍ al-Bāsim*, al-Malaṭī says that he was known as Taghrībirdī Ṭaṭar because he was a Tatar (*maʿrūf bi-ṭaṭar li-kawnihi tatarī al-jins*),[217] but shortly afterwards says that "he was a Turk, as I mentioned, and a Muslim" (*wa-huwā turkī ka-mā qultu muslim al-aṣl*).[218] This case suggests that for al-Malaṭī describing a person as "Tatar" is equivalent to describing him as a "Muslim Turk." Later Arabic sources quoting Raḍī al-Dīn Ibn al-Ḥanbalī (d. 1563) report on a person named Qujā who was a treasurer (*khāzindār*) in the household of Yashbak al-Yūsufī al-Jarkasī (d. 1421) who was one of the "free Muslim Tatars" (*min muslimī al-tatār al-aḥrār*).[219]

As mentioned, except for Shāhīn al-Ẓāhirī (no. 2 in Table A) all the other *mamlūks* labeled as "Tatar" in their biographical entries arrived in Egypt circa 1400 or later (nos. 8–18 in Table A). Kūkāy min Ḥamza al-Ẓāhirī (d. 1465) [no. 8] is the only one of them who was a slave of al-Ẓāhir Barqūq. He was 70 years old or more when he died in 1465, so it is quite clear that he arrived in Egypt towards the

213 According to Ayalon, "[t]he *Tatar*... especially under the Circassians, were very often synonymous with *Turk*. The reason for this alternation is obvious. The more the Tatars advanced in the steppe, the greater was the Turkish element which they subjugated, included in their armies and mingled with. Since the Turks were much more numerous, it was they who absorbed their conquerors. Already Ibn Faḍl Allāh al-'Umarī says that the Tatars were completely assimilated by the Ḳipchāḳīs and had lost their own identity": Ayalon, "Mamlūk: Military Slavery," 8–9. This explanation does not make much sense. Had it been the case we would have expected that the Tatar conquerors will gradually be labeled "Turks" and not the other way around. The fact that the label "Tatar" became associated with Islam, strongly suggests that Islamization begun with the Mongol (Tatar) ruling elite of the Golden Horde and not the Qipchaqi inhabitants, and see below at note 223.

214 Al-Malaṭī, *al-Rawḍ al-Bāsim*, 4: 120.

215 Ibid., 2: 174–5.

216 Idem, *al-Majmaʿ al-Mufannan*, 741.

217 Idem *al-Rawḍ al-Bāsim*, 2: 235.

218 Ibid., 2: 236.

219 ʿAbd al-Ḥayy ibn Aḥmad ibn Muḥammad Ibn al-ʿImād, *Shadharāt al-Dhahab fī Akhbār Man Dhahab*, ed. Maḥmūd al-Arnāʾūṭ (Beirut, Damascus: Dār Ibn Kathīr, 1986), 10: 318; Najm al-Dīn Muḥammad ibn Muḥammad al-Ghazzī, *al-Kawākib al-Sāʾira bi-Aʿyān al-Miʾa al-al-ʿĀshira*, ed. Khalīl Manṣūr (Beirut: Dār al-Kutub al-ʿIlmiyya, 1997), 2: 255. On Yashbak al-Yūsufī al-Jarkasī, see al-Sakhāwī, *al-Ḍawʾ al-Lāmiʿ*, 10: 279.

end of al-Ẓāhir Barqūq's reign in 1399. Four were *mamlūks* of al-Ẓāhir Barqūq's son al-Nāṣir Faraj or his amirs (nos. 9–12), and according to their ages at death they arrived in Egypt in all likelihood circa 1400. The others (nos. 13–18) clearly arrived in Egypt circa 1400 or later. It suggests that in the Mamluk Sultanate circa 1400 "Tatar" became a label for *mamlūks* originating from the Golden Horde. While the evidence we have on the usages of the label "Tatar" in reference to *mamlūks* from the Golden Horde comes only from late sources (al-Malaṭī and Ibn Taghrībirdī) there is evidence that they reflect earlier usages. The first time in the Circassian period that "Tatars" are enumerated as one of the major ethnic groups instead of "Turks" is related to the reign of al-Ẓāhir Barqūq (1382–1399). Ibn Taghrībirdī reports that after a revolt of a Circassian amir in 1398, the "Turkish" wife of al-Ẓāhir Barqūq recommended him to buy *mamlūks* from four origins: "Tatars," Circassians, Rūmīs, and Turkmen.[220] Although also this reference comes from the late Ibn Taghrībirdī, he is clearly quoting an earlier text or informant, and it remarkably fits the information we have regarding *mamlūks* labeled as "Tatars." Moreover, to the best of my knowledge, the first Mamluk historian who explicitly refers to the Golden Horde as "the land of the Tatars among the Turks (i. e. Tatar Turks)" (*arḍ al-tatariyya min al-turk*) is Ibn Khaldūn (d. 1406) who flourished during the reign of al-Ẓāhir Barqūq.[221] In addition, circa 1400 the Islamization of the Golden Horde seems to have reached a critical point.

While Islamization has started during the days of Uzbek (1312–1341),[222] his son Jānī Bek (1342–1357) is linked with even greater support for Islam than his father and is said to have ordered his "Tatar" commanders to wear Muslim garb and forbade the export of slaves from his country to Egypt in what seems to be an Islamizing measure.[223] Important figures in the history of the Golden Horde are

220 David Ayalon, "The Circassians in the Mamlūk Kingdom," *Journal of the American Oriental Society* 69 (1949): 141; Ibn Taghrībirdī, *al-Nujūm*, 12: 88.

221 ʿAbd al-Raḥmān ibn Muḥammad Ibn Khaldūn, *Muqaddimat Ibn Khaldūn wa-Huwa al-Juzʾ al-Awwal min Taʾrīkh Ibn Khaldūn al-Musammá Dīwān al-Mubtadaʾ wal-Khabar fī Taʾrīkh al-ʿArab wal-ʿAjam wal-Barbar wa-Man ʿĀṣarahum min Dhawī al-Shaʾn al-Akbar*, ed. Khalīl Shaḥḥāda (Beirut: Dār al-Fikr, 1988), 101. For al-Malaṭī's references to the Golden Horde as "the Land of the Tatars," see above at notes 206–7. Ibn Taghrībirdī refers to the ruler of the Golden Horde as the king of the "Tatars" (*ṣāḥib al-Dasht wal-tatar*), see Ibn Taghrībirdī, *al-Manhal al-Ṣāfī*, 4: 107.

222 Peter B. Golden, *An Introduction to the History of the Turkic Peoples. Ethnogenesis and State-Formation in Medieval and Early Modern Eurasia and the Middle East* (Wiesbaden: Otto Harrassowitz, 1992), 237–8.

223 Devin DeWeese, *Islamization and Native Religion in the Golden Horde: Baba Tükles and Conversion to Islam in Historical and Epic Tradition* (Pennsylvania: Penn State Press, 1994), 95; and see al-Shujāʿī, *Taʾrīkh al-Malik al-Nāṣir Muḥammad*, 214, 234; but see Amalia Levanoni, "*Awlad al-Nas* in the Mamluk Army during the Bahri Period," in *Mamlūks and Ottomans: Studies in Honour of Michael Winter*, ed. David Wasserstein and Ami Ayalon (London and New York: Routledge, 2006), 101.

said to have taken measures of Islamization until the days of Edigü (1397–1419),[224] who also forbade the selling of slaves to Egypt.[225] The descendants of Edigü legitimized their position by claiming descent from the early leaders of Islam.[226] It seems that while Islamization during the days of Uzbek was only partial in its extent and depth,[227] it gained momentum during the reign of Jānī Bek,[228] reaching a critical point during the days of Edigü.

As mentioned, according to their ages at death and masters, all the *mamlūks* labeled "Tatars" in the historical narrative, that seem to have originated from Timurid territories (nos. 1, 3–7 in Table A), seem to have arrived in Egypt in the early days of al-Ẓāhir Barqūq, and no later than 1393 (no. 6 in Table A).[229] It would seem thus, that circa 1400 after the wave of *mamlūks* that arrived to the Sultanate due to the Timurid expansion has ended, after the Persianization and de-Tatarization of the Timurids gained momentum, and after the Islamization of the inhabitants of the Golden Horde reached a critical point, it became common to label the latter as "Tatars" and to label *mamlūks* that originated from Timurid territories as "Turks" (and "Persians") and not as "Tatars." Notwithstanding this, it seems that roughly between 1400 and 1420 the label "Tatar" continued at times to be used in reference to *mamlūks* that originated from Timurid territories.

It should be mentioned that in Europe "Tatar" became a common label for slaves originating from the Golden Horde earlier than in the Mamluk Sultanate. Most of the information comes from Italian notarial records and documents. There is much information starting from the 1360s. Starting from the 1360s and

224 Devin DeWeese, *Islamization and Native Religion*, 95.

225 Halperin, "The Kipchak Connection," 237; Barker, "Egyptian and Italian Merchants," 183.

226 Golden, "Migration, Ethnogenesis," 115.

227 In *Taqwīm al-Buldān* written between 1316 and 1321, Abū al-Fidāʾ (d. 1331) reports that the inhabitants of the Golden Horde were still practicing their native religion; see Peter B. Golden, "The Shaping of the Cuman-Qïpčaqs and Their World," in *Studies on the Peoples and Cultures of the Eurasian Steppes*, ed. Peter B. Golden and Cătălin Hriban (Bucharest-Braila: Editura Academiei Române, 2011), 329; in *Masālik al-Abṣār* written in 1338, Ibn Faḍl Allāh al-ʿUmarī (d. 1349) says that the religion of Islam has started to spread in the Golden Horde and some of the Qipchaqs became Muslims but others were still not Muslims (*kuffār*); see al-ʿUmarī, *Masālik al-Abṣār*, 3: 182, 190; Ayalon, "Mamlūk: Military Slavery," 4.

228 Yossef Rapoport mentions that in a query sent to Taqī al-Dīn al-Subkī (d. 1355), an anonymous questioner said that "in our days, everyone, including the scholars and the virtuous, take slave-girls as concubines," but these men are committing a crime, for "they all know with certitude that these slave-girls must have been Muslims in their countries of origin"; see Yossef Rapoport, "Women and Gender in Mamluk Society: An Overview," *Mamlūk Studies Review* 11/2 (2007): 12. Most of the dated *fatwás* in al-Subkī's *Kitāb al-Fatāwá* are from circa 1350. The query seems to refer also to slave-girls and concubines of the Mamluk ruling elite, which originated at that period mostly from the Golden Horde. It implies that by 1350 many of them were Muslim.

229 This is also true for other *mamlūks* who seem to have originated from Timurid territories but not labeled "Tatar" (see Tables B and C).

until the 1400s most of the slaves sold in Italy (in Florence, Venice, and Genoa), were labeled "Tatar" and no "Cumans" (i. e. Qipchaqs) are mentioned. On rare occasions "Turks" are mentioned, but these may well be Anatolian (Ottoman) slaves.[230] In that period in Venice for example 410 Tatars are mentioned but no Cumans or Turks. In the 1360s alone 95 Tatars are mentioned.[231] In documents produced by Venetian notaries in Tana in the Black Sea region between 1359 and 1363, 251 slaves are mentioned. Among these slaves 169 "Tatars" and 21 "Mongols" are mentioned (82 percent of the slaves) but no "Turks" or "Cumans."[232] In 47 slave-related documents produced in Famagusta between 1360 and 1362 by the Venetian notary Nicola De Boateriis, 8 "Tatars" are mentioned but no "Turks" or "Cumans."[233]

Unfortunately, in the late thirteenth century and the first half of the fourteenth century, Italian notarial records from the Black Sea are practically limited to one notary, Lamberto de Sambuceto, who was active in Caffa during the years 1289–1290. His records mention 70 slaves; almost all are from the Caucasus, two are labeled "Cumans" and none is labeled "Tatar."[234] Lamberto de Sambuceto was also active in Famagusta between 1296 and 1307.[235] In 77 slave-related documents from that period, 13 "Turks," two "Cumans," three "Mongols," and only one "Tatar" are mentioned.[236] One out of two slave-related documents that survived from Caffa in the Black Sea region dated to 1351 mentions the sale of a Cuman woman.[237] In general, it has been concluded that during this period, the most important groups among slaves from the Black Sea region were Russians, Circassians, and Cuman Turks, but not Tatars.[238]

It is clear that in Europe by 1360 the term "Tatar" became the common label for slaves originating from the Golden Horde and that it replaced the label "Cuman" (or "Turk"). However, the scarcity of documents from earlier periods makes it difficult to pinpoint the exact time of this change in terminology. According to István Vásáry, "In the 14th century the term *Tatar*… came to mean

230 Sally McKee, "Domestic Slavery in Renaissance Italy," *Slavery and Abolition* 29/3 (2008): 309–11, 313; and see also Barker, "Egyptian and Italian Merchants," 134–5, 177–8.

231 McKee, "Domestic Slavery," 311.

232 Barker, "Egyptian and Italian Merchants," 176–7. The label "Mongol" perhaps refers to ethnic Mongols.

233 Benjamin Arbel, "Slave Trade and Slave Labor in Frankish Cyprus (1191–1571)," *Studies in Medieval and Renaissance History* 14 (1993): 156, 184–90.

234 Barker, "Egyptian and Italian Merchants," 170–1; and see also ibid., 174–6; and see also Reuven Amitai, "Diplomacy and the Slave Trade in the Eastern Mediterranean: A Re-Examination of the Mamluk Byzantine-Genoese Triangle in the Late Thirteenth Century in Light of the Existing Early Correspondence," *Oriente Moderno* 88/2 (2008): 355.

235 Arbel, "Slave Trade," 152.

236 Ibid., 152–4, 176–83.

237 Barker, "Egyptian and Italian Merchants," 176. The other mentions an Alan woman.

238 Ibid., 136.

the nationality and language of the Qumans. The terms *Quman* and *Tatar* for a long time lived side by side, until in the second half of the 14th century the term Quman finally disappeared" and was irrevocably replaced by the term *Tatar*. The "Cuman language" is last mentioned in written sources in 1338.[239] So it seems, that at some point between 1338 and 1359 the term "Tatar" totally replaced the term "Cuman."[240] This roughly overlaps the days of Jānī Bek (1342–1357). It thus seems, that in Europe the term "Tatar" begun to be used commonly when Islamization in the Golden Horde gained momentum. About fifty years passed until it became a common label for slaves originating from the Golden Horde also in the Mamluk Sultanate.[241]

The reasons for this should be clear. The Mamluk Sultanate was troubled by its Mongol (Tatar) Ilkhanid neighbors until 1323. In 1304 the Ilkhanid ruler Öljeitü declared that al-Nāṣir Muḥammad was a "Tatar" like himself (*huwa tatarī mithlī*),[242] in what was a clear demand for subjugation.[243] The Mamluks remembered the days of al-ʿĀdil Kitbughā (1294–1296) and the Oirat *wāfidiyya* as a "Mongol State" (*Dawlat al-Mughul*).[244] Even when a Turco-Mongol identity was constructed during al-Nāṣir Muḥammad's third reign (1310–1341) it was the Mongols who became Turks and not the other way around, and the state was deemed a "Turkish State."[245] During the days of Jānī Bek and even later, these memories were still fresh and the "Turkish" identity of the Sultanate still extremely important. In *Kitāb Uns al-Malā bi-Waḥsh al-Falā* Muḥammad Ibn Manjlī (fl. 1362–1376) compares between "Persian" (*ʿajam*) horsemen and "Tatar" (*tatār*) horsemen and says that the "Persians" are better than the "Tatars." Then he explains that by "Tatar" horsemen he refers to the "Tatars" that are now in their homeland (*wa-aʿnī bi-fursān al-tatār hum alladhīna al-ān fī bilādihim*). He continues and says that the "Turk" (*turkī*) trained in "our land" (*bilādinā*), that is Egypt, becomes an excellent horseman.[246] The fact that he is comparing between eastern horsemen ("Persians") and "Tatar" ones, and the time in which he is writing, seems to suggest that by "Tatar" he refers to the inhabitants of the Golden Horde. It seems then that in the 1360s Mamluk writers were aware that the Golden Horde has become the "Land of the Tatars." Once

239 István Vásáry, "Orthodox Christian Qumans and Tatars of the Crimea in the 13th-14th centuries," *Central Asiatic Journal* 32/3–4 (1988): 269–70.
240 Note that in 1351 a document mentions a Cuman slave-girl, see above.
241 For a possible unique early usage see David Ayalon, "Baḥrī Mamlūks, Burjī Mamlūks – Inadequate Names for the Two Reigns of the Mamlūk Sultanate," *Tārīḫ* 1 (1990): 41.
242 Al-Yūnīnī, *Dhayl Mirʾāt al-Zamān: Taʾrīkh al-Sanawāt 697–711*, 2: 810.
243 See above at note 37; and see Broadbridge, *Kingship and Ideology*, 95.
244 See above at notes 83–5.
245 See section 1.4 above.
246 Muḥammad Ibn Manjlī, *Kitāb Uns al-Malā bi-Waḥsh al-Falā*, ed. Muḥammad ʿĪsá Ṣāliḥiyya (Amman: Dār al-Bashīr, Beirut: Muʾassasat al-Risāla, 1993), 101.

these "Tatars" arrived in the Sultanate, however, they immediately became "Turks." The Timurid expansion (roughly 1370–1400) made latent ethnic and political animosities resurface. Only circa 1400, after the Timurid expansion, the Persianization and de-Tatarization of the Timurids, the more complete Islamization of the Golden Horde, and perhaps no less important, the becoming of the "Turks" a minority group, "Tatar" became an accepted label for Turco-Mongol inhabitants of the Golden Horde, originally mostly Qipchaq. In *Nuzhat al-Asāṭīn fī Man Waliya Miṣr min al-Salāṭīn*, al-Malaṭī surveys states in the history of Egypt. Amazingly, according to al-Malaṭī, after "the Kurdish Ayyūbid State" (*al-Dawla al-Ayyūbiyya al-Kurdiyya*)[247] came a "Turkish Tatar state" (*al-Dawla al-Turkiyya al-Tatāriyya*),[248] after which came a "Circassian State" (*al-Dawla al-Jarkasiyya*).[249] For al-Malaṭī "Tatars" and "Turks" were united from the beginning of the Sultanate.

2. Islamization and Transition

It has been suggested that the transfer of the *mamlūks*' purchasing-center from the Golden Horde to the Caucasus had to do with the decline of the Golden Horde. In the second half of the fourteenth century the Golden Horde could no longer supply slaves in sufficient numbers due to a dwindling population, caused by excessive selling of young boys and girls, plagues, and wars.[250] Additionally, some scholars have suggested that in the long run the Islamization of the inhabitants of the Golden Horde must have made the enslavement of *mamlūks* from that area more difficult.[251] Therefore, the Mamluk Sultanate had to search for alternative sources for slaves. The Timurid expansion had brought some slaves from territories once held by the Ilkhans or from Central Asia to the slave markets and from there to Egypt,[252] and some Central Asian slaves arrived in Egypt as war captives.[253] Some of these *mamlūks* would have been originally

247 ʿAbd al-Bāsiṭ ibn Khalīl ibn Shāhīn al-Ẓāhirī al-Malaṭī, *Nuzhat al-Asāṭīn fī Man Waliya Miṣr min al-Salāṭīn*, ed. Muḥammad Kamāl al-Dīn ʿIzz al-Dīn (Cairo: Maktabat al-Thaqāfa al-Dīniyya, 1987), 49, 64.

248 Ibid., 65.

249 Ibid., 114.

250 Ayalon, "The Circassians," 136; idem, "Mamlūk: Military Slavery," 6–7; Levanoni, "*Awlad al-Nas*," 101; idem, "Al-Maqrīzī's Account of the Transition from Turkish to Circassian Mamluk Sultanate: History in the Service of Faith," in *The Historiography of Islamic Egypt (c. 950–1800)*, ed. Hugh Kennedy (Leiden: Brill, 2001), 100–1; and see also Barker, "Egyptian and Italian Merchants," 135.

251 Ayalon, "Mamlūk: Military Slavery," 4, 7; Golden, *Introduction*, 350; idem, "The Shaping," 331.

252 See item no. 7 in Table A, item no. 2 in Table B, and possibly also item no. 3 in Table B.

253 See item no. 6 in Table A.

Muslims,[254] and in any case these *mamlūks* could not supply the demand for slaves in the Mamluk Sultanate. Thus, the Caucasus gradually became the main source for slaves, and the historical territories of the Byzantine Empire and Europe became a secondary source.

Starting from the 1350s or 1360s an increase in the number of non-Turkish *mamlūks* can be detected, mainly Circassians, but also Rūmīs (i.e. *mamlūks* originating from the historical territories of the Byzantine Empire [*Bilād al-Rūm*], who were probably mainly Greeks and Slavs).[255] As mentioned, in this article I use the label "non-Turks" to refer to European ("Rūmīs" and "Franks") and Caucasian *mamlūks*. The Mongols are not included in the ethnic group labeled "non-Turks," because, as mentioned, even when they were the Sultanate's enemies they were considered to be ethnically related to the Turks, and, more importantly, starting from al-Nāṣir Muḥammad's third reign, Turks and Mongols were considered to belong to the same ethnic group, that is, the Turco-Mongols. It is well known that whereas al-Ṣāliḥ Ayyūb and al-Ẓāhir Baybars restricted recruitment largely to Qipchaqs, al-Manṣūr Qalāwūn purchased *mamlūks* from a wide variety of ethnic origins. Except for Turks and Mongols, al-Manṣūr Qalāwūn purchased Circassians, Georgians, Armenians, Greeks and other European people.[256] After the death of al-Manṣūr Qalāwūn in 1290 and until the inauguration of al-Nāṣir Muḥammad's third reign in 1310, specifically the Circassians formed coalitions based on ethnic solidarity resented by the Turks and Mongols.[257] However, after al-Nāṣir Muḥammad took back in 1310 the reins of power from the Circassian sultan al-Muẓaffar Baybars al-Jāshankīr (d. 1310), he seems to have turned against non-Turks and specifically against the Circassians. Non-Turks, and specifically Circassians, are hardly noticeable from that time until the 1350s or 1360s, when, as mentioned, an increase in their numbers is again detected. During the Turkish period of the Sultanate (1250–1382) the Turks and Mongols (or Turco-Mongols) constituted the majority of the Mamluk army,

254 See item no. 7 in Table A, item no. 2 in Table B, and item no. 5 in Table C.

255 In that period, names given exclusively to "Rūmīs" and others given exclusively to Circassians appear for the first time in the history of the Sultanate, see Yosef, "The Names of the *Mamlūks*"; idem, "Ethnic Groups," 1: 96–100. The label "Rūmī" was sometimes used interchangeably with the label "Frank" (*faranjī*), thus it may refer by extension to practically all European origins. The label "Rūmī" may also refer to Turkmen originating from Asia Minor. The position of Turkmen originating from Asia Minor among the ethnic groups of the *mamlūks* is a complicated issue which cannot be addressed in detail in the scope of this article.

256 Robert Irwin, *The Middle East in the Middle Ages: The Early Mamluk Sultanate 1250–1382* (London: Croom Helm, 1986), 70; for Armenians, see Aḥmad ibn ʿAlī al-Maqrīzī, *Kitāb al-Mawāʿiẓ wal-Iʿtibār bi-Dhikr al-Khiṭaṭ wal-Āthār* (Beirut: Dār Ṣadr, n.d.), 2: 214.

257 See for example Linda S. Northrup, "The Baḥrī Mamlūk Sultanate, 1250–1390," in *The Cambridge History of Egypt*. Vol. 1: *Islamic Egypt, 640–1517*, ed. Carl F. Petry (Cambridge: Cambridge University Press, 1998), 258–9.

but starting from the 1350s or 1360, and especially starting from the days of al-Ẓāhir Barqūq (1382–1399) and his son al-Nāṣir Faraj (1399–1412)[258] they gradually became the minority and lost their leading position to the Circassians.[259] It may be said that during the Turkish period of the Sultanate, and especially starting from al-Nāṣir Muḥammad's third reign, the non-Turks where perceived as the "ultimate other." How did this come to be?

3. Attitudes towards Non-Turks

3.1. The Mamluk Sultanate and the Christian World

Even though the Crusader states in Syria were vanquished by the fourteenth century, Christianity was and remained the eternal enemy of Islam.[260] The fall of Acre and other Christian strongholds on the Syrian coast to the Mamluks in 1291 marked the end of western military presence in Syria but did not signify the end of the crusading movement.[261] Crusading ideology, the belief that Christians had an obligation to defend their Christian brethren overseas, and enthusiasm for holy war against the infidels continued to exist.[262] After 1291 the kingdom of Cyprus under the Lusignans (1192–1489) remained a western outpost in the Levant, and Cilician Armenia a Christian-controlled point in southeastern Anatolia. The Hospitallers seized between 1306 and 1310 the island of Rhodes from the Byzantines.[263] The Cypriots attempted to join forces with the Mongols (supported by Armenians and Georgians) in their invasions to Syria in 1299 and 1301. The Mamluks led several campaigns against Cilician Armenia in 1298, 1302, 1304, 1320, and 1322. In 1322 the Mamluks briefly occupied the Armenian town Ayas which was finally taken in 1337.[264] In 1365, Peter I of Cyprus invaded Alexandria and begun a war with the Mamluks.[265] Although a peace treaty was signed in 1370, the island continued to serve "as a naval basis for regular attacks

258 Ayalon, "The Circassians," 138–40; Yosef, "Ethnic Groups," 1: 111–15, 118–20; and see also Barker, "Egyptian and Italian Merchants," 135–6.

259 There is not even one biographical entry of a *mamlūk* labeled "Tatar" or "Turk" who arrived in the Sultanate after the days of al-Ẓāhir Jaqmaq (1438–1453). For such *mamlūks* until the days of al-Ẓāhir Jaqmaq, see Table A above.

260 See for example Ayalon, "The Great Yāsa (C1)," 144.

261 Peter Edbury, "Christians and Muslims in the Eastern Mediterranean," in *The New Cambridge Medieval History:* Vol. 6: *C. 1300-c. 1415*, ed. Michael Jones (Cambridge: Cambridge University Press, 2008), 864.

262 Ibid., 884.

263 Ibid., 864.

264 Ibid., 871.

265 Ibid., 876.

on Muslim shores by pirates and corsairs of various origins, culminating in a massive counter attack by Sultan al-Ashraf Barsbāy in 1427," after which Cyprus remained under Mamluk suzerainty until 1487.[266]

In addition to the struggles with Cyprus and European (mainly Catalan) pirates, during the fifteenth century a Genoese fleet under the French Marshal Jean de Boucicault raided the Syrian coasts in 1402.[267] Between 1440 and 1444 the Mamluks attacked Rhodes.[268] Another "Christian enemy that threatened Mamluk power was the Portuguese, who had already reconquered all Muslim dominions in their country in the 13th century." By the end of the fifteenth century they threatened Mamluk economic interests, and the resulting war ended "in a resounding victory for the Portuguese, who destroyed the Egyptian fleet in the Arabian Sea (1508) and even threatened the shores of the Red Sea."[269]

Neither the Crusades nor the post-Crusades confrontations between the Mamluks and the Christian world prevented commercial relations, and diplomatic and cultural exchanges; however these did not have "significant bearing on mental frontiers," did not entail a deeper affinity to the Christian culture, and "did not introduce any perceptible change in the image of Europe that had taken shape in Mamluk narratives since the Crusades." The Mamluk's political identity and legitimacy remained connected to their victory over the Crusades.[270] The image of Europe "remained marked by the experience of the Crusades and perpetuated by the repeated Christian raids on Mamluk coastal cities, notably by the devastating sack of Alexandria... in 1365 which remained for a long period deeply carved in the minds of Mamluk historians, even after it was avenged by the conquest" of Cyprus in 1427.[271] The growing Portuguese influence in the Indian

---

266 Herman G. B. Teule, "Introduction: Constantinople and Granada. Christian-Muslim interaction 1350–1516," in *Christian-Muslim Relations A Bibliographical History: Volume 5 (1350–1500)*, ed. David Thomas and Alex Mallett (Leiden, Boston: Brill, 2013), 6; on Catalan piracy against Mamluk ships, see also Nicholas Coureas, "Commerce between Mamluk Egypt and Hospitaller Rhodes in the Mid-Fifteenth Century: The Case of Sidi Galip Ripolli," in *Egypt and Syria in the Fatimid, Ayyubid and Mamluk Eras VI*, ed. Urbain Vermeulen and Kristof D'hulster (Leuven: Uitgeverij Peeters, 2010); on Latin Cyprus and the Mamluk Sultanate see idem, "Latin Cyprus and its Relation with the Mamluk Sultanate: 1250–1517," in *The Crusader World*, ed. Adrian J. Boas (London and New York: Routledge, 2016).

267 Albrecht Fuess, "Prelude to a Stronger Involvement in the Middle East: French Attacks on Beirut in the Years 1403 and 1520," *Al-Masāq* 17/2 (2005).

268 Anthony Luttrell, "The Latin East," in *The New Cambridge Medieval History*, Vol. 7: *C. 1415-c. 1500*, ed. Christopher Allmand (Cambridge: Cambridge University Press, 2008), 800.

269 Teule, "Introduction: Constantinople and Granada," 6.

270 Doris Behrens-Abouseif, "Mamluk Artistic Relations with Latin Europe," in *La frontière méditerranéenne du XVe au XVIIe siècle: Échanges, circulations et affrontements*, ed. Bernard Heyberger and Albrecht Fuess (Turnhout: Brepols Publishers, 2014), 370; idem, "Mamluk Perceptions of Foreign Arts," in *The Arts of the Mamluks in Egypt and Syria – Evolution and Impact*, ed. Doris Behrens-Abouseif (Bonn: Bonn University Press, 2012), 314.

271 Ibid., 315; and see also idem, *Practicing Diplomacy in the Mamluk Sultanate: Gifts and*

Ocean in the second half of the fifteenth century, "perpetuated the image of the European as a Crusader to the last days of the Sultanate."[272]

3.2. Attitudes towards the Christian World

Carole Hillenbrand has emphasized "the longevity and unchanging nature of the negative perceptions of the peoples of western Europe which can be found at least from the tenth century in Islamic literature."[273] Even before the Crusades, the Franks were perceived as filthy, stupid, and treacherous savages, more beasts than men, which are lacking in sexual morality. These negative qualities became rooted in the Muslim mind.[274] The role of religion of Islam was very significant in constructing the image of the Frankish Crusaders as a non-Muslim barbarian "other."[275] The Crusaders became known by a variety of stereotyped pejoratives ("devils," "pigs," "dogs") and were deemed "heretics" and "accursed."[276] They were perceived as untrustworthy, dishonorable, and extremely cruel enemy.[277] These perceptions continued to exist well into the Mamluk period, and lingered on even after the Crusader states were vanquished.[278]

In the Mamluk period, negative attitudes were not restricted to Franks and Crusaders, but extended to other Christian peoples. In popular literature written in part during the Mamluk period the Byzantines and Portuguese are also depicted negatively and Christians in general are shown hostility.[279] In Mamluk history books, at least starting from the second half of the fourteenth century the Byzantines were suspected of collaboration with Latin Europe, and were deemed "accursed" Christian heretics.[280] Peter of Castile (d. 1319) the Spanish lord is

Material Culture in the Medieval Islamic World (London: I.B. Tauris, 2014), 103 (the sack of Alexandria "was neither forgiven nor forgotten").

272 Idem, "Mamluk Artistic Relations," 369.

273 Hillenbrand, *The Crusades*, 257.

274 Ibid., 270–4.

275 Ibid., 282.

276 Ibid., 303.

277 Wadīʿ Z. Haddad, "The Crusaders through Muslim Eyes," *The Muslim World* 73/3-4 (1983): 237.

278 See for example Frédéric Bauden, "Taqī al-Dīn Aḥmad ibn ʿAlī al-Maqrīzī," in *Medieval Muslim Historians and the Franks in the Levant*, ed. Alex Mallett (Leiden: Brill, 2014), 181.

279 Irwin, "The Image of the Byzantine and the Frank," 231–5.

280 Ibn Kathīr, *al-Bidāya wal-Nihāya*, 14: 320; al-Malaṭī, *al-Rawḍ al-Bāsim*, 1: 321. Nadia Maria El-Cheikh argued that during the twelfth and thirteenth centuries "the new political alliance between the Byzantines and Saladin, and later on between the Byzantine and Mamluk states, redirected Muslim animosity toward the Franks, while the Byzantines came to be viewed in much friendlier terms"; see El-Cheikh, "Byzantium through the Islamic Prism," 68; and see also Irwin, "The Image of the Byzantine and the Frank," 228; Behrens-Abouseif, "Mamluk Perceptions," 314. During the fourteenth century, however, the Ottoman conquest of the

depicted as an evil Christian who tried to harm the Muslims.[281] The Christian Armenians and Georgians, who collaborated with the Mongol Ilkhans against the Mamluk Sultanate, were also represented in a negative manner. They are said to be "accursed" (*malāʿīn*), and specifically the Georgians are depicted as a rough (*ghalīẓīn* [!] *al-ṭibāʿ*) and heretic (*ʿaẓīmīn* [!] *al-kufr*) people, who tend to have massive bodies (*shadīdīn* [!] *al-ajsām*) and large beards (*kibār al-liḥá*).[282] According to a chapter dedicated to the description of the nations of mankind (*waṣf ajnās al-nās*) in al-ʿAbbāsī's (flourished in the days of al-Nāṣir Muḥammad's third reign) mirror for princes *Āthār al-Uwal*, the Armenians are known for their untrustworthiness (*qillat amāna*).[283]

Not only the "wrong" religion of the Christian peoples, but also their pale physical appearance (light complexion, blond/red hair, and blue or green eyes), were connected to their negative qualities.[284] Kristina Richardson has recently shown how ubiquitous were negative representations of blue (and green) eyes in Arab and Muslim history.[285] According to al-Zamakhsharī (d. 1144), blue (or green) eyes "are the ugliest eye color for Arabs, because the people of Rūm are their enemies" and they have such a color of eyes.[286] Pale appearance and blue eyes were also linked to deceitfulness and treachery ("beware of every blond and blue eyed person"), and stupidity.[287] These representations of "physical otherness" were meant to construct an image of a non-Arab and non-Muslim

Byzantine areas of Asia Minor "meant that western opinion had now swung firmly in favour of supporting the Byzantine regime against further Muslim losses and away from the idea of overthrowing it," and already in 1334 the Byzantine empire became part of the Christian league, see Edbury, "Christians and Muslims," 868. In late fourteenth century, Italian slave-owning societies viewed the enslavement of Greeks as illegitimate as their own enslavement, see McKee, "Domestic Slavery," 309. Moreover, as mentioned, the label "Rūmī" was sometimes used interchangeably with the label "Frank," see Ayalon, "Mamlūk: Military Slavery," 9. Both terms were sometimes used to mean Europeans or Christians in general, see El-Cheikh, "Byzantium through the Islamic Prism," 56; Koray Durak, "Who Are the Romans? The Definition of Bilād al-Rūm (Land of the Romans) in Medieval Islamic Geographies," *Journal of Intercultural Studies* 31/3 (2010): 293–5. Latin communities in Greek lands must have made the differentiation between "Franks" and "Rūmīs" even more complicated. On these Latin communities, see Luttrell, "The Latin East." It is therefore not surprising that Mamluk historians were sometimes not sure if a *mamlūk* was Frank or Rūmī, see for example Ibn Taghrībirdī, *al-Manhal al-Ṣāfī*, 3: 435.

281 Al-Ṣafadī, *Aʿyān al-ʿAṣr*, 2: 361–2.

282 Ibn al-Dawādārī, *Kanz al-Durar*, 8: 204; 9: 255.

283 Al-Ḥasan ibn ʿAbd Allāh al-ʿAbbāsī, *Āthār al-Uwal fī Tartīb al-Duwal*, ed. ʿAbd al-Raḥmān ʿUmayra (Beirut: Dār al-Jīl, 1989), 292.

284 See Hillenbrand, *The Crusades*, 270–1; Irwin, "The Image of the Byzantine and the Frank," 231.

285 Kristina Richardson, "Blue and Green Eyes in the Islamicate Middle Ages," *Annales islamologiques* 48/1 (2014): 15.

286 Ibid., 17.

287 Ibid., 21, 25.

"other."[288] In the Mamluk period the image of the "blue-eyed enemy" continued to exist.[289] The "Bashqurd," a mostly Christian Turkish people living in Eastern Europe (perhaps the Hungarians are meant here) who allegedly had a pale appearance (*ṣufr al-wujūh, shuqr al-shuʿūr wal-wujūh, zurq al-ʿuyūn*) were depicted as evil.[290] According to Qaraṭāy al-ʿIzzī al-Khāzindārī, they collaborated with the Franks against the Muslim Mamluks during the reign of al-Ẓāhir al-Baybars, and he labels them as "an accursed nation known for its evilness and its bad behavior" (*jins malʿūn maʿrūf bil-sharr wal-naḥs/jins malʿūn wa-khalq ashrār*), as "evil and troublesome" (*maʿrūfūn bil-sharr wal-fitan*), and as "the worst of nations and of colors" (*anḥas mā yakūnu min al-alwān wal-ajnās*).[291]

3.3. Attitudes towards Christian Subjects and Christian Bureaucrats in the Mamluk Sultanate

The hatred and suspicion towards Christian external enemies infiltrated into the territories of the Sultanate. The autochthon Christian population of the Mamluk Sultanate was generally mistrusted and suspected or accused of collaboration with the Sultanate's European enemies.[292] European attacks on the Mamluk Sultanate fueled "a pervasive sense of a Christian fifth column,"[293] and had devastating consequences for the Christian subjects of the Mamluk Sultanate.[294]

Christian bureaucrats, even those who converted to Islam, were disliked, their Christian past was never forgotten, and their Islamization not considered sincere.[295] The Coptic officials were said to have had an insufficient knowledge in the Arabic language,[296] and such accusations in fact labeled them as not Muslims

288 Ibid., 13, 25, 27.

289 Ibid., 26.

290 See Abū al-Fidāʾ, *al-Mukhtaṣar*, 1: 93; and see also Qaraṭāy al-ʿIzzī al-Khāzindārī, *Taʾrīkh Majmūʿ al-Nawādir*, 242; Yāqūt al-Ḥamawī, *Muʿjam al-Buldān*, ed. Farīd ʿAbd al-ʿAzīz al-Jundī (Beirut: Dār al-Kutub al-ʿIlmiyya, 1990), 1: 383–5; and see Irwin, "The Image of the Byzantine and the Frank," 238–9.

291 Qaraṭāy al-ʿIzzī al-Khāzindārī, *Taʾrīkh Majmūʿ al-Nawādir*, 237, 242.

292 Ashtor, *Toldot ha-Yehudim*, 1: 337–9; al-Maqrīzī, *al-Sulūk*, 3: 106.

293 Carl F. Petry, "Crime and Scandal in Foreign Relations," in *La frontière méditerranéenne du XVe au XVIIe siècle: Échanges, circulations et affrontements*, ed. Bernard Heyberger and Albrecht Fuess (Turnhout: Brepols Publishers, 2014), 152.

294 Johannes Pahlitzsch, "Mediators between East and West: Christians under Mamluk Rule," *Mamlūk Studies Review* 9/2 (2005): 39; A. S. Atiya "Ḳibṭ," *The Encyclopaedia of Islam*, 2nd Edition (Leiden: Brill, 1985), 5: 90–5.

295 Moshe Perlmann, "Notes on Anti-Christian Propaganda in the Mamlūk Empire," *Bulletin of the School of Oriental and African Studies* 10 (1940–1942): 858.

296 Ashtor, *Toldot ha-Yehudim*, 346.

even if converted to Islam. Al-Malaṭī accuses a Copt for advising al-Ẓāhir Jaqmaq to take un-Islamic measures because it is natural for the Copt "to be leaning towards his original religion" (*mā'il ilá dīn ābā'ihi al-awwal*).[297] According to Ibn Taghrībirdī, the *wazīr* ʿAbd al-Ghanī ibn ʿAbd al-Razzāq ibn Abī al-Faraj ibn Naqūlā al-Armanī al-Qibṭī (d. 1418) was an evil person, "because he was from a household of exploitation and injustice. He had the tyranny of the Armenians, the guile of the Christians, the devilry of the Copts and the exploitation of the customs officials. It was because his ethnic origin was Armenian, he was brought up by Christians, trained by Copts, and grew up with the customs officials" (*fa-innahu min bayt ẓulm wa-ʿasf wa-kāna ʿindahu jabrūt al-arman wa-dahāʾ al-naṣārá wa-shayṭanat al-aqbāṭ wa-ẓulm al-makasa fa-inna aṣluhu min al-arman wa-rubbiya maʿa al-naṣārá wa-tadarraba bil-aqbāṭ wa-nashaʾa maʿa al-makasa*).[298] Al-Sakhāwī (d. 1497), who probably did not want "to discriminate" against anyone, mentions that his evil character was also the result of his having been brought up by Jews.[299]

In the course of the thirteenth and fourteenth centuries, a large number of polemics against the employment of non-Muslim officials were written in Syria and Egypt.[300] In these polemical treatises, it is said that it is normal for the Christians to hate and deceive the Muslims because of their religious hate.[301] They are accused of being anti-Muslim, treacherous, and dishonest, and of collaborating with the enemies of Islam.[302] They are held responsible for the spread of wine drinking and moral laxity, and the seduction of Muslim women.[303]

3.4. Attitudes towards Non-Turkish *mamlūks*

3.4.1. The Identity of Non-Turks – Christian Background

The non-Turkish *mamlūks* were also, generally, Christians in their past. Although, as Ulrich Haarmann already indicated, European travelers who visited the Sultanate probably exaggerated when they claimed that all *mamlūks* were Christian renegades longing to return to Christianity,[304] it is clear that European,

297 Al-Malaṭī, *al-Rawḍ al-Bāsim*, 1: 150.
298 Ibn Taghrībirdī, *al-Manhal al-Ṣāfī*, 7: 314–18.
299 Al-Sakhāwī, *al-Ḍawʾ al-Lāmiʿ*, 4: 248–51.
300 See Luke Yarbrough, "'A Rather Small Genre': Arabic Works Against Non-Muslim State Officials," *Der Islam* 93/1 (2016): 139–69.
301 Perlmann, "Notes on Anti-Christian Propaganda," 847, 850.
302 Ibid., 851; Ashtor, *Toldot ha-Yehudim*, 319.
303 Perlmann, "Notes on Anti-Christian Propaganda," 851.
304 Ulrich Haarmann, "The Mamluk System of Rule in the Eyes of Western Travelers," *Mamlūk*

Armenian and Georgian *mamlūks* were indeed Christians in their past. As noted by Robert Irwin, "many of the governing elite in Egypt and Syria in the late Middle Ages had been born and raised in Christian Europe."[305] Irwin added that while Mamluk sources rarely mention *mamlūks* of Western European origin ("Franks"), it can be deduced that an important section of the Mamluk elite were of Greek origin ("Rūmīs").[306] Doris Behrens-Abouseif who found some more Franks in Mamluk sources, spoke about a "well-known presence of Europeans within the Mamluk establishment since the early fifteenth century,"[307] and noted that "Europeans at the Mamluk court were not an unusual sight in late fifteenth century."[308] Like scholars before her, she notes that most of the European *mamlūks* are mentioned in European travel accounts and only occasionally in Arabic sources,[309] and concludes that "[t]here is more research to be done on this subject, for which it will be necessary to consult European sources and archives."[310] In fact, Mamluk sources offer more information about *mamlūks* of European origin (mainly Rūmīs but also Franks). The presence of European *mamlūks* in the Mamluk Sultanate can also be examined by following names that were given to European *mamlūks* even when there is no explicit information regarding the ethnic origin of these *mamlūks*.[311] As mentioned, European *mamlūks* (mainly Rūmīs) started to arrive to the Sultanate in relatively large numbers already during the second half of the fourteenth century. They filled high-ranking positions during the days of al-Nāṣir Faraj (1399–1412) who was a son of a Rūmī slave-girl.[312] It seems that European *mamlūks* started playing a more important role during the reign of al-Ẓāhir Jaqmaq (1438–1453), at about the time when the Turco-Mongols were hardly arriving anymore to the Sultanate.

Studies Review 5 (2001): 6–22; and see also Irwin, "The Image of the Byzantine and the Frank," 227.

305 Ibid.

306 Ibid. For *mamlūks* of Western European origin mentioned by European travelers who visited the Sultanate, see Haarmann, "The Mamluk System of Rule," 6–9; Irwin, "The Image of the Byzantine and the Frank," 227; Doris Behrens-Abouseif, "European Arts and Crafts at the Mamluk Court," *Muqarnas: An Annual on the Visual Culture of the Islamic World* 21 (2004): 49–50.

307 Idem, "Mamluk Artistic Relations," 364.

308 Idem, *Practicing Diplomacy*, 107; for Frankish *mamlūks* in Mamluk sources, see idem, "Mamluk Perceptions," 313–14; idem, "Mamluk Artistic Relations," 364–7.

309 Idem, "Mamluk Perceptions," 313.

310 Idem, "European Arts," 53. For a research using European archives for this end, see Benjamin Arbel, "Venetian Cyprus and the Muslim Levant, 1473–1570," in *Cyprus and the Crusades/Kypros kai oi Staurophories*, ed. Nicholas Coureas and Jonathan Riley-Smith (Nicosia: Cyprus Research Centre and Society for the Study of the Crusades and the Latin East, 1995), 174–7.

311 I cannot elaborate on this in the scope of this article.

312 Ayalon, "The Circassians," 141–2.

Moreover, there is some evidence that during the fourteenth and fifteenth centuries the Circassians were Christians in their homeland. According to contemporary Arab historians and geographers, and European travelers who visited the Caucasus at that time, the Circassian people were mostly Christians.[313] There is much evidence that al-Ẓāhir Barqūq (d. 1399) and his father Anaṣ (d. 1381) were originally Christians,[314] and there is information that al-Ashraf Qaytbāy (d. 1496) was Christian.[315] There is also indirect evidence for the link between Circassians and the Christian religion. During the Turkish period of the Sultanate, Ciracassian *mamlūks* were given names that were given also to Rūmīs, Armenians and other Christian *mamlūks*.[316] Moreover, many times Mamluk historians found it hard to decide whether a *mamlūk* was Circassian or of another Christian ethnic origin (such as Armenian or Rūmī).[317] The practice of giving non-Turkish *mamlūks* of many ethnic origins a set of names different from that of Turks and Mongols (and later on from that of Turco-Mongols) was a mechanism that was used by Qipchaq sultans to construct their identity as the "other."

During the Turkish period of the Sultanate, many of the non-Turkish *mamlūks* were captured in raids,[318] or were war captives,[319] and, therefore, their enslavement was more traumatic than that experienced by Turco-Mongol *mamlūks*. In the course of the fifteenth Century, Cypriots arrived to the Sultanate as war captives,[320] and Christian Europeans (mainly Rūmīs but also Franks) captured by the Ottomans were regularly sent as gift to Mamluk sultans.[321]

313 See for example Abū al-Fidā', *al-Mukhtaṣar*, 1: 92; Lajos Tardy, "The Caucasian Peoples and their Neighbors in 1404," *Acta Orientalia Academiae Scientiarum Hung.* 32/1 (1978): 92; Ayalon, "The Circassians," 136–7.

314 Haarmann, "The Mamluk System of Rule," 9–10.

315 Behrens-Abouseif, "European Arts," 50.

316 Yosef, "The Names of the *Mamlūks*"; idem, "Ethnic Groups," 1: 17–19, 68–70.

317 See for example ibid., 1: 132–3, 159–60. The label "Rūmī" in such cases may well refer to the Greek religion; see Barker, "Egyptian and Italian Merchants," 67.

318 The Circassians, Alans, and Russians were captured in raids and brought to the slave markets, see al-ʿUmarī, *Masālik al-Abṣār*, 3: 178.

319 For Armenian war captives, see Behrens-Abouseif, "European Arts," 48; idem, "Mamluk Perceptions," 311–12; al-Yūnīnī, *Dhayl Mir'āt al-Zamān: Ta'rīkh al-Sanawāt 697–711*, 2: 724, 768–70. For Georgian and "Christian" war captives, see ibid., 2: 724. For Frankish war captives, see Julien Loiseau, "Frankish Captives"; Behrens-Abouseif, "European Arts," 48; for Christian war captives from Qārā in Syria, see al-ʿUmarī, *Masālik al-Abṣār*, 27: 409.

320 Arbel, "Venetian Cyprus," 174; Johannes Pahlitzsch, "The Mamluks and Cyprus: Transcultural Relations between Muslim and Christian Rulers in the Eastern Mediterranean in the Fifteenth Century," *Acteurs des transferts culturels en Méditerranée médiévale. Ateliers des Deutschen Historischen Instituts Paris*, ed. R. Abdellatif, Y. Benhima, D. König, and E. Ruchaud (Paris: Deutsches Historisches Institut Paris, 2010), 115–17; Coureas, "Latin Cyprus," 409; Behrens-Abouseif, "Mamluk Perceptions," 313–14; idem, *Practicing Diplomacy*, 107.

321 Ibid., 85–93. The Ottoman expansion into Europe (mainly to territories held or once held by the Byzantines) became noticeable already in the 1350s and continued throughout the

3.4.2. The Identity of the Non-Turks – Physical Appearance and Stereotypical Attributes

Physically, the non-Turkish *mamlūks* were typically characterized as being pale and tall,[322] thus, for example, Lājīn al-Manṣūrī (d. 1299) was said to have been "blond with blue eyes… tall and it was said that he was a Circassian" (*kāna ashqar azraq al-ʿaynayn… ṭawīl wa-dhukira annahu kāna jarkasī al-jins*).[323] It seems that because the non-Turks were considered to be relatively tall, and because tallness was related to fearsomeness,[324] during the days of Qalāwūn (1279–1290) as members of the *Burjiyya* unit they were given the posts of *ṣilāḥdāriyya* (arms-bearers) and *jumaqdāriyya* (mace-bearers),[325] which probably contributed to their perception as cruel and fearsome.

As with the bureaucrats, the fact that the non-Turkish *mamlūks* were Christians in their past was held against them.[326] Sometimes a clear link was made between their Christian background and their distinct physical appearance which resembled that of the Sultanate's Christian enemies, and their bad traits. Because of their Christian origin and pale appearance, they were perceived as not (true) Muslims, as inclined towards un-Islamic practices (wine drinking and illicit or immoral sexual behavior), disloyal, untrustworthy and treacherous, cruel, evil, exploitative, frivolous, stupid and sometimes even ugly.[327]

---

second half of the fourteenth century, see Teule, "Introduction: Constantinople and Granada," 2–3; Edbury, "Christians and Muslims," 882–3. Due to this expansion Rūmīs probably arrived in great numbers to the slave markets, which may explain the increase in their presence in the Mamluk Sultanate already during that period. It has also been suggested that Catalan and Genoese piracy was responsible for the enslavement of Rūmīs during the second half of the fourteenth century, see Arbel, "Slave Trade," 156.

322 Ayalon briefly mentioned the "different physiognomy" of the non-Turkish *mamlūks* without elaborating on the matter, see Ayalon, "Baḥrī Mamlūks, Burjī Mamlūks," 44; for the full analysis, see Yosef, "Ethnic Groups," 1: 167–70.

323 Al-ʿAynī, *ʿIqd al-Jumān*, 3: 432; for the opinion that he was "a blond Rūmī" (*ashqar rūmī*), see for example al-Dhahabī, *Duwal al-Islām*, 2: 202.

324 See for example al-Ṣafadī, *Aʿyān al-ʿAṣr*, 4: 364–5.

325 Yosef, "The Names of the *Mamlūks*"; idem, "Ethnic Groups," 1: 36–42. The post of *jumaqdār* seems to have been filled by tall people, see Fatima Sadeque, "The Court and Household of the Mamlūks of Egypt (13th-15th centuries)," *Journal of the Asiatic Society of Pakistan* 49 (1969): 248; on the *ṣilāḥdāriyya* see notes 118–19 above.

326 Ayalon considered the pre-Muslim monotheistic (that is, Christian) background that some of the *mamlūks* had as a "dividing line within a Mamlūk group" that could have undermined the foundations of the Mamlūk system, see Ayalon, "Baḥrī Mamlūks, Burjī Mamlūks," 45–6.

327 After the days of al-Nāṣir Muḥammad no Turco-Mongol is explicitly said to have been drinking wine or to have practiced illicit sex (*zinā/liwāṭ/mayl lil-aḥdāth*). For example, until al-Nāṣir Muḥammad's third reign sexual inclination towards young men was attributed mainly to Mongols. After the disappearance of the Mongol *mamlūks* during al-Nāṣir Muḥammad's third reign we do not hear on *mamlūks* attributed such an inclination until the Circassian period when it is attributed only to non-Turks, see Yosef, "Ethnic Groups," 1: 157. From about fifty *mamlūks* labeled "Turks" during the Circassian period only one is said to

In a part of his mirror for princes treatise *Āthār al-Uwal* in which he enumerates the characteristics of the various ethnic groups of *mamlūks*, al-ʿAbbāsī writes that the Armenians and Georgians slaves are characterized by treachery (*khiyāna/ghadr*).[328] According to books of advice for those interested in buying slaves, the disadvantage of the Armenian slaves is that they are cruel, disobedient, liars, they have a filthy mouth, and, most importantly, they are fond of non-Muslims and their rulers.[329] The amir Ughurlū al-Sayfī (d. 1348) who is said to have been an Armenian or Circassian, is said to have led a Circassian faction and turned against the Turks. He is said to have been a very cruel and exploitative person. The people hated him so much that after he had been buried they took his body out of his grave and crucified it.[330] The Georgian amir Asandamur Kurjī (d. 1311) is depicted in Mamluk sources as a tall and extremely cruel person whom the people feared because he used to execute people in all sorts of ways. Some Mamluk historians make a link between his Georgian origin and his cruelty.[331]

According to books of advice for those interested in buying slaves, the Franks have pale appearance and usually have blue eyes, they are stupid, uneducated, and they are loyal to their religion (i. e. Christianity).[332] Taghrībirdī al-Armanī al-Manṣūrī (d. 1469) a Florentine Frank (*min al-faranj al-farantiyyīn*) who was promoted by the Rūmī sultan al-Ẓāhir Tamurbughā (d. 1475) is said to have been a bad person (*ghayr mashkūr al-sīra*).[333] Damurdāsh al-Iqrīṭishī a Frank from Crete used to sell wine.[334] A Frank *mamlūk* from Tripoli was lynched by a mob

have been blond (*ashqar*) and only two are said to have been tall. One of these "Turks" Aqbirdī al-Qijmāsī (d. 1438) is said to have been blond and tall and uncharacteristically for "Turks" (who were not "Tatar" or "Persians" from the east) he is described in a very negative manner. Immediately after Ibn Taghrībirdī says that he was blond and tall he adds that he was not known for being a good Muslim (*lam yushhar bi-dīn*), see Ibn Taghrībirdī, *al-Manhal al-Ṣāfī*, 2: 489. Other historians add that he was exploitative and greedy, see al-Malaṭī, *Nayl al-Amal*, 5: 29. This shows how pale appearance was closely related to negative perceptions, and how important it was in constructing the image of the non-Turks as the "other."

328 Al-ʿAbbāsī, *Āthār al-Uwal*, 229–230. Al-ʿAbbāsī probably did not mention in this context the Circassian *mamlūks* because his treatise was dedicated to the Circassian sultan al-Muẓaffar Baybars al-Jāshankīr.

329 Müller, *Die Kunst des Sklavenkaufs*, 87. Although the description of Armenian slaves comes from an eleventh century treatise it fits the general description of Armenians in Mamluk sources. There is no reason to believe that the perceptions reflected in this text have changed. The following descriptions of Franks and Circassians come from a Mamluk treatise.

330 Al-Maqrīzī, *Kitāb al-Muqaffá*, 2: 224–6; Ibn Ḥajar al-ʿAsqalānī, *al-Durar*, 1: 228.

331 Al-Ṣafadī, *Aʿyān al-ʿAṣr*, 1: 535; Ibn Ḥajar al-ʿAsqalānī, *al-Durar*, 1: 226; al-Maqrīzī, *Kitāb al-Muqaffá*, 2: 190.

332 Müller, *Die Kunst des Sklavenkaufs*, 132.

333 Al-Malaṭī, *al-Majmaʿ al-Mufannan*, 734; idem, *al-Rawḍ al-Bāsim*, 4: 111–12.

334 Muḥammad ibn Aḥmad Ibn Iyās, *Badāʾiʿ al-Zuhūr fī Waqāʾiʿ al-Duhūr*, ed. P. Kahle and Muḥammad Muṣṭafá (Istanbul: Maṭbaʿat al-Dawla, 1931), 4: 466.

because he was said to have killed several persons and taken their money, and attacked women.[335] Al-Malaṭī reports that he had a Frankish slave from Sardinia (*min ʿulūj Sardīnya*) who converted to Islam and was manumitted by him. Al-Malaṭī says that he treated the slave kindly and trusted him, and the slave acted as if he loved al-Malaṭī a lot and as if he was his obedient servant. But all this was just a deceit. At some point he convinced al-Malaṭī to let him go to Beirut to sell al-Malaṭī's slaves but after leaving he renounced Islam (*irtadda*) and returned to Sardinia.[336] Later on al-Malaṭī found out that "this dog my slave in fact remained a Christian all the time keeping his infidel belief to himself and pretending that he was a Muslim" (*hādhā al-kalb mamlūkī kāna bāqiyan ʿalá dīn al-naṣrāniyya mubṭin al-kufr muẓhir al-islām*).[337] Al-Malaṭī adds that a Jew cooperated with the Frankish slave in the scheme.[338]

As for Rūmīs, Bahādur Ḥalāwa (d. 1343) is described as blond with blue eyes and cruel.[339] Al-Kāmil Shaʿbān (d. 1346), al-Nāṣir Muḥammad's son from a Rūmī slave-girl, was said to be the only one of his brothers who was blond with blue eyes (*ḥilyatuhu dūna ikhwatihi annahu ashqar azraq al-ʿaynayn*),[340] and that "he combined between ugly looks and ugly deeds" (*jamaʿa bayna qabīḥ al-shikl wal-fiʿl*).[341] It was also said that he drank wine and entertained himself with women.[342] In 1349 a Rūmī slave-girl was executed because she killed her master. No slave-girl before her was known to have killed her master.[343] In 1490 a group of Rūmī *mamlūks* was caught drinking wine in the middle of the day.[344] The Rūmī amir Iyās al-Muḥammadī al-Nāṣirī (d. 1472) known as "the tall" (*al-ṭawīl*) is said to have been an exploitative person and a sinner who used to drink wine and practice pederasty. He even made a special glass from gold for wine drinking. Al-Malaṭī's father reported that he saw him on a Friday in the Mosque of Tripoli smelling of wine.[345] Taghrībirdī al-Sayfī Lājīn (d. 1487) a blond Rūmī is said to have been a Ḥurūfī Shīʿī, a heretic, and a godless person (*mulḥid*), who claimed to be Messiah and even God. He believed that pederasty, wine drinking, and illicit

335 Shams al-Dīn Muḥammad ibn ʿAlī Ibn Ṭūlūn, *Mufākahat al-Khillān fī Ḥawādith al-Zamān*, ed. Khalīl al-Manṣūr (Beirut: Dār al-Kutub al-ʿIlmiyya, 1998), 191.
336 Al-Malaṭī, *al-Rawḍ al-Bāsim*, 2: 229–30.
337 Ibid., 2: 294.
338 Ibid., 2: 295.
339 Al-Ṣafadī, *Aʿyān al-ʿAṣr*, 2: 65.
340 Ibid., 2: 522.
341 Ibn Iyās, *Badāʾiʿ al-Zuhūr*, 1: 159.
342 Al-Malaṭī, *Nayl al-Amal*, 1: 131.
343 Ibid., 1: 185.
344 Ibid., 8: 199.
345 Idem, *al-Majmaʿ al-Mufannan*, 608, 610.

sex (*zinā*) are all permissible. When asked on what his beliefs are based he replied that a Christian scholar from Tripoli told him so.[346]

As for Circassians, according to books of advice for those interested in buying slaves, the pale among the Circassians are said to be cruel, disloyal and ugly.[347] The blond hair of the Circassian Lājīn al-Manṣūrī (d. 1299) was related to his treachery and untrustworthiness.[348] He is also said to have been drinking wine excessively in his youth.[349] At least according to al-Malaṭī, already during the Turkish period the Ciracssians were considered to be stupid (*qalīlū al-ʿaql*) and very troublesome people (*kathīrū al-fitan*), who harmed the religion of Islam and the Muslims.[350] Al-Maqrīzī attributed al-Ẓāhir Barqūq the introduction of pederasty and bribery into the Mamluk Sultanate.[351] The Circassian amir ʿAlībāy min Amīr ʿAlam (d. 1421) was said to have had "the lightheadedness of the Circassians" (*khiffat al-jarākisa*);[352] thus we learn that the Circassans were also considered to be frivolous. Uzbak al-Naṣrānī (d. 1479), who was most probably a Circassian,[353] is depicted as an evil sinner (*fājir*).[354] According to Ayalon, his nickname ("the Christian") was given to him because of his bad deeds, and therefore he was not necessarily a Christian.[355] In light of the afore-mentioned evidence, however, it may well be another case of negative attitudes towards a Christian *mamlūk* (at least in his past). The amir Jānibak al-Nāṣirī (d. 1467) was known as "the apostate" (*al-murtadd*). Some said that he was nicknamed *al-murtadd* only because after the death of his master al-Nāṣir Faraj he returned to Circassia, and later on returned once again to Egypt. Others have insisted, however, that he renounced Islam and converted to Islam once again upon his return to Egypt.[356] Be that as it may, it is clear that some have suspected the sincerity of the Islam of the Circassians. The biographical entry of the Circassian amir Iyāz al-Jurjāwī (d. 1396) in the history book of Ibn Ḥijjī (d. 1413) is probably the best example for the negative attitudes towards Circassian *mamlūks*:

346 Ibid., 745–6, 748.
347 Müller, *Die Kunst des Sklavenkaufs*, 131.
348 Al-ʿAynī, *ʿIqd al-Jumān*, 3: 267, 434.
349 Al-Maqrīzī, *al-Sulūk*, 1: 861.
350 Al-Malaṭī, *Nayl al-Amal*, 1: 156; for other examples of negative attitudes towards the Circassians, apparently already during the Turkish period, see Ayalon, "The Circassians," 138; and see also al-Ṣafadī, *al-Wāfī*, 10: 296.
351 Levanoni, "Al-Maqrīzī's Account," 101; Sami G. Massoud, "Al-Maqrīzī as a Historian of the Reign of Barqūq," *Mamlūk Studies Review* 7/2 (2003): 121.
352 Ibn Taghrībirdī, *al-Manhal al-Ṣāfī*, 8: 252–5; and see Ayalon, "The Circassians," 144.
353 Yosef, "Ethnic Groups," 1: 123, 160.
354 Al-Malaṭī, *Nayl al-Amal*, 8: 145–6.
355 Ayalon, "Names," 223.
356 Al-Malaṭī, *al-Rawḍ al-Bāsim*, 3: 227.

> The high-ranking amir Iyāz the Circassian… he was unjust (*ẓālim*) and exploiting (*ghāshim*)… he spent five years [in Damascus] exploiting the people in all manner of exploitation, unheard of in other people. Not only that, he was also a dubious Muslim (*muttaham fī dīnihi*). He respected the Christians and associated with the Franks. He gave them respect and preferred them over the Muslims. It was said that he had seven wives simultaneously and some of his deeds may indicate that he even stopped being a Muslim.[357]

Other historians also mention that he was ugly (*bashiʿ al-manẓar*).[358]

3.4.3. The Identity of Non-Turks – Lack of Knowledge of the Arabic Language

There is much evidence that non-Turkish *mamlūk*s tended not to know Arabic.[359] For example, we are informed that Aqqūsh al-Mawṣilī (d. 1293) "did not speak Turkish much because he was Armenian" (*kāna qalīlan yataḥaddathu bi-lisān al-turkiyya fa-innahu kāna jinsuhu armanī*).[360] It is clear that a non-Turkish *mamlūk* who was struggling to learn the Turkish language[361] would have been hard put to also learn Arabic. As for Circassians, it is said that the Circassian Burdbak al-Ẓāhirī Jaqmaq al-Mashṭūb (d. 1470) did not know much Arabic, and that in this respect "he was like all the Circassians" (*wa-huwa ʿalá ḥālat al-jarākisa*).[362] Some Circassian amirs could not speak Turkish, not to mention Arabic.[363] It is reported that a Turkmen from Aleppo who wanted to pretend that he was a Circassian, deliberately spoke broken Arabic.[364] As for Rūmīs, the amir Taghrībirdī al-Maḥmūdī al-Rūmī (d. 1432) "spoke somewhat deficient Arabic, like the Rūmīs usually do" (*wa-kāna bi-lisānihi baʿḍ ʿujma ka-mā huwa ʿādat jins al-rūm*).[365] The amir Taghrībirdī al-Mu'dhī al-Baklamushī (d. 1442) spoke eloquent Arabic (*kāna faṣīḥ fī kalāmihi bi-lughat al-ʿarab*), and although he was a Rūmī pretended that he was a "Turk" (*wa-kāna rūmī al-jins wa-yaddaʿī huwa*

357 Aḥmad ibn ʿAlāʾ al-Dīn Ibn Ḥijjī, *Taʾrīkh Ibn Ḥijjī*, ed. Abū Yaḥyá ʿAbd Allāh al-Kundarī (Beirut: Dār Ibn Ḥazm, 2003), 1: 204.

358 Ibn Taghrībirdī, *al-Nujūm*, 12: 156.

359 For the full analysis, see Yosef, "Ethnic Groups," 1: 154–6; 2: 176. Until al-Nāṣir Muḥammad's third reign, lack of knowledge of the Arabic language seems to have been connected mainly to Mongols but also to non-Turks. During the Circassian period, lack of knowledge of the Arabic language is attributed only to non-Turks.

360 Qaraṭāy al-ʿIzzī al-Khāzindārī, *Taʾrīkh Majmūʿ al-Nawādir*, 308.

361 Ayalon mentioned the "deficient Turkish speech" of the non-Turkish *mamlūk*s as a factor that may have contributed to the differentiation between them and the Turks: see Ayalon, "Baḥrī Mamlūks, Burjī Mamlūks," 44.

362 ʿAlī ibn Dāʾūd al-Ṣayrafī, *Inbāʾ al-Haṣr bi-Abnāʾ al-ʿAṣr*, ed. Ḥasan Ḥabashī (Cairo: Dār al-Fikr al-ʿArabī, 1970), 302.

363 Ibn Taghrībirdī, *al-Nujūm*, 15: 555, 69.

364 Al-Malaṭī, *al-Majmaʿ al-Mufannan*, 754.

365 Ibn Taghrībirdī, *al-Manhal al-Ṣāfī*, 4: 54.

annahu turkī).[366] It implies that normally Rūmīs did not know Arabic properly, and no less importantly that Turco-Mongols did.

It is well known that "the production of literary works in Turkish mostly seems to have been a late development that reached its peak in the Circassian period."[367] The fact that more works in Turkish have been produced during the Circassian period than in the earlier Qipchaq Turkish period has been considered "one of the curious features of the Circassian period."[368] What may explain this phenomenon, it has been suggested, is that some form of Turkish remained the military *lingua franca*.[369] This, however, does not explain why specifically during the Circassian period more works have been produced in Turkish. What may well explain this is that non-Turks, and more specifically Circassians, tended not to know Arabic and thus more inclined towards Turkish as a literary language.

The fact that non-Turks tended not to know Arabic only worsened their situation. During the fifteenth century, the Circassian ruling elite preferred to sponsor non-Arab foreign Turkish (or Persian)-speaking Ḥanafī scholars[370] and this made the local Arab Shāfiʿīs turn against them.[371] A relation of Mamluk amirs to Ḥanafī or foreign (*ʿajam*) scholars was sometimes linked to lack of faith in Islam or un-Islamic behavior.[372] It has been noted that by and large, Circassian-

366 Al-Malaṭī, *al-Majmaʿ al-Mufannan*, 737.

367 Robert Irwin, "Mamluk Literature," *Mamlūk Studies Review* 7 (2003): 3; and see also Haarmann, "Arabic in Speech," 90; Reuven Amitai, "Echoes of the Eurasian Steppe in the Daily Culture of Mamluk Military Society," *Journal of the Royal Asiatic Society* 26/1–2 (2016): 264.

368 Irwin, "Mamluk Literature," 3; and see also Amitai, "Echoes of the Eurasian Steppe," 264.

369 Irwin, "Mamluk Literature," 3.

370 See for example Jonathan P. Berkey, *The Transmission of Knowledge in Medieval Cairo: A Social History of Islamic Education* (Princeton: Princeton University Press, 1992), 147; Carl F. Petry, *The Civilian Elite of Cairo in the Later Middle Ages* (Princeton: Princeton University Press, 1981), 70–2; Leonor E. Fernandes, "Mamluk Politics and Education: The Evidence from Two Fourteenth Century Waqfiyya," *Annales islamologiques* 23 (1987): 87–98 (esp. 89); Ulrich Haarmann, "The Late Triumph of the Persian Bow: Critical Voices on the Mamluk Monopoly on Weaponry," in *The Mamluks in Egyptian Politics and Society*, ed. Thomas Philipp and Ulrich Haarmann (Cambridge: Cambridge University Press, 1998), 178; Amalia Levanoni, "A Supplementary Source for the Study of Mamluk Social History: The *Taqārīẓ*," *Arabica* 60/1–2 (2013): 149, 155, 170–5.

371 Anne F. Broadbridge, "Academic Rivalry and the Patronage System in Fifteenth-Century Egypt: al-ʿAynī, al-Maqrīzī, and Ibn Ḥajar al-ʿAsqalānī," *Mamlūk Studies Review* 3 (1999): 86–7, 93–7; Amalia Levanoni, "Who Were the 'Salt of the Earth' in Fifteenth-Century Egypt?," *Mamlūk Studies Review* 14 (2010): 79, 82; Irwin, "Mamluk History and Historians," 168; Little, "Historiography," 437–8; Holt, "Literary Offerings," 8.

372 According to al-Maqrīzī, a Ḥanafī scholar (who functioned as an envoy to Tīmūr) told al-Ẓāhir Barqūq that wine drinking is licit according to his school of law, see Ibn Qāḍī Shuhba, *Taʾrīkh Ibn Qāḍī Shuhba*, 4: 427; al-Maqrīzī says that the amir Baysaq al-Shaykhī (d. 1418) was an enthusiastic supporter of the Ḥanafī school, and then mentions that he was an evil and exploitative person, al-Maqrīzī, *al-Sulūk*, 4: 474; According to Ibn Qāḍī Shuhba, Buzlār al-ʿUmarī al-Nāṣirī (d. 1389) was lacking in faith (*fasād ʿaqīda*) because he associated with

period historians maintained some distance from the regime.[373] The sharpest critics of the Circassian regime and by extension of the Circassian ethnic group and non-Turks in general, were local Arab Shāfiʿī historians who dominated historical writing during that era, notably al-Maqrīzī (d. 1442),[374] but also Ibn Ḥajar al-ʿAsqalānī (d. 1449)[375] and al-Sakhāwī (d. 1497).[376] It has been noted that the chronicle of the Turkish-speaking Ḥanafī historian al-ʿAynī who enjoyed the patronage of several Circassian sultans took a more favorable view of the Circassian regime.[377] It would be interesting to check if his chronicle also shows more favorable views towards Circassians and non-Turks in general. Modern scholars usually maintain that the negative perception of the Sultanate's Circassian period which predominates in the writings of Circassian-period authors has to do with the latter's perception of the Turkish period as a golden era and their period as one of decline.[378] It should be added, however, that, as we have seen, negative perceptions towards non-Turks, and specifically Circassians, existed already in the Turkish period. The growing cultural-linguistic barrier between the *mamlūk* ruling elite and the local Arab Shāfiʿī civilian elite, and the loss of patronage which it entailed, must have encouraged Circassian-period Arab Shāfiʿī historians to preserve negative perceptions towards non-Turks, and more specifically the Circassians, which existed already during the Turkish period of the Sultanate.

---

foreigners (*li-kathrat mulāzamatihi al-ʿajam*), Ibn Qāḍī Shuhba, *Taʾrīkh Ibn Qāḍī Shuhba*, 1: 307.

373 Li Guo, "History Writing," in *The New Cambridge History of Islam*, Vol. 4: *Islamic Cultures and Societies to the End of the Eighteenth Century*, ed. Robert Irwin (Cambridge: Cambridge University Press, 2010), 450.

374 Irwin, "Mamluk History and Historians," 167; Levanoni, "al-Maqrīzī's Account," 94–5, 102–3; Massoud, "Al-Maqrīzī as a Historian," 129–30.

375 Irwin, "Mamluk Literature," 26.

376 Idem, "Mamluk History and Historians," 169. Other prominent Shāfiʿī historians during the Circassian period were al-Qalqashandī (d. 1418) and al-Biqāʿī (d. 1480) in Egypt, and Ibn Ḥijjī (d. 1413 or 1414) and Ibn Qāḍī Shuhba (d. 1448) in Syria.

377 Donald P. Little, "A Comparison of al-Maqrīzī and al-ʿAynī as Historians of Contemporary Events," *Mamlūk Studies Review* 7/2 (2003): 207, 215; Irwin, "Mamluk History and Historians," 168.

378 See for example David Ayalon, "Some Remarks on the Economic Decline of the Mamlūk Sultanate," *Jerusalem Studies in Arabic and Islam* 16 (1993): 110, 113; Irwin, "Mamluk History and Historians," 168; Little, "Historiography," 440; Anne F. Broadbridge, "Royal Authority, Justice, and Order in Society: The Influence of Ibn Khaldūn on the Writings of al-Maqrīzī and Ibn Taghrībirdī," *Mamlūk Studies Review* 7/2 (2003): 233–4; Nasser Rabbat, "Was al-Maqrīzī's Khiṭaṭ a Khaldūnian History?," *Der Islam* 89/1–2 (2012): 130.

Concluding Words: Social and Political Consequences of the Attitudes towards Non-Turkish *mamlūks*

As already mentioned, the reason for these perceptions during the Turkish period was cross-boundary hatred towards Christians, which resulted in the discrimination of non-Turkish *mamlūks* and possibly had critical implications for the Sultanate. There is some evidence that already in the Turkish period non-Turkish *mamlūks* started families at a later age than their Turkish peers, and this may be related to evidence that they were manumitted at a later age.[379] More importantly, during the Turkish period as soon as the non-Turkish *mamlūks* entered the Sultanate, their connection to their families was severed forever. Whereas the Turkish *mamlūk* had the option of becoming a favored *mamlūk*, marrying into the Qalāwūnid family, establishing a family while still young, and of bringing his relatives into the Sultanate, this option was almost totally closed to non-Turkish *mamlūks*, at least starting from the days of al-Nāṣir Muḥammad. Since the creation of a family was the only way to ultimately shed one's slave status, the non-Turkish *mamlūks* could not fully leave behind this status even after manumission, and were probably perceived by their contemporaries as being "more slaves" than the Turkish *mamlūks*.[380] In the absence of a family the non-Turkish *mamlūks* started ascribing greater importance to *mamlūk* ties.[381] Not only was the Mamluk Sultanate connected to its surroundings and affected by its ever-changing circumstances, but these circumstances perhaps eventually contributed to make it what it is so famous for, that is, *mamlūk*.

379 Yosef, "The Term *Mamlūk*," 24–7; and see idem, "Ethnic Groups," 1: 215–23, 246–50, 272–3.

380 Idem, "Mamluks and Their Relatives," 56–69 (especially 56–60). During the Turkish period we also find expressions of contempt and disrespect towards non-Turkish *mamlūks*. When the Circassian amir Qarā Sunqur al-Manṣūrī (d. 1327) was pursued by al-Nāṣir Muḥammad, he was advised to turn himself in. He refused, claiming that al-Nāṣir Muḥammad would surely kill him, because he was originally just "a piece of Circassian slave" (*qiṭʿat mamlūk jarkasī*), Ibn al-Dawādārī, *Kanz al-Durar*, 9: 224. It should also be noted that during the days of al-Manṣūr Qalāwūn, only four names are attested to have been commonly given to non-Turkish *mamlūks*, and starting from al-Nāṣir Muḥammad's third reign and until the Circassian period they were given significantly less names than Turco-Mongols, see Yosef, "The Names of the *Mamlūks*"; idem, "Ethnic Groups," 1: 30–80. This may be yet another indication for feelings of contempt and disrespect towards non-Turks during the Turkish period. When one gives the same four names to hundreds of *mamlūks* of different ethnic origins he actually treats them as chattel and not as human beings. The fact that non-Turks tended not to know Arabic must have also contributed to their perception as "more slaves" than the Turkish *mamlūks*.

381 Koby Yosef, "*Ikhwa*, *Muwākhūn* and *Khushdāshiyya* in the Mamlūk Sultanate," *Jerusalem Studies in Arabic and Islam* 40 (2013): 335–58 (especially 355–8); idem, "Ethnic Groups," 1: 203–32; and see also idem, "Masters and Slaves: Substitute Kinship in the Mamluk Sultanate," in *Egypt and Syria in the Fāṭimid, Ayyūbid and Mamlūk Eras VIII*, ed. Urbain Vermeulen, Kristof D'hulster, and Jo Van Steenbergen (Leuven: Peeters, 2016), 576–9.

Bibliography

Primary Sources

al-ʿAbbāsī, al-Ḥasan ibn ʿAbd Allāh. *Āthār al-Uwal fī Tartīb al-Duwal*. Ed. ʿAbd al-Raḥmān ʿUmayra. Beirut: Dār al-Jīl, 1989.

Abū al-Fidāʾ, ʿImād al-Dīn Ismāʿīl ibn ʿAlī. *Al-Mukhtaṣar fī Akhbār al-Bashar*. Cairo: Al-Maṭbaʿa al-Ḥusayniyya al-Miṣriyya, 1907. 4 vols.

Abū al-Fidāʾ, ʿImād al-Dīn Ismāʿīl ibn ʿAlī. *Kitāb Taqwīm al-Buldān*. Ed. Raynūd and al-Barūn Māk Kūkīn Dīslān. Paris: Dār al-Ṭibāʿa al-Sulṭāniyya, 1840.

al-ʿAynī, Badr al-Dīn Maḥmūd. *ʿIqd al-Jumān fī Taʾrīkh Ahl al-Zamān*. Ed. Muḥammad Muḥammad Amīn. Cairo: Dār al-Kutub wal-Wathāʾiq al-Qawmiyya, 2009–2010. 5 vols.

al-ʿAynī, Badr al-Dīn Maḥmūd. *ʿIqd al-Jumān fī Taʾrīkh Ahl al-Zamān*. Ed. ʿAbd al-Razzāq al-Ṭanṭāwī al-Qarmūṭ. Cairo: al-Zahrāʾ lil-Iʿlām al-ʿArabī, 1989.

al-ʿAynī, Badr al-Dīn Maḥmūd. *Al-Sulṭān Barqūq Muʾassis Dawlat al-Mamālīk al-Jarākisa 1382–1398 Mīlādī/784–801 Hijrī: min khilāl Makhṭūṭ ʿIqd al-Jumān fī Taʾrīkh Ahl al-Zamān li-Badr al-Dīn al-ʿAynī*. Ed. Īmān ʿUmar Shukrī. Cairo: Maktabat Madbūlī, 2002.

Baybars al-Manṣūrī al-Dawādār. *Al-Tuḥfa al-Mulūkiyya fī al-Dawla al-Turkiyya*. Ed. ʿAbd al-Ḥamīd Ṣāliḥ Ḥamdān. Beirut: Al-Dār al-Miṣriyya al-Lubnāniyya, 1987.

al-Dhahabī, Shams al-Dīn Muḥammad ibn Aḥmad. *Kitāb Duwal al-Islām*. Ed. Fahīm Muḥammad Shaltūt. Egypt: Al-Hayʾa al-Miṣriyya al-ʿĀmma lil-Kitāb, 1974. 2 vols.

al-Dhahabī, Shams al-Dīn Muḥammad ibn Aḥmad. *Al-ʿIbar fī Khabar Man Ghabar*. Ed. Abū Hājar Muḥammad al-Saʿīd ibn Basyūnī Zaghlūl. Beirut: Dār al-Kutub al-ʿIlmiyya, 1985. 4 vols.

al-Dhahabī, Shams al-Dīn Muḥammad ibn Aḥmad. *Al-Mukhtār min Taʾrīkh Ibn al-Jazarī*. Ed. Khuḍayr ʿAbbās Muḥammad Khalīfa al-Munshadāwī. Beirut: Dār al-Kitāb al-ʿArabī, 1988.

al-Dhahabī, Shams al-Dīn Muḥammad ibn Aḥmad. *Siyar Aʿlām al-Nubalāʾ*. Ed. Muḥammad Ayman. Cairo: Dār al-Ḥadīth, 2006. 18 vols.

al-Dhahabī, Shams al-Dīn Muḥammad ibn Aḥmad. *Taʾrīkh al-Islām wa-Wafayāt al-Mashāhīr wal-Aʿlām*. Ed. ʿUmar ʿAbd al-Salām Tadmurī. Beirut: Dār al-Kitāb al-ʿArabī, 1989–2004. 53 vols.

al-Ghazzī, Najm al-Dīn Muḥammad ibn Muḥammad. *Al-Kawākib al-Sāʾira bi-Aʿyān al-Miʾa al-ʿĀshira*. Ed. Khalīl Manṣūr. Beirut: Dār al-Kutub al-ʿIlmiyya, 1997. 3 vols.

Ibn ʿAbd al-Ẓāhir, Muḥyī al-Dīn ʿAbd Allāh. *Tashrīf al-Ayyām wal-ʿUṣūr fī Sīrat al-Malik al-Manṣūr*. Ed. Murād Kāmil. Cairo: Al-Sharika al-ʿArabiyya lil-Ṭibāʿa wal-Nashr, 1961.

Ibn ʿArabshāh, Shihāb al-Dīn Aḥmad ibn Muḥammad. *Kitāb ʿAjāʾib al-Maqdūr fī Akhbār Tīmūr*. Ed. Aḥmad ibn Muḥammad ibn ʿAlī al-Anṣārī al-Yamanī al-Shirwānī. Calcutta: no publisher, 1232 [1817].

Ibn al-Dawādārī, Abū Bakr ibn ʿAbd Allāh. *Kanz al-Durar wa-Jāmiʿ al-Ghurar*. Ed. H.R. Roemer. Cairo: Qism al-Dirāsāt al-Islāmiyya bil-Maʿhad al-Almānī lil-Āthār, 1960–1982. 9 vols.

Ibn Duqmāq, Ṣārim al-Dīn Ibrāhīm ibn Muḥammad ibn Aydamur. *Nuzhat al-Anām fī Taʾrīkh al-Islām*. Ed. Samīr Ṭabbāra. Beirut: Al-Maktaba al-ʿAṣriyya, 1999.

Ibn al-Furāt, Nāṣir al-Dīn Muḥammad. *Taʾrīkh al-Duwal wal-Mulūk*. Ed. Q. Zurayk and N. ʿIzz al-Dīn. Vols. 7–9. Beirut: Al-Maṭbaʿa al-Amrīkāniyya, 1936–1942.

(pseudo) Ibn al-Fuwaṭī. *Kitāb al-Ḥawādith li-Muʾallif min al-Qarn al-Thāmin al-Hijrī wa-Huwa al-Kitāb al-Musammá Wahman bil-Ḥawādith al-Jāmiʿa wal-Tajārib al-Nāfiʿa wal-Mansūb li-Ibn al-Fuwaṭī*. Ed. Mahdī al-Najm. Beirut: Dār al-Kutub al-ʿIlmiyya, 1997.

Ibn Ḥajar al-ʿAsqalānī, Aḥmad ibn ʿAlī. *Al-Durar al-Kāmina fī Aʿyān al-Miʾa al-Thāmina*. Ed. ʿAbd al-Wārith Muḥammad ʿAlī. Beirut: Dār al-Kutub al-ʿIlmiyya, 1997. 4 vols.

Ibn Ḥajar al-ʿAsqalānī, Aḥmad ibn ʿAlī. *Dhayl al-Durar al-Kāmina fī Aʿyān al-Miʾa al-Thāmina*. Ed. Aḥmad Farīd al-Mazīdī. Beirut: Dār al-Kutub al-ʿIlmiyya, 1998.

Ibn Ḥijjī, Aḥmad ibn ʿAlāʾ al-Dīn. *Taʾrīkh Ibn Ḥijjī*. Ed. Abū Yaḥyá ʿAbd Allāh al-Kundarī. Beirut: Dār Ibn Ḥazm, 2003. 2 vols.

Ibn al-ʿImād, ʿAbd al-Ḥayy ibn Aḥmad ibn Muḥammad. *Shadharāt al-Dhahab fī Akhbār Man Dhahab*. Ed. Maḥmūd al-Arnāʾūṭ. Beirut, Damascus: Dār Ibn Kathīr, 1986. 11 vols.

Ibn Iyās, Muḥammad ibn Aḥmad. *Badāʾiʿ al-Zuhūr fī Waqāʾiʿ al-Duhūr*. Cairo: Maṭābiʿ al-Shaʿb, 1960. 2 vols.

Ibn Iyās, Muḥammad ibn Aḥmad. *Badāʾiʿ al-Zuhūr fī Waqāʾiʿ al-Duhūr*. Ed. P. Kahle and Muḥammad Muṣṭafá. Vol. 4. Istanbul: Maṭbaʿat al-Dawla, 1931.

Ibn Kathīr, Abū al-Fidāʾ Ismāʿīl ibn ʿUmar. *Al-Bidāya wal-Nihāya fī al-Taʾrīkh*. Beirut: Dār al-Maʿārif, 1966. 14 vols.

Ibn Khaldūn, ʿAbd al-Raḥmān ibn Muḥammad. *Muqaddimat Ibn Khaldūn wa-Huwa al-Juzʾ al-Awwal min Taʾrīkh Ibn Khaldūn al-Musammá Dīwān al-Mubtadaʾ wal-Khabar fī Taʾrīkh al-ʿArab wal-ʿAjam wal-Barbar wa-Man ʿĀṣarahum min Dhawī al-Shaʾn al-Akbar*. Ed. Khalīl Shaḥḥāda. Beirut: Dār al-Fikr, 1988.

Ibn Manjlī, Muḥammad. *Kitāb Uns al-Malā bi-Waḥsh al-Falā*. Ed. Muḥammad ʿĪsá Ṣāliḥiyya. Amman: Dār al-Bashīr, Beirut: Muʾassasat al-Risāla, 1993.

Ibn Qāḍī Shuhba, Abū Bakr ibn Aḥmad. *Taʾrīkh Ibn Qāḍī Shuhba*. Ed. ʿAdnān Darwīsh. Damascus: Institut français de Damas, 1977–1997. 4 vols.

Ibn Shaddād, Muḥammad ibn ʿAlī ibn Ibrāhīm. *Taʾrīkh al-Malik al-Ẓāhir*. Ed. Aḥmad Ḥuṭayṭ. Wiesbaden: Franz Steiner Verlag, 1983.

Ibn Taghrībirdī, Yūsuf. *Ḥawādith al-Duhūr fī Madá al-Ayyām wal-Shuhūr*. Ed. Muḥammad Kamāl al-Dīn ʿIzz al-Dīn. Beirut: ʿĀlam al-Kutub, 1990. 2 vols.

Ibn Taghrībirdī, Yūsuf. *Kitāb al-Nujūm al-Zāhira fī Mulūk Miṣr wal-Qāhira*. Ed. Fahīm Muḥammad Shaltūt et al. Cairo: Dār al-Kutub al-Miṣriyya, 1963–1972. 16 vols.

Ibn Taghrībirdī, Yūsuf. *Al-Manhal al-Ṣāfī wal-Mustawfá baʿda al-Wāfī*. Ed. Muḥammad Muḥammad Amīn. Cairo: Al-Hayʾa al-Miṣriyya al-ʿĀmma lil-Kitāb, 1984–2006. 12 vols.

Ibn Ṭūlūn, Shams al-Dīn Muḥammad ibn ʿAlī. *Mufākahat al-Khillān fī Ḥawādith al-Zamān*. Ed. Khalīl al-Manṣūr. Beirut: Dār al-Kutub al-ʿIlmiyya, 1998.

al-Malaṭī, ʿAbd al-Bāsiṭ ibn Khalīl ibn Shāhīn al-Ẓāhirī. *Al-Majmaʿ al-Mufannan bil-Muʿjam al-Muʿanwan*. Ed. ʿAbd Allāh Muḥammad al-Kundarī. Kuwait: Dār al-Nashr al-Islāmiyya, 2011.

al-Malaṭī, ʿAbd al-Bāsiṭ ibn Khalīl ibn Shāhīn al-Ẓāhirī. *Nayl al-Amal fī Dhayl al-Duwal*. Ed. ʿUmar ʿAbd al-Salām Tadmurī. Beirut and Ṣaydā: Al-Maktaba al-ʿAṣriyya, 2002. 9 vols.

al-Malaṭī, ʿAbd al-Bāsiṭ ibn Khalīl ibn Shāhīn al-Ẓāhirī. *Nuzhat al-Asāṭīn fī Man Waliya Miṣr min al-Salāṭīn*. Ed. Muḥammad Kamāl al-Dīn ʿIzz al-Dīn. Cairo: Maktabat al-Thaqāfa al-Dīniyya, 1987.

al-Malaṭī, ʿAbd al-Bāsiṭ ibn Khalīl ibn Shāhīn al-Ẓāhirī. *Al-Rawḍ al-Bāsim fī Ḥawādith al-ʿUmur wal-Tarājim*. Ed. ʿUmar ʿAbd al-Salām Tadmurī. Beirut: Al-Maktaba al-ʿAṣriyya, 2014. 4 vols.

Mandeville, John. "The Book of Sir John Maundeville. A.D. 1322–1356." In *Early Travels in Palestine, Comprising the Narratives of Arculf, Willibald, Bernard, Säwulf, Sigurd, Benjamin of Tudela, Sir John Maundeville, De la Brocquière, and Maundrell*. Ed. Thomas Wright. London: Henry G. Bohn, 1848. 127–182.

al-Maqdisī, Abū Ḥāmid Muḥibb al-Dīn Muḥammad ibn Khalīl. *Kitāb Duwal al-Islām al-Sharīfa al-Bahiyya wa-Dhikr mā Ẓahara lī min Ḥikam Allāh al-Khafiyya fī Jalb Ṭāʾifat al-Atrāk ilá al-Diyār al-Miṣriyya*. Ed. Ṣubḥī Labīb and Ulrich Haarmann. Beirut: Orient-Institut der Deutschen Morgenländischen Gesellschaft, 1997.

al-Maqrīzī, Taqī al-Dīn Aḥmad ibn ʿAlī. *Durar al-ʿUqūd al-Farīda fī Tarājim al-Aʿyān al-Mufīda*. Ed. Maḥmūd al-Jalīlī. Beirut: Dār al-Gharb al-Islāmī, 2002. 4 vols.

al-Maqrīzī, Taqī al-Dīn Aḥmad ibn ʿAlī. *Kitāb al-Mawāʿiẓ wal-Iʿtibār bi-Dhikr al-Khiṭaṭ wal-Āthār*. Beirut: Dār Ṣadr, n.d. 2 vols.

al-Maqrīzī, Taqī al-Dīn Aḥmad ibn ʿAlī. *Kitāb al-Muqaffá al-Kabīr*. Ed. Muḥammad al-Yaʿlāwī. Beirut: Dār al-Gharb al-Islāmī, 1991. 8 vols.

al-Maqrīzī, Taqī al-Dīn Aḥmad ibn ʿAlī. *Kitāb al-Sulūk li-Maʿrifat Duwal al-Mulūk*. Ed. Muḥammad Muṣṭafá Ziyāda and Saʿīd ʿAbd al-Fattāḥ ʿĀshūr. Cairo: Dār al-Kutub al-Miṣriyya, 1934–1973. 4 vols.

al-Nuwayrī, Shihāb al-Dīn Aḥmad ibn ʿAbd al-Wahhāb. *Nihāyat al-Arab fī Funūn al-Adab*. Ed. Fahīm Muḥammad Shaltūt et al. Cairo: Al-Muʾassasa al-Miṣriyya al-ʿĀmma lil-Taʾlīf wal-Nashr, 1964–1998. 33 vols.

al-Qalqashandī, Shihāb al-Dīn Aḥmad ibn ʿAlī. *Ṣubḥ al-Aʿshá fī Ṣināʿat al-Inshāʾ*. Cairo: al-Maṭbaʿa al-Amīriyya, 1913–1919. 14 vols.

Qaraṭāy al-ʿIzzī al-Khāzindārī. *Taʾrīkh Majmūʿ al-Nawādir mimmā Jará lil-Awāʾil wal-Awākhir*. Ed. ʿUmar ʿAbd al-Salām Tadmurī. Ṣaydā and Beirut: al-Maktaba al-ʿAṣriyya, 2005.

al-Ṣafadī, Khalīl ibn Aybak. *Aʿyān al-ʿAṣr wa-Aʿwān al-Naṣr*. Ed. ʿAlī Abū Zayd. Beirut: Dār al-Fikr al-Muʿāṣir, 1998. 6 vols.

al-Ṣafadī, Khalīl ibn Aybak. *Al-Wāfī bil-Wafayāt*. Ed. Helmut Ritter et al. Wiesbaden: Franz Steiner Verlag, 1962–2004. 30 vols.

al-Sakhāwī, Muḥammad ibn ʿAbd al-Raḥmān. *Al-Ḍawʾ al-Lāmiʿ li-Ahl al-Qarn al-Tāsiʿ*. Beirut: Dār al-Jīl, 1992. 12 vols.

al-Ṣayrafī, ʿAli ibn Dāʾūd. *Inbāʾ al-Haṣr bi-Abnāʾ al-ʿAṣr*. Ed. Ḥasan Ḥabashī. Cairo: Dār al-Fikr al-ʿArabī, 1970.

Shāfiʿ ibn ʿAlī, *al-Faḍl al-Maʾthūr min Sīrat al-Sulṭān al-Malik al-Manṣūr*. Ed. ʿUmar ʿAbd al-Salām Tadmurī. Beirut: Al-Maktaba al-ʿAṣriyya, 1998.

al-Shujāʿī, Shams al-Dīn. *Taʾrīkh al-Malik al-Nāṣir Muḥammad b. Qalāwūn al-Ṣāliḥī wa-Awlādihi*. Ed. Barbara Schäfer, *Die Chronik aš-Šujāʿīs*. Wiesbaden: Franz Steiner Verlag, 1977.

al-ʿUmarī, Ibn Faḍl Allāh. *Kitāb Masālik al-Abṣār wa-Mamālik al-Amṣār*. Ed. ʿAbd Allāh ibn Yaḥyá al-Sarīḥī et al. Abu Dhabi: al-Majmaʿ al-Thaqāfī, 2001–2004. 14 vols.

Yāqūt al-Ḥamawī. *Muʿjam al-Buldān*. Ed. Farīd ʿAbd al-ʿAzīz al-Jundī. Beirut: Dār al-Kutub al-ʿIlmiyya, 1990. 7 vols.

al-Yūnīnī, Quṭb al-Dīn Mūsá ibn Muḥammad ibn Aḥmad. *Dhayl Mir'āt al-Zamān*. Hyderabad: Dā'irat al-Ma'ārif al-'Uthmāniyya, 1954–1961. 4 vols.

al-Yūnīnī, Quṭb al-Dīn Mūsá ibn Muḥammad ibn Aḥmad. *Dhayl Mir'āt al-Zamān: Ta'rīkh al-Sanawāt 697–711 H/1297–1312 M.* Ed. Ḥamza Aḥmad 'Abbās. Abu Dhabi: Hay'at Abū Ẓabī lil-Thaqāfa wal-Turāth, al-Majma' al-Thaqāfī, 2007. 3 vols.

al-Yūsufī, Mūsá ibn Muḥammad ibn Yaḥyá. *Nuzhat al-Nāẓir fī Sīrat al-Malik al-Nāṣir*. Ed. Aḥmad Ḥuṭayṭ. Beirut: 'Ālam al-Kutub, 1986.

Modern Studies

Aigle, Denise. "The Mongol Invasions of Bilād al-Shām by Ghāzān Khān and Ibn Taymīyah's Three 'Anti-Mongol' Fatwas." *Mamlūk Studies Review* 11/2 (2007): 89–120.

Aigle, Denise. *The Mongol Empire between Myth and Reality: Studies in Anthropological History*. Leiden: Brill, 2014.

Amitai, Reuven. "Diplomacy and the Slave Trade in the Eastern Mediterranean: A Re-Examination of the Mamluk Byzantine-Genoese Triangle in the Late Thirteenth Century in Light of the Existing Early Correspondence."*Oriente Moderno* 88/2 (2008): 349–368.

Amitai, Reuven. "Echoes of the Eurasian Steppe in the Daily Culture of Mamluk Military Society." *Journal of the Royal Asiatic Society* 26/1–2 (2016): 261–270.

Amitai, Reuven. "Ghazan, Islam and Mongol Tradition: A View from the Mamlūk Sultanate." *Bulletin of the School of Oriental and African Studies* 59/1 (1996): 1–10.

Amitai, Reuven. "Mamluks of Mongol Origin and Their Role in Early Mamluk Political Life." *Mamlūk Studies Review* 12/1 (2008): 119–137.

Amitai, Reuven. *Mongols and Mamluks: The Mamluk-Īlkhānid War, 1260–1281*. Cambridge: Cambridge University Press, 1995.

Amitai, Reuven. "Mongol Imperial Ideology and the Ilkhanid War against the Mamluks." In *The Mongol Empire and its Legacy*, ed. Reuven Amitai-Preiss and David Morgan. Leiden: Brill, 1999. 57–72.

Amitai, Reuven. "The Mongol Occupation of Damascus in 1300: A Study of Mamluk Loyalties." In *The Mamluks in Egyptian and Syrian Politics and Society*, ed. Amalia Levanoni and Michael Winter. Leiden: Brill, 2004. 21–41.

Amitai, Reuven. "Northern Syria between the Mongols and Mamluks: Political Boundary, Military Frontier, and Ethnic Affinities." In *Frontiers in Question: Eurasian Borderlands c. 700–1700*, ed. Naomi Standen and Daniel Power. London: Macmillan, 1999. 128–152.

Amitai, Reuven. "The Remaking of the Military Elite of Mamlūk Egypt by al-Nāṣir Muḥammad b. Qalāwūn." *Studia Islamica* 72 (1990): 145–163.

Amitai, Reuven. "The Resolution of the Mongol-Mamluk War." In *Mongols, Turks, and Others: Eurasian Nomads and the Sedentary World*, ed. Reuven Amitai and Michal Biran. Leiden: Brill, 2005. 359–390.

Arbel, Benjamin. "Slave Trade and Slave Labor in Frankish Cyprus (1191–1571)." *Studies in Medieval and Renaissance History* 14 (1993): 151–190.

Arbel, Benjamin. "Venetian Cyprus and the Muslim Levant, 1473–1570." In *Cyprus and the Crusades/Kypros kai oi Staurophories*, ed. Nicholas Coureas and Jonathan Riley-Smith.

Nicosia: Cyprus Research Centre and Society for the Study of the Crusades and the Latin East, 1995. 159–185.

Ashtor, Eliyahu. *Toldot ha-Yehudim bi-Mitsrayim ve-Suriya taḥat Shilton ha-Mamlukim* [The History of the Jews in Egypt and Syria und the Rule of the Mamluks]. Jerusalem: Mosad ha-Rav Quq she-ʿal Yad ha-Mazraḥi ha-ʿOlami, 1944, 1951 and 1970. 3 vols.

Atiya, A.S. "Ḳibṭ." *The Encyclopaedia of Islam.* 2nd Edition. Leiden: Brill, 1985. 5: 90–95.

Ayalon, David. "Baḥrī Mamlūks, Burjī Mamlūks – Inadequate Names for the Two Reigns of the Mamlūk Sultanate." *Tārīḫ* 1 (1990): 3–53.

Ayalon, David. "The Circassians in the Mamlūk Kingdom." *Journal of the American Oriental Society* 69 (1949): 135–147.

Ayalon, David. "The Great Yāsa of Chingiz Khān: A Re-examination." *Studia Islamica* 36 (1972): 113–158.

Ayalon, David. "Mamlūk: Military Slavery in Egypt and Syria." In D. Ayalon, *Islam and the Abode of War.* Aldershot: Variorum, 1994. Article II, 1–21.

Ayalon, David. "Names, Titles, and 'Nisbas' of the Mamluks." *Israel Oriental Studies* 5 (1975): 189–232.

Ayalon, David. "Some Remarks on the Economic Decline of the Mamlūk Sultanate." *Jerusalem Studies in Arabic and Islam* 16 (1993): 108–124.

Ayalon, David. "The Wafidiya in the Mamluk Kingdom." *Islamic Culture* 25 (1951): 89–104.

Barker, Hannah. "Egyptian and Italian Merchants in the Black Sea Slave Trade, 1260–1500." PhD dissertation, Columbia University, 2014.

Bauden, Frédéric. "Taqī al-Dīn Aḥmad ibn ʿAlī al-Maqrīzī." In *Medieval Muslim Historians and the Franks in the Levant*, ed. Alex Mallett. Leiden: Brill, 2014. 161–200.

Behrens-Abouseif, Doris. "The Baptistère de Saint Louis: A Reinterpretation." *Islamic Art* 3 (1988–1989): 3–13.

Behrens-Abouseif, Doris. "European Arts and Crafts at the Mamluk Court." *Muqarnas: An Annual on the Visual Culture of the Islamic World* 21 (2004): 45–54.

Behrens-Abouseif, Doris. "Mamluk Artistic Relations with Latin Europe." In *La frontière méditerranéenne du XVe au XVIIe siècle: Échanges, circulations et affrontements*, ed. Bernard Heyberger and Albrecht Fuess. Turnhout: Brepols Publishers, 2014. 351–374.

Behrens-Abouseif, Doris. "Mamluk Perceptions of Foreign Arts." In *The Arts of the Mamluks in Egypt and Syria – Evolution and Impact*, ed. Doris Behrens-Abouseif. Bonn: Bonn University Press, 2012. 307–318.

Behrens-Abouseif, Doris. *Practicing Diplomacy in the Mamluk Sultanate: Gifts and Material Culture in the Medieval Islamic World.* London: I.B. Tauris, 2014.

van den Bent, Josephine. "'None of the Kings on Earth is Their Equal in *ʿAṣabiyya*': The Mongols in Ibn Khaldūn's Works."*Al-Masāq* 28/2 (2016): 171–186.

Berkey, Jonathan P. "Mamluks and the World of Higher Islamic Education in Medieval Cairo, 1250–1517." In *Modes de transmission de la culture religieuse en Islam*, ed. Hassan Elboudrari. Cairo: Institut français d'archéologie orientale, 1993. 93–116.

Berkey, Jonathan P. *The Transmission of Knowledge in Medieval Cairo: A Social History of Islamic Education.* Princeton: Princeton University Press, 1992.

Berkey, Jonathan P. "The Mamluks as Muslims: The Military Elite and the Construction of Islam in Medieval Egypt." In *The Mamluks in Egyptian Politics and Society*, ed. Thomas Philipp and Ulrich Haarmann. Cambridge: Cambridge University Press, 1998. 163–173.

Birtalan, Agnes. "An Oirat Ethnogenetic Myth in Written and Oral Traditions." *Acta Orientalia Academiae Scientiarum Hung.* 55/1–3 (2002): 69–88.

Broadbridge, Anne F. "Academic Rivalry and the Patronage System in Fifteenth-Century Egypt: al-ʿAynī, al-Maqrīzī, and Ibn Ḥajar al-ʿAsqalānī." *Mamlūk Studies Review* 3 (1999): 85–107.

Broadbridge, Anne F. *Kingship and Ideology in the Islamic and Mongol Worlds.* Cambridge: Cambridge University Press, 2008.

Broadbridge, Anne F. "Mamluk Legitimacy and the Mongols: The Reigns of Baybars and Qalāwūn." *Mamlūk Studies Review* 5 (2001): 91–118.

Broadbridge, Anne F. "Royal Authority, Justice, and Order in Society: The Influence of Ibn Khaldūn on the Writings of al-Maqrīzī and Ibn Taghrībirdī." *Mamlūk Studies Review* 7/2 (2003): 231–245.

Broadbridge, Anne F. "Sending Home for Mom and Dad: The Extended Family Impulse in Mamluk Politics." *Mamlūk Studies Review* 15 (2011): 1–18.

Coureas, Nicholas. "Commerce between Mamluk Egypt and Hospitaller Rhodes in the Mid-Fifteenth Century: The Case of Sidi Galip Ripolli." In *Egypt and Syria in the Fatimid, Ayyubid and Mamluk Eras VI*, ed. Urbain Vermeulen and Kristof D'hulster. Leuven: Uitgeverij Peeters, 2010. 207–217.

Coureas, Nicholas. "Latin Cyprus and its Relation with the Mamluk Sultanate: 1250–1517." In *The Crusader World*, ed. Adrian J. Boas. London and New York: Routledge, 2016. 391–418.

DeWeese, Devin. *Islamization and Native Religion in the Golden Horde: Baba Tüklesand Conversion to Islam in Historical and Epic Tradition.* Pennsylvania: Penn State Press, 1994.

DeWeese, Devin. "Islamization in the Mongol Empire."In *The Cambridge History of Inner Asia. The Chinggisid Age*, ed. Nicola Di Cosmo, Allen J. Frank, and Peter B. Golden. Cambridge: Cambridge University Press, 2009. 120–134.

Durak, Koray. "Who are the Romans? The Definition of Bilād al-Rūm (Land of the Romans) in Medieval Islamic Geographies." *Journal of Intercultural Studies* 31/3 (2010): 285–298.

Edbury, Peter. "Christians and Muslims in the Eastern Mediterranean." In *The New Cambridge Medieval History.* Vol. 6: *C. 1300-c. 1415*, ed. Michael Jones. Cambridge: Cambridge University Press, 2008. 864–884.

El-Cheikh, Nadia Maria. "Byzantium through the Islamic Prism from the Twelfth to the Thirteenth Century." In *The Crusades from the Perspective of Byzantium and the Muslim World*, ed. Angeliki E. Laiou and Roy Parviz Mottahedeh. Washington: Dumbarton Oaks Research Library and Collection, 2001. 54–69.

Fernandes, Leonor E. "Mamluk Politics and Education: The Evidence from Two Fourteenth Century Waqfiyya." *Annales islamologiques* 23 (1987): 87–98.

Fuess, Albrecht. "Prelude to a Stronger Involvement in the Middle East: French Attacks on Beirut in the Years 1403 and 1520." *Al-Masāq* 17/2 (2005): 171–192.

Golden, Peter B. *An Introduction to the History of the Turkic Peoples. Ethnogenesis and State-Formation in Medieval and Early Modern Eurasia and the Middle East.* Wiesbaden: Otto Harrassowitz, 1992.

Golden, Peter B. "Migration, Ethnogenesis." In *The Cambridge History of Inner Asia. The Chinggisid Age*, ed. Nicola Di Cosmo, Allen J. Frank, and Peter B. Golden. Cambridge: Cambridge University Press, 2009. 109–119.

Golden, Peter B. "The Shaping of the Cuman-Qïpčaqs and Their World." In *Studies on the Peoples and Cultures of the Eurasian Steppes*, ed. Peter B. Golden and Cătălin Hriban. Bucharest-Braila: Editura Academiei Române, 2011. 303–332.

Guo, Li. "History Writing." In *The New Cambridge History of Islam*. Vol. 4: *Islamic Cultures and Societies to the End of the Eighteenth Century*, ed. Robert Irwin. Cambridge: Cambridge University Press, 2010. 444–457.

Haarmann, Ulrich. "Arabic in Speech, Turkish in Lineage: Mamluks and Their Sons in the Intellectual Life of Fourteenth-Century Egypt and Syria." *Journal of Semitic Studies* 33/1 (1988): 81–114.

Haarmann, Ulrich. "The Late Triumph of the Persian Bow: Critical Voices on the Mamluk Monopoly on Weaponry." In *The Mamluks in Egyptian Politics and Society*, ed. Thomas Philipp and Ulrich Haarmann. Cambridge: Cambridge University Press, 1998. 174–187.

Haarmann, Ulrich. "The Mamluk System of Rule in the Eyes of Western Travelers." *Mamlūk Studies Review* 5 (2001): 1–24.

Haddad, Wadīʿ Z. "The Crusaders through Muslim Eyes." *The Muslim World* 73/3–4 (1983): 234–252.

Halperin, Charles J. "The Kipchak Connection: The Ilkhans, the Mamluks and Ayn Jalut." *Bulletin of the School of Oriental and African Studies* 63/2 (2000): 229–245.

Herzog, Thomas. "La mémoire des invasions mongoles dans la Sīrat Baybars. Persistances et transformations dans l'imaginaire populaire arabe." In *Le Bilād al-Šām face aux Mondes Extérieurs: La perception de l'Autre et la représentation du Souverain*, ed. Denise Aigle. Damascus-Beirut: Presses de l'ifpo, 2012. 345–362.

Hillenbrand, Carole. *The Crusades: Islamic Perspectives*. New York: Routledge, 2000.

Hirschler, Konrad. "Studying Mamluk Historiography. From Source-Criticism to the Cultural Turn." In *Ubi Sumus? Quo Vademus? Mamluk Studies – State of the Art*, ed. Stephan Conermann. Bonn: Bonn University Press, 2012. 159–186.

Hofer, Nathan. "The Origins and Development of the Office of the "Chief Sufi" in Egypt, 1173–1325." *Journal of Sufi Studies* 3/1 (2014): 1–37.

Holt, P.M. "An-Nāṣir Muḥammad b. Qalāwūn (684–741/1285–1341): His Ancestry, Kindred, and Affinity." In *Egypt and Syria in the Fatimid, Ayyubid and Mamluk Eras, Proceedings of the 1st, 2nd, and 3rd International Colloquium*, ed. Urbain Vermeulen and Daniel De Smet. Leuven: Uitgeverij Peeters, 1995. 313–324.

Holt, P.M. "Literary Offerings: A Genre of Courtly Literature." In *The Mamluks in Egyptian Politics and Society*, ed. Thomas Philipp and Ulrich Haarmann. Cambridge: Cambridge University Press, 1998. 3–16.

Humphreys, Stephen R. "Ayyubids, Mamluks, and the Latin East in the Thirteenth Century." *Mamlūk Studies Review* 2 (1998): 1–17.

Irwin, Robert. "The Image of the Byzantine and the Frank in Arab Popular Literature of the Late Middle Ages." In *Latins and Greeks in the Eastern Mediterranean after 1204*, ed. Benjamin Arbel, Bernard Hamilton, and David Jacoby. London: Frank Cass and Company Limited, 1989. 226–242.

Irwin, Robert. "Mamluk History and Historians." In *Arabic Literature in the Post-Classical Period*, ed. Allen Richards. Cambridge: Cambridge University Press, 2006. 159–170.

Irwin, Robert. "Mamluk Literature." *Mamlūk Studies Review* 7 (2003): 1–29.
Irwin, Robert. *The Middle East in the Middle Ages: The Early Mamluk Sultanate 1250–1382.* London: Croom Helm, 1986.
Jackson, Peter. *The Mongols and the West, 1221–1410.* London and New York: Routledge, 2014.
Landa, Ishayahu. "Oirats in the Ilkhanate and the Mamluk Sultanate in the Thirteenth to the Early Fifteenth Centuries: Two Cases of Assimilation into the Muslim Environment." *Mamlūk Studies Review* 19 (2016): 149–191.
Levanoni, Amalia. "Al-Maqrīzī's Account of the Transition from Turkish to Circassian Mamluk Sultanate: History in the Service of Faith." In *The Historiography of Islamic Egypt (c. 950–1800)*, ed. Hugh Kennedy. Leiden: Brill, 2001. 93–105.
Levanoni, Amalia. "*Awlad al-Nas* in the Mamluk Army during the Bahri Period." In *Mamlūks and Ottomans: Studies in Honour of Michael Winter*, ed. David Wasserstein and Ami Ayalon. London and New York: Routledge, 2006. 96–105.
Levanoni, Amalia. "A Supplementary Source for the Study of Mamluk Social History: The *Taqārīẓ*." *Arabica* 60/1–2 (2013): 146–177.
Little, Donald P. "A Comparison of al-Maqrīzī and al-ʿAynī as Historians of Contemporary Events." *Mamlūk Studies Review* 7/2 (2003): 205–215.
Little, Donald P. "Diplomatic Missions and Gifts Exchanged by Mamluks and Ilkhans." In *Beyond the Legacy of Genghis Khan*, ed. Kinda Komoroff. Leiden: Brill, 2006. 30–42.
Little, Donald P. "Historiography of the Ayyūbid and Mamlūk Epochs." In *The Cambridge History of Egypt.* Vol. 1: *Islamic Egypt, 640–1517*, ed. Carl F. Petry. Cambridge: Cambridge University Press, 1998. 412–444.
Little, Donald P. "Notes on Aitamiš, a Mongol Mamlūk." In *Die islamische Welt zwischen Mittelalter und Neuzeit: Festschrift für Hans Robert Roemer zum 65. Geburtstag*, ed. Ulrich Haarmann and Peter Bachman. Beirut: Orient-Institut der Deutschen Morgenländischen Gesellschaft, and Wiesbaden: Franz Steiner, 1979. 387–401.
Loiseau, Julien. "Frankish Captives in Mamlūk Cairo." *Al-Masāq* 23/1 (2011): 37–52.
Luttrell, Anthony. "The Latin East." In *The New Cambridge Medieval History*. Vol. 7: *C. 1415–c. 1500*, ed. Christopher Allmand. Cambridge: Cambridge University Press, 2008. 796–811.
Martinez, Arsenio Peter. "Institutional Development Revenues and Trade." In *The Cambridge History of Inner Asia. The Chinggisid Age*, ed. Nicola Di Cosmo, Allen J. Frank, and Peter B. Golden. Cambridge: Cambridge University Press, 2009. 89–108.
Massoud, Sami G. "Al-Maqrīzī as a Historian of the Reign of Barqūq." *Mamlūk Studies Review* 7/2 (2003): 119–136.
May, Timothy. "Tatars." In *The Mongol Empire: A Historical Encyclopedia*, ed. Timothy May. Santa Barabara, California: ABC-CLIO, 2017. 1: 249–251.
Mazor, Amir. *The Rise and Fall of a Muslim Regiment. The Manṣūriyya in the First Mamluk Sultanate 678/1279–710/1341.* Bonn: Bonn University Press, 2015.
McKee, Sally. "Domestic Slavery in Renaissance Italy." *Slavery and Abolition* 29/3 (2008): 305–326.
Morgan, David. *The Mongols.* Oxford: Basil Blackwell, 1986.
Müller, Hans. *Die Kunst des Sklavenkaufs nach arabischen, persischen and türkischen Ratgebern vom 10. bis zum 18. Jahrhundert.* Freiburg-im-Breisgau: Klaus Schwarz Verlag, 1980.

Nakamachi, Nobutaka. "The Rank and Status of Military Refugees in the Mamluk Army: A Reconsideration of the *Wāfidīyah.*" *Mamlūk Studies Review* 10/1 (2006): 55–81.

Northrup, Linda S. "The Baḥrī Mamlūk Sultanate, 1250–1390." In *The Cambridge History of Egypt.* Vol. 1: *Islamic Egypt, 640–1517*, ed. Carl F. Petry. Cambridge: Cambridge University Press, 1998. 242–289.

Northrup, Linda S. *From Slave to Sultan: The Career of al-Manṣūr Qalāwūn and the Consolidation of Mamluk Rule in Egypt and Syria (678–689 A.H./1279–1290 A.D.).* Stuttgart: Franz Steiner Verlag, 1998.

Pahlitzsch, Johannes. "The Mamluks and Cyprus: Transcultural Relations between Muslim and Christian Rulers in the Eastern Mediterranean in the Fifteenth Century." In *Acteurs des transferts culturels en Méditerranée médiévale. Ateliers des Deutschen Historischen Instituts Paris*, ed. R. Abdellatif, Y. Benhima, D. König, and E. Ruchaud. Paris: Deutsches Historisches Institut Paris, 2010. 111–119.

Pahlitzsch, Johannes. "Mediators between East and West: Christians under Mamluk Rule." *Mamlūk Studies Review* 9/2 (2005): 31–47.

Paul, Jürgen. "Mongols Aristocrats and Beyliks in Anatolia. A Study of Astārādī's *Bazm va Razm.*" *Eurasian Studies* 9/1–2 (2011): 105–158.

Perlmann, Moshe. "Notes on Anti-Christian Propaganda in the Mamlūk Empire." *Bulletin of the School of Oriental and African Studies* 10 (1940–1942): 843–861.

Petry, Carl F. *The Civilian Elite of Cairo in the Later Middle Ages.* Princeton: Princeton University Press, 1981.

Petry, Carl F. "Crime and Scandal in Foreign Relations." In *La frontière méditerranéenne du XVe au XVIIe siècle: Échanges, circulations et affrontements*, ed. Bernard Heybergerand and Albrecht Fuess. Turnhout: Brepols Publishers, 2014. 145–161.

Popper, William. *Egypt and Syria under the Circassian Sultans 1382–1468 A.D.: Systematic Notes to Ibn Taghrī Birdī's Chronicles of Egypt.* Berkeley: University of California Press, 1955.

Rabbat, Nasser O. "The Changing Concept of *Mamlūk* in the Mamlūk Sultanate in Egypt and Syria." In *Slave Elites in the Middle East and Africa: A Comparative Study*, ed. Toru Miura and John Edward Philips. London and New York: Kegan Paul International, 2000. 81–98.

Rabbat, Nasser O. "In Search of a Triumphant Image: The Experimental Quality of Early Mamluk Art." In *The Arts of the Mamluks in Egypt and Syria: Evolution and Impact*, ed. Doris Behrens-Abouseif. Bonn: Bonn University Press, 2012. 21–36.

Rabbat, Nasser O. "Representing the Mamluks in Mamluk Historical Writing." In *The Historiography of Islamic Egypt (c. 950–1800)*, ed. Hugh Kennedy. Leiden: Brill, 2001. 59–75.

Rabbat, Nasser O. "Was al-Maqrīzī's Khiṭaṭ a Khaldūnian History?" *Der Islam* 89/1–2 (2012): 118–140.

Rapoport,Yossef. "Women and Gender in Mamluk Society: An Overview." *Mamlūk Studies Review* 11/2 (2007): 1–47.

Richardson, Kristina. "Blue and Green Eyes in the Islamicate Middle Ages." *Annales islamologiques* 48/1 (2014): 13–29.

Rice, David Storm. *Le Baptistère de Saint Louis: A Masterpiece of Islamic Metal Work.* Paris: Éditions du Chêne, 1951.

Rice, David Storm. "The Blazons of the 'Baptistere de Saint Louis'." *Bulletin of the School of Oriental and African Studies* 13/2 (1950): 367–380.

Sadeque, Fatima. "The Court and Household of the Mamlūks of Egypt (13th–15th Centuries)." *Journal of the Asiatic Society of Pakistan* 49 (1969): 271–288.

Shoshan, Boaz. *Popular Culture in Medieval Cairo.* Cambridge: Cambridge University Press, 2002.

Stewart, Angus. "If the Cap Fits: Going Mongol in Thirteenth Century Syria." *Journal of the Royal Asiatic Society* 26/1–2 (2016): 137–146.

Tardy, Lajos. "The Caucasian Peoples and their Neighbors in 1404." *Acta Orientalia Academiae Scientiarum Hungaricae* 32/1 (1978): 83–111.

Spuler, Bertold. "Ilkhāns." *The Encyclopaedia of Islam.* 2nd Edition. Leiden: Brill, 1971. 3: 1120–3.

Teule, Herman G.B. "Introduction: Constantinople and Granada. Christian-Muslim interaction 1350–1516." In *Christian-Muslim Relations A Bibliographical History: Volume 5 (1350–1500)*, ed. David Thomas and Alex Mallett. Leiden, Boston: Brill, 2013. 1–16.

Troadec, Anne. "Baybars and the Cultural Memory of Bilād al-Shām: The Construction of Legitimacy." *Mamlūk Studies Review* 18 (2014–15): 113–148.

Van Steenbergen, Jo. "Is Anyone my Guardian…? Mamlūk Under-age Rule and the Later Qalāwūnids." *Al-Masāq* 19/1 (2007): 55–65.

Van Steenbergen, Jo. *Order out of Chaos. Patronage, Conflict and Mamluk Socio-Political Culture. 1341–1382.* Leiden: Brill, 2006.

Vásáry, István. "Orthodox Christian Qumans and Tatars of the Crimea in the 13th–14th Centuries." *Central Asiatic Journal* 32/3–4 (1988): 260–271.

Vásáry, István. *Cumans and Tatars. Oriental Military in the Pre-Ottoman Balkans, 1185–1365.* Cambridge: Cambridge University Press, 2005.

Wing, Patrick. "The Decline of the Ilkhanate and the Mamluk Sultanate's Eastern Frontier." *Mamlūk Studies Review* 11/2 (2007): 77–88.

Yarbrough, Luke. "'A Rather Small Genre': Arabic Works Against Non-Muslim State Officials." *Der Islam* 93/1 (2016): 139–169.

Yosef, Koby. "*Dawlat al-Atrāk* or *Dawlat al-Mamālīk?* Ethnic Origin or Slave Origin as the Defining Characteristic of the Ruling Elite in the Mamluk Sultanate." *Jerusalem Studies in Arabic and Islam* 39 (2012): 387–410.

Yosef, Koby. "Ethnic Groups, Social Relationships and Dynasty in the Mamluk Sultanate (1250–1517)." PhD dissertation, University of Tel-Aviv, 2011 [in Hebrew]. 2 vols.

Yosef, Koby. "*Ikhwa*, *Muwākhūn* and *Khushdāshiyya* in the Mamlūk Sultanate." *Jerusalem Studies in Arabic and Islam* 40 (2013): 335–362.

Yosef, Koby. "Mamluks and Their Relatives in the Period of the Mamluk Sultanate (1250–1517)." *Mamlūk Studies Review* 16 (2012): 55–69.

Yosef, Koby. "Masters and Slaves: Substitute Kinship in the Mamluk Sultanate." In *Egypt and Syria in the Fāṭimid, Ayyūbid and Mamlūk Eras VIII*, ed. Urbain Vermeulen, Kristof D'hulster, and Jo Van Steenbergen. Leuven: Peeters, 2016. 557–579.

Yosef, Koby. "The Names of the *Mamlūks* – Ethnic Groups and Ethnic Solidarity in the Mamluk Sultanate (1250–1517)." In *Egypt and Syria under Mamluk Rule: Political, Social and Cultural Aspects*, ed. Amalia Levanoni (forthcoming).

Yosef, Koby. "The Term *Mamlūk* and Slave Status during the Mamluk Sultanate." *Al-Qantara* 19/1 (2013): 7–34.

Georg Christ (University of Manchester)

The Sultans and the Sea: Mamluk Coastal Defence, Dormant Navy and Delegation of Maritime Policing (14th and Early 15th Centuries)

Introduction

After the fall of Acre and the end of the Crusader States in the Levant, the Mamluk Empire claimed control over the Mediterranean coast from Asia Minor to Libya. How did the Mamluks protect this coast? How did they protect merchantmen calling on its ports and the respective maritime trade routes? How did they keep pirates out while letting merchantmen come, in order to maximise their profit from the fiscally pivotal transit trade between India/the Far East and the wider Mediterranean area? This source of revenue had arguably become even more important after the external shocks of the 14th century, which had affected the empire's fiscal base significantly. Thus, the Mamluk Empire had to control the nodes of this trade: its ports. The 1365 Cypriot attack on Alexandria and subsequent raids on the Levantine coast underlined the pertinence of these questions: the Mamluk Empire sometimes had a problem with controlling its Mediterranean shores. Why was that? Did they simply not care or did they not have the means to protect their coasts?

That the Mamluks did not maintain a permanent navy is uncontroversial and their naval weakness has been repeatedly stated. David Ayalon explained this weakness with the lack of resources, mainly wood, the absence of an adequate sea-based enemy outside of the Mediterranean, and the land-based mentality of Mamluk rule characterized by the primacy of cavalry.[1] Albrecht Fuess compre-

1 David Ayalon, *The Mamluks and Naval Power: A Phase of the Struggle Between Islam and Christian Europe.* Jerusalem: (s.n.), 1965), 1. and passim; cf. idem, "Bahriyya, II. The Navy of the Mamluks," in *EI^2*, vol. 1, 945–947. Ayalon argues that the Arabs in their home waters, which would be the Red Sea and the Indian Ocean, did not face an enemy and therefore did not develop naval prowess. He argues that in the Mediterranean they always delegated maritime matters to other, i. e. non-Arab, people; Ayalon, *The Mamluks and Naval Power*, 2. This is only moderately convincing; the western North African shores featured much Arab naval prowess. On the strategic decision to favour heavy cavalry, Reuven Amitai: "Dealing with Reality: Early Mamluk Military Policy and the Allocation of Resources". In *Crossroads between Latin Europe and the Near East: Corollaries of the Frankish Presence in the Eastern Mediterranean (12th–14th*

hensively analysed Mamluk naval policies on the Syrian coast and concluded that the Mamluk maritime policy was essentially a non-maritime policy. Fuess describes the Mamluk approach to sea power as three-pronged: Razing coasts and harbours (scorched earth), building of transient fleets if needed, and alliances with European powers, chiefly, for the period in question, with the Venetians. The Mamluks, he argues, razed the coasts and withdrew their defences and with them their main economic activities inland; the Mamluk coastguard was a detachment of cavalry rushing to the coast from an inland stronghold that typically came too late.[2] Reuven Amitai came more recently to a similar verdict.[3] Both Ayalon and Fuess analyse how the Mamluks succeeded several times in building and operating fleets. They emphasize the transient and very limited success of these attempts.[4] Fuess explains how the Mamluks with regard to proper maritime policing, for instance against pirates, relied on 'foreign' actors – chiefly the Venetians.[5]

The apparent non-existence of a Mamluk coastal defence system and the existence of an, at best, transient fleet as well as aspects of the Veneto-Mamluk symbiosis thus have been studied.[6] The focus on the Mamluk policies as a failure to protect sea lanes and coasts including ports, however, is somewhat at odds with the fact that, generally speaking, merchantmen felt it safe to call on Mamluk ports; not only on the major ports of Alexandria and Beirut but also on smaller ports, such as Acre. This raises the question of how the Mamluks, in the sense of

centuries), edited by Stefan Leder, Istanbuler Texte und Studien 24. Würzburg: Ergon Verlag, 2011, 127–144, here 135.

2 Albrecht Fuess, *Verbranntes Ufer: Auswirkungen mamlukischer Seepolitik auf Beirut und die syro-palästinensische Küste (1250–1517)*. Leiden: Brill, 2001; Albrecht Fuess: "Rotting Ships and Razed Harbours: The Naval Policy of the Mamluks," *Mamlūk Studies Review* 5 (2001): 45–71; cf. Albrecht Fuess: "Prelude to a Stronger Involvement in the Middle East: French Attacks on Beirut in the Years 1403 and 1520," *Al-Masaq: Studia Arabo-Islamica Mediterranea* 17/2 (2005): 171–192; id.: "From the Sea to the Foot of the Hill. The Dislocation of Tripoli by the Mamluks after 1289," *Burgen und Schlösser* 4 (2009): 218–223.

3 Amitai, "Dealing with Reality", 139.

4 Ayalon, *The Mamluks and Naval Power*, 6, 9; Fuess, "Rotting Ships," 46, 60.

5 Albrecht Fuess: "Why Venice, not Genoa? How Venice Emerged as the Mamluks' Favourite European Trading Partner After 1365," in *Union in Separation: Diasporic Groups and Identities in the Eastern Mediterranean (1100–1800)*, ed. by Georg Christ et al. Roma: Viella, 2015, 251–266.

6 For the financial side of this symbiosis in the Circassian period, see Francisco Javier Apellániz Ruiz de Galarreta: *Pouvoir et finance en Méditerranée pré-moderne: Le deuxième état Mamelouk et le commerce des épices (1389–1517)*. Barcelona: CSIC, 2009; Georg Christ: "Settling Accounts with the Sultan: Cortesia, Zemechia and Fiscal Integration of Venice into the Mamluk Empire," in *The Flux and Reflux of Late Medieval State Formations: Integration, Negotiation and Political Order across Fifteenth-century Eurasia – Parallels, Connections, Divergences*, ed. by Jo van Steenbergen, *Rulers and Elites*. Leiden: Brill, forthcoming.

the ruling sultans in Cairo,[7] managed to keep coast and ports safe; how they projected power into those areas, which presumably remained, at least partially, outside of their direct military, political and economic control. The following sketch tries to propose some preliminary answers. While previous studies chiefly relied on evidence from chronicles, I seek to contribute to a deeper understanding of the late 14th-century Mamluk maritime and naval policy by reconsidering the evidence from a military-economical perspective, while enriching the source base by Latin textual sources and archaeological evidence. I argue that the Mamluk Empire had a comprehensive and sophisticated naval and coastal defence policy based on older precedents, rooted in a long tradition of Islamic and pre-Islamic imperial maritime policy. I will suggest that Mamluk naval policy rested on four pillars: 1) a coastal defence system based on *ribāṭ*s, 2) defence of ports as access points in this maritime frontier, 3) maintenance of a reduced/dormant naval capability, and 4) delegation of sea power to Latin maritime actors. This last mentioned policy fostered close Veneto-Mamluk relations. One might even say that this symbiosis would amount to a delegation of sea power to the Venetians. I will then suggest that, although sophisticated and well-suited to manage the ongoing normal matters, the Mamluk Sultanate was ill-equipped to deal with an entirely new threat: the Portuguese.

I will first review the Mamluk coastal defence system. Strongly relying on archaeological evidence, I will argue that the *ribāṭ* system was (at least partially) restored and operational under the Mamluks as a first line of defence at the coastline. Mindful of military principles of beachhead versus coastline defence, I suggest that the Mamluks razed fortifications selectively and did not retreat from the razed places but rather reconverted the defensive system to the new purpose, which was defence of the coast. In the next section I will analyse ports as the official gateways or entry points within this defence system – focusing on Alexandria and Acre – and will again rely on archaeological evidence to suggest that the differences between Alexandria, one of the main ports of the empire, and the supposedly razed port of Acre are not as fundamental as it might first appear. Finally, I will reconsider the evidence on the but transient Mamluk fleet pro-

7 Van Steenbergen has recently discussed the problematic implications of the "Mamlukisation" of late medieval Syro-Egyptian history, i.e. the tendency to interpret the multiple forms of statehood and power deployment but also cultural expression, social life etc. within the core realm and wider rim of the sultanate as "Mamluk"; Jo van Steenbergen: "'Mamlukisation' between Social Theory and Social Practice: An Essay on Reflexivity, State Formation, and the Late Medieval Sultanate of Cairo," *ASK Working Paper* 22 (2015) = https://www.mamluk.uni-bonn.de/publications/working-paper/ask-wp-22-vansteenbergen.pdf. I agree with him not least because of the evidence from Venetian sources speaking of the sultan and his "state" rather than of the Mamluk Empire. I will retain the term here as a nevertheless convenient short-hand to refer to sultanal-imperial policies and their exponents, i.e. mostly directly appointed governors as well as for the standing cavalry forces of manumitted military slaves.

posing that is was not so much incapability or cultural reluctance but rather fiscal-economical considerations that led the Mamluks to adopt the model of a dormant navy. They thus relied on a minimal permanent structure and the capability to generate additional resources in case of need (*Aufwuchsfähigkeit*) while they outsourced (Fuess) or delegated some of the permanent naval tasks to Venice.

Coastal Defence: Razing vs. Re-converting Beachheads

The razing of the Levantine coast by the Mamluks seems somewhat overstated.[8] The military logic of defending a coast is very different from the defence of a beachhead or coastal stronghold. Its spatial logic, in fact, is the opposite of the coastal stronghold. The Crusader states' centres of gravity were heavily fortified portal towns such as Acre. Or rather, these ports were the lifeline connecting the remnants of the Crusader states to Europe or Cyprus, which were the actual centres of gravity and hinterlands of the Crusading movement. The core of the defences typically was a castle around which wider rings of concentric defensive systems were arranged, most importantly the walls of the surrounding city. From these strongholds the crusaders could project military power further inland. The late Crusader states' military structures in the Levant thus pretty much followed the tactical principles to secure a beachhead (fig. 1). The Mamluks faced a very different military challenge. They had to defend the coast against attacks from the sea. Their centre of gravity was not overseas or in a coastal stronghold but in the imperial cities of Cairo and Damascus (and to a lesser degree in provincial cities) situated inland. The coast thus became the outer rim of a defensive system; it was not its core anymore. The Mamluk defences, consequently, gravitated around the major cities of the empire and a wider ring of capitals of provinces (*qāʾida, mamlaka*, lit. kingdom; formerly also *jund*) and much less the regions/governorates (*safaqa/barr*) and districts (*ʿamal/niyāba*).[9] The military logic went hand

8 Fuess, "Rotting Ships."

9 Jørgen S. Nielsen: "The Political Geography and Administration of Bahri Mamluk Palestine: The Evidence of al-Qalqashandi," in *Studia Palaestina: Studies in Honour of Constantine K. Zurayk*, ed. by Hisham Nashabe. Beirut: Institute for Palestine Studies, 1988, 114–133, here 119–122. The terminology is not quite clear and the hierarchical, "rational" taxonomy is broken by districts (*niyāba*), where the governor, then called *nāʾib*, would be directly appointed by the sultan. *Safaqa* and *barr* seem to be on the same hierarchical level, the former being rural and the latter urban. The district would be divided into *wilāyāt*, administred by a *wālī* (rural districts), Richard Hartmann: "Die politische Geographie des Mamlukenreiches. Kapitel 5 und 6 des Staatshandbuches des Ibn Fad'lallâh al-ʿOmarîs," *Zeitschrift der Deutschen Morgenländischen Gesellschaft* 70, 71 (1916, 1917): 1–40, 477–511; 429–430, here 13, 17, 21–25. Alexandria and Damietta and probably the respective coastal zones would have yet another

in hand with the political framework: power projection from the centres of power through sub-centres or nodes to the periphery. For the permanent Mamluk military forces were expensive, thus small, but relatively mobile. They were, therefore, best concentrated in neuralgic points – not least in order to be prepared against internal threats such as rival emirs.[10] Naturally, the number of garrisons (and not only in the coastal regions) thus declined.[11] The Mamluks could, therefore, only in theory but not in practice, have spread their forces along the coast.[12] Yet even so that would have allowed an amphibious invader to concentrate all his forces on one spot and gain local superiority. He thus could have formed a beachhead from which to further expand inland. The late Crusader strongholds comprising port, castle and city with some *avant-terrain* such as Acre, Arsuf, Caesarea, Ashkelon or ʿAtlīt were such potential beachheads and therefore had to be disabled.[13] Fig. 2 and 3 show the lay-out of the fortress of Arsuf which was surrounded by a walled-city. This is the design typical for a beachhead fortification, which is primarily concerned with a threat from the landside (see fig. 4 of Venetian Chania for comparison). ʿAtlīt castle (Château des Pèlerins) is another example although features of round defence are here more pronounced (fig. 5).[14] The defender of a coast, however, usually prefers to con-

status: they would as *thaghr*, "Islamic"/imperial ports, some sort of rump-provinces, directly respond to the sultan. This model seems to have been reserved, however, to Egypt only; TAVO B VIII 13, on Alexandria and its *thaghr* status see more below.

10 This is a bigger issue that cannot be covered in detail here. The standing Mamluk army was not only a defense but also a police force dealing with matters of interior security.

11 Hannes Möhring: "Die muslimische Strategie der Schleifung fränkischer Festungen und Städte in der Levante," *Burgen und Schlösser* 50/4 (2009): 211–217, here 216; on Mamluk concentration of resources, Amitai, "Dealing with Reality," 136.

12 For this would have been too costly, ibid., 137.

13 Cf. Möhring, "Muslimische Strategie," 216.

14 The small harbour it commanded was not suitable for major amphibious landings and might have been used by Mamluk naval units. Khalilieh lists ʿAtlīt as a *ribāṭ*, yet his main focus is on the pre-Crusader period, Hassan Salih Khalilieh: "The Ribāṭ System and its Role in Coastal Navigation," *Journal of the Economic and Social History of the Orient* 42/2 (1999): 212–225, here 224. Underwater archaeological exploration detected the wreck of a Mamluk warship, E. Galili: "Atlit," *Hadashot Arkheologiyot: Excavations and Surveys in Israel (HA-ESI)* 5 (1986): 6. ʿAtlīt is also listed by Qalqashandī as a *wilāya*; Nielsen, "Political Geography", 124, cf. 131; The castle itself, however, might have been destroyed: Pīrī Reis described it as such in the early 15th century; Uriel Heyd: "A Turkish Description of the Coast of Palestine in the Early Sixteenth Century," *Israel Exploration Journal* 6,4 (1956): 201–216, here 210, also *Archaeological Survey of Israel*, ʿAtlit – 26, site 82 ʿAtlit, http://www.antiquities.org.il/survey/new/default_en.aspx?pid=8586, does not mention any Mamluk remains but there are Arabic tombs in the vicinity (sites 79, 84). That might have to do with the focus of the digs, which was the crusader castle and the detailed literature would perhaps give more details (C.N. Johns: "Reports on the Excavations at Pilgrims' Castle, ʿAtlit," *Quarterly of the Department of Antiquities in Palestine* 1 (1932), 111–129; 2 (1933), 41–104; 3 (1934), 145–164; 4 (1935), 122–137; 5 (1936), 31–60; 6 (1938), 121–152; F.M. Abel, *Géographie de la Palestine*, Paris 1938, II, 22, 122; B. M. Benvenisti: *The Crusaders in the Holy Land.* Jerusalem, 1970, 175–185 all n.v.

centrate mobile, armoured reserves further inland which are able to reach potential landing zones quickly enough to engage invading enemy forces while they are landing and thus most vulnerable. Time is crucial; in order to alert/trigger the reserve in a timely manner, the coast cannot be abandoned but has to be guarded by an early warning system and a first line of defence only strong enough to retard the attacker so that the mobile reserves could arrive in time. Ayalon already noted that the Mamluks replaced the Crusader strongholds by a system of look-outs and small-garrisons.[15] In the light of the rational explained above, this, however, would not suggest a withdrawal from or razing of the coast but rather that the Mamluks re-structured the coast for coastal defence.

The military-political reality of the Mamluk Empire, entirely different from that of the Crusader states, required different fortifications. The crusaders' coastal fortresses were not suitable for the defence of the coast from attacks from the sea and even posed a threat as they could easily be re-occupied by a returning amphibious force of crusaders. They thus had to be removed or converted to the new purpose of coastal defence.

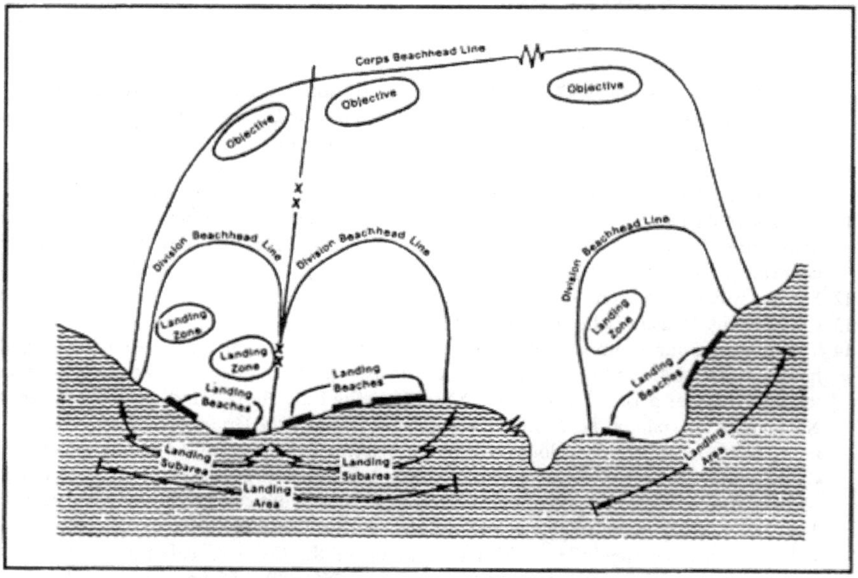

Figure 8-6. Beachheads and landing areas (schematic)

Fig. 1 Beachhead and landing areas (schematic).[16]

15 Ayalon, *The Mamluks and Naval Power*, 8 seq.

16 US field manual 71–100–2 Infantry Division Operations, http://www.globalsecurity.org/military/library/policy/army/fm/71-100-2/Ch8.htm – amphibious operations, fig. 8–6, accessed 17 August 2016.

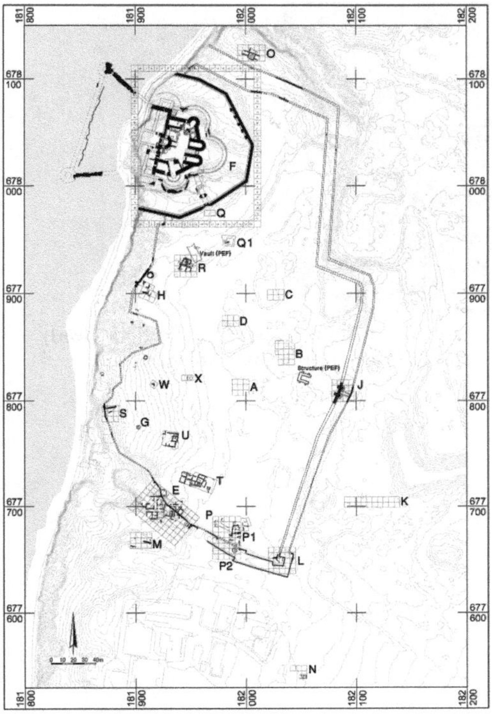

Fig. 2 Arsuf castle (plan)[17]

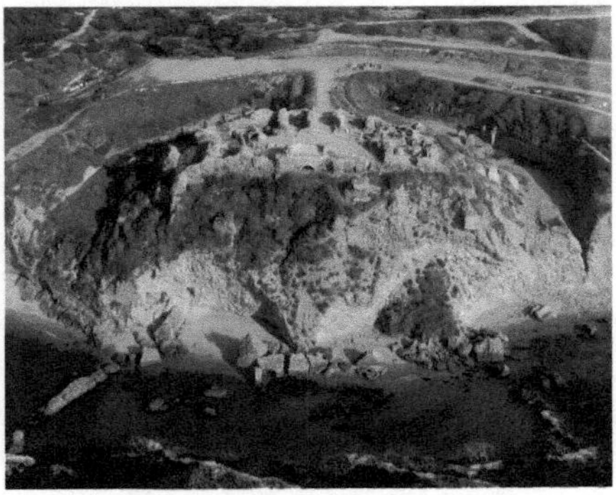

Fig. 3 Arsuf castle (aerial photograph)[18]

17 http://archaeology.tau.ac.il/wp-content/uploads/2015/01/FIG02_New.jpg, accessed 17 August 2016.

18 Arsuf, Wikimedia commons, https://commons.wikimedia.org/wiki/File:Arsuf_fortress_2.JPG, accessed 7 October 2018.

Fig. 4 Fortifications of Chania, Venetian Crete. Note that the harbour fortifications clearly subordinate to the defences against the mainland were significantly strengthened later.[19]

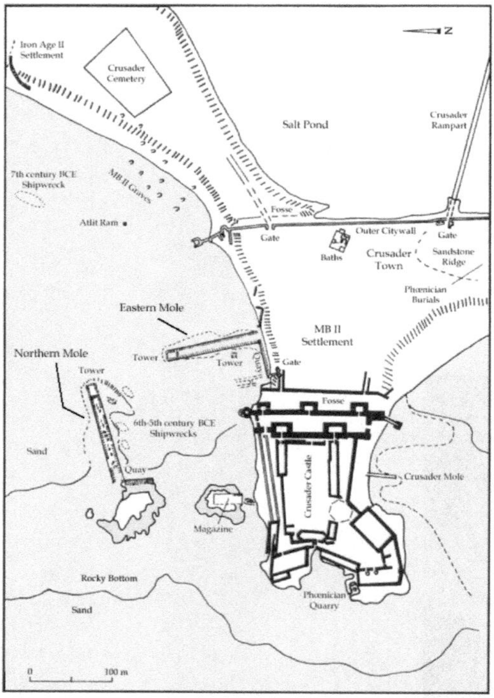

Plan of the Phœnician harbor and other ancient sites at Atlit

Fig. 5 ʿAtlīt[20]

19 Pianta della Canea, Marco Boschini (1613–1678), Biblioteca Nacional de Portugal, cota CC-68-P2, http://purl.pt/1622/3/, accessed 7 October 2018.

20 Plan of ʿAtlīt fortress, Zaraza Friedman, NAVIS II, https://www2.rgzm.de/Navis2/Harbours/Friedman/Atlit/fig03Plan.jpg, accessed 7 October 2018.

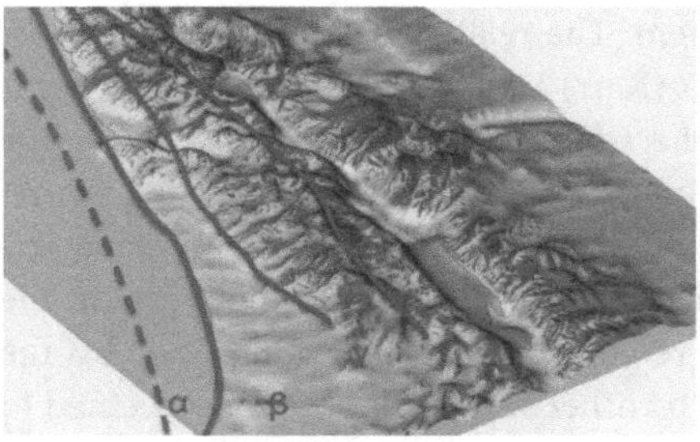

Fig. 6 Lines of coastal defence[21]

The Mamluks, therefore, usually did not repair crusader castles which they had destroyed in the course of conquest and they also razed remaining intact parts. They invested instead in military structures to support a mobile-defence of the coast. Their coastal defence system seems to confirm to the tactical elements detailed above and was based on three elements (cf. fig. 6): a fleet, which we will discuss below, as the active most forward component (α), a line of *ribāṭ* castles along the coast as a line of outposts serving as early warning system, for intelligence gathering and as a first line of land-based defence (β), a line of garrisoned outposts a few miles removed from the coast (γ), and more substantial castles in the provincial centres in the hinterland garrisoned with highly mobile Mamluk cavalry of high shock-power (δ).

The line of *ribāṭ*s hemming the Palestine coast has been studied by Hassan Khalilieh.[22] However, he does not explicitly address the question to which extent the *ribāṭ* system of the pre-Crusader period was revived by the Mamluks. He adduces, however, a reference to portal fortresses in a Florentine privilege as evidence for the existence of *ribāṭ*s in the Mamluk period.[23] Yet this is neither compelling nor conclusive. Fortress (in the Arab version of the privilege: *ḥuṣn*) does in this context of assistance to ships in distress not necessarily imply *ribāṭ* but could mean any secure installation and might indeed rather refer to a fortified port as we shall discuss below.[24] We can nevertheless assume that the

21 Original image from http://www.searchingthescriptures.net/images/maps/007b.jpg, accessed 24 August 2016, lines of defence added GC.

22 Khalilieh, "The Ribāṭ System."

23 Ibid., 217 seq., cf. John E. Wansbrough: "Venice and Florence in the Mamluk Commercial Privileges," *Bulletin of the School of Oriental and African Studies* 28 (1965): 483–523, here 505, 519.

24 Ibid., 505, § 24; in the model probably used, a privilege from 1488 (?) preserved in Italian, the text is even less specific: "qualunque sia luogo", Michele Amari: *Diplomi arabi nel R. Archivio Fiorentino.* Firenze: Reale Soprintendenza Generale agli Archivi/Le Monnier, 1863, § 45, 639, ca XX. It has to be read in the context of the preceding ca XIX of which it is merely a further (unnecessary and redundant) specification. That would also explain why the stipulation is lacking from the so-called Correr document published by Wansbrough in his "Venice and

Mamluks restored the former *ribāṭ* system. The relatively good state of preservation of the *ribāṭ*s of Ashdod and Kefer (Kafr) Lām/Ha-bonīm till today might imply continuity in their usage.[25] For the *ribāṭ* in Kefer Lām continued usage from the Umayyad to the Ottoman periods seems to be corroborated by archaeological evidence.[26] More systematic investigation of the available archaeological evidence would be needed to appreciate to which extent the Mamluks systematically converted or re-converted installations used by the crusaders which is, however, confirmed by other sources.[27] The *ribāṭ*s seemed to adhere to a blueprint comprising a square structure with towers reinforcing the

---

Florence," 486. Why unnecessary and redundant? Ca XIX stipulates that Florentine ships have the right to call any Mamluk port in case of necessity and should be assisted etc. but that they pay for their expenses (which is part of the standard content of privileges for Latin nations). XX merely explicates a particular case of such assistance, which was already implied in XIX, namely the case of a pirate attack. That it is indeed implied seems uncontroversial to me as the privileges, in terms of Islamic law, are merely the explication and transmission (in the form of a sultanic decree to his subordinates) of the sultan taking the Florentines under his personal and official protection, i. e. granting *amān*; cf. Joseph Schacht: "Amān," in *EI*², vol. 1, 429a–430a; Hans Peter Alexander Theunissen, "Ottoman Venetian Diplomatics: The ʿAhd-names. The Historical Background and the Development of a Category of Political-Commerical Instruments together with an Annotated Edition of a Corpus of Relevant Documents," *Arabica* I/2 (1998): 1–698. This of course raises the question why, then, the passus was included. Besides the obvious explanation that neither amirs (as a rule) nor Venetian officials were trained in Islamic law, we can presume that such assistance in case of pirates' attacks had not been granted in a way that was satisfactory to Venetians or Florentines and thus seemed to require further affirmation and explication of the principle of assistance and salvage. Why is that indeed plausible and reflects a problem in the construction of the Mamluk framework for international trade based on parallel unilateral grants of *amān*? Coastal defence against pirates as understood and practiced by *ghāzī*s but also by the governors within the cultural and legal framework of the *thaghr* is directed against Christians attacking collectively. The pirates are not a priori, *hostes humani generis*, but either a Muslim sea-borne *ghāzī* or a Christian crusader/attacker. Piracy by Christians and chiefly directed against other Christians does not really fit into this framework. That might, other than the very limited offensive naval capabilities of the *thaghr* governors, explain why they perhaps preferred not to get involved in inner-Christian quarrels or even take regress on other Christians under their control in the event of pirate attacks. Yet the *amān* although there are some rhetorical tricks employed to make it ambiguous enough to cover other (Latin) Christians is essentially a privilege enjoyed by a defined group (*Privilegiengemeinschaft*): the Venetians (or Florentines, Genoese or to whomever it was granted).

25 Khalilieh, "Ribāṭ," 216.

26 The Archaeological Survey of Israel, Dor 30, site 54, http://www.antiquities.org.il/survey/new/default_en.aspx?pid=1166 accessed 19 August 2016, cf. Hervé Barbé, Yoav Lehrer and Miriam Avissar, "Ha-Bonim," *HA-ESI* 114 (2002), 30 2 A–33 2 A [34–38 Hebrew] n.v., but cf. Kareem Sa'id, "Ha-Bonim," *HA-ESI* 120 (2008). http://www.hadashot-esi.org.il/report_detail_eng.aspx?id=825&mag_id=114 accessed 25/11/2016.

27 Yehoshua Frenkel: "Jihâd in the Medieval Mediterranean Sea", in *Crossroads between Latin Europe and the Near East: Corollaries of the Frankish Presence in the Eastern Mediterranean (12th-14th Centuries)*, ed. by Stefan Leder, Istanbuler Texte und Studien 24. Würzburg: Ergon Verlag, 2011, 103–125, here 105 seq., 113.

corners, a watchtower for observation and signalling, storerooms, an armoury and often a small harbour in the vicinity. This blueprint conformed to their function as an early warning station assuring good visibility of the coastal waters and communications with the hinterland as well as some limited defensive capability. They were thus polyvalent installations and it is likely that the crusaders continued to use existing *ribāṭs*, not for coastal defence but as fortified residences. For the *ribāṭ* of Kefer Lām/Ha-bonīm a crusader origin was suggested but it is clearly older. Perhaps a previous installation continued to be used by crusader lords and then the Mamluks.[28] The first line of defence along the *ribāṭs* was reinforced by the settlement of Turkomans, for instance in the area between Beirut and Tripoli (Ṭarābulus ash-shām in today's Lebanon), who then were entrusted with coastal defence.[29] This delegation was problematic though; the Turkomans' naval units also engaged in piracy and could thus harm trade.[30] They also occasionally rebelled against the Mamluks.[31]

For the further lines of defences inland it seems useful to distinguish between smaller garrisons or rather military outposts in the vicinity of the coast (3rd line of defence – γ) and the stronger garrisons in the governorate and provincial capitals (4th line of defence – δ). The 3rd line of defence was composed of outposts/castles, located about 10–20 km inland and able to reach the coast within a short time. Ramla, for instance, is situated ca. 18 km inland from the pilgrims' port of Jaffa (of which the fortifications were destroyed by the Mamluks).[32] To the north, garrisons may have been stationed in Qāqūn[33] and in other locations situated at a similar distance depending on the terrain, while the Crusader Red Tower was

28 Khalilieh, "Ribāṭ," 216.

29 Albrecht Fuess: "Déplacer une ville au temps des Mamelouks: Le cas de Tripoli," *Chronos* 19 (2009): 157–172, here 159.

30 "Anchora have arecordado che l'è algune galie de Turchomani e d'altri, li qual va scorsizando e rompendo i caminj: et esse di porti, e si dà briga ai Venitiani, e si i taia la via in mar e deroba le lor marchadantie, haver e altre cosse", Mamluk privilege issued to Venice in 1415, Georg Martin Thomas and Riccardo Predelli (eds.): *Diplomatarium veneto-levantinum sive acta et diplomata res venetas graecas atque levantis illustrantia, pars II, a. 1351–1454.* Deputazione veneta di storia patria. Venice, 1899, 313.

31 Fuess, "Déplacer une ville," 159, 167; Gustav Weil: *Das Chalifat unter den Bahritischen Mamlukensultanen.* Stuttgart: Metzler, 1860, 534, 538 seq., they were also involved in the many contests for power, some leaders/tribes on one side, some on the other, ibid., 534, 546, 549 seq., 552, 568.

32 Heyd, "A Turkish Description", 207 seq.; for Jaffa under the Crusader States: Denys Pringle: *Secular Buildings in the Crusader Kingdom of Jerusalem: An Archaeological Gazetteer.* Cambridge: Cambridge Univ. Press, 1997, 25, 60–63; for Ramla, see M. Rosen-Ayalon: "Ramla," in: *The New Encyclopedia of Archaeological Excavations in the Holy Land*, ed. by Ephraim Stern. Jerusalem: The Israel Map and Publishing Co. Ltd, 1992, vol. 4, 1269–1271.

33 Hebrew: Ḥorvat Burgata; Denys Pringle: *The Red Tower (al-Burj al-Ahmar): Settlement in the Plain of Sharon at the Time of the Crusaders and Mamluks A.D. 1099–1516.* London: British School of Archaeology in Jerusalem, 1986, 25, 60–63.

probably destroyed.[34] The 4th line of defence would have been the governorate and provincial capitals further inland such as the Krak des Chevaliers, Damascus, Safed, later also Jerusalem (cf. fig. 6).[35]

There is a notable asymmetry in the system though. Gaza, head of a governorate since the 14th century, is basically a coastal town and seems to conflate 2nd, 3rd and, to an extent, 4th line of defence (β-δ).[36] It thus hosted a slightly more substantial garrison.[37] The flat hinterland of Gaza does not provide dominating heights and in southern to western direction there is essentially desert.[38] The area was thus not suitable to sustain a garrison and the fact that the coast was shallow and therefore not suitable for the landing of an amphibious force did not necessitate it either.[39] Tripoli was a portal town that remained head of a province (contrary to, say, Alexandria, which had lost this status earlier).[40] Albrecht Fuess has analysed how Tripoli was relocated from the coast to the foothills of Mt. Lebanon about four kilometres inland.[41] Thus the portal area as the first line of

34 Ibid., 25; for instance Tel Yoqne'am, cf. http://www.antiquities.org.il/survey/new/default_en.aspx?pid=3411, or Ḥorvat Eleq (Ramat ha nadiv) http://www.antiquities.org.il/survey/new/default_en.aspx?pid=1972, Zeror (Zrur, Tel ed-dhrur/dhurer) http://www.antiquities.org.il/survey/new/default_en.aspx?pid=3365; possibly there were also other, smaller outposts between those stations and the coast, such as Tel Nahal near Haifa, http://www.antiquities.org.il/survey/new/default_en.aspx?surveynum=56, site 33, all accessed 17 August 2016; see also Bethany J. Walker: "Militarization to Nomadization: The Middle and Late Islamic Periods," *Near Eastern Archaeology* 62/4 (1999): 202–232, here 225.

35 Ibid., on Safed, which became head of a new province, albeit a rather small and not very important one, (*mamlaka*, lit.=kingdom), see Joseph Drory: "Founding a New Mamlaka," in *The Mamluks in Egyptian and Syrian Politics and Society*, ed. by Michael Winter and Amalia Levanoni. Leiden: Brill, 2004, 167, passim. Further removed but no provincial centres would be Beaufort (25–30 km) and Krak des Chevaliers (40 km); Möhring, "Muslimische Strategie," 216; on the Krak's continuous use see also below.

36 On the administrative status of Gaza, see Amitai, "Development of a Muslim City"; Nielsen, "Political Geography," 121 seq.; Johann Büssow: "Gaza", in: *EI*^{3}, ed. by Kate Fleet et al., s.v. consulted online 02 September 2016, first published online 2014; see also Richard Hartmann: "Die politische Geographie," 24 seq.; for Gaza's architecture M. M. Sadek: *Die mamlukische Architektur der Stadt Gaza.* Berlin: K. Schwarz, 1991, n.v.

37 Reuven Amitai: "The Development of a Muslim City in Palestine: Gaza under the Mamluks". *ASK Working Paper* 28 (Aug 2017).

38 Heinz Gaube (ed.): *Tübinger Atlas des Vorderen Orients (TAVO).* Tübingen: Reichert, 1977, sheet A VI 8.

39 Heyd, "A Turkish Description," 207; Tel el-Hesi further inland bears also a cemetery which probably is from the Mamluk period; Lawrence Toombs: *Tell el-Hesi: Modern Military Trenching and Muslim Cemetery in Field I, Strata I–II.* Waterloo, ON: Wilfrid Laurier Univ. Press, 1985, 116; yet this is hardly proof of the presence of a regular Mamluk force; cf. TAVO A I 15.

40 Christian Décobert: "Alexandrie au XIIIe siècle. Une nouvelle topographie," in *Alexandrie médiévale 1*, ed. by id. and Jean-Yves Empereur, Cairo: IFAO, 1998, 71–100, here 74.

41 Fuess, "Déplacer une ville," 159, 162–165, cf. also his "From the Sea".

defence was henceforth separated from the town as the second line of defence.[42] In the north, from Tyre onwards, the lines of defence would tend to converge because of the changing topography, i.e. because of a much smaller coastal strip.[43] The model of coastal defence adopted by the Mamluks does not seem to fundamentally differ from late Roman, earlier Islamic or Ottoman coastal defence systems.[44]Also in more recent wars coastal defence had been organized along similar lines.[45] The repeated attacks and subsequent plundering by Cypriot and other crusader forces in the 14th century also suggest that the coast was inhabited and that there was something to plunder.[46]

Protection of Ports: Alexandria and Acre

Seaborne trade and especially the intercontinental transit trade between India and the Mediterranean required harbours that could accommodate a substantial number of merchantmen. Harbours for that very reason were naturally susceptible to amphibious assaults and thus the most vulnerable parts of the coastal defence system. How could coastal defence and trade be reconciled? How could the Mamluks control and negotiate access; i.e. allow traders to come in while keeping pirates and invaders out? As the revenues from sea-borne transit trade were crucial for the Mamluks, they took whatever measure necessary to foster this

42 H. Salam-Liebich: *The Architecture of the Mamluk City of Tripoli.* Cambridge, MA: Aga Khan Program for Islamic Architecture at Harvard University and the Massachusetts Institute of Technology, 1983.

43 TAVO A I 15; as a result more Crusader fortresses were re-used: e.g. Krak des Chevalier (although possibly only until the first half of the 14th century), Ross Burns: *Monuments of Syria. An Historical Guide.* London: I.B. Tauris, 1999, 144, 148; Werner Meyer, John Zimmer, and Maria-Letizia Boscardin: "Krak de Chevaliers. Zwischenbericht über das Projekt 2005/7," *Burgen und Schlösser* 4 (2009): 242–245, here 243; Marqab, Burns, *Monuments*, 185; Möhring, "Muslimische Strategie," 216.

44 Chester G. Starr: "Coastal Defence in the Roman World," *The American Journal of Philology* 64/1 (1943): 56–70, here 56, 69 seq. although remaining vague regarding the actual disposition and staggering of defences; for Islamic coastal defence prior to the Mamluks, cf. Khalilieh, "The Ribāṭ System," 213 seqq. and passim; for similar medieval English coastal defences Randall Moffett: "Defense Schemes of Southampton in the Late Medieval Period, 1300–1500," *Journal of Medieval Military History* 11 (2013): 215–58.

45 Cf. the German coastal defences in northern France in 1944 and the failure to deploy their mobile reserves in time. A new problem appearing at this time is air superiority as a precondition for mobile defence, Liddell Hart: *Geschichte des Zweiten Weltkriegs*, Wiesbaden: Fourier Verlag, 1970, 679 seq.; Janusz Piekalkiewic: *Krieg der Panzer 1939–1945*, Eltville am Rhein: Bechtermünz Verlag, 1989, 258.

46 The narrative sources informing us about these events, however, are hardly reliable on this question and this caveat needs to be taken into account, cf. Werner Krebs: *Innen- und Aussenpolitik Ägyptens 741–784/1341–1382.* Hamburg, 1980, 280 seq. Sidon 1356; 301–316 Tripoli and Ayas 1367.

trade and thus to keep ports open despite of the risk of enemy attacks. Alexandria was the main Egyptian port on the Mediterranean. In Palestine, the port of Jaffa catered to the needs of the pilgrim-tourists.[47] Acre was the terminal for the shipping of Palestinian cotton.[48] Beirut remained important and even gained in importance in the second half of the 14th century as the port of Damascus and was crucial for the shipping of both goods of the transit trade (pepper) and the (although by then declining) domestic industrial production.[49] Tripoli remained similarly important as the port for the central Syrian plain and the Orontes valley.[50] Latakia, finally, was vital as the port of Aleppo, another crucial hub in the intercontinental spice transit trade and an industrial centre.[51] These ports differed with regard to their defensive arrangements. Fuess has highlighted, how in the case of Tripoli, harbour and city were detached in order to make the latter more secure. While the harbour was hardly defended, the city was so located as to prevent an attacker from exiting his beachhead in the port area. A cavalry shock force deployed from the city could perfectly develop in the plain between city and harbour and thus present a formidable deterrent. This was exactly what happened, when Jean le Meingre (Boucicaut) attacked in 1403 and triggered his hasty retreat.[52] In Egypt, Alexandria was the only natural harbour that was well-suited to accommodate bigger merchantmen and was thus without alternative. Cairo's ports, south-facing Miṣr and north-facing Būlāq, although they arguably were the biggest ports in Egypt, could not replace Alexandria.[53] This, for sure, would have

47 Cf. David Jacoby: "Ports of Pilgrimage to the Holy Land, Eleventh-Fourteenth Century: Jaffa, Acre, Alexandria," in *The Holy Portolano. Le portulan sacré. The Sacred Geography of Navigation in the Middle Ages. Fribourg Colloquium 2013. La géographie religieuse de la navigation au moyen âge. Colloque fribourgeois 2013,* ed. by Michele Bacci and Martin Rohde. Berlin: de Gruyter, 2014, 51–72.

48 Möhring, "Muslimische Strategie," 216 seq. and see below.

49 For Beirut, see Albrecht Fuess: "Beirut in Mamluk Times (1291–1517)," *Aram* 9–10 (1997–1998): 85–101.

50 Salam-Liebich, *Architecture.*

51 Eliyahu Ashtor: *Levant Trade in the Later Middle Ages.* Princeton: Princeton University Press, 1983, 247, 461; Ira Marvin Lapidus: *Muslim Cities in the Later Middle Ages.* Cambridge, Mass: Harvard University Press, 1984, 41; Jean Richard: "Le royaume de Chypre et l'embargo sur le commerce avec l'Égypte (fin XIIIe – début XIVe siècle)," *Comptes rendues de l'Académie des inscriptions et belles lettres* 128 (1984): 120–134, here 129; see also letter by Alvise Soranzo to Donado Soranzo, 04.09.1402, ASVe, *Miscellanea di carte non appartenenti a nessun archivio,* b. 15, fasc. 3, f. 5.

52 Fuess, "Déplacer une ville," 166; for Boucicaut's operations see in more detail Joseph Delaville le Roulx: *La France en Orient au XIVe siècle: Expéditions du Maréchal Boucicaut,* 2 vol. Paris: E. Thorin, 1885 and more recently Denis Lalande: *Jehan II le Meingre, dit Boucicaut (1366–1421). Étude d'une biographie héroïque.* Genève: Droz, 1988.

53 On Būlāq and Miṣr, see Nelly Hanna: *An Urban History of Būlāq in the Mamluk and Ottoman Periods.* Cairo: Institut français d'archéologie orientale, 1983, mainly 3–8, 11. Al-Maqs, the older north-facing port, due to the Nile changing course, had become a canal port by the 13th century and could be used only during the flood, 4. Hanna argues that Būlāq eclipsed Miṣr

been safer (and such inland ports on the banks of great rivers were thriving in London, Hamburg, Lübeck etc.). Yet to call on Alexandria was already difficult enough for big sailing ships (cogs, *navi*) and sailing up the Nile was only an option for much smaller craft all year long and for bigger craft like galleys only during the flood.[54] In any case, the Mamluks did not allow foreign ships to sail up the Nile. At least in theory, foreign ships were not even allowed to call on the port of Rosetta at the mouth of the Nile branch that leads to Cairo. Important but mainly for regional trade was the port of Damietta. Alexandria thus remained without alternative for international trade.[55]

The Mamluks tried to protect Alexandria and its harbour by stationing a nominally substantial force in the city composed of a Mamluk detachment, *ḥalqa* cavalry and further *ghāzī* volunteers in the *ribāṭ*s outside of the town.[56] The sea-facing fortifications were reinforced by a double wall, a moat and strong gate towers with the entrances positioned at right angles to the city wall. The defenders of the city could rely on a well-filled armoury including high-tech weapons such as equipment to launch naphtha (*midfāʿ, pl. madāfiʿ, an-naft*), possibly artillery[57] and conventional ballistic weapons (mangonels, trebuchets: *manjānīq*,

over the course of the 15th century. By the late 14th and early 15th century, the two ports were used. Hanna also provides evidence for Būlāq's portal infrastructure in the 14th century, 22 seq., 25, 42, 78 seq., cf. Georg Christ: *Trading Conflicts. Venetian Merchants and Mamluk Officials in Late Medieval Alexandria.* Leiden: Brill, 2012, 28 seq., for the ongoing importance of Miṣr: Letter by Angelo qd. Luca Michiel to Biagio qd. Lorenzo Dolfin, 13.09.1419, ASVe, *Procuratori di San Marco*, Commissarie miste, b. 181, fasc. 15, int. d, f. [59]: "Io son sta (…) in Babillonia trovo le spezie entro ieri (…). Dapuò partì da Babilonie sento che intra spezie domani; serò ly et ancor ve n'avixerò."

54 Cf. Hanna, *Urban History*, 27.

55 For Venetian merchants using the port of Rosetta, see Christ, *Trading Conflicts*, 172 seqq.; more generally on Alexandria and other Egyptian ports on the Mediterranean, see idem: "Collapse and Continuity: Alexandria as a Declining City with a Thriving Port (13th–16th centuries)," in *The Routledge Handbook of Maritime Trade Around Europe, 1300–1600: Commercial Networks and Urban Autonomy*, ed. by Wim Blockmans, Mikhail Krom, Justyna Wubs-Mrozewicz. London: Routledge, 2017, 121–140.

56 For Ayalon the fact that part of the garrison is *ḥalqa* is indicative of the secondary importance of Alexandria, Ayalon, *The Mamluks and Naval Power*, 11. This, and the assessments of the *ḥalqa*'s military capability in general, might need modification. The *ḥalqa* was probably better suited to cope with the specific challenges posed by the defence of Alexandria than temporarily posted Mamluks specialized in mainly two military roles: civil disturbance, including internal power struggles and tax enforcement, and mounted cavalry attacks in pitched battles. Ibn Mänglī's treatise could perhaps be seen as an indication of this; see note 126 below.

57 *Naft* from the mid-fourteenth century onward seems to be ambiguous, meaning either artillery or naphta; Robert Irwin: "Gunpowder and Firearms in the Mamluk Sultanate Reconsidered," in *The Mamluks in Egyptian and Syrian Politics and Society*, ed. by Michael Winter and Amalia Levanoni. Leiden: Brill, 2004, 117–139, here 120 seq., cf. David Ayalon: *Gunpowder and Firearms in the Mamluk Kingdom. A Challenge to a Mediaeval Society.* London: Frank Cass, 1978, 24 seqq.

or *mirmā*).[58] After the devastating (if ultimately futile) Cypriot conquest of the city in 1365, the fortifications were restored, strengthened and the garrison reinforced.[59] The attack had also shown how the harbour area north of the city was particularly exposed and only poorly defended by the *ribāṭs* located in the area. Therefore the harbour was further reinforced by a tower guarding the entrance to the port to the east while on the west the remnants of the famous lighthouse of Alexandria served as a watchtower. There were also watch towers in the city and a pigeon post connection to Cairo. The early warning system was completed by boats of the customs administration which identified ships before entering the harbour. Later the harbour area was further strengthened by the monumental fortress of Qāytbāy, which's layout could seem to be inspired by the classic *ribāṭ* blueprint rather than other examples of Mamluk military architecture – some sort of super-*ribāṭ*.[60] This was accompanied by a slow shift of the main settlement areas from the old, walled city to the port. Administratively and ideologically Alexandria was a *thaghr*,[61] a frontier town/port, where *ghāzīs* could earn rewards for defending Islam thus underlining the importance of defence and programmatically compensating for a very different reality. In reality, it seems, piratic incursions into the port were numerous. Often they were not directed against the Mamluks but Latin merchantmen.[62] In 1365 a Cypriot led crusading force conquered and sacked the city. The success of a merely passive system of portal defence was obviously limited and highlights the Mamluk need for a fleet, which we shall discuss below. Yet the fact that, even after the attack of 1365, trade quickly resumed shows that the Mamluks were not willing to jeopardize their international trade at the expense of tightened security measures.

Acre presents a different case, which recently has been discussed by Reuven Amitai.[63] Undoubtedly the city was widely destroyed and plundered during and

58 Muḥammad Ibn Qāsim al-Nuwayrī: *Kitāb al-Ilmām bi-al-iʿlām fīmā jarat bihī al-aḥkām wa-al-umūr al-maqḍīya fī waqʿat al-Iskandarīya*, vol. 3. Hyderabad: Osmania Oriental Publications Bureau, 1970, 87 simply speaks of the leader of the arsenal and the throwers "qiyād as-ṣināʿa wa-rumāt."

59 Décobert, "Alexandrie au XIIIe siècle," 75.

60 On this fortress, see Kathrin Machinek: *Das Fort Qaitbay in Alexandria – Baugeschichte und Architektur einer mamlukischen Hafenfestung im mittelalterlichen Stadtbefestigungssystem von Alexandria.* Karlsruhe: Thesis faculty of architecture, KIT, 2014.

61 (Frontier) port; lit. front tooth, for Alexandria cf. Christ, "Collapse and Continuity".

62 Ashtor, *Levant Trade*, 111, 221, 234.

63 Reuven Amitai: "Post-Crusader Acre in Light of a Mamluk Inscription and a Fatwā Document from Damascus," in *Developing Perspectives in Mamluk History. Essays in Honour of Amalia Levanoni*, edited by Yuval Ben-Bassat. Islamic History and Civilization 143. Leiden: Brill, 2017. Amitai focuses mainly on the *burj* inscription and the fatwa published by Atiya. This essay came out only after I had drafted this article in summer 2016; Amitai's and our conclusions were reached independently but essentially match. In note 37 Amitai rightly notices my reluctance to altogether reject the traditional assessment of the late Mamluk

after the Mamluk conquest.[64] Most of its inhabitants had immigrated to Cyprus in the years before the conquest or during the siege of 1291.[65] Supposedly, its fortifications were razed although one wonders, to which extent this meant systematic razing rather than not repairing the destructions the city had suffered during the siege.[66] Nevertheless, trade with the Levantine coast including Acre continued after 1291. Although Cyprus cultivated cotton since the late 12th century for its textile industry and perhaps also export,[67] the Cypriot output was not sufficient to cover the demand for cotton of the expanding European textile industries. Francesco di Balducci Pegolotti's merchant manual, reflecting conditions of the 1320s,[68] lists cotton besides potash (sodium or potassium carbonate) as the main goods purchased in Acre.[69] In return finished cloths were sold; Pegolotti lists conditions for the sale of Cypriot fabrics in Acre.[70] This is also attested by other sources.[71] Therefore, contrary to what is often assumed, Acre's port remained central both for the marketing of the products of the Cypriot textile industry and for the purchase of raw materials, especially cotton and it continued to be frequented.[72]

There might have been a lull during the time of reinforced embargos in the first half of the 14th century although it is not very likely in light of the evidence here adduced. Certainly in the second half of the 14th century, Latin trade with

economy; this is still the case yet with some important modifications and caveats, see my "Decline or Deindustrialization? Notes on the Entangled Histories of Levantine and European Industries in the Late Middle Ages," *Comparativ* 26, no. 3 (2016): 25–44.

64 "ʿAkko," *HA-ESI* 13 (1995): 22–24, here 23, cf. David Nicolle: *Acre 1291.* Oxford: Osprey Publishing, 2005; Nathan Schur, *תולדות עכו – A History of Acre* (Tel Aviv: Dvir, 1990), n.v.

65 David Jacoby: "Refugees from Acre in Famagusta around 1300," in *The Harbour of all this Sea and Realm: Crusader to Venetian Famagusta*, ed. by Michael J. K. Walsh, Tamás Kiss, and Nicholas S.H. Coureas. Budapest: Central European University Press, 2014, 53–67, here 56 and passim.

66 Fuess, "Rotten Ships," 47 seq.

67 David Jacoby: "The Venetians in Byzantine and Lusignan Cyprus: Trade, Settlement, and Politics," in *La Serenissima and la Nobilissima: Venice in Cyprus and Cyprus in Venice*, ed. by Angel Nicolaou-Konnari. Nicosia, 2009, 59–100, here 75, cf. 71, 73.

68 Francesco di Balducci Pegolotti: *La pratica della mercatura*, ed. by Allan Evans. Cambridge, Mass.: The Mediaeval Academy of America, 1936, XXI.

69 "Al cantare tabarani si vende cotone, e cenere grevellera, e altre cose grosse," Ibid., 69, § 55. For the *cenere grevellera* interpreted as sodium or potassium carbonate (or a mix of the two), see Anne Françoise Cannella and Jean des Prés: *Gemmes, verre coloré, fausses pierres précieuses au Moyen Âge: le quatrième livre du "Trésorier de philosophie naturelle des pierres précieuses" de Jean d'Outremeuse.* Genève: Librairie Droz, 2006, 132 seq.

70 Pegolotti, *Pratica*, 69, § 55.

71 Jacoby, "Camlet Manufacture," 25 seqq.; for a later period 31.

72 Generally, Crusader Acre is much better studied (cf. for instance the numerous studies by David Jacoby, http://opac.regesta-imperii.de/lang_en/suche.php?qs=David+Jacoby&ts=Acre&ps=&tags=&sprache=&objektart=alle&pagesize=20&sortierung=d&ejahr= accessed 19 August 2016) than Mamluk Acre.

Acre resumed. The main export good was raw cotton, which fuelled the Upper German and Venetian textile industries producing blended fustian fabrics.[73] A 1353 *fatwā* complains vociferously about Frankish religious rituals that continued to be held in Acre thus marking a continuity of Latin-Christian presence and even a certain control; it was almost as if the conquest and destruction had never happened.[74] Also the Datini accounts contain a reference to Acre's cotton trade.[75] For the 15th century, Benjamin Arbel provides rich evidence for intense Venetian trading activity in Acre.[76] Archaeological evidence points in the same direction. While it is scarce for Acre proper (the investigations, however, seem to have focused predominantly on Crusader Acre and no comprehensive survey has been conducted yet),[77] the hinterland seems to have thrived.[78] While the city of

73 Eliyahu Ashtor: "L'apogée du commerce vénitien au Levant. Un nouvel essai d'explication," in *Venezia. Centro di Mediazione tra Oriente e Occidente (secoli XV–XVI) Aspetti e Problemi*, ed. by Agostino Pertusi et al. Firenze: Leo S. Olschky, 1977, 307–326, here 313.

74 Aziz Suryal Atiya: "An Unpublished 14th Century Fatwa on the Status of Foreigners in Mamluk Egypt and Syria," in *Studien zur Geschichte und Kultur des Nahen und Fernen Ostens: Paul Kahle zum 60. Geburtstag überreicht von Freunden und Schülern aus dem Kreise des Orientalischen Seminars der Universität Bonn*, ed. by Willi Heffening and Willibald Kirfel. Leiden: Brill, 1935, see also Amitai, "Post-crusader Acre".

75 Letter by Gaddi Zanobi di Taddeo (Venice) to Agli Manno di Albizo (Pisa) 09.08.1399, Archivio di Stato di Prato, *Fondo Datini*, Fondaco di Pisa/Carteggio ricevuto dal fondaco/ proveniente da Venezia, b. 550, inserto 14, codice 407250, online http://datini.archiviodistato.prato.it/la-ricerca/scheda/ASPO00046802/ accessed 19 August 2016.

76 Benjamin Arbel: "Venetian Trade in Fifteenth-Century Acre: The Letters to Francesco Bevilaqua, 1471–72," *Asian and African Studies: Journal of the Israel Oriental Society* 22 (1988): 227–288, cf. Ashtor, *Levant Trade*, 253 seq.

77 On the Israeli Antiquities survey database the area of Acre (19) is marked as not surveyed, http://www.antiquities.org.il/survey/new/default_en.aspx accessed 19 August 2016. The little evidence presented by Stern and in smaller notes in the *Ḥadashot Arkheologiyot* does not provide significant evidence on Mamluk Acre. This can, of course, be interpreted in different ways: that there was not much of a Mamluk Acre, or that there was but that the remains were significantly disturbed by Ottoman and/or recent construction activity [cf. Ayelet Tatcher: "ʿAkko," *HA-ESI* 117 (2005)], or that it is ultimately difficult to differentiate between Crusader and Mamluk evidence, e. g. regarding ceramics as Levantine ceramics were also used in Crusader Acre and Frankish ceramics continued to be used in the Mamluk period, cf. "Akko," *HA-ESI* 13 (1995): 22–24; A Druks: "Akko," *HA-ESI* 3 (1984): 2–4, Edna J. Stern: "The Fatimid, Crusader and Mamluk – Early Ottoman Ceramic Finds from the ʿAkko Marina: Some Insights into Medieval Maritime Activity," *ʿAtiqot* 76 (2013): 139–168. On the importation of ceramics from the hinterland in the Crusader period, see David Jacoby: "The Trade of Crusader Acre in the Levantine Context: an Overview," *Archivio storico del Sannio: rivista semestrale del Centro Interdipartimentale per gli Studi Aziendali, Economici e Sociali della Facoltà di Economia di Benevento*, no. 3 (1998): 103–120, here 108. One might even argue that Mamluk evidence has been willfully under-reported or even discarded, cf. Nadia Abu El-Haj: *Facts on the Ground: Archaeological Practice and Territorial Self-Fashioning in Israeli Society.* Chicago: The University of Chicago Press, 2001. That such things can happen is confirmed by an independent source. Nevertheless, I would not overrate it. Salvage excavations have to make painful, rapid decisions of what to prioritize; the feel of the publications of Israeli Antiquities is one of

Acre may have been widely uninhabited in the Mamluk period, a new settlement developed on a different location, 2 miles away, from the late 14th century onward.[79] Ceramic finds point at trade connections with Venice, Tuscany and Genoa/the Ligurian coast.[80] In 1469, the Mamluks created additional infrastructure by endowing a khan (caravanserai).[81] The exact lay-out of the port is unclear but there is evidence for the existence of a tower (Burj as-Sulṭān) carrying an inscription from 1436–7 (Sultan Barsbāy r. 1438–53) supposedly inhabited by Venetians, which could have been part of a defensive system protecting the port.[82] A tower, constructed by the "Egyptians," i. e. Mamluks, guarding the port is also mentioned by Pīrī Reis at the beginning of the 16th century and identified as the Burj as-Sulṭān by Uriel Heyd.[83]

Acre thus did decline as a city but it reinvented itself as a port with some facilities and a village attached. Yet this was not necessarily the result of the Mamluk conquest. A similar shift occurred in Alexandria which was never officially razed or abandoned: The city declined, the harbour thrived and the centre of activity and subsequently the core of the settlement moved into the harbour area.[84] Historians, naturally, have connected this decline to another hallmark date of crusading history: the sack of Alexandria by Peter of Lusignan and his

pedantic professionalism, a cultural trait that would do much to mitigate a possible political bias. Finally, the problem seems rather to be one of source interpretation, of a simple confirmation bias: as historians based on chronicles state, say, the razing of coasts, that is what archaeologists expect to find and indeed did "find." This is natural enough and does not have to be interpreted politically.

78 Yaʿaqov Olami and Zvi Gal, *Shefarʿam* 24, 2011 (online) [The Archaeological Survey of Israel] http://www.antiquities.org.il/survey/new/default_en.aspx?surveynum=9 accessed 5 September 2016, "Introduction, Mamluk and Ottoman periods": "'Akko rose to predominance during the Mamluk and Ottoman periods. Apparently this development led to renewed efflorescence throughout the region. Noteworthy among the important settlements from the Mamluk period are H. Gahosh, H. Galemat, H. Zefat ʿAdi, Iʿbillin, Shefarʿam and H. Shur (Sites 1, 16, 34, 41, 123)"; cf. Gunnar Lehmann and Martin Peilstöcker, *Ahihud – 20*, 2012 [The Archaeological Survey of Israel online], Introduction, http://www.antiquities.org.il/survey/new/default_en.aspx?surveynum=12, accessed 01.12.2016; the number of identifiable sites rose from 14 in the Crusader to 18 in the Mamluk period.

79 Stern, "Fatimid, Crusader," 140, confirms this for the 15th century but the economic upswing and the other evidence discussed would suggest that the formation of this settlement happened earlier.

80 Ibid., 157–161.

81 Ibid., 140.

82 Ibid., 140, erroneously attributing to Baybars. and referencing Moshe Sharon: *Corpus Inscriptionum Arabicarum Palaestinae (CIAP)* 1. Leiden: Brill, 1997, 26, 31–34. On the inscription now conclusively Amitai, "Post-Crusader Acre"; the *burj* is probably older, as the fortifications were reused (the exact Mamluk input is difficult to determine), Jacob Sharvit and Dror Planer: "'Akko, the Southern Seawall," *HA-ESI* 126 (2014).

83 Heyd, "A Turkish Description," 212.

84 Georg Christ: "Eine Stadt wandert aus. Kollaps und Kontinuität im spätmittelalterlichen Alexandria," *Viator* 42 (2011): 145–168.

army in 1365. This is, however, not convincing. The decline of Alexandria started in all likelihood earlier and had more to do with the decline of the Alexandrian industries, the plague, the city's declining political importance and the decline of its hinterland.[85] Decline of settlements or rather their transformation especially in peripheral zones of the Mamluk Empire should not be read in isolation. To interpret such phenomena as the result of deliberate central government action would be misleading.[86]

Fig. 7 Burj as-Sulṭān[87]

Acre, except for the Burj as-Sulṭān, did not dispose of any substantial defence systems and was thus probably defended in the same way as any other part of the Palestine coast: The crews of the towers and nearby *ribāṭ*s would signal for help and an armoured cavalry detachment from a nearby garrison, i. e. Safed (garrisoned by up to thousand Mamluks and the same number of *ḥalqa* troops)[88], or closer but much weaker garrisoned ash-Shāghūr (of merely *wilāya* status and governed by a Mamluk of the lowest rank, *jundī*) could come to help.[89] Appa-

85 Christ, "Collapse and Continuity," cf. id., "Eine Stadt wandert aus," 147 and passim.
86 Cf. Walker, "Militarization to Nomadization," 202–232.
87 https://commons.wikimedia.org/wiki/Category:Burj_al-Sultan,_Acre#/media/File:Akko-2-840.jpg, accessed 24 August 2016.
88 These numbers might be exaggerated, Nielsen, "Political Geography," 128 seq.
89 Ibid., 124; the identification is not clear – is this Sajur, the Crusader Seisor, Saor? Cf. Rafael Frankel: "Topographical Notes on the Territory of Acre in the Crusader Period," *Israel Exploration Journal* 38 (1988): 249–272, here 254 seq., 267. Was there perhaps also a small military outpost at "turon de Saladin" today's Khirbat/ras/jabal et-tantūr or Horvat Turit dominating the Acre-Safed road? The archaeological evidence remains too weak to assert it and the written sources seem not to confirm such an assumption. Israel Archaeological Survey, map Ahihud – 20, site 14, http://www.antiquities.org.il/survey/new/default_en.aspx?pid=2085 accessed 19 August 2016; Frankel, "Topographical Notes," 271–272 for the iden-

rently no Mamluk naval units of substance were stationed in Acre. Probably the nearest more substantially garrisoned port was Beirut in the north with perhaps a small naval installation in ʿAtlīt in the south.[90] In any case, it seems that no major attacks on Acre occurred.[91] It is ultimately difficult to assess to which extent this was due to the effectiveness of the defensive system or to the relatively lesser importance of the port of Acre.

The Mamluks took various steps to protect their ports but where only moderately successful. Their portal defence system might have coped with some incidents while in other cases, most notoriously the attack on Alexandria in 1365, the system failed. Although this might be over-reflected in the Western sources, the Mamluk inability to maintain law and order in the moorings of the port illustrated by numerous pirate attacks and skirmishes between ships is palpable.

Dormant Mamluk Naval Capabilities

It might seem uncontroversial that the Mamluks needed a navy in the Mediterranean in order to combat pirates and bolster Mamluk mercantile navigation. Studies in Mamluk naval policy, however, unanimously argued that the Mamluks were neither willing nor able to maintain a permanent fleet. Yet on the second glance we find evidence suggesting that there was more permanent naval infrastructure than we first might think. Different explanations have been put forward for the supposed Mamluk incapability to maintain a fleet. It was argued that the Mamluks, and in fact Muslim warriors generally, did not like the sea and seaborne warfare. Ibn Khaldūn exempts the Maghreb somewhat, slipping in a prophecy that a great sea-borne attack on the Christians would occur in the future (and this was indeed to happen soon with the rise of the Barbary pirates).[92] Yet for the 14th century he notes a decline and explains the naval weakness with a quote from Ibn ʿAmr stating that "the sea is a great creature upon which weak creatures ride – like worms upon a piece of wood."[93] This fits nicely with the findings of Ayalon, Fuess and Amitai, who all stress the land-based imperial mode of the Mamluks based on chivalric ideals favouring pitched battles and

tification of *Turon de Saladin* with Horvat Turit; Denys Pringle, *Secular Buildings in the Crusader Kingdom*, 99 no. 217.

90 See note 14 above.

91 For 1417 an attack by the pirate San Pere is recorded, Ashtor, *Levant Trade*, 226, cf. 250.

92 ʿAbd ar-Raḥmān Ibn Khaldūn: *The Muqaddimah: An Introduction to History*, ed. and trans. by Franz Rosenthal. New York: Pantheon Books, 1958, vol. 2: 39–46.

93 Ibid., 39.

horse-mounted sabre blanche/lance attacks.[94] One might be tempted to add the Mamluks' alleged reluctance to use artillery, which supposedly was to be the harbinger of their doom, further contributed to their weakness at sea.[95]

Fuess and Ayalon highlighted that there was no permanent Mamluk fleet.[96] They describe how Mamluk sultans would not maintain the fleets of their predecessors.[97] The occasional Mamluk war fleets indeed were usually financed by the sultan's personal purse. When the sultan died and his kin haggled with his successor and various power groups over the split of the heritage, the fleet would not find a lobby to support its up-keep. The Mamluks thus constructed fleets occasionally but did not keep them permanently.[98] This seems to prove the Mamluks' inability to maintain a fleet. Yet the evidence of transient fleets warrants a second thought. It seems a remarkable feat to build a fleet from scratch and in a short time long after a previous fleet had disintegrated. After the Cypriot attack on Alexandria, emir Yalbughā al-Khāṣṣakī ordered the construction of a fleet to take revenge for the attack. After only one year a fleet of 100 galleys (*aghriba*) and bigger transport ships (*ṭarā'id*) was allegedly ready to be reviewed on the Nile where they displayed their prowess involving also the use of naphtha (Greek fire), possibly also artillery.[99] Even if this report might be exaggerated, it remains a notable achievement. This fleet, however, was not really put to the test as only its smallest part saw action in the Mediterranean after its *spiritus rector*, Yalbughā al-Khāṣṣakī, was killed in an uprising of his Mamluks.[100] His fleet was

94 Ayalon, "The Mamluks and Naval Power", 5 seq., Fuess, "Rotting Ships", 69; Amitai: "Post-Crusader Acre", 338.

95 Early modern navies, it is true, were basically moving platforms of amassed artillery and it is also true that this development started, slowly to be sure, in the 14th century; cf. Carlo M. Cipolla: *Guns, Sails and Empires: Technological Innovation and the Early Phases of European Expansion 1400–1700.* New York: Pantheon Books, 1965. Yet for the Eastern Mediterranean and perhaps also for the Red Sea the situation was different. Due to climatic conditions, galleys dominated sea-borne warfare and they could only load a limited amount of guns. Naval warfare was hybrid and marked as much by amphibious enterprises as by ship-to-ship duels. Therefore, the Mamluks' alleged reluctance to use artillery, if it then would be conclusively substantiated, would not necessarily be directly related to their naval policy. For a revised view on Mamluks and guns, see above, note 57.

96 Fuess, "Rotting Ships," 45 and passim; Ayalon, *The Mamluks and Naval Power.*

97 Fuess, "Rotting Ships," 46; cf. Ayalon, *The Mamluks and Naval Power*, 5 seq.

98 Ibid., 60; see also Ayalon, *The Mamluks and Naval Power*; idem: "Bahriyya, II. The Navy of the Mamluks," in *EI*², vol. 1: 945–947.

99 Krebs, *Innen- und Aussenpolitik Ägyptens*, 100 seq.; on the types of ships cf. Hans Kindermann: *"Schiff" im Arabischen. Untersuchung über Vorkommen und Bedeutung der Termini.* Zwickau: PhD Dissertation, University of Bonn, 1934; on Greek fire used by Arab navies, Tarek M. Muhammad: "Ibn Mangli and Naval Warfare: The Question of Greek Fire between the Muslims and Byzantines," *International Journal of Maritime History* 21/1 (2009): 55–80 and see also above note 57.

100 Krebs, *Innen- und Aussenpolitik*, 101 seq., 318 seq.

thus "left to rot."[101] This expression is implying human agency, for which, however, there was no need. Wooden ships rot quite naturally; they disintegrate so to say by themselves. They are under constant attack from ship worms (*teredo navalis*) thriving in the Mediterranean and Red Sea's ideal temperatures and salinity. The worms find fair game in the wood alternatively exposed to warm, highly saline water and air and attacked by algae. Wooden ship hulls, in general, did not survive long and had to be constantly maintained and regularly replaced.[102] It made only sense to have a fleet, if one would use it constantly (or preserve it under ideal conditions protected against vermin in dry storage). If one did not regularly use it (and we shall come back to this point later), it could easily seem wasteful to maintain a fleet. This problem was further aggravated by the necessity to import a substantial amount of the timber from abroad. This is a stereotype in crusading projects against the Mamluks but might have been overstated.[103] The Mamluks managed to find timber when they needed it as the episodes of Mamluk fleet building show. Wood supply clearly did not present unsurmountable problems.[104] Yet the scarcity of wood in Egypt and thus the necessity to ship wood from other parts of the empire or the Mediterranean would certainly have contributed to the prohibitively high expenses of maintaining a permanent navy. Piloti seems to confirm that wood supply per se was not a problem but emphasizes that there was a lack of specific types of woods, namely high-quality beech required to produce good oars.[105] The latter also

101 Fuess, "Rotting Ships," 52 quoting Ṣāliḥ Ibn Yaḥyā's *Tārīkh Bayrūt.*

102 Gluzman estimates an average life-expectancy of c. 10 years for Venetian ships, Renard Gluzman: "Venice Overseas Afloat: Private Shipping in Renaissance Venice," paper presented at the workshop *Venice Overseas, 1400–1800. Second International Workshop for Young Scholars*, Venice 27–28 May 2011.

103 E.g. Louis Comte de Mas Latrie: *Histoire de l'île de Chypre sous le règne des princes de la maison de Lusignan*, vol. 2. Paris, 1852, 120 seq. (treatise by Henry II of Cyprus).

104 Fuess, "Rotting Ships,", 52–60, 67 seq., focusing only on the Mediterranean; for the Red Sea, see Ulrich Haarmann and Bettina Zantana: "Zwischen Suez und Aden: Pilger und Fernhändler im Roten Meer vom zehnten bis zum sechzehnten Jahrhundert," in *Der Indische Ozean in historischer Perspektive*, ed. by Stephen Conermann. Hamburg: E.B. Verlag, 1998, 109–142. For an earlier period: David Jacoby: "The Supply of War Materials to Egypt in the Crusader Period," *Jerusalem Studies in Arabic and Islam* 25 (2001): 102–132.

105 Emmanuele Piloti: *Traité d'Emmanuel Piloti sur le passage en Terre Sainte*, edited by Pierre-Herman Dopp. Louvain: Éditions E. Nauwelaerts, 1958, 224, § 150: "Se le souldain de Babilonne avoit le chemin de povoir avoir rièmes de galées, il porroit aussi bien armer .iij.C. galées comme une: pourquoy il peut avoir tout lez aultrez chosez nécessaires à galées"; for the wood required for oars in Venice: Karl Richard Appuhn: "Inventing Nature: Forests, Forestry, and State Power in Renaissance Venice," *The Journal of Modern History* 72/4 (2000): 861–89, here 867.

insinuates that Rhodes, although officially a Crusader state, supplied wood to Egypt in the 15th century, which is also confirmed by notarial documents.[106]

There were other factors that contributed to the high costs of a permanent navy. The Mamluks had to deal with two seas not just one. This would have meant that they needed two fleets (unless they dug a Suez Canal to link the two theatres of operation).[107] Also, the Mamluks could not mitigate the costs of maintaining navies by preying on enemies. Adversaries such as the Mongols or the Ottomans had no fleet to speak of in this period and most of the richer Christian ships would belong to the Mamluks' trading partners. The Mamluks lacked a sea-borne nemesis such as the Venetians were for the Genoese (or the Romans for the Carthaginians) and vice versa.[108] A Mamluk navy could thus only have preyed on smugglers and pirates. These, including raids from the kings of Cyprus, were obnoxious, to be sure, but they did not ever challenge the Mamluk sultan's power as crucially as a rivalling emir would. Indeed internally, i.e. with regard to the power struggle between emirs aspiring to become sultan, the fleet did not matter much.[109] The other perceived main threat were rather a massive Mongol invasion and insurgent Bedouins – both incentives to invest in heavy cavalry.[110] Therefore, naval armament could not be a priority for the sultan, certainly not for a young sultan, who was not very well established. Furthermore, the Mamluks had no serious competitor with regard to their staple policy that would justify the costs. After the collapse of the Mongol Empire the Mamluks controlled the bulk of the transit trade between India/the Far East and the Near East/the Mediterranean including Europe. One might argue, of course, that the ports of the Levantine coast, such as Acre, Beirut and Latakia would have constituted such rival emporia. The sultan's control over these ports was certainly not as tight and direct as over Alexandria. Yet these "internal" competitors could be dealt with more effectively in a land-based way by controlling the Hijaz and the hinterland emporia of Damascus and Aleppo respectively. The most important node in this transit trade, however, was Cairo and the sultan's aim was to channel as much of the

106 Piloti, *Traité*, 139; Theresa M. Vann: "Christian, Muslim and Jewish Mariners in the Port of Rhodes, 1453–1480,"*Medieval Encounters* 13/2 (2007): 158–173, here 162, 168–173.

107 The old canals linking the two seas via the river Nile ceased to exist by probably the late 8th century, C. H. Becker, "Miṣr," section 2. ii, *EI*², vol. 7, 149. Another canal project was considered in some seriousness as the Portuguese appeared in the Indian Ocean but was finally materialized only in the 19th century with the opening of the Suez Canal in 1869; Rinaldo Fulin: "Il canale di Suez e la Repubblica di Venezia (MCIV),"*Archivio Veneto* 2/1 (1871): 175–213.

108 Ayalon, "The Mamluks and Naval Power," 3.

109 As illustrated by Shaʿbān's fight against Yalbughā and his counter-sultan of the island. Weil does not mention any naval units; Weil, *Geschichte*, vol. 4, 516 seq.

110 Amitai, "Dealing with Reality," 135 and passim.

transit trade as possible tither. A firm control of Cairo and the regional centres in Syria was thus not only a political but also a fiscal necessity.

Also, the Mamluks could not mitigate the costs of maintaining a fleet by building dual-use ships and drawing on an autochthonous merchant fleet. The established division of labour in the transit trade attributed the shipping of spices both in the Mediterranean and the Red Sea chiefly to allochthonous players, the Venetians (and other Latin, Greek and Maghribi traders) in the Mediterranean and the Rasulids/Kârimîs in the Red Sea. Only the fleets connecting the Hijaz with Egypt and on the Nile could be somewhat identified as 'Mamluk'.[111] The deployment of Mamluk merchantmen/men-o-war for spice transport would have meant to fundamentally shake-up and re-organize trade in both seas. Under these circumstances a system that allowed to build a fleet if needed and dispose of it afterwards and thus avoiding high maintenance costs seems sensible.

So the Mamluks constructed a fleet only when needed; in just-in-time production so to say. They did this by maintaining a permanent naval force in the main port cities. This force was so small that it rather accounts for a coastguard than a navy. European travellers mention such boats that inspected incoming ships.[112] Also the afore-mentioned *ribāṭs* might have maintained some rudimentary naval units or naval capabilities.[113] The immediate response to the Cypriot sack of Alexandria in 1365 likewise indicates that the Mamluks were capable of mounting limited naval action with only short preparation and thus disposed of some more permanent structures. For instance in 1366, only a few month after the attack, Emir Ibrāhīm at-Tāzī, embarked on a prodding or reconnaissance mission.[114] At-Tāzī's operation was financed by the *dīwān al-khāṣṣ*, but that was within the particular context of the 1365 attack on Alexandria.[115] Fuess mentions a naval expedition launched from Damietta 1439.[116] Central coordination and financing of naval armament seems to have been transient and exceptional. Hints in Venetian sources might be interpreted as evidence for the existence of a permanent commander of this rudimentary Mamluk naval infrastructure: Ibn Khaldūn informs us that the position of admiral had been

111 Éric Vallet: *L'Arabie marchande : état et commerce sous les sultans Rasulides du Yémen (626–858/1229–1454)*, Bibliothèque historique des pays d'Islam 1. Paris: Publications de la Sorbonne, 2010; Georg Christ: *A King of Two Seas? Mamluk Maritime Trade Policy in the Wake of the Crisis of the 14th Century*, Ulrich Haarmann Memorial Lecture. Berlin: EB-Verlag, 2017.

112 Christ, *Trading Conflicts*, 192.

113 Khalilieh, "Ribāṭ," 217.

114 Krebs, *Innen- und Aussenpolitik Ägyptens*; Martina Müller-Wiener: *Eine Stadtgeschichte Alexandrias von 564/1169 bis in die Mitte des 9./15. Jahrhunderts: Verwaltung und innerstädtische Organisationsformen*. Berlin: Klaus Schwarz, 1992, 56–58.

115 Krebs, *Innen- und Aussenpolitik Ägyptens*, 56–58.

116 Fuess, "Rotting Ships," 67.

discontinued by the mid-14th century.[117] Yet it seems that at the beginning of the 15th century, at least, regionally, the emir of Alexandria fulfilled this task.[118] Venetian sources indicate the official title of the emir of Alexandria that was used in internal Mamluk correspondence. Among other titles the emir is addressed as the "signior alto, l'armiraio grande, (...), homo di bataia che senpre abudo vitoria, signior di l'oste dil soldan, signior di mamaluchi dil soldan".[119] The title "signior di l'oste dil soldan" does not make much sense in Italian (lord of the host/innkeeper/publican of the sultan). This could mean either Lat. *ostium* (entrance, estuary, gate) probably for Arab. *thaghr* or, less likely, *usṭūl* (from Greek στόλος, cf. Latin *stolus*), that is fleet.[120] It seems that only the emirs in charge of portal towns bore the title.[121] It was neither part of the title of the viceroy of Greater Syria, nor, to my best knowledge, of any particular officer at the court in Cairo.[122] In one letter to the doge of Venice, after the sultan's titles, blessing is invoked not only for the sultans reign/realm but also his army and fleet/gateways (again *oste* in the [only preserved] Italian translation).[123] This sparse formal evidence, the occasional financial contributions and the occasional and transient attention from the centre, such as after the 1365 sack of Alexandria, could suggest that there was the idea of a sultanic, i. e. imperial fleet but that the responsibility for it was usually delegated to the governors of the ports. Naval matters were regarded as subordinate and were part of the duties of the governors of the *thughūr al-islāmiyya* or "ports of Islam", which were also the mercantile access nodes, the emporia of the empire.[124]

The permanent naval staff, therefore, was at best regional. The Egyptian chronicler al-Nuwayrī refers to *qiyād al-ṣināʿa wa-rumāt* (leadership of industries, i. e. of the arsenal and throwers/shooters [of naphtha or cannonball, i. e.

117 Ibn Khaldūn, *The Muqaddimah*, vol. 2, 46; cf. Fuess "Rotting Ships," 69: under the Ayyubids there apparently existed a *dīwān al-usṭūl* = bureau of the fleet.

118 Later there would also be a unit stationed in Suez/Qulzum.

119 Missive by the Mamluk Sultan (Muʾayyad Shaykh) to the Venetian community in Alexandria containing a copy of a letter to the emir of Alexandria and a safe conduct in translation, 9 April 1418, ASVe, *Procuratori di San Marco*, Commissarie miste, b. 180, Commissaria Biagio Dolfin, fasc. IX, f. [1].

120 As becomes clear from the use of the term in many other documents, see below; for the use of Latin *stolus* in this context, see Amari, *Diplomi*, 268, 276, 278.

121 Again as a title of governors addressed by the sultan: "protectori de le riviere e de le marine, (...), conductori de li hoste," Thomas/Predelli, *Diplomatarium*, II, § 168, 309; Amari, *Diplomi*, 288 (§ XXV) "alle sue portora dell'oste forti".

122 Wansbrough, "Venice and Florence," 497 a decree directed to the viceroy of Greater Syria residing in Damascus does not contain this title.

123 "Mantegna Dio so regname e so cavalaria e so oste," 6 Aug 1345, Thomas, *Diplomatarium*, I, 297.

124 Cf. Wansbrough, "Venice and Florence," 498/510.

gunners]) or what we might call masters of ordnance.[125] Last but not least military literati kept the knowledge in naval matters alive. Ibn Mängli, a *ḥalqa* officer stationed in Alexandria (and this is hardly a coincidence), wrote a treatise on naval warfare including a partial translation and explication of the classic Byzantine naval treatise *Naumakhia* by Leo VI.[126] There was thus a corps of specialist, who maintained some crucial naval knowledge. The problem was that they had no permanent fleet to train with. The fact that Mamluk officers, unexperienced in naval affairs, were nominal commanders of fleets should not be overrated though; also Venetian galleys were commanded by only more or less experienced patrician *patroni* but the difference was that they were seconded by professional and non-patrician naval officers.[127] A similar system of appointments was known in the not so unsuccessful British navy of the 17th century.[128] Naval infrastructure was maintained in Būlāq (near Cairo), in Alexandria, in Beirut, later (and earlier) also in Qulzum/Suez.[129] These bases must have operated more continuously than the transient fleets and thus provided the institutional underpinning of the dormant Mamluk naval capability. To which extent the Mamluks stockpiled raw materials such as wood, iron, tar pitch, coco and other fibres etc. is not clear.[130] Nor is it clear to which extent this was necessary as the main inland ports of Egypt, Būlāq and Miṣr near Cairo, disposed of a substantial

125 Nuwayrī, Kitāb al-Ilmām, 87.

126 Muḥammad ibn Mänglī: *al-Aḥkām al-mulūkiyya wal-ḍawābit al-nāmūsiya fī fann al-qitāl*, partly edited and transl. in *The Age of the Dromôn: The Byzantine Navy ca. 500–1204*, ed. by Elizabeth M. Jeffreys and John H. Pryor. Leiden: Brill, 2005, 645–666; Vassilios Christides: "New Light on Navigation and Naval Warfare in the Eastern Mediterranean, the Red Sea and the Indian Ocean, 6th–14th Centuries A.D.," *Nubica* 3/1 (1989/93): 3–42, here 3–26; idem: "Naval Warfare in the Eastern Mediterranean (6th–14th Centuries): An Arabic Translation of Leo VI's Naumachia," *Graeco-Arabica* 3 (1984): 137–148 n.v.; idem: "Ibn al-Manqlī (Manglī) and Leo VI: New Evidence on Arab-Byzantine Ship Construction and Naval Warfare," *Byzantinoslavica* 56 (1995): 83–96; cf. G. Zoppoth: "Muhammad Ibn Mängli: Ein ägyptischer Offizier und Schriftsteller des 14. Jh.," *Wiener Zeitschrift für die Kunde des Morgenlandes* 53 (1957): 288–99.

127 Cf. Alan M Stahl: "Michael of Rhodes: Mariner in Service to Venice (chapter 2)," in *The Book of Michael of Rhodes*, ed. by Pamela O. Long, David McGee, and Alan M Stahl. 3 vols. Cambridge, MA: MIT Press, 2009, 35–98, here 71 seq.; cf. Giovanni Italo Cassandro: "Formazione del diritto marittimo veneziano," in *Venezia e il Levante fino al secolo XV*, vol. 1, ed. by Agostino Pertusi. Firenze: Leo S. Olschki Editore, 1973, 147–184.

128 Cf. Norbert Elias: "Studies in the Genesis of the Naval Profession," *The British Journal of Sociology* 1/4 (1950): 291–309, here 298–300.

129 Būlāq: Fuess "Rotting Ships," 54; Alexandria: Krebs, *Innen- und Aussenpolitik*, 318 seq.; Beirut: Ayalon, *The Mamluks and Naval Power*, 9; Suez, Christides, "Milāḥa" in EI², s.v.

130 The importance of iron should not be overstated for shipbuilding proper, as the wooden planks were joined by coco fibres rather than with iron nails if using the technique common in Red Sea and Indian Ocean; cf. John L Meloy: *Mamluk Authority, Meccan Autonomy and Red Sea Trade, 797–859/1395–1455*. PhD thesis, University of Chicago, 1998, 59.

private ship construction sector on which's material resources and know-how the Mamluk naval efforts could rely.[131]

Indeed, Būlāq and Miṣr were pivotal for raising a fleet. The Mamluks did probably not build all units from scratch but commandeered ships from the Nile's merchant fleet in case of need. Riverine boats, however, were optimised for use on the Nile and of but limited use in the high sea. Also, ship-owners were probably mostly members of the local élite, the *'ulamā'*, and might have objected to commandeering on the basis of the Islamic legal view that dynastic military governance (*sulṭa*) responsible for defence and internal stability should be financed by regular, canonical taxes.[132] The segregation of Mamluk slave soldiers as the military élite from the rest of the population of the empire may have further complicated the mustering of civilian resources for the war effort. It was done, however, for the conquest of Cyprus; Piloti indeed states that Cyprus was taken by Nile boats.[133]

The Mamluks thus disposed of a system that allowed them to create fleets quasi ex nihilo in case of need. This reveals a baffling dormant naval capability, which today defence politicians would boldly market as expandability (*Aufwuchsfähigkeit*), i.e. the capability to generate additional forces when needed, while thus camouflaging a decline in combat power due to continuous down-sizing of the armed forces.[134] Looked at it from this perspective, we would perhaps see this system not as indicative of incapacity to maintain a fleet but as a sensible and cost-effective solution to the logistical-economic problem inherent to the maintenance of fleets –the prohibitively high operating costs. It probably reflects a preference to invest in other policy fields rather than a lack of know-how. Indeed, the phenomenon of rump and temporary fleets is not specifically Mamluk but similarly occurred earlier in the late Roman period[135] and occurs again in the 21th century.[136]

131 Cf. Būlāq, see Hanna, *Urban History*, 23 seq.

132 As reflected, for instance, in Ibn Khaldūn's *Muqaddimah*.

133 Piloti, *Traité*, 224, § 150: "Et si vous dis certainement que dedans le flume du Caire se treuve le nombre de plus de .xv.M. sermes, entre grandes et petites. Et avecques celle puissance de cerme mist sez gens dessus l'isole de Cipre, et si conquesta le roy avecquez le demorant de tout le peuple, nonobstant que il avoit aulcune galiottes et naves, mais avecques celles avroit peu pou faire."

134 UK: National Security Strategy and Strategic Defence and Security Review 2015 (NSS SD Review 2015), https://www.gov.uk/government/uploads/system/uploads/attachment_data/file/478933/52309_Cm_9161_NSS_SD_Review_web_only.pdf, 76, accessed 23 August 2016; cf. Michael Grünenfelder: "Die Aufwuchsfähigkeit der Luftwaffe," *Air Power Revue* [Schweizer Armee] 4 (Oct 2015) http://www.isn.ethz.ch/Digital-Library/Publications/Detail/?lang=en&id=14096.

135 "They had to prepare a fleet in great haste for each new conflict and on its completion allowed the ships to rot away in dry-dock." Starr, "Coastal Defense," 60.

136 On the down-sizing of European navies while maintaining high levels of technological

In light of these considerations we might re-consider the Mamluk dormant naval capability as a solution, rather than a failing. The governing élite, consciously or not, did not maintain a fleet because they appreciated that its benefits would not have justified its costs. It was perhaps not so much the alleged horse man's despise for the sea but the bureaucrats' calculating fury in saving money. A dormant fleet meant that hardly any investments in naval hardware or permanent naval staff had to be budgeted. The dormant fleet saved a great deal of tax dinars. But this system had its severe shortcomings. This fleet was not permanently available to complement the very limited capabilities and the not more than local reach of the small permanent coast guard units. The Mamluks could not control maritime sea lanes or protect convoys and thus pursue an active maritime commercial policy. The war fleets built in Būlāq/Miṣr, Beirut or Alexandria essentially must have been based on the transferable skills from civilian ship building. The designs were thus probably similar to merchant ships and not perfected for military use (higher speed and manoeuvrability, reinforced ram-bow, platforms for ballistic weapons etc.).[137] The Mamluks probably managed to muster civilian crews to row and operate their ships; they, for instance, enrolled North African sailors.[138] More difficult it must have been to recruit experienced naval officers able to manoeuvre warships in naval combat. The necessary level of expertise and institutional sophistication necessary for complex naval operations could hardly be achieved through training of cavalry officers during the few months within which the Mamluks built their temporary fleets, especially as the more advanced combined/manoeuvre training had to be effected with the whole fleet, i.e. could be started only upon completion of the building programme.[139] Sultan Baybars famously argued that no skills were needed to row a boat.[140] He was wrong; while rowing per se might seem simple; rowing in unison and in battle requires training.[141] The dormant navy's sole purpose seems to have been to pose a sufficiently strong threat and deterrent to keep subordinates – Cyprus but perhaps also Venice – in check. The "sub-

sophistication, see Lawrence Sondhaus: *Navies of Europe: 1815–2002.* Harlow: Longman, 2002, 323–335; the UK MOD announces in the last review to slightly increase the navy's size but there still seems to be some reliance on dormant capabilities, NSS SD Review 2015, 76.

137 Cf. note 133.

138 Fuess, "Rotting Ships."

139 This is a problem not unfamiliar to modern historians of war. The German armed forces in WW2, for instance, although disposing of a great quantity of military matériel could not train tank or air crews to keep up with the speed of production (esp. from 1944), Richard Overy: *War and Economy in the Third Reich.* Oxford: Clarendon Press, 1994, 343–375.

140 Ayalon, *The Mamluks and Naval Power*, 5 seq.

141 Cf. how the Venetians trained their naval reserves in the lagoon during the war of Chioggia; Frederic Chapin Lane: *Venice – A Maritime Republic.* Baltimore: The Johns Hopkins University Press, 1973, 193.

ordinate" ruler of Cyprus had to be disciplined several times and the Mamluks did this successfully. The very system of dormant or just-in-time-produced naval capability seems responsible for the rather mixed success of Mamluk fleets. The fleets suffered naval defeat against the Franks of Cyprus in 1270 and later against the Portuguese.[142] Even the ultimately successful operations such as against Cyprus in 1425 or Rhodes in 1443 reveal a serious lack of experience and leadership. The action of 1443, although having some limited success, illustrates how the ill-coordinated, hap-hazard navigating and difficult weather hampered the progress of the fleet and hailed its early return.[143] It was apparently not so much the seaworthiness of the ships than the seaworthiness of the crews and especially the naval officers causing the problems. It was arguably the lack of an adequately trained and respected naval officer corps, rather than hard-ware, i. e. artillery (which, in any case, the Mamluk navy did dispose of),[144] which decided the fate of the Mamluks against the Portuguese in the Indian Ocean.[145] Even a small permanent naval staff led by respected and well-trained officers could have made a difference. Even if only equipped with a small and shabby range of ships they could have trained properly and could have built an esprit de corps, trained, gained experience and know-how. And that is what the Mamluk fleet, although adequately equipped and staffed, was badly lacking: combat power. This extra that decides whether a unit is more or less than the sum of its material parts is somewhere in the fluid and not easily assessable realm of soft-skills such as morale, leadership, esprit the corps, discipline, training and experience.[146]

Delegation of Naval Interdiction to Venice

Could the Mamluks really forfeit all forward maritime defence and capacity to protect protection of trade routes that needed a blue-water and permanent, rather than merely brown- (riverine) or green-water (littoral) navy? How did they

142 Ayalon, *The Mamluks and Naval Power*, 5 (1270), 7 (Portuguese); Fuess, "Rotting ships," 57–60.

143 Yehoshua Frenkel: "Al-Biqāʿī's Naval War Report," in *History and Society during the Mamluk Period (1250–1517): Studies of the Annemarie Schimmel Research College I*, ed. by Stephan Conermann. Göttingen: V&R unipress, 2014, 9–19; cf. C. Edmund Bosworth: "Arab Attacks on Rhodes in the Pre-Ottoman Period," *Journal of the Royal Asiatic Society* 6/2 (July 1996): 157–164, here 162 seqq.

144 See above, regarding the warship found in ʿAtlīt harbor, note 14.

145 Differences in training (drill) remain more important than differences in technical fire power even in the early modern period, Jeremy Black: *European Warfare, 1660–1815*, Warfare and History. London: UCL Press, 1994, 2.

146 Cf. for the concept and similar shortcoming in the US army during WW2, Martin Creveld: *Fighting Power: German and U.S. Army Performance, 1939–1945*. London: Arms and Armour Press, 1983.

organise naval interdiction and forward coastal defence without maintaining a proper permanent fleet?

Fuess showed how the Mamluks outsourced these services to Venice.[147] I would even argue that they adopted the Venetian fleet as their own permanent blue-water navy; that they delegated rather than outsourced naval interdiction and protection of the commerce bound for Mamluk ports. For Venice was not an external actor but a subordinate of the sultan and thus an entity within the wider Mamluk Empire. The emir of Alexandria, addressed as the commander of the fleet/imperial gateway, was also the superior of the Venetian consul and the Venetian community. The Venetians could call directly on the sultan and did so occasionally.[148] The privileges of 1415 do not explicitly formulate such a right to immediate access. They emphasize, however, that only the sultan and by him appointed officials could administer justice in cases involving Venetians.[149] Therefore, the Venetians often took regress to the emir of Alexandria. In a document from 1418, the sultan, while clearly affirming the privileges granted, rejected the Venetian request to intervene on their behalf against supposedly incurred injuries and referred them to the emir of Alexandria.[150] We can, of course, hardly argue that the emir of Alexandria had nominal let alone practical say in Venetian maritime operations. The term admiral for a naval commander, however, enters Venetian parlance in that period. It denominates inspectors of Venetian ports and chief naval engineers (cf. the early modern English "master") seconding the commander of the fleet (rather than the commander himself).[151] This seems to indicate that the Venetians perceived the emir of Alexandria as the commander of the port rather than a naval commander.[152]

147 Albrecht Fuess, "Why Venice, not Genoa?" 251–266.

148 This is certainly implied by the 1344/45 privileges, cf. the preamble: "Franchi (…) qui veniunt ante ostium nostrum, (…) aliquis venit coram nobis," Thomas, *Diplomatarium* I, 292; for Venetian embassies to Cairo, see for instance, Christ, *Trading Conflicts*, 273–280.

149 "Anchora è entro i pacti de Venitiani che quando lo intravegnirà che i bexogna esser al conspecto de algun zudixio, per haver over per altra differentia, zoè sì in civil chomo in criminal, da sarain a venitian, over da venitian a sarain, che queli che die zudegar o termenar si facte caxon sia de queli che è deputadi per nome del soldan; e siando dentro dal Chayro, diebia esser a la presentia del soldan over del naybo de la cità, over de lo azebo, over de i offitiali messi per nome del soldan in chadaun luogo del so reame"; Thomas/Predelli, *Diplomatarium*, II, 311.

150 Missive by the Mamluk Sultan (Mu'ayyad Shaykh) to the Venetian community in Alexandria containing a copy of a letter to the emir of Alexandria and a safe conduct in translation, 9 April 1418, ASVe, *Procuratori di San Marco*, Commissarie miste, b. 180, Commissaria Biagio Dolfin, fasc. IX, f. [1].

151 Probably this is a secondary usage derived from the title's application in Sicily, Genoa and/or Aragon.

152 Giuseppe Boerio: *Dizionario del dialetto veneziano* reprint Venezia: Giunti, 1993. (Venezia: Giovanni Cecchini, 1867) s.v. "almirante" does not give any etymological explanation and does only mention the admirals of ports of Venice (Lido, Malamocco, Chioggia) not the

The delegation of sea-power to the Venetians was part and parcel of the contract underlying the safe-conduct, *amān*, which was the base of the privileged status the Venetians enjoyed. The Venetians, similar to any other community (*ṭāʾifa*) enjoying an *amān* had to agree to a financial contribution. Although the Venetians enjoyed overall a more privileged position than the regular *dhimmī* communities, there was still a Venetian *quid pro quo.* The counter-service comprised tax and other quasi-tributary payments as well as the regularity of trade (especially of gold and copper imports). It also included Venetian naval services, such as the clearing of eastern Mediterranean sea-lanes from pirates and the ransoming of Muslims taken prisoner by such pirates[153] as well as the providing of naval intelligence on maritime or, rather, amphibious threats to the Mamluk Empire.[154] In Piloti's crusading treatise we find a particularly revealing example of how the Venetian fleet could parade as Mamluk fleet. The Venetian consul conducted a mission to liberate Muslim captives in the Aegean in 1409/10.[155] Piloti describes how they were sent to the sultan in Cairo parading under a Venetian banner and claims to have addressed the sultan with these words:

> Seigneur souldain, le beau present que je apporte à la Vostre Seigneurie si est cest penon d'or, qui est l'enseigne que portent Venitians, lezquelx sont seigneurs de la mer. Et tous coursaires qui voyent ceste enseigne s'enfuyent et ne s'acostent pour le peur qu'il ont de lui. Et avecque ceste seurté nous avons passés la mer salée, et arivâmes en Alexandrie saulvement; de quoy le grant Dieu en soit loé.[156]

According to Piloti, the sultan took no offence but was pleased and lavishly compensated Piloti for his services. Of course this is just Piloti's narrative and not

naval officer, cf. for the latter, Doris Stöckly: *Le système de l'incanto des galées du marché à Venise.* Leiden: Brill, 1995, 290–94; Christ, *Trading Conflicts*, 127, 134 n. 82.

153 Georg Christ: "Transkulturelle Pirateriebekämpfung? Venezianisch-Mamlukische Kooperation und Gefangenenbefreiung im östlichen Mittelmeerraum im Spätmittelalter," in *Seeraub im Mittelmeerraum. Piraterie, Korsarentum und maritime Gewalt von der Antike bis zur Neuzeit*, ed. by Nikolas Jaspert and Sebastian Kolditz. Paderborn: Ferdinand Schöningh, 2013, 363–375.

154 Privileges for Venetians in Syria from 1375, "Comanda meser lo Soldam chel consolo di Veneciani diebia esser liale con tutta la soa generacion d'avanti la porta del soldam Syriph, che in caso chel consolo ho alguno de la soa generacione sentiseno ho avesse nuova che armata alguna si fesse per alguna generacione, la qual fosse per dannificare le terre del Soldam, che in quella fiata il consolo o altri de so generacion diebia far asaver le nuove al naybo del Soldam che serà in Damasco; et quando lui sentisse questo et no<n e>l fesse asaver al naybo, che li diebia portar quella pena che plaserà al Soldam." This clearly was not on the Venetian draft of privileges they sought and so is stated by the scribe/translator preceding the clause: "Nota como questo capitolo infrascripto de commandamento de meser lo Soldam fo scripto, ma non fo de mio consentimento." Thomas/Predelli, *Diplomatarium*, II, 171. But it seems to have worked; the Venetians subsequently did provide such intelligence, Fuess, "Prelude," 176.

155 Piloti, *Traité*, 201–206.

156 Piloti, *Traité*, § 137, 207.

confirmed by other sources. Yet the message, inserted into a compilation posing as a crusading treatise, sits rather too uncomfortably to be invented. The Venetian fleet was the fleet of the Mediterranean and as Venice was part of the Mamluk Empire, the Venetian flag presented no offense to the sultan but as the ensign of the Venetian fleet was also an ensign of his imperial fleet.[157]

Conclusion

These few considerations widely confirm Ayalon's and Fuess' findings. They might give rise, however, to a slightly different interpretation. The Mamluks wanted to control transit trade and thus they needed to somehow control the sea and to provide safe ports. If they wanted their lands to prosper, they had to defend their coasts. And they did. For sure, pirate attacks happened and happened again. But is that evidence for the absence of a Mamluk coastal defence system? We could of course argue that the main reason why the Mamluks were not attacked more ferociously was that they controlled the main routes of the Indian trade to the Mediterranean; that the Turks increasingly came to the fore as objects of Crusade. It is precisely because of that situation that it was rational to save costs and slim-down coastal defences, which, after all, were robust enough to successfully protect the coast, for instance against the likes of Boucicaut. It was not their priority, to be sure, and often haphazardly executed but there was a concept and it was a basically sound one. The Mamluks knew that they had to provide good ports. The fact that the system did not always work, that Latin nations fought each other in the harbour of Alexandria, cannot be interpreted as a Mamluk withdrawal from the sea. It is rather indicative that those incidents did not seem to harm trade enough to justify additional investments in the harbours' security infrastructure. Rather, they seemed to be the unavoidable consequence of dealing with traditionally predatory maritime traders-raiders. Similarly, with regard to the fleet, Mamluk suffering was apparently not pronounced and continuous enough to justify more costly and more direct naval preparations. The combination of the delegation of naval policing to Venice (similar to later Ottoman-French arrangements e.g. regarding Crete[158]) while maintaining a dormant naval capability mainly based on autochthonous civilian naval resources, presented an apparently sufficient and certainly cost-effective solution. A fleet could be constructed, outfitted and paraded in front of the sultan on relatively short notice. This would be a most remarkable feat indeed and raise the question

157 Cf. my "Transkulturelle Pirateriebekämpfung," 369–373.

158 Molly Greene: "Ruling an Island without a Navy. A Comparative View of Venetian and Ottoman Crete," *Oriente moderno* 20 (81), no. 1 (2001): 193–207, here 206.

of how the Mamluks managed the necessary knowledge to make this possible.[159] More research would be needed into the Mamluk naval substructure: the arsenals in Miṣr/Būlāq and the Mamluk naval administration in order to better understand this astonishing dormant naval capability. Yet once the fleet hit the waters of the Mediterranean or later the Indian Ocean, the performance was not satisfactory. The main problem was not to build a fleet; it was to operate it. Delegation of naval power and the consequent absence of a permanent fleet made adequate group-formation, disciplining and training of crews and especially of naval officers of the dormant navy difficult, nay impossible. This is the reason for the naval inferiority of the Mamluks. Similar phenomena are plaguing armed forces today. Military planners bending to political pressure to cut costs do so and speak of "smart power" in order to justify the reduction of armed forces to mere shadows of their former selves. Thereby they uphold old ambitions of grandeur (and marshal's positions). Particularly affected are the notoriously expensive navies. The claim that a reduced core of a fleet (of tanks, guns, planes or ships) could preserve the know-how and be able to generate more forces as needed is bureaucratically convincing yet treacherous. Force generation, even if supported by sufficient logistical and industrial power, is not enough. It is not enough to have the planned number of units manned with the appropriate number of sailors. Even if nominally trained in all the different bureaucratically defined modules, this is not enough. For to operate a fleet successfully, we need more than just sailors who "given an oar, can row well."[160] Crews and especially officers have to be trained holistically, as crews, as entire fleets. They have to be respected and experienced in order to turn a bunch of ships and their crews into a successful fleet. The Mamluk example can serve as an example for the relaxed and elegant efficacy of a system which worked reasonably well despite (or perhaps even because) being part of a waning empire in a context of economic transformation-cum-decline. Yet it should also be a warning. The Mamluk fleet, as many other features of the empire, might remind us comfortably or uncomfortably of our own world; mirror conditions, problems and challenges of a post-national, saturated and happily retiring society. Highly skilled professionalism and sophisticated armament could ultimately not camouflage that the military provision, although sophisticated, was not exactly robust. The fleet had all it needed but not enough substance to withhold unexpected shocks. It was perfectly well-suited to deal with the routine problems military planners envisaged but it struggled to cope with the reality of complex naval operations such as

159 It would nevertheless seem that the Mamluk naval technology was somewhat inferior or less practical; Frenkel, "Al-Biqāʿī's Naval War Report," 5.

160 Baybars according to Ayalon, *The Mamluks and Naval Power*, 5.

attacking Rhodes and failed when it had to cope with a new and unexpected challenge – the Portuguese emerging in the Indian Ocean and the Red Sea.

Bibliography

Archival and Archaeological Sources

Archivio di Stato di Venezia (ASVe):
Miscellanea di carte non appartenenti a nessun archivio.
Procuratori di San Marco, Commissarie miste.
Archivio di Stato di Prato:
Fondo Datini.
The Archaeological Survey of Israel http://www.antiquities.org.il/survey/new/default_en.aspx#12.

Edited Material and Studies

ʿAbd al-Raḥmān Ibn Khaldūn, ʿAbd al-Raḥmān: *The Muqaddimah: An Introduction to History,* vol. 2, ed. by Franz Rosenthal. New York: Pantheon Books, 1958.

Abel, F. M.: *Géographie de la Palestine*, vol. II, Paris 1938.

Abu El-Haj, Nadia: *Facts on the Ground: Archaeological Practice and Territorial Self-Fashioning in Israeli Society.* Chicago: The University of Chicago Press, 2001.

Amari, Michele: *Diplomi arabi nel R. Archivio Fiorentino.* Firenze: Reale Soprintendenza Generale agli Archivi/Le Monnier, 1863.

Amitai, Reuven: "Dealing with Reality: Early Mamluk Military Policy and the Allocation of Resources". In *Crossroads between Latin Europe and the Near East: Corollaries of the Frankish Presence in the Eastern Mediterranean (12th–14th centuries)*, edited by Stefan Leder. Istanbuler Texte und Studien 24. Würzburg: Ergon Verlag, 2011.

Amitai, Reuven: "Post-Crusader Acre in Light of a Mamluk Inscription and a Fatwā Document from Damascus". In *Developing Perspectives in Mamluk History. Essays in Honour of Amalia Levanoni*, edited by Yuval Ben-Bassat. Islamic History and Civilization 143. Leiden: Brill, 2017.

Amitai, Reuven: "The Development of a Muslim City in Palestine: Gaza under the Mamluks". *ASK Working Paper* 28 (Aug 2017).

Apellániz Ruiz de Galarreta, Francisco Javier: *Pouvoir et finance en Méditerranée pré-moderne: Le deuxième état Mamelouk et le commerce des épices (1389–1517).* Barcelona: CSIC, 2009.

Appuhn, Karl Richard: "Inventing Nature: Forests, Forestry, and State Power in Renaissance Venice," *The Journal of Modern History* 72/4 (2000): 861–889.

Arbel, Benjamin: "Venetian Trade in Fifteenth-Century Acre: The Letters to Francesco Bevilaqua, 1471–72," *Asian and African Studies: Journal of the Israel Oriental Society* 22 (1988): 227–288.

Ashtor, Eliyahu: "L'apogée du commerce vénitien au Levant. Un nouvel essai d'explication," in *Venezia. Centro di Mediazione tra Oriente e Occidente (secoli XV–XVI) Aspetti e Problemi*, ed. by Agostino Pertusi, Hans-Georg Beck, Manoussos I. Manoussacas, Florence: Leo S. Olschky, 1977, 307–326.

Ashtor, Eliyahu: *Levant Trade in the Later Middle Ages.* Princeton, N.J.: Princeton University Press, 1983.

Atiya, Aziz Suryal: "An Unpublished 14th Century Fatwa on the Status of Foreigners in Mamluk Egypt and Syria," in *Studien zur Geschichte und Kultur des Nahen und Fernen Ostens: Paul Kahle zum 60. Geburtstag überreicht von Freunden und Schülern aus dem Kreise des Orientalischen Seminars der Universität Bonn*, ed. by Willi Heffening and Willibald Kirfel. Leiden: Brill, 1935.

Ayalon, David: "Bahriyya, II. The Navy of the Mamluks", in *EI²*, vol. 1, 945–947.

Ayalon, David: *Gunpowder and Firearms in the Mamluk Kingdom. A Challenge to a Mediaeval Society.* London: Frank Cass, 1978.

Ayalon, David: *The Mamluks and Naval Power: A Phase of the Struggle between Islam and Christian Europe.* Jerusalem: [s.n.], 1965.

Barbé, Hervé, Lehrer, Yoav, Avissar, Miriam: "Ha-Bonim", *Hadashot Arkheologiyot: Excavations and Surveys in Israel* (HA-ESI) 114 (2002), 30 2 A-33 2 A [34–38 Hebrew].

Becker, C. H.: "Miṣr", section 2. ii, in *EI²*, vol. VII, 149.

Benvenisti, B. M.: *The Crusaders in the Holy Land.* Jerusalem, 1970.

Black, Jeremy: *European Warfare, 1660–1815.* London: UCL Press, 1994.

Boerio, Giuseppe: *Dizionario del dialetto veneziano.* Venice: Giovanni Cecchini, 1867 (reprint Venice: Giunti, 1993).

Bosworth, Edmund: "Arab Attacks on Rhodes in the Pre-Ottoman Period," *Journal of the Royal Asiatic Society* 6/2 (1996): 157–164.

Burns, Ross: *Monuments of Syria. An Historical Guide.* London: I.B. Tauris, 1999.

Büssow, Johann: "Gaza", in: EI³, ed. by Kate Fleet, Gudrun Krämer, Denis Matringe, John Nawas, Everett Rowson, consulted online on 02 September 2016 <http://dx.doi.org/10.1163/1573-3912_ei3_COM_27380> first published online: 2014.

Cannella, Anne Françoise and Jean des Prés: *Gemmes, verre coloré, fausses pierres précieuses au Moyen Age: le quatrième livre du "Trésorier de philosophie naturelle des pierres précieuses" de Jean d'Outremeuse.* Geneva: Librairie Droz, 2006.

Cassandro, Giovanni Italo: "Formazione del diritto marittimo veneziano," in *Venezia e il Levante fino al secolo XV*, vol. 1, ed. by Agostino Pertusi. Firenze: Leo S. Olschki Editore, 1973, 147–184.

Christ, Georg: "Collapse and Continuity: Alexandria as a Declining City with a Thriving Port (13th–16th Centuries)," in *The Routledge Handbook of Maritime Trade Around Europe, 1300–1600: Commercial Networks and Urban Autonomy*, ed. by Wim Blockmans, Mikhail Krom, Justyna Wubs-Mrozewicz. London: Routledge, 2017, 121–140.

Christ, Georg: "Settling Accounts with the Sultan: Cortesia, Zemechia and Fiscal Integration of Venice into the Mamluk Empire," in *The Flux and Reflux of Late Medieval State Formations: Integration, Negotiation and Political Order across Fifteenth-century Eurasia – Parallels, Connections, Divergences*, ed. by Jo van Steenbergen, Rulers & Elites. Leiden: Brill, forthcoming.

Christ, Georg: "Transkulturelle Pirateriebekämpfung? Venezianisch-Mamlukische Kooperation und Gefangenenbefreiung im östlichen Mittelmeerraum im Spätmittelalter," in

Seeraub im Mittelmeerraum. Piraterie, Korsarentum und maritime Gewalt von der Antike bis zur Neuzeit, ed. by Nikolas Jaspert and Sebastian Kolditz. Paderborn: Ferdinand Schöningh, 2013, 363–375.

Christ, Georg: "Eine Stadt wandert aus. Kollaps und Kontinuität im spätmittelalterlichen Alexandria," *Viator* 42 (2011): 145–168.

Christ, Georg: *Trading Conflicts. Venetian Merchants and Mamluk Officials in Late Medieval Alexandria.* Leiden: Brill, 2012.

Christides, Vassilios: "Ibn al-Manqlī (Manglī) and Leo VI: New Evidence on Arab-Byzantine Ship Construction and Naval Warfare," *Byzantinoslavica* 56 (1995): 83–96.

Christides, Vassilios: "Milâh'a (navigation)". In *Encyclopaedia of Islam*, edited by P.J. Bearman et al. 2nd ed. Leiden: Brill.

Christides, Vassilios: "Naval Warfare in the Eastern Mediterranean (6th–14th Centuries): An Arabic Translation of Leo VI's Naumachia," *Graeco-Arabica* 3 (1984): 137–148.

Christides, Vassilios: "New Light on Navigation and Naval Warfare in the Eastern Mediterranean, the Red Sea and the Indian Ocean, 6th-14th Centuries A.D.," *Nubica* 3/1 (1989/93): 3–42.

Cipolla, Carlo M.: *Guns, Sails and Empires: Technological Innovation and the Early Phases of European Expansion 1400–1700.* New York: Pantheon Books, 1965.

Creveld, Martin: *Fighting Power: German and U.S. Army Performance, 1939–1945.* London: Arms and Armour Press, 1983.

Décobert, Christian: "Alexandrie au XIIIe siècle. Une nouvelle topographie," in *Alexandrie médiévale 1*, ed. by Christian Décobert and Jean-Yves Empereur. Cairo: IFAO, 1998, 71–100.

Delaville le Roulx, Joseph: *La France en Orient au XIVe siècle. Expéditions du Maréchal Boucicaut.* 2 vols. Paris: E. Thorin, 1885.

Drory, Joseph: "Founding a New Mamlaka," in *The Mamluks in Egyptian and Syrian Politics and Society*, ed. by Michael Winter and Amalia Levanoni. Leiden: Brill, 2004, 163–187.

Druks, A.: "Akko," *Hadashot Arkheologiyot: Excavations and Surveys in Israel* 3 (1984): 2–4.

Elias, Norbert: "Studies in the Genesis of the Naval Profession," *The British Journal of Sociology* 1/4 (1950): 291–309.

Frankel, Rafael: "Topographical Notes on the Territory of Acre in the Crusader Period," *Israel Exploration Journal* 38 (1988): 249–272.

Frenkel, Yehoshua: "Jihâd in the Medieval Mediterranean Sea", in *Crossroads between Latin Europe and the Near East: Corollaries of the Frankish Presence in the Eastern Mediterranean (12th–14th Centuries)*, ed. by Stefan Leder, Istanbuler Texte und Studien 24. Würzburg: Ergon Verlag, 2011, 103–125.

Frenkel, Yehoshua: "Al-Biqāʿī's Naval War Report," in *History and Society during the Mamluk Period (1250–1517): Studies of the Annemarie Schimmel Research College I*, ed. by Stephan Conermann. Göttingen: V&R unipress, 2014, 9–19.

Fuess, Albrecht: "Beirut in Mamluk Times (1291–1517)", *Aram* 9–10 (1997–1998): 85–101.

Fuess, Albrecht: "Déplacer une ville au temps des Mamelouks: Le cas de Tripoli," *Chronos* 19 (2009): 157–172.

Fuess, Albrecht: "From the Sea to the Foot of the Hill. The Dislocation of Tripoli by the Mamluks after 1289," *Burgen und Schlösser* 4 (2009): 218–223.

Fuess, Albrecht: "Prelude to a Stronger Involvement in the Middle East: French Attacks on Beirut in the Years 1403 and 1520," *Al-Masaq: Studia Arabo-Islamica Mediterranea* 17/2 (2005): 171–192.

Fuess, Albrecht: "Rotting Ships and Razed Harbours: The Naval Policy of the Mamluks," *Mamlūk Studies Review* 5 (2001): 45–71.

Fuess, Albrecht: "Why Venice, not Genoa? How Venice Emerged as the Mamluks' Favourite European Trading Partner After 1365," in *Union in Separation: Diasporic Groups and Identities in the Eastern Mediterranean (1100–1800)*, ed. by Georg Christ, Roberto Zaugg, Franz-Julius Morche, Wolfgang Kaiser, Stefan Burkhardt. Rome: Viella, 2015, 251–266.

Fuess, Albrecht: *Verbranntes Ufer: Auswirkungen mamlukischer Seepolitik auf Beirut und die syro-palästinensische Küste (1250–1517)*. Leiden: Brill, 2001.

Fulin, Rinaldo: "Il canale di Suez e la Repubblica di Venezia (MCIV)," *Archivio Veneto* II/1 (1871): 175–213.

Gaube, Heinz (ed.): *Tübinger Atlas des Vorderen Orients* (TAVO). Tübingen: Reichert, 1977.

Gluzman, Renard: "Venice Overseas Afloat: Private Shipping in Renaissance Venice," paper presented at the workshop *Venice Overseas, 1400–1800. Second International Workshop for Young Scholars*, Venice 27–28 May 2011.

Greene, Molly: "Ruling an Island without a Navy. A Comparative View of Venetian and Ottoman Crete," *Oriente moderno* 20/1 (2001): 193–207.

Grünenfelder, Michael: "Die Aufwuchsfähigkeit der Luftwaffe," *Air Power Revue* [Schweizer Armee] 4 (Oct 2015) http://www.isn.ethz.ch/Digital-Library/Publications/Detail/?lang=en&id=14096.

Haarmann, Ulrich and Bettina Zantana, "Zwischen Suez und Aden: Pilger und Fernhändler im Roten Meer vom zehnten bis zum sechzehnten Jahrhundert," in *Der Indische Ozean in historischer Perspektive*, ed. by Stephan Conermann. Hamburg: E.B.-Verlag, 1998, 109–142.

Hanna, Nelly: *An Urban History of Būlāq in the Mamluk and Ottoman Periods*. Cairo: Institut français d'archéologie orientale, 1983.

Hart, Liddell: *Geschichte des Zweiten Weltkriegs*. Wiesbaden: Fourier Verlag, 1970.

Hartmann, Richard: "Die politische Geographie des Mamlukenreiches. Kapitel 5 und 6 des Staatshandbuches des Ibn Fad'lallâh al-'Omarîs", *Zeitschrift der Deutschen Morgenländischen Gesellschaft* 70, 71 (1916, 1917): 1–40, 477–511; 429–430.

Heyd, Uriel: "A Turkish Description of the Coast of Palestine in the Early Sixteenth Century," *Israel Exploration Journal* 6/4 (1956): 201–216.

Irwin, Robert: "Gunpowder and Firearms in the Mamluk Sultanate Reconsidered," in *The Mamluks in Egyptian and Syrian Politics and Society*, ed. by Michael Winter and Amalia Levanoni. Leiden: Brill, 2004, 117–139.

Jacoby, David: "Ports of Pilgrimage to the Holy Land, Eleventh-fourteenth Century: Jaffa, Acre, Alexandria," in *The Holy Portolano. Le portulan sacré. The Sacred Geography of Navigation in the Middle Ages. Fribourg Colloquium 2013. La géographie religieuse de la navigation au moyen âge. Colloque fribourgeois 2013*, ed. by Michele Bacci and Martin Rohde. Berlin: de Gruyter, 2014, 51–72.

Jacoby, David: "Refugees from Acre in Famagusta around 1300," in *The Harbour of all this Sea and Realm: Crusader to Venetian Famagusta*, ed. by Michael J. K. Walsh, Tamás Kiss, and Nicholas S. H. Coureas. Budapest: Central European University Press, 2014, 53–67.

Jacoby, David: "The Supply of War Materials to Egypt in the Crusader Period," *Jerusalem Studies in Arabic and Islam* 25 (2001): 102–132.

Jacoby, David: "The Trade of Crusader Acre in the Levantine Context: an Overview," *Archivio storico del Sannio: rivista semestrale del Centro Interdipartimentale per gli Studi Aziendali, Economici e Sociali della Facoltà di Economia di Benevento* 3 (1998): 103–120.

Jacoby, David: "The Venetians in Byzantine and Lusignan Cyprus: Trade, Settlement, and Politics," in *La Serenissima and la Nobilissima: Venice in Cyprus and Cyprus in Venice*, ed. by Angel Nicolaou-Konnari. Nicosia, 2009, 59–100.

Johns, C. N.: "Reports on the Excavations at Pilgrims' Castle, ʿAtlit", *Quarterly of the Department of Antiquities in Palestine* I (1932), 111–129; II (1933), 41–104; III (1934), 145–164; IV (1935), 122–137; V (1936), 31–60; VI (1938), 121–152.

Khalilieh, Hassan Salih: "The Ribāṭ System and its Role in Coastal Navigation," *Journal of the Economic and Social History of the Orient* 42/2 (1999): 212–225.

Kindermann, Hans: *"Schiff" im Arabischen. Untersuchung über Vorkommen und Bedeutung der Termini.* Zwickau: Diss. Univ. Bonn, 1934.

Krebs, Werner: *Innen- und Aussenpolitik Ägyptens 741–784/1341–1382.* Hamburg; Diss. Univ. Hamburg, 1980.

Lalande, Denis: *Jehan II le Meingre, dit Boucicaut (1366–1421). Étude d'une biographie héroïque.* Geneva: Librairie Droz, 1988.

Lane, Frederic Chapin: *Venice – A Maritime Republic.* Baltimore: The Johns Hopkins University Press, 1973.

Lapidus, Ira Marvin: *Muslim Cities in the Later Middle Ages.* Cambridge, Mass: Harvard University Press, 1984.

Machinek, Kathrin: *Das Fort Qaitbay in Alexandria – Baugeschichte und Architektur einer mamlukischen Hafenfestung im mittelalterlichen Stadtbefestigungssystem von Alexandria.* Karlsruhe: Thesis faculty of architecture, KIT, 2014.

Mänglī, Muḥammad ibn: *al-Ahkām al-mulūkija wa ḍ-ḍawābit an-nāmūsiya fī fann al-qitāl*, partly ed. in *The Age of the Dromôn: The Byzantine Navy ca. 500–1204*, ed. by Elizabeth M. Jeffreys and John H. Pryor. Leiden: Brill, 2005.

Mas Latrie, Louis Comte de: *Histoire de l'île de Chypre sous le règne des princes de la maison de Lusignan*, vol. 2. Paris, 1852.

Meloy, John L.: *Mamluk Authority, Meccan Autonomy and Red Sea Trade, 797–859/1395–1455.* Chicago: PhD thesis University of Chicago, 1998.

Meyer, Werner, John Zimmer and Maria-Letizia Boscardin: "Krak de Chevaliers. Zwischenbericht über das Projekt 2005/7", *Burgen und Schlösser* 4 (2009): 242–245.

Moffett, Randall: "Defense Schemes of Southampton in the Late Medieval Period, 1300–1500," *Journal of Medieval Military History* 11 (2013): 215–58.

Möhring, Hannes: "Die muslimische Strategie der Schleifung fränkischer Festungen und Städte in der Levante," *Burgen und Schlösser* 50/4 (2009): 211–217.

Muhammad, Tarek M.: "Ibn Mangli and Naval Warfare: The Question of Greek Fire between the Muslims and Byzantines," *International Journal of Maritime History* 21/1 (2009): 55–80.

Müller-Wiener, Martina: *Eine Stadtgeschichte Alexandrias von 564/1169 bis in die Mitte des 9./15. Jahrhunderts Verwaltung und innerstädtische Organisationsformen.* Berlin: Klaus Schwarz, 1992.

Nicolle, David: *Acre 1291.* Oxford: Osprey Publishing, 2005.

Nielsen, Jørgen S.: "The Political Geography and Administration of Bahri Mamluk Palestine: The Evidence of al-Qalqashandi," in *Studia Palaestina. Studies in Honour of Constantine K. Zurayk*, ed. by Hisham Nashabe. Beirut: Institute for Palestine Studies, 1988, 114–133.

al-Nuwayrī, Muḥammad Ibn Qāsim: *Kitāb al-Ilmām bi-al-iʿlām fīmā jarat bihī al-aḥkām wa-al-umūr al-maqḍīya fī waqʿat al-Iskandarīya.* Hyderabad: Osmania Oriental Publications Bureau, 1970.

Overy, Richard J.: *War and Economy in the Third Reich.* Oxford: Clarendon Press, 1994.

Pegolotti, Francesco di Balducci: *La pratica della mercatura*, ed. by Allan Evans. Cambridge, Mass.: The Mediaeval Academy of America, 1936.

Piekalkiewicz, Janusz: *Krieg der Panzer 1939–1945.* Eltville am Rhein: Bechtermünz Verlag, 1989.

Piloti, Emmanuele: *Traité d'Emmanuel Piloti sur le passage en Terre Sainte*, edited by Pierre-Herman Dopp. Louvain: Éditions E. Nauwelaerts, 1958.

Pringle, Denys: *Secular Buildings in the Crusader Kingdom of Jerusalem: an Archaeological Gazetteer.* Cambridge: Cambridge Univ. Press, 1997.

Pringle, Denys: *The Red Tower (al-Burj al-Ahmar): Settlement in the Plain of Sharon at the Time of the Crusaders and Mamluks A.D. 1099–1516.* London: British School of Archaeology in Jerusalem, 1986.

Richard, Jean: "Le royaume de Chypre et l'embargo sur le commerce avec l'Égypte (fin XIIIe – début XIVe siècle," *Comptes rendues de l'Académie des inscriptions et belles lettres* 128 (1984): 120–134.

Rosen-Ayalon, M.: "Ramla," in: *The New Encyclopedia of Archaeological Excavations in the Holy Land* ed. by Ephraim Stern, Israel Exploration Society & Carta. Jerusalem: The Israel Map and Publishing Co. Ltd, 1992, vol. 4, 1269–1271.

Sadek, M. M.: *Die mamlukische Architektur der Stadt Gaza.* Berlin: K. Schwarz, 1991.

Salam-Liebich, H.: *The Architecture of the Mamluk City of Tripoli.* Cambridge (Mass.): Aga Khan Program for Islamic Architecture at Harvard University and the Massachusetts Institute of Technology, 1983.

Schacht, Joseph: "Amān," in *EI*[2], vol. I, 429a–430a.

Schur, Nathan: *תולדות עכו – A History of Acre.* Tel Aviv: Dvir, 1990.

Sharvit, Jacob and Planer, Dror: "'Akko, the Southern Seawall," *Hadashot Arkheologiyot: Excavations and Surveys in Israel* 126 (2014).

Sharon, M.: *Corpus Inscriptionum Arabicarum Palaestinae (CIAP) 1.* Leiden: Brill, 1997.

Sondhaus, Lawrence: *Navies of Europe: 1815–2002.* Harlow: Longman, 2002.

Stahl, Alan M.: "Michael of Rhodes: Mariner in Service to Venice (chapter 2)," in *The Book of Michael of Rhodes*, ed. by Pamela O. Long, David McGee and Alan M. Stahl, 3 vols. Cambridge (Mass.): MIT Press, 2009, 35–98.

Starr, Chester G.: "Coastal Defense in the Roman World," *The American Journal of Philology* 64/1 (1943): 56–70.

Stern, Edna J.: "The Fatimid, Crusader and Mamluk. Early Ottoman Ceramic Finds from the ʿAkko Marina: Some Insights into Medieval Maritime Activity," *ʿAtiqot* 76 (2013): 139–168.

Stöckly, Doris: *Le système de l'incanto des galées du marché à Venise.* Leiden: Brill, 1995.

Tatcher, Ayelet: "ʿAkko," *Hadashot Arkheologiyot: Excavations and Surveys in Israel* 117 (2005).

Theunissen, Hans Peter Alexander: "Ottoman Venetian Diplomatics: The ʿAhd-names. The Historical Background and the Development of a Category of Political-Commerical Instruments together with an Annotated Edition of a Corpus of Relevant Documents," *Arabica* 1/2 (1998): 1–698.

Thomas, Georg Martin and Predelli, Riccardo (eds.): *Diplomatarium veneto-levantinum sive acta et diplomata res venetas graecas atque levantis illustrantia, pars II, a. 1351–1454.* Deputazione veneta di storia patria. Venice 1899.

Toombs, Lawrence: *Tell el-Hesi: Modern Military Trenching and Muslim Cemetery in Field I, Strata I–II.* Waterloo, ON: Wilfrid Laurier Univ. Press, 1985.

Van Steenbergen, Jo: "'Mamlukisation' between Social Theory and Social Practice: An Essay on Reflexivity, State Formation, and the Late Medieval Sultanate of Cairo," *ASK Working Paper* 22 (2015) (= https://www.mamluk.uni-bonn.de/publications/working-paper/ask-wp-22-vansteenbergen.pdf.

Vann, Theresa M.: "Christian, Muslim and Jewish Mariners in the Port of Rhodes, 1453–1480," *Medieval Encounters* 13/2 (2007): 158–173.

Walker, Bethany J.: "Militarization to Nomadization: The Middle and Late Islamic Periods," *Near Eastern Archaeology* 62/4 (1999): 202–232.

Wansbrough, John. E.: "Venice and Florence in the Mamluk Commercial Privileges," *Bulletin of the School of Oriental and African Studies* 28 (1965): 483–523.

Weil, Gustav: *Das Chalifat unter den Bahritischen Mamlukensultanen.* Stuttgart: Metzler, 1860.

Zoppoth, G.: "Muhammad Ibn Mängli: Ein ägyptischer Offizier und Schriftsteller des 14. Jh.," *Wiener Zeitschrift für die Kunde des Morgenlandes* 53 (1957): 288–99.

Bethany J. Walker (University of Bonn)

The "Liquid Landscapes" of the Late Mamluk Mediterranean: Rural Perspectives on the Ever-Evolving Sultanate

Introduction

It would be natural, in studying rural landscapes, to turn to the Arab geographers, who give us convenient descriptions of green spaces (gardens and orchards and the fruit they produced), sweet water, and topography (they seem to have been fond of castles perched on high hills). For the purposes of this paper, though, we go beyond the tropes of the geographical accounts to consider the "socialized landscapes" of Mamluk Syria (Wilkinson 2010). These landscapes are where the natural and the social meet. Our concern is how rural communities understood, connected with, tried to tame, and moved within their physical environment. These relationships with the natural world were constantly changing, particularly in the fifteenth century. The concept of "liquid landscapes" provides us with a convenient framework for asking a range of questions related to the fluid, frequently unpredictable ways in which communities have historically engaged with their physical environment (Sutton 2000; Forbes 2007; Walker 2016). For Jordan, a country that the World Health Organization has ranked as the fifth most water-starved in the world, the choice of words may seem strange. The term was originally coined by historians of Ottoman Greece, to describe the traditional mobility of rural populations and the attempt to isolate the factors that propelled peasants, in particular, to leave their villages, such as economic opportunities, marriage and kinship ties, and crises of various kinds. For archaeologists, it is a particularly useful concept to identify the possible triggers in settlement growth and decline. The land of modern Jordan is the focus of this paper. Three elements of the Transjordan's rural landscape (as defined sociologically) experienced the greatest change at the end of the Mamluk period: settlement structures (reflecting the growing rural mobility of the period), field systems (which are the manifestation of land use and tenure), and agricultural markets (and the communication, economic, and social networks that supported them). We will focus here on settlement and land.

The Fifteenth and Sixteenth Centuries: A Global Turning Point

A growing body of scholarship on rural society in the late medieval Mediterranean and Europe has demonstrated ways in which lives of peasants, and the landscapes in which they lived, were transformed by the greater interconnectedness of the fifteenth and sixteenth centuries (Vassberg 1996; Davis and Davies 2007). Changes in land tenure and use (made possible by administrative developments), ever expanding agricultural markets, and a greater physical mobility of rural communities together contributed to important changes in village and sub-village society. The "capitalist expansion" of this period, which Braudel traces for the Mediterranean, is only one factor, of course, in these developments (Braudel 1979). Not all regions, of course, were caught up in the internationalization made possible by imperial expansion and inter-regional trade. Uniquely local factors – such as the nature of local-imperial relations and imperial programs (which were as impacted by matters as much internal to their territories as external forces) – would have also come to play. Historians of medieval European peasantry have made important contributions in this regard. Scholarship on village society in late medieval and Early Modern Europe is replete with descriptions of "peasant agency," the "resilience of rural society," and narratives about "rural populations fully conscious of the resources at [their] disposal." Citing increased rural mobility, the vitality of local and regional markets, diversification of agricultural production, and privatization of land as the local outcomes of the internationalization of the period, such studies present a picture of rural society that is largely autonomous and constantly on the move; in control, to some degree, of its resources; and with greater relative affluence. The opportunities that brought wealth were made possible by the international networks that developed at the time (Braudel 1979; Vassberg 1979).[1] This scholarship, of course, relies on a body of sources that we simply do not have at our disposal as Mamlukists, such as church records of births and deaths, census records, family documents, and tax registers. Even court records are rare for our period. It is difficult to write a demographic history without these. There are few local studies in Mamluk historiography, not to mention anything on village society, as a result. Acknowledging these limitations of the textual record, some information about rural society in the fifteenth and sixteenth centuries under Mamluk control can be pulled from the contemporary Arabic sources, if they are carefully mined and creatively combined.[2] They include not only narrative

1 For the ways that incorporation into the Ottoman Empire had a positive economic impact on rural communities, at least for a time, through the agrarian sphere, see Given and Hadjianastasis 2010; and Walker 2009 (and sources cited therein), 2014a, and 2017a.

2 For a fuller methodological discussion, see Walker 2015.

sources, but the contemporary documents that record, in at times surprising detail, the lay of the land, who is planting what, and who lives where. Archival sources such as endowment documents (*waqfiyyāt*), legal records, and tax registers provide a high chronological and geographical resolution not legible in the narrative sources alone.

For the Transjordan, these three sources – scattered throughout archives in four countries – are invaluable for recreating the conditions under which rural societies and landscapes developed. *Waqfiyyāt*, for example, directly allude to private ownership of land, as only private property could be legally set aside in this manner. For agricultural lands, they can describe borders of fields and of the village, the road system, public buildings, the numbers of houses occupied and derelict, locations of mosques and shrines, the types of crops planted, the kinds and development of water resources, and the nature and location of nearby markets. Court records relevant to Mamluk Jordan are found in Jerusalem and at St. Catherine's Monastery in the Sinai; these are rich sources of information about property exchanges and disputes and the value of land. The sixteenth-century Ottoman *defters* (tax registers) are equally informative, recording anticipated tax revenues from agriculture, animal husbandry, markets, and the poll tax on non-Muslims. As the Ottomans taxed religious endowments (at the rate of 10%), the maintenance of many Mamluk-era *awqāf*, of both large and small scale, is attested and described. Archaeologists have been increasingly turning to these registers in recent years for information on place names in southern Syria after the Ottoman conquest. All of these sources, of course, document practices but do not describe local impact. The archaeological record has the benefit of physically documenting such practices, describing broader spatial and deeper chronological contexts of their impact and development, and raising new issues about land use that are not readily apparent (or were not documented at all) in the written sources. This obvious point is relevant to mention: what we think we know about financial, and particularly land, reform in this period pulls from the archives themselves; how we understand the ways these reforms impacted local society in terms of village life, settlement, and land use is generated by the archaeological record. The two kinds of sources, used in tandem with and in complement to one another, have the potential to write a rural history that would otherwise not be possible from one source alone. And together they present a scenario of rural transformation of the period, that while it mirrors quite closely contemporary trends in the Mediterranean and Europe, may be triggered by other forces.

Transjordan in Late Mamluk Period

The rural societies of Egypt and Bilad al-Sham were caught up in the same trends in rural mobility and growing economic and social opportunities that swept the Mediterranean basin and beyond in the fifteenth century. Important demographic changes – resulting from a greater mobility than was typical of rural society and a concomitant abandonment of some of the larger villages – can be documented in regions of the Transjordan in this period. The same trends, though less pronounced, appear to have characterized the history of settlement throughout Bilād al-Shām, as indicated by archaeological surveys.

Settlement Shifts.[3] By the end of the Mamluk period, the Transjordan experienced a 30–75 % decline in settlement (as indicated by the number of settlements that continued to be occupied into the Ottoman period). Certain regions were hit harder than others. Archaeological surveys document the large-scale abandonment of the highland plateaus and the Jordan River Valley. Placed against the backdrop of land use and landscape variables, an interesting pattern becomes clear: there was a general movement of people from regions reliant on state-funded irrigation and the rain-fed plateaus dedicated to grains to better-watered lands where small-scale (and traditional systems) of run-off irrigation had been practiced. Parallel to this is another pattern: many of the newly settled regions were in lands that had been recently privatized and no longer under the control of the state. The large villages in the "grain belt" of the plateaus were hardest hit. These include such sites as Hisban, which one could describe as a "mega-village," the creation, to a large degree, of imperial fiat – a bloated settlement that was quickly reduced in size and importance once state funds were withdrawn from agriculture and defense. The new settlements that replaced these were smaller, more ephemeral in construction, and connected to smaller fields, garden, and orchards. They can be best described a hamlets and isolated farmsteads. It is likely that a confluence of factors drove this migration of people from the larger villages to smaller ones: climatic, political, and economic change. The dispersal of settlement in Transjordan in the late Mamluk period may have been the combined result of: 1. new economic opportunities (such as the privatization of land), which pushed farmers further afield to live and farm; 2. climatic trends (drier conditions favoring small-scale irrigation regimes and diversified agriculture); and 3. the withdrawal of state investment from the rural sector, under which conditions smaller, more widely dispersed plots had a greater possibility to survive the new political and climatic conditions than the large, contiguous grain fields of the fourteenth century.

3 The following section summarizes arguments made in Walker 2011: 211–232.

This demographic pattern is usually described archaeologically as "settlement dispersal." It is an important phenomenon in social history and one impacted by political systems and institutions, community structure, kinship, and land tenure and use. Archaeological and ethnographic studies suggest that certain conditions are conducive for settlement dispersal: changes in land tenure and use (namely the opportunity for private land-holding and the changes in cropping that might go with it), changes in state structure that once controlled land (and more local control over land management and agricultural marketing), and the character of the local community (Does it rely on communal labor?, have kinship ties dissolved?, does tribal structure allow for the formation of new ties?, etc.). Many of these conditions were in place in the fifteenth century. Of course, rural society was always mobile to some degree, regardless of what narrative sources may lead us to believe. The image of the "immobile village" is a myth (Vassberg 1996). The state was never able to completely prevent peasants from leaving their land for other places. The chronicles also illustrate quite clearly patterns of mobility that were always part of rural society: seasonal migration for the harvest and pilgrimage, migration resulting from marriage outside the community, the movements of itinerant scholars and artisans, temporary abandonment of a place until a threat has passed (a military conflict or a Bedouin raid), and nomadic migrations, to name only a few. This kind of migration was normal and was part of the healthy pulse of rural society. Full-scale and permanent abandonment of the largest villages was not.Leaving one's village for good was a last resort (and generally tied to insupportable taxes or repeated drought). The scale of the migratory patterns of the fifteenth century are something new for the region, but appear to have been characteristic of the period, as we will address shortly.

Changes in Land Use and Tenure. Clearly, one cannot separate settlement from land use and tenure: they are part of the same system. Intimately related to settlement dispersal in the fifteenth century are important changes in who "owned" the land and decided what and when to plant. These changes make sense only against the backdrop of the economic decline.

Historical Background – The Mamluk Fiscal Crisis of the Late Fourteenth Century

The fiscal crisis of the late fourteenth century is well documented in all textual sources of the period and finds compelling evidence "on the ground" in archaeological fieldwork in some regions of Bilād al-Shām (Porter 2010; Walker 2011, 2014b, 2917a; Walker et al 2014–2015). Archaeological surveys throughout the country support the image of demographic growth and economic prosperity over the course of the century, with decline in both sectors from the fifteenth century on. The specifically economic factors behind this slide are described by both narrative and documentary sources and can possibly be traced to the cadastral survey of al-Nāṣir Muḥammad, which was applied in southern Syria in 714/1314. The survey officially served two purposes: to regain revenues lost in some of the provinces and to reassert governmental control over tax collection. It was a radical restructuring of the *iqṭāʿ* system (of tax grants), which paid salaries to numerous officials, defined relations between those officers and the sultan, and regularized relations between the officers and local peasants. The ultimate result of al-Nāṣir's *rawk* was to lay the economic foundations for Mamluk society by reallocating *iqṭāʿ*s and regularly rotating them – empowering and enriching the sultan at the expense of his officers and "free"-soldiers; this system essentially remained in place until the reign of Sultan Barqūq.The state system established by al-Nāṣir Muḥammad's surveys began to collapse in mid-century. Such a centralized structure needed a strong political leader in order to properly function; the young and weak sultans that succeeded al-Nāṣir Muḥammad were unable to stem the tide of privatization that was gradually undermining the financial foundations of the state. The role of the Black Death in mid-century accelerated this process, as *iqṭāʿ*s left vacant by deceased amirs could be surreptitiously acquired by others through semi-legal means. The transformation of *iqṭāʿ* and royal lands into private property (*milk*) was accomplished in one of two ways: 1. through low-cost "rental" of state lands by amirs and 2. through the purchase of land from the Treasury and its subsequent endowment for charitable purposes (*waqf*). To cite one example from Jordan, Amir Sarghatmish, a prominent officer under Sultans al-Nāṣir Muḥammad and al-Nāṣir Ḥasan, purchased the town (*madīna*) of Amman directly from the Treasury in 757/1356, presumably to fund the construction and operation of his *madrasa* built in Cairo earlier that year (Ibn Qāḍī Shuhba 1:550). The creation of private estates in this manner secured an income for amirs at the expense of the state as a whole, which depended on revenues from agricultural land to pay army and government officials. Unlike the Ottomans, endowments under the Mamluks were tax-exempt.

By comparison, endowments of rural lands in Syria by Mamluk sultans were modest and infrequent. I have been able to document only twoin Jordan and the Jordan Valley that pre-date Barquq's pivotal reign:[4] 1. Sultan Baybars – two shares of the village Bayt Ramah in the Jordan Valley, for his *madrasa* complex in Cairo,

4 One notes, as well, the occasional sultanic endowment in this manner in Palestine. Sultan Qalāwūn, for example endowed the village of Tayba (or Tayyibat) near Caesarea in Palestine – which was awarded to him as *milk* in 1265 by Baybars. I am grateful to Reuven Amitai for this reference. See also Northrup 1998: 86, n. 150.

no date given (Bakhit and Hmoud 1991: 32); 1 ½ *qirāt* of the village of al-Turra in the northern plains for his khan in Jerusalem in 662/1263, its revenues to be used for bread, cash, and sandal-repair for travelers staying there (al-Yūnīnī 1: 553; Ghawanmeh 1979: 61).[5] 2. Sultan Shaʿbān – the village of Ādar near Karak, in its entirety, for the cities of Mecca and Medina, in 777/1375 (Ghawanmeh 1979: 243–244; Ghawanmeh 1982). It was the endowments of former state lands by the officers themselves (the amirs) that robbed the Treasury of much needed tax revenues in the post-plague period. Contemporary historians also bemoaned the impact of these officers' endowments on local peasants, who were not protected by state financial officers from the abuses of *waqf* managers.

Jordan as a Solution

Thus, by the last quarter of the fourteenth century, the imperial finances were in a dire state. The *iqṭāʿ* system, which was the financial underpinning of the state's entire military apparatus, and the cornerstone of the regime itself, was on the verge of collapse, as the best of the agricultural lands that had once been distributed to military officers were now in private hands or tied up in mortmain endowments. The sultan of the time, Barqūq (r. 1382–89, 1390–99), devoted much of his first reign to solving this fiscal-political-military crisis. Current scholarship in Mamluk studies has focused on the development of the sultan's private fisc and the restructuring of government bureaus to put funds under his personal control (Igarashi 2006, 2009, 2010, and 2015). The endowment system (*awqāf*) may have played an equally important role in this regard. In Egypt, the revenues from lands confiscated from amiral endowments were placed into a newly created bureau used for the support of the Royal Mamluks. This was done in a largely piecemeal process, one portion of a village's land at a time. In Syria, however, it seems the sultan aggressively endowed villages in their entirety, largely to fund his pet projects in Egypt. Exactly how he initially acquired them is unclear from the *waqfiyyāt.*

Barqūq's endowments of agricultural land in the Transjordan included contiguous lands and villages and were concentrated in the Jordan Valley and the northern hill country (some of the richest farmland in the region); the earliest

5 After the sultan's death his son al-Malik al-Saʿīd endowed shares of the village, along with village of Baḥmayn in the Jordan Valley, for his father's mausoleum in Damascus and the two attached *madrasas* (al-Yūnīnī 3: 247–248; Ghawanmeh 1979: 84). Al-Turra experienced a revival from the mid-nineteenth century, acquiring adjacent lands and experiencing population growth through population transfer from the Hawrani town of Darʿa (Wetzstein 1860). This village and its lands were subject to archaeological survey by the author in 2010 (Walker et al 2011).

recorded endowments consisted of entire villages, not merely shares. They include: 1. In the Jordan Valley – the villages of Nimrīn, Kafrīn, and Zarrāʿa, in their entirety, for his *madrasah*-mausoleum complex in Cairo, no date given [Ibshirlī and al-Ṭamīmī 1982: 94; Bakhit and Hmoud 1991: 32; an unnamed village near Karak and miscellaneous properties along the King's Highway south to Shawbak (Waqfiyya 704, Wizārat al-Awqāf, Cairo)]. 2. In the North – the village of Malkā, for his *madrasah*-mausoleum complex in Cairo, in 796/1393 (Waqfiyya 9/51, Dār al-Wathāʾiq, Cairo).[6] 3. In the South – an unnamed village near Karak and miscellaneous properties along the King's Highway south to Shawbak(Waqfiyyah 704, Wizārat al-Awqāf, Cairo).

Barqūq's aggressive royal "waqfization" of Jordanian land continued unabated by later sultans throughout the Circassian period, though the estates created in this process were comparatively smaller. They include: 1. Sultan Khushqadam – three shares each of the Sawād villages of Marw and Harhār, for his *madrasa* complex in Cairo, no date given (Bakhit 1989: 38 and 45); twelve shares of an unnamed *mazraʿa* (isolated farm) in the Jordan Valley for the same complex, no date given (Bakhit and Hmoud 1991: 32). 2. Sultan Qāytbāy – the village of Mājid of Banī Juhma district in the North, to buy shredded wheat to feed the poor and needy in Mecca and Medina (Bakhit 1990: 188, citing *tapu defterleri* 430 and 431).[7]

The lands endowed in the Circassian period were located in the most fertile regions of Jordan and fall into three categories: grain fields of the plains, sugar plantations of the Jordan Valley, and the orchards of the northern hills (which produced high quality olive oil, as they do today). Wheat, sugar, and olive oil – these were the staples of the average person's diet in this period – and were, moreover, vulnerable to state monopolies in this period.These properties remained productive and profitable long after Ottoman annexation, in spite of the changes in cropping that came with it (Walker 2011: 260–264). As former sultanic endowments, the lands were retained as whole units by the Ottoman state, in some cases the taxes on them assigned to the sultan or the provincial governor. Today there is a growing consensus that these kinds of sultanic endowments, which essentially created landed estates, were a form of investment strategy meant to generate income on the long-term and in a stable way (Petry 2000).

6 This village and its farmland was the focus of surveys directed by the author in 2003 (Walker 2005). For a fuller discussion of this and other unpublished *waqfiyyāt* in this articles, see Walker 2011.

7 The ruins of Khirbat Mājid, near the modern village of Shajra in northern Jordan, were surveyed archaeologically as part of the Northern Jordan Project by the author in 2010 (Walker et al 2012).

The "Waqfization" of the Jordanian Countryside[8]

It was not only the ruling elite that became active in the land-grab of the Circassian Mamluk period. The most tangible response of local society to the increasing availability of formerly public lands was their purchase by members of the rural elite - merchants, local officials, and tribal leaders - and their subsequent endowment. The written sources that document a rise in rural endowments in Jordan among sultans and amirs in this period also attest to the development of private property among enterprising, and more affluent, members of these communities. The *waqfiyyāt* on which this study of sultanic *awqāf* relies identify properties that by law had to be excluded from the sultans' endowments. These include private lands and preexisting endowments, which are located within the borders of the estate described in the *waqfiyya*. For these preexisting endowments to have been made legally, they must have originally been the private property of the donor; endowments of adjacent land made earlier by other patrons would be excluded. While some degree of small-scale land ownership, in one form or another, had likely always existed (the fruit-bearing trees in orchards and groves, for example, could be bought and sold), there is documentation in this period of full-scale land sales and endowments by local peoples. The sultanic *waqfiyyāt* of the mid-fourteenth through fifteenth centuries attest time and again to farmland in private hands (*bi-yad* of so-and-so), and in many cases their subsequent endowment. Shawbakis owned many of the gardens and orchards surrounding the local monastery, and which had, as a result, to be excluded from Sultan Shaʿbān's endowment of 777/1375 (Waqfiyya 40, Dār al-Wathāʾiq, Cairo). Every *waqfiyya* I have identified for the Karak region has noted the same. Time and again the same kind of land is described: irrigated property (namely gardens and orchards), dry-farmed fields of modest dimensions (for the cultivation of grains), and nothing in the open plains.

Beyond the *waqfiyyāt*, there is further documentary evidence for the growth in privately-owned, rural property in Jordan in the closing decades of the Mamluk period. Of the many contemporary documents that have survived in the St. Catherine's Monastery archive, a surprisingly number (20 %) of the deeds record transactions initiated by people of Transjordanian background (Atiya 1955; Walker 2011: 171–178). The properties, in this case, were bought and sold by Christian entrepreneurs from Karak and Shawbak and located in and around the town of al-Ṭūr in the Sinai. However, one petition in the collection, from the reign of Sultan Khushqadam, requests the sultan to intervene in the illegal taxation by Mamluk officials of a long-established local *waqf* – a garden (*bustān*) in the Karak

8 There is a growing body of published scholarship on this phenomenon. See, in particular, Petry 1994, 1998, 2000; Abu Ghazi 2000; Walker 2011; and Igarashi 2015.

District endowed for St. Catherine's monastery (Atiya 1955: 53; Ibrahim 1963: 101–103). The petition does not attest to when the garden was originally endowed, but it is likely that it was sometime in the Mamluk period. We should mention, as well, the numerous and specific references to privately-held land in the early Ottoman tax registers. Because the Ottomans required proof of purchase to support land claims, some information on local land-holding has been retained in tax registers from documents that are now long gone. For Jordan, these properties are largely located in the region of Karak, a phenomenon that still eludes explanation. The properties thus described are never very large: small plots of land (*mazraʿas*, *qiṭʿas*) or shares in farmland, gardens, orchards, mills, houses, and shops. Some of the register entries document with certitude the status of these properties as privately held, by including the date of "purchase" (*taʾrīkh al-mushtārī*) or "certification" (*muṣādaqa*) (Bakhit and Hmoud 1991: 334–337; Walker 2011: 246). Most purchases were certified during the late fifteenth and early sixteenth century, thus at the end of Mamluk rule. These entries reflect the requirement by Ottoman officials that taxpayers provide documentation of ownership, such as a purchase document, a requirement with which few could comply (Johansen 1988: 81–82, 87–88). We cannot know, though, whether these properties were purchased directly from the Treasury, although that is likely.

Some of the entries in the registers referred to family endowments, where farm land was registered in court for the continued benefit of the family until it died out. For example, according to the register of 945/1538 for Liwāʾ ʿAjlūn, one Badr al-Dīn Ḥasan b. Sharaf al-Dīn had acquired a garden below Karak in 906/1500. Likewise, a Ḥasan b. Badr al-Dīn b. Ḥasan Sharaf al-Dīn Abu Bakr Zafān purchased three pieces of land (one of which was a garden) in 899/1493. The Ottoman authorities recognized their families' claims on this land and registered it as such for tax purposes (Bakhit and Hmoud 1989: 33 and 35). This information had been recovered in 945/1538 from the older survey of 932/1525–6, at which point the original documentation would have been presented to Ottoman officials (Walker 2011: 268). The family endowments of local people had as much staying power as the large sultanic endowments of the Mamluk era, attesting to the economic impact that the shift from state lands to private property had on the long term. The registers, moreover, list numerous, though relatively modest, charitable endowments (for local mosques, churches, and shrines), suggesting that much of the land acquired by local officials and families in the last century of Mamluk rule was eventually converted into *waqf*. Although taxed by the Ottoman state, it appears, at least for a while, that some of the endowments in Jordan were honored by the Ottoman government and remained in local hands, escaping confiscation. In short, once the opportunity to do so was recognized, the local elites took full advantage of the poor state of the Mamluk Treasury to acquire land for themselves and safeguard it through endowment. To cite only one example: the *waqf* of ʿAlī al-Karakī al-Barīdī for al-Kāʾin mosque in Karak was financially supported by shares of small plots of land (*qiflaʿ*) in the village of al-Duqayr, purchased in 832/1428 but endowed in 925/1519, according to the tax register of 1005/1596 for the District of Ajlūn (Bakhit and Hmoud 1991: 335).

What impact, ultimately, did this growing trend of privatization have on local society and on the Mamluk state? Recent scholarship on fifteenth-century *waqfiyyāt* for rural lands in Egypt suggests that by broadening the base of private ownership, the agricultural base of the Mamluk economy could be revived. The maintenance of the sultanic estates in Jordan, for example, by the Ottoman state in the sixteenth century would certainly argue for the fiscal viability of the largest landed endowments in Jordan well beyond the Ottoman conquest. Is there archaeological evidence for any of these trends?

Archaeological Correlates of This Phenomenon

The changes in land tenure and use that followed the privatization, endowment, and estate-building in the fourteenth century directly impacted rural lands and village communities. It was the regions where land had been privatized, where irrigated agricultural regimes dominated, and where communities were economically self-sufficient that outlived the Ottoman conquest and the chaos that followed the eventual withdrawal of Ottoman personnel from the Transjordan at the end of the sixteenth century. Archaeological surveys have supported such patterns, which indirectly reflect a localized form of land management. As for direct archaeological evidence for the privatization of land, Carol Palmer, ever with an eye towards nuanced changes in the agricultural landscapes of northern Jordan, suggests ways in which shifts in land tenure may be recognized "on the ground." In a recent ethnographic-historical study of traditional patterns of land use in Jordan, Palmer suggests ways in which private and collective ownership (*mushaʿ*) of land leave a physical imprint, comparing the two forms of land tenure in terms of the organization of work and general use of the land (Palmer 1998). Specific forms of tenure offer different possibilities for development of the land. In private, or individually-held, land the individual makes decisions about cropping and crop rotation and can base these decisions on market and environmental factors; new crops (or an emphasis on high-profit ones, such as olive trees and summer vegetables) are introduced as local production is commercialized. Grazing land tends to be freed up for cultivation. There are significant financial incentives for the individual to invest in the land, through terracing and irrigation; there is flexibility in the location of fields vis-à-vis the village, and villages can expand and contract accordingly; and farming is intensive. On the other hand, the system also tends towards absentee landownership (which can result in land not being cultivated for long periods of time), indebtedness (through forced land sales), labor shortages, and the increase of rented land (leading, in turn, to disinterested oversight and management). In short, while private ownership can be very profitable, it can also lead to abandonment of the land, when in the hands of apathetic, distant land owners. Different forms of land tenure may also be recognized in field patterns. The communal system of ownership, which was characteristic of the late Ottoman and Mandate eras, could, according to Palmer, be identified with large tracts of cropped, alternating with tracts of fallow, land, as prime and sub-prime fields were regularly rotated among local families to cultivate. Private ownership on the village level, on the other hand, may be recognized by patchwork patterns of smaller fields and continuous cropping. Sometimes these patterns can be identified in old aerial photos, combined with archaeological survey. Changes in land tenure also have implications for cropping: what to plant, when, and for what purposes. With privatization of land, the new land owner was free to plant as (s)he chose. Imperial pressures for the production of cash crops, as characterized the Jordanian agricultural regime before the fifteenth century, waned during the final centuries of Mamluk rule, with a more diversified production of summer and winter crops and production for local markets, as suggested by Ottoman tax registers. Sugar production, for example, essentially disappeared from the Jordan Valley with the Mamluk state.[9] Although archaeologists are at a relatively early stage of studying such patterns "on the ground" through their surveys, both kinds of field patterns, for example, have been identified in northern Jordan for the Mamluk and Ottoman periods.[10]

Local Scale – The Case of Ḥisbān.[11] Many of the patterns of demographic and land use change noted for the fifteenth and sixteenth centuries have been

9 Sugar does not appear as a taxable commodity in Ottoman tax registers in the region for the sixteenth century, and the Jordan Valley experienced by the sixteenth century some of the highest rates of settlement abandonment in all of southern Bilād al-Shām. For more on both phenomena, see Kareem 2000 and Walker 2011.

10 The Northern Jordan Project, launched by the author in 2003, is a regional archaeological-environmental research initiative focused on the northern highlands near the Jordanian-Syrian border. The Historical Land Use and Landscape Change in the Decapolis Project, an extension of the Northern Jordan Project funded by the German Research Foundation from 2013–2016, has documenting changes of such field systems and their associated settlements against the backdrop of changes in climate and land use (together measured by soil morphology). For project publications, see http://www.mamluk.uni-bonn.de/islamic-archaeology/field-projects/north-jordan-project.

11 The following pulls from reports on the 2013 and 2014 seasons, published as Walker 2014b and Walker et al 2014–2015, as well as unpublished project files at the University of Bonn. The

documented in some detail at the archaeological site of Tall Ḥisbānin central Jordan. The site is located in the heart of the Madaba Plains – a highland plateau that produced grains for export since the Roman period – and some 20 kilometers south of Amman. It is one of the best preserved rural sites of the Mamluk period in Bilād al-Shām and consists of the Citadel, which was excavated from 1968 to 2010, and the medieval village below, which has been the focus of multidisciplinary investigations since 2013. The site, which served as both a frontier fortress and rural administrative center (capital of *wilāyat al-Balqāʾ*) was supported by a small town/urbanized village with a very long history of more or less continuous occupation that spans the Iron Age until today. The village grew practically overnight at the beginning of the fourteenth century, with its promotion to a district capital and the stationing there of a small garrison of soldiers under a low-ranking Mamluk commander. It is an ideal test case for studying changes in settlement, land use, and relationship with "the state" during this important period of political transition from Mamluk to Ottoman rule. Stratigraphic contexts in both Citadel and village dated to the fourteenth-sixteenth centuries attest to changes in village structure and eventual settlement dispersal. The imperial decision to relocate the garrison, administrative personnel, the marketplace and court, and even some of the residents (through forced population transfer) in the middle of the fourteenth century led to the abandonment of the Citadel and its storage spaces on the upper slopes of the tell, the burial of financial assets(silver coins and imported apothecary-style jars, the content of which are currently under analysis), and the physical and functional transformation of the Mamluk-era town to a village of more regionally traditional form (complexes of barrel-vaulted, single-room houses clustered around a common courtyard and cistern). These farmhouse complexes of the lower slopes were gradually abandoned over the course of the fifteenth and early sixteenth centuries, leaving behind only a scatter of more ephemeral sites in the vicinity (dispersal of population).[12] This pattern of gradual village abandonment and settlement dispersal has been recently noted at other sites in central Jordan in the same period, such as the village of Dhibān to the south.[13]

A multifaceted environmental and agricultural research conducted since 2013 – combining palynological, phytolith, zooarchaeological, palaeobotanical analysis, and textual analysis on Ottoman tax registers – has provided evidence for

scientific excavations today are directed by the author and are part of the larger Ḥisbān Cultural Heritage Project led by Øystein LaBianca of Andrews University in Michigan.

12 For the results of the Ḥisbān hinterland surveys, see Ibach 1987 and the Madaba Plains Project Hinterland Survey web publications by Gary Christopherson at: http://www.casa.arizona.edu/MPP/.

13 A list of project publications can be found via Open Access at: http://opencontext.org/projects/01D080DF-2F6B-4F59-BCF0-87543AC89574.

diversification of agriculture and animal husbandry concomitant with the gradual demographic decline of the village in the fifteenth and sixteenth centuries. The project environmental analysts have interpreted these changes as a transition to a more resilient form of agriculture (and a buffer against drought), which was more appropriate to self-sufficient village life, and a greater reliance on local markets (for the phytolith component of the study, see Laparidou and Rosen 2015 and Laparidou in Walker et al 2017). Water use, apparently, changed in like manner, with a shift from large and complex imperially controlled irrigation systems to smaller scale systems based on a combination of traditional run-off irrigation and dry farming (Walker 2017b).[14] Land tenure is more difficult to extract from the archaeological record. While field lines, as we have seen above, may reflect different patterns of land holding, the best evidence of tenure and right to use comes from the textual (documentary) record. The Ḥisbān excavations have spearheaded in Jordan a long-term program of integrated archaeological and traditional archival textual analysis for the later Islamic periods. The on-going study of Mamluk *waqfiyyāt*, early Ottoman (sixteenth-century) tax registers, and Tanzimat-era land registers by the author and project staff holds promise for reconstructing the history of land tenure in the Madaba Plains over *la longue durée.*

Europe and the Ottoman Empire in the Fifteenth–Sixteenth Centuries

The same trends towards dispersal of settlement, privatization of land, and agricultural diversification can be identified in Europe and the larger Mediterranean in the fifteenth and sixteenth centuries. In England the old Roman-style pattern of "small, enclosed settlements with localized … field systems" broke down and was replaced by the fifteenth and fifteenth centuries. There were regionalized responses to the collapse of the old system, and in the southwest, settlement dispersal was the norm. It created a demographic and settlement pattern that would lay the foundations for the landscape one sees there today: hamlets and isolated villages "set in a … continuous field-scape and supported by agricultural diversification and development" (Rippon et al 2006: 31). It is not entirely clear what initially drove these changes, but disintegration of land-

14 The water study at Ḥisbān has relied on a combination of phytolith analysis (to differentiate irrigated from rain-watered crops); low-flying aerial photography by drones to identify ancient terraces, field lines, and irrigation systems; previous hinterland surveys; a recent pedestrian water survey; 3-D mapping of subterranean water systems; and geomorphological studies.

holding (partible inheritance) and an expanding economy may have played a role. Rural landscapes of Ottoman Rumelia, Anatolia, and Syria were transformed in a similar manner. The expansion of the empire, and the international networks of trade that came with it, created new opportunities for peasants. Though the Ottoman authorities tried (half-heartedly) to control it, there was remarkable peasant mobility in the fifteenth and sixteenth centuries, with regular migration from villages to other villages and into the towns (for Palestine, see Singer 1992 and 1994). This mobility did not, apparently, create a financial problem for the state. Quite the contrary: tax registers and provincial codes of regulations attest to agricultural diversification and expansion (particularly into "marginal lands"), population growth and greater settlement density and the growth of medium-sized towns (all networked by regional markets), and the growing privatization of land. The management of rural endowments was done in relative autonomy from the state. Agricultural growth was, in part, driven by the needs of an ever-expanding military and its frequent campaigns, urbanization, and both trans-Mediterranean and short-haul trade. Rural taxation was gradually monetarized, with a shift from payment in kind to payment in coin (Pamuk 2000). One could even make cash payments to "buy one's way out of" labor service (İslamoğlu-İnan 1994). Post-Mamluk Syria presents an even more poignant example of such trends. Here there was expansion of settlement into the "marginal zones" of the Ḥawrān, for example, reaching population levels not attained again until the 1960s (Walker et al 2011)! The tax registers attest to the development of *mazrāʿas* (cultivated land unattached to settlements) into proper villages. They also document the degree to which the countryside was becoming "privatized," with greater peasant free-hold property in village buildings, vineyards, and orchards, and the corresponding rights to sell, bequeath, and endow, as well as transfer usufruct and organize agricultural production. The high degree of continuity between pre-Ottoman and Ottoman systems of landholding, regulations, services and taxes suggests that these trends have their roots in late Mamluk practice.

Conclusions

The Mamluk economy was in poor condition in the late fourteenth century. Under the combined weight of political and economic pressures, the Mamluk sultans began a series of reforms to salvage the regime and regain power over the state's physical frontiers. Among the most important actions in this regard were efforts by the state to regain control of public lands lost to private entrepreneurs, who had bought them earlier from the Treasury through mechanisms considered only quasi-legal by the juridical authorities of the day. Subsequent endowments of agricultural land by indigenous elites, to prevent confiscation, effected a transformation of rural society, as local communities (both Muslim and Christian) carved out their own physical and functional spaces in the rural hinterland – one free from taxation and imperial agrarian programs – and a new class of independent, small landowners emerged. The ultimate legacy of these changes in land tenure in the history of late medieval Jordan is difficult to ascertain. In revisiting the archaeological record from the perspective of the textual record, certain patterns in settlement and land use become apparent. After the Ottoman conquest, the frontier of settlement retracted and shifted west, reflecting the new geography illustrated by the *waqfiyyāt*. The open plains, whose grains fields were once so important to the Mamluk economy, were largely emptied of permanently settled villages. The agricultural economy shifted from imperially directed planting of cash crops to a combination of subsistence production with cropping more appropriate to local markets. Entire communities appear to have moved – but to where and for what purpose remains to be determined. The dispersal of once large village communities is a characteristic of post-medieval Jordan that may be related to these changes in land tenure and use. It could be argued, but cannot yet be confirmed, that these developments foreshadowed the great tribal migrations and restructuring of village communities over the Ottoman centuries that laid the foundations for modern Jordanian society. The emptying out of the highland plateaus, for example, may have facilitated the migration of tribes into these regions from the Hijaz in the seventeenth and eighteenth centuries (Johns 1994). As a concluding thought, we may ask whether the Mamluk state was in any sense unique in the way its rural sector was transformed in the fifteenth century. Settlement dispersal, high rural mobility, privatization of land, and agricultural diversification seem to have been characteristic responses to the economic opportunities and political transitions of this period. The specific and immediate triggers for these developments, however, appear to have been culturally and politically (or institutionally) specific. The potential of *waqf* to mold rural society is one (underdeveloped) line of research that offers great promise for Mamluk studies in the future.

Bibliography

Manuscripts

Waqfiyya 40, Ḥajāj ʿumarāʾ wa-salāṭīn, microfilm #15, folia 1–3 – endowments near Karak supporting Sultan Hasan's monumental madrasa complex at base of Citadel, Cairo, 762/1360, Dār al-Wathāʾiq, Cairo.

Waqfiyya 8/49, Ḥajāj ʿumarāʾ wa-salāṭīn – endowments of Sultan Shaʿban for his madrasa in Cairo, 777/1375, Dār al-Wathāʾiq, Cairo.

Waqfiyya 9/51, Ḥajāj ʿumarāʾ wa-salāṭīn – endowments of Sultan Barquq for his madrasa complex in Cairo, Bayn al-Qasrayn, 796/1393, Dār al-Wathā'iq, Cairo.

Waqfiyya 704– endowments of Sultan Barqūq for his mosque-madrasa complex in Cairo, 792/1389, Wizārat al-Awqāf, Cairo.

Secondary sources and edited manuscripts

Abū Ghāzī, ʿImād Badr al-Dīn 2000, *Taṭawwur al-Ḥiyāza al-Zirāʿiyya fī Miṣr Zaman al-Mamālīk al-Jarākisah: Dirāsa fī Bayʿ Amlāk Bayt al-Māl.* Cairo ʿAyn lil-Dirāsāt wal-Buḥūth al-Insāniyya wal-Ijtmāʿiyya.

Atiya, Aziz Suryal 1955, *The Arabic Manuscripts of Mount Sinai: A Hand-list of the Arabic Manuscripts and Scrolls Microfilmed at the Library of the Monastery of St. Catherine, Mount Sinai.* Baltimore: The Johns Hopkins Press.

al-Bakhit, Muhammad Adnan, ed. 1989a, *Nāḥiyat Banī Kināna (Shamālī al-Urdunn) fī al-Qarn al-ʿĀshir al-Hijrī/al-Sādis ʿĀshir al-Milādī.* Amman: University of Jordan. (in Turkish with Arabic commentary).

al-Bakhit, Muhammad Adnan, ed. 1990, "Awqaf during the Late Mamluk Period and the Early Ottoman Times in Palestine and Jordan. In *Urbanism in Islam*," ed. The Editorial Committee of the Research Project "Urbanism in Islam, a Comparative Study." Tokyo: Middle Eastern Culture Center.

al-Bakhit, Muhammad Adnan and Noufan Raja Hmoud, eds. 1989 *The Detailed Defter of Liwāʾ ʿAjlūn (The District of Ajlun) Tapu Defteri No. 970.* Amman: University of Jordan. (In Turkish with Arabic commentary).

al-Bakhit, Muhammad Adnan and Noufan Raja Hmoud, eds. 1991, *The Detailed Defter of Liwāʾ ʿAjlūn (The District of Ajlun) Tapu Defteri No. 185, Ankara 1005 A.H./1596 A.D.* Amman: University of Jordan. (In Turkish with Arabic commentary).

Braudel, Fernand 1979, *Civilisation matérielle, économie et capitalisme, XVe–XVIIIe siècle* (3 vols.). Paris: A. Colin.

Davis, Siriol and Jack Davies (eds.) 2007, *Between Venice and Istanbul: Colonial Landscape in Early Modern Greece* (Hesperia Supplements 40). Princeton: American School of Classical Studies at Athens.

Forbes, Hamish 2007, "Early Modern Greece: Liquid Landscapes and Fluid Populations." In *Between Venice and Istanbul: Colonial Landscape in Early Modern Greece*, edited by Siriol Davis and Jack Davies. Princeton: Princeton University Press. Pp. 111–135.

Ghawanmeh, Yusuf 1979, *Taʾrīkh Sharqī al-Urdunn fī ʿAṣr Dawlat al-Mamālīk al-Ulā (al-Qism al-Ḥaḍarī).* Amman: Wizārat al-Thaqāfa wal-Shabāb.

Ghawanmeh, Yusuf 1982, "Al-Qaryafī Junūb al-Shām (al-Urdunn wa-Filisṭīn) fī al-ʿAṣr al-Mamlūkifī Ḍawʾ Waqfiyyat Ādar." *Studies in the History and Archaeology of Jordan.* 1: 363–371.

Given, Michael and Marios Hadjianastasis 2010, "Landholding and Landscape in Ottoman Cyprus." *Byzantine and Modern Greek Studies.* 34: 38–60.

Ibach, Robert 1987, *Archaeological Survey of the Hesban Region: Catalogue of Sites and Characterization of Periods.* Hesban 5. Berrien Springs, MI: Andrews University Press.

Ibn Qāḍī Shuhba, Tāqī al-Dīn (d. 851/1448) 1997, *Ta'rīkh Ibn Qāḍī Shuhba*, ed. Adnan Darwish. Damascus: L'Institut Français du Proche Orient, 1997.

Ibrāhīm, ʿAbd al-Laṭīf 1963, "Thalātha Wathā'iq Faqahiyya." *Majallat Kulliyat al-Adab (Jāmiʿat al-Qāhira)* 25.1: 95–105.

Ibshirlī, Muḥammad and Muḥammad Dāwūd al-Ṭamīmī, eds. 1982, *Awqāf wa-Amlāk al-Muslimīn fi Filisṭīn fī Awliyāt Ghazza, al-Quds al-Sharīf, Ṣafad, Nāblūs, ʿAjlūn.* Istanbul: Markaz al-Abḥāth lil-Ta'rīkh al-Funūn wal-Thaqāfa al-Istilaqīyya bi-Istanbūl.

Igarashi, Daisuke 2006, "The Establishment and Development of al-Diwan al-Mufrad: Its Background and Implications." *Mamlūk Studies Review.* 10.1: 117–140.

Igarashi, Daisuke 2009, "The Financial Reforms of Sultan Qaytbay." *Mamlūk Studies Review.* 13.1: 27–51.

Igarashi, Daisuke 2010, "The Evolution of the Sultanic Fisc and al-Dhakhirah during the Circassian Mamluk Period." *Mamlūk Studies Review.* 14: 65–108.

Igarashi, Daisuke 2015, *Land Tenure, Fiscal Policy and Imperial Policy in Medieval Syro-Egypt.* Chicago: Middle East Documentation Center, University of Chicago.

İslamoğlu-İnan, Huri 1994, *State and Peasant in the Ottoman Empire: Agrarian Power Relations and Regional Economic Development in Ottoman Anatolia during the Sixteenth Century.* Leiden: E.J. Brill.

Johansen, Barber 1988, *The Islamic Law on Land Tax and Rent: The Peasants' Loss of Property Rights as Interpreted in the Hanafite Legal Literature of the Mamluk and Ottoman Periods* London: Croom Helm.

Johns, Jeremy 1994, "The *Longue Durée:* State and Settlement Strategies in Southern Transjordan across the Islamic Centuries." In *Village, Steppe and State: The Social Origins of Modern Jordan*, eds. E.L. Rogan and T. Tell. London: British Academic Press. Pp. 1–31.

Kareem, J.M.H. 2000, *The Settlement Patterns in the Jordan Valley in the Mid- to Late Islamic Period.* Oxford: BAR Series.

Laparidou, Sofia and Arlene Rosen 2015, "Intensification of Production in Medieval Islamic Jordan and its Ecological Impact: Towns of the Anthropocene." *Holocene.*25: 1685–1697.

Northrup, Linda 1998, *From Slave to Sultan: The Career of al-Mansur Qalawun and the Consolidation of Mamluk Rule in Egypt and Syria (678–689 A.H./1279–1290 A.D.).* Stuttgart: Franz Steiner Verlag.

Palmer, Carol 1998, "'Following the Plough': The Agricultural Environment of Northern Jordan." *Levant* 30: 129–165.

Pamuk, Şevket 2000, *A Monetary History of the Ottoman Empire.* Cambridge: Cambridge University Press.

Petry, Carl 1994, *Protectors or Praetorians? The Last Mamluk Sultans and Egypt's Waning as a Great Power* Albany: SUNY Press.

Petry, Carl 1998, "Fractionalized Estates in a Centralized Regime: The Holdings of al-Ashraf Qaytbay and Qansuh al-Ghawri According to their Waqf Deeds." *Journal of the Social and Economic History of the Orient.* 41.1: 96–117.

Petry, Carl 2000, "Waqf as an Instrument of Investment in the Mamluk Sultanate: Security or Profit?" In *Slave Elites in the Middle East and Africa: A Comparative Study*, ed. M. Toru and J. E. Philips. N.Y.: Kegan Paul International. Pp. 95–115.

Porter, Benjamin 2010, "Locating Middle Islamic Dhiban on the Mamluk Imperial Periphery, 2010." *Fondation Max van Berchem Bulletin* 24: 5–7

Rippon, S.J., R.M. Fyfe, and A.G. Brown 2006, "Beyond Villages and Open Fields: The Origins and Development of a Historic Landscape Characterised by Dispersed Settlement in South-West England." *Medieval Archaeology.* 50: 31–70.

al-Shqour, Reem 2015, "Aqaba Castle – Origin, Development, and Evolution of Khans in Jordan: An Archaeological Approach." Unpublished PhD dissertation, University of Ghent.

Singer, Amy 1992, "Peasant Migration: Law and Practice in Early Ottoman Palestine." *New Perspectives on Turkey.* 8: 49–65.

Singer, Amy 1994, *Palestinian Peasants and Ottoman Officials: Rural Administration around Sixteenth-century Jerusalem.* Cambridge: Cambridge University Press.

Sutton, Susan Buck 2000, "Liquid Landscapes: Demographic Transitions in the Ermionidha." In *Contingent Countryside: Settlement, Economy, and Land Use in the Southern Argolid Since 1700*, ed. Susan Sutton. Stanford, CA: Stanford University Press. Pp. 84–106.

Vassberg, David E. 1996, *The Village and the Outside World in Golden Age Castile: Mobility and Migration in Everyday Rural Life.* Cambridge: Cambridge University Press.

Walker, Bethany J. 2005, "The Northern Jordan Survey 2003 – Agriculture in Late Islamic Malka and Hubras Villages: A Preliminary Report on the First Season." *Bulletin of the American Schools of Oriental Research.* 339: 67–111.

Walker, Bethany J. 2009, "Defining the Levant." In *Reflections of Empire: Archaeological and Ethnographic Studies on the Pottery of the Ottoman Levant*, ed. Bethany J. Walker, Boston: American Schools of Oriental Research. Pp. 1–6.

Walker, Bethany J. 2011, *Jordan in the Late Middle Ages: Transformation of the Mamluk Frontier.* Chicago: Middle East Documentation Center, University of Chicago.

Walker, Bethany J. 2014a, "Ottoman Archaeology: Localizing the Imperial." In *Encyclopedia of Global Archaeology*, vol. 12, ed. C. Smith. New York: Springer. Pp. 5642–5653.

Walker, Bethany J. 2014b, "Planned Villages and Rural Resilience on the Mamluk Frontier: A Preliminary Report on the 2013 Excavation Season at Tall Hisban." In *History and Society during the Mamluk Period (1250–1517)*, ed. Stephan Conermann. Göttingen: Bonn UP. Pp. 157–192.

Walker, Bethany J. 2015, "On Archives and Archaeology: Reassessing Mamluk Rule from Documentary Sources and Jordanian Fieldwork." In *Material Evidence and Narrative Sources: Interdisciplinary Studies of the History of the Middle East*, eds. Daniella Talmon-Heller and Katia Cytryn-Silverman. Leiden: Brill. Pp. 113–143.

Walker, Bethany J. 2016, "The Northern Jordan Project and the 'Liquid Landscapes' of Late Islamic Bilad al-Sham." In *The Materiality of the Islamic Rural World*, ed. Stephen McPhillips and Paul Wordworth. Philadephia: University of Pennsylvania Press. Pp. 184–199.

Walker, Bethany J. 2017a, "Early Ottoman/Late Islamic I/Post-Mamluk: What Are the Archaeological Traces of the 16thCentury in Syria?" In *The Mamluk-Ottoman Tran-*

sition: Continuity and Change in Egypt and Bilad al-Sham in the Sixteenth Century, ed. Stephan Conermann and Gül Şen. Bonn: University of Bonn Press. Pp. 321–344.

Walker, Bethany J. 2017b, "The Struggle over Water: Evaluating the 'Water Culture' of Syrian Peasants under Mamluk Rule." In *Developing Perspectives in Mamluk History*, ed. Yuval Ben-Bassat. Leiden: Brill. Pp. 287–310.

Walker, Bethany J., Robert Bates, Jeff Hudon, and Øystein LaBianca 2014–2015, "Tall Hisban 2013 and 2014 Excavation Seasons: Exploration of the Medieval Village and Long-Term Water Systems." *Annual of the Department of Antiquities of Jordan* 58: 483–523.

Walker, Bethany J., Sofia Laparidou, Annette Hansen, and Chiara Corbino 2017, "Did the Mamluks Have an Environmental Sense? Natural Resource Management in Syrian Villages." *Mamlūk Studies Review*. 20: 167–245.

Walker, Bethany J., Mohammed Shunnaq, David Byers, Muwafaq al-Bataineh, Sofia Laparidou, Bernhard Lucke, and Atef Shiyab 2011, "Northern Jordan Project 2010: The al-Turra Survey," *Annual of the Department of Antiquities of Jordan*. 55: 509–536.

Wetzstein, Johann Gottfried 1860, *Reisebericht über Hauran und die Trachonen*. Berlin: Dietrich Reimer.

Wilkinson, Tony 2010, "The Tell: Social Archaeology and Territorial Space." In *Development of Pre-State Communities in the Ancient Near East*, ed. Diana Bolger and Louise C. Maguire/. Oxford: Oxbow. Pp. 55–62.

al-Yūnīnī, Quṭbal-Dīn Mūsā b. Muḥammad b. Aḥmad (d. 726/1326) 1954–60, *Dhayl Mirʿāt al-Zamān*, vols. 1, 3. Hyderabad: Osmania Oriental Publications Bureau.

Zarinebaf, Fariba, John Bennet and Jack L. Davis 2005, *A Historical and Economic Geography of Ottoman Greece: The Southwestern Morea in the 18th Century*. Athens: American School of Classical Studies at Athens.

III. Mediterranean Connections

Amar S. Baadj (Bonn and Trier Universities)

Travel by Sea and Land between the Maghrib and the Mamluk Empire

Introduction

During the Mamluk period (1250–1517) there was a considerable amount of travel between the western Islamic lands (the Maghrib, al-Andalus, and Bilād al-Sūdān) and the Mamluk Empire. A substantial community of Maghāriba (people from the Maghrib) was established in Cairo and the cities of the Hijaz and Syria. Among the luminaries from the west who traveled to Mamluk Cairo were Ibn Baṭṭūṭa (d. 779/1377) and Ibn Khaldūn (d. 808/1406). Maghāriba traveled to the Mamluk sultanate for a variety of reasons: pilgrimage, study, trade, or even from a sense of adventure and a desire to see the world as in Ibn Baṭṭūṭa's case.

The two most important genres of Arabic sources which shed light on travel between the Maghrib and the Mashriq during the late medieval period are the Mamluk biographical dictionaries (*tarājim*) and the travel books (*riḥlāt*) written by Maghribī and Andalusī authors. Such sources have some inherent limitations. They are disproportionately concerned with recording the lives of members of the ulema including the scholars under whom they studied, the students whom they taught, and the books that they read. We find very little information in these sources about merchants or military men from the Maghrib who may have traveled to the Mashriq. Trade, seafaring, and travel conditions were not primary concerns for most of the authors of these works.

In contrast, we have a wealth of information about commerce between Ifrīqiya and Egypt from the Fatimid period, especially during the eleventh and twelfth centuries, thanks to the Geniza letters.[1] These documents portray a flourishing trade between both regions by land and sea. As a result the standard modern study of Maghribī-Egyptian relations during the Fatiṃid period gives adequate

1 S.D. Goitein, "Medieval Tunisia, the Hub of the Mediterranean," in idem., *Studies in Islamic History and Institutions* (Leiden: Brill, 2010), pp. 308–328.

attention to the commercial sphere and recognizes the importance of trade in this period.[2]

On the other hand, many modern studies on Mamluk relations with the Maghrib focus largely on the cultural and diplomatic aspect of relations, reflecting the bias of the Arabic sources. Ḥabīb's study of Mamluk trade relations with Africa is disappointing in its coverage of Egyptian trade with the Maghrib, West Africa, and the Saharan regions because of his over-reliance on very early authors such as al-Bakrī (d. 487/1094) and Ibn Ḥawqal (d. 367/977) and his failure to take into account Mamluk authors other than al-ʿUmarī (d. 786/1384).[3] In an article about the relations between Ifrīqiya and Mamluk Egypt, Chapoutot-Remadi has observed that our picture of these relations is incomplete due to the paucity of information about trade and economic matters. Furthermore, she notes that while we have many accounts of Maghāriba who traveled to the Mamluk lands we rarely find descriptions of journeys by easterners to the Maghrib.[4]

Nonetheless, the situation is not as bleak as it may appear at first glance. There are itineraries of ship and caravan voyages between Tunis and Alexandria from the Mamluk period buried in the Arabic sources from which we can extract valuable information about trade routes, the conditions of travel, seafaring, and even a few references to mercantile activity. Furthermore, the Arabic sources can be supplemented by the rich testimony of the Venetian and Genoese archives. Scholars such as Valerian, Jehel, and Doumerc have demonstrated the importance of the Italian sources to late medieval Maghribī history in general.[5] The merchant fleets of the Italian city-states played a major role in the transport of goods and passengers between Ifrīqiya and Alexandria throughout the Mamluk period and this is reflected in some of the surviving documents.

I have managed to collect several late medieval Arabic accounts of land and sea voyages between the Maghrib and Egypt which I have summarized and presented in chronological order in part one. All of these sources except for one date from

---

2 Ḥasan Khuḍayrī Aḥmad, *ʿAlaqāt al-Fāṭimīyīn fī Miṣr bi-Duwal al-Maghrib: 362/973–567/1171* (Cairo: Madbouli, 1996), pp. 93–151.

3 Shawqī ʿAbd al-Qawī ʿUthmān Ḥabīb, *Al-Tijāra bayna Miṣr wa-Afrīqīyā ʿAṣr Salāṭīn al-Mamālīk: 648/1250–922/1517* (Cairo: Al-Majlis al-Aʿlā lil-Thaqāfa, 2000), pp. 65–71.

4 Mounira Chapoutot-Remadi, "Les relations entre l'Égypte et l'Ifriqya aux XIIIe et XIVe siècle d'après les auteurs Mamlûks," in *Actes du premier congrès d'histoire et de la civilisation du Maghreb / Ashghāl al-Muʾtamar al-Awwal li-Taʾrīkh al-Maghrib al-ʿArabī wa-Ḥaḍāratihi*, vol. 1: 139–159. Tunis, December 1974 (Tunis: Université de Tunis, Centre d'études et de recherches économiques et sociales, 1979), p. 159.

5 See Bernard Doumerc, *Venise et l'émirate hafside de Tunis (1231–1535)* (Paris: L'Harmattan, 1999); George Jehel, *Les Gênois en Méditerranée occidentale: (fin XIème – début XIVème siècle: ébauche d'une stratégie pour un empire)* (Amiens [Somme, France]: Centre d'histoire des sociétés, Université de Picardie, 1993); Dominique Valérian, *Bougie, port maghrébin, 1067–1510* (Rome: École française de Rome, 2006).

the Mamluk period. In part two I have analyzed these sources in the light of recent studies including those based on the Italian archives in order to make some observations about the conditions of sea and land travel between Mamluk Egypt and the Maghrib and in order to answer the question of whether trade was as important a factor in Maghribī-Egyptian relations during the Mamluk period as it was during the earlier Fatimid period.

Part I: Summaries of Late Medieval Voyages between the Maghrib and Egypt

Ibn Jubayr (540/1145–614/1217)

The celebrated Valencian traveler Ibn Jubayr made three voyages to the Mashriq, the first of which was described in his *Riḥla*. In 578/1183 he traveled in a Genoese ship on a thirty day voyage from Ceuta (Sabta) to Alexandria. His vessel passed by the eastern coast of Spain, Ibiza, Majorca, and Minorca. It put ashore in Cape St. Mark in western Sardinia where a local Christian ruler greeted the ship's crew and Ibn Jubayr saw eighty Muslim captives who were being sold into slavery there. Off the Sardinian coast the ship encountered harrowing storms before continuing to Sicily, Byzantine Crete, and finally the port of Alexandria.[6]

In 580/1184 Ibn Jubayr commenced his return journey from the east. He considered traveling in a ship anchored in the Crusader-held port of Tyre that was headed to Bijāya, however, he decided that this vessel was too small for the journey. In the nearby port of Acre he boarded a large Genoese ship bound for Messina in Sicily.[7] The passengers included Maghāriba as well as European Christian pilgrims returning from Palestine. Though they had expected the voyage to last for no more than two weeks they reached Messina only after two difficult months as a result of adverse winds and severe storms.[8] On the way they stopped in Crete and some smaller islands under Byzantine control. Ibn Jubayr spent four months in the Norman kingdom of Sicily where he visited Messina,

6 Abū al-Ḥasan Muḥammad b. Aḥmad b. Jubayr, *Riḥlat Ibn Jubayr* (Beirut: Dār al-Kutub al-ʿIlmīya, 2003), pp. 28–31.

7 He makes mention of two wealthy Muslim merchants of Maghribī origin in Acre, Naṣr b. Qawwām and Abū al-Durr Yāqūt. These men engaged in long-distance international trade and were respected by both the Christian and Muslim rulers of the time. They used their wealth and connections to ransom Maghribī captives in Acre of whom there seem to have been quite a few. See Ibn Jubayr, *Riḥla*, pp. 238–239; Claude Cahen, "Ibn Jubayr et les Maghrébins de Syrie," *Revue de l'Occident Musulman et de la Méditerranée*, vol. 13, no. 1 (1973): 207–209.

8 Ibn Jubayr, *Riḥla*, pp. 240–250.

Cefalu, Termini, Palermo, and Trapani.[9] He set sail from the latter city in 581/1185 in a Genoese ship with a party of fifty other Muslims. While at sea they briefly encountered another Genoese vessel that was carrying two hundred Muslim pilgrims who were returning to al-Andalus from Alexandria. After sailing past the southern tip of Sardinia and the Balearic islands, Ibn Jubayr's ship anchored in the port of Cartagena where he disembarked.[10]

Al-ʿAbdarī (fl. c. 688/1289)

Al-ʿAbdarī was born in Ḥaḥa in southern Morocco. The biographical dictionaries supply very little information about him, even his birth and death dates are unknown. His *Riḥla*, an account in ornate rhyming prose of his voyage to and from the Hijaz, is one of the most important surviving descriptions of a land journey between Ifrīqiya and Egypt during the Mamluk period.[11] Few other texts shed as much light on conditions in late medieval Libya. His voyage combined pilgrimage and study. Like most of the Maghribī travel works, al-ʿAbdarī's *Riḥla* also furnishes accounts of the many scholars whom he met and studied under in the cities along his route.

Al-ʿAbdarī set out from Ḥaḥa in 688/1289. He crossed the Tāza gap between Morocco and Algeria and continued onwards to Tilimsān, Milyāna, Algiers, Bijāya, Constantine, Annaba, Bāja and Tunis. He described these places as prosperous, large, and well-fortified towns surrounded by fertile countryside.[12] He paints a bleak picture of the route between Qayrawān and Alexandria. According to him, Qayrawān was a shadow of its former self, inhabited by uncivilized, boorish people. Qābis had an unhealthy climate. The inhabitants of Zawāra and Zawāgha, two towns in western Tripolitania, were unfriendly to travelers and their practice of raising swine horrified al-ʿAbdarī. Tripoli itself had no gardens, trees, or streams. The Arabs threatened it by land and the Christians by sea. Sirt, described by the eleventh century geographer al-Bakrī as a great city in his day, was all but abandoned when al-ʿAbdarī visited.[13]

His harshest words were saved for Barqa. The Arab tribes in this region were rude and savage. Money and precious metals had no value to them and barter was the norm. Al-ʿAbdarī criticized the dress of their women. He wrote a long di-

9 Ibid., pp. 250–264.

10 Ibid., pp. 264–267.

11 Abū ʿAbdallāh Muḥammad b. Muḥammad b. ʿAlī b. Aḥmad b. Suʿūd al-ʿAbdarī, *Riḥlat al-ʿAbdarī*, ed. ʿAlī Ibrāhīm al-Kurdī (Damascus: Saʿd al-Dīn lil-Ṭibāʿa wal-Nashr wal-Tawzīʿ, 2005).

12 Al-ʿAbdarī, *Riḥla*, pp. 40–156.

13 Ibid., pp. 157–202.

gression about their speech, remarking that they spoke the purest and most eloquent Arabic for they pronounced the case-endings and the full verb endings. He attributes this to their utter isolation. Between Barqa and Alexandria there was only barren desert.[14] In approximately 691/1292 al-ʿAbdarī made his return journey by land from Egypt to the Maghrib.[15] Curiously enough, his account of Libya on the return voyage is more positive than his first description of the country. He praises two towns in Barqa, Suwaysa and Berenice (Barnīq), for their prosperity and the fertility of their districts. On the other hand, he notes that Ajdābiya, an important town in former times, was largely uninhabited and lacked a good water supply when he visited it.[16]

Ibn Rushayd (657/1259–721/1321)

Ibn Rushayd was a native of Sabta. He wrote a lengthy account of his journey to the east for the pilgrimage entitled *Milʾ al-ʿAyba bi- mā Jumiʿa bi-Ṭūl al-Ghayba fī al-Wajha al-Wajīha ilā Makka wa-Ṭība.* The work consisted of seven parts of which the first and fourth parts are missing.[17] Unfortunately for our purposes, the work is mainly concerned with recording the lives of the scholars whom the author encountered in the various cities on his route and it lacks the rich information on geography, itineraries, and nautical matters that one encounters in Ibn Jubayr's book. In 683/1284 Ibn Rushayd set out from Almeria. We know that he went to Tilimsan, Bijaya, Annaba, Tunis, Tripoli and Alexandria though the portion of his writings that covers this stage of his journey is lost.[18]

In 685/1286 he returned to Ifrīqiya by ship from Alexandria with stops in Ṭubruq, Marsā Hawwāra (Qaṣr Aḥmad), and Tripoli (whose inhabitants, he notes, feared attack by sea) before arriving in al-Mahdīya, which he said was largely in ruins in his time. Then he traveled by land to various places until he reached Tunis. He remained in Tunis for a while due to the absence of any ships

14 Ibid., pp. 203–209.

15 Kurdī, *Adab al-Riḥal*, p. 87.

16 Al-ʿAbdarī, *Riḥla*, pp. 481–484.

17 ʿAlī Ibrāhīm Al-Kurdī, *Adab al-Riḥal fī al-Maghrib wal-Andalus* (Damascus: Wizārat al-Thaqāfa, 2013), pp. 47–48; Abū ʿAbdallāh Muḥammad b. ʿUmar b. Rushayd, *Milʾ al-ʿAyba bi-mā Jumiʿa bi-Ṭūl al-Ghayba fī al-Wajha al-Wajīha ilā Makka wa-Ṭība: Al-Juzʾ al-Thānī, Tūnis ʿinda al-Wurūd*, Ed. Muḥammad al-Ḥabīb Ibn al-Khūja (Tunis: Al-Dār al-Tūnisīya lil-Nashr, 1982); idem, *Milʾ al-ʿAyba bi-mā Jumiʿa bi-Ṭūl al-Ghayba fī al-Wajha al-Wajīha ilā Makka wa-Ṭība: Al-Juzʾ al-Khāmis, Al-Ḥaramayn al-Sharīfayn wa-Miṣr wa al-Iskandarīya ʿinda al-Ṣudūr*, Ed. Muḥammad al-Ḥabīb Ibn al-Khūja (Beirut: Dār al-Gharb al-Islāmī, 1988).

18 Unfortunately, I was only able to consult the second and fifth parts of Ibn Rushayd's travels. Therefore, I have relied on the summaries of his itinerary contained in the following works: Aḥmad Ḥaddādī, *Riḥlat b. Rushayd al-Sabtī: Dirāsa wa-Taḥlīl*, 2 vols. in 1, (Morocco: Wizārat al-Awqāf wal-Shuʾūn al-Islāmīya, 2003), pp. 244–249; Kurdī, *Adab al-Riḥal*, pp. 48–49.

sailing to al-Andalus. Finally, in 686/1287 he boarded a Christian ship. There was a group of Muslim merchants traveling with him who had a dispute with the ship's owner. He reports that the merchant ship (*jafn* or large round shaped galley) of a certain al-Dalāʾī was captured by the enemy (presumably Christian privateers).[19] Ibn Rushayd disembarked in Malaga and made his way back to his native Sabta.[20]

Mamluk Embassy to the Merinids (706/1306–709/1309) in *Zubdat al-Fikra*

The Mamluk historian Baybars al-Manṣūrī (d. 725/1324) gives an account of a Mamluk embassy that traveled overland to the Merinid sultanate and back.[21] In 706/1306 two Mamluk ambassadors named ʿAlāʾ al-Dīn Aydughdī al-Talīlī and ʿAlāʾ al-Dīn Aydughdī al-Khwārazmī set out for the west. Their itinerary was Alexandria-Ṭulmaytha-Sirt-Misrāta-Ṭajūra-Tripoli-Qābis-Safāqus-al-Mahdīya-Sūsa-Tunis-Bāja-Annaba-Qusanṭīna-al-Midīya-Milyāna-Tilimsān.[22] Near the latter city they had an audience with the Merinid ruler Abū Yaʿqūb Yūsuf (685/1286–706/1307) who was besieging Tilimsān from his base at al-Manṣūra. After delivering their gifts to the sultan the ambassadors were sent onwards to Fez. They were detained there for fourteen months, during which time Abū Yaʿqūb was assassinated and succeeded by Abū Thābit who reigned for only one year.[23]

Eventually the ambassadors were allowed to return home to Egypt. They traveled in the company of a caravan of Maghribī pilgrims which included many merchants and notables. When they reached Tilimsān they received a very cool reception from the Ziyānid sultan Abū Ḥammū I (707/1308–718/1318), who refused to provide a military escort for the caravan to fend off attacks by the Bedouin who were a serious threat to travelers in this region. Near al-Midīya Arabs from the tribe of Ḥuṣayn attacked the caravan, killing and scattering its members and despoiling them of all their goods including the clothes on their backs. The ambassadors survived the attack and were sheltered and clothed by a sympathetic local. They made their way to Hafsid Bijāya where they were received

19 Ḥaddādī, *Riḥlat Ibn Rushayd*, p. 248. For more information on the term *jafn* see Dionisius A. Agius, *Classic Ships of Islam from Mesopotamia to the Indian Ocean* (Leiden: Brill, 2008), pp. 338–340, 342–343.

20 Ḥaddādī, *Riḥlat Ibn Rushayd*, p. 249.

21 Rukn al-Dīn Baybars al-Manṣūrī, *Zubdat al-Fikra fī Tārīkh al-Hijra*, ed. Donald S. Richards (Beirut: al-Shārika al-Muttahida lil-Tawzīʿ, 1998), pp. 410–412; for a French summary see, Chapoutot, "Les Relations," pp. 156–157.

22 Baybars al-Manṣūrī, *Zubda*, p. 411. Chapoutot suggests that the ambassadors preferred the land route even though it was longer and difficult because sea travel was more hazardous due to the activities of the Christian fleets and privateers, see "Les Relations," p. 156.

23 Baybars al-Manṣūrī, *Zubda*, p. 411.

with honor by the local amir. In Tunis the Hafsid caliph Abū ʿAbdallāh (Abū ʿAṣīda) Muḥammad al-Muntaṣir II (694/1295–709/1309) furnished them with guides who took them to Tripoli where his cousin Ibn al-Liḥyānī (d. 727/1327) was the amir. The latter accompanied them to Egypt, ostensibly to make the pilgrimage but in reality to escape from Tripoli for political reasons. They returned to Cairo in 709/1309 after an absence of over three years.[24]

Ibn Baṭṭūṭa (704/1303–779/1377)

Ibn Baṭṭūṭa, a native of Tangier (Ṭanja) was the most famous of medieval Muslim travelers. He left Tangier in 725/1324 with the intention of making the pilgrimage. He traveled eastward by land to Tilimsān, Milyāna, Algiers, Bijāya, Constantine, Annaba, Tunis (where he joined a large pilgrim caravan), Sūsa, Safāqus, and Qābis. His caravan traveled between Qābis and Tripoli accompanied by one hundred horsemen and there were archers in the caravan itself as well. These precautions were taken due to fear of attack by the Bedouin. He reached Tripoli in 726/1325. Then he continued on to Maslāta, Masrāta and Quṣūr Sirt. Near the latter place the Arabs tried to attack them but they escaped. Later his caravan passed through Qaṣr Barṣīṣ al-ʿĀbid, Qubbat Salām, and al-Zaʿāfīya (places not far from Sirt). Unfortunately he has nothing to say regarding his travels between Sirt and Alexandria and the conditions in Cyrenaica at this time.[25]

In 750/1349 Ibn Baṭṭūṭa returned from the east and he took passage from Alexandria to Tunis via Jirba in a vessel of the type known as a *qarqūra* which belonged to some Tunisians.[26] Then he took another ship to Safāqus and Bilyāna after which he returned to land and traveled back to Tunis with some Arabs. From Tunis he boarded a Catalonian ship which took him to Cagliari in Sardinia. He marveled at this fine port city but he feared capture by the natives. From Sardinia his ship took him to the port of Tinis (in western Algeria) where he disembarked

24 Baybars al-Manṣūrī, *Zubda*, pp. 411–412.

25 Abū ʿAbdallāh Muḥammad b. ʿAbdallāh b. Baṭṭūṭa, *Riḥlat Ibn Baṭṭūṭa*, ed. Ṭalāl Ḥarb (Beirut: Dār al-Kutub al-ʿIlmīya, 2002), pp. 31–36.

26 The text mentions a small *qarqūra* (pl.*qarāqīr*), however, studies on the medieval *qarqūra* suggest that it was one of the larger ships of the time. According to Pryor, the *qarāqīr* were large three-masted and three-decked sailing ships that could only anchor in deep water due to their great size. Agius mentions the great height of these ships while al-Sukhnī describes them as great triple-masted cargo ships. John H. Pryor and Sergio Bellabarba, "Medieval Muslim Ships of the Pisan *Bacini*," *The Mariner's Mirror*, vol. 76, no. 2 (1990): 107–109; Dionisius A. Agius, "Maqrīzī's Evidence for the Gurāb," in *Law, Christianity, and Modernism in Islamic Society: Proceedings of the Eighteenth Congress of the Union Européene des Arabisants et Islamisants*, ed. U. Vermeulen and J.M.F. Van Reeth (Leuven: Peeters, 1998), pp. 188–189; Maḥmūd Khālid al-Sukhnī, *Al-Nashāṭ al-Baḥrī li Dawlat al-Mamālīk fī al-Baḥr al-Mutawassiṭ: 690/1291–923*/1517, (MA thesis, University of Damascus, 2012), p. 84.

and continued by land to Māzūna, Mustaghānim, Tilimsān, Nadrūma, Tāzā and finally Fez.[27]

Khālid b. ʿIṣā al-Balawī (713/1313–755/1354?)

Al-Balawī was a judge and scholar from the city of Cantoria (Qantūriya) near Almeria. He made a four-year journey to the east for study and pilgrimage that he recorded in his book entitled *Tāj al-Mafriq*.[28] His journey began in 736/1335 when he took a ship from Almeria to the port of Hunayn in what is now western Algeria. He then made his way by land to Tunis. In 737/1336 he boarded a great Alexandria-bound vessel in Tunis that carried one thousand passengers. The ship sailed past Pantellaria (Qawsara) and Malta without incident. Then strong winds carried it to Crete where it remained for five days. Once it left Crete and entered the open sea again it was overtaken by a violent storm. The crew attempted to ride out the storm by anchoring in Karpathos (Arabic *Ashqarbāṭa*, an island in the Dodecanese lying northeast of Crete) but conditions only grew worse and the anchors were cut by the strength of the undersea current, forcing the ship back out into the open sea.[29] Water broke in nearly reaching the top deck of the ship. The able-bodied passengers operated a rope-drawn bucket nonstop for an entire day and they bailed enough water to keep their ship afloat. They passed by Cyprus but were unable to land there. Their thirst was intolerable as the water supplies were nearly exhausted and some passengers resorted to drinking seawater. The captain ordered his crew to share their remaining water with the passengers through a strict system of rationing. Finally, the wind picked up and carried them into the harbor of Alexandria after a journey of over eleven weeks.[30]

In the fall of 738/1337, after completing the pilgrimage, al-Balawī returned to Alexandria intending to sail back to Tunis in the company of his brother. They boarded a ship which belonged to a certain Ibn Khulāṣ and which was captained by a man named *Alfunsh* (Alfonso).[31] It was evidently a fairly large vessel which carried two hundred Muslim and Christian passengers. Soon after departing the

27 Ibn Baṭṭūṭa, *Riḥla*, pp. 663–667.

28 Khālid b. ʿIṣā al-Balawī, *Tāj al-Mafriq fī Taḥlīyat ʿUlamāʾ al-Mashriq*, ed. Al-Ḥasan al-Sāʾiḥ, (Rabat, 1964), 2 vols. A Spanish summary of and commentary on al-Balawī's sea voyages can be found in the useful article by Jorge Lirola-Delgado, "Travesias Nauticas en la *Riḥla* del Almeriense Jālid al-Balawī (siglo XIV)," in *Actas del II Congreso de Historia de Andalucía* (Córdoba, 1991), pp. 85–92.

29 Al-Balawī, *Tāj*, vol. 1, pp. 193–196; Lirola-Delgado, "Travesias," pp. 87–88.

30 Ibid.

31 Al-Balawī, *Tāj*, vol. 2, pp. 28–29. Perhaps this is an example of a ship that was owned by a Muslim merchant but operated by a European Christian crew. More research must be done to determine whether this was a common occurrence.

ship encountered violent storms which imposed great hardships on the crew and passengers alike. Just as Tripoli came into sight strong winds from the west blew the ship back in the very direction from which it had come. As the situation did not improve and the ship was dangerously short on water and provisions, the captain announced that he had decided to winter in the small, remote port of al-ʿImāra.[32] One day the captain persuaded al-Balawī and his brother to disembark for some relaxation while leaving their baggage on board and then he abruptly set sail, stranding them along with other passengers. Al-Balawī and his brother made their way back to Alexandria by land facing hunger and great danger. When they reached the port they found that their ship had preceded them and was at anchor. Al-Balawī confronted the captain and recovered his possessions.[33]

When spring came al-Balawī and his brother tried again to reach Tunis. They sailed from Alexandria in a *qarqūra* but once again unfavorable winds prevented them from reaching their intended destination. They were forced to anchor in the port of Ṭubruq in Barqa, some ninety miles west of Marsā al-ʿImāra. Some of the passengers returned to Alexandria by land while al-Balawī and the others waited with the ship. As the situation did not improve they eventually sailed back to Alexandria.[34] Al-Balawī waited until the next year (739/1339) before trying again. He boarded a vessel owned by a Muslim named Sayf al-Dīn with a large number of Muslim passengers. This time they successfully completed their voyage to the port of Ḥammāmāt near Tunis.[35] He continued traveling by land to Tunis and then westward to Bāja, Annaba, Constantine, Bijāya, Algiers, and Tilimsān before finally reaching the port of Hunayn. He sailed from Hunayn in a qarqūra to the port of Mojacar on the coast of Spain near Almeria. From there he returned to his native town of Cantoria by land.[36]

Ibn Khaldūn (732/1332–808/1406)

The great historian ʿAbd al-Raḥmān Ibn Khaldūn recorded some important information about his move from Ifrīqiya to the Mamluk sultanate in a travel account (*riḥla*) that was appended to his universal history, the *Kitāb al-ʿIbar*. In 784/1382 he boarded a ship in Tunis which belonged to some Egyptian merchants

32 Al-Balawī, *Tāj*, vol. 2, pp. 28–29; Lirola-Delgado, "Travesias," pp. 88–89. According to Lirola-Delgado, al-ʿImāra is located near the modern Libyan-Egyptian border, sixty miles west of Alexandria.
33 Al-Balawī, *Tāj*, vol. 2, pp. 29–36; Lirola-Delgado, "Travesias," pp. 88–89.
34 Al-Balawī, *Tāj*, vol. 2, pp. 66–68; Lirola-Delgado, "Travesias," p. 89.
35 Al-Balawī, *Tāj*, vol. 2, p. 93, Lirola-Delgado, "Travesias," p. 89.
36 Al-Balawī, *Tāj*, vol. 2, pp. 115, 138, 150–151, 154–156; Lirola-Delgado, "Travesias," p. 89.

from Alexandria. Together they sailed for forty days before reaching the port of Alexandria. He then made his way to Cairo where he started a new career.[37]

Ibn Khaldūn arranged for his family, who were still in Tunis, to join him in Cairo. In 786/1384 his wife and children boarded a large ship called "Rubʿ al-Dunyā" in Tunis. With them were the great historian's prized possessions including his private library. Tragically, the ship sank in a storm off the coast of Tunisia. Ibn Khaldūn's wife and five daughters lost their lives. Two of his sons survived and joined him in Egypt.[38]

Muḥammad b. Abī l-Qāsim al-Mashaddālī al-Zawāwī (also known as Ibn Abī l-Faḍl, born 821/1418 or 822/1419, died 864 /1459)[39]

Al-Mashaddālī was a native of Bijāya. He was a polymath who enjoyed great renown both in his native Maghrib and in the Mamluk east where he lived the last half of his life. Al-Sakhāwī included an exceptionally long and detailed entry on al-Mashaddālī in his biographical dictionary, *Al-Daw' al-Lāmiʿ*.[40] Fortunately, it includes mention of the itinerary which he followed during his voyage from the Maghrib to Egypt.

Al-Mashaddālī was educated in Bijāya and Tilimsān by the greatest scholars of his day whom he eventually surpassed. Then he traveled to Constantine, Annaba, and finally Tunis where he arrived in 845/1441.[41] Some time before the end of 845/1441 he set sail for Egypt in a Genoese ship. First his ship anchored in a place called "the Land of Pitch" (Bilād al-Qatrān) on the northern shore of the Mediterranean.[42] Later in the voyage storm winds carried the ship off course to Cyprus. It anchored in Famagusta and al-Mashaddālī traveled inland to Nicosia, which was the capital of the Kingdom of Cyprus. There he engaged in debate with some of the bishops. Then he sailed to Beirut and from there he traveled to Damascus.[43] He spent the next few years journeying throughout Bilād al-Shām. He visited Tripoli and Ḥamā, and settled for an extended period in Jerusalem. In

37 ʿAbd al-Raḥmān b. Khaldūn, *Riḥlat Ibn Khaldūn*, ed. Muḥammad b. Tāwīt (Beirut: Dār al-Kutub al-ʿIlmīya, 2004), p. 199.

38 See Ibn Khaldūn, *Riḥla*, p. 208 and especially note 3 on the same page; Taqī al-Dīn b. Abī Bakr b. Aḥmad b. Qāḍī Shuhba, *Tārīkh Ibn Qāḍī Shuhba*, ed. ʿAdnān Darwīsh (Damascus: Al-Maʿhad al-Fransī, 1977), vol. 3, p. 138.

39 I am grateful to Dr. Lameen Souag (CNRS, Paris), a specialist in North African linguistics, for informing me of the correct spelling of this name.

40 Muḥammad b. ʿAbd al-Raḥmān al-Sakhāwī, *Al-Ḍawʾ al-Lāmiʿ li Ahl al-Qarn al-Tāsiʿ* (Beirut: Dār Maktabat al-Ḥayāt), vol. 9, pp. 180–188.

41 Ibid., pp. 180–183.

42 Perhaps this is a reference to Calabria.

43 Al-Sakhāwī, vol. 9, pp. 182–183.

849/1445 he made the pilgrimage to Mecca and then traveled to Cairo.[44] He died during the course of a voyage to Syria and Asia Minor in ʿAyn Tāb in 864 /1459 while he was still in his forties.[45]

Naṣrid embassy to Cairo (844/1440)

In the fifteenth century the Nasrid rulers of Granada sent numerous embassies to Cairo requesting military assistance, all of which were without success. An anonymous, incomplete manuscript from the Escorial records the story of one of these embassies. It was discovered and published by the Egyptian scholar ʿAbd al-ʿAzīz al-Ahwānī in the journal *Kullīyat al-Ādāb* in 1954.[46] The Spanish orientalist Luis Seco de Lucena Paredes produced an annotated translation of the text.[47] It concerns a Granadan embassy from the Nasrid Sultan al-Ghālib Billāh Muḥammad IX "el Zurdo" (822/1419–831/1427, 833/1430–835/1432, 835/1432–848/1445, 851/1457–858/1454) to the Mamluk sultan al-Ẓāhir Jaqmaq (842/1438–857/1453) in Cairo in 844/1440. The author was evidently one of the ambassadors.[48]

The surviving portion of the account begins *in medias res.* The ambassadors were already at sea in a Christian ship of unspecified nationality sailing in a convoy that was under attack by Muslim vessels. As Muslims themselves this put the ambassadors and other passengers in a particularly difficult position. The other Muslims on board took refuge in the hull but the Granadans watched the battle from the deck. Rough sea separated the Christian vessels from the corsairs and from each other. By the end of the combat the crew had suffered six dead and many wounded, only their fatigue kept them from taking out their anger on the Muslim passengers. They headed to shore and made repairs at some unspecified place for two days. Then they sailed to Rhodes. As they approached its port they almost hit a sandbank. The author says he would have been made prisoner by the Rhodians had the ship been wrecked.[49]

---

44 Ibid., 182–183.

45 Ibid., 188.

46 ʿAbd al-ʿAzīz al-Ahwānī, "Sifāra Siyāsīya min Gharnāṭa ilā al-Qāhira fī al-Qarn al-Tāsiʿ al-Hijrī (sanat 844)" *Majallat Kullīyat al-Ādāb*, vol. 16/ No. 1 (1954): 95–121. I am grateful to my colleague Dr. Josef Zenka (Charles University, Prague) for providing me with a copy of this very difficult to obtain article. Dr. Zenka told me that he has searched for the original manuscript that al-Ahwānī used but he was unable to locate it and he fears that it may have been lost or misplaced in the decades following its discovery.

47 Luis Seco de Lucena Paredes, "Viaje a Oriente: Embajadores granadinos en el Cairo," in *Miscelánea de estudios Árabes y Hebraicos*, 4 (1955): 5–30.

48 Seco de Lucena Paredes, "Viaje," pp. 5–7.

49 Al-Ahwānī, "Sifāra," p. 98; Seco de Lucena Paredes, "Viaje," pp. 8–9.

The author then gives us a detailed and remarkably well-informed account of conditions in Rhodes under the rule of the Knights of St. John. He describes Rhodes as great base for the Christians. The knights received 150,000 gold pieces a year in charitable donations and their fortifications were manned by volunteers from throughout Europe.[50] He notes that it was a rallying point for Christian pirates from the neighboring islands. Typically they would capture Muslims from the coastal districts of Bilād al-Shām. At the time of writing sixteen Rhodian ships were out raiding the Muslims, and two hundred Muslims were held captive in Rhodes. The Muslims on the ships were not allowed access to these captives out of fear that they would try to ransom them. The governor of Rhodes wanted to keep the Muslim captives as hostages for negotiations with the Mamluk sultan whom he greatly feared since the latter had recently attacked Rhodes with sixteen ships.[51]

Shortly before the author's arrival in Rhodes a major naval battle had taken place between the Christians and the Mamluk fleet.[52] Twenty-four Christian ships (from Rhodes and other Christian islands or cities) opposed the Mamluk fleet in a fiercely contested naval battle resulting finally in the retreat of the Mamluk ships.[53] The son of the governor of Rhodes and five hundred Christians died in this battle. Many were wounded as well, and since the church bells were sounded whenever one died, the author could tell that many of the wounded died during his stay. The Rhodian corsair fleet had set out only ten days before our author's arrival. The grand master issued an order forbidding Muslims who were in port from leaving their ships to visit the city of Rhodes so that they could not report on the weak points of the city and the number of defenders. Nonetheless the author and his companions managed to clandestinely obtain some information from the Muslim captives inside the city. The author was very impressed by Rhodes' fortifications.[54]

After twenty-two days in Rhodes, during which time the crew of the ambassadors' ship made good their losses, undertook repairs, and ascertained that there was no threat from the Egyptian fleet, they took on a Rhodian guide and set sail for Alexandria. Unfortunately the wind changed, blowing in their faces, and they were forced to take shelter on the Rhodian coast for twelve days. Then they

50 Ibid.

51 Al-Ahwānī, "Sifāra," p. 99; Seco de Lucena Paredes, "Viaje," p. 10.

52 The Mamluks under Jaqmaq sent three expeditions against Rhodes which all ended in defeat: the first in 844/1440, the second in 846/1442, and the last in 848/1444. The ambassadors from Granada must have witnessed the aftermath of the first expedition. For a good discussion of Sultan Jaqmaq's conflict with the knights of Rhodes see Saʿīd ʿAbd al-Fattāḥ ʿĀshūr, *Al-ʿAṣr al-Mamālīkī fī Miṣr wal-Shām* (Cairo: Dār al-Nahda al-ʿArabīya, 1976), pp. 177–180.

53 Al-Ahwānī, "Sifāra," p. 99; Seco de Lucena Paredes, "Viaje," p. 10.

54 Al-Ahwānī, "Sifāra," pp. 99–100; Seco de Lucena Paredes, "Viaje," pp. 10–11.

sailed for two days and once again encountered strong winds blowing against them. They were forced to take shelter in Venetian controlled Candia (in Crete) for four days. Then they continued on their course. They came within sight of Rosetta and a day later approached Alexandria but were forced to anchor fifteen miles outside of Alexandria's harbor due to unfavorable winds. They could taste the sweet Nile water as it was flood season and reached them out at sea. One day with high waves and bad winds the rudder broke, and the sailors with great difficulty made it safely to Alexandria.[55]

After disembarking, the ambassadors were honored by the governor of Alexandria and then taken to Cairo for an audience with Jaqmaq. He apologized for having no men to spare to aid the Muslims of Granada but offered to send some money and war supplies. Some poetry that the ambassadors composed in honor of Jaqmaq is included. Then the ambassadors decided to make the pilgrimage and the rest of the manuscript is an account of their visit to the Hijaz.[56]

Aḥmad b. Saʿīd b. Muḥammad b. Masʿūd al-Jarīrī (810/1407–849/1445)

Al-Jarīrī was born in a village outside of Qayrawān. He received a thorough education from the greatest scholars of the day in Ifrīqiya. In 844/1440 he boarded a "ship of the Franj" that was bound for Alexandria. During the course of al-Jarīrī's voyage some Genoese vessels attacked his ship and damage it. They anchored in Rhodes where they spent twenty days making repairs before continuing onwards to Egypt. Then from Egypt he traveled to the Hijaz in another boat. After making the pilgrimage he settled permanently in Medina where he was known for his scholarship and great piety.[57]

Al-Qalaṣādī (815/1413–891/1486)

Al-Qalaṣādī was a famous mathematician born in Baza (Basṭa) in southwestern Spain. In addition to his works on mathematics he composed a Riḥla in which he recounts his travels in the Maghrib, Egypt and the Hijaz which he undertook in order to further his studies and perform the pilgrimage.[58] In 840/1436–1437 he sailed from the port of Almuñecar (al-Munakkab) to Oran and traveled overland

55 Al-Ahwānī, "Sifāra," pp. 100–101; Seco de Lucena Paredes, "Viaje," p. 12.

56 Al-Ahwānī, "Sifāra," pp. 101–121; Seco de Lucena Paredes, "Viaje,", pp. 12–20.

57 Shams al-Dīn Muḥammad b. ʿAbd al-Raḥmān al-Sakhāwī, *Al-Ḍawʾ al-Lāmiʿ li-Ahl al-Qarn al-Tāsiʿ* (Beirut: Dār Maktabat al-Ḥayāt, 1966), vol. 1, pp. 305–306.

58 Abū al-Ḥasan ʿAlī al-Qalaṣādī, *Riḥlat al-Qalaṣādī*, ed. Muḥammad Abū al-Ajfān (Tunis: Al-Shārika al-Tūnisīya li al-Tawzīʿ, 1978).

to Tilimsān where he continued the studies that he had commenced in his native Baza. In 848/1444 he left Tilimsān and traveled to Oran.[59] From there he took a ship to Tunis (the journey lasted twelve days).[60] In 851/1447 he took a ship from Tunis to Alexandria that stopped in Jirba and Tripoli. During the journey between Tripoli and Alexandria al-Qalaṣādī's ship was buffeted by terrible storms and he feared that he would drown.[61]

In the spring of 853/1449 he began his return voyage to the west from Egypt. He took a boat from Būlāq in Cairo to Alexandria. Then he boarded a Muslim ship in Silsila (a port of Alexandria) that was bound for Tunis. The vessel stopped in al-ʿImāra and in Barqa where it remained for eight days due to unfavorable winds. There was consternation and confusion among the passengers. Some wanted to continue their journey by land to Tunis or simply to return to Alexandria. Others wanted to wait in Barqa until next autumn when the new sailing season would begin. Fortunately, the winds improved and they set out again in a convoy with three other Muslim ships. After another stop in Tripoli they arrived in Tunis. In 854/1450 al-Qalaṣādī sailed from Tunis to Oran. He visited Tilimsān, then returned to Oran and sailed from there to Almeria in 855/1451.[62] Afterwards al-Qalaṣādī became a distinguished teacher in his native Baza and in Granada. In 888/1483, when the fall of the Nasrid kingdom appeared inevitable, he emigrated to Bāja in Ifrīqiya where he lived the last four years of his life.[63]

Muḥammad al-Zawāwī (d. 882/1477)

Muḥammad al-Zawāwī was a colorful and eccentric Sufi from Bijāya. He left to posterity a "dream diary" entitled *Tuḥfat al-Nāẓir wa-Nuzhat al-Manāẓir* which recounts 109 dreams, scattered throughout a ten year period between 851/1447 and 861/1457 in which he claimed to have encountered the Prophet Muḥammad.[64] He traveled to the Mashriq to perform the pilgrimage and then he resided in Cairo for several months from 855/1451 until 856/1452. It is interesting to note that al-Zawāwī had a great fear of sea voyages thus he made the journey between the Maghrib and Egypt by land.[65] One of his dreams involved a caravan lost without water in the desert of eastern Libya which he saved in his capacity as a

59 Al-Qalaṣādī, *Riḥla*, pp. 109–110.
60 Ibid., pp. 112–115.
61 Ibid., pp. 122–125.
62 Ibid., pp. 158–162.
63 *Adab al-Riḥla*, p. 75.
64 Jonathan G. Katz, "The Vision of the Prophet in Fifteenth Century North Africa: Muḥammad az-Zawāwī's Tuḥfat an-Nāẓir," (Ph.D. Dissertation, Princeton 1990).
65 Katz, "Vision," p. 240, note 51.

holy man.[66] This may be indicative of some of the dangers faced by pilgrim caravans that traversed Libya between the Maghrib and Egypt during this period.

ʿAbd al-Bāsiṭ b. Khalīl b. Shāhīn al-Malaṭī al-Ḥanafī (844/1440–920/1514)

ʿAbd al-Bāsiṭ was born in Melitene (Malaṭya) in Asia Minor to a family of Tatar or Qipchaq extraction. His father, Khalīl b. Shāhīn, was a high ranking official of the Mamluk state who held several governorships as well as the office of vizier. He was also a great scholar and historian who wrote a famous work entitled *Zubdat Kashf al-Mamālik*. According to Brunschvig, ʿAbd al-Bāsiṭ did not follow his father's path into the civil service but rather became a merchant-scholar.[67] Like his father he had a great passion for learning and knowledge. He studied under more than fifty scholars in various fields including the religious and linguistic sciences as well as medicine. He was a prolific author with twenty works to his credit on a variety of subjects. His most important historical works include the eight volume *Nayl al-Amal fī Dhayl al-Duwal* and *Al-Rawḍ al-Bāsim fī Ḥawādith al-ʿUmur wa al-Tarājim* which has only partially survived.[68] ʿAbd al-Bāsiṭ undertook a journey to the Maghrib and al-Andalus between the years 866/1462 and 871/1467. He left a detailed account of this voyage in *Al-Rawḍ al-Bāsim* which is summarized below.

Brunschvig says that the purpose of ʿAbd al-Bāsiṭ's voyage was to study medicine in the western Islamic world under the great masters of the day.[69] The Rawḍ al-Bāsim contains an important detail that leaves us in no doubt about the equally important commercial aspect of this voyage. ʿAbd al-Bāsiṭ mentions that he bought great quantities of linen (*kuttān*) in Upper Egypt in 866/1462 which he brought with him to trade in the Maghrib.[70] Evidently then the purpose of the voyage was both trade and learning. It is interesting to note that ʿAbd al-Bāsiṭ was accompanied throughout his voyage by his wife, children, and slaves.[71]

Later in the same year ʿAbd al-Bāsiṭ departed Alexandria in a convoy of Venetian *shawānī* along with other Muslim merchants who brought with them

66 Ibid., pp. 247–8.

67 Robert Brunschvig, *Deux Récits de Voyage inédits en Afrique du Nord au XVe siècle* (Paris: Larose, 1936), p. 7.

68 Zayn al-Dīn ʿAbd al-Bāsiṭ b. Khalīl b. Shāhīn al-Ẓāhirī, *Nayl al-Amal fī Dhayl al-Duwal*, ed. ʿUmar ʿAbd al-Salām al-Tadmurī (Beirut: Al-Maktaba al-ʿAṣrīya, 2002), 9 vols.; Idem, *Al-Rawḍ al-Bāsim fī Ḥawādith al-ʿUmur wa al-Tarājim*, ed. ʿUmar ʿAbd al-Salām al-Tadmurī (Beirut: Al-Maktaba al-ʿAṣrīya, 2014), 4 vols.

69 Brunschvig, *Deux récits*, p. 8.

70 ʿAbd al-Bāsiṭ, *Rawḍ*, vol. 2, p. 155.

71 ʿAbd al-Bāsiṭ, *Rawḍ*, vol. 2, p. 332, vol. 3, p. 112; Brunschvig, *Deux récits*, pp. 8–9.

their merchandise including large amounts of linen.[72] He reports that the ships briefly stopped in Rhodes due to unfavorable weather conditions and a need to refresh their drinking water supplies.[73] They arrived in Tunis after thirty-three days.[74] While they were in port some Frankish ships arrived bearing Muslim captives who were offered for ransom. ʿAbd al-Bāsiṭ, who was a fluent Turkish speaker, ransomed a Qipchaq Turk who could not speak Arabic and who was ignored by the locals. Later he met with the chief merchant (*kabīr al-tujjār*) in Tunis who was an Andalusī from Granada.[75] Afterwards, ʿAbd al-Bāsiṭ set sail from Tunis in another convoy of Venetian galleys intending to return to Alexandria. His vessel stopped in Jirba where he noted that the merchants took onboard great quantities of olive oil and garments. When the convoy reached Tripoli ʿAbd al-Bāsiṭ had a change of heart and he decided to stay there as a guest of the city's chief merchant rather than returning to Egypt.[76]He noted that the ruler of Tripoli paid an annual tribute of 100,000 dinars to the Hafsid caliph in Tunis and his account leaves the impression of a prosperous city.[77]

From Tripoli he returned to Tunis by land.[78] He passed by Qābis, which was largely in ruins according to him, and then visited Qayrawān. There he studied with various shaykhs and visited the famous cemeteries.[79] He noted the great water basins of the Qayrawān region of which only one was still in use in his day.[80] After passing through Tunis and Bāja he reached Constantine where he stayed for three days while admiring the fineness of its buildings and fertility of its countryside. He continued on to Bijāya and Algiers and he visited some scholars in these cities. Then he passed through Māzūna, Qalʿat Hawwāra, and al-Baṭḥāʾ before he finally reached Tilimsān, the goal of his journey.[81] In Tilimsān he visited the tomb of the famous sufi saint Abū Madyān and studied with eminent religious scholars and physicians. Among the latter was the Jewish chief physician Mūsā b. Samūyal b. Yahūdā al-Mālaqī, for whom he had great admiration.[82]

Then he traveled to Oran on the coast where he studied with several scholars.[83] After visiting Tilimsān a second time he returned to Oran and boarded a large

72 ʿAbd al-Bāsiṭ, *Rawḍ*, vol. 2, p. 163.
73 ʿAbd al-Bāsiṭ, *Rawḍ*, vol. 2, p. 167.
74 ʿAbd al-Bāsiṭ, *Rawḍ*, vol. 2, pp. 171–172.
75 ʿAbd al-Bāsiṭ, *Rawḍ*, vol. 2, pp. 174–175.
76 ʿAbd al-Bāsiṭ, *Rawḍ*, vol. 2, pp. 220–223.
77 ʿAbd al-Bāsiṭ, *Rawḍ*, vol. 2, p. 311.
78 ʿAbd al-Bāsiṭ, *Rawḍ*, vol. 2, p. 312.
79 ʿAbd al-Bāsiṭ, *Rawḍ*, vol. 2, p. 318.
80 ʿAbd al-Bāsiṭ, *Rawḍ*, vol. 2, p. 322.
81 ʿAbd al-Bāsiṭ, *Rawḍ*, vol. 2, pp. 329–332.
82 ʿAbd al-Bāsiṭ, *Rawḍ*, vol. 3, pp. 23–25.
83 ʿAbd al-Bāsiṭ, *Rawḍ*, vol. 3, p. 37.

Genoese ship that was bound for Malaga.[84] On board were a great number of Muslim merchants from Oran, Tilimsān, and al-Andalus. He met the Qāḍī al-Jamāʿa (chief judge of the Nasrid kingdom) in Malaga along with other dignitaries.[85] Later he traveled inland to Granada by mule.[86] After returning to the coast he sailed back to Oran.[87] He intended to continue traveling in the same ship to Tunis but an illness forced him to remain behind. While he was there four Christian ships approached from the west. The local inhabitants were frightened because there was a rumor that these ships were full of fighting men who had come to raid Oran and take captives. The ships passed by Oran without incident but later news was received that they had attacked Bijāya where they caused great destruction and enslaved many Muslims.[88]

ʿAbd al-Bāsiṭ had recovered from his illness and he was ready to continue his return voyage to the east. At this moment a big Genoese merchant-galley (*shūna*) arrived in port.[89] It had come from Flanders and it carried a cargo of cloth (*jūkh*). ʿAbd al-Bāsiṭ and many Maghribī merchants boarded this vessel to travel to Tunis. At one point during the voyage the wind fell calm and the galley continued under the power of its oars though due to its great weight it made little progress. After a short stop in Bijāya they reached Tunis.[90] ʿAbd al-Bāsiṭ stayed onboard with his luggage and family for the four days that the ship was anchored in Tunis.[91] They continued to Tripoli where they disembarked. He rented a house in Tripoli and stayed there with his family for several months.[92]

While he was in Tripoli, ʿAbd al-Bāsiṭ met a *ḥajj* caravan consisting of Maṣmūda Berbers and local pilgrims. He decided to travel with them to Egypt and he bought a camel and supplies for the journey. They stopped in Misrāta and Qaṣr Aḥmad before reaching Barqa (Cyrenaica).[93] In the latter province they traveled through the interior of the country, avoiding the coastal route which was considered more dangerous due to the Arab tribes. ʿAbd al-Bāsiṭ noted that Barqa was a strange, desolate land with no mountains, hills or traces of civilization. He saw the remains of a great ancient city called *Labna*. Then he and his companions came across a large well called Sāwaknā where some Bedouin threatened them. Upon arriving in eastern Barqa they reached the abode of the Arabs of Labīd. These were friendly people who lived in a fertile area. They were kind to the

84 ʿAbd al-Bāsiṭ, *Rawḍ*, vol. 3, pp. 51–52, 111–112.
85 ʿAbd al-Bāsiṭ, *Rawḍ*, vol. 3, pp. 112–113.
86 ʿAbd al-Bāsiṭ, *Rawḍ*, vol. 3, pp. 117–118, 120–122.
87 ʿAbd al-Bāsiṭ, *Rawḍ*, vol. 3, pp. 125–126.
88 ʿAbd al-Bāsiṭ, *Rawḍ*, vol. 3, p. 131.
89 ʿAbd al-Bāsiṭ, *Rawḍ*, vol. 3, p. 189.
90 ʿAbd al-Bāsiṭ, *Rawḍ*, vol. 3, p. 190.
91 ʿAbd al-Bāsiṭ, *Rawḍ*, vol. 3, p. 193.
92 ʿAbd al-Bāsiṭ, *Rawḍ*, vol. 3, p. 199.
93 ʿAbd al-Bāsiṭ, *Rawḍ*, vol. 3, pp. 202–205.

pilgrims and held markets for them. They continued into the desert lying west of Alexandria where they endured considerable hardship and many of their camels died, forcing them to walk great distances.[94] Finally, they reached Alexandria and ʿAbd al-Bāsiṭ continued on to Cairo. He had hoped to meet his father there, but unfortunately the latter had just left Cairo for the pilgrimage before ʿAbd al-Bāsiṭ's arrival.[95]

Part II: Analysis

Observations on Travel by Land and Sea

Goitein remarks that during the eleventh and twelfth centuries travel by ship between the Maghrib and Mashriq was much preferred to travel by caravan along the North African coast. He estimates that the ratio of references to sea travel compared to references to caravan travel in the Geniza documents is 20:1 from the period before the Hilālī migration (when presumably the land routes were disrupted) and 50:1 afterwards.[96] Mūsā says that travelers between Ifrīqiya and Egypt had to go by sea during the Almohad period because the land route between Tripoli and Alexandria was not secure.[97]

It is not possible to make such generalizations about the preference for one mode of transportation over the other based on the evidence that we have from the Mamluk period. Certainly both land and sea travel presented unique dangers: attack by nomads or loss in the desert in the case of the former and piracy or shipwreck in the case of the latter. While sea travel was much faster under normal circumstances, storms could force a ship off course for weeks on end and during the winter season most ships could not sail at all.

We have seen that Muḥammad al-Zawāwī feared sea voyages and insisted on traveling by land between Tripoli and Alexandria.[98] Many voyages were mixed, combining travel by ship with travel by caravan. In the Venetian archives there is mention of an Egyptian merchant who was returning home from Ifrīqiya in a Genoese ship which was too slow for his liking. As a result, he disembarked and

94 ʿAbd al-Bāsiṭ, *Rawḍ*, vol. 3, pp. 204–207.

95 ʿAbd al-Bāsiṭ, *Rawḍ*, vol. 3, p. 212.

96 S.D. Goitein, "The Unity of the Mediterranean World in the 'Middle' Middle Ages," in idem, *Studies in Islamic History and Institutions* (Leiden: Brill, 2010), pp. 300–301.

97 ʿUmar Aḥmad ʿIzz al-Dīn Mūsā, *Al-Nashāṭ al-Iqtiṣādī fī al-Maghrib khilāl al-Qarn al-Sādis al-Hijrī* (Beirut: Dār al-Shurūq, 1983), p. 311.

98 Katz, "Vision," p. 240.

completed his journey to Alexandria by land.[99] ʿAbd al-Bāsiṭ traveled by ship as far as Tripoli during his return voyage to Egypt and completed his journey on land in the company of a *ḥajj* caravan.[100] When al-Qalaṣādī's ship was forced to remain in Barqa due to unfavorable winds the passengers were divided with some wishing to continue by land to Tunis while others preferred to wait for the winds to change.[101]

Muslim Ships on the East-West Routes

Some scholars have maintained that from the late twelfth century onwards maritime traffic between the eastern and western Mediterranean was almost wholly in the hands of the Christians, particularly the Italian city-states.[102] In the travel accounts from the Mamluk period that we have examined above there are many references to Muslim ships, both Egyptian and Maghribī, which plied the routes between Alexandria and Ifrīqiya. In the mid-fourteenth century both Ibn Baṭṭūṭa and al-Balawī sailed from Alexandria to Tunis in Muslim vessels.[103] Ibn Khaldūn traveled from Tunis to Alexandria in an Egyptian ship and his family followed him several years later in a large Muslim vessel which tragically sank.[104] In the middle of the fifteenth century al-Qalaṣādī sailed from Alexandria to Tunis in a convoy of Muslim vessels.[105] From the eyewitness account of the ambassador from Granada it appears that as late as the 1440s the Mamluks maintained a formidable fleet which threatened the very existence of the principality of Rhodes.[106] We can conclude then that though the foremost maritime powers in the late medieval Mediterranean were Christian states (namely Venice, Genoa, and Aragon), there was also a Muslim maritime presence in the western and eastern Mediterranean throughout the period in question. The merchant fleets of the Christian powers certainly played a large role in maritime trade between the Maghrib and Egypt but they never succeeded in removing this trade entirely from the hands of local North African seafarers.

99 Bernard Doumerc, *Venise et l'émirate hafside de Tunis (1231–1555)* (Paris: L'Harmattan, 1996). pp. 48–49.
100 ʿAbd al-Bāsiṭ, *Rawḍ*, vol. 3, pp. 199, 202–205, 207.
101 Al-Qalaṣādī, *Riḥla*, pp. 158–162.
102 Claude Cahen, *Orient et occident au temps des Croisades* (Paris: Aubier, 1983), p. 137, quoted in Agius, "Maqrizi's Evidence," p. 186.
103 Ibn Baṭṭūṭa, *Riḥla*, p. 664; Al-Balawī, *Tāj*, vol. 2, p. 93.
104 Ibn Khaldūn, *Riḥla*, p. 199; Ibn Qāḍī Shuhba, *Tārīkh*, vol. 3, p. 138.
105 Al-Qalaṣādī, *Riḥla*, pp. 158–159.
106 Al-Ahwānī, "Sifāra."

Christian Ships on the East-West Routes

The Arabic sources that we have examined usually refer to Christian ships as "Frankish" ships, which was a generic term for any of the western (Latin) European states. Occasionally, they specify the nationality of the ship. Ibn Jubayr and al-Mashaddalī traveled in Genoese ships.[107] ʿAbd al-Bāsit traveled in a Venetian ship from Egypt to Ifrīqiya and he took a Genoese vessel from Oran to Tripoli on his return voyage.[108] There were two broad categories of ships used on these voyages: galleys which were powered by both rowers and sails and sailing ships which had no oarsmen. Most merchant vessels relied on wind power alone. The largest of these included the cog (*jafn*) with its wide, round hull and the carrack (*qarqūra*) with its triple decks and triple masts. The larger sailing ships had small crews since they did not carry oarsmen, thus they could carry more passengers and bulk cargo than the galleys. The major disadvantage of these ships was that they were entirely dependent on the winds. They were also slower and more difficult to maneuver than galleys. These factors together with their relatively small crew sizes made them tempting targets for corsairs and hostile navies. Galleys (*shawānī*) were primarily used as war vessels, however, large modified galleys with a wider hull were also used to carry passengers and precious cargo. These ships could move under the power of oars when the wind was unfavorable. Furthermore, due to their maneuverability and their large, well-armed crews, such vessels were capable of fending off all but the most determined corsair attacks.[109]

Most ships were privately owned but the Venetians developed a system of state merchant galleys which regularly sailed on certain fixed routes in convoys of two to five vessels called the *mude* (singular *muda*). Shares in these galleys were sold by the state to patricians who became the sponsors of the galleys and these in turn sold space on the vessel to merchants who wished to transport their goods in the ship. The commanding officers of the galleys were always appointed by the state. These state galleys were perhaps the safest and most reliable means of transportation in the Mediterranean.[110] The Muda of Flanders, established in the early fourteenth century, sometimes followed the North African coast from the straits of Gibraltar to Alexandria.[111] In the 1400s the Venetian senate created the Muda al Trafego, a line whose sole purpose was to connect Tunis to Alexandria via some

107 Ibn Jubayr, *Riḥla*, pp. 28–31, 240–250; Al-Sakhāwī, *Ḍaw'*, vol. 9, pp. 182–183.
108 ʿAbd al-Bāsiṭ, *Rawḍ*, vol. 2, p. 163, vol. 3, p. 189.
109 Frederic C. Lane, *Venice: A Maritime Republic* (Baltimore: John Hopkins University Press, 1973), pp. 337–339.
110 Lane, *Venice*, pp. 337–342; Doumerc, *Venise*, pp. 79–81.
111 Doumerc, *Venise*, pp. 101–103.

intermediary ports such as Tripoli.[112] It is evident from ʿAbd al-Bāsiṭ's account that he sailed from Alexandria to Tunis in such an organized convoy comprised of three Venetian galleys.[113] After seeing the success of the Venetian Muda al Trafego, the Genoese established their own Tunis-Alexandria line at the end of the 1400s.[114]

Piracy

During the late medieval period Muslim pilgrims and merchants routinely traveled on the Christian ships which sailed between North Africa and the Levant. For these passengers corsairs, both Muslim and Christian, were an ever-present danger. On occasion the passengers experienced tension with their European crews as well. The ambassadors from Granada were in the delicate position of being Muslim passengers on a Christian ship that came under attack by Muslim corsairs. They narrowly avoided being attacked by the ship's crew.[115] Al-Jarīrī was a passenger on a Christian ship of unspecified nationality that came under attack by the Genoese in 1440.[116] The Venetian government was careful to ensure the safety of the Muslim passengers who embarked on their galleys as they did not want to jeopardize their trade relations with the Mamluks and Hafsids nor to risk reprisals against their consuls and overseas communities in Islamic port cities. In 1464 two galleys of the Trafego line were attacked and captured by the fleet of the Knights of Rhodes while *en route* to Tunis. The knights seized 220 Muslim merchants who were travelling aboard the vessels along with their wares of linen. The Hafsid and Mamluk rulers blamed Venice and imprisoned the Venetian consuls. The Venetian senate reacted energetically by dispatching its main fleet to Rhodes and compelling the Grand Master to release his Muslim prisoners.[117] In 1489 the Venetian crew of a Trafego galley kidnapped and sold into slavery a Maghribī slave trader who had taken passage on their vessel. This provoked outrage in Tunis and the Venetian government intervened by punishing the culprits very harshly.[118]

112 Ibid., pp. 103–106.
113 ʿAbd al-Bāsiṭ, *Rawḍ*, vol. 2, pp. 168–169.
114 Doumerc, *Venise*, p. 64.
115 Al-Ahwānī, "Sifāra," p. 98; Seco de Lucena, "Viaje," pp. 8–9.
116 Al-Sakhāwī, *Ḍaw'*, vol. 1, pp. 305–306.
117 ʿAbd al-Bāsiṭ, *Rawḍ*, vol. 3, pp. 35–36; Lane, *Venice*, pp. 349–350; Doumerc, *Venise*, p. 60.
118 Lane, *Venice*, p. 350; Doumerc, *Venise*, p. 62.

Land Travel between Ifrīqiya and Egypt

The most popular land route between Ifrīqiya and Egypt closely followed the Mediterranean coast between Qābis in southeastern Tunisia and Alexandria. Neither the Mamluks nor the Hafsids managed to exercise effective control over the Libyan coast. Three major tribes of the Arab Banū Sulaym dominated northern Libya. The Dabbāb were found in Tripolitania between Qābis and Sirt, while the Hayb and Labīd were found in Cyrenaica (Barqa) where they roamed from Sirt to Alexandria.[119] These tribes were further sub-divided into many feuding smaller tribes. Baybars sent military expeditions to Barqa and attempted to extend Mamluk authority over the region, however, by the fifteenth century if not earlier it appears that Barqa had slipped completely out of Mamluk control.[120] Barghūthī says that during this period Barqa was an impoverished region dominated by the incessantly quarrelling Sulaymī tribes who lived through raiding and plunder.[121] Al-ʿAbdarī complained about the barbarity of the inhabitants of eastern Libya while the geographer Ibn Saʿīd (d. 673/1274) remarked that between Tripoli and Alexandria there was not to be found a single town with a bath and a baker.[122]

Tripoli was controlled by the Hafsids from the end of Almohad rule in Ifrīqiya in the early thirteenth century until 724/1323. From 724/1323 to 803/1400 it was ruled by a local Arab family of Sulaymī (Dabbābī) origin called the Banū Thābit. In 803/1400 it returned to Hafsid rule which continued at least nominally until the Spaniards occupied Tripoli in 916/1510.[123] Curiously, Ibn Saʿīd praised Tripoli for the fertility and wealth of its countryside while al-ʿAbdarī, who wrote only a decade later, claimed that the countryside of Tripoli was barren and that no gardens or orchards were to be found in its vicinity.[124]

Due to the often unsettled, anarchic conditions along the Libyan coastal route, attack by local tribesmen and bandits posed a serious threat to travelers. Ibn Baṭṭūṭa traveled in a heavily armed and well-escorted caravan that narrowly escaped a clash with the Bedouin near Sirt.[125] ʿAbd al-Bāsiṭ's caravan also escaped hostile Bedouin in Barqa.[126] Leo Africanus, writing in the early sixteenth century, said that the Arabs of Barqa were impoverished and had a habit of robbing

119 ʿAbd al-Laṭīf Maḥmūd al-Barghūthī, *Tārīkh Lībīyā al-Islāmī min al-Fatḥ al-Islāmī ḥattā Bidāyat al-ʿAṣr al-ʿUthmānī* (Beirut: Dār Ṣādir, 1973), pp. 460–461.

120 Ibid., p. 467.

121 Ibid., pp. 472–473.

122 Abū al-Ḥasan ʿAlī b. Mūsā b. Saʿīd, *Kitāb al-Jughrāfīyā*, ed. Ismāʿīl al-ʿArabī (Beirut: Al-Maktab al-Tijārī, 1970), p. 146; Al-ʿAbdarī, *Riḥla*, pp. 203–209.

123 Barghūthī, *Tārīkh*, pp. 385–426.

124 Ibn Saʿīd, *Jughrāfīyā*, pp. 145–146; Al-ʿAbdarī, *Riḥla*, pp. 184–186.

125 Ibn Baṭṭūṭa, *Riḥla*, p. 36.

126 ʿAbd al-Bāsiṭ, *Rawḍ*, vol. 3, pp. 204–205.

passersby.[127] On the other hand, there are also accounts which mention that at least some of the tribes in Libya were kind and helpful to pilgrims.[128] ʿAbd al-Bāsiṭ remarks that the Sulaymī tribe of the Labīd treated him and his companions well when their caravan passed through eastern Cyrenaica.[129]

Trade between Ifrīqiya and Mamluk Egypt

The importance of land and sea trade between Ifrīqiya and Egypt during the Fatimid period (especially between 1000 and 1150 A.D.) has been firmly established thanks to the abundant evidence furnished by the Geniza documents. The standard study of relations between Fatimid Egypt and the Maghrib by Aḥmad gives ample space and consideration to the commercial aspect of these relations.[130] Regrettably, studies concerning Mamluk-Maghribī relations focus overwhelmingly on cultural and religious exchanges, and to a lesser extent political relations, while largely ignoring the subject of trade between the Maghrib and Egypt during this period. Chapoutot-Remadi says that we have an incomplete picture of Mamluk relations with Ifrīqiya due to the paucity of economic data.[131] A recent Ph.D. thesis on the relations between the Mamluks and the Maghribī dynasties has nothing to say about trade and economic relations, the same can be said of Musʿad's work on the role of the Maghāriba in Mamluk Egypt.[132] Khalafallāh's study on Almohad and Hafsid relations with the Mashriq and Ḥabīb's work on Mamluk trade with Africa offer surprisingly little information about trade between the Maghrib and Egypt that is specific to the Mamluk period.[133] An exception is Bin Mīlād's important study on relations between Ifrīqīya and the Mashriq from the eleventh to sixteenth centuries which takes into account all dimensions of the contacts between these two regions during the late Middle Ages, including the economic aspect.[134]

127 Quoted in Barghūthī, *Tārīkh*, p. 475.
128 For example see Ibn Saʿīd, *Jughrāfīyā*, p. 146.
129 ʿAbd al-Bāsiṭ, *Rawḍ*, vol. 3, pp. 205, 207.
130 Aḥmad, *Al-ʿAlāqāt.*
131 Chapoutot, "Les Relations," p. 159.
132 ʿAbd al-Raḥmān Bi'l Aʿraj, "ʿAlāqāt Duwal al-Maghrib al-Islāmī bi Dawlat al-Mamālīk Sīyāsīyān wa-Thaqāfīyān bayna al-Qarnayn al-Sābiʿ wa al-Tāsiʿ Hijrīyayn," (Ph.D. thesis, Tlemcen University, 2012–2013); Sāmiya Muṣṭafā Musʿad, *Al-Maghāriba wa Dawruhum al-Thaqāfī fī Miṣr ʿAṣr Salāṭīn al-Mamālīk* (Cairo: Ein for Human and Social Sciences, 2002).
133 Ibtisām Marʿī Khalafallāh, *Al-ʿAlaqāt bayna al-Khilāfat al-Muwaḥḥidīya wal-Mashriq al-Islāmī: 524/1130–936/1529* (Cairo: Dār al-Maʿārif, 1980); Ḥabīb, *Al-Tijāra.*
134 See Luṭfī bin Mīlād, *Ifrīqīya wa al-Mashriq al-Mutawassiṭī min Awāsiṭ al-Qarn 5 h./11 m. ilā Maṭlaʿ al-Qarn 10 h./16 m.*, (Tunis: al-Maghāribīya, 2011).

The relative lack of attention given to commercial relations between the Mamluks and the Maghrib in modern studies is probably due to the nature of the Arabic primary sources from this period. There are many entries about Maghribī scholars who traveled to the east in the great biographical dictionaries of the Mamluk period as well as in the *ṭabaqāt* of the Mālikī scholars. As we have seen above, there are also quite a few travel books (*riḥlāt*) written by Maghribī and Andalusī scholars who made the pilgrimage during the era of Mamluk domination in the Mashriq. It is important to note, however, that these works were written by the ulema for the ulema. The biographical dictionaries largely recount the lives of scholars, mentioning the teachers under whom they studied and the books that they read. Such information is far more useful to intellectual and cultural historians than to economic historians. It is extremely rare to come across the biography of a merchant with details of his travels and his commercial activities in these sources.

Most of the travel books are similarly concerned with describing the scholars whom the author met and studied with during his journey and the various books that he read with them. The popularity of Ibn Jubayr and Ibn Baṭṭūṭa with modern readers is no doubt due to the fact that their *Riḥlas* incorporate a great deal of material that is of general interest (such as information on ethnology, geography, local politics, and most importantly, their personal adventures) whereas other travel works such as the books of al-Qalaṣādī and al-Balawī are closer to the genre of scholarly biographical dictionaries. Nonetheless, even from the latter works it is possible to extract some information about travel and seafaring in the Mamluk period as we have attempted to do here.

It is also worth noting that historians of the Fatimid period have at their disposal a wealth of contemporary merchants' documents from the Geniza which discuss the details of trade, travel, and communication between Ifrīqiya and Egypt in the eleventh and twelfth centuries.[135] If similar Geniza letters exist from the Mamluk period they have not yet been published and translated. Furthermore, the Fatimid period coincided with the golden age of the Arabic geographical tradition, particularly in the Islamic west where scholars such as Ibn Ḥawqal (d. 367/977), al-Bakrī (d. 487/1094), and al-Idrīsī (d. 560/1165) left detailed accounts of the routes which connected Egypt to the Maghrib as well as the towns, tribes, and resources that awaited a traveler. From the Mamluk period there is no surviving geographical work of this caliber apart from that of al-ʿUmarī (d. 786/1384). At first glance one might conclude from the surviving sources that performance of the pilgrimage and study were the main motivations for Maghāriba who traveled to the Mamluk empire. It will be shown here that

135 Goitein, "Medieval Tunisia."

trade was at least an equally important factor behind travel during the period in question.

There are some hints in the Arabic sources that we have summarized above which point to brisk trade between the Maghrib and Mamluk Egypt. ʿAbd al-Bāsiṭ sailed from Alexandria to Tunis with a ship full of Egyptian merchants who had, like himself, bought large quantities of Egyptian linen to sell in the markets of the Maghrib. On his return voyage he traveled in a large Genoese ship that had arrived from northern Europe and which was continuing its journey to the eastern Mediterranean with stops along the coast of North Africa. He notes that many Maghribī and Andalusī merchants boarded the ship with him.[136] Ibn Khaldūn sailed from Tunis to Alexandria in a ship owned by Egyptian merchants.[137] The Mamluk ambassadors to the Merinids, al-Khwārazmī and al-Talīlī, returned to Egypt in the company of a caravan consisting of Maghribī pilgrims and merchants.[138] Lirola-Delgado reminds us that the pilgrimage was often combined with commercial activities.[139]

Perhaps the strongest evidence for the importance of Maghribī-Egyptian trade during this period comes from the Venetian archives. In 1460 the Venetians established the *Muda al Trafego*, a shipping line which connected Tunis to Alexandria via Tripoli. From Alexandria the convoys followed the eastern and northern coasts of the Mediterranean back to the Adriatic and Venice. According to Doumerc, the creation of this line was due in great part to the demand of the Maghribī merchants and the Hafsid government in Tunis for a regular service that would link the ports of Ifrīqiya with Alexandria.[140] Pressure from the Hafsids on the Venetian senate was decisive in bringing about this decision since maintaining good relations with Tunis was a pillar of Venetian foreign and commercial policy. As mentioned above, the Venetian state galleys of the *mude* offered greater security and speed than private merchant ships though this came at a higher cost. Doumerc says that it was the participation of the Maghribī and Egyptian merchants which ensured the success of the Trafego line.[141] The Venetian documents mention that black slaves were brought to Egypt in the state galleys by Maghribī slave-traders and they also mention that Maghribī and Egyptian merchants brought Egyptian linen to the Maghrib in the galleys.[142] We can safely assume that there was simultaneously a much greater volume of

136 ʿAbd al-Bāsiṭ, *Rawḍ*, vol. 2, p. 163, vol. 3, p. 189.
137 Ibn Khaldūn, *Riḥla*, p. 199.
138 Baybars al-Manṣūrī, *Zubda*, pp. 411–412.
139 See Lirola Delgado, "Travesias," p. 86.
140 Doumerc, *Venise*, p. 105.
141 Ibid.
142 On the slave trade see Lane, *Venice*, p. 350. For linen see Doumerc, *Venise*, p. 60 and Lane, *Venice*, p. 349.

merchandise carried between Ifrīqiya and Egypt by private merchant ships whether Venetian, non-Venetian Christian, or Muslim.[143]

In light of the evidence above there can be no doubt that there was large-scale direct trade between Ifrīqiya and Egypt during the Mamluk period and that it was no less important a factor in the relations between these two regions than it had been during the time of the Fatimids. It is to be hoped that future research in the archives of the Italian maritime cities and in unpublished Arabic manuscript collections will shed more light on this vital, but neglected aspect of relations between the Mashriq and the Maghrib in the late Middle Ages.

Bibliography

Primary Sources

ʿAbd al-Bāsiṭ b. Khalīl b. Shāhīn al-Ẓāhirī, Zayn al-Dīn. *Nayl al-Amal fī Dhayl al-Duwal.* Ed. ʿUmar ʿAbd al-Salām al-Tadmurī. Beirut: Al-Maktaba al-ʿAṣrīya, 2002. 9 vols.

–. *Al-Rawḍ al-Bāsim fī Ḥawādith al-ʿUmur wa al-Tarājim.* Ed. ʿUmar ʿAbd al-Salām al-Tadmurī. Beirut: Al-Maktaba al-ʿAṣrīya, 2014. 4 vols.

Al-ʿAbdarī, Abū ʿAbdallāh Muḥammad b. Muḥammad b. ʿAlī b. Aḥmad b. Suʿūd. *Riḥlat al-ʿAbdarī.* Ed. Ibrāhīm al-Kurdī. Damascus: Majmaʿ al-Lughat al-ʿArabīya, 1999.

Al-Ahwānī, ʿAbd al-ʿAzīz. "Sifāra Siyāsīya min Gharnāṭa ilā al-Qāhira fī al-Qarn al-Tāsiʿ al-Hijrī (sanat 844)." *Majallat Kullīyat al-Ādāb.* Vol. 16/ No. 1 (1954), 95–121.

Al-Balawī, Khālid b. ʿIsā. *Tāj al-Mafriq fī Taḥlīyat ʿUlamāʾ al-Mashriq.* Ed. Al-Ḥasan al-Sāʾiḥ. Muḥammadīya [Morocco]: Maṭbaʿat Faḍḍāla, 1980. 2 vols.

Ibn Baṭṭūṭa, Muḥammad b. ʿAbdallāh b. Muḥammad al-Ṭanjī. *Riḥlat Ibn Baṭṭūṭa.* Ed. Ṭalāl Ḥarb. Beirut: *Dār al-Kutub al-ʿIlmīya*, 2002. 2 vols. in 1.

Baybars al-Manṣūrī, Rukn al-Dīn. *Zubdat al-Fikra fī Tārīkh al-Hijra.* Ed. Donald S. Richards. Beirut: al-Shārika al-Muttaḥida lil-Tawzīʿ, 1998.

Brunschvig, Robert. *Deux Récits de Voyage inédits en Afrique du Nord au XVe siècle.* Paris: Larose, 1936.

Ibn Jubayr, Muḥammad b. Aḥmad. *Riḥlat Ibn Jubayr.* Ed. Ibrāhīm Shams al-Dīn. Beirut: Dār al-Kutub al-ʿIlmīya, 2003.

Ibn Khaldūn. ʿAbd al-Raḥmān. *Riḥlat Ibn Khaldūn.* Ed. Muḥammad b. Tāwīt. Beirut: Dār al-Kutub al-ʿIlmīya, 2004.

Ibn Qāḍī Shuhba, Taqī al-Dīn b. Abī Bakr b. Aḥmad. *Tārīkh Ibn Qāḍī Shuhba.* Ed. ʿAdnān Darwīsh. Damascus: Al-Maʿhad al-Fransī, 1977. 4 vols.

Al-Qalaṣādī, Abū al-Ḥasan ʿAlī. *Riḥlat al-Qalṣādī.* Ed. Muḥammad Abū al-Ajfān. Tunis: Al-Sharika al-Tūnisīya lil-Tawzīʿ, 1978.

Ibn Rushayd, Abū ʿAbdallāh Muḥammad b. ʿUmar. *Milʾ al-ʿAyba bi-mā Jumiʿa bi-Ṭūl al-Ghayba fī al-Wajha al-Wajīha ilā Makka wa-Ṭība: Al-Juzʾ al-Khāmis, Al-Ḥaramayn al-*

143 Doumerc, Venise, p. 80.

Sharīfayn wa-Miṣr wal-Iskandarīya ʿinda al-Ṣudūr. Ed. Muḥammad al-Ḥabīb b. al-Khūja. Beirut: Dār al-Gharb al-Islāmī, 1988.

–. *Milʾ al-ʿAyba bi-mā Jumiʿa bi Ṭūl al-Ghayba fī al-Wajha al-Wajīha ilā Makka wa-Ṭība: Al-Juzʾ al-Thānī, Tūnis ʿinda al-Wurūd.* Ed. Muḥammad al-Ḥabīb b. al-Khūja. Tunis: Al-Dār al-Tūnisīya li al-Nashr, 1982.

Ibn Saʿīd, Abū al-Ḥasan ʿAlī b. Mūsā. *Kitāb al-Jughrāfīyā.* Ed. Ismāʿīl al-ʿArabī. Beirut: Al-Maktab al-Tijārī, 1970.

Al-Sakhāwī, Muḥammad b. ʿAbd al-Raḥmān. *Al-Ḍawʾ al-Lāmiʿ li-Ahl al-Qarn al-Tāsiʿ.* 12 Vols. Beirut: Dār Maktabat al-Ḥayāt, 1966.

Seco de Lucena Paredes, Luis. "Viaje a Oriente: Embajadores granadinos en el Cairo." *Miscelánea de estudios Árabes y Hebraicos.* 4 (1955), 9–30.

Modern Studies

Agius, Dionisius A. *Classic Ships of Islam from Mesopotamia to the Indian Ocean.* Leiden: Brill, 2008.

–. "Maqrīzī's Evidence for the Gurāb." In *Law, Christianity, and Modernism in Islamic Society: Proceedings of the Eighteenth Congress of the Union Européene des Arabisants et Islamisants.* Ed. U. Vermeulen and J.M.F. Van Reeth. Leuven: Peeters, 1998. Pp. 185–197.

Aḥmad, Ḥasan Khuḍayrī. *ʿAlaqāt al-Fāṭimīyīn fī Miṣr bi-Duwal al-Maghrib: 362/973–567/1171.* Cairo: Madbouli, 1996.

ʿĀshūr, Saʿīd ʿAbd al-Fattāḥ. *Al-ʿAṣr al-Mamālīkī fī Miṣr wal-Shām.* Cairo: Dār al-Nahda al-ʿArabīya, 1976.

Al-Barghūthī, ʿAbd al-Laṭīf Maḥmūd. *Tāʾrīkh Lībīyā al-Islāmī min al-Fatḥ al-Islāmī ḥattā Bidāyat al-ʿAṣr al-ʿUthmānī.* Beirut: Dār Ṣādir, 1973.

Biʾl Aʿraj, ʿAbd al-Raḥmān. "ʿAlāqāt Duwal al-Maghrib al-Islāmī bi-Dawlat al-Mamālīk Sīyāsīyān wa-Thaqāfīyān bayna al-Qarnayn al-Sābiʿ wa al-Tāsiʿ Hijrīyayn." Ph.D. thesis, Tlemcen University, 2012–2013.

Bin Mīlād, Luṭfī. *Ifrīqīya wa al-Mashriq al-Mutawassiṭī min Awāsiṭ al-Qarn 5 h./11 m. ilā Maṭlaʿ al-Qarn 10 h./16 m.* Tunis: al-Maghāribīya, 2011.

Cahen, Claude. *Orient et occident au temps des Croisades.* Paris: Aubier, 1983.

–. "Ibn Jubayr et les Maghrébins de Syrie." *Revue de l'Occident Musulman et de la Méditerranée.* Vol. 13/ No. 1 (1973), 207–209.

Chapoutot-Remadi, Mounira. "Les relations entre l'Égypte et l'Ifriqya aux XIIIe et XIVe siècle d'après les auteurs Mamlûks." In *Actes du premier congrès d'histoire et de la civilisation du Maghreb / Ashghāl al-Muʾtamar al-Awwal li-Tārīkh al-Maghrib al-ʿArabī wa-Ḥaḍāratih.* Tunis, December 1974. Tunis: Université de Tunis, Centre d'études et de recherches économiques et sociales, 1979. Vol. 1 : 139–159.

Doumerc, Bernard. *Venise et l'émirate hafside de Tunis (1231–1535).* Paris: L'Harmattan, 1999.

Goitein, S.D. "Medieval Tunisia, the Hub of the Mediterranean." In idem. *Studies in Islamic History and Institutions.* Leiden: Brill, 2010. Pp. 308–328.

–. "The Unity of the Mediterranean World in the 'Middle' Middle Ages." In idem. *Studies in Islamic History and Institutions.* Leiden: Brill, 2010. Pp. 296–307.

Jehel, George. *Les Gênois en Méditerranée occidentale: (fin XIème – début XIVème siècle : ébauche d'une stratégie pour un empire)*. Amiens [Somme, France] : Centre d'histoire des sociétés, Université de Picardie, 1993.

Ḥabīb, Shawqī ʿAbd al-Qawī ʿUthmān. *Al-Tijāra bayna Miṣr wa-Afrīqīyā ʿAṣr Salāṭīn al-Mamālīk: 648/1250–922/1517*. Cairo: Al-Majlis al-Aʿlā li al-Thaqāfa, 2000.

Ḥaddādī, Aḥmad. *Riḥlat b. Rushayd al-Sabtī: Dirāsa wa-Taḥlīl*. Morocco: Wizārat al-Awqāf wa al-Shuʾūn al-Islāmīya, 2003. 2 vols. in 1.

Katz, Jonathan G. "The Vision of the Prophet in Fifteenth Century North Africa: Muḥammad al-Zawāwī's Tuḥfat al-Nāẓir." Ph.D. Dissertation, Princeton University, 1990.

Khalafallāh, Ibtisām Marʿī. *Al-ʿAlāqāt bayna al-Khilāfat al-Muwaḥḥidīya wa al-Mashriq al-Islāmī: 524/1130–936/1529*. Cairo: Dār al-Maʿārif, 1980.

Al-Kurdī, ʿAlī Ibrāhīm. *Adab al-Riḥal fī al-Maghrib wal-Andalus*. Damascus: Wizārat al-Thaqāfa, 2013.

Lane, Frederic C. *Venice: A Maritime Republic*. Baltimore: John Hopkins University Press, 1973.

Lirola-Delgado, Jorge. "Travesias Nauticas en la *Riḥla* del Almeriense Jālid al-Balawī (siglo XIV)." In *Actas del II Congreso de Historia de Andalucía*. (Córdoba, 1991). Pp. 85–92.

Mūsā.ʿUmar Aḥmad ʿIzz al-Dīn. *Al-Nashāṭ al-Iqtiṣādī fī al-Maghrib khilāl al-Qarn al-Sādis al-Hijrī*. Beirut: Dār al-Shurūq, 1983.

Musʿad, Sāmiya Muṣṭafā. *Al-Maghāriba wa-Dawruhum al-Thaqāfī fī Miṣr ʿAṣr Salāṭīn al-Mamālīk*. Cairo: Ein for Human and Social Sciences, 2002.

Pryor, John and Sergio Bellabarba. "Medieval Muslim Ships of the Pisan *Bacini*." *The Mariner's Mirror*. Vol. 76/ No. 2 (1990), 99–113.

Al-Sukhnī, Maḥmūd Khālid. "Al-Nashāṭ al-Baḥrī li-Dawlat al-Mamālīk fī al-Baḥr al-Mutawassiṭ: 690/1291–923/1517." MA thesis, University of Damascus, 2012.

Valérian, Dominique. *Bougie, port maghrébin, 1067–1510*. Rome: École française de Rome, 2006.

Nikolas Jaspert (Heidelberg University)

The Crown of Aragon and the Mamluk Sultanate: Entanglements of Mediterranean Politics and Piety[1]

The Mamluk Empire may be conceived as a sharply contoured physical and political entity, as a geographical territory with borders which were defended or shifted. The Sultanate, however, can (and should) also be envisaged in a more dynamic way as a node of communication and exchange through which commodities – be they material or intellectual – flowed, or it can even be seen as a hub that forcefully attracted and invigorated such processes.[2] The same holds true for the other polities that are put into relation with the Mamluk Sultanate in this volume, amongst them the medieval Crown of Aragon. In fact, this confederation of several principalities (comprised of the Catalan counties, the kingdoms of Aragon, Valencia and – for the most part of the 13th to 15th centuries – Mallorca) is particularly apt for such an understanding of spatial interaction, because, over the course of the later Middle Ages, it not only rose to a major trade emporium, but in fact to a transmarine Mediterranean empire.[3] Within this realm processes

1 Many thanks for suggestions and assistance to Viktor Gottesmann, Elisabeth Luy, Julian Reichert, Rebecca Sauer, Sandra Schieweck and Wolf Zöller (all Heidelberg), as well as Damien Coulon (Strasbourg) and Jo Van Steenbergen (Ghent).

2 See Stephan Conermann, ed. *Everything is on the Move: The Mamluk Empire as a Node in (Trans-)Regional Networks* (Göttingen: Bonn University Press, 2014) and particularly programmatic: Idem. "Networks and Nodes in Mamluk Times: some introductory remarks." *Ibidem*, 9–24. On the concept of nodes and hubs see Alex Cowan. "Nodes, Networks and Hinterlands." In *Cities and Cultural Exchange in Europe, 1400–1700*, ed. Donatella Calabi and Stephen Turk Christensen (Cambridge: Cambridge University Press, 2007), 28–41; Marc von der Höh, Nikolas Jaspert and Jenny Rahel Oesterle. "Courts, Brokers and Brokerage in the Medieval Mediterranean." In *Cultural Brokers at Mediterranean Courts in the Middle Ages*, ed. Marc von der Höh, Nikolas Jaspert and Jenny Rahel Oesterle (Paderborn: Fink-Schöningh, 2013), 10–31, particularly 15–18; Nikolas Jaspert. "Mendicants, Jews and Muslims at Court in the Crown of Aragon: Social Practice and Inter-Religious Communication." *Ibid.*, 107–147, particularly 107–109.

3 General overviews: Thomas Noel Bisson. *The Medieval Crown of Aragon: A Short History* (Oxford: Clarendon, 1986); María Teresa Ferrer i Mallol and Damien Coulon, ed. *L'Expansió catalana a la Mediterrània a la baixa edat mitjana* (Barcelona: CSIC, 1999); José-Luis Martín. *Historia de la Corona de Aragón* (Madrid: Universiad Nacional de Educación a Distancia, 2002) and the many volumes of the nineteen "Congresos de Historia de la Corona de Aragón."

of transculturation took place on many levels and were reinforced by its mobile agents abroad, as a number of recent studies have demonstrated.[4] Most of these works focus on the realm's military or economic history, highlighting the widespread commercial networks established throughout the Mediterranean, predominantly by Catalan merchants.

The present article will specifically deal with the political and diplomatic relations between the Mamluk Sultanate and the Crown of Aragon. This by no means represents a new field of research. One need only call to mind the seminal studies by Girolamo Golubovich,[5] Aziz Atiya,[6] and more recently Peter Holt.[7] Frequently overlooked on an international level, yet significant are Spanish contributions to the history of Aragonese diplomatic relations with the Muslim Levant.[8] A good case in point is the relative neglect of the edition of 166 original

4 Coral Cuadrada. *La Mediterrània, cruïlla de mercaders (segles XIII–XV)* (Barcelona: Rafael Dalmau Editor, 2001); Josefina Mutgé i Vives, Roser Salicrú i Lluch and Carles Vela Aulesa, ed. *La Corona catalano aragonesa, l'Islam i el món mediterrani. Estudis d'història medieval en homenatge a la Doctora María Teresa Ferrer i Mallol* (Barcelona: CSIC, 2013). Exemplary: Damien Coulon, *Barcelone et le grand commerce d'Orient au Moyen Age. Un siècle de relations avec l'Egypte et la Syrie-Palestine (ca. 1330–ca. 1430)* (Madrid: Casa de Velázquez, 2004), Christian Neumann, *Venedig und Aragon im Spätmittelalter (1280–1410): Eine Verflechtungsgeschichte* (Paderborn: Fink-Schöningh 2017).

5 Girolamo Golubovich, *Biblioteca bio-bibliografica della Terra Santa e dell'Oriente Francescano* (Quaracchi: Tipografia del Collegio di S. Bonaventura, 1906–1927), particularly: Idem, Biblioteca bio-bibliografica della Terra Santa e dell'Oriente Francescano. 3: *Dal 1300 al 1332* (Quaracchi: Tipografia del Collegio di S. Bonaventura, 1919), 73–85, 185–189, 232–237.

6 Aziz Suryal Atiya, *Egypt and Aragon: Embassies and Diplomatic Correspondence between 1300 and 1330 A.D.* (Leipzig: Brockhaus, 1938); idem, *The Crusade in the Later Middle Ages* (London: Methuen, 1938).

7 Peter Malcolm Holt. "Al-Nasir Muḥammad's Letter to a Spanish Ruler in 699/1300." *Al-Masaq* 3 (1990): 23–29; idem. "The Mamluk Sultanate and Aragon: The Treaties of 689/1290 and 692/1293." *Tārīḫ* 2 (1992): 105–118; idem, *Early Mamluk Diplomacy (1260–1290): Treaties of Baybars and Qalawun with Christian Rulers* (Leiden: Brill, 1995). More recently on Mamluk diplomacy with Christian powers Dimitri A. Korobeinikov. "Diplomatic Correspondence between Byzantium and the Mamluk Sultanate in the Fourteenth Century." *Al-Masaq* 16 (2004): 53–74; Anne F. Broadbridge, "Diplomatic Conventions in the Mamluk Sultanate." *Annales Islamologiques* 41 (2007): 97–118; Deborah Howard, "Venice and the Mamluks." In: *Venice and the Islamic World*, ed. Stefano Carboni (New Haven: Yale University Press, 2007), 72–89; Georg Christ, *Trading Conflicts: Venetian Merchants and Mamluk Officials in Late Medieval Alexandria* (Leiden: Brill, 2012).

8 Ángeles Masiá de Ros. *La corona de Aragón y los estados del norte de África: política de Jaime II y Alfonso IV en Egipto, Ifriquía y Tremecén* (Barcelona: Instituto español de estudios mediterráneos, 1951); more recently: Gabriel González Maurazos. "La documentación diplomática entre la Corona de Aragón y el Sultanato Mameluco durante el reinado de Jaime II: un ejemplo de las transformaciones en las relaciones internacionales del ámbito mediterráneo en la Baja Edad Media." In *Anales de la Universidad de Alicante. Historia medieval* 11 (1996): 395–403; Ministerio de Cultura, ed. *El perfume de la amistad: correspondencia diplomática árabe en archivos españoles (siglos XIII–XVII)* (Madrid: Secretaria General Técnica, 2009). On Aragonese-Ifriqiyan and Aragonese-Maghrebi relations see: Charles Emmanuel Dufourcq. *L'*

Arabic documents kept in the *Archivo de la Corona de Aragón* (*Arxiu de la Corona d'Aragó*) in Barcelona published by Maximiliano Alarcón Santón and Ramón García de Linares in 1940.[9] This collection is extremely valuable due to the dearth of extant original documentation in Northern Africa,[10] so much so that a modern, up-to-date edition of the Barcelonese holdings is currently under progress.[11] Such an enterprise is all the more necessary, because the archival situation in Barcelona is more complex than the edition by Alarcón and García suggests.

When studying Aragonese administrative sources concerned with the Mamluk Sultanate, a distinction has to be made between at least four different types of texts. First, original Arabic Mamluk documents (mostly letters and treaties). Eleven of the 182 such Arabic documents kept at the Archivo de la Corona de

---

Espagne catalane et le Maghrib aux XIIIe et XIVe siècles: de la bataille de Las Navas de Tolosa (1212) à l'avènement du sultan mérinide Abou-l-Hasan (1331) (Paris: Presses Universitaires de France, 1966); María Dolores López Pérez. *La Corona de Aragón y el Magreb en el siglo XIV: (1331–1410)* (Barcelona: Institut Milá y Fontanals, 1995); Henri Bresc and Yusuf Rāġib. *Le sultan mérinide Abū l-Ḥasan ʿAli et Jacques III de Majorque: du traité de paix au pacte secret* (Cairo: Institut Français d'Archéologie Orientale 2011). Cf. the first major contribution: Antoni Capmany y de Montpalau. *Memorias históricas sobre la marina, comercio y artes de la antigua ciudad de Barcelona* (Madrid, 1779–1792), 3 vols.

9 Maximiliano A. Alarcón Santón and Ramón García de Linares. *Los documentos árabes diplomáticos del Archivo de la Corona de Aragón: editados y traducidos* (Madrid: Estanislao Maestre, 1940). Earlier references to this archival collection: Wilhelm Heyd. *Histoire du commerce du Levant au moyen âge 2* (Leipzig: Hakkert, 1886), 30–32; Atiya, *Egypt and Aragon* (note 6). All in all, the Archivo de la Corona de Aragon holds 182 original Arabic documents: Alberto Torra Pérez. "Las relaciones diplomáticas entre la Corona de Aragón y los países musulmanes (siglos XIII–XV). Las fuentes documentales del Archivo de la Corona de Aragón." In *El perfume de la amistad: correspondencia diplomática árabe en archivos españoles (siglos XIII–XVII)*, ed. Ministerio de Cultura (Madrid: Secretaria General Técnica, 2009), 13–39, here: 17.

10 Frédéric Bauden. "Mamluk Era Documentary Studies: The State of the Art." *Mamlūk Studies Review* 9 (2005): 15–60; Nuria Martínez de Castilla Muñoz, María Jesús Viguera Molins and Pascal Buresi, ed. *Documentos y manuscritos árabes del Occidente musulmán medieval* (Madrid, 2010); Frédéric Bauden. "Du destin des archives en Islam. Analyse des données et éléments de réponse." In *La correspondance entre souverains, princes et cités-états: approches croisées entre l'Orient musulman, l'Occident latin et Byzance (XIIIe-début XVIe siècle)*, ed. Denise Aigle and Stephane Péquignot (Turnhout: Brepols, 2013), 27–49; Lucian Reinfandt. "Mamluk Documentary Studies." In *Ubi sumus? Quo vademus? Mamluk Studies – State of the Art*, ed. Stephan Conermann (Göttingen: Bonn University Press, 2013), 285–310.

11 The project "The diplomatic exchanges between Islamic Mediterranean and Christian European powers in the Middle Ages: New methods for the analysis of documents" is led by Roser Salicrú i Lluch (CSIC, Institut Milà i Fontanals, Barcelona), Maria Mercè Viladrich Grau (Universitat de Barcelona), Mohamed Ouerfelli (Université d'Aix-Marseille) and Frédéric Bauden (Université de Liège). The Barcelonese collection is also being studied in Germany: Daniel Potthast. "Drei Fragmente von arabischen Staatsbriefen (14. Jahrhundert) im Archivo de la Corona de Aragón/Barcelona." *Der Islam.* 92 (2015): 367–412.

Aragón stem from Egypt.[12] They are particularly valuable for specialists in Mamluk history and diplomatics. Second, there are a number of translations of these documents into Latin or the vernacular, that is Catalan. Around a third of the extant originals were translated and copied into the royal registers, including four Mamluk texts.[13] Such documents are of particular interest to cultural historians and specialists in international relations, because one can employ them to study which elements of the Arabic formulary were omitted or changed in the translated text.[14] Even more significant than these renditions of existing sources is the third type of sources, namely translations of now lost Arabic documents. They were not included in the edition by Alarcón and García and have therefore often been ignored by later scholars. This group of deperdita comprises 80 documents, two of them from Egypt.[15] They are of minor interest to specialists in medieval diplomatics, but nevertheless valuable for Mamlukologists. Fourth and finally, the many hundreds of royal registers still extant in Barcelona contain numerous entries referring to Egypt, usually written in Latin or in the vernacular. They have not been collected systematically and exhaustively, but some important headway has been made since Atiya's ground-breaking study thanks to Spanish historians working on the 14th century. For example, Àngels Masià de Ros identified over 50 relevant documents dating from the 14th century.[16] Some of them refer to the activities of Mamluk ambassadors in Aragon, thus complementing the official documents such as letters and peace treaties.[17]

All four types of sources will form the basis for this article. Its approach is admittedly one-sided, for it draws heavily on the above mentioned 14th century royal, that is Christian, registers, and it is written by a historian of Latin and European history, not by an Orientalist. Nevertheless, the very rich Aragonese documentation raises some points which might be of interest to Mamlukologists and to historians of medieval Europe alike.[18] Amongst these is the question of the

12 Torra Pérez. "Las relaciones diplomáticas entre la Corona de Aragón y los países musulmanes" (note 9), 18.

13 Ibid. 32.

14 For this approach see: Pascal Buresi. "Traduttore, traditore. À propos d'une correspondance arabe-latine entre l'Empire almohade et la cité de Pise (début XIIIe siècle)." In *Les relations diplomatiques entre le monde musulman et l'Occident latin: (XIIe–XVIe siècle)*, ed. Denise Aigle and Pascal Buresi (Rome: Istituto per l'Oriente C. A. Nallino, 2008), 297–309.

15 Torra Pérez. "Las relaciones diplomáticas entre la Corona de Aragón y los países musulmanes" (note 9), 19.

16 Masiá de Ros, *La corona de Aragón y los estados del norte de África* (note 8).

17 On the ambassadors see ibid., 100–132; Damien Coulon. "Négocier avec les sultans de Méditerranée orientale à la fin du moyen âge. Un domaine privilegié pour les hommes d'affaires?" In *Negociar en la Edad Media = Négocier au Moyen Âge*, ed. María Teresa Ferrer i Mallol (Barcelona: Consejo Superior de Investigaciones Científicas, 2005), 503–526.

18 On the trans-disciplinary turn in Mamluk Studies see Stephan Conermann. "Quo vadis,

defining factors that influenced diplomatic relations between Egypt and Aragon. In this article, I will largely disregard the arguably most momentous of these features, namely commerce and economic interests, in order to concentrate on two other fields: piety and domestic affairs.

Mediterranean diplomatic networks

Of late, the historical disciplines of diplomacy and foreign relations, which form the analytical framework of this study, have received vital impulses thanks to new and innovative approaches and studies,[19] some of which focus on the medieval Crown of Aragon.[20] Recent works not only deal with the issues that were negotiated, but rather concentrate on the agents of diplomacy and their modes of action. Social history and prosopography have been employed at a profit, and consuls, ambassadors, messengers and other envoys are currently not only considered as political agents, but also as cultural brokers.[21] The ceremonies,

Mamlukology? (A German Perspective)." In *Ubi sumus? Quo vademus? Mamluk Studies – State of the Art*, ed. Stephan Conermann (Göttingen: Bonn University Press, 2013), 7–22.

19 Dieter Berg, Martin Kintzinger and Pierre Monnet, ed. *Auswärtige Politik und internationale Beziehungen im Mittelalter: 13. bis 16. Jahrhundert* (Bochum: Winckler, 2002); Claudia Zey and Claudia Märtl, ed. *Aus der Frühzeit europäischer Diplomatie: zum geistlichen und weltlichen Gesandtschaftswesen vom 12. bis zum 15. Jahrhundert* (Zurich: Chronos-Verlag, 2008); John Watkins. "Toward a New Diplomatic History of Medieval and Early Modern Europe." *Journal of Medieval and Early Modern Studies* 38 (2008): 1–14; Rainer Christoph Schwinges and Klaus Wriedt, ed. *Gesandtschafts- und Botenwesen im spätmittelalterlichen Europa* (Ostfildern: Thorbecke, 2003); Hillard von Thiessen and Christian Windler, ed. *Akteure der Außenbeziehungen: Netzwerke und Interkulturalität im historischen Wandel* (Cologne: Böhlau, 2010); Thierry Kouamé, ed. *Les relations diplomatiques au Moyen Âge: Formes et enjeux* (Paris: Publications de la Sorbonne, 2011); *Le relazioni internazionali nell'alto medioevo* (Spoleto: Fondazione Centro Italiano di Studio sull'Alto Medioevo, 2011). Cf. the overview by Stéphane Péquignot. "Europäische Diplomatie im Spätmittelalter. Ein historiographischer Überblick." *Zeitschrift für Historische Forschung* 39 (2012): 65–96; Nikolas Jaspert and Sebastian Kolditz. "Christlich-muslimische Außenbeziehungen im Mittelmeerraum: Zur räumlichen und religiösen Dimension mittelalterlicher Diplomatie." *Zeitschrift für Historische Forschung* 41 (2014): 1–88.

20 María Teresa Ferrer i Mallol, ed. *Negociar en la Edad Media = Négocier au Moyen Âge* (Barcelona: Consejo Superior de Investigaciones Científicas, 2005); Stéphane Péquignot. *Au nom du roi: pratique diplomatique et pouvoir durant le règne de Jacques II d'Aragon (1291–1327)* (Madrid: Casa de Velázquez, 2009); Nikolas Jaspert. "Interreligiöse Diplomatie im Mittelmeerraum. Die Krone Aragón und die islamische Welt im 13. und 14. Jahrhundert." In *Aus der Frühzeit europäischer Diplomatie. Zum geistlichen und weltlichen Gesandtschaftswesen vom 12. bis zum 15. Jahrhundert*, ed. Claudia Märtl and Claudia Zey (Zurich: Chronos, 2008), 151–190.

21 Claudia Moatti and Wolfgang Kaiser, ed. *Gens de passage en Méditerranée de l'Antiquité à l'époque moderne: procédures de contrôle et d'identification* (Paris: Maisonneuve et Larose, 2007); Michael Borgolte. "Experten der Fremde. Gesandte in interkulturellen Beziehungen

rituals and other forms of symbolic communication employed in foreign relations are beginning to receive the attention they deserve, and Christian-Muslim medieval diplomacy is turning into a vibrant field of research which is being opened up to transcultural approaches.[22] Yet dealing with bilateral diplomacy also has its pitfalls. One of them, and this is a first point worth stressing, is the all too often overlooked fact that foreign relations are seldom detached from domestic politics and should be studied accordingly. A second impediment to adequately understanding Christian-Muslim diplomacy is that it was rarely as bilateral a form of communication as historiography is prone to claim – and as medieval sources would make us believe. Rather, Mediterranean diplomacy between Christian and Muslim powers must be understood as a complex and multipolar network.

To give an example: in 1290, Sultan Qalāwūn agreed to a far reaching treaty, even an alliance with King Alfonso III of Aragon and his brothers, which was confirmed the same year by Alfonso's successor James II.[23] The Aragonese ruler promised peace and safety for the sultan's subjects on land and at sea, swore to return the goods of any deceased merchant from the sultanate and assured he would hand over any fugitive arriving to his kingdom from the sultanate to the sultan. The latter pledged similar rights and promised to allow Aragonese pilgrims to access Jerusalem freely. Most surprisingly, both rulers vowed military assistance to each other in case they were to be attacked by third parties. This astonishing document can only be explained adequately by taking its signees' contemporary interests and needs into account. As Peter Holt emphasised correctly some years ago, the Crown of Aragon was under extreme pressure in April 1290: eight years before, Alfonso's brother Peter had seized power over Sicily in a

des frühen und hohen Mittelalters." In *Le relazioni internazionali nell'alto medioevo* (Spoleto: Fondazione Centro Italiano di Studio sull'Alto Medioevo, 2011), 945–992; Rania Abdellatif, Yassir Benhima et al., ed. *Acteurs des transferts culturel en Méditerranée médiévale* (Munich: Oldenbourg, 2012); Marc von der Höh, Nikolas Jaspert and Jenny Rahel Oesterle, ed. *Cultural Brokers at Mediterranean Courts in the Middle Ages* (Paderborn: Schöningh-Fink, 2013).

22 Nicolas Drocourt. "Christian-Muslim diplomatic relations. An overview of the main sources and themes of encounter (600–1000)." In *Christian Muslim relations: a bibliographical history Vol. 1: (600–900)*, ed. David Thomas, Barbara Roggema and Juan Pedro Monferrer-Sala (Leiden: Brill, 2009), 29–72; Denise Aigle and Pascal Buresi, ed. *Les relations diplomatiques entre le monde musulman et l'Occident latin: (XIIe–XVIe siècle)* (Rome: Istituto per l'Oriente C. A. Nallino, 2008); Jocelyne Dakhlia and Wolfgang Kaiser, ed. *Les Musulmans dans l'histoire de l'Europe II: Passages et contacts en Méditerranée* (Paris: Albin Michel, 2012); Jaspert und Kolditz. "Christlich-muslimische Außenbeziehungen im Mittelmeerraum" (note 19).

23 Holt, *Early Mamluk Diplomacy* (note 7) 129–140; Linda Stevens Northrup. *From Slave to Sultan: The Career of Al-Manṣūr Qalāwūn and the Consolidation of Mamlūk Rule in Egypt and Syria (678–689 A.H./1279–1290 A.D.)* (Stuttgart: Franz Steiner, 1998), 155; Albrecht Fuess, *Verbranntes Ufer: Auswirkungen mamlukischer Seepolitik auf Beirut und die syro-palästinensische Küste (1250–1517)* (Leiden: Brill, 2001), 71–73.

coup de main triggered by the popular uprising known as the Sicilian Vespers, and the resulting enmity of the papacy and French king - a crusade against Aragon was officially launched in 1285 - drove him to an alliance with the Mamluks.[24] But Sultan Qalāwūn's interest in this agreement has not been sufficiently realised to date. Several contemporary sources mention that precisely in 1290 the Ilkhanid Sultan Arghun had employed 800 Genoese to build ships in Baghdad for a planned naval attack on Egypt.[25] Qalāwūn thus appears to have signed a truce and military alliance with Aragon, the third most potent naval power in the Mediterranean - and one of Genoa's major rivals - to counter the Mongol threat. Tellingly, the Sultanate reached an agreement with Genoa shortly after and thus temporarily averted the danger of a Genoese-Mongol alliance.[26] Thus, in order to understand the treaty of 1290 adequately, one should consider both the Egyptian and Aragonese contexts, but also take Genoa, the Mongols, France, Naples, Byzantium and the Papacy into the equation.

The same holds true for subsequent intensifications of Aragonese-Mamluk relations. The peace treaty signed with Aragon in 1292 was not only a bilateral agreement: James II's envoys also acted on behalf of the Kings of Castile and Portugal, as the document clearly states, thus conveying a certain predominance to the Aragonese ruler over the Iberian Christian Monarchs active in the Eastern

24 Holt, *Early Mamluk Diplomacy* (note 7), 25–28, 130–131. On the war of the Vespers see: Santi Correnti, *La Guerra dei novant'anni e le ripercussioni europee della Guerra del Vespro* (Catania: Muglia, 1973); Francesco Giunta, ed. *XI Congresso di Storia della Corona d'Aragona: "'La società mediterranea all'epoca del Vespro.*" (Palermo: Accad. di Scienze Lettere e Arti, 1983), 4 vols.; Lawrence V. Mott, *Sea Power in the Medieval Mediterranean: The Catalan-Aragonese Fleet in the War of the Sicilian Vespers* (Gainesville: University Press of Florida, 2003). Significantly, when the Crown of Aragon reached an agreement with the papacy in 1295, the Aragonese ruler ordered that the papal ban on travelling to Egypt's be complied; trade however continued: Coulon, *Barcelone et le grand commerce d'Orient* (note 4), 87–97. Cf. José Trenchs Odena. "'De Alexandrinis' (El comercio prohibido con los musulmanes y el Papado de Aviñón durante la primera mitad del siglo XIV)." *Anuario de estudios medievales* 10 (1980): 237–320.

25 Friedrich Baethgen, ed. *Die Chronik Johanns von Winterthur* (Berlin: Berolini, 1924), 58; Ernest A. Wallis Budge, ed. and trans. *The Chronography of Gregory Abû'l Faraj, the Son of Aaron, the Hebrew Physician Commonly Known as Bar Hebraeus, Being the First Part of his Political History of the World* (London: Oxford University Press, 1932), 486; cf. Sylvia Schein, *Fideles Crucis: The Papacy, the West, and the Recovery of the Holy* (Oxford: Clarendon Press, 1991), 43–44, 88; Giles Constable, *William of Adam: How to Defeat the Saracens = Guillelmus Ade: Tractatus quomodo Sarraceni sunt expugnandi* (Washington: Dumbarton Oaks Research Library and Collection, 2012), 105.

26 Holt, *Early Mamluk Diplomacy* (note 7), 141–151; Northrup, *From Slave to Sultan* (note 23), 155–156; Peter Jackson, *The Mongols and the West, 1221-1410* (Harlow: Pearson Longman, 2005), 169–70; Alexander Markus Schilling. "Der Friedens- und Handelsvertrag von 1290 zwischen der Kommune Genua und dem Sultan Qalawun von Ägpyten." *Quellen und Forschungen aus italienischen Archiven und Bibliotheken* 95 (2015): 63–109.

Mediterranean.[27] After a certain lull in diplomatic contacts, new initiatives were undertaken around 1315,[28] and not by chance: That year, James II of Aragon married Maria of Lusignan, a possible heiress to the Cypriot throne. This union increased Aragonese political interests in Levantine affairs that had already been kindled due to the Staufen heritage and the Catalonian merchants' commercial expansion into the eastern Mediterranean.[29] Even the extensive peace treaty signed in 1430 can only be explained by considering wider contexts – here the political networks that King Alfonso the Magnanimous's new and active policy in the eastern Mediterranean had created with regional powers such as the Hospitallers of Rhodes.[30]

That being said, Mamluk-Aragonese diplomacy also needs to be evaluated against the backdrop of Christian Iberian contacts with the entire Dār al-Islām, markedly intensified with the rise of the Crown of Aragon to a major Mediterranean power at the turn of the 13th century. The Crown's widespread political and commercial activities made sure that its diplomatic relations with Muslim powers were certainly not limited to Egypt, but also comprised the Hafsids, Abdalwadids, Marinids as well as Nasrids. Mamluk-Aragonese diplomacy therefore has to be regarded within a wider Mediterranean framework.

In order to fully appraise the relevance of the Crown of Aragon's diplomatic contacts to the Mamluk Sultanate, it is of great importance to correlate Arago-

27 Antonio de Capmany Surís de Montpaláu, *Antiguos tratados de paces y alianzas entre algunos reyes de Aragón y diferentes príncipes infieles de Asia y Africa, desde el siglo XIII hasta el XV* (Valencia: Anúbar Ed. 1974 – first printed 1786), 26–31; Alarcón Santón und García de Linares, *Los documentos árabes diplomáticos del Archivo* (note 9), 335–344 (doc. 153); Ministerio de Cultura, *El perfume de la amistad* (note 8), 105–109. Cf. on Mamluk perceptions of Castile: Pedro Martínez Montávez. "Relaciones castellano-mamelucas 1283–1382." *Hispania. Revista española de historia* 23 (1963): 505–523.

28 Capmany Surís de Montpaláu, *Antiguos tratados de paces y alianzas* (note 27), 32–35; Atiya, *Egypt and Aragon* (note 6), 35, 36–41; Alarcón Santón und García de Linares, *Los documentos árabes diplomáticos del Archivo* (note 9), 360–365 (doc. 149); Ministerio de Cultura, *El perfume de la amistad* (note 8), 185–187.

29 Eugenio Sarrablo. "La Reina que vino de Oriente (María de Chipre, esposa de Jaime II, Rey de Aragón)." *Boletín de la Real Academia de la Historia* 148 (1961): 13–160.

30 Reginaldo Ruiz Orsatti. "Tratado de paz entre Alfonso V de Aragón y el Sultán de Egipto, al-Malik al Ašraf Barsbay." *Al-Andalus* 4 (1939): 333–390; Constantin Marinescu, *La politique orientale d'Alfonse V d'Aragon, roi de Naples (1416–1458)* (Barcelona: Institut d'Estudis Catalans, 1994); Mercè Viladrich. "Jaque al sultán en el 'Damero maldito'. Edición y traducción de un tratado diplomático entre los mercaderes catalanes y el sultanato mamluco (1429)." In *L'Expansió catalana a la Mediterrània a la baixa edat mitjana*, ed. María Teresa Ferrer i Mallol and Damien Coulon (Barcelona: CSIC, 1999), 161–206; Damien Coulon. "Un tournant dans les relations de Barcelone avec la Méditerranée orientale: la nouvelle politique d'Alphonse le Magnanime (1415–1442)." In *Atti del XVI Congresso Internazionale di Storia della Corona d'Aragona*, ed. Guido d'Agostino (Napoli: Paparo, 2000), 2: 1055–1079; Maria Mercé Viladrich. "Solving the 'Accursed Riddle' of the Diplomatic Relations between Catalonia and Egypt around 1430." *Al-Masaq* (2002): 25–31.

Egyptian relations with those the Crown upheld with other Muslim realms, for example with Hafsid Ifriqiya and Marinid Maghreb. One way to do so is by comparing the sheer quantities of documents extant in Aragonese archives referring to each polity. The result of such a survey is telling: of almost 600 documents dating from 1328 to 1386 and referring to the Crown of Aragon's dealings with the Dār al-Islām, one half concern Nasrid Granada. Of the remaining half, around 35% refer to the Marinids and Hafsids, whilst the Abdalwadids and the Mamluks together take up around 15%. In concrete numbers: 51 of ca. 600 documents refer to Mamluk Egypt.[31] On the field of diplomacy at least, Mamluk Egypt appears to have been of secondary relevance to the Crown of Aragon when compared to the Muslim realms situated in closer proximity to the Iberian coasts. It would be interesting, but hardly feasible, to conduct a similar survey of the Mamluk sultanate's dealings with Latin Europe. Where would the Crown of Aragon stand in such a comparative perspective? We cannot tell precisely, but it is safe to say that the easternmost Iberian realm was deemed a significant regional player by the Mamluks. As late as 1412, al-Qalqashandī elaborated on details of Aragonese history and laid down the quite complaisant wording of documents that were to be sent to the "King of Barcelona," as the Aragonese monarchs were sometimes termed in his handbook on chancery practices.[32] One hundred years earlier, the Mamluk Sultan's administration clearly had a very exact notion of the King of Aragon's titles: Arabic letters to James II reflected the Christian King's factual titulature by referring to him as "King of Aragon, Valencia, Sardinia and Corsica, count of Barcelona and standard-bearer of the Roman Church."[33] Some years before, Muḥyī al-Dīn ʿAbd al-Ẓāhir (d. 1292) had already reported on the Aragonese takeover in Sicily and the

31 Torra Pérez. "Las relaciones diplomáticas entre la Corona de Aragón y los países musulmanes" (note 9), 15–16.

32 Golubovich, *Biblioteca bio-bibliografica della Terra Santa e dell'Oriente Francescano 3* (note 5), 73; Henri Lammens. "Correspondances diplomatiques entre les sultans mamluks d'Egypte et les puissances chrétiennes."*Revue de l'Orient chrétien* 9 (1904): 151–187, 359–392, especially 163, 166–167. On the author's perception of the Iberian realms: Luis Seco de Lucena Paredes. "Un tratado árabe del siglo XV sobre España extraido del 'Subh al-Aʿša' de Al-Qualquasandi." *Boletín de la universidad de Granada* 14 (1942): 87–126; and now: Daniel König. *Arabic-Islamic Views of the Latin West. Tracing the Emergence of Medieval Europe* (Oxford: Oxford University Press, 2015), 319–322.

33 Alarcón Santón und García de Linares, *Los documentos árabes diplomáticos del Archivo* (note 9), 362 (doc. 149); Catalán translation: Ministerio de Cultura, *El perfume de la amistad* (note 8), 185. Similarly: Alarcón Santón and García de Linares, *Los documentos árabes diplomáticos del Archivo* (note 9), 365 (doc. 150). Cf. Michele Amari. *De' titoli che usava la cancelleria de' Sultani di Egitto nel 14 secolo scrivendo a' reggitori di alcuni stati italiani* (Rome, 1886), especially 25, and the Castilian case: Martínez Montávez, *Relaciones castellano-mamelucas 1283–1382* (note 27). The quite substantial knowledge of Christian polities and people in the middle ages has now been convincingly brought to our attention: König, *Arabic-Islamic Views of the Latin West* (note 32).

Mamluk-Aragonese alliance of 1290, and al-ʿUmarī (d. 1349) even spoke of the Catalans as the "Arabs amongst the Franks," praising them as vigorous people active on land and sea who were obedient to their King and who "do not commit evil as long as they are not aroused."[34] On both sides, rulers went to pains to furnish their embassies with extravagant gifts.[35] Lists of the presents given to James II by Egyptian ambassadors in 1306, 1315, and 1319 are still extant[36] – they comprise valuable cloths such as linen and silk, bows, crossbows, sables, balsam, incense, ginger marmalade, honey etc. On the Aragonese side, the rulers sent falcons, textiles and furs.[37] Thus, by analysing the Mamluk and Aragonese chancery records not only with respect to the sheer number of documents issued, but also with regard to the language and symbolism of communicative measures employed, we may cross the line from quantitative to qualitative research. In order to further pursue this line of study the following remarks aim at highlighting particularities of Mamluk-Aragonese relations by scrutinizing the diplomatic issues dealt with as well as the cultural brokers that conducted negotiations between both powers.

On a purely quantitative level, a statistical overview of the extant documentation reveals that there were periods of intensified contact and others of relative diplomatic lull. During the years 1290–1293, 1300–1306, 1315, 1323–1330, 1353–1356, 1373–1374, 1429–1430, the rulers of Aragon and Egypt appear to have maintained closer relations than in other periods. This means that diplomatic exchanges were particularly lively during the second and third reins of al-Nāṣir

34 *Kitāb tashrīf al-ayyām walʿuṣūr fi sīrat al-malik al-Manṣūr*, ed. Michele Amari, Leipzig 1857, 546–68; Michele Amari. *Condizioni degli stati cristiani dell'occidente secondo una relazione di Domenichino Doria da Genova: testo arabo con versione italiana* (Rome: Salviucci, 1883), 17; see König, *Arabic-Islamic Views of the Latin West* (note 32), 321.

35 In general on gift exchange see: Gadi Algazi, Valentin Groebner and Bernhard Jussen, ed. *Negotiating the Gift: Pre-modern Figurations of Exchange* (Göttingen: Vandenhoeck & Ruprecht, 2003); Anthony Cutler. "Significant Gift: Patterns of Exchange in Late Antique, Byzantine, and Early Islamic Diplomacy." *Journal of Medieval and Early Modern Studies* 38 (2008): 79–101; Elias I. Muhanna. "The Sultan's New Clothes: Ottoman-Mamluk Gift Exchange in the Fifteenth Century." *Muqarnas* 27 (2010): 189–207; Catarina Schmidt Arcangeli and Gerhard Wolf, ed. *Islamic Artefacts in the Mediterranean World: Trade, Gift Exchange and Artistic Transfer* (Venice: Marsilio, 2010); Michael Grünbart, ed. *Geschenke erhalten die Freundschaft. Gabentausch und Netzwerkpflege im europäischen Mittelalter* (Berlin: LIT-Verlag, 2011).

36 Atiya, *Egypt and Aragon* (note 6), 29–32; Alarcón Santón and García de Linares, *Los documentos árabes diplomáticos del Archivo* (note 9), 360–365 (doc. 149); Ministerio de Cultura, *El perfume de la amistad* (note 8), 185–187; Masiá de Ros, *La corona de Aragón y los estados del norte de África* (note 8), 114, 117, 314–315 (doc. 42). Cf. Coulon. "Négocier avec les sultans de Méditerranée orientale à la fin du moyen âge" (note 17), 518.

37 Alarcón Santón und García de Linares, *Los documentos árabes diplomáticos del Archivo* (note 9), 370–371 (doc. 152); Atiya, *Egypt and Aragon* (note 6), 62–64; Ministerio de Cultura, *El perfume de la amistad* (note 8), 193; Masiá de Ros, *La corona de Aragón y los estados del norte de África* (note 8), 112, 116, 119, 304–307 (doc. 37), 311–313 (doc. 41), 322–325 (doc. 51).

Muḥammad (ruled 1293–1341) and the reign of James II (1291–1327).[38] Needless to say, commercial interaction and also diplomacy on the part of economic urban agents such as the town council of Barcelona (the Consell de Cent and other urban institutions) continued notwithstanding the waning or even stagnation of royal political contacts. Indeed, Iberian trade interests were so strong that the agents chosen by the King to represent his interests before the Sultan were frequently merchants. For example, Ramon Alemany (1292), Gerart Olivera (1322), Pere Mitjavila (1327) or Francesc Saclosa (1373, 1379), Rafael Ferrer and Lluis Sirvent (1429/30) combined their short-term activities as diplomats with their long-term profession as traders.[39] When the King sent an embassy to the Sultan, the ship to Egypt not only carried the King's ambassador. Rather, it was loaded with goods and transported many merchants chosen under the strict supervision of the ambassador and the King's officials, as the documents preparing the embassies sent in 1305 and 1318 reveal.[40] Tellingly, Aragonese monarchs requested papal permission before despatching such "embassies" to the East: these major commercial-diplomatic trips threatened to undermine the papal ban on strategic material.[41]

38 On both rulers see: Heinrich Finke. *Acta Aragonensia. Quellen zur deutschen, italienischen, französischen und spanischen, zur Kirchen- und Kulturgeschichte aus der diplomatischen Korrespondenz Jaumes II. (1291–1327)* (Berlin: Rotschild, 1908–1922), 3 vols.; Amalia Levanoni. *A Turning Point in Mamluk History: The Third Reign of al-Naṣīr Muḥammad Ibn Qalāwūn (1310–1341)* (Leiden: Brill, 1995); see Hayat Nasser al-Hajji. *The Internal Affairs in Egypt during the Third Reign of Sultan al-Nāṣir Muḥammad B. Qalawun 709–741/1309–1341* (Kuwait: Dar al-Qalam, 1995); José Hinojosa Montalvo. *Jaime II y el esplendor de la Corona de Aragón* (San Sebastián: Nerea, 2006); Juan Manuel del Estal. *Itinerario de Jaime II de Aragón (1291–1327)* (Zaragoza: Institución Fernando el Católico, 2009); Stéphane Péquignot. *Au nom du roi: pratique diplomatique et pouvoir durant le règne de Jacques II d'Aragon (1291–1327)* (Paris: Casa de Velázquez, 2009).

39 Masiá de Ros, *La corona de Aragón y los estados del norte de África* (note 8), 110–132; See the list in Miguel Ángel Ochoa Brun. *Historia de la diplomacia española. Apéndice 1: Repertorio diplomático, listas cronológicas de representantes, desde la Alta Edad Media hasta el año 2000* (Madrid: Ministerio de Asuntos Exteriores, 2002), 59–60; Jaspert. "Interreligiöse Diplomatie im Mittelmeerraum" (note 20), 174–177, 186–189; Coulon. "Négocier avec les sultans de Méditerranée orientale à la fin du moyen âge" (note 17), particularly 511–518.

40 Atiya, *Egypt and Aragon* (note 6), 26–34; similarly in 1327: ibid., S. 54–60; Masiá de Ros, *La corona de Aragón y los estados del norte de África* (note 8), 104, 116; Miguel Ángel Ochoa Brun. *Historia de la diplomacia española*, vol. 3 (Madrid: Ministerio de Asuntos Exteriores, 1991), S. 223–225; Coulon. "Négocier avec les sultans de Méditerranée orientale à la fin du moyen âge" (note 17); Damien Coulon. "Lluis Sirvent, homme d'affaires et ambassadeur barcelonais (vers 1385–1444)." In *Les échanges en Méditerranée médiévale: marqueurs, réseaux, circulations, contacts*, ed. Élisabeth Malamut and Mohamed Ouerfelli (Aix-en-Provence: Presses universitaires de Provence, 2012), 215–242.

41 Francisco Javier Miquel Rosell. *Regesta de letras pontificias del Archivo de la Corona de Aragón: sección Cancilleria Real (pergaminos)* (Madrid: Góngora 1948), doc. 398, 414, 444; Trenchs Odena, "De Alexandrinis" (note 24); Ochoa Brun, *Historia de la diplomacia española* (note 40), 221–222; Damien Coulon. "La documentation pontificale et le commerce avec les

Sometimes, the envoy's concurrency between economic and political tasks could prove detrimental to the King's interests: In 1327, the Aragonese ambassador cum merchant Pere Mitjavila caused a major international outrage, because his economic concerns resulted in a clash with the French envoy in Alexandria, Guillaume de Bonnesmains, he too a merchant. The quarrel escalated to such a degree that Pere de Mitjavila accused Guillaume de Bonnesmains of being an imposter who carried false credentials and officially slandered the French King at the Court in Cairo claiming he was a heretic whose marriage was void. Significantly, and this throws a light on the functioning of the Mamluk chancery, pertinent French credentials could not be found in the archives, and Guillaume was expulsed from Egypt, which in turn had serious diplomatic repercussions on Franco-Aragonese relations.[42]

Complications such as these could and did affect diplomacy with Muslim powers. There were setbacks to Aragonese trade with the Mamluk Levant due to military conflicts between both polities – for example the incursion organized by Alfonso V (the Magnanimous) against Alexandria as retribution for the ill-treatment of a Catalan consul in 1416.[43] From time to time, minor irritations had detrimental consequences – see for example the scandal caused by the Aragonese ambassador Pere Dusay in 1306 when he forced his Egyptian counterpart and all Muslims accompanying him to disembark from his vessel in mid-voyage,[44] or the naval battle between Catalan and Genoese merchant ships fought in the port of Alexandria in Summer 1409.[45] Yet despite political tensions, trade continued throughout the 14th and 15th centuries. Between 1349 and 1408, no less than 224 Catalan ships anchored in the harbour of Beirut, third only to the number of

musulmans." In *Les territoires de la Méditerranée VIe-XVIe siècle*, ed. Annliese Nef (Rennes: Presses Universitaires de Rennes, 2013), 161–192.

42 Golubovich, *Biblioteca bio-bibliografica della Terra Santa e dell'Oriente Francescano* 3 (note 5), 320; Atiya, *Egypt and Aragon* (note 6), S. 54–60; Masiá de Ros, *La corona de Aragón y los estados del norte de África* (note 8), 124–126, 333–334 (doc. 58–59); Josep María Madurell Marimón. "Les activitats diplomàtiques i mercantils de Pere de Mitjavila." In *La corona de Aragon en el siglo XIV. VIII Congreso de Historia de la Corona de Aragón* (Valencia, 1973), 3: 177–188.

43 Coulon, *Barcelone et le grand commerce d'Orient* (note 4), 54–62. See in general Damien Coulon. "Formas de violencia entre la Corona de Aragón y el sultanato Mameluco en los siglos XIV y XV." *Anales de la Universidad de Alicante. Historia medieval* 16 (2009/10): 277–288.

44 Golubovich, *Biblioteca bio-bibliografica della Terra Santa e dell'Oriente Francescano* 3 (note 5), 80–85; Finke, *Acta Aragonensia* (note 38), 2: 744–745 (doc. 461); Masiá de Ros, *La corona de Aragón y los estados del norte de África* (note 8), 105–110, 296–302 (doc. 31).

45 Pierre-Herman Dopp. "Les relations egypto-catalanes et les corsaires au commencement du quinzième siècle." *Bulletin de la Faculte des Arts. Fouad I University* 11/1 (1949): 1–14; María Teresa Ferrer i Mallol. "Incidència dels cors en les relacions catalanes amb l'Orient (segles XIII–XV)." In *Els catalans a la Mediterrània oriental a l'edat mitjana*, ed. María Teresa Ferrer i Mallol (Barcelona: Institut d'Estudis Catalans, 2003), 259–307, especially 294–300.

Venetian and Genoese vessels,[46] and recent studies have shown the intensity of Barcelona's trade with Egypt during this period.[47]

Therefore, on a qualitative level and perhaps not surprisingly, a comparative analysis of the topics that Muslim and Christian envoys were ordered to negotiate shows a clear bias towards matters of commerce and war. The resolution of individual cases of maritime violence, but also more general negotiations designed at curbing naval assaults and raids, repeatedly emerge in the documentation. Time and again the containment of maritime marauding figures prominently in diplomatic correspondence and treaties. These negotiations should make us wary of the use of terms like Mediterranean "piracy." Precisely the fact that these occurrences were the object of political intervention shows that more often than not they were acts of "corsairing" rather than of "piracy."[48] For the Aragonese and the Mamluk rulers, semi-official forms of maritime violence were just another political instrument that complemented acts of overt warfare. These too, that is official conflicts in the central and western Mediterranean, frequently appear as issues of diplomacy. Even more numerous were initiatives undertaken in order to liberate groups of captives or individual prisoners.[49] Both

46 Federigo Melis. "Nota sul movimento del porto di Beirut secondo la documentazione fiorentina intorno al 1400." In *Idem: I trasporti e le comunicazioni nel medioevo* (Florence: Le Monnier, 1984), 77–79.

47 Coulon, *Barcelone et le grand commerce d'Orient* (note 4). Still valuable: Francesco Giunta, *Aragonesi e Catalani nel Mediterraneo. II: La presenza catalana nel Levante dalle origini a Giacomo II* (Palermo: U. Manfredi, 1959), especially 68–78, 107–122.

48 For discussions on these issues and related questions see: Nikolas Jaspert and Sebastian Kolditz, ed. *Seeraub im Mittelmeerraum. Piraterie, Korsarentum und maritime Gewalt von der Antike bis zur Neuzeit* (Munich-Paderborn: Fink-Schöningh, 2013). In general on piracy in the Mediterranean: Emilio Sola Castaño, *Un mediterráneo de piratas: corsarios, renegados y cautivos* (Madrid: Ediciones Tecnos, 1988); López Pérez, La Corona de Aragón y el Magreb en el siglo XIV (note 8), 577–812; Antonello Savaglio, ed. *Atti del Convegno Internazionale di Studi su "Guerra di Corsa e Pirateria nel Mediterraneo"* (Cosenza: Orizzonti Meridionali, 1999); Anna Unali, *Marineros, piratas y corsarios catalanes en la Baja Edad Media* (Sevilla: Renacimiento, 2007); Ferrer i Mallol. "Incidència dels cors en les relacions catalanes amb l'Orient" (note 45); Gérard Chastagnaret, ed. *Les sociétés méditerranéennes face au risque: disciplines, temps, espaces* (Cairo: Institut Français d'Archéologie Orientale, 2008); Vito Piergiovanni, ed. *Corsari e riscatto dei captivi: garanzia notarile tra le due sponde del Mediterraneo* (Milano: Giuffrè, 2010).

49 José María Ramos Loscertales, *El Cautiverio en la corona de Aragón durante los siglos XIII, XIV, y XV* (Zaragoza, 1915); María Teresa Ferrer Mallol. "Els redemptors de captius: mostolafs eixees o alfaquecs (segles XII–XIII)." *Medievalia* 9 (1990): 85–106; Jarbel Rodriguez, *Captives and their saviors in the medieval crown of Aragon* (Washington, DC: Catholic University of America Press, 2007); Wolfgang Kaiser, ed. *Le commerce des captifs: les intermédiaires dans l'échange et le rachat des prisonniers en Méditerranée, XVe–XVIIIe siècle* (Rome: École Française de Rome, 2008); Georg Christ. "Transkulturelle Pirateriebekämpfung? Venezianisch-Mamlukische Kooperation und Gefangenenbefreiung im östlichen Mittelmeerraum im Spätmittelalter." In *Seeraub im Mittelmeerraum. Piraterie, Korsarentum und maritime Gewalt von der Antike bis zur Neuzeit*, ed. Nikolas Jaspert and Sebastian Kolditz

in Islam and Christianity, commitment and efforts to free imprisoned subjects were charitable assignments a good ruler was expected to fulfil, which is why these formed part of practically every case of official diplomatic exchange between Cairo and Barcelona studied in this article. Men and women captured during coastal raids, at high sea or during battle are sometimes individually named in the documents, in other cases prisoners are only referred to generically.

By and large, economic interests played a major role for Mamluk-Aragonese relations. Considering the intense commercial activities of Catalonian merchants in the Levant, this, too, comes as no surprise. Indeed, long-distance trade and its agents have traditionally been a primary objective of historical research when dealing with the Crown of Aragon in the late Middle Ages. But merchants were by no means the only cultural brokers that crossed the religious border between the Dār al-Islām and the Christian Iberian realms. A comparative survey of a lesser known group of agents – mercenaries – might help to highlight particularities of Mamluk-Aragonese diplomacy. For many reasons, medieval mercenaries are an especially intriguing group of cultural brokers; not least because many of them might be termed "trans-imperial subjects" in that they rendered service to foreign rulers while maintaining ties to their motherland.[50] Christian mercenaries took on military expatriation to other realms within Latin Europe,[51] but they also crossed the Mediterranean: nearly every North African power from the 12th to 15th century employed Christian mercenaries, and Aragon was one of their prime suppliers.[52]

(Munich-Paderborn: Fink-Schöningh, 2013), 363–375; Nikolas Jaspert. "Gefangenenloskauf in der Krone Aragon und die Anfänge des Mercedarierordens: Institutionelle Diversität, religiöse Kontexte, mediterrane Verflechtungen." In *Gefangenenloskauf im Mittelmeerraum. Ein interreligiöser Vergleich*, ed. Heike Grieser and Nicole Priesching (Hildesheim: Olms, 2015), 99–121.

50 Stephen Morillo. "Mercenaries, Mamluks and Militia: towards a Crosscultural Typology of Military Service." In *Mercenaries and Paid Men: The Mercenary Identity in the Middle Ages*, ed. John France, HW (Leiden: Brill, 2008), 243–259 and the titles named in footnote 52. The term "trans-imperial subject" was coined by Ella Natalie Rothman, *Brokering Empire: Trans-imperial Subjects between Venice and Istanbul* (Ithaca: Cornell University Press, 2012).

51 Kenneth Alan Fowler. *Medieval Mercenaries 1: The Great Companies* (Oxford: Blackwell, 2001); Stephan Selzer. *Deutsche Söldner im Italien des Trecento* (Tübingen: Niemeyer, 2001); John France, ed. *Mercenaries and Paid Men: The Mercenary Identity in the Middle Ages* (Leiden: Brill, 2008); Hunt Janin and Ursula Carlson. *Mercenaries in Medieval and Renaissance Europe* (Jefferson, N.C: McFarland Company, Inc., Publishers, 2013).

52 Simon Barton. "Traitors to the Faith? Christian Mercenaries in al-Andalus and the Maghreb, c. 1100–1300." In *Medieval Spain. Culture, Conflict and Coexistence. Studies in Honour of Angus MacKay*, ed. Roger Collins and Anthony Goodman (Basingstoke, 2002), 23–45; María Dolores López Pérez. "Marchands, esclaves et mercenaires: les transferts de populations dans le Maghreb médiéval." In *Migrations et diasporas méditerranéennes (Xe–XVIe siècles)*, ed. Michel Balard and Alain Ducellier (Paris: Publications de la Sorbonne, 2002), 399–415; Roser Salicrú Lluch. "Mercenaires castillans au Maroc au début du XVe siècle."; *ibid.*, 417–434; María Teresa Ferrer i Mallol. "Marruecos y la Corona catalano-aragonesa: mercenarios cat-

Paid warriors were contracted in conflicts against competing Muslim powers, but they were also hired as a protective force for tax collectors in Northern Africa. Muslim sources relate that several sultans in Ifriqiya and the Maghreb maintained foreign soldiers under the leadership of Castilian and Arago-Catalan captains. From the little we know about such Christian militias of the Almoravid and Almohad periods, their activities were confined to an intra-religious, that is inner-Islamic context. Just as other praetorians before and after, these foreign fighters stabilised the power of local potentates since they were less easily won for court intrigues and dynastic struggles. Due to their particular military and tactical training, these foreign warriors could effectively strengthen local forces on the battlefield. Such were the reasons why Christian rulers on the Iberian Peninsula in turn contracted Muslim corps during the Middle Ages.[53] The practice of employing Christian militiamen to defend the interests of Muslim rulers against internal and external threats continued until the end of the Middle Ages.

As intriguing as such Christian mercenaries are: what needs to be stressed is the fact that from a perspective of Mamluk-Aragonese relations things were different: No Aragonese mercenaries appear to have been employed in the Mamluk Sultanate, rather understandably considering the very nature of this polity and its ruling class. This, however, does not mean that Catalans, Aragonese or other Iberian Christians did not convert to Islam and become Mamluks. We know that North African rulers also employed former Christians as mercenaries, and such converts have also been attested in the Mamluk Sultanate.[54] But it

alanes al servicio de Marruecos (1396–1410)." In *Homenaje al profesor Eloy Benito Ruano* (Murcia: Universitad de Murcia, 2010), 251–272; Javier Albarrán Iruela. "De la conversión y expulsión al mercenariado: los cristianos en las fuentes almohades." In *La Península Ibérica en tiempos de Las Navas de Tolosa*, ed. Carlos Estepa and María Antonia Carmona Ruiz (Madrid: Sociedad Española de Estudios Medievales, 2014), 79–91; Michael Lower. "The Papacy and Christian Mercenaries of Thirteenth-Century North Africa." *Speculum* 89 (2014): 601–631; Nikolas Jaspert. "Zur Loyalität interkultureller Makler im Mittelmeerraum: Christliche Söldnerführer (alcayts) im Dienste muslimischer Sultane." In *Loyalty in the Middle Ages. Ideal and Practice of a Cross-Social Value*, ed. Jörg Sonntag and Coralie Zermatten (Turnhout: Brepols, 2016), 235–274.

53 Brian Aivars Catlos. "Mahomet Abenadalill: A Muslim Mercenary in the Service of the Kings of Aragon (1290–1291)." In *Jews, Muslims, and Christians in and around the Crown of Aragon: Essays in Honour of Professor Elena Lourie*, ed. Harvey J. Hames (Leiden: Brill, 2004), 257–302; Ana Echevarría. *Knights in the Frontier: The Moorish Guard of the Kings of Castile (1410–1467)* (Leiden: Brill, 2009); Hussein Fancy. *The Mercenary Mediterranean: Sovereignty, Religion, and Violence in the Medieval Crown of Aragon* (Chicago: University of Chicago Press, 2016).

54 François Clément. "Reverter et son fils, deux officiers catalans au service des sultans de Marrakech." *Medieval Encounters* 9 (2003): 79–107, 82. On apostasy see Robert Ignatius Burns. "Renegades, Adventurers, and Sharp Businessmen: The Thirteenth Century Spaniard in the Cause of Islam." *The Catholic Historical Review* 58 (1972): 341–366; José Vicente Cabezuelo Pliego. "Cristiano de Alá, renegado de Cristo. El caso de Abdalla, fill d'en Domingo

remains an open question, how many of these apostates might have heralded from the Iberian Peninsula. As the subject of Christian mercenaries in Muslim service shows, the specific character of the Mamluk state had a marked impact on the Sultanate's diplomatic relations with the Crown of Aragon. But what else made Egypt special? There was one particularly relevant factor which, for Christian powers, singled out the Mamluk sultanate from amongst the Muslim realms: its possession of Jerusalem. I will elaborate on this point in the second part of my article.

Christian and Muslim Pilgrimage

During the entire Middle Ages, men and women from Eastern Iberia undertook pilgrimages to Jerusalem. From the 11th century onwards, the number of Christians who took sail for the Holy Land grew considerably,[55] and even after the demise of the Crusader States at the end of the 13th century, Catalano-Aragonese pilgrimage to Jerusalem continued, as sources of the 14th and 15th centuries corroborate.[56] For example, the Royal registers contain late medieval requests for safe conducts presented to the Chancery by Christian pilgrims.[57] Admittedly, medieval Jerusalem pilgrimage was not confined to the Iberian Peninsula. Yet the Crown of Aragon showed one marked characteristic that distinguished it from most other Christian realms: two kingdoms within this confederation – Aragon proper and Valencia – were home to substantial Muslim populations. Nowhere in Latin medieval Europe did as many Muslims live in as large communities and for

Vallés, un valenciano al servicio del islam." *Sharq al-Andalus* 13 (1996): 27–46; Roser Salicrú Lluch. "En busca de una liberación alternativa: fugas y apostasía en la Corona de Aragón bajomedieval." In *La liberazione dei "captive"' tra Cristianità e Islam: oltre la crociata e il Gihad: tolleranza e servizio umanitario*, ed. Giulio Cipollone (Città del Vaticano: Archivio Segreto Vaticano, 2000), 703–713; Ulrich Haarmann. "The Mamluk System of Rule in the Eyes of Western Travelers." *Mamlūk Studies Review* 5 (2001): 1–24, particularly 6–16.

55 Josep Gudiol. "De peregrins i peregrinatges religiosos catalans." *Analecta sacra tarraconensia* 3 (1927): 93–120; Pierre-Vincent Claverie. "La dévotion envers les Lieux saints dans la Catalogne médiévale." In *Chemins d'outre-mer. Études d'histoire sur la Méditerranée médiévale offertes à Michel Balard*, ed. Damien Coulon (Paris: Publications de la Sorbonne, 2004), 127–137; Nikolas Jaspert. "Eleventh-Century Pilgrimage from Catalonia to Jerusalem: New Sources on the Foundations of the First Crusade." *Crusades* 14 (2015): 1–48.

56 Josep M. Marquès. "Sis-cents pidolaires (1368–1540). Captius, esclaus i pelegrins." *Estudis del Baix Empordà* 13 (1994): 137–165; María T. Ferrer i Mallol. *Els catalans a la Mediterrània oriental a l'edat mitjana* (Barcelona: Institut d'Estudis Catalans, 2003).

57 Masiá de Ros, *La corona de Aragón y los estados del norte de África* (note 8), 118, 123; Maria Teresa Ferrer i Mallol. "Els viatges piadosos de cristians, jueus i musulmans per la Mediterrània medieval." In *Un mar de lleis, de Jaume I a Lepant, catàleg de l'exposició*, ed. María Teresa Ferrer and Josep Giralt (Barcelona: Institut Europeu de la Mediterrània, 2008), 101–118, particularly 101–109.

as long a period of time as in the Iberian realms. This also had effects on pilgrimage in this area.

The *mudéjares* or *sarraïns* (as they are termed in Catalan documents) have been the object of much research, past as well as present, and lately, archaeological findings are teaching us even more about the everyday life of these politically and socially underprivileged minorities.[58] Usually, studies as these centre on the legal and social aspects of Mudéjar life, while recent years have shown a marked interest in interfaith contacts.[59] The following deliberations aim at contributing to this lively field of research by paying special attention to aspects of religious mobility.

The subjected *mudéjares* were not free to move wherever they wanted. Muslims who intended to leave the country were obliged to ask local authorities for permission to do so. Most of these requests referred to Muslim men, women or even entire families who wanted to emigrate to the Dār al-Islām, usually either to the Kingdom of Granada or to Northern Africa.[60] Scholarship on the deterioration of Muslim life in the Iberian realms has focused on this phenomenon of

58 Overviews of the abundant bibliography and syntheses: David Nirenberg. "The Current State of Mudejar Studies." *Journal of Medieval History* 24 (1998): 381–389; María Blanca Basáñez Villaluenga. *Las morerías aragonesas durante el reinado de Jaime II: catálogo de la documentación de la Cancillería Real* (Teruel: Centro de Estudios Mudéjares, Instituto de Estudios Turolenses, 1999); José Hinojosa Montalvo. *Los mudéjares: la voz del Islam en la España cristiana* (Teruel: Centro de Estudios Mudéjares, Instituto de Estudios Turolenses, 2002), 2 vols.; Manuel Ruzafa, ed. *Los mudéjares valencianos y peninsulares* (Valencia: Universitat de València, 2003); Ana Echevarría Arsuaga. *Biografías mudéjares o La experiencia de ser minoría: biografías islámicas en la España cristiana* (Madrid: Consejo Superior de Investigaciones Científicas, 2008); José Hinojosa Montalvo. "Mudejaren im Königreich Aragón: Integration und Segregation." In *Integration – Segregation – Vertreibung: Religiöse Minderheiten und Randgruppen auf der Iberischen Halbinsel (7.–17. Jh.)*, ed. Klaus Herbers and Nikolas Jaspert (Münster: LIT-Verlag, 2011), 293–336 and the volumes of the – so far – twelve "Simposio Internacional de Mudejarismo."

59 Besides the studies cited in footnote 58, see David Nirenberg. *Communities of Violence. Persecution of Minorities in the Middle Ages* (Princeton: Princeton University Press, 1996); Brian A. Catlos. *The Victors and the Vanquished: Christians and Muslims of Catalonia and Aragon, 1050–1300* (Cambridge: Cambridge University Press, 2004).

60 David Romano. "Musulmanes residentes y emigrantess en la Barcelona de los siglos xiv–xv." *Al-Andalus* 40 (1976): 49–86; José Enrique López de Coca Castañer. "Sobre la emigración mudéjar al reino de Granada." *Revista d'Històrica Medieval* 12 (2001/2002): 241–258; Maria Teresa Ferrer i Mallol. "Les phénomènes migratoires entre les musulmans soumins à la couronne catalo-aragonaise pendant le Moyen Âge." In *Migrations et diasporas méditerranéennes (Xe–XVIe siècles)*, ed. Michel Balard and Alain Ducellier (Paris: Publications de la Sorbonne, 2002), 259–284; Vaca Lorenzo and Jean-Pierre Molénat, ed. *Minorías y migraciones en la historia: XV Jornadas de Estudios Históricos* (Salamanca: Ediciones Universidad de Salamanca, 2004); Isabel O'Connor. "Mudejars Helping Other Mudejars in the Kingdom of Valencia." *Al-Masaq* 17 (2005): 99–108; Alan Verskin. *Islamic Law and the Crisis of the Reconquista: The Debate on the Status of Muslim Communities in Christendom* (Leiden: Brill, 2015).

flight and emigration (often enough to Egypt). Specifically addressing pilgrimage (*ḥajj*) to Mecca by Iberian Muslims might help to complement the picture while necessarily directing the analytical focus towards Mamluk territories.

Even though subjected *mudéjares* developed regional centres of pilgrimage, the *ḥajj* certainly remained a paramount obligation for Iberian Muslims.[61] Generally, permission to conduct the *ḥajj* was issued on a regional or even local level by royal officers, which means that only few references to safe conducts and travel authorizations have come down to us. Consequently there is no way of acquiring trustworthy, let alone statistically relevant quantitative information.[62] In some cases, however, royal permits survive. Several decades ago, David Romano identified several such instances from the middle of the 14th century,[63] and María Teresa Ferrer i Mallol, who has done outstanding work on editing relevant source material on the *sarraïns* in the Crown of Aragon, collected many more documents relating to Muslim pilgrimages, mostly from the Royal Treasury (*llibres de Batllia*) and from the series *Gratiarum* of the Chancery.[64] These records contain references to almost 600 pilgrims, sometimes with very concrete personal information about the travellers in question. For example, on 1 June 1375 Peter IV, the Ceremonious, of Aragon allowed seven Muslims from Lleida – Acer Abenferre and his wife Azize, Acer's daughter Fatima and her husband Azmet Abenferre, Juce Alcodi and his wife Aziz as well as Moferriç Alguaxqui – to "travel over the sea in order to visit the house of Mecca" (*apud partes ultramarinas pro visitando domum de Mecha*). The pilgrims were allowed to bear arms

61 Olivia Remie Constable. "Regulating Religious Noise: The Council of Vienne, the Mosque Call and Muslim Pilgrimage in the Late Medieval Mediterranean World." *Medieval Encounters* 16 (2010): 64–95, particularly 81–90; Maria Teresa Ferrer i Mallol. *Els sarraïns de la corona catalano-aragonesa en el segle XIV: segregació i discriminació* (Barcelona: Consell Superior d'Investigacions Científiques, 1987), 95–99, 144–146; Josef W. Meri. "The Etiquette of Devotion in the Islamic Cult of Saints." In *The Cult of Saints in Late Antiquity and the Middle Ages: Essays on the Contribution of Peter Brown*, ed. James Howard-Johnston and Paul Antony Hayward (Oxford: Oxford University Press, 1999), 263–286; idem. *The Cult of Saints among Muslims and Jews in Medieval Syria* (Oxford: Oxford University Press, 2002); Michael Alan Ryan. "Power and Pilgrimage: The Restriction of Mudéjares' Pilgrimage in the Kingdom of Valencia." *Essays in Medieval Studies* 25 (2008): 115–128; Xavier Casassas Canals. "La Rihla de Omar Patún: el viaje de peregrinación a la Meca de un musulmán de Ávila a finales del siglo XV (1491–1495)." *Espacio, Tiempo y Forma* 3-28 (2015): 221–254.

62 On the composition of the archival holdings see María Teresa Ferrer i Mallol. "Documentación sobre mudéjares del Archivo de la Corona de Aragón." In *Fuentes documentales para el estudio de los mudéjares*, ed. María Teresa Ferrer i Mallol, Isabel Romero Camacho et al. (Teruel: Centro de Estudios Mudéjares, Instituto de Estudios Turolenses, 2005), 9–53.

63 Romano. "Musulmanes residentes y emigrantes en la Barcelona" (note 60), 63, 74: Seven free mudejars from Saragossa who left for Mecca in 1358.

64 Ferrer i Mallol, *Els sarraïns de la corona catalano-aragonesa en el segle XIV* (note 61), 144–146; idem. "Els viatges piadosos de cristians, jueus i musulmans" (note 57), particularly 112–117. See also Coulon, *Barcelone et le grand commerce d'Orient* (note 4), 90–97.

and carry certain goods (*cum armis et bonis mobilibus*).[65] A document from 1431 reveals that pilgrims appear to have left their real estate as a surety on departure in order to pledge their return. Moreover, this text demonstrates that pilgrimage could well be connected with commerce, because Alí Benxarnit, a Valencian Muslim, was allowed to take bales of cloth and silk worth 1500 Valencian pounds to Bejaia in present-day Algeria on his way to Mecca, thus combining a commercial trip with a religious one.[66]

Certain, albeit few, permits appear to reflect processes of religious transfer in that some royal permits applied standard Christian imagery or wording – for example when Muslims were allowed to travel "due to the devotion they feel towards the Holy Land and Jerusalem" (*ob devotionem quam habent ad Terram Sanctam et Iherusalem*) as stated in a document from 1362.[67] Muslim pilgrimage was set into a Christian context even more glaringly in a document from 1361, when Peter the Ceremonious extended a safe conduct in favour of a group of twelve Muslims so they might conduct a "pilgrimage to the Holy Sepulchre" as the document states quite clearly: *Per faciendo peregrinagium apud Sanctum Sepulcrum.*[68] Of course, we cannot say for certain if these *sarraïns* really visited Christ's tomb in Mamluk Jerusalem.[69] Possibly they wanted to pray at the Dome of the Rock, or only used Jerusalem as a cover-up on their way to Mecca. In any way it is telling that the scribes noted the Sepulchre as the Pilgrims' destination, possibly echoing the words the Muslims used when pleading permission to leave. Either the scribes or the travellers themselves must have presented Muslim voyages to the East as pilgrimages to the Holy Sepulchre. Thus, Jerusalem figured as a goal of pilgrimage for Aragonese Christians and Muslims alike – at least it was depicted as such. Mudéjar pilgrims to the Mamluk Sultanate thus seem to have been able to count on the support of their Christian lord, if only by paying him money for permits to travel abroad. Mamluk sultans in contrast are not known to have put themselves out on behalf of foreign Muslim pilgrims when dealing with the Aragonese monarchs. However, this does not mean that the

65 Ferrer i Mallol, *Els sarraïns de la corona catalano-aragonesa en el segle XIV* (note 61), 319–320 (doc. 104); see also Josefa Mutgé Vives. *L'aljama sarraïna de Lleida a l'Edat Mitjana: aproximació a la seva història* (Barcelona: Consell Superior d'Investigacions Científiques, Institut Milà i Fontanals, 1992), 98.

66 José Hinojosa Montalvo. *Los mudéjares: la voz del Islam en la España Cristiana* (Teruel: Centro de Estudios Mudéjares), 2: 320–321 (doc. 253).

67 Archivo de la Corona de Aragón, Cancillería, Reg. 1183, fol. 127v; Ferrer i Mallol, *Els sarraïns de la corona catalano-aragonesa en el segle XIV* (note 61), 145.

68 Archivo de la Corona de Aragón, Cancillería, Reg. 950, fol. 220r-v; Ferrer i Mallol, *Els sarraïns de la corona catalano-aragonesa en el segle XIV* (note 61), 145.

69 Yehoshua Frenkel. "Muslim Pilgrimage to Jerusalem in the Mamluk Period." *Studies in Jewish Civilization* 7 (1996): 63–87; for early Islam see Amikam Elad. *Medieval Jerusalem and Islamic Worship: Holy Places, Ceremonies, Pilgrimage* (Leiden and Cologne: Brill, 1995).

Mamluks did not back coreligionists at certain periods in time, as the final part of this article will try to underscore.

Piety as an Element of Aragonese-Mamluke Diplomacy: Minority Rights

Since the extensive peace treaty of 1290 between King Alfonso III of Aragon and Sultan Qalāwūn, diplomatic relations between both realms had been maintained on a constant basis. During the reign of James II of Aragon, embassies were sent from Catalonia to Cairo in 1293, 1303, 1305, 1314 and 1319.[70] The Crown Archive in Barcelona still contains Arabic letters sent from Egypt dating to 1300, 1304, 1306, and 1315 relating to bilateral diplomatic negotiations. As stated above, most of these revolved around topics such as commercial rights, the liberation of captives and the freedom of Christian pilgrims. The Kings of Aragon repeatedly put themselves out in favour of short term visitors (pilgrims) and even strove to stabilise the situation of Christians permanently living under Muslim rule.[71] In 1303 they championed the Copts and other oriental Christians, successfully pleading for the reopening of their churches.[72] Later initiatives in 1305 and 1314/1315 equally attempted to achieve free access to Jerusalem for Aragonese pilgrims, combined with efforts to improve the situation of all Christians in the Levant.[73]

Eight years later, in 1322/23, King James for the first time sought to gain the sultan's permission to establish a house of religious brethren in Jerusalem in

70 Atiya, *Egypt and Aragon* (note 6); Masiá de Ros, *La corona de Aragón y los estados del norte de África* (note 8); Giunta, *Aragonesi e Catalani nel Mediterraneo* (note 47), 114–115.

71 On the situation of the Christian minority in Egypt during these years see Nasser al-Hajji, *The Internal Affairs* (note 38), 112–147.

72 Golubovich, *Biblioteca bio-bibliografica della Terra Santa e dell'Oriente Francescano* 3 (note 5), 73–77; Atiya, *Egypt and Aragon* (note 6), 20–24. Al-Maqrīzī relates that the churches were reopened thanks to diplomatic initiatives by the "King of Barcelona": Masiá de Ros, *La corona de Aragón y los estados del norte de África* (note 8), 102; al-Hajji, *The Internal Affairs in Egypt* (note 38), 124–127. On the situation of the Copts also see Johannes Pahlitzsch. "Mediators between East and West: Christians under Mamluk Rule." *Mamlūk Studies Review* 9/2 (2005): 32–47; Tamer El-Leithy. "Sufis, Copts and the Politics of Piety: Moral Regulation in Fourteenth-Century Upper Egypt." In *Le développement du soufisme en Égypte à l'époque mamelouke*, ed. Richard J. A. McGregor and Adam Abdelhamid Sabra (Cairo: Institut Français d'Archéologie Orientale, 2006), 75–119; hopefully soon in print: Tamer El-Leithy. *Coptic Culture and Conversion in Medieval Cairo: 1293–1524 A.D* (PhD Diss., Princeton University, 2005).

73 Golubovich, *Biblioteca bio-bibliografica della Terra Santa e dell'Oriente Francescano* 3 (note 5), 77–85, 185–187; Atiya, *Egypt and Aragon* (note 6), 27–41; Masiá de Ros, *La corona de Aragón y los estados del norte de África* (note 8), 304–307, doc. 37.

order to permanently provide spiritual care to the Christian pilgrims who visited the town and the holy sites.[74] The backdrop for this initiative might have been anti-Christian violence that had broken out in Cairo in May 1321.[75] In the subsequent embassy, James invested a good deal of diplomatic energy on behalf of establishing a mendicant convent at the Holy Sepulchre. In 1322/23 he approached the sultan in favour of the Dominicans,[76] only to champion the Franciscans four years later.[77] The Minorites in fact finally achieved permission to maintain a house in Jerusalem – the nucleus of their guard of the holy places later to be known as the "Custodia di Terra Sancta" that exists to this very day.[78] The Aragonese King's commitment to the holy places of Christianity and his initiatives to secure their administrative and spiritual maintenance by Latin clerics were not driven by religious zeal alone. Here, too, the complex power relations between Christian realms in the Mediterranean need to be taken into account. For the backdrop to the Aragonese diplomatic enterprise was without a doubt the rivalry between the house of Barcelona and the Capetians that had reached new heights since the Sicilian Vesper of 1282. It is no coincidence that the nominal King of Sicily and member of a side-line of the Capetian dynasty, Robert of

74 Atiya, *Egypt and Aragon* (note 6), 45, 47–52; Alarcón Santón und García de Linares, *Los documentos árabes diplomáticos del Archivo* (note 9), 365–367 (doc. 150).

75 Heyd, *Histoire du commerce du Levant au moyen âge* (note 9), 2: 385; Masiá de Ros, *La corona de Aragón y los estados del norte de África* (note 8), 119; al-Hajji, *The Internal Affairs in Egypt* (note 38), 131–139. On attacks and reprisals against Christian merchants in Egypt in general and Cairo in particular see: Denis Gril. "Une émeute anti-chrétienne à Quṣ au début du VIIIe/XIVe siècle." *Annales islamologiques* 16 (1980): 241–274; Mohamed Tahar Mansouri. "Les communautés marchandes occidentales dans l'espace mamlouk (XIIIe–XVe siècle)." In *Coloniser au moyen âge*, ed. Michel Balard (Paris: Colin, 1995), 89–114, especially, 92–95; Pierre Moukarzel. "Les marchands européens dans l'espace urbain mamelouk: un groupe minoritaire privilégié?" In *Minorités et régulations sociales en Méditerranée médiévale*, ed. Stéphane Boissellier, François Clément and John Tolan (Rennes: Presses Universitaires de Rennes, 2010), 181–206.

76 Golubovich, *Biblioteca bio-bibliografica della Terra Santa e dell'Oriente Francescano* 3 (note 5), 232–237; Atiya, *Egypt and Aragon* (note 6), 44–52.

77 Atiya, *Egypt and Aragon* (note 6), 53–54.

78 Samuel Eijan. *El Real Patronato de los Santos Lugares en la historia de la Tierra Santa* (Madrid, 1945–1946), 2 vols.; Kaspar Elm. "La Custodia di Terra Santa. Franziskanisches Ordensleben in der Tradition der lateinischen Kirche Palästinas." In *I Francescani nel Trecento: Assisi 16–17–18 ottobre* 1986 (Assisi: Univ. degli Studi di Peruga, Centro di Studi Francescani, 1988), 127–166; Sabino De Sandoli. *The Peaceful Liberation of the Holy Places in the XIV Century: the third return of the Frankish or Latin clergy to the custody and service of the holy places through official negotiations in 1333* (Cairo: Franciscan Center of Christian Oriental Studies, 1990); Eugenio Alliata. "Evoluzione delle memorie storiche in Terra Santa tra la fine del Regno Crociato e l'insediamento dei Francescani a Gerusalemme (1292–1332)." In *Il cammino di Gerusalemme: atti del 2. Convengo internazionale di studio (Bari-Brindisi-Trani, 18–22 maggio 1999)*, ed. María S. Calò Mariani (Bari: Adda, 2002), 211–222; Félix del Buey and Cristóforo Alvi. "Orígenes de la custodia de Tierra Santa: ayuda de los Reinos de Aragón, Nápoles y Castilla." *Archivo Ibero-Americano* 65 (2005): 7–96.

Anjou, simultaneously launched a competing initiative in order to establish the Franciscans at the Holy Sepulchre. Indeed, the creation of the "Custodia di Terra Sancta" was finally brought about by the Angevin ruler rather than by James II of Aragon. Religious diversity in Mamluk Egypt thus provided Christian rulers – here the Aragonese and the Angevin monarchs – with a base for fashioning their own identity as champions of subdued coreligionist minorities in distant lands.[79] *En passant*, the kings' religious zeal could be put to use in order to acquire relics which, too, heightened the monarchs' prestige at home. During the course of the 14th century, several Aragonese rulers negotiated the surrender of relics – of the True Cross, St Barbara, St Simon and Christ's chalice – with Cairo.[80]

These activities are not unknown to historians of medieval Latin Europe. But what needs to be stressed is that similar forms of "political piety" can also be observed on the part of the Mamluk sultans. A careful reading of their correspondence kept in the Barcelonese archives shows to which extent they, too, advocated the interests of subdued coreligionists, in this case those of Muslims in Aragon. In September 1314, King James promised that *mudéjares* in his realm (or *sarraïns*, as he put it) would be able to conduct their prayers in their mosques as they were accustomed to and without any impediment.[81] Nine years later, this right was no longer a matter of course. In February 1323, Sultan al-Nāṣir Muḥammad officially requested that King James of Aragon respect the customs of the Muslims living in his realm, just as the Sultan himself claimed to respect those of the Christians in the Mamluk Empire. He explicitly singled out the difficulties the *mudéjares* were encountering in reciting the *adhān:*

> We inform him, however, that it has come to our knowledge that a community of Muslims who have remained in his territories after the disturbance of their conditions

79 See King Peter the Ceremonious' donation to restore the Coenaculum in Jerusalem in 1366: Eijan, *El Real Patronato de los Santos Lugares* (note 78), 62. On the political implications of pilgrimage see – with references to prior scholarship: Sebastian Kolditz. "Der Herrscher als Pilger im westlichen und östlichen Mittelalter. Eine Skizze." In *Transkulturelle Komparatistik. Beiträge zu einer Globalgeschichte der Vormoderne*, ed. Wolfram Drews and Jenny Rahel Oesterle, Comparativ 18 (Leipzig, 2008), 73–94.

80 Heinrich Finke. *Acta Aragonensia: Quellen zur deutschen, italienischen, französischen, spanischen, zur Kirchen- und Kulturgeschichte aus der diplomatischen Korrespondenz Jaymes II; 1291–1327* (Leipzig: Rothschild, 1908), 2: 756; Atiya, *Egypt and Aragon* (note 6), 45; Masiá de Ros, *La corona de Aragón y los estados del norte de África* (note 8), 124, 322–325 (doc. 51). Cf. Johannes Vincke. "Die Gesandtschaften der aragonesischen Könige um die Reliquien der heiligen Barbara (1322–1337)." *Historisches Jahrbuch* 60 (1940): 115–124; Amada López de Meneses. "Pedro el Ceremonioso y las reliquias de Santa Bárbara." *Estudios de Edad Media de la Corona de Aragón* 7 (1962): 299–357; Vicent Baydal Sala. "Santa Tecla, San Jorge y Santa Bárbara: los monarcas de la Corona de Aragón a la búsqueda de reliquias en Oriente (siglos XIV–XV)." *Anaquel de estudios árabes* 21 (2010): 153–162.

81 Masiá de Ros, *La corona de Aragón y los estados del norte de África* (note 8), 304–307, doc. 37 (here 306).

have been accustomed of old to honour, protection and non-aggression in the mosques where they abide. Now these customs have often changed for the worse, and they are no longer able to call for and hold prayers in their mosques. It is desired of his [i. e. King James'] true affection that he should issue a comprehensive order regarding all Muslims residents in his country so that they might be allowed to enjoy the practice of all their customs and their tenets undiminished, that no aggressor might attack them in their mosques, that they might proclaim their prayers, and that they might be secured from harm and remain under protection. He [i. e. King James] is aware that God the High has entrusted us with the management of the affairs of all the people of Islam in whatever place they may be. So wherever any of the Muslims is to be found, he has held himself to be dependent on us and it is therefore our duty to provide him with protection. Let him [i. e. King James] therefore deal with them in a way that will secure for him our fullest affection and best friendship. His zeal, however, saves us further emphasis in this respect; and may the Almighty repay his friendliness and ensure the success of his endeavour, by the grace of God![82]

Clearly then, the Mamluk Sultan used his connections to Aragon to claim a special link to the subjected Muslims of the Crown of Aragon and position himself as champion of Islam, just as the Aragonese King did concerning the holy sites in Jerusalem. Aziz Atiya phrased it many years ago: "Hegemony over the rest of the Muhammedan world is here re-claimed for Egypt,"[83] because the Mamluk rulers now were not only the Lords of Mecca and Medina and defenders of Islam against the Mongols, but also protectors of subdued Muslims in Christian lands. This was only possible due to the intensive commercial, trans-Mediterranean ties between Aragon and Egypt that facilitated information about the living conditions and environments of coreligionists abroad and thus intensified translocal interaction on different levels, including that of political and religious ideas.

Sultan al-Nāṣir Muḥammad's initiative of 1323 raises the question why none of his predecessors used this opportunity to strengthen their position within the Dār al-Islām. Perhaps domestic policy, that is inner-Islamic developments, might have been influential in this respect,[84] but arguably, so were the dynamics of diplomacy between the Mamluk Sultanate and its Christian neighbours.

In the Medieval Crown of Aragon, surrender treaties and other pacts between the rulers and subdued Muslims expressly allowed the latter to practice their religion, as long as they did not belittle the Christian faith.[85] Praying was per-

---

82 Alarcón Santón und García de Linares, *Los documentos árabes diplomáticos del Archivo* (note 9), 367 (doc. 150); Atiya, *Egypt and Aragon* (note 6), 51; Ministerio de Cultura, *El perfume de la amistad* (note 8), 189–190.

83 Atiya, *Egypt and Aragon* (note 6), 52.

84 Tellingly, in these very years the rivalling dynasty of the Nasrids also claimed patronage over Aragonese Muslims – Alarcón Santón und García de Linares, *Los documentos árabes diplomáticos del Archivo* (note 9), 35 (doc. 15), 58 (doc. 27); cf. López de Coca Castañer, *Sobre la emigración mudéjar* (note 60), 243–246.

85 See the syntheses: Ferrer i Mallol, *Els sarraïns de la corona catalano-aragonesa en el segle XIV*

mitted, even though particularly loud calls to prayer – for example by sounding horns – was prohibited in 1303.[86] At the Church Council of Vienne celebrated in 1311, however, the assembled Christian prelates issued a canon forbidding Muslims living under Christian rule to recite the *adhān*, the call to prayer.[87] Al-Nāṣir Muḥammad's reference to freedom of Muslim prayer in 1314 might already have been a reaction to these rulings. Some years after the Council of Vienne, this prohibition was widely proclaimed in the Crown of Aragon by order of King James II, who in 1318 officially announced that any perpetrator would be condemned to death.[88] Apparently, the situation of subjected Muslims indeed experienced a marked deterioration during these years.

Yet, this prohibition was not heeded by all Muslims. In the summer of 1322, in the region of Xàtiva,[89] a man by the name of *Abdala Abenxando* (ʿAbd Allāh Ibn Khandū/ō?) publicly and loudly proclaimed the Prophet's name despite the royal prohibition: on 20 July 1322, king James II wrote to Bernat Sanou, a royal officer of the Kingdom of Valencia. He acknowledged receipt of a letter in which Bernat had reported the arrest of a certain Muslim named *Abdala Abenxando*, who was now imprisoned in the town of Xàtiva. This Muslim had "loudly proclaimed in the name of Mohammad in spite of the King's prohibition and contrary to his orders" (*contra inhibicionem et ordinationem nostrum alta voce nomine Mafometi clamavit*), an offence he had confessed to having committed. The king ordered that if indeed *Abdala Abenxando* admitted to having loudly proclaimed the name of Mohammed, he was to be sentenced to death according to the aforementioned rulings and as a warning to other Muslims.[90]

This case has gone practically unnoticed in modern research. If mentioned at all, it is simply read as a sign of Christian oppression of Muslims in the Crown of Aragon. But what if we suppose that *Abdala Abenxando* was acting in full knowledge of the consequences? The royal ruling left no doubt: whoever broke it was to die. *Abdala Abenxando* might in fact have been seeking religious martyrdom by knowingly and voluntarily provoking his death by the hands of

(note 61), 85–101; Basáñez Villaluenga, *Las morerías aragonesas* (note 58); Hinojosa Montalvo, *Los mudéjares: la voz del Islam en la España Cristiana* (note 58), 1: 115–126.

86 Constable. "Regulating Religious Noise" (note 61), 73.

87 Giuseppe Alberigo et al., ed. *Conciliorum oecumenicorum generaliumque decreta II/1* (Turnhout: Brepols, 2013), 438–439 (do. 25). Constable. "Regulating Religious Noise" (note 61), particularly 74–76.

88 Ferrer i Mallol, *Els sarraïns de la corona catalano-aragonesa en el segle XIV* (note 61), 88, 233 (doc. 24).

89 On the mudéjars of Xàtiva see Isabel A. O'Connor. *A Forgotten Community: The Mudejar Aljama of Xàtiva, 1240–1327* (Leiden: Brill, 2003).

90 Ferrer i Mallol, *Els sarraïns de la corona catalano-aragonesa en el segle XIV* (note 61), 236 (doc. 27). The issue continued to be dealt with at court and at church Councils: Constable. "Regulating Religious Noise" (note 61), 77–81; Ferrer i Mallol, *Els sarraïns de la corona catalano-aragonesa en el segle XIV* (note 61), 92–95.

Christians. In a recent scholarly overview on Muslim martyrdom, the author states that on the Iberian Peninsula there was "no galvanising action to rally the believers to stand firm. Probably the reason for this lies in the close identification of martyrdom with fighting in Islam that left few practical examples as to how martyrdom in such circumstances could be best utilised or whether it should even be carried out."[91] But perhaps the events surrounding *Abdala Abenxando* of Xàtiva were precisely such a galvanising action. Seen from this perspective, his behaviour would have been a deliberate attempt to rally coreligionists, knowing full well that by publically calling the prophet's name he was in fact calling death upon himself. Whatever *Abdala Abenxando*'s motives, his case seems to have had stark effects on Aragonese-Mamluk relations, because immediately after the crisis of 1322 triggered by the Valencian *mudéjar*'s infringement of royal rulings, communication between both powers was suddenly marked by the novel diplomatic issue of the *adhān.*We are probably not wrong in assuming that the case of *Abdala Abenxando* of Xàtiva – and possible similar cases that have not come down to us – lay at the heart of this diplomatic initiative discussed on both sides of the Mediterranean.

Conclusion

This paper attempted to substantiate three points: first, that Mamluk-Aragonese relations were in no ways bipolar, instead forming part of complex and dynamic trans-regional networks. Second, that competition between powers of one and the same religious affiliation was a basic motive behind the engagement for religious minorities in foreign lands on the part of Christian and Muslim rulers alike. And finally, that domestic issues related to the situation of Christian minorities in Egypt and Muslim minorities in the Crown of Aragon had profound effects on foreign affairs. The unusually concrete information provided by the documents kept in Catalonian archives allows us to uncover these correlations with much greater detail than anywhere else in Latin Europe. The discussed episodes of the Muslim pilgrims to Jerusalem and the religious zealot *Abdala Abenxando* disclose an interrelated international as well as domestic dimension. Domestic affairs and intra-religious rivalry therefore have to be employed as helpful tools capable of shedding new light on the traditional research field of Mamluk-Christian relations.

91 David Cook. *Martyrdom in Islam* (Cambridge: Cambridge University Press, 2007), 86.

Bibliography

Le relazioni internazionali nell'alto medioevo. (Spoleto: Fondazione Centro Italiano di Studio sull'Alto Medioevo, 2011).

Abdellatif, Rania et al., ed. *Acteurs des transferts culturels en Méditerranée médiévale* (Munich: Oldenbourg, 2012).

Aigle, Denise, and Pascal Buresi, ed. *Les relations diplomatiques entre le monde musulman et l'Occident latin: (XIIe–XVIe siècle)* (Rome: Istituto per l'Oriente C. A. Nallino, 2008).

Aivars Catlos, Brian. "Mahomet Abenadalill: A Muslim Mercenary in the Service of the Kings of Aragon (1290–1291)." In *Jews, Muslims, and Christians in and around the Crown of Aragon: Essays in Honour of Professor Elena Lourie*, ed. Harvey J. Hames (Leiden: Brill, 2004), 257–302.

Alarcón Santón, Maximiliano A., and Ramón García de Linares. *Los documentos árabes diplomáticos del Archivo de la Corona de Aragón: editados y traducidos* (Madrid: Estanislao Maestre, 1940).

Albarrán Iruela, Javier. "De la conversión y expulsión al mercenariado: los cristianos en las fuentes almohades." In *La Península Ibérica en tiempos de Las Navas de Tolosa*, ed. Carlos Estepa and María Antonia Carmona Ruiz (Madrid: Sociedad Española de Estudios Medievales, 2014), 79–91.

Algazi, Gadi, Valentin Groebner and Bernhard Jussen, ed. *Negotiating the Gift: Pre-modern Figurations of Exchange* (Göttingen: Vandenhoeck & Ruprecht, 2003).

al-Hajji, Hayat Nasser. *The Internal Affairs in Egypt during the Third Reign of Sultan al-Nāṣir Muḥammad B. Qalawun 709–741/1309–1341* (Kuwait: Dar al-Qalam, 1995).

Alliata, Eugenio. "Evoluzione delle memorie storiche in Terra Santa tra la fine del Regno Crociato e l'insediamento dei Francescani a Gerusalemme (1292–1332)." In *Il cammino di Gerusalemme: atti del 2. Convengo internazionale di studio (Bari-Brindisi-Trani, 18–22 maggio 1999)*, ed. María S. Calò Mariani (Bari: Adda, 2002), 211–222.

Amari, Michele. *Condizioni degli stati cristiani dell'occidente secondo una relazione di Domenichino Doria da Genova: testo arabo con versione italiana* (Rome: Salviucci, 1883).

Amari, Michele. *De' titoli che usava la cancelleria de' Sultani di Egitto nel 14 secolo scrivendo a' reggitori di alcuni stati italiani* (Rome: Salviucci, 1886).

Atiya, Aziz Suryal. *Egypt and Aragon: Embassies and Diplomatic Correspondence between 1300 and 1330 A.D.* (Leipzig: Brockhaus, 1938).

Atiya, Aziz Suryal. *The Crusade in the Later Middle Ages* (London: Methuen, 1938).

Baethgen, Friedrich, ed. *Die Chronik Johanns von Winterthur* (Berlin: Berolini, 1924).

Barton, Simon. "Traitors to the Faith? Christian Mercenaries in al-Andalus and the Maghreb, c. 1100–1300." In *Medieval Spain. Culture, Conflict and Coexistence. Studies in Honour of Angus MacKay*, ed. Roger Collins and Anthony Goodman (Basingstoke: Palgrave Macmillan, 2002), 23–45.

Basáñez Villaluenga, María Blanca. *Las morerías aragonesas durante el reinado de Jaime II: catálogo de la documentación de la Cancillería Real* (Teruel: Centro de Estudios Mudéjares, Instituto de Estudios Turolenses, 1999).

Bauden, Frédéric. "Du destin des archives en Islam. Analyse des données et éléments de réponse." In *La correspondance entre souverains, princes et cités-états: approches croisées entre l'Orient musulman, l'Occident latin et Byzance (XIIIe-début XVIe siècle)*, ed. Denise Aigle and Stephane Péquignot (Turnhout: Brepols, 2013), 27–49.

Bauden, Frédéric. "Mamluk Era Documentary Studies: The State of the Art." *Mamlūk Studies Review* 9 (2005): 15–60.

Baydal Sala, Vincent. "Santa Tecla, San Jorge y Santa Bárbara: los monarcas de la Corona de Aragón a la búsqueda de reliquias en Oriente (siglos XIV–XV)." *Anaquel de estudios árabes* 21 (2010): 153–162.

Berg, Dieter, Martin Kintzinger and Pierre Monnet, ed. *Auswärtige Politik und internationale Beziehungen im Mittelalter: 13. bis 16. Jahrhundert* (Bochum: Winckler, 2002).

Bisson, Thomas Noel. *The Medieval Crown of Aragon: A Short History* (Oxford: Clarendon, 1986).

Borgolte, Michael. "Experten der Fremde. Gesandte in interkulturellen Beziehungen des frühen und hohen Mittelalters." In *Le relazioni internazionali nell'alto medioevo* (Spoleto: Fondazione Centro Italiano di Studio sull'Alto Medioevo, 2011), 945–992.

Bresc, Henri, and Yusuf Rāġib. *Le sultan mérinide Abū l-Ḥasan ʿAli et Jacques III de Majorque: du traité de paix au pacte secret* (Cairo: Institut Français d'Archéologie Orientale 2011).

Broadbridge, Anne F. "Diplomatic Conventions in the Mamluk Sultanate." *Annales Islamologiques* 41 (2007): 97–118.

Budge, Ernest A. Wallis, ed. and trans. *The Chronography of Gregory Abû'l Faraj, the Son of Aaron, the Hebrew Physician Commonly Known as Bar Hebraeus, Being the First Part of his Political History of the World* (London: Oxford University Press, 1932).

Buey, Félix del, and Cristóforo Alvi, "Orígenes de la custodia de Tierra Santa: ayuda de los Reinos de Aragón, Nápoles y Castilla." *Archivo Ibero-Americano* 65 (2005): 7–96.

Buresi, Pascal. "Traduttore, traditore. À propos d'une correspondance arabe-latine entre l'Empire almohade et la cité de Pise (début XIIIe siècle)." In *Les relations diplomatiques entre le monde musulman et l'Occident latin: (XIIe–XVIe siècle)*, ed. Denise Aigle and Pascal Buresi (Roma: Istituto per l'Oriente C. A. Nallino, 2008), 297–309.

Burns, Robert Ignatius. "Renegades, Adventurers, and Sharp Businessmen: The Thirteenth Century Spaniard in the Cause of Islam." *The Catholic Historical Review* 58 (1972): 341–366.

Cabezuelo Pliego, José Vicente. "Cristiano de Alá, renegado de Cristo. El caso de Abdalla, fill d'en Domingo Vallés, un valenciano al servicio del islam." *Sharq al-Andalus* 13 (1996): 27–46.

Capmany y de Montpaláu, Antonio de. *Antiguos tratados de paces y alianzas entre algunos reyes de Aragón y diferentes príncipes infieles de Asia y Africa, desde el siglo XIII hasta el XV* (Valencia: Anúbar Ed., 1974 - first printed 1786).

Capmany y de Montpalau, Antoni. *Memorias históricas sobre la marina, comercio y artes de la antigua ciudad de Barcelona* (Madrid, 1779–1792), 3 vols.

Casassas Canals, Xavier. "La Rihla de Omar Patún: el viaje de peregrinación a la Meca de un musulmán de Ávila a finales del siglo XV (1491–1495)." *Espacio, Tiempo y Forma* 3–28 (2015): 221–254.

Catlos, Brian A. *The Victors and the Vanquished: Christians and Muslims of Catalonia and Aragon, 1050–1300* (Cambridge: Cambridge University Press, 2004).

Chastagnaret, Gérard, ed. *Les sociétés méditerranéennes face au risque: disciplines, temps, espaces* (Cairo: Institut Français d'Archéologie Orientale, 2008).
Christ, Georg. "Transkulturelle Pirateriebekämpfung? Venezianisch-Mamlukische Kooperation und Gefangenenbefreiung im östlichen Mittelmeerraum im Spätmittelalter." In *Seeraub im Mittelmeerraum. Piraterie, Korsarentum und maritime Gewalt von der Antike bis zur Neuzeit*, ed. Nikolas Jaspert and Sebastian Kolditz (Munich-Paderborn: Fink-Schöningh, 2013), 363–375.
Christ, Georg. *Trading Cconflicts: Venetian Merchants and Mamluk Officials in Late Medieval Alexandria* (Leiden: Brill, 2012).
Claverie, Pierre-Vincent. "La dévotion envers les Lieux saints dans la Catalogne médiévale." In *Chemins d'outre-mer. Études d'histoire sur la Méditerranée médiévale offertes à Michel Balard*, ed. Damien Coulon, Catherine Otten-Froux et al. (Paris: Publications de la Sorbonne, 2004), 127–137.
Clément, François. "Reverter et son fils, deux officiers catalans au service des sultans de Marrakech." *Medieval Encounters* 9 (2003): 79–107.
Conermann, Stephan, ed. *Everything is on the Move: The Mamluk Empire as a Node in (Trans-)Regional Networks* (Göttingen: Bonn University Press, 2014).
Conermann, Stephan. "Networks and Nodes in Mamluk Times: Some Introductory Remarks." In: *Everything is on the Move: The Mamluk Empire as a Node in (Trans-) Regional Networks*, ed. Stephan Conermann (Göttingen: Bonn University Press, 2014), 9–24.
Conermann, Stephan. "Quo vadis, Mamlukology? (A German Perspective)." In *Ubi sumus? Quo vademus? Mamluk Studies - State of the Art*, ed. Stephan Conermann (Göttingen: Bonn University Press, 2013), 7–22.
Constable, Giles. *William of Adam: How to Defeat the Saracens = Guillelmus Ade: Tractatus quomodo Sarraceni sunt expugnandi* (Washington: Dumbarton Oaks Research Library and Collection, 2012).
Cook, Davis. *Martyrdom in Islam* (Cambridge: Cambridge University Press, 2007).
Correnti, Santi. *La Guerra dei novant'anni e le ripercussioni europee della Guerra del Vespro* (Catania: Muglia, 1973).
Coulon, Damien. "Formas de violencia entre la Corona de Aragón y el sultanato Mameluco en los siglos XIV y XV." *Anales de la Universidad de Alicante. Historia medieval* 16 (2009/10): 277–288.
Coulon, Damien. "La documentation pontificale et le commerce avec les musulmans." In *Les territoires de la Méditerranée VIe–XVIe siècle*, ed. Annliese Nef (Rennes: Presses Universitaires de Rennes, 2013), 161–192.
Coulon, Damien. "Lluis Sirvent, homme d'affaires et ambassadeur barcelonais (vers 1385–1444)." In *Les échanges en Méditerranée médiévale: marqueurs, réseaux, circulations, contacts*, ed. Élisabeth Malamut and Mohamed Ouerfelli (Aix-en-Provence: Presses universitaires de Provence, 2012), 215–242.
Coulon, Damien. "Négocier avec les sultans de Méditerranée orientale à la fin du moyen âge. Un domaine privilegié pour les hommes d'affaires?" In *Negociar en la Edad Media = Négocier au Moyen Âge*, ed. María Teresa Ferrer i Mallol, Anuario de Estudios Medievales (Barcelona: Consejo Superior de Investigaciones Científicas, 2005), 503–526.
Coulon, Damien. "Un tournant dans les relations de Barcelone avec la Méditerranée orientale: la nouvelle politique d'Alphonse le Magnanime (1415–1442)." in *Atti del XVI*

Congresso Internazionale di Storia della Corona d'Aragona, ed. Guido d'Agostino (Napoli: Paparo, 2000), 2:1055–1079.

Coulon, Damien. *Barcelone et le grand commerce d'Orient au Moyen Age. Un siècle de relations avec l'Egypte et la Syrie-Palestine (ca. 1330-ca. 1430)* (Madrid: Casa de Velázquez, 2004).

Cowan, Alex. "Nodes, Networks and Hinterlands." In *Cities and Cultural Exchange in Europe, 1400–1700*, ed. Donatella Calabi and Stephen Turk Christensen (Cambridge: Cambridge University Press, 2007), 28–41.

Cuadrada, Coral. *La Mediterrània, cruïlla de mercaders (segles XIII–XV)* (Barcelona: Rafael Dalmau Editor, 2001).

Cutler, Anthony. "Significant Gift: Patterns of Exchange in Late Antique, Byzantine, and Early Islamic Diplomacy." *Journal of Medieval and Early Modern Studies* 38 (2008): 79–101.

Dakhlia, Jocelyne, and Wolfgang Kaiser, ed. *Les Musulmans dans l'histoire de l'Europe II: Passages et contacts en Méditerranée* (Paris: Albin Michel, 2012).

De Sandoli, Sabino. *The Peaceful Liberation of the Holy Places in the XIV Century: the third return of the Frankish or Latin clergy to the custody and service of the holy places through official negotiations in 1333* (Cairo: Franciscan Centerof Christian Oriental Studies, 1990).

Dopp, Pierre-Herman. "Les relations egypto-catalanes et les corsaires au commencement du quinzième siècle." *Bulletin de la Faculte des Arts. Fouad I University* 11/1 (1949): 1–14.

Drocourt, Nicolas. "Christian-Muslim Diplomatic Relations. An Overview of the Main Sources and Themes of Encounter (600–1000)." In Christian Muslim Relations: a Bibliographical History Vol. 1: *(600–900)*, ed. David Thomas, Barbara Roggema and Juan Pedro Monferrer-Sala (Leiden: Brill, 2009), 29–72.

Dufourcq, Charles Emmanuel. *L' Espagne catalane et le Maghrib aux XIIIe et XIVe siècles: de la bataille de Las Navas de Tolosa (1212) à l'avènement du sultan mérinide Abou-I-Hasan (1331)* (Paris: Presses Universitaires de France, 1966).

Echevarría Arsuaga, Ana. *Biografías mudéjares o La experiencia de ser minoría: biografías islámicas en la España cristiana* (Madrid: Consejo Superior de Investigaciones Científicas, 2008).

Echevarría Arsuaga, Ana. *Knights in the Frontier: The Moorish Guard of the Kings of Castile (1410–1467)* (Leiden: Brill, 2009).

Eijan, Samuel. *El Real Patronato de los Santos Lugares en la historia de la Tierra Santa* (Madrid, 1945–1946), 2 vols.

Elad, Amikam. *Medieval Jerusalem and Islamic Worship: Holy Places, Ceremonies, Pilgrimage* (Leiden and Cologne: Brill, 1995).

El-Leithy, Tamer. "Sufis, Copts and the Politics of Piety: Moral Regulation in Fourteenth-Century Upper Egypt." In *Le développement du soufisme en Égypte à l'époque mamelouke*, ed. Richard J. A. McGregor and Adam Abdelhamid Sabra (Cairo: Institut Français d'Archéologie Orientale, 2006), 75–119.

El-Leithy, Tamer. *Coptic Culture and Conversion in Medieval Cairo: 1293–1524 A.D* (PhD Diss., Princeton University, 2005).

Elm, Kaspar. "La Custodia di Terra Santa. Franziskanisches Ordensleben in der Tradition der lateinischen Kirche Palästinas." in *I Francescani nel Trecento: Assisi 16–17–18 ot-*

tobre 1986 (Assisi: Univ. degli Studi di Peruga, Centro di Studi Francescani, 1988), 127–166.

Estal, Juan Manuel del .*Itinerario de Jaime II de Aragón (1291–1327)* (Zaragoza: Institución Fernando el Católico, 2009).

Fancy, Hussein. *The Mercenary Mediterranean: Sovereignty, Religion, and Violence in the Medieval Crown of Aragon* (Chicago: University of Chicago Press, 2016).

Ferrer i Mallol, María Teresa. *Els catalans a la Mediterrània oriental a l'edat mitjana* (Barcelona: Institut d'Estudis Catalans, 2003).

Ferrer i Mallol, María Teresa, and Damien Coulon, ed. *L'Expansió catalana a la Mediterrània a la baixa edat mitjana* (Barcelona: CSIC, 1999).

Ferrer i Mallol, María Teresa, ed. *Negociar en la Edad Media = Négocier au Moyen Âge* (Barcelona: Consejo Superior de Investigaciones Científicas, 2005).

Ferrer i Mallol, María Teresa. "Documentación sobre mudéjares del Archivo de la Corona de Aragón." In *Fuentes documentales para el estudio de los mudéjares*, ed. María Teresa Ferrer i Mallol, Isabel Romero Camacho et al. (Teruel: Centro de Estudios Mudéjares, Instituto de Estudios Turolenses, 2005), 9–53.

Ferrer i Mallol, María Teresa. "Els viatges piadosos de cristians, jueus i musulmans per la Mediterrània medieval." In *Un mar de lleis, de Jaume I a Lepant, catàleg de l'exposició*, ed. María Teresa Ferrer and Josep Giralt (Barcelona, Institut Europeu de la Mediterrània, 2008), 101–118.

Ferrer i Mallol, María Teresa. "Incidència dels cors en les relacions catalanes amb l'Orient (segles XIII–XV)." in *Els catalans a la Mediterrània oriental a l'edat mitjana*, ed. María Teresa Ferrer i Mallol, Jornades científiques 11 (Barcelona: Institut d'Estudis Catalans, 2003), 259–307.

Ferrer i Mallol, María Teresa. "Les phénomènes migratoires entre les musulmans soumins à la couronne catalo-aragonaise pendant le Moyen Âge." In *Migrations et diasporas méditerranéennes (Xe–XVIe siècles)*, ed. Michel Balard and Alain Ducellier (Paris: Publications de la Sorbonne, 2002), 259–284.

Ferrer i Mallol, María Teresa. "Marruecos y la Corona catalano-aragonesa: mercenarios catalanes al servicio de Marruecos (1396–1410)." In *Homenaje al profesor Eloy Benito Ruano* (Murcia: Universitad de Murcia, 2010), 251–272.

Ferrer i Mallol, María Teresa. *Els sarraïns de la corona catalano-aragonesa en el segle XIV: segregació i discriminació* (Barcelona: Consell Superior d'Investigacions Científiques, 1987).

Ferrer Mallol, María Teresa. "Els redemptors de captius: mostolafs eixees o alfaquecs (segles XII–XIII)." *Medievalia* 9 (1990): 85–106.

Finke, Heinrich. *Acta Aragonensia. Quellen zur deutschen, italienischen, französischen und spanischen, zur Kirchen- und Kulturgeschichte aus der diplomatischen Korrespondenz Jaumes II. (1291–1327)* (Berlin: Rotschild, 1908–1922), 3 vols.

Finke, Heinrich. *Acta Aragonensia: Quellen zur deutschen, italienischen, französischen, spanischen, zur Kirchen- und Kulturgeschichte aus der diplomatischen Korrespondenz Jaymes II; 1291–1327* (Leipzig: Rothschild, 1908).

Fowler, Kenneth Alan. *Medieval Mercenaries 1: The Great Companies* (Oxford: Blackwell, 2001).

France, John, ed. *Mercenaries and Paid Men: The Mercenary Identity in the Middle Ages* (Leiden: Brill, 2008).

Frenkel, Yehoshua. "Muslim Pilgrimage to Jerusalem in the Mamluk Period." *Studies in Jewish Civilization* 7 (1996): 63–87.

Fuess, Albrecht. *Verbranntes Ufer: Auswirkungen mamlukischer Seepolitik auf Beirut und die syro-palästinensische Küste (1250–1517)* (Leiden: Brill, 2001).

Giunta, Francesco, ed. *XI Congresso di Storia della Corona d'Aragona: "'La società mediterranea all'epoca del Vespro"* (Palermo: Accad. di Scienze Lettere e Arti, 1983), 4 vols.

Giunta, Francesco. *Aragonesi e Catalani nel Mediterraneo. II: La presenza catalana nel Levante dalle origini a Giacomo II* (Palermo: U. Manfredi, 1959).

Golubovich, Girolamo. *Biblioteca bio-bibliografica della Terra Santa e dell'Oriente Francescano* (Quaracchi: Tipografia del Collegio di S. Bonaventura, 1906–1927).

Golubovich, Girolamo. Biblioteca bio-bibliografica della Terra Santa e dell'Oriente Francescano. 3: *Dal 1300 al 1332* (Quaracchi: Tipografia del Collegio di S. Bonaventura, 1919).

Gril, Denis. "Une émeute anti-chrétienne à Quṣ au début du VIIIe/XIVe siècle." *Annales islamologiques* 16 (1980): 241–274.

Grünbart, Michael ed. *Geschenke erhalten die Freundschaft. Gabentausch und Netzwerkpflege im europäischen Mittelalter* (Berlin: LIT-Verlag, 2011).

Gudiol, Josep. "De peregrins i peregrinatges religiosos catalans." *Analecta sacra tarraconensia* 3 (1927): 93–120.

Haarmann, Ulrih. "The Mamluk System of Rule in the Eyes of Western Travelers." *Mamluk Studies Review* 5 (2001): 1–24.

Heyd, Wilhelm. *Histoire du commerce du Levant au moyen- âge 2* (Leipzig: Hakkert, 1886).

Hinojosa Montalvo, José. "Mudejaren im Königreich Aragón: Integration und Segregation." In *Integration – Segregation – Vertreibung: Religiöse Minderheiten und Randgruppen auf derIberischen Halbinsel (7.–17. Jh.)*, ed. Klaus Herbers and Nikolas Jaspert (Münster: LIT-Verlag, 2011), 293–336.

Hinojosa Montalvo, José. *Jaime II y el esplendor de la Corona de Aragón* (San Sebastián: Nerea, 2006).

Hinojosa Montalvo, José. *Los mudéjares: la voz del Islam en la España cristiana* (Teruel: Centro de Estudios Mudéjares, Instituto de Estudios Turolenses, 2002), 2 vols.

Hinojosa Montalvo, José. *Los mudéjares: la voz del Islam en la España Cristiana* (Teruel: Centro de Estudios Mudéjares).

Holt, Peter Malcolm. "Al-Nasir Muḥammad's Letter to a Spanish Ruler in 699/1300." *Al-Masaq* 3 (1990): 23–29.

Holt, Peter Malcolm. "The Mamluk Sultanate and Aragon: The Treaties of 689/1290 and 692/1293." *Tārīḫ* 2 (1992): 105–118.

Holt, Peter Malcolm. *Early Mamluk Diplomacy (1260–1290): Treaties of Baybars and Qalawun with Christian Rulers* (Leiden: Brill, 1995).

Howard, Deborah. "Venice and the Mamluks." In *Venice and the Islamic World*, ed. Stefano Carboni (New York, 2007), 72–89.

Jackson, Peter. *The Mongols and the West, 1221–1410* (Harlow: Pearson Longman, 2005).

Janin, Hunt, and Ursula Carlson. *Mercenaries in Medieval and Renaissance Europe* (Jefferson, N.C: McFarland Company, Inc., Publishers, 2013).

Jaspert, Nikolas, and Sebastian Kolditz, ed. *Seeraub im Mittelmeerraum. Piraterie, Korsarentum und maritime Gewalt von der Antike bis zur Neuzeit* (Munich-Paderborn: Fink-Schöningh, 2013).

Jaspert, Nikolas, and Sebastian Kolditz. "Christlich-muslimische Außenbeziehungen im Mittelmeerraum: Zur räumlichen und religiösen Dimension mittelalterlicher Diplomatie." *Zeitschrift für Historische Forschung* 41 (2014): 1–88.

Jaspert, Nikolas. "Eleventh-Century Pilgrimage from Catalonia to Jerusalem: New Sources on the Foundations of the First Crusade." *Crusades* 14 (2015): 1–48.

Jaspert, Nikolas. "Gefangenenloskauf in der Krone Aragon und die Anfänge des Mercedarierordens: Institutionelle Diversität, religiöse Kontexte, mediterrane Verflechtungen." In *Gefangenenloskauf im Mittelmeerraum. Ein interreligiöser Vergleich*, ed. Heike Grieser and Nicole Priesching (Hildesheim: Olms, 2015), 99–121.

Jaspert, Nikolas. "Interreligiöse Diplomatie im Mittelmeerraum. Die Krone Aragón und die islamische Welt im 13. und 14. Jahrhundert." In *Aus der Frühzeit europäischer Diplomatie. Zum geistlichen und weltlichen Gesandtschaftswesen vom 12. bis zum 15. Jahrhundert*, ed. Claudia Märtl and Claudia Zey (Zurich: Chronos, 2008), 151–190.

Jaspert, Nikolas. "Mendicants, Jews and Muslims at Court in the Crown of Aragon: Social Practice and Inter-Religious Communication." In *Cultural Brokers at Mediterranean Courts in the Middle Ages*, ed. Marc von der Höh, Nikolas Jaspert and Jenny Rahel Oesterle (Paderborn: Fink-Schöningh, 2013), 107–147.

Jaspert, Nikolas. "Zur Loyalität interkultureller Makler im Mittelmeerraum: Christliche Söldnerführer (alcayts) im Dienste muslimischer Sultane." In *Loyalty in the Middle Ages. Ideal and Practice of a Cross-Social Value*, ed. Jörg Sonntag and Coralie Zermatten (Turnhout: Brepols, 2016), 235–274.

Kaiser, Wolfgang. ed. *Le commerce des captifs: les intermédiaires dans l'échange et le rachat des prisonniers en Méditerranée, XVe–XVIIIe siècle* (Rome: École Française de Rome, 2008).

Kolditz, Sebastian. "Der Herrscher als Pilger im westlichen und östlichen Mittelalter. Eine Skizze." In *Transkulturelle Komparatistik. Beiträge zu einer Globalgeschichte der Vormoderne*, ed. Wolfram Drews and Jenny Rahel Oesterle (Leipzig: leipziger Universitätsverlag, 2008), 73–94.

König, Daniel. *Arabic-Islamic Views of the Latin West. Tracing the Emergence of Medieval Europe* (Oxford: Oxford University Press, 2015).

Korobeinikov, Dimitri A. "Diplomatic Correspondence between Byzantium and the Mamluk Sultanate in the Fourteenth Century." *Al-Masaq* 16 (2004): 53–74.

Kouamé, Thierry, ed. *Les relations diplomatiques au Moyen Âge: Formes et enjeux* (Paris: Publications de la Sorbonne, 2011).

Lammens, Henri. "Correspondances diplomatiques entre les sultans mamluks d'Egypte et les puissances chrétiennes."*Revue de l'Orient chrétien* 9 (1904): 151–187, 359–392.

Levanoni, Amalia. *A Turning Point in Mamluk History: The Third Reign of al-Naṣīr Muḥammad Ibn Qalāwūn (1310–1341)*(Leiden: Brill, 1995).

López de Coca Castañer, José Enrique. "Sobre la emigración mudéjar al reino de Granada." *Revista d'Històrica Medieval* 12 (2001/2002): 241–258.

López de Meneses, Amanda. "Pedro el Ceremonioso y las reliquias de Santa Bárbara." *Estudios de Edad Media de la Corona de Aragón* 7 (1962): 299–357.

López Pérez, María Dolores. "Marchands, esclaves et mercenaires: les transferts de populations dans le Maghreb médiéval." In *Migrations et diasporas méditerranéennes (Xe–XVIe siècles)*, ed. Michel Balard and Alain Ducellier (Paris: Publications de la Sorbonne, 2002), 399–415.

López Pérez, María Dolores. *La Corona de Aragón y el Magreb en el siglo XIV: (1331–1410)* (Barcelona: Institut Milá y Fontanals, 1995).

Lorenzo, Vaca, and Jean-Pierre Molénat, ed. *Minorías y migraciones en la historia: XV Jornadas de Estudios Históricos* (Salamanca: Ediciones Universidad de Salamanca, 2004).

Lower, Michael. "The Papacy and Christian Mercenaries of Thirteenth-Century North Africa." *Speculum* 89 (2014): 601–631.

Lucena Paredes, Luis Seco de. "Un tratado árabe del siglo XV sobre España extraido del 'Subh al-Aʿša' de Al-Qualquasandi." *Boletín de la universidad de Granada* 14 (1942): 87–126.

Madurell Marimón, Josep María. "Les activitats diplomátiques i mercantils de Pere de Mitjavila." In *La corona de Aragon en el siglo XIV. VIII Congreso de Historia de la Corona de Aragón* (Valencia, 1973), 3: 177–188.

Mansouri, Mohamed Tahar. "Les communautés marchandes occidentales dans l'espace mamlouk (XIIIe–XVe siècle)." In *Coloniser au moyen âge*, ed. Michel Balard (Paris: Colin, 1995), 89–114.

Marinescu, Constantin. *La politique orientale d'Alfonse V d'Aragon, roi de Naples (1416–1458).* (Barcelona: Institut d'Estudis Catalans, 1994).

Marquès, Josep M. "Sis-cents pidolaires (1368–1540). Captius, esclaus i pelegrins." *Estudis del Baix Empordà* 13 (1994): 137–165.

Martín, José-Luis. *Historia de la Corona de Aragón* (Madrid: Universiad Nacional de Educación a Distancia, 2002).

Martínez de Castilla Muñoz, Nuria, María Jesús Viguera Molins and Pascal Buresi, ed. *Documentos y manuscritos árabes del Occidente musulmán medieval* (Madrid, 2010).

Martínez Montávez, Pedro. "Relaciones castellano-mamelucas 1283–1382." *Hispania. Revista española de historia* 23 (1963): 505–523.

Masiá de Ros, Ángeles. *La corona de Aragón y los estados del norte de África: política de Jaime II y Alfonso IV en Egipto, Ifriquía y Tremecén* (Barcelona: Instituto español de estudios mediterráneos, 1951).

Maurazos, Gabriel González. "La documentación diplomática entre la Corona de Aragón y el Sultanato Mameluco durante el reinado de Jaime II: un ejemplo de las transformaciones en las relaciones internacionales del ámbito mediterráneo en la Baja Edad Media." *Anales de la Universidad de Alicante. Historia medieval* 11 (1996): 395–403.

Melis, Federigo. "Nota sul movimento del porto di Beirut secondo la documentazione fiorentina intorno al 1400." In *I trasporti e le comunicazioni nel medioevo*, ed. Federigo Melis (Florence: Le Monnier, 1984), 77–79.

Meri, Josef W. "The Etiquette of Devotion in the Islamic Cult of Saints." In *The Cult of Saints in Late Antiquity and the Middle Ages: Essays on the Contribution of Peter Brown*, ed. James Howard-Johnston and Paul Antony Hayward (Oxford: Oxford University Press, 1999), 263–286.

Meri, Josef W. *The Cult of Saints among Muslims and Jews in Medieval Syria* (Oxford: Oxford University Press, 2002).

Ministerio de Cultura, ed, *El perfume de la amistad: correspondencia diplomática árabe en archivos españoles (siglos XIII–XVII)* (Madrid: Secretaria General Técnica, 2009).

Miquel Rosell, Francisco Javier. *Regesta de letras pontificias del Archivo de la Corona de Aragón: sección Cancilleria Real (pergaminos)* (Madrid: Góngora 1948).

Moatti, Claudiaa, and Wolfgang Kaiser, ed. *Gens de passage en Méditerranée de l'Antiquité à l'époque moderne: procédures de contrôle et d'identification* (Paris: Maisonneuve et Larose, 2007).
Morillo, Stephen. "Mercenaries, Mamluks and Militia: towards a Crosscultural Typology of Military Service." In *Mercenaries and Paid Men: The Mercenary Identity in the Middle Ages*, ed. John France, HW (Leiden: Brill, 2008), 243–259.
Mott, Lawrence V. *Sea Power in the Medieval Mediterranean: The Catalan-Aragonese Fleet in the War of the Sicilian Vespers* (Gainesville: University Press of Florida, 2003).
Moukarzel, Pierre. "Les marchands européens dans l'espace urbain mamelouk: un groupe minoritaire privilégié?" In *Minorités et régulations sociales en Méditerranée médiévale*, ed. Stéphane Boissellier, François Clément and John Tolan (Rennes: Presses Universitaires de Rennes, 2010), 181–206.
Muhanna, Elias I. "The Sultan's New Clothes: Ottoman-Mamluk Gift Exchange in the Fifteenth Century." *Muqarnas* 27 (2010): 189–207.
Mutgé i Vives, Jodefina, Roser Salicrú i Lluch and Carles Vela Aulesa, ed. *La Corona catalanoaragonesa, l'Islam i el món mediterrani. Estudis d'història medieval en homenatge a la Doctora María Teresa Ferrer i Mallol* (Barcelona: CSIC, 2013).
Mutgé Vives, Josefa. *L'aljama sarraïna de Lleida a l'Edat Mitjana: aproximació a la seva història* (Barcelona: Consell Superior d'Investigacions Científiques, 1992).
Neumann, Christian. *Venedig und Aragon im Spätmittelalter (1280–1410): Eine Verflechtungsgeschichte* (Paderborn: Fink-Schöningh 2017).
Nirenberg, David. "The Current State of Mudejar Studies." *Journal of Medieval History* 24 (1998): 381–389.
Nirenberg, David. *Communities of Violence. Persecution of Minorities in the Middle Ages* (Princeton: Princeton University Press, 1996).
Northrup, Linda S. *From Slave to Sultan: The Career of Al-Manṣūr Qalāwūn and the Consolidation of Mamlūk Rule in Egypt and Syria (678–689 A.H./1279–1290 A.D.)* (Stuttgart: Franz Steiner, 1998).
Ochoa Brun, Miguel Ángel. *Historia de la diplomacia española. Apéndice 1: Repertorio diplomático, listas cronológicas de representantes, desde la Alta Edad Media hasta el año 2000* (Madrid: Ministerio de Asuntos Exteriores, 2002).
Ochoa Brun, Miguel Ángel. *Historia de la diplomacia española.* Vol. 3 (Madrid: Ministerio de Asuntos Exteriores, 1991).
O'Connor, Isabel. "Mudejars Helping Other Mudejars in the Kingdom of Valencia." *Al-Masaq* 17 (2005): 99–108.
O'Connor, Isabel. A. *A Forgotten Community: The Mudejar Aljama of Xàtiva, 1240–1327* (Leiden: Brill, 2003).
Pahlitzsch, Johannes. "Mediators between East and West: Christians under Mamluk Rule." *Mamlūk Studies Review* 9/2 (2005): 32–47.
Péquignot, Stéphane. *Au nom du roi: pratique diplomatique et pouvoir durant le règne de Jacques II d'Aragon (1291–1327)* (Madrid: Casa de Velázquez, 2009).
Péquignot, Stéphane. "Europäische Diplomatie im Spätmittelalter. Ein historiographischer Überblick." *Zeitschrift für Historische Forschung* 39 (2012): 65–96.
Piergiovanni, Vito, ed. *Corsari e riscatto dei captivi: garanzia notarile tra le due sponde del Mediterraneo* (Milano: Giuffrè, 2010).

Potthast, Daniel. "Drei Fragmente von arabischen Staatsbriefen (14. Jahrhundert) im Archivo de la Corona de Aragón/Barcelona." *Der Islam* 92 (2015): 367–412.

Ramos Loscertales, José María. *El Cautiverio en la corona de Aragón durante los siglos XIII, XIV, y XV* (Zaragoza, 1915).

Reinfandt, Lucian. "Mamluk Documentary Studies." In *Ubi sumus? Quo vademus?: Mamluk Studies – State of the Art*, ed. Stephan Conermann (Göttingen: Bonn University Press, 2013), 285–310.

Remie Constable, Olivia. "Regulating Religious Noise: The Council of Vienne, the Mosque Call and Muslim Pilgrimage in the Late Medieval Mediterranean World." *Medieval Encounters* 16 (2010): 64–95.

Rodriguez, Jarbel. *Captives and their saviors in the medieval crown of Aragon* (Washington, DC: Catholic University of America Press, 2007).

Romano, David. "Musulmanes residentes y emigrantess en la Barcelona de los siglos xiv–xv." *Al-Andalus* 40 (1976): 49–86.

Rothman, Ella Nathalie. *Brokering Empire: Trans-imperial Subjects between Venice and Istanbul* (Ithaca: Cornell University Press, 2012).

Ruiz Orsatti, Reginaldo. "Tratado de paz entre Alfonso V de Aragón y el Sultán de Egipto, al-Malik al Ašraf Barsbay." *Al-Andalus* 4 (1939): 333–390.

Ruzafa, Manuel ed., *Los mudéjares valencianos y peninsulares* (Valencia: Universitat de València, 2003).

Ryan, Michael Alan. "Power and Pilgrimage: The Restriction of Mudéjares' Pilgrimage in the Kingdom of Valencia."*Essays in Medieval Studies* 25 (2008): 115–128.

Salicrú Lluch, Roser. "En busca de una liberación alternativa: fugas y apostasía en la Corona de Aragón bajomedieval." In *La liberazione dei "captive"' tra Cristianità e Islam: oltre la crociata e il Gihad: tolleranza e servizio umanitario*, ed. Giulio Cipollone (Città del Vaticano: Archivio Segreto Vaticano, 2000), 703–713.

Salicrú Lluch, Roser. "Mercenaires castillans au Maroc au début du XVe siècle." In: *Migrations et diasporas méditerranéennes (Xe–XVIe siècles)*, ed. Michel Balard and Alain Ducellier (Paris: Publications de la Sorbonne, 2002), 417–434.

Sarrablo, Eugenio. "La Reina que vino de Oriente (María de Chipre, esposa de Jaime II, Rey de Aragón)." *Boletín de la Real Academia de la Historia* 148 (1961): 13–160.

Savaglio, Antonello, ed. *Atti del Convegno Internazionale di Studi su "Guerra di Corsa e Pirateria nel Mediterraneo"* (Cosenza: Orizzonti Meridionali, 1999).

Schein, Sylvia. *Fideles Crucis: The Papacy, the West, and the Recovery of the Holy* (Oxford: Clarendon Press, 1991).

Schilling, Alexander Markus. "Der Friedens- und Handelsvertrag von 1290 zwischen der Kommune Genua und dem Sultan Qalawun von Ägpyten." Quellen und Forschungen aus italienischen Archiven und Bibliotheken 95 (2015): 63–109.

Schmidt Arcangeli, Catarina, and Gerhard Wolf, ed. *Islamic Artefacts in the Mediterranean World: Trade, Gift Exchange and Artistic Transfer* (Venice: Marsilio, 2010).

Schwinges, Rainer Christoph, and Klaus Wriedt, ed. *Gesandtschafts- und Botenwesen im spätmittelalterlichen Europa* (Ostfildern: Thorbecke, 2003).

Selzer, Stephan. *Deutsche Söldner im Italien des Trecento* (Tübingen: Niemeyer, 2001).

Sola Castaño, Emilio. *Un mediterráneo de piratas: corsarios, renegados y cautivos* (Madrid: Ediciones Tecnos, 1988).

Torra Pérez, Alberto. "Las relaciones diplomáticas entre la Corona de Aragón y los países musulmanes (siglos XIII–XV). Las fuentes documentales del Archivo de la Corona de Aragón." In *El perfume de la amistad: correspondencia diplomática árabe en archivos españoles (siglos XIII–XVII)*, ed. Ministerio de Cultura (Madrid: Secretaria General Técnica, 2009), 13–39.

Trenchs Odena, José. "'De Alexandrinis' (El comercio prohibido con los musulmanes y el Papado de Aviñón durante la primera mitad del siglo XIV)." *Anuario de estudios medievales* 10 (1980): 237–320.

Unali, Anna. *Marineros, piratas y corsarios catalanes en la Baja Edad Media* (Seville: Renacimiento, 2007).

Verskin, Alan. *Islamic Law and the Crisis of the Reconquista: The Debate on the Status of Muslim Communities in Christendom* (Leiden: Brill, 2015).

Viladrich, María Mercè. "Jaque al sultán en el 'Damero maldito'. Edición y traducción de un tratado diplomático entre los mercaderes catalanes y el sultanato mamluco (1429)." In *L'Expansió catalana a la Mediterrània a la baixa edat mitjana*, ed. María Teresa Ferrer i Mallol and Damien Coulon (Barcelona: CSIC, 1999), 161–206.

Viladrich, María Mercé. "Solving the 'Accursed Riddle' of the Diplomatic Relations between Catalonia and Egypt around 1430." *Al-Masaq* 14/1 (2002): 25–31.

Vincke, Johannes. "Die Gesandtschaften der aragonesischen Könige um die Reliquien der heiligen Barbara (1322–1337)." *Historisches Jahrbuch* 60 (1940): 115–124.

von der Höh, Marc, Nikolas Jaspert and Jenny Rahel Oesterle, ed. *Cultural Brokers at Mediterranean Courts in the Middle Ages* (Paderborn: Schöningh-Fink, 2013).

von der Höh, Marc, Nikolas Jaspert and Jenny Rahel Oesterle. "Courts, Brokers and Brokerage in the Medieval Mediterranean." In *Cultural Brokers at Mediterranean Courts in the Middle Ages*, ed. Marc von der Höh, Nikolas Jaspert and Jenny Rahel Oesterle (Paderborn: Fink-Schöningh, 2013), 10–31.

von Thiessen, Hillard and Christian Windler, ed. *Akteure der Außenbeziehungen: Netzwerke und Interkulturalität im historischen Wandel* (Cologne: Böhlau, 2010).

Watkins, Joh,. "Toward a New Diplomatic History of Medieval and Early Modern Europe." *Journal of Medieval and Early Modern Studies* 38 (2008): 1–14.

Zey, Claudia, and Claudia Märtl, ed. *Aus der Frühzeit europäischer Diplomatie: zum geistlichen und weltlichen Gesandtschaftswesen vom 12. bis zum 15. Jahrhundert* (Zürich: Chronos-Verlag, 2008).

IV. Looking North and East

Marie Favereau (University of Oxford)

The Mamluk Sultanate and the Golden Horde. Tension and Interaction During the Mongol Peace

"The Mongol Peace" is an old paradigm originally modeled on the notion of Pax Romana.[1] It refers to the post-conquest stability of the Mongol dominions and supposedly peaceful relationships between the descendants of Chinggis Khan. During the Mongol Peace a commercial boom transformed the human landscape in western Eurasia, connecting the Mediterranean Sea to India and China. The ways Mongols stimulated the exchanges resulted in a new form of long-distance trade. The agreements they established with the Mamluks, the Byzantines, the Italians, and others, led to the transformation of the trade networks. A new economic order emerged, which cannot be seen as the mere revival of the continental silk roads of the ancient world. A major change was that it deeply connected for the first time Egypt and the Volga basin. The phenomenon of the Mongol Peace lasted roughly a century: from the 1260s, when the old Chinggisid empire split into four Khanates, to the late 1360s. At that time, the Ming have replaced the Mongols in China, Tibet and Mongolia; the Ilkhanate, once covering Iran, Azerbaijan, Iraq and Eastern Anatolia, has fallen apart. Only the Chagatay Horde in Central Asia and the Golden Horde in western Kazakhstan, Southern Siberia, Russia and Eastern Europe, resisted and adapted to the new geopolitical situation. From its inception, the descendants of Jöchi, the eldest son of Chinggis Khan, ruled over the Golden Horde. The Jöchids had their main winter camp in the lower Volga. For summer, they moved west towards the Don or south towards the Caucasus. In the lower Volga, region of modern Astrakhan, two major routes were passable: the eastern one through Central Asia towards north India and China, and the western one through the Black Sea steppes and the Crimean Peninsula towards the Mamluk Sultanate and the Mediterranean markets.

1 The so-called Pax Mongolica had nothing to do with peace in the modern sense of term. I define it as a new economic space in which the Mongols changed the rules of exchange and created a kind of "global market." During this period, wars and military clashes occured, but did not prevent the implementation of joint policies and multilateral agreements on routes, diplomatic conventions, monetary and weight exchange systems as well as the use of common scripts and languages to communicate.

The first alliance between the Mamluk Sultans and the Jöchid Khans dated back to 1262. Almost a century after, Ibn Faḍl Allāh al-ʿUmarī noted about the Golden Horde:

> [Its Khan] rules over Saray, Khwarazm, Qrim (Crimea) and the Dašt al-Qibjaq (Qipchaq). This kingdom is known as the House (*bayt*) of Berke *qān*. In ancient times, during the reign of the caliphs and before, this ruler was called the Master of the Throne (*ṣāḥib sarīr*). At the time of al-Nāṣir's reign, this ruler was the sultan Özbek Khan. The sultan [Özbek Khan] chose a spouse for him [al-Nāṣir Muḥammad] and made him marry his daughter to get closer to him. And until today, between the kings of this kingdom and our kings, there is an alliance, with sincerity and friendship; [this lasts] since the first days of the reign of al-Ẓāhir Baybars until recently.[2]

The alliance was renewed under Toqtamish and Barqūq and both empires kept in touch through embassies until the first half of the fifteenth century, until their exchanges lost their *raison d'être*. Not surprisingly, their intensive period of alliances coincided with the Mongol Peace. The academic literature has focused on the role of the Venetians and the Genoese whose mercantile activities developed enormously during this period. The Maritime Republics were indeed part of the Eurasian economic breakthrough until the great rupture of the Black Death. Yet, as recent scholarship demonstrates, the Mongol rulers and the heads of the nomadic groups played the leading role in the new inter-regional order.[3]

In this paper, I argue further that the alliances between the Mamluk Sultans and the Jöchids of the Golden Horde were a key component of the Mongol Peace. At that period, the Khans and the Sultans of Egypt and Syria introduced a new form of partnership. Some research has established that they exchanged religious books for slave girls and Qipchaq mamluks.[4] Yet, the dynamics of the relations between the Golden Horde and the Mamluks cannot be reduced to an exchange based on two commodities. They did also circulate a wide range of luxury goods, animals, food and weapons as well as technical skills, knowledge, court fashion

2 Ibn Faḍl Allāh al-ʿUmarī, *al-Taʿrīf fī al-muṣṭalaḥ al-šarīf* (Cairo, 1312/1894–95), 47–48; see also al-Qalqašandī, *Ṣubḥ al-aʿšā fī ṣināʿat al-inšāʾ* (Cairo, 1963–1972), 7: 292.

3 Michal Biran, "The Mongol Empire and Inter-civilizational Exchange," in *The Cambridge World History*, ed. Benjamin Z. Kedar and Merry E. Wiesner-Hanks (Cambridge: Cambridge University Press, 2015), 534–558. For a case study in the mid-fourteenth-century Golden Horde, see: Marie Favereau, "Venecianskie istochniki po istorii Zolotoj Ordy: novye perspektivy izuchenija," *Golden Horde Review/Zolotoordynskoe obozrenie* 1 (2016): 39–54.

4 As far as I know Salikh Zakirov, *Diplomatičeskie otnošenija Zolotoj Ordy s Egyptom (XIII–XIV vv.)*, (Moscow: Nauka, 1966) was the first monograph entirely devoted to the Mamluk-Jöchid relationship. Since then major studies were published, among them: David Ayalon, "The Great Yāsa of Chingiz Khān," Part A, *Studia Islamica* 33 (1971): 97–140; Part B, *Studia Islamica* 34 (1971): 151–180; Part C1, *Studia Islamica* 36 (1972) 113–158; Part C2, *Studia Islamica* 38 (1973): 107–156. Reuven Amitai-Preiss, *Mongols and Mamluks. The Mamluk-Īlkhānid War 1260–1281* (Cambridge, Cambridge University Press, 1995) and Anne Broadbridge, *Kingship and Ideology in the Islamic and Mongol Worlds* (Cambridge: Cambridge University Press, 2008).

and ideas. People used to travel from one territory to another, especially craftsmen and merchants. As I hope to demonstrate, their diplomatic relations were only one side of their interactions, hiding a more complex economic interdependence. I will look at three episodes to show how both powers were deeply connected. First, the debate over conversion between Khan Berke and Sultan Baybars (1262–1264); second, how Khan Tokta prohibited the mamluk slave trade (*c.* 1300–1312); third, the dispute between Khan Özbek and al-Malik al-Nāṣir Muḥammad b. Qalāwūn (1312–41). These episodes coincide with diplomatic clashes. But these clashes, instead of breaking the commercial dynamics, had the opposite effect to trigger the exchanges. By putting these three episodes within their wider geopolitical context, we may understand better this global economic *momentum* and explain how the Mongol-Mamluk encounter played a key role in the Mongol Peace phenomenon.[5]

Berke and Baybars: First Agreement and Debate over Conversion

A Context for an Agreement. The Mongols not only attacked the caliphate and executed the Abbasid caliph in 1258, they annihilated the rulers of the most important Islamic dynasties to establish a new order based on their imperial legitimacy. The Qara-Khitai, Khwarazmshahs, Abbasids, Ayyubids, and Seljuqs were destroyed, which created a power vacuum with significant political legacies to claim. Berke (1257–1267), the first Muslim Khan of the Mongol empire and the founder of the Golden Horde, seized the opportunity to claim the Islamic leadership. After the death of the Great Khan Möngke in 1259, the underlying tensions among the descendants of Chinggis Khan turned into open conflicts. Berke refused to pay allegiance to the new Great Khan and chose to support another candidate.[6] Hülegü (1256–1265), appointed by the new Great Khan, was leading successful conquests into the West. He threatened the Jöchids on their borders, cut their external sources of income, from Herat and Tabriz, and perhaps even tried to be elevated on the throne of the descendants of Jöchi. Hülegü was about to create a new empire of his own. He annexed the territories from the Mughan plain, in today's Azerbaijan, up to the Lake Van; a *continuum* of steppes that covered the fertile pastures of Arran, which would later constitute the heartland

5 This essay revisits some of the themes and arguments put forward in Marie Favereau, *La Horde d'Or et le sultanat mamelouk. Naissance d'une alliance* (Cairo: Ifao, 2018) and "Zolotaja Orda i Mamljuki (The Golden Horde and the Mamluks)" in *Zolotaja Orda v Mirovoj Istorii* (*The Golden Horde in World History*), co-edited with Roman Hautala, Ilnur Mirgaleev and Vadim Trepavlov (Kazan: Sh. Marjani Institute of History, 2016). I would like to thank Prof. Reuven Amitai and Prof. Stephan Conermann for their insightful comments and patient support.

6 Arigh-Böke, who was definitely defeated in 1264.

of the Ilkhanate and the southern frontier of the Jöchid empire. During the winter 1261–62, Khan Berke broke with the Mongol empire by declaring war on Hülegü. Berke's military attacks in Azerbaijan were only part of a larger strategy. He also sent his envoys to the ruler of the Delhi Sultanate who refused to pledge allegiance to the Great Khan Qubilai and wrote to General Negüder, head of the Jöchid contingent in eastern Iran, to protect Jöchid interests in Khorasan.[7] At roughly the same time, he allied with the Mamluks, the new rulers of Egypt and Syria, against the Great Khan and Hülegü. Berke and his followers maintained their control on the Crimean Peninsula but had lost the market beyond it as the Sultanate of Rūm was in the hands of their Mongol enemies. They were blocked in the Caucasus as well and could not access the trade centers of Tabriz and Baghdad. Local and long-distance merchants could not get into the Golden Horde. Commercial isolation was part of the Mongols' war strategy; opening routes with controlling posts and flooded passages were, thus, crucial to the Jöchids. The only way to penetrate the blockade was to push through the Black Sea to Constantinople and from there to the Mediterranean and further to Egypt.

The Content of the Agreement. Therefore, in 1262–1263 Khan Berke entered into an agreement with the Mamluk Sultan, Baybars, and the Byzantine emperor, Michael Palaiologos, and his allies, the Genoese. Michael agreed to let envoys and merchants sent by the Khan and the Sultan pass through the Bosphorus and ship goods and slaves. The Sultan needed manpower for his armies to fight both the Crusaders and the Mongols in Syria and over the Euphrates. The Mamluks had the same enemy as the Golden Horde and the same problem: they need to bypass the Seljuq markets where slaves were sent from Crimea. Berke agreed to sell young nomads from the heartland of the Horde to the Sultanate. At that time, the most appreciated warriors were taken from the Qipchaq Turks, a tribal federation living in the steppes stretching from the Caspian Sea to the northern shores of the Black sea. These boys, widely considered to have great potential to become superior mounted warriors, were part of the nomadic populations the Mongols subjugated in the first half of the thirteenth century. The Khan and the *noyans* (members of the Mongol elite) fought to keep the Constantinople route open and forced the Byzantines to comply. The first alliance between the Mamluks and the Jöchids established the trade route from Cairo to the lower Volga, a trip that took approximately two months.[8]

7 On the warlike struggles before the Mongol empire split up, see the classical study of Peter Jackson, "The Dissolution of the Mongol Empire", *Central Asiatic Journal* 32 (1978): 186–244. On Berke's attempt to set up an alliance with the Negūderis (or Qara'unas) and the Delhi Sultanate in 1259–1261, see Jean Aubin, "L'ethnogenèse des Qaraunas", *Turcica* 1 (1969): 65–94.

8 Ibn ʿAbd al-Ẓāhir, *al-Rawḍ al- zāhir fī sīrat al-malik al-Ẓāhir*, ed. ʿAbd al-ʿAzīz al-Ḫuwayṭir

The *dār al-islām* in the 1260s: An Acephalous Order. This first agreement was not only about military coordination; rulers' legitimacy and reputation mattered as well.[9] The Khan and the Sultan needed each other, as they had a common enemy, but they were also Islamic leaders in competition. Between 1261 and 1262 (660 H.), Baybars entrusted his first letter for Berke to Alan merchants (*ʿAllān*). The Sultan congratulated the Khan on his recent conversion to Islam and urged him to fight Hülegü in the name of *jihād*. In his *al-Rawḍ al-zāhir fī sīrat al-malik al-Ẓāhir*, Ibn ʿAbd al-Ẓāhir includes the reconstructed texts of the letters Baybars sent to Berke. The Sultan acted as a "senior in Islam" and his letters were pieces of advice on how to be a true Muslim leader. Obviously the Sultan placed himself above the Khan because he was the first who converted: he was, then, a teenager; while, when Berke announced his conversion, he was in his forties. The notion of precedence in Islam was crucial since the formative period of the *dār al-islām*. Precedence and excellence in Islam are key aspects in the Islamic discourse about legitimate leadership and it developed through the *manāqib* literature – a genre that directly inspired Ibn ʿAbd al-Ẓāhir in his royal biography of Baybars.[10] Berke's conversion had a great impact in his own time. Indeed, he was the first Mongol ruler to become a "Sultan." The Mamluks had nothing to do with his decision. His spiritual influence came from the Khwarazm where he received his religious education. His mentor was the Sufi sheikh Sayf al-Dīn Bāḫarzī, from Bukhara. According to Jūzjānī, Berke was raised a Muslim.[11] His so-called conversion when he was elected Khan was a significant act of politics: a new symbolic allegiance and a change of orientation. He broke with the great Mongol empire, where he was an outsider, and he entered the *umma* – to be a leader. In his first letter to Baybars, he said that he converted along with his four brothers, his wife, his companions, several *noyans*, the *tümen* (military regiment) of Khorasan and with the men of Baiju, the leader of the conquests in the Seljuq lands, whom Hülegü sent to death because he was too close to the Jöchids. In the debate about precedence and excellence in Islam, the key criterion was not only precedence in conversion, but also the way the conversion was made and the moral excellence of

(al-Riyāḍ, 1976), 215. For further details on the Nile-Volga route, see Marie Favereau, "The Golden Horde and the Mamluks: The Birth of a Diplomatic Set-up (1261–67)," in *Mamluk Cairo, a Crossroad for Embassies*, ed. Frédéric Bauden & Malika Dekkiche (Leiden and Boston: Brill, 2019), 320–321.

9 Ibid., 284–289.

10 Marie Favereau, *La Horde d'Or et le sultanat mamelouk*, 34–39. On the question of hierarchy in conversion and the significance of the *manāqib* literature, see Asma Afsaruddin, "In Praise of the Caliphs: Re-Creating History from the Manaqib Literature," *International Journal of Middle East Studies* 31/3 (1999): 329–350.

11 In the *Ṭabaqat-i Nāṣirī*, composed in 1260. See Devin DeWeese, *Islamization and Native Religion in the Golden Horde: Baba Tükles and Conversion to Islam in Historical and Epic Tradition* (University Park, PA: Pennsylvania State University Press, 1994), 83–86.

the leader. The public conversion of a male adult could be more valued than the conversion of a child or a teenager because the impact on the *umma* and on the outside world was much higher, especially if the leader's conversion came with the collective conversion of his family and companions – which was precisely what the Khan answered the Sultan. Berke claimed the Seljuq and Abbasid political legacies. The Khan's Islamic entourage (qadis, muftis, sheikhs) developed new theories on legitimacy and leadership, which were different from the Mamluks' ideological constructions. Yet, the Mamluks had a huge advantage: they controlled the access to the pilgrimage and the holy places. Therefore, in exchange for selling some of his subjects as military slaves, Berke demanded the Mamluks to recognize him as supreme Sultan by the new Abbasid caliph, then residing in Cairo, and to grant free access to the holy cities of Mecca and Medina. From this time onwards, the Jöchids were allowed to send their people to the Ḥejaz to perform the *ḥajj*.[12]

The First Crisis between the Mamluks and the Jöchids (*c.* 1300–1312)

At the dawn of the fourteenth century, the Mamluk-Jöchid relation took a different shape. Their exchanges were exposed to new inter-regional competition and tensions were palpable through their diplomatic correspondence. Clashes between the two courts never led to direct military conflicts because the Golden Horde and the Mamluk Sultanate had no common borders but, as we will see, the consequences were significant for their go-betweens and intermediaries.[13]

The Mongol Empire Reborn?

When Toqta inherited the lands which used to belong to Möngke-Temür,[14] envoys were exchanged and diplomatic correspondence was re-established among the Mongol rulers, so that the roads were once again open to merchants and licensed traders (*ortāqān*). Provisions for the immunity and safety of travellers were made. The region of

12 On Berke's claims as Sultan and on what he asked in exchange for selling Qipchaq slaves: Marie Favereau, *La Horde d'Or et le sultanat mamelouk,* 31–40. On the traffic over the Mongol-Mamluk frontier and the *ḥajj* caravans in the second half of the thirteenth century, see Amitai-Preiss, *Mongols and Mamluks*, 212–213.

13 On Toqta's reign, see Bertold Spuler, *Die Goldene Horde. Die Mongolen in Russland, 1223–1502* (Wiesbaden: Otto Harrassowitz, 1965), 77–85. On the relations between the Mamluks and the Ilkhanid ruler Öljeitu, see Broadbridge, *Kingship and Ideology*, 94–98. On the Black Sea context during Toqta's reign: Virgil Ciocîltan, *The Mongols and the Black Sea Trade in the Thirteenth and Fourteenth Centuries* (Leiden and Boston: Brill, 2012), 163–173.

14 Toqta (1291–1312) was the son of Möngke-Temür (1266–1280). Both were Khans of the Golden Horde.

> Arran [on the Caucasian frontier between the Golden Horde and the Ilkhanate] became replete with the constant movement of carriages, tents, horses and sheep. Rare commodities from those lands became plentiful again after an interruption of some years.[15]

The early fourteenth century was a period of alliance at the level of the entire Mongol empire. In 1301, after the Khan of the *ulus* of Ögödei died, his heirs and allies from the Chagatay Khanate opened peace negotiations with the Great Khan and the Jöchids. The "Qaidu wars" had been in full swing for a quarter of a century.[16] Peace was finally declared and a joint mission sent by the parts involved in the process came to the Ilkhanid ruler Öljeitu (r. 1304–16) in 1304. At the end of the year, an agreement was concluded between the four Mongol Khanates and the formal unity of the Chinggisid Empire was apparently restored.[17] Öljeitü wrote to the king of France, Philip the Fair, that the Mongol nations have achieved peace:

> Now under the inspiration of the Sky (*Tengri*), we Tëmur Qaan [the Great Khan], Toqta, Chapar, Du'a, and others, descendants of Chinggis Khan, while since forty five years until recently we used to recriminate against each other, now, under the protection of the Sky, [we] elder brothers and younger brothers, reached a mutual agreement; our states are but one from southern China, where the sun rises, as far as the Talu Sea [the legendary ocean surrounding Eurasia] and now our postal stations (*yam*) are connected once more.[18]

Yet "peace" in this case meant the submission of the heirs of Chagatay and Ögödei to the Yuan order and paved the way for the rise of old territorial claims.[19]

15 Persian text in *Geschichte Wassaf's*, Persisch herausgegeben und Deutsch übersetzt von Hammer-Purgstall (Vienna: Hof- und Staatsdruckerei, 1856), 99, translated by Marie Favereau and Maya Petrovich.

16 On Qaidu (1236–1301), see Michal Biran, *Qaidu and the Rise of the Independent Mongol State in Central Asia* (Richmond: Curzon, 1997).

17 Interestingly, at the end of the thirteenth century the Ilkhanid ruler Ghazan already claimed that peace with the Great Khan, the Golden Horde (Toqta and Nogay), and Qaidu had been established. See Broadbridge, *Kingship and Ideology*, 78.

18 Antoine Mostaert and Francis W. Cleaves, *Les lettres de 1289 et 1305 des Ilhan Arghun et Öljeitu à Philippe le Bel* (Cambridge, MA.: Harvard University Press, 1962), 55–56 (Mongolian Text), 56–57 (French Translation). This is a quotation of lines 21–29. I have translated from both the Mongolian original and the French modern translation. See also the remarks in Peter Jackson, "World Conquest and Local Accommodation: Threat and Blandishment in Mongol Diplomacy," in *History and Historiography of Post-Mongol Central Asia and the Middle East. Studies in Honor of John E. Woods*, ed. Judith Pfeiffer and Sholeh Quinn (Wiesbaden: Harrassowitz Verlag, 2006), 15–16.

19 In 1306, Du'a and Chapar clashed again with each other for territorial reasons. See Hsiao Ch'i-Ch'ing, "*Mid-Yuan Politics*," in *The Cambridge History of China*, Volume 6: *Alien Regimes and Border States*, ed. Herbert Franke and Denis Twitchett (Cambridge: Cambridge University Press, 1994), 501–504. As Hsiao Ch'i-Ch'ing noticed, the peace of 1303–1304 is mainly described in al-Qāshānī, *Tārīkh-i Ūljāytū Sulṭān*, ed. Mahīn Hambalī (Tehran: Bungāh-i

Thus, the same year, the Khan of the Golden Horde sent his first embassy to Sultan al-Nāṣir Muḥammad. In his letter, Khan Toqta said that he had asked the Ilkhan to surrender the lands from Khorasan to Tabriz. He sent also two hundred slave girls and four hundred mamluks (most of whom died during the journey).[20] In exchange, the Khan asked al-Nāṣir Muḥammad to fight with him against the Ilkhanids.[21] At that time, Khan Toqta was at the peak of his power. He had eliminated Nogay (d. 1299), the powerful *beglerbeg* who had ruled over Crimea and southeastern Europe. He had pacified the local tensions in the Dnieper and Dniester areas and in the Crimean Peninsula. He also wanted to control Transcaucasia. In May 1301, he had sent his envoys to the Ilkhanid ruler Ghazan. We do not know the exact mission of this embassy nor the content of the letters brought by the Jöchid messengers; yet after being received at court "they soon withdrew." A few months later, Jöchid warriors met some Ilkhanid imperial troops in the area of Derbent. The clashes ended with a status-quo agreement between the Khan and the Ilkhan and the Transcaucasian trade route was re-opened.[22] In January 1303, at the Ilkhanid court in Hilla, Ghazan held a meeting with Mamluk ambassadors and Jöchid envoys – the latter came under the protection of three hundred cavalrymen. According to Rashīd al-Dīn, the letters the Mamluks brought "were not pleasing," but the envoys were finely treated as well as Toqta's messengers who "were shown much favor."[23] Obviously this was the Ilkhanid perspective, as Rashīd al-Dīn was writing for the Ilkhan. In another version, the Mamluk embassy came to answer Ghazan's provocation: he had asked the Sultan to pay taxes and had even ordered to mention the Ilkhan's name in the *khuṭba*

Tarǧuma va Našr-i Kitāb, 1969), 32–35. Other sources, especially Chinese, are mentioned on p. 503, n. 58.

20 Doris Behrens-Abouseif, *Practising Diplomacy in the Mamluk Sultanate: Gifts and Material Culture in the Medieval Islamic World* (London and New York: I.B. Tauris, 2014), 64.

21 Al-Nuwayrī, *Nihāyat al-Arab fī funūn al-adab*, ed. Fāhim Muḥammad ʿAlawī Shaltūt (Cairo: al-Muʾassasat al-Miṣriyya al-ʿĀmma lil-Taʾlīf wal-Tarjama wal-Ṭibāʿa wal-Našr, 1998), 32: 86; Baybars al-Dawādār, *Zubdat al-fikra fī taʾrīḫ al-ḥijra*, ed. D.S. Richards (Beirut and Berlin: Orient-Institut der DMG- and Das Arabische Buch, 1998) 381; Ibn al-Dawādārī, *Kanz al-Durar wa-jāmiʿ al-Ġurar*, ed. Hans Robert Roemer (Cairo, Wiesbaden: al-Maʿhad al-Almānī lil-Āthār bil-Qāhira, Otto Harrassowitz, 1960), 9: 128; al-ʿAynī, *ʿIqd al-jumān fī tawārīḫ ahl al-zamān*, ed. Muḥammad Muḥammad Amīn (Cairo: Dār al-Kutub, 1987–92), 4: 345; Ibn Abī al-Faḍāʾil, *Al-Nahǧ al-sadīd wal-durr al-farīd fīmā baʿd Taʾrīḫ Ibn al-ʿAmīd*, in *Histoire des sultans Mamlouks*, ed. and trans. Edgar Blochet (Paris, 1932) 3: 106–107. See also Broadbridge, *Kingship and Ideology*, 131.

22 Rašīd al-Dīn, *Rashiduddin Fazlullah's Jamiʿu't-tawarikh. Compendium of Chronicles: A History of the Mongols*, trans. Wheeler Thackston, (Cambridge, MA: Harvard University, The Department of Near Eastern Languages and Civilizations 1998–1999), 3: 649–651. See Ciocîltan, *The Mongols and the Black Sea*, 168–169. This clash was perhaps incidental. It occurred at a time when the Ilkhan was about to leave his winter quarters in Arran, while the Khan was coming to the north of the same area for summer.

23 Rašīd al-Dīn, *Compendium of Chronicles*, 3: 654.

and on the Sultan's coins. As for the mission of the Khan's envoys, it was to reassert the old Jöchid rights on Arran and Azerbaijan.[24] The three rulers had aggressive imperial discourses and ambitions. Exchanging embassies did not necessarily mean that they sought peace, but rather that they provoked each other. The Ilkhanate had tense relations with its neighbours. Ghazan led three campaigns on the Syrian borders during his rule, the region being still a disputed zone between Ilkhanids and Mamluks. With the Jöchids, clashes occurred not only in the area of Derbent but also in Gurjistan where King David, although under the suzerainty of the Ilkhan, tried to ally with the Khan.[25]

After Ghazan died, and despite the "Mongol Peace," Toqta planned to attack the Ilkhanate. The only way to really break the power of his Mongol neighbour was to open several military fronts at the same time and to attack the Ilkhanate not only from north Caucasus but also on his Syrian border. The Mamluks were, therefore, crucial allies for the Jöchids. But when Toqta sent his envoys to al-Nāṣir Muḥammad, the Sultan refused to comply arguing that "Allāh had called Ghāzān to him and that his brother Kharbandā [Öljeitü] was already asking for peace."[26] At this time, the emirs Sayf al-Dīn Salār and Baybars al-Jāshnakīr who were ruling in the name of al-Nāṣir Muḥammad dictated the political orientation of the Sultanate. For the Mamluk emirs economic cooperation with the Ilkhan had huge financial advantages and allowed them to secure the transit of young slave-warriors via Tabriz. On the Ilkhanid side, the foreign policy has changed with the enthronement of Öljeitü. Thus, as early as 1305 an embassy came to inform the Sultan that the Ilkhan allowed Mamluk merchants into Persia and offered that both sides release and exchange war captives. In other words, a truce was proclaimed.[27] This political overture was in line with the switch of the trade route:

24 Vaṣṣāf, *Taʾrīḫ-i Vaṣṣāf al-Ḥażrat*, (Bombay, 1269 H./1853; repr. Tehran, 1338 H./1959–1960), 397; Mīrkhwānd, *Rawḍat al-Ṣafāʾ fī sīrat al-anbiyāʾ wal-mulūk wal-ḫulafāʾ*, ed. Jamšīd Kiyānfar (Tehran: Intišārāt-i Asāṭīr, 2001/2002), 8: 4243–4244 quoted in John A. Boyle, "*Dynastic and Political History of the Il-Khans,*" in *The Cambridge History of Iran, Vol. 5: The Saljuq and Mongol Periods, ed. John A. Boyle,* (Cambridge: The University Press, 1968) 392–393. Judith Kolbas, *The Mongols in Iran: Chingiz Khan to Uljaytu, 1220–1309*, (London-New York: Routledge, 2006), 354–355, apparently based on Boyle with some misreading, does not give her sources. For a complete picture and additional sources on the meeting between the Mamluk envoys and the Ilkhan, see Broadbridge, *Kingship and Ideology*, 87–90.

25 Kolbas, *The Mongols in Iran*, 338–339, 355.

26 Quoted from al-Maqrīzī, *al-Sulūk* in Ciocîltan, *The Mongols and the Black Sea*, 170. The main sources on this embassy are: al-Nuwayrī, *Nihāyat al-Arab*, 32: 86; Baybars al-Dawādār, *Zubdat al-fikra*, 381; idem, *Kitāb al-Tuḥfat al-mulūkīya fī-l-dawlat al-turkīya* (638–711), ed. ʿAbd al-Ḥamīd Ṣāliḥ Ḥamadān (Cairo: Dār al-Miṣriyya al-Lubnāniyya, 1987),176; Ibn al-Dawādārī, *Kanz al-Durar*, 9: 127–128, 130; Ibn Abī al-Faḍāʾil, *al-Nahǧ*, 3: 117; see also Spuler, *Die Goldene Horde*, 81–82; Zakirov, *Diplomatičeskie otnošenija*, 70; Broadbridge, *Kingship and Ideology*, 95.

27 Qāshānī, *Tārīkh-i Ūljāytū*, 42, 48. Vaṣṣāf, *Taʾrīḫ-i Vaṣṣāf*, 472; Ibn Abī al-Faḍāʾil, *al-Nahǧ*, 3: 104–107.

during the first years of Öljeitü's reign, northern Anatolia and sites in connection with the Black Sea commercial circuits became more active than stations on the southern route across Jazira, such as Mardin and Mosul.[28] This indicated a substantial increase in the contacts between locals and merchants from the Crimea, north-east Anatolia and the Caucasus. To enhance the fluidity of trade flows, like Ghazan had done, Öljeitü practiced very low taxation on commercial exchanges within the Ilkhanate. *Ortaq* (licensed traders working for the Ilkhan and the elite) were not taxed and foreign merchants – like the Venetians – benefited from huge advantages as well. Trade, at local and international levels, made vital contributions to the Ilkhanid finances.[29] But for the Ilkhanate, this meant to live with a strong dependency on its surrounding world, including its archenemies, the Mamluks and the Jöchids. In 1306/07, Khan Toqta sent the same message to al-Nāṣir Muḥammad who again refused to support any military operation against the Ilkhan.[30] A few weeks after, the Khan ordered to expel the Genoese from the Golden Horde and to confiscate their goods. Caffa was besieged for eight months and the Genoese had to abandon their fortified settlement in May 1308.[31] Since the formation of the Golden Horde, the Jöchids had blocked the activities of the Italian merchants only once.[32] The Khans' policies combined state control (treaties, currency issue, taxes, roads supervision) and liberal exchange (fluidity in partnership, alliances based on common interest and not on ethnic or religious affiliation, low taxation regime). They did not interrupt the exchanges except in the case of warlike situation. Only very serious reasons could have led to Khan Toqta's decision. Historians, who often presented the Khan's actions as brutal and unexpected, struggled to provide convincing in-

28 This change and the decline of the Jazira route may be a consequence of the last campaign led by Ghazan in Syria. Minting was usually done in the main cities on trade routes to facilitate the exchanges; see Kolbas, *The Mongols in Iran*, 366, on the basis of numismatic evidence.

29 Kolbas, *The Mongols in Iran*, 367–368. She mentions that customs dues were paid only by foreign merchants. Yet some foreign traders were also granted protected status, such as the Venetians, for instance, and most likely the Genoese. See the text of the Ilkhanid ruler Abū Saʿīd to the Venetians (dated 1320, but showing the significant state of Venetian trade after years of experience within the Ilkhanate): Louis de Mas-Latrie, "Privilège commercial accordé en 1320 à la République de Venise par un roi de Perse, faussement attribué à un roi de Tunis," *Bibliothèque de l'école des Chartes* 31 (1870): 95–102.

30 Baybars al-Dawādār, *Kitāb al-Tuḥfat al-mulūkīya*, 180; *Zubdat al-fikra*, 388; al-ʿAynī, *ʿIqd al-jumān*, 4: 421–22; see also Broadbridge, *Kingship and Ideology*, 95, 131.

31 Ciocîltan, *The Mongols and the Black Sea*, 164, quoting Vincenzo Promis, "Continuazione della Cronaca di Jacopo da Varagine dal 1297 al 1332," *Atti della societa' ligure di storia patria* 10 (1874): 500–501.

32 At the end of the thirteenth century, when Nogay fought with the Genoese, it had nothing to do with the Mamluks; tax issues and political struggles within the Horde were at stake: Ciocîltan, *The Mongols and the Black Sea*, 161–162; Baybars al-Dawādār, *Zubdat al-fikra*, 260, 285–286, 327; Ibn Abī al-Faḍāʾil, *al-Nahǧ*, 2: 629–631.

terpretations of what happened.[33] Let us go back to the explanations given in the sources of the time.

The Reasons for the First Genoese-Mamluk-Jöchid Crisis. According to both Mamluk and Christian sources, Toqta took his revenge because the Genoese "stole" Tatar and Qipchaq children to sell them on the slave markets.[34] The Franciscans argued further that the Genoese were acting too independently and were not respectful of the imperial laws.[35] Indeed, kidnapping was illegal and merchants had to pay taxes on selling and purchasing. Yet, these taxes were very low and we know cases of pure robbery involving Genoese, or others, that were not punished by the sword.[36] Finally, we might ask if Khan Toqta was against the slave trade or against selling local children – why was this happening in 1307 and not before? We should remember that in 1304 he had sent two-hundred slave-girls and four-hundred mamluks to the Sultan. Therefore, selling local children cannot be considered the reason for the tension between the Genoese and the Golden Horde.[37] Some historians argued that Khan Toqta was a "shamanist" and not a Muslim – which would explain the misunderstandings and disagreements he had with the Mamluk Sultan.[38] We may counter-argue that the Mamluks had fine diplomatic relations with Khan Möngke-Temür (1267–1280) who was not Muslim. Besides, depending on the sources, Toqta was a sky-worshipper, a Christian baptized by the Franciscans under the name of Iohannes and buried in a Franciscan monastery near Saray, and a Muslim, bearing the name of Ghiyāṯ al-Dīn, as can be seen on series of coins that were minted under his name in Saray and Ukek.[39] Thus, it is hard to believe that religion had anything to do with the crisis between the Khan and the merchants. Obviously, the Genoese paid for al-

33 Ciocîltan offers an overview of the historiography and its limits: *The Mongols and the Black Sea*, 163–173, and esp.166, note 93.

34 See for instance Nicola Di Cosmo, "Mongols and Merchants on the Black Sea Frontier in the Thirteenth and Fourteenth Centuries: Convergences and Conflicts," in *Mongols, Turks and Others: Eurasian Nomads and the Sedentary World*, ed. Reuven Amitai and Michal Biran (Leiden and Boston: Brill, 2005), 412–413.

35 Girolamo Golubovich, *Biblioteca bio-bibliografica della terra santa dell'oriente francescano* (Florence: Collegio di S. Bonaventura, 1919) 3: 173–174; Promis, "Continuazione della Cronaca," 500–501.

36 In the Golden Horde, at that period, the commercium/commerclum tax was only 3% of the price of the sold goods. I do not know if there existed a special tax on the purchase of slaves, but I assume that the commerclum applied to slave trade as well.

37 See the remarks by Ciocîltan, *The Mongols and the Black Sea*, 165–167.

38 Especially Zakirov, *Diplomatičeskie otnošenija*, 72. See also Spuler, *Die Goldene Horde*, 216; Broadbridge, *Kingship and Ideology*, 131; Ciocîltan, *The Mongols and the Black Sea*, 172.

39 Ibn Abī al-Faḍā'il called him a Muslim (*al-Nahǧ*, 3: 101). The Franciscans claimed that they converted Khan Toqta and other members of the Tatar elite: Golubovich, *Biblioteca bio-bibliografica*, 3: 182.

Nāṣir Muḥammad's refusal to organize a joint attack against the Ilkhanids. The timing of the Khan's decision is a revealing indication: right after the Sultan's third refusal, Toqta expelled the Genoese (November 1307).[40] The Genoese were not only key intermediaries between the Sultanate and the Golden Horde, they were also responsible of the most strategic slave-market places, at Caffa especially. In the wake of his order to expulse the Genoese, the Khan stopped all diplomatic exchanges with the Mamluks, despite the conciliation attempt of the Sultan who wrote to Toqta in September-October 1308, that having heard of military clashes between Ilkhanids and Jöchids, he took the decision to prepare a military contingent, but since the news came that the fight had stopped, he cancelled the whole operation.[41]

The Consequences of the Crisis. Mamluks and Jöchids had no common border, so they could not fight on the battlefield but they could fight on the market arena. Striking the slave merchants was striking the Sultanate. For the first time, the Jöchids tried to stop the slave trade; but the trade could not be stopped because there were other slave traders besides the Genoese (Venetians, Greeks and local merchants, such as Alans and Turkmens) and alternative networks.[42] As the Byzantine historian Nicophorus Gregoras (*c.* 1292–*c.* 1360) noticed: every year one or two ships would cross the Black Sea to bring slave-warriors to serve in the Mamluk army and nothing could be done to end this trade which had become so significant.[43] Even the most powerful empires cannot control their surrounding world. In this specific case, the use of embargo had two effects. On the one hand, the Genoese and Venetians merchants living in the Golden Horde sought for a new legal and institutional framework that would provide better protection to their business.[44] On another hand, the Mamluks looked for alternative solutions to secure the supply of military-slaves, which meant to cooperate further with the Ilkhanids, masters of the trade route via Tabriz. Yet, even if there was a short detente, the war had not ended; the Ilkhanids were still the enemies of the

40 This is also suggested in Ciocîltan, *The Mongols and the Black Sea*, 171.

41 Baybars al-Dawādār, *Zubdat al-fikra*, 381–382; Ciocîltan, *The Mongols and the Black Sea*, 171–173.

42 As far as I know, there is no indication in the sources that the slave trade from the Qipchaq steppes went down at that time.

43 Reuven Amitai, "Diplomacy and The Slave Trade in The Eastern Mediterranean: A Re-examination of The Mamluk-Byzantine-Genoese Triangle in The Late Thirteenth Century in Light of The Existing Early Correspondance," *Oriente Moderno* 88/1 (2008): 364–366; Nicephorus Gregoras, *Nicephori Gregorae Byzantina historia graece et latine*, ed. L. Schopen (Bonn: E. Weber, 1829), 1: 101–102.

44 On this new legal and institutional framework, see Marie Favereau, "Convention constitutive. L'approche historique des contrats: le cas des Vénitiens et de la Horde d'Or," in *Dictionnaire des conventions*, ed. Ph. Batifoulier *et alii* (Villeneuve d'Ascq: Presses Universitaires du Septentrion, 2016), 82–87.

Sultanate, welcoming Mamluk rebels and conducting lateral diplomacy with European kings. In 1310/11, al-Nāṣir Muḥammad sent his envoys to the Khan to announce his third enthronement – actually the beginning of his personal and autonomous rule. Toqta sent his envoys back to Cairo with the Mamluk messengers to congratulate the Sultan.[45] At approximately the same period, Öljeitü was gathering an army to invade Syria.[46] The Mamluks and the Jöchids still needed to collaborate. In 1311/1312, before he died, Khan Toqta exchanged eighty mamluks, twenty slave-girls, and furs for a Mamluk gift of one thousand suits of armour including helmets, the same number of horse armour, textiles, belts and headgear.[47]

How Özbek and al-Malik al-Nāṣir Muḥammad b. Qalāwūn Divorced (1312–41)[48]

Khan Özbek's first embassy arrived in Cairo in March-April 1314.[49] His letter informed the Sultan of his throne accession and conversion to Islam. Al-Nāṣir Muḥammad sent his congratulations of his accession to the throne and a long list of gifts. In December 1315, he made a special request to the Khan's envoys: he asked for a Jöchid bride.[50] After three years of negotiations, Ṭulunbāy Khatun, a Khan's close relative, was ready to be married to the Sultan.[51] To pay the dowry and the wedding parties, the Khan forced the Mamluk ambassadors to borrow 27,000 dinars from his merchants. Ṭulunbāy Khatun and her huge retinue (up to three thousand people depending on the sources) departed from the lower Volga

45 Baybars al-Dawādār, *Kitāb al-Tuḥfat al-mulūkīya*, 220.

46 Broadbridge, *Kingship and Ideology*, 96; Reuven Amitai, "Resolution of the Mamluk-Mongol War," in *Mongols, Turks and Others: Eurasian Nomads and the Sedentary World*, ed. Reuven Amitai and Michal Biran (Leiden and Boston: Brill, 2005), 362–64.

47 Behrens-Abouseif, *Practising Diplomacy*, 64–65 quoting Ibn al-Dawādārī, *Kanz al-durar*, 9: 280–281. There is some confusion in this source between the last convoy of Toqta and the first of Özbek. On the last embassy sent by Khan Toqta, see also Nuwayrī, *Nihāyat al-Arab*, 32: 173–174, 180.

48 On the relationship between Khan Özbek and al-Nāṣir Muḥammad, see Broadbridge, *Kingship and Ideology*, 131–137. I also learnt a lot from Evgeniya Yudkevich, *Diplomatic Relations and Commerce between the Mamluk Sultanate and the Golden Horde during the Third Reign of Sultan al-Nāṣir Muḥammad b. Qalāwūn (709/1310–741/1341)*, Master Thesis (Faculty of Humanities, The Hebrew University of Jerusalem, December 2011), 70 pages. The academic literature on Özbek Khan is extensive and cannot be listed here; in English the reference work is DeWeese, *Islamization*, see esp. 67–158.

49 Nuwayrī, *Nihāyat al-Arab* (Cairo, 1985–1998), 27: 375; on this first embassy, see also Ibn Abī all-Faḍā'il, *al-Nahğ*, 3: 238.

50 Nuwayrī, *Nihāyat al-Arab*, 32: 224–225, 323.

51 She was either the daughter or the sister or the niece of the Khan. See the remarks in Broadbridge, *Kingship and Ideology*, 132 n. 142.

in 1319 and arrived in Egypt in early May 1320.[52] Among the persons of the princess escort, we should mention the sheikh Nuʿman Khwarazmī, who was the Khan's chief physician, the qadi of Saray (a religious precaution for the establishment of the wedding contract), the Genoese merchant Segurano Salvaygo, nicknamed Sakrān (a wealthy go-between, expert in slave trade) and Qūṣūn who was then a young ambitious merchant from the Qipchaq steppes.[53] The Sultan received Ṭulunbāy Khatun like a queen – according to the emphatic description of the Mamluk sources – and a marriage contract was established at once (on the 16th of May) for a dowry of 30,000 dinars.[54] This was not an extravagant bride-price if we consider that a year later, the Sultan sent a gift package that was worth 40,000 dinars to "thank" the Ilkhanid ruler Abū Saʿīd for his series of gifts equivalent to 25,000 dinars.[55] For Özbek Khan, this wedding alliance was a re-assessment of the Mamluk-Jöchid alliance, and it implied commercial exchange and military action against the Ilkhanids. Not surprisingly, as early as 1320/1321 the Khan asked al-Nāṣir Muḥammad to join him on the battlefield against their common enemy. Yet, the Sultan refused to do as told and even attempted to inform the Ilkhan of Özbek's plan. At that time, peace negotiations between the Mamluks and the Ilkhanids had started and, for al-Nāṣir Muḥammad, it was worth a diplomatic clash with the Khan. In 1322, when the Mamluk messenger carrying this negative answer went back from the Golden Horde, he complained of Özbek's treatment. The Khan received him only once. During the meeting, he did not inquire of al-Nāṣir Muḥammad's health. Besides, the Sultan's envoy was prevented from purchasing slaves and slave-girls.[56]

The Khan had two major reasons to complain as it was expressed in his messages to the Sultan: first, al-Nāṣir Muḥammad had sent no army to Iraq while he, Özbek, had faced the enemy for a month and, so far, has received no news of any advance from the Mamluk side. Second, the sheikh Nuʿman, who had very high status in the Golden Horde, was ill-treated by the Sultan and his entourage. The sheikh wished to visit Jerusalem and Hebron (al-Khalīl) and to build in

52 Nuwayrī, *Nihāyat al-Arab* , 32: 324–325.

53 On the Sufi sheikh and physician ʿAlāʾ al-Dīn al-Nuʿman al-Khwārazmī al-Ḥanafī, see DeWeese, *Islamization,* 125–127. On Segurano Salvaygo, see Benjamin Z. Kedar, "Segurano-Sakrān Salvaygo: un mercante Genovese al servizio dei Sultani Mamalucchi, c. 1303–1322," in *Fatti e idée di storia economica nei secoli XII–XX. Studi dedicati a Franco Borlandi* (Bologna: Il Mulino, 1976) [Reprinted in B.Z. Kedar, *The Franks in the Levant, 11th to 14th Centuries* (Aldershot: Ashgate, 1993) Art. XXI]; on the emir Qūṣūn al-Nāṣiri, see Jo Van Steenbergen, "The Amir Qawṣūn, Statesman or Courtier? (720–741 AH/1320–1341 AD)," in *Egypt and Syria in the Fatimid, Ayyubid and Mamluk Eras,* III (Orientalia Lovaniensia Analecta 102), ed. Urbain Vermeulen and Jo Van Steenbergen (Leuven: Peeters, 2001), 449–466.

54 Nuwayrī, *Nihāyat al-Arab,* 32: 325; Broadbridge, *Kingship and Ideology,* 133.

55 Behrens-Abouseif, *Practising Diplomacy,* 67.

56 Nuwayrī, *Nihāyat al-Arab* (Cairo, 1985–1998), 33: 28–29; Broadbridge, *Kingship and Ideology,* 134–135.

Jerusalem a pious endowment, but the Sultan had not let him to do so. The Khan was particularly displeased with this issue, as he had provided the sheikh with the necessary funds. It meant no respect for someone close to him and considered as a holy figure in the Golden Horde.[57] Moreover, the Khans had always allowed the Sultans, and people from their entourage, to patronize the construction of religious buildings in the Crimea. For instance, in 1287 Qalāwūn ordered his envoys to carry 2000 dinars in goods for a mosque being built in Solkhat (Qrim). He was allowed to send his own workers with their material and paint and to have his name and titles carved on the mosque.[58] Between Sultans of the same standing, reciprocity in the exchanges was expected. Al-Nāṣir Muḥammad acted as if he was despising the Khan or as if they did not have the same status. To retaliate, the Khan killed Segurano Salvaygo, a rich Genoese merchant who was close to the Sultan and used to purchase slaves in the Golden Horde. When al-Nāṣir Muḥammad complained, the Khan said that this merchant was killed by one of the kings of al-Jazā'ir (the islands); openly lying to the Sultan's envoys.[59] A few years after, al-Nāṣir Muḥammad took his revenge by making a fool of the Khan's messengers. In 1327–1328, al-Nāṣir Muḥammad had divorced Ṭulunbāy Khatun and married her to one of his Mamluk commanders.[60] When the Khan complained that she should be sent back to the Golden Horde, the Sultan answered the messengers she had died and asked a judge to produce the legal proof for it.[61]

The inter-regional context has evolved since the time of Baybars and Berke. Al-Nāṣir Muḥammad was in a strong position to negotiate with the Khan: the Bosphorus route was not the sole access to the Sultanate for the slave traders; the Anatolian and the Syrian land routes were then passable.[62] As Reuven Amitai has pointed out, in 1320 "a series of negotiations commenced which resulted some three years later in the resolution of the 60 plus year war between the Mamluk

---

57 Ibid., 135. DeWeese, *Islamization*, 128–129.

58 Ibn al-Furāt, *Ta'rīḫ Ibn al-Furāt*, ed. Qusṭanṭīn Zurayq (Beirut: al-Maṭbaʿa al-Amīrkānīya, 1939) 8: 51 quoted in Behrens-Abouseif, *Practising Diplomacy*, 64 (the place where the mosque was to be built was not Saray, but Solkhat, the local capital of the Jöchids, called also Qrim in the Arabic sources, today Staryj Krym). There were several Mamluk mosques in Solkhat and Ibn Baṭṭūṭa seemed to describe another one. As far as I know the only "Mamluk mosque" in the Crimea preserved until today is the so-called "Özbek mosque" founded in 1314 in Solkhat which shows Mamluk features on its portal: Osman Akchokrakly, "Starokrymskie i otuzskie nadpisi XIII–XIV vv.", *Izvestija Tavricheskovo Obshchestva Istorii Arkheologii i E'tnografii*, 1/58, (1927) 16.

59 Kedar, " Segurano-Sakrān Salvaygo," 86. Salvaygo's activities as a merchant and a diplomat are also discussed in detail in Evgeniya Yudkevich, *Diplomatic Relations* (chapter 3), 45–56.

60 Al-Ṣafadī, *Aʿyān al-ʿAṣr wa-aʿwān al-naṣr*, ed. ʿAlī Abū Zayd, (Beirut and Damascus: Dār al-Fikr al-Muʿāṣir, 1998), 1: 482.

61 Broadbridge, *Kingship and Ideology*, 136.

62 In 1321, the Mamluk troops occupied Ayas (Laiazzo) in Cilician Armenia, one of the greatest commercial hubs of the area.

Sultanate of Egypt and Syria and the Ilkhanid kingdom." The peace treaty between the Sultan and the Ilkhan concerned not only the end of military violence but also trading between both empires: "The roads between the two kingdoms would be opened and merchants would travel without restriction."[63] Besides, we see a clear evolution in the status of the Genoese between the reigns of Toqta and Özbek. Under Toqta, the clash with the Mamluks led to a massive expulsion of the Genoese merchants. The entire community living in the Golden Horde was held responsible for it. Under Özbek, the Genoese, as an intermediary group between the Jöchids and the Mamluks, could not be held responsible anymore for any diplomatic struggles with the Mamluks. In fact, when Özbek arrived on the throne, the Khan agreed on the reconstruction of Caffa, which started in 1316 on the basis of a new agreement:

> Anno domini MCCCXVI redificata fuit civitas Caffa per dominum Antoniun gallum et dominum Nicolaum de pagana sindicos comunis Janue per gratiam sibi concessam per Usbech impratorem tartarorum.[64]

The detailed content of this agreement was not preserved, but for the same period we can rely on the contract concluded between Özbek Khan and the Venetians. Dated in 1333, it covered the crucial questions of the liability (collective and individual) and protected status of the trading community.[65] It is highly probable that the same rights were granted to the Genoese and their most important settlement in Caffa.[66] If Segurano Salvaygo paid for the diplomatic clash between the Khan and the Sultan, it was not because he was Genoese. Indeed, this Italian community was left in peace and the Khan did not confiscate their goods. Neither was it for the divorce with Ṭulunbāy Khatun, that Özbek learnt later, nor because of the military defection of the Mamluks against the Ilkhanids. Segurano Salvaygo, a close friend of the Sultan, paid with his life for the sheikh Nuʿman's ill-treatment. The Sultan has scorned the image of the Khan as a powerful Islamic ruler, influential beyond the Golden Horde. The Khan had to reply, for his internal and external legitimacy was at stake. Like the messages the diplomatic gifts suggested, actions towards rulers' representatives (ambassadors, close relations) required appropriate reactions. It was a matter of reputation for the

63 Amitai, "Resolution of the Mamluk-Mongol War", 359, 368. On the process of the softening of hostilities and "organized negotiations" between the Mamluks and the Ilkhanids, see especially pages 366 *sqq*. See also Broadbridge, *Kingship and Ideology*, 101–114.

64 Promis, "Continuazione della Cronaca," 500–501, quoted in Ciocîltan, *The Mongols and the Black Sea*, 178 n.141.

65 Favereau, "Venecianskie istochniki."

66 Except the chronicles, the oldest agreements passed between the Genoese and the Golden Horde that were preserved are from the 1380s, but fortunately they included older contracts. On the Black Sea policies implemented by Özbek, see Ciocîltan, *The Mongols and the Black Sea*, 173–199.

rulers of the time. Yet, Özbek Khan and al-Nāṣir Muḥammad continued to exchange embassies and gifts even during this "cold war." The main source of young mamluks was still the core territory of the Golden Horde. The interdependence between both empires was too strong to be stopped and could not even be limited on the decision of their rulers.

Conclusive Remarks: On the Meaning of "Peace"

In this paper, I tried to identify the reasons why the Mamluks and the Jöchids, though officially allied, struggled at times. I focused on three historical episodes when tension and exchange intermingled. By way of conclusion I raise the following questions which may open some paths for further research:

1. How does an emperor address an emperor? By definition imperial discourse is hegemonic as an empire has no alter ego. How does an emperor address an equal ruler without compromising his own supposedly overarching position? How to express competition without jeopardizing a vital alliance with a trade partner? Internal and external legitimacies are always intertwined, especially in imperial context. The evolving relationship between the Jöchids and the Mamluks is a case in point. Both the Sultanate and the Golden Horde were empires, which had, yet, to acknowledge each other's sovereignty. The Mamluk sources show how secretaries of the *dīwān al-inshā'* learnt to master the subtle art of diplomacy. For that reason, the *kuttāb* needed to be aware as much as possible of the political situations of the Sultanate's neighbors, allies and enemies. Despite the angelic description of their first diplomatic exchange in the Mamluk sources, we saw that Baybars and Berke struggled over the question of what was Islamic legitimate leadership and provided antagonistic answers. Yet, interestingly, the rulers' competition for status did not prevent military and mercantile collaborations.[67]

2. What was the Mongol Peace? It is necessary to rethink this old paradigm. Scholarship has established that the Mongol Peace was a continent-scale phenomenon. But what did "peace" mean for the Mongols?[68] I argue that they created a new form of economic entente which allowed small-scale military conflicts and

67 While there is significant scholarship on the ideological competition between Mamluks and Mongols (especially, Broadbridge, *Kingship and Ideology*), the debate over Islam between Mamluks and Jöchids is often obscured by the better-known disputes among Mamluks, Ilkhanids, Turkmen, Timurids and Ottomans.

68 This question can be linked to the debate on the meaning of the term *il* or *el* (peace, people, subservient). See, for instance, Reuven Amitai-Preiss, "Evidence for the early use of the title *il-khan* among the Mongols," *Journal of the Royal Asiatic Society*, 3rd series, 1/3 (1991): 353–362; Amitai-Preiss, *Mongols and Mamluks*, 13–15.

internal competition. To accept this "peace" meant to submit to a new economic order, which was supple, mobile and organized. This brief article shows that the Mongol Peace did not only link up the Chinggisid Khanates to the Italian Republics and the Byzantine Empire but also to the Mamluk Sultanate.

3. Did Mongol and Mamluk politics change economics in their own time? Politics has the power to change economics, yet governments and rulers' decisions are not enough to implement policies and change old practices on the ground. How to control (and predict) the multiple effects of a new policy? "The unintended consequences of intentional behaviors" is an old debate in the social sciences, extensively studied since Karl Popper's groundbreaking work. This conceptual framework shed new light on the episodes of crisis between the Mamluk Sultanate and the Golden Horde. For instance, the "institutionalization" of the military slave market through treaties and diplomatic negotiations changed the scale for human trafficking to a point that the main political actors were not even able to reduce it. Mongol and Mamluk political elites intentionally implemented new policies and reforms. Yet the use of embargo, the manipulation of money, credit and tax, the temporary expulsion of traders, as well as royal weddings, had unintended effects such as improving the legal status of the foreign merchants and increasing dramatically market competition among Ilkhanids, Jöchids, Mamluks and others.

Bibliography

Primary Sources

al-ʿAynī, Badr al-Dīn. *ʿIqd al-jumān fī tawārīḫ ahl al-zamān.* Ed. Muḥammad Muḥammad Amīn Cairo: Dār al-Kutub, 1987–92.

Baybars al-Dawādār. *Zubdat al-fikra fī taʾrīḫ al-ḥijra.* Ed. D.S. Richards. Beirut and Berlin: Orient-Institut der DMG and Das Arabische Buch, 1998.

Baybars al-Dawādār. *Kitāb al-Tuḥfat al-mulūkīya fīʾl-dawlat al-turkīya* (638–711). Ed. ʿAbd al-Ḥamīd Ṣāliḥ Ḥamadān. Cairo: Dār al-Miṣrīya al-Lubnānīya, 1987.

Golubovich, Girolamo. *Biblioteca bio-bibliografica della terra santa dell'oriente francescano.* Florence: Collegio di S. Bonaventura, 1919.

Ibn ʿAbd al-Ẓāhir. *Al-Rawḍ al-zāhir fī sīrat al-malik al-Ẓāhir.* Ed. ʿAbd al-ʿAzīz al-Ḫuwayṭir. Al-Riyāḍ, 1976.

Ibn Abī al-Faḍāʾil. *Al-Nahǧ al-sadīd wal-durr al-farīd fīmā baʿd Taʾrīḫ Ibn al-ʿAmīd.* In *Histoire des sultans Mamlouks.* Ed. and trans. Edgar Blochet. Paris, 1932.

Ibn al-Dawādārī. *Kanz al-durar wa-jāmiʿ al-ġurar.* Ed. Hans Robert Roemer. Cairo and Wiesbaden: al-Maʿhad al-Almānī lil-Āthār bil-Qāhira and Otto Harrassowitz, 1960. Vol. 9.

Ibn Faḍl Allāh al-ʿUmarī. *Al-Taʿrīf fī al-muṣṭalaḥ al-šarīf.* Cairo, 1312/1894–95.

Ibn al-Furāt, *Taʾrīḫ Ibn al-Furāt*. Ed. Qusṭanṭīn Zuray. Beirut: al-Maṭbaʿa al-Amīrkānīya, 1939. Vol. 8.

Mīrkhwānd. *Rawḍat al-Ṣafāʾ fī sīrat al-anbiyāʾ wal-mulūk wal-ḫulafāʾ*. Ed. Jamšīd Kiyānfar. Tehran: Intišārāt-i Asāṭīr, 2001/2002.

Nicephorus Gregoras. *Nicephori Gregorae Byzantina historia graece et latine*. Ed. L. Schopen. Bonn: E. Weber, 1829.

al-Nuwayrī. *Nihāyat al-Arab fī funūn al-arab*. Cairo, 1985–1998.

al-Qalqašandī. *Ṣubḥ al-aʿšā fī ṣināʿat al-inšāʾ*. Cairo, 1963–1972.

Qāshānī. *Tārīkh-i Ūljāytū Sulṭān*. Ed. Mahīn Hambalī. Tehran: Bungāh-i Tarǧuma va Našr-i Kitāb, 1969.

Rašīd al-Dīn, *Rashiduddin Fazlullah's Jamiʿu't-tawarikh. Compendium of Chronicles: a history of the Mongols*, trans. Wheeler Thackston, (Cambridge, MA: Harvard University, Dept. of Near Eastern Languages and Civilizations, 1998–1999.

al-Ṣafadī, Khalīl b. Aybak. *Aʿyān al-ʿAṣr wa-aʾwān al-naṣr*. Ed. ʿAlī Abū Zayd. Beirut and Damascus: Dār al-Fikr al-Muʿāṣir, 1998.

Vaṣṣāf. *Taʾrīḫ-i Vaṣṣāf al-Ḥażrat*. Bombay, 1269 H./1853; reprinted Tehran, 1338 H./1959–1960. Partial translation in *Geschichte Wassaf's, Persisch herausgegeben und Deutsch übersetzt von Hammer-Purgstall.* Vienna: Hof- und Staatsdruckerei, 1856.

Secondary Literature

Afsaruddin, Asma. "In Praise of the Caliphs: Re-Creating History from the Manaqib Literature." *International Journal of Middle East Studies*. 31/3 (1999): 329–350.

Amitai, Reuven. "Diplomacy and The Slave Trade in The Eastern Mediterranean: A Re-examination of the Mamluk-Byzantine-Genoese Triangle in the Late Thirteenth Century in Light of the Existing Early Correspondence." *Oriente Moderno*. NS. 87/1 (2008): 349–368.

Amitai, Reuven. "Resolution of the Mamluk-Mongol War." In *Mongols, Turks and Others: Eurasian Nomads and the Sedentary World*. Ed. Reuven Amitai and Michal Biran. Leiden and Boston: Brill, 2005: 359–390.

Amitai-Preiss, Reuven. "Evidence for the early use of the title *il-khan* among the Mongols." *Journal of the Royal Asiatic Society*. 3rd series. 1:3 (1991). 353–362.

Amitai-Preiss, Reuven. *Mongols and Mamluks: The Mamluk-Ilkhanid War 1260–1281*. Cambridge: Cambridge University Press, 1995.

Aubin, Jean. "L'ethnogenèse des Qaraunas." *Turcica*. 1 (1969): 65–94.

Ayalon, David. "The Great Yāsa of Chingiz Khān." Part A, *Studia Islamica* 33 (1971): 97–140; Part B, *Studia Islamica*34 (1971): 151–180; Part C1, *Studia Islamica* 36 (1972) 113–158; Part C2, *Studia Islamica* 38 (1973): 107–156.

Behrens-Abouseif, Doris. *Practising Diplomacy in the Mamluk Sultanate: Gifts and Material Culture in the Medieval Islamic World*. London and New York: I.B. Tauris, 2014.

Biran, Michal. "The Mongol Empire and Inter-civilizational Exchange." *The Cambridge World History*. Ed. Benjamin Z. Kedar and Merry E. Wiesner-Hanks. Cambridge: Cambridge University Press, 2015. 534–558.

Boyle, John A. "Dynastic and Political History of the Il-Khans." In *The Cambridge History of Iran. Volume 5: The Saljuq and Mongol Periods.* Ed. John A. Boyle. Cambridge: The University Press, 1968. 303–421.

Broadbridge, Anne. *Kingship and Ideology in the Islamic and Mongol Worlds.* Cambridge: Cambridge University Press, 2008.

Ciocîltan, Virgil. *The Mongols and the Black Sea Trade in the Thirteenth and Fourteenth Centuries.* Leiden and Boston: Brill, 2012.

DeWeese, Devin. *Islamization and Native Religion in the Golden Horde: Baba Tükles and Conversion to Islam in Historical and Epic Tradition.* University Park, PA: Pennsylvania State University Press, 1994.

Di Cosmo, Nicola. "Mongols and Merchants on the Black Sea Frontier in the Thirteenth and Fourteenth Centuries: Convergences and Conflicts." In *Mongols, Turks and Others: Eurasian Nomads and the Sedentary World.* Ed. Reuven Amitai and Michal Biran. Leiden and Boston: Brill, 2005. 391–424.

Favereau, Marie. "Convention constitutive. L'approche historique des contrats: le cas des Vénitiens et de la Horde d'Or." In *Dictionnaire des conventions.* Ed. Ph. Batifoulier *et alii.* Villeneuve d'Ascq: Presses Universitaires du Septentrion, 2016. 82–87.

Favereau, Marie. "Venecianskie istochniki po istorii Zolotoj Ordy: novye perspektivy izuchenija." *Golden Horde Review/Zolotoordynskoe obozrenie.* 1 (2016): 39–54.

Favereau, Marie. *La Horde d'Or et le sultanat mamelouk. Naissance d'une alliance.* Cairo: Ifao, 2018.

Favereau, Marie. "The Golden Horde and the Mamluks: The Birth of a Diplomatic Set-up (1261–67)." In *Mamluk Cairo, a Crossroad for Embassies.* Ed. Frédéric Bauden and Malika Dekkiche. Leiden-Boston: Brill, 2019.

Hsiao Ch'i-Ch'ing. "*Mid-Yuan Politics.*" In *The Cambridge History of China.* Volume 6: *Alien Regimes and Border States.* Ed. Herbert Franke and Denis Twitchett. Cambridge: Cambridge University Press, 1994. 490–562.

Jackson, Peter. "The Dissolution of the Mongol Empire." *Central Asiatic Journal.* 32 (1978): 186–244.

Jackson, Peter. "World Conquest and Local Accommodation: Threat and Blandishment in Mongol Diplomacy." In *History and Historiography of Post-Mongol Central Asia and the Middle East. Studies in Honour of John E. Woods.* Ed. Judith Pfeiffer and Sholeh Quinn Wiesbaden: Harrassowitz Verlag, 2006. 3–22.

Kedar, Benjamin Z. "Segurano-Sakrān Salvaygo: un mercante Genovese al servizio die Sultani Mamalucchi, c. 1303–1322." In *Fatti e idée di storia economica nei secoli XII–XX. Studi dedicati a Franco Borlandi.* Bologna: Il Mulino, 1976. Reprinted in B.Z. Kedar, *The Franks in the Levant, 11th to 14th Centuries.* Aldershot: Ashgate, 1993.

Kolbas, Judith. *The Mongols in Iran: Chingiz Khan to Uljaytu, 1220–1309.* London-New York: Routledge, 2006.

Mas-Latrie, Louis de. "Privilège commercial accordé en 1320 à la République de Venise par un roi de Perse, faussement attribué à un roi de Tunis." *Bibliothèque de l'école des Chartes.* 31 (1870): 95–102.

Mostaert, Antoine and Francis W. Cleaves, *Les lettres de 1289 et 1305 des Ilhan Arghun et Öljeitu à Philippe le Bel.* Cambridge, MA: Harvard University Press, 1962.

Promis, Vincenzo. "Continuazione della Cronaca di Jacopo da Varagine dal 1297 al 1332," *Atti della societa' ligure di storia patria.* 10 (1874): 493–512.

Spuler, Bertold. *Die Goldene Horde. Die Mongolen in Russland, 1223–1502.* Wiesbaden: Otto Harrassowitz, 1965.

Van Steenbergen, Jo. "The Amir Qawṣūn, Statesman or Courtier? (720–741 AH/1320–1341 AD)." In *Egypt and Syria in the Fatimid, Ayyubid and Mamluk Eras*, III (Orientalia Lovaniensia Analecta 102). Ed. Urbain Vermeulen and Jo Van Steenbergen. Leuven: Peeters, 2001. 449–466.

Yudkevich, Evgeniya. *Diplomatic Relations and Commerce between the Mamluk Sultanate and the Golden Horde during the Third Reign of Sultan al-Nāṣir Muḥammad b. Qalāwūn (709/1310–741/1341).* Master Thesis, Faculty of Humanities, The Hebrew University of Jerusalem, December 2011.

Zakirov, Salikh. *Diplomatičeskie otnošenija Zolotoj Ordy s Egyptom (XIII–XIV vv.).* Moscow: Nauka, 1966.

Michal Biran (The Hebrew University of Jerusalem)

The Mamluks and Mongol Central Asia[1]

Unlike the other Mongol khanates, Mongol Central Asia, usually known as the Chaghadaid Khanate (1260–1370), was rather marginal to the Mamluk Sultanate in terms of politics, economy and culture, at least until Tamerlane's attacks on the latter (1389–1401). Yet the Chaghadaid Khanate did play a certain role in the Sultanate's world, both as another front that could indirectly help the Mamluks during their wars against the Ilkhanate, and as a source for migrants, including both mamluks and scholars – mainly Hanafi lawyers and Sufis – who became part of Mamluk society and intellectual life. These migrating scholars, in turn, provided Mamluk historians with information about Mongol Central Asia, especially regarding religious circles in Transoxania. This information is of negligible scope in comparison to the voluminous Mamluk sources. However, it is of great value for the history of the poorly-documented Chaghadaid Khanate. This paper reviews the political and diplomatic relations of Mongol Central Asia with the Sultanate up to the death of Tamerlane; dedicates a few words to their sparsely documented economic relations, and analyzes their cultural connections, especially in the field of Hanafi law. Finally, it gives a short summary of the aspects in which Mamluk sources shed some light on the Khanate's culture, mainly in the fields of islamization and Islamic culture.

Political and Diplomatic Relations

The Mamluks were of course aware of Chinggis Khan's invasion of Central Asia that initiated the Mongol advance into the Islamic world, and recognized Chaghadai (known as Jaghaday/Jaqaṭāy/Jadāy in the Arabic sources) as one of Chinggis Khan's sons who ruled in Central Asia – from the Oxus to the far ends of

1 This study was supported by the Israel Science Foundation (grant 602/12) and made use of the database prepared with the funding of the European Research Council under the European Union's Seventh Framework Programme (FP/2007–2013)/ERCGrant Agreement no. 312397.

the land of the Turks and the borders of Cathay (Khatā) – and was an expert on the *Yasa*, the law ascribed to Chinggis Khan.[2] Yet they did not show much interest in the Mongol state in Central Asia, naturally giving much more attention to their major rival, the Ilkhanate, and their main ally and source of mamluks, the Golden Horde. Chaghadaid Central Asia became relevant to the Mamluks in the late 1260s, due to the invasion of Ilkhanid Khurasan by the Chaghadaid Khan Baraq (r. 1266–70), an invasion that culminated in the battle of Herat (in present-day Afghanistan) in 1270 between the Chaghadaids and the Ilkhanid army led by Abaqa (r. 1265–82). Abaqa won the day, but his preoccupation in the east cost him on his western front. Being busy in the north and east in 1268–70, chasing a prince who had tried to defect to Baraq's forces, Abaqa did not send troops to aid Antioch, an Ilkhanid vassal state that in 1268 had passed into the hands of the Mamluk Sultan Baybars. For the same reason Abaqa also did not take steps to prevent Baybars's advance against the Crusaders in 1269. Moreover, Abaqa's involvement in Herat, and his awareness of the eastern threat to his lands, probably contributed to his failure to implement a real joint campaign with the Franks against the Mamluks. When the crusade of the future Edward I of England reached Acre in spring 1271, Abaqa sent to his aid merely a small and ineffective force that raided north Syria in October 1270, only to withdraw at the first indications of the Mamluks' approach.[3] This battle, and especially Abaqa's retaliatory campaign against Bukhara in 1273, also resulted in a huge wave of emigration from the city. Some of those refugees found their way into the Sultanate, as will be discussed below.

Soon after Baraq's defeat in Herat, the Ögödeid prince Qaidu (r. 1271–1301) took over Mongol Central Asia and became the Chaghadaids' overlord. It was under Qaidu, probably on the initiative of his then ally and patron, the Khan of the Golden Horde Möngke Temür (r. 1267–80), that the Mamluks established diplomatic contacts with Mongol Central Asia. Although there were rumors that the first contacts with Qaidu began already under Sultan Baybars (r. 1260–77),

2 E.g. Shihāb al-Dīn al-Nuwayrī, *Nihāyat al-arab fī funūn al-adab*, ed. S. ʿA. ʿĀshūr (Cairo: Dār al-kutub al-miṣriyya, 1985), 27: 336–7; Ibn Faḍlallāh al-ʿUmarī, *Das Mongolische Weltreich: Al-ʿUmarī's Darstellung der mongolischen Reiche in seinem Werk Masālik al-abṣār fī mamālik al-amṣār*, ed. and trans. Klaus Lech (Wiesbaden: Harrassowitz, 1968), 36 [hereafter: ʿUmarī/Lech].

3 For the battle of Herat and its relevance to the Mamluks see Michal Biran, "The Battle of Herat (1270): A Case of Inter-Mongol Warfare," in *Warfare in Inner Asia*, ed. Nicola Di Cosmo (Leiden: E.J. Brill, 2002), 175–220; also Reuven Amitai-Preiss, *Mongols and Mamluks: The Mamluk-Ilkhanid War 1260–1281* (Cambridge: Cambridge University Press, 1995), 98–9, 119–20; Reuven Amitai, "Edward of England and Abagha Ilkhan: A Reexamination of a Failed Attempt at Mongol-Frankish Cooperation," in *Tolerance and Intolerance: Social Conflict in the Age of the Crusades* eds. Michael Gervers and James M. Powell (Syracuse, NY: Syracuse University Press, 2001), 75–82 (notes: 160–163).

the first documented Mamluk embassy to Qaidu was sent by Qalāwūn (r. 1279–90) in 1281–2, when he notified his allies of his accession. Qalāwūn's envoys to Qaidu, who, like all future attested Mamluk embassies to Mongol Central Asia, were sent together with emissaries to the Golden Horde, called upon Qaidu to "support his (i.e. Qalāwūn's) friends and oppose his enemies," namely to support the Golden Horde and oppose the Ilkhanate.[4] While rumors about a possible alliance between the Golden Horde, Mamluk Egypt and Mongol Central Asia sometimes haunted Ilkhanid chroniclers,[5] there is no evidence that such an alliance was ever discussed in earnest, let alone implemented. Qaidu sent back emissaries, who again arrived by sea via the Golden Horde, and Mamluk envoys were dispatched again in 1284, but relations seemed to have cooled down afterwards.[6] In the following decades, however, the Mamluks again benefitted from Qaidu's rivalry with the Ilkhans: A month after they finally vanquished the Mamluks at Wādī Khaznadār (December 1299) and conquered Damascus, the Ilkhans were obliged to retreat and return home, apparently in order to deal with the incursion of the troops of the Chaghadaid prince Qutluq Qocha, acting under Qaidu's command. In this case, the Armenian historian Het'um explicitly states that Ghazan's troops retreated because of the advance of Qaidu's army,[7] even though in the *amān* he gave the people of Damascus in 1300 Ghazan claimed that he was at peace with Qaidu and the other Mongol branches.[8] The fact that in 1303 Ghazan did not lead the incursion to Syria personally, not even pursuing the siege of Raḥba, and opting instead to return to Iran, may very well be related to the invasion of Khurasan by Qaidu's son Sarban at that time.[9] Yet while Mamluk

4 Baybars al-Manṣūrī, *Zubdat al-fikra fī taʾrīkh ahl al-hijra*, ed. D.S. Richards (Beirut and Berlin: Orient-Institut der Deutschen Morgenländischen Gesellschaft and "Das Arabische Buch", 1998), 206; Mufaḍḍal b. Abī al-Faḍāʾil, *al-Nahj al-sadīd wa-l-durr al-farīd fī mā baʿda ibn al-ʿamīd (Histoire des sultans mamloukes)*, ed. and trans. E. Blochet (Paris: Firmin Didot, 1919–28), 3: 631–2; Michal Biran, "Chaghadaid Diplomacy and Chancellery Practices: Some Preliminary Remarks," *Oriente Moderno* 88 (2008): 375; on Qaidu see Michal Biran, *Qaidu and the Rise of the Independent Mongol State in Central Asia* (Richmond, Surrey: Curzon Press, 1997).

5 E.g. Abū al-Qāsim Qāshānī, *Taʾrīkh-i Ūljāytū*, ed. M. Hambly (Tehran: Bangah-i tarjumah wa-nashr-i kitāb, 1969), 212.

6 Ibn al-Furāt, *Taʾrīkh al-duwal wa-l-mulūk*, ed. K. Zurayk and N. Izzedin (Beirut: American University Press, 1939), 8: 1; Baybars al-Manṣūrī, *Zubdat al-fikra*, 206, 239; al-Nuwayrī, *Nihāyat al-arab*, 27: 376.

7 Het'um (Hayton/Hetoum), "La Flor des estories de la Terre d'Orient," in *Receuil des historiens des croisades, documents armeniens* (Paris: L'Imprimérie Nationale, 1869–1906), 2: 196; Peter Jackson, "Chaghatayid Dynasty," *Encyclopedia Iranica*, http://www.iranicaonline.org/articles/chaghatayid-dynasty (last accessed 17 July 2016); 45; Biran, *Qaidu*, 62; on the battle of Wādī Khazandār see Reuven Amitai, "Whither the Ilkhanid Army? Ghazan's First Campaign into Syria (1299–1300)," in *Warfare in Inner Asian History (500–1800)*, ed. Nicola Di Cosmo (Leiden-Boston-Köln: Brill, 2002), 221–64.

8 Baybars al-Manṣūrī, *Zubdat al-fikra*, 336.

9 Biran, *Qaidu*, 62.

sources retained bits and pieces of information about Qaidu - including his struggle against Qubilai Khan and his involvement in the affairs of the White Horde at the end of the thirteenth century - they were not even in accord regarding which branch of the Chinggisids he belonged to, sometimes defining him as Tuloid and sometimes (correctly) as Ögödeid.[10] This, too, suggests that the contacts between the two polities were not close and that while they benefitted from each other's acts, there was no actual cooperation between them. The lack of communication is also apparent from the fact that long after Qaidu was dead and his kingdom dissolved, Mamluk historians still defined him and his son Chapar as ruling over Central Asia. According to al-Nuwayrī, Qaidu ruled until 709/1309, eight years after his death, while his son Chapar is described as ruling until 717/1317, long after he had submitted to the Yuan. Chapar was allegedly followed by another son, Alwīn Bughā, unattested elsewhere.[11] This also suggests that the Chaghadaids, who after Qaidu's death took over Mongol Central Asia, were even less known than Qaidu in the Mamluk realm. Indeed, even in 1315 the Mamluks still record an embassy from Qaidu.[12] This mission, probably sent by the Chaghadaids, may have been connected to the attempts of the Chaghadaid Khan Esen Boqa (r. 1310–20) to secure allies to counter the alleged Yuan-Ilkhanid coalition against him.[13] Al-Nuwayrī, writing in the 1320s, clearly states at the end of his short chapter on "the rulers of Transoxania from the seed of Chinggis Khan," that "We received no information about them due to the distance of their country [from our own] and the cutting of the [exchange of] messengers between us and them."[14]

However, Mamluk-Chaghadaid relations improved considerably due to the Islamization of Tarmashirin, who from 1326 was the Chaghadaid viceroy in Ghazna under his various brothers, and later ascended the Chaghadaid throne (r. 1331–34). Tarmashirin, the only Chaghadaid Khan who merited a biography in Mamluk biographical dictionaries,[15] had been on friendly terms with the Mamluk

10 Nuwayrī, *Nihāyat al-arab*, 27: 376; Baybars al- Manṣūrī, *Zubdat al-fikra*, 262, 269, 365.

11 Nuwayrī, *Nihāyat al-arab*, 27: 376; see also Mufaḍḍal, *Histoire*, 631–2; Ibn al-Dawādārī, *Kanz al-durar wa-jāmiʿ al-ghurar*, ed. H.R. Roemer et al. (Cairo: Deutsches Archäologisches Institut Kairo, 1960–94), 9: 207.

12 G. Tizengauzen, *Sbornik materialov, otnosjashchikhsia k istorii Zolotoi Ordy*, (St. Petersburg: Izd. na izhdivenīe grafa S.G. Stroganova, 1884), 1: 270 (citing the British Museum manuscript of *Taʾrīkh al-Ṣafadī*, which he considers equivalent to *al-Wāfī*, fol. 96r. In fact the reference is to a work of another historian known as al-Ṣafadī: al-Ḥasan ibn Abī Muḥammad ʿAbdallāh al-Hāshimī al-ʿAbbāsī al-Ṣafadī, *Nuzhat al-mālik wa-al-mamlūk: fī mukhtaṣar sīrat man waliya Miṣr min al-mulūk* , ed. ʿU.ʿA. Tadmūrī (Sidon: al-Maktabah al-ʿAṣrīyah, 2003), 227.

13 Qāshānī, *Taʾrīkh-i Ūljaytū*, 212–13.

14 Al-Nuwayrī, *Nihāyat al-arab*, 27: 376.

15 Al-Dhahabī, *Taʾrīkh al-islām*, ed.ʿU.ʿA.Tadmurī (Beirut: Dār al-kitāb al-ʿarabī, 1995–2004), 61: 329–30; al-Ṣafadī, *al-Wāfī bi-l-wafayāt*, ed. Helmut Ritter (Beirut: Orient-Institut,2008), 10: 382–3; idem, *Aʿyān al-ʿaṣr wa-aʿwān al-naṣr*, ed. ʿA. b. Abū Zayd (Beirut and Damascus:

Sultan al-Naṣīr Muḥammad b. Qalāwūn (r. 1293–4, 1299–1309, 1310–41), exchanging letters and embassies with him, and was even reported to carry al-Naṣīr's banners (sing. *sanjaq* or *ʿalam*) on his head during his royal procession (*mawkib*), an act that implied submission.[16] Al-ʿUmarī indeed remarks in his chancellery guide that the letters to Tarmashirin were written in the same format as the letters to the Ilkhanate, thereby attesting that such letters existed.[17] Tarmashirin certainly showed interest in al-Nāṣir Muḥammad and his realm, especially the holy cities of Mecca, Medina, Jerusalem and Hebron, when he met Ibn Baṭṭūṭa in 1333, although he was also interested in other polities.[18] Indeed, in a letter Tamerlane sent to the Mamluk Sultan Barqūq in the mid-1390s, he declares that a historical Mamluk-Chaghadaid alliance coalesced during the reign of al-Nāṣir Muḥammad, who allegedly acknowledged the Chaghadaid rights over Iran and their role in hampering Ilkhanid attacks on the Mamluks. According to Tamerlane, letters and embassies were frequently exchanged between the two sides,[19] a statement that seems, however, highly exaggerated. Yet the improved relations with Tarmashirin, led, just like in Qaidu's case, to prolonging his reign, and in some Mamluk sources he remained in power until 738/1337–8 or even 741/1340–1.[20] However, al-ʿUmarī, by far the most knowledgeable Mamluk source on

---

Dār al-fikr, 1998), 2: 105; abridged in Ibn Ḥajar, *al-Durar al-kāmina* (Cairo: Dār al-kutub al-ḥadītha, 1966), 2: 51; al-Maqrīzī, *Kitāb al-suluk li-maʿrifat duwal al-muluk* (Cairo: Maṭbaʿat dār al-kutub, 1934–73), 2: 389. On Tarmashirin, see Michal Biran, "The Chaghadaids and Islam: The Conversion of Tarmashirin Khan (1331–34)," *Journal of the American Oriental Society* 122 (2002): 742–52.

16 Mufaḍḍal, *Histoire*, 1: 389 (in Blochet's introduction); Mufaḍḍal, *Ägypten und Syrien zwischen 1317 und 1341 in der Chronik des Mufaḍḍal b. Abī l-Faḍāʾil*, ed. and trans. S. Kortantamer (Freiburg im Breisgau: Klaus Schwarz, 1973), 63–4 and 90. Blochet explained that the banner(s) were probably a piece of silk embroidered with al-Naṣīr's name and tied around the khan's forehead, and suggested that their use as a sign of submission might have been related to the presence of the Abbasid Caliph in Cairo (*ibid).* Mufaḍḍal's assertion (*Histoire*, 631–2) that Qaidu wore such banners, both of Baybars and of Qalāwūn, is even less plausible. Al-Jazarī, *Taʾrīkh ḥawādith al-zamān wa-anbāʾihā wa-wafayāt al-akābir wa-l-aʿyān min abnāʾihā*, ed. ʿU.ʿA. Tadmūrī (Beirut and Sidon: al-Maṭbaʿa al-baṣariyya, 1998), 3: 751, 851, 922–3; Biran, "Chancellery," 376.

17 Ibn Faḍlallāh al-ʿUmarī, *al-Taʿrīf bi-l-muṣṭalaḥ al-sharīf* (Beirut: Dār al-kutub, 1988), 70.

18 Ibn Baṭṭūṭa, *Voyages d'Ibn Baṭṭūṭa*, ed. and trans. C. Defrémery and B.R. Sanguinetti (Paris: L'Imprimérie Nationale, 1969), 3: 35–6; H.A.R. Gibb, trans., *The Travels of Ibn Baṭṭūṭa* (Cambridge: The Hakluyt Society, 1958–94), 3: 558.

19 ʿAbd al-Ḥusayn Nawāʾī, *Asnād wa-mukātabāt-i taʾrīkhī-i Īrān az Tīmūr tā Shāh Ismāʿīl* (Tehran: Bungāh-i tarjamah wa nashr-i kitāb, 1962), 75–79, as cited in Anne F. Broadbridge, *Kingship and Ideology in the Islamic and Mongol Worlds* (Cambridge: Cambridge University Press, 2008), 179. I was unable to locate in the Mamluk chronicles, which dutifully recorded many foreign embassies, even a single reference to Chaghadaid emissaries, despite the mentions of the exchange of letters.

20 Mufaḍḍal, *Ägypten und Syrien*, 63–4 (738), 90 (741); al-Jazarī, *Ḥawādith al-zamān*, 3: 751 (735), 851 (736), 922–3 (737); al-Shujāʿī, *Taʾrīkh al-malik al-nāṣir Muḥammad b. Qalāwūn al-ṣāliḥī wa-awlādihi*, ed. B. Schäfer (Wiesbaden: Franz Steiner, 1985), 1: 17 (738).

Mongol Central Asia, who provided a rather detailed genealogy of the Chaghadaids, was also aware of the deterioration of Chaghadaid rule after Tarmashirin's reign. Al-ʿUmarī followed the Central Asian upheavals up to the reign of Khan Changshi (r. 1335–7).[21]

The Chaghadaids appear again in the Mamluk sources with the rise of Tamerlane (r. 1370–1405). Then "Chaghatay" is used as a general term related either to Tamerlane himself ("the Lame Chaghatay"),[22] or – more often – to his troops, also referred to as the Tatars or even the Timūriyya.[23] Contemporaneous Mamluk writers were aware of the connection between the Chaghadaid Khanate – or rather, the Chinggisids of Transoxiana – to Tamerlane,[24] but the exact relation was not clear even to a man of Ibn Khaldūn's stature. Ibn Khaldūn, who showed great interest in the conqueror who could prove his theory of nomadic power, and who is famous for his meeting with Tamerlane to which I will return below, tried to collect the materials on the Chaghadaids in the Mamluk sources, though he adds little to al-ʿUmarī's materials.[25] Ibn Khaldūn admits that he is not clear about the relationship between Temür and the Chaghadaids, only that the latter was not one of them, and he appeared in Transoxania after the kingdoms of the descendants of Chinggis Khan had been dissolved.[26] After his meeting with Tamerlane, however, he described him both as an amīr (military commander)

21 ʿUmarī/Lech, 22 (Janghaṣū), who gives no dates for the post-Tarmashirin upheavals; hence al-Qalqashandī, *Ṣubḥ al-aʿshā fī ṣināʿat al-inshāʾ* (Cairo: al-Maṭbaʿa al-amīriyya, 1913–19), 7: 328; Ibn Khaldūn, *Kitāb al-ʿibar* (Beirut: Dār al-kitāb al-lubnānī, 1957), 5: 1128. For the Chaghadaids after Tarmashirin see Michal Biran, "The Mongols in Central Asia from Chinggis Khan's Invasion to the Rise of Temür: The Ögödeid and Chaghadaid Realms," in *The Cambridge History of Inner Asia: The Chinggisid Age*, ed. Nicola Di Cosmo, Allen J. Frank and Peter B. Golden (Cambridge: Cambridge University Press, 2009), 58–60.

22 Ibn ʿArabshāh, *ʿAjāʾib al-maqdūr fī nawāʾib Tīmūr*, text available at http://www.al-mostafa.info/data/arabic/depot/gap.php?file=001405-www.al-mostafa.com.pdf, last accessed 20 July 20, 2016), 22 (*al-Aʿraj al-Jaghatāyī*) [hereafter: Ibn ʿArabshāh/Calcutta]; Ibn ʿArabshāh, *Tamerlane; or Timur the great amir*, tr. J.H. Sanders (London: Luzac, 1936), 33 [hereafter: Ibn ʿArabshāh/Sanders]; see also al-Sakhāwī, *Al-Dawʾ al-lāmiʿ li-ahl al-qarn al-tāsiʿ* (Cairo: Maktabat al-Quds, 1353–5/1934–36), 3: 46, where Chaghatay (Ḥafaṭāy) is described as Tamerlane's *nisba.*

23 E.g. Ibn ʿArabshah/Sanders, 6, 41, 54, 64, 84,140; Ibn Khaldūn, *al-ʿIbar*, 7: 1221.

24 E.g. al-Qalqashandī, *Ṣubḥ*, 7: 328–9; Ibn Khaldūn, *al-ʿIbar*, 5: 1129–1131.

25 Ibn Khaldūn, *al-ʿIbar*, 5: 1127–1129. He is the only Mamluk source I have seen who acknowledged the fact that Qaidu overran the Chaghadaids, though he follows al-ʿUmarī in recording the Chaghadaids as back in power in Baraq's days.

26 Ibn Khaldūn, *al-ʿIbar*, 5: 1129–31. His sources on Tamerlane included "someone he met from the people of China (*ahl al-Ṣīn*)," and the Khwārizmian lawyer Burhān al-Dīn al-Khwārazmī. As he finishes his description of Tamerlane in 1398 with the battles against Toqtamish, this part was written before Ibn Khaldūn himself met Tamerlane. After their meeting, his information was improved, though not necessarily accurate. See Walter J. Fischel, *Ibn Khaldūn and Tamerlane: Their Historic Meeting in Damascus, 1401 A.D. (803 A.H.)* (Berkeley : University of California Press, 1952), 46, and below.

acting in the name of the Chaghadaid Khan, whose mother he married, his only mistake here was that the puppet khan was Ögödeid; or as a paternal cousin of the Chaghadaids acting as a guardian for the khan.[27]

The Mamluks' contacts with Tamerlane were of a completely different scale and importance. Temür's three major invasions of the Middle East in 1386–88, 1392–96 and 1399–1404, culminating from the Mamluk perspective in his 1401 conquest of Damascus, took place during the reigns of the first Circassian sultans, Barqūq (r. 1382–9, 1390–9) and his son Faraj (first r. 1399–1405). Already in 1384–5, when Temür invaded Iran, Barqūq's allies in the east began to ask for his help against the new force. In 1387 Barqūq even sent troops to assist his ally the Qara Qoyunlu against Temür, but before they left Syria, the Timurid troops had already retreated to Samarqand. In the same year, Temür already reached Iraq, threatening the Sultanate's allies, and prompting (vain) Mamluk attempts to create a coalition against him with the Ottomans and the Golden Horde. In 1394 Barqūq offered asylum to the Jalāyirid ruler of Iraq, Aḥmad b. Uways, who fled before Temür, leading an army to al-Bīra on the Euphrates to confront him. Temür, however, withdrew, and Barqūq died before the former resumed his plans to invade Syria.[28] As showed by Anne Broadbridge,[29] Barqūq used Tamerlane's threat to enhance his legitimation, both as a regional leader heading the opposition against Temür and as the Guardian of Islam against the allegedly Muslim infidel. The letters he sent Temür, retained in al-Qalqashandī's chancellery guide, nicely expressed his sense of superiority (e.g. when he addressed Tamerlane saying: "Oh Amīr Temür, how can you claim to be a Muslim while doing such acts [i.e. killing and torturing Muslims]? Let us know according to which Islamic school this is allowed (*ḥalāl*)?").[30] During the recurrent correspondence, Temür also used Chinggisid claims to legitimize his conquest of the Middle East, but as those were mainly based on Ilkhanid precedents, they did not lead to more interest in Chaghadaid history.

Tamerlane's third invasion occurred while the Mamluks were preoccupied with the civil war that erupted after Barqūq's death. The eleven-year-old sultan, Barqūq's son Faraj, set out for Syria to expel the Timurid forces, but a rebellion fomented by a rival faction compelled the prominent amīrs in the force to return

27 Ibn Khaldūn, *al-ʿIbar*, 7: 1197–1199 for Tamerlane's career; see also 7:1219ff. as he recalls Mongolian and Timurid history in his letter to Ṣāḥib al-Maghrib; trans. in Fischel, 46.

28 Amalia Levanoni, "The Mamlūks in Egypt and Syria: the Turkish Mamlūk Sultanate (648–784/1250–1382) and the Circassian Mamlūk Sultanate (784–923/1382–1517)," in *The New Cambridge History of Islam*. Vol. 2, ed. Maribel Fierro (Cambridge: Cambridge University Press, 2010), 263–4.

29 Broadbridge, *Kingship and Ideology*, 168–187.

30 Qaqashandī, *Ṣubḥ*, 7: 336; see there pp. 329–55 for various examples of letters.

to Egypt with him, leaving Damascus to Temür's depredations.[31] When Tamerlane left the city in summer 1401 – after burning its famous Umayyad mosque to ashes and massacring its population – he made Faraj his governor, thereby striking a harsh blow to Mamluk legitimation claims. The submissive tone of Faraj's letters, in sharp contrast to his father's ones, certainly make this clear, as does the tribute mission Faraj had to send to Samarqand (famous mainly for the giraffe that it brought). After Temür's death, however, Faraj's humiliating stint as a governor was soon forgotten. As Tamerlane's invasions weakened not only the Mamluks but their neighbors as well – notably the Ottomans – and as Temür's successors did not have their father's ambitions and stature, the Mamluks were able to restore their power and prestige. While future Mamluk sultans continued to exchange letters with the Timurids, and contested Tamerlane's successor, Shāh Rukh (r. 1409–47), on the position of guardian of the holy places – or at least on the issue of providing a cover (*kiswa*) for the Kaʿba – relations returned to being formal. Once more, the two states were separated by various intermediaries, and their relations are outside the scope of this paper.[32]

Economic Relations

The economic connections between Mongol Central Asia and the Mamluk Sultanate are even less documented than the political ones, and this alone suggests that they were of a very limited scope. Basically, we are told that as a result of the battles between Qaidu and Qubilai Khan from the late 1270s onwards, many slaves were brought to Egypt.[33] Indeed, all the (few!) recorded embassies from Central Asia brought slaves with them, and this is especially stressed in relation to the 1315 embassy.[34] By that time it seems that the Central Asian trade was closely connected to the Golden Horde's extensive slave trade with the Mamluks, and the merchants of both realms arrived at the Sultanate by sea. Al-ʿUmarī, however, indicates that until the reign of Tarmashirin Khan (r. 1331–4), Transoxania was not open to the traders of the Sultanate, although due to the khan's great respect for, and many benefits to, merchants, Mongol Central Asia became a popular route for Mamluk traders moving from East to West.[35] Al-ʿUmari's informant in this case was *al-ṣadr* Badr al-Dīn Ḥasan al-Isʿirdī, himself a trader (otherwise

31 Levanoni, "The Mamluks," 264.

32 See e. g. Broadbridge, *Kingship and Ideology*, 198–200; Peter M. Holt, *The Age of the Crusades: the Near East from the Eleventh Century to 1517* (London and New York: Longman, 1986), 184ff. For letters expressing Mamluk humiliation see Qalqashandī, *Ṣubḥ*, 7: 343–55.

33 Baybars al-Manṣūrī, *Zubdat al-fikra*, 262; Nuwayrī, *Nihāyat al-arab*, 27: 354–5.

34 Tizengauzen, *Sbornik*, 270; al-Ṣafadī, *Nuzhat*, 227.

35 ʿUmarī/Lech, 41.

unidentified), who seems to be speaking from his own experience.[36] Indeed, the 1320s and 1330s were the heyday of the *Pax Mongolica* in Central Asia, when European (mostly Italian) and Muslim (Iraqi, Syrian, Indian) traders crowded its continental routes. This was not only due to Tarmashirin's policies, such as abolishing the commercial duties not sanctioned by the *sharīʿa* (Muslim law), enhancing relations with Mamluk Egypt and the Delhi Sultanate, and showing great respect to traders, but also due to the Chaghadaids' improved relations with China from the mid-1320s, and the Mamluk-Ilkhanid peace since 1323, all developments that made the continental routes safer and more profitable.[37] It therefore makes sense that the commercial connections between the Mamluks and the Chaghadaids at this stage were mainly continental, not maritime. However, the post-Tarmashirin upheavals in the Chaghadaid realm, especially from the 1340s, combined with the fall of the Ilkhanate in 1335, the affliction of the Black Death in the mid-fourteenth century and later the "time of troubles" in the Golden Horde (1359–80), must have had a negative effect on this trade as well.[38] In Barqūq's times, captives from Samarqand, probably captured during Tamerlane's invasions, reached the Sultanate and were sold as mamluks,[39] but their number seems to have been negligible. It is tempting to suggest that at least part of the Mamluks known as Khitāʾī, who allegedly comprised the *Khāṣṣakiyya* (bodyguard, servants) of Qalāwun (r. 1279–90),[40] originated in, or at least arrived through, Central Asia, perhaps as a result of Qaidu and the Chaghadaids' invasions of North China (*Khitā*-Cathay), but there is no conclusive evidence to support this. Most of the few Mamluks described as *Khitāʾī* or *Ṣīnī* that I was able to locate, died in the late fourteenth century,[41] and could therefore have been bought during Tarmashirin's reign, but at this stage this is mere speculation.

---

36 Ibid.

37 Biran, "The Chaghadaids and Islam," 747–8; idem, "The Mongols in Central Asia," 62.

38 For the Chaghadaid upheavals, see Biran, "The Mongols in Central Asia," 58–60; for the Golden Horde, see István Vásáry, "The Jochid Realm: The Western Steppe and Eastern Europe", in *The Cambridge History of Inner Asia: The Chinggisid Age*, 79–81.

39 Sakhāwī, *al-Ḍawʾ*, 10: 289.

40 Al-Maqrīzī, *Al-Mawāʿiẓ wa-l-iʿtibār bi-dhikr al-khiṭaṭ wa-l-āthār fī miṣr wa-l-qāhira*, ed. M.Q. al-ʿAdawī (Bulaq: Dār al-ṭibāʿa al-miṣriyya, 1854), 2: 214; Linda Northrup, *From Slave to Sultan: The Career of Al-Manṣūr Qalāwūn and the Consolidation of Mamluk rule in Egypt and Syria (678–689 A.H./1279–1290 A.D.)* (Stuttgart: F. Steiner, 1998), 192; Amir Mazor, *The Rise and Fall of a Muslim Regiment: the Mansūriyya in the First Mamluk Sultanate, 678/1279–741/1341* (Göttingen: V&R unipress, 2015), 35–6.

41 See, e.g., ʿAlāʾ al-Dīn Abū Aḥmad al-Kushtardī al-Khitāʾī (633–744), who could have been bought in Qalāwun's time (al-Ṣafadī, *Aʿyān*, 4: 158); Aydamir b. Ṣadīq al-Khitāʾī, d. 785 (Ibn Ḥajar, *Inbāʾ al-ghumr bi-anbāʾ al-ʿumr*, ed. Ḥ. Ḥabashī [Cairo: s.n., 1969], 1: 282; Ibn Taghrī Birdī, *al-Manhal al-ṣāfī wa-l-mustawfā baʿd al-wāfī* [Cairo: al-Hayʾa al-miṣriyya al-ʿāmma lil-kitāb, 2005], 3: 171; Ibn Taghrī Birdī, *al-Nujūm al-zāhira fī mulūk miṣr waʾl-qāhira* [Cairo: Dār al-kutub al-miṣriyya, 1929–72], 11: 44); Shams al-Dīn b. al-Jandī al-Khitāʾī, d. 788 (Ibn Ḥajar, *Inbāʾ al-ghumr*, 1: 330); Ghārib al-Khitāʾī, fl. 790s (Ibn al-Taghrī Birdī, *Nujūm*, 11: 345).

Cultural Relations

While the picture of sparse diplomatic and commercial relations described above does not look promising in terms of cultural contacts, a certain level of such exchange existed, mainly due to the presence of emigrants from Mongol Central Asia in the Mamluk Sultanate, and to Mamluk interest in the scholarly community of Bukhara due to the city's eminence in the pre-Mongol Muslim world. Most of the identified migrants from Mongol Central Asia – coming principally from Bukhara and its environs, but also from Khotan, Kashgar, Ghazna, Nasaf, Sighnāq, Samarqand and Khujand – were religious scholars, notably Hanafi lawyers, or Sufis (some of them itinerant), and often both. None of them was particularly prominent, but quite a few taught in the colleges and khānqāhs of Damascus and Cairo, and one was even appointed judge.[42] Luckily for present-day scholars, some of these migrants also befriended Mamluk historians, notably al-Dhahabī (d. 1349), who therefore included a considerable number of the migrants' teachers in their works. The most renowned migrant by far, who was also the major source on Mongol Central Asia's scholarly community, was ʿAlāʾ al-Dīn al-Faraḍī (1246–1300), whose life demonstrates the perils of the Mongol period, on the one hand, and the highly personal character of knowledge transmission in this age, on the other. Al-Faraḍī was a scholar and sufi, born and raised in Bukhara, where he received his education and later taught *ḥadīth.* After Abaqa's attack on Bukhara in 1273, he immigrated to Baghdad, settling there for more than a decade during which he studied also in Khurasan and al-Jazīra and performed the *ḥajj.* In the early 1280s, after the fall of the Juwaynī family, notable patrons of Baghdadi scholars, al-Faraḍī migrated to the Mamluk Sultanate, dividing his time between Egypt and Syria. When the Ilkhan Ghazan attacked Syria in 1299, al-Faraḍī, "worried about the high cost of living" following the invasions, chose to join the Mongols. He planned to return to Iraq, but died in Mārdīn on his way back. During his stay in the Sultanate, al-Faraḍī befriended several prom-

Arghūn Shāh al-Nāṣiri al-Ṣīnī, brought from China with other Mamluks to the Ilkhan Abū Saʿīd by the trader Kamāl al-Khitāʾī, apparently from Abū Saʿīd's appanages in China (al-Ṣafadī, *Aʿyān*, 1: 475) is probably irrelevant; the Mamluk historian, Baybars al-Manṣūrī (d. 1325), is often called al-Khitāʾī, perhaps a reference to his Qara Khitai origin (see Li Guo, "Baybars al-Manṣūrī", in *EI3*, ed. Kate Fleet et al., <http://referenceworks.brillonline.com/entries/encyclopaedia-of-islam-3/baybars-al-mansuri>, accessed on 21 July 2016); and the grandmother of the historian Ibn al-Dawādārī (fl. fourteenth century) is defined as ethnically Kitan (*Khitāʾīyya al-jins*; Ibn al-Dawādārī, *Kanz al-Durar*, 7: 372).

42 E.g. ʿAbd al-Qādir b. Muḥammad al-Qurashī, *al-Jawāhir al-muḍiyya fī ṭabaqāt al-ḥanafiyya*, ed. ʿA. M. al-Ḥilw, (Cairo: Hajar, 1993), 1: 507; 2: 204, 294, 428; 3: 318, 431–4; Ibn Ḥajar, *Durar*, 2: 352, 360; 3: 110–111, 154–5; ʿUmarī/Lech, 41; Ibn Rāfiʿ al-Sulāmī, *Taʾrīkh ʿulamāʾ Baghdād al-musammā muntakhab al-mukhtār* (Baghdad: Maṭbaʿat al-ahālī, 1938), 50, 66; and see next note.

inent Mamluk historians, notably al-Dhahabī, and also wrote a dictionary of his teachers, which included 700 entries. He and his dictionary were by far the main source of Mamluk information on Transoxanian scholars.[43]

Another form of transmission of knowledge was through the *ijāza*, permission to transfer what was heard or read from a certain person. Most of the Central Asian *ijāzas* that are recorded in the Mamluk sources originated with Central Asian migrants who settled in Ilkhanid Baghdad: Throughout Ilkhanid rule, even during the heyday of the war between the Mamluks and the Ilkhans, scholarly and commercial connections between the Sultanate and the Arabic-speaking community of Ilkhanid Iraq, especially Baghdad, were retained, and Syrian scholars greatly appreciated *ijāzas* received from the former Abbasid capital, including those of migrants scholars who settled there.[44] The extensive book trade between Baghdad and the Sultanate also meant that Ilkhanid materials, which included *inter alia* knowledge about Mongol Central Asia, were also available in the Sultanate.[45] Of primary importance for Central Asian information (and much more) was the work of the important Baghdadi historian and librarian Ibn al-Fuwaṭī (1244–1323), whose biographical dictionary *Talkhīṣ majmaʿ al-ādāb fī muʿjam al-alqāb* was well known in the Sultanate – and was available there in its full form, in contrast to the partial and abridged version that exists today.[46] Ibn al-Fuwaṭī's information also often originated in the writings and sayings of Transoxanian emigrants who had settled in Baghdad.[47] Ilkhanid mediation

43 See e.g. al-Dhahabī, *Taʾrīkh*, 53: 392–3; 56: 167–8; 57: 86, 266; 58: 87, 116–17, 344–5, 354; 59: 77–8, 97, 100, 117, 153, 181, 212, 224, 226, 247–8, 326, 336; 60: 115–16, 233, 308, 328–30, 365, 435, 490–1; 61: 76, 258–9; al-Birzālī, *Taʾrīkh al-Birzālī (al-Muqtafī ʿalā kitāb al-rawḍatayn)* (Beirut: al-Maktaba al-ʿaṣriyya, 2006), 1: 529; 2: 366; 3: 129, 384; al-Ṣafadī, *Aʿyān*, 5: 365; 1: 17. Al-Faraḍī was also a major source on Baghdadi scholars as is obvious from his mentions in 36 biographies (!) in Ibn Rāfiʿ's work, see Ibn Rāfiʿ, *Tārīkh ʿulamāʾ*, 18–20, 20–3, 36, 37–8, 42–3, 75–7, 78–9, 79–80, 83–4, 87–9, 91–3, 114–15, 116–17, 127–8, 129–30, 134–5, 135–6, 139–40, 165–7, 177–9, 179–80, 181, 182–3, 183–5, 195–6, 201, 203–4, 205–7, 207–8, 213–15, 231–2, 32–4, 240, 242–3. See also Michal Biran, "The Mental Maps of Mongol Central Asia as Seen from the Mamluk Sultanate," *Journal of Asian History* 49 (2015): 36–7.

44 E.g., Ibn Hajar, *Durar*, 3: 405–6; al-Dhahabī, *Taʾrīkh*, 60: 213; al-Ṣafadī, *Wāfī*, 1: 282–3; al-Qurashī, *Jawāhir*, 3: 290, 351.

45 For the book trade see Michal Biran, "Libraries, Books, and Transmission of Knowledge in Ilkhanid Baghdad," *Journal of the Economic and Social History of the Orient*, forthcoming.

46 On Ibn al-Fuwaṭī, see e.g. F. Rosenthal, "Ibn al-Fuwaṭī," *EI2*, ed. P. Bearman et al., consulted online on 24 July 2016 <http://dx.doi.org/10.1163/1573-3912_islam_SIM_3165>; M.R. Shabībī, *Muʾarrikh al-ʿIrāq Ibn al-Fuwaṭī* (Baghdād: al-Majmaʿ al-ʿilmī al-ʿirāqī, 1950); Devin DeWeese, "Cultural Transmission and Exchange in the Mongol Empire: Notes from the Biographical Dictionary of Ibn al-Fuwaṭī," in *Beyond the Legacy of Genghis Khan, ed. Linda Komaroff* (Leiden: Brill, 2006), 11–29.

47 E.g. al-Dhahabī, *Siyar aʿlām al-nubalāʾ* (Beirut: Muʾassasat al-risāla, 1982–88), 23: 364–7; Ibn al-Fuwaṭī, *Talkhīṣ majmaʿ al-ādāb fī muʿjam al-alqāb* (Tehran: Muʾassasat al-ṭibāʿa wa-l-nashr, 1995), 1: 72–73.

therefore played quite a considerable role in the cultural contacts between the Mamluks and Mongol Central Asia.

The Mamluk interest in Central Asian scholarship mainly derives from the religious prestige of Transoxania and especially Bukhara in the pre-Mongol Muslim world. More specifically, Bukhara was the hometown of Abū ʿAbdallāh Muḥammad b. Ismāʿīl al-Bukhārī (d. 870), the compiler of *Ṣaḥīḥ al-Bukhārī*, the most prominent canonical *ḥadīth* collection. This text was second only to the Qurʾān in its popularity in Mamluk Egypt, where numerous commentaries, abridgements and studies of it were compiled.[48] For this reason, Transoxanian scholars were greatly respected by the Mamluk scholarly community, which retained information on their life and works, preferred to read Eastern works according to Eastern scholars, and continued to study Transoxanian masterpieces of the pre-Mongol and early Mongol period such the main twelfth-century legal compilations, notably *al-Hidāya* by al-Marghīnānī (d. 1197) and the *Fatāwā* of Qāḍī Khān (d. 1196), or *Miftāḥ al-ʿulūm* by al-Sakkakī (d. 1229), compiled in the early thirteenth century.[49] This certainly improved the Transoxanian migrants' chances of finding a job in the Sultanate.

It is harder to appreciate the impact of the Sufi presence on the Mamluk scene: the Sufis I encountered in the texts were not referred to as belonging to a specific order nor did I find any material about their doctrines. They were rather orthodox Sufis (or at least I did not find any references to non-orthodox behavior or belief) and many were also religious scholars. Sayf al-Dīn al-Bākharzī, the prominent Sufi sheikh of Mongol Central Asia in the first half of the thirteenth century, certainly aroused interest, but I did not find any reference to Kubrawī activity in the Sultanate. McChesney recently suggested that Ibn ʿArabshāh, who while staying in Timurid Samarqand was in contact with Muḥammad Parsā, a notable link in the Naqshbandī *silsila*, might have been the first to bring Naqshbandī teachings to Egypt and Syria, but this is again undocumented.[50] Religious and cultural connections obviously intensified under Tamerlane, first as a result of the direct connections that became possible due to the gigantic

48 See, e.g., the ample references to the *Ṣaḥīḥ* in *al-Durar al-kāmina* by Ibn Ḥajar, who wrote a commentary on the *Ṣaḥīḥ* — more than 70 mentions in the online edition! On *Ṣaḥīḥ al-Bukhari* see, e.g., Christopher Melchert, "al-Bukhārī," in *EI3*, ed. Kate Fleet et al., <http://referenceworks.brillonline.com/entries/encyclopaedia-of-islam-3/al-bukha-ri-COM_24024>, last accessed 10 December 2014; Biran, "Mental Maps," 37.

49 E.g. al-Qurashī, *Jawāhir*, 2: 428, 619, 648; 3: 318; 4: 147, 210; Ibn Ḥajar, *Durar*, 1: 307–8, 414–16; 2: 255, 360; 3: 154–5; Ibn Taghrī Birdī, *Manhal*, 2: 174–5; al-Ṣafadī, *Wāfī*, 3: 172–4; Ibn Rajab, *al-Dhayl ʿalā ṭabaqāt al-ḥanābila*, ed. ʿA. al-ʿUthaymīn (Riyadh: Maktabat al-ʿUbaykān, 2005), 4: 39, 5: 1–7.

50 Robert D. McChesney, "A Note on the Life and Works of Ibn ʿArabshāh," in *History and Historiography of Post-Mongol Central Asia and the Middle East: Studies in Honor of John E. Woods*, eds. Judith Pfeiffer and Sholeh A. Quinn (Wiesbaden: Harrassowitz Verlag, 2006), 245.

dimensions of Temür's empire – that is, while Chaghadaid Central Asia was far away from the Sultanate, Tamerlane's empire nearly bordered the Mamluk realm – and second due to the high level of human mobility that characterized Temür's reign. Temür's custom of having scholars accompany him during his campaigns, either as translators or as entertainers who debated with local scholars, as well as his assembling the best scholars of the Muslim world in his capital Samarqand, were major stimulants to such contacts, as were the myriad captives taken by Temür in his invasions, many of whom returned home after his death. Two famous outcomes of such contacts are the record of Tamerlane's meeting with Ibn Khaldūn in Damascus in 1401and Ibn ʿArabshāh's biography of Tamerlane. Ibn Khaldūn's meeting with Tamerlane resulted in a history of the Maghrib that he dedicated to the conqueror, which did not survive, and in a unique description of their meeting in the scholar's autobiography, which he concluded by saying that Tamerlane, despite his cruelty, is "the greatest and mightiest of kings," highly intelligent and addicted to debate and argumentation as well as favored by Allah.[51] Unlike him, Ibn ʿArabshāh (d. 1450), who as a young boy was taken captive with his family and spent several years in Temür's Samarqand, retained a rather negative view of the conqueror and his career. However, he did describe the learned circles of Samarqand, as well as the challenges posed by Temür to the scholars of Damascus and Aleppo (where their acquaintance with the *Hidāya* proved useful).[52] Moreover, such contacts also assured that the luminaries of Temür's realm, such as Taftāzānī (d. 1390) and ʿAlī Jurjānī (1339–1434), both of whom visited the Sultanate, and Shams al-Dīn Ibn al-Jazarī (1350–1429) – born and raised in the Sultanate, than migrated to the Ottomans, captured in 1402 during Temür's battle against them and taken eastwards – were well known and highly respected in the Mamluk realm, just as they were among the Timurids and Ottomans.[53] Their works were available in the Sultanate, and they, as well as a plethora of their students, are recorded in the Mamluk biographical dictionaries.[54] This was partly due to the highly itinerant lives of these scholars, that enabled people from various places to study under them, and created a more united curriculum in the Muslim world.

In addition to religious scholars, Mamluk writers were aware of non-religious Central Asian talents, from physicians to chess players,[55] who are absent from the

51 Ibn Khaldūn, *al-ʿIbar*, 7: 1129; Fischel, *Ibn Khaldūn and Tamerlane*, 46–7.

52 Ibn ʿArabshāh/Calcutta, 185–90; Ibn ʿArabshāh/Sanders, 125–36, citing Ibn al-Shiḥna; see also the biographies of ʿAbd al-Jabbār b. Nuʿmān al-Khwārazmī, Tamerlane's translator, e.g. Ibn Ṭaghrī Birdī, *Manhal*, 7: 143.

53 See the chapters on the Timurids and Ottomans in this volume.

54 E.g. Ibn Hajr, *Durar*, 4: 350, 2: 322–3; idem, *Inbāʾ al-ghumr*, 1: 183, 389–90; Ibn Ṭaghrī Birdī, *Manhal*, 2: 172–5; al-Sakhāwī, *Ḍawʾ*, 3: 110, 10: 68, 339; 5: 328ff; 8: 256ff and many more.

55 E.g. Ibn ʿArabshāh/Sanders, 312–15.

Mamluk record of the Chaghadaid khanate. Ibn Khaldūn acknowledged the Timurid realm as the only contemporaneous polity comparable to the Mamluk Sultanate in terms of its scientific output and scholarly stature.[56]

Mongol Central Asia in the Mamluk Sources

The interest that Mamluk scholars showed in Mongol Central Asia and their voluminous historical and biographical output means that the Sultanate can shed some light for us on Muslim society in Mongol Transoxania and its relations with the Mongols. The accumulated information, culled mainly from Mamluk biographical dictionaries, encyclopedias and chronicles, enables us to reconstruct in part the learning community of Bukhara across several generations, as well as to review the city's relations with the Mongols, and gather a few insights with regard to early Mongol Islamization in Central Asia. Thus, prominent Hanafi teachers of the first generations of scholars in Mongol Central Asia included *Ṣāḥib al-Hidāya* al-Marghīnānī (d. 1197); Qāḍī Khān (d. 1196); the Banū Māza, also known as the Burhān family, who led the city religiously and politically throughout the twefth-early thirteenth century, and the Maḥbūbī family who succeeded them. Most of these scholars remained respected and their work was studied throughout Mongol rule. While the Burhān family was eliminated – by local rebels not by the Mongols – in 1238,[57] other families continued to lead the scholarly community well into the fourteenth century, and sometimes even afterwards. A good example is *Ṣāḥib al-Hidāya* al-Marghīnānī, whose family took part in Chaghadai's administration and held religious posts in Samarqand well into the Timurid period.[58] Moreover, even in late fourteenth-century Egypt, scholars of Central Asian origin retained the exact chain of transmissions that connected them to *Ṣāḥib al-Hidāya*, thereby attesting to the prestige ascribed to the text and its author in the Mamluk Sultanate.[59]

56 Ibn Khaldūn, *The Muqaddimah: An Introduction to History*, tr. Franz Rosenthal, 2nd ed. (Princeton: Princeton University Press, 1967), 3: 117, 315.

57 On the Burhān family, see O. Pritsak, "Āl-i Burhān," *Der Islam* 30 (1950): 81–96, rpt. in his *Studies in Medieval Eurasian History* (London: Variorum, 1981), Art. XX. For the importance of these scholars and families in pre-Mongol Central Asia, see Michal Biran, *The Empire of the Qara Khitai in Eurasian History: Between China and the Islamic World* (Cambridge: Cambridge University Press, 2005), 181–6; for the various generations see also idem, "Mental Maps," 34–5.

58 Juwaynī, *History of the World Conqueror*, trans. J.A. Boyle (rpt., Manchester: Manchester University Press, 1997), 273–6; Maria Eva Subtelny and Anas B. Khalidov, "The Curriculum of Islamic Higher Learning in Timurid Iran in the Light of the Sunni Revival under Shāh-Rukh," *Journal of the American Oriental Society* 115/2 (1995), 210–36, esp. 219.

59 E.g al-Sakhāwī, *Daw'*, 2: 194–5; al-Qurashī, *Jawāhir*, 2: 619, 4: 147, 4: 210; Ibn Rāfi', *Muntakhab*, 50; Ibn Ḥajar, *Durar*, 2:360.

The luminaries of the second generation, who experienced the Mongol conquest in the 1220s and were active in the United Mongol Empire, included Abū Rashīd al-Ghazzāl al-Isfahānī (d. 1233–4),[60] Shams al-Aʾimā al-Kardārī (d. 1244), who attracted the largest number of students,[61] and Sayf al-Dīn al-Bākharzī (d. 1261), the famous Kubrawī Sufi mentioned already, who was also a jurist and transmitter of prophetic tradition (*muḥaddith*; student of al-Ghazzāl), and whose family remained in Bukhara for most of the period of Mongol rule.[62] Members of the Maḥbūbī family, who replaced the Banū Māza as Bukhārā's leading Ḥanafi family (*Ṣadr al-Sharīʿa*) in 1238, are attested in the city up to the mid-fourteenth century.[63]

The brightest student of al-Kardārī and al-Maḥbūbī was Ḥāfiẓ al-Dīn al-Kabīr (d. 1294), whose family continued its prominence in the scholarly community up to the Timurid period.[64] Information about the fourteenth century is sporadic, and apart from the above-mentioned families, it is not easy to identify new intellectual leadership. However, a unique biography of a Khujandi scholar who settled in Medina[65] allows us to reconstruct the scholarly training in the western Chaghadaid realm in the early fourteenth century and to get some insight into its academic activities. Aḥmad b. Muḥammad al-Khujandī al-Madanī al-Akhawī

60 E. g., al-Dhahabī, *Taʾrīkh al-islām*, 54:80–81 (biography) and many references in his students' biographies, e. g. ibid., 56: 387, 58: 116–17, 117–18; 60: 490–1; al-Birzālī, *Muqtafa*, 2: 366; Ibn Rāfiʿ, *Muntakhab*, 213–15; al-Ṣafadī, *Aʿyān*, 5: 365.

61 E. g., Dhahabī, *Siyar*, 23: 112–13 (biography); al-Qurashī, *Jawāhir*, 3: 228–30 (biography) and the many references, mainly in his students' biographies: idem, 1: 299, 329, 330, 440; 2: 94, 115, 627, 641, 667; 3: 61, 101, 290, 312, 318, 319, 333, 337, 350, 362, 363, 426, 515; 4: 147, 148, 149, 204, 210, 297, 359, 376, 402; also e. g. al-Dhahabī, *Taʾrīkh al-islām*, 58: 116–17, 60:168–9; Ibn Ḥajar, *Durar*, 2: 360.

62 On al-Bākharzī see e. g. al-Dhahabī, *Siyar*, 23: 364–7; Hamid Algar, "Sayf al-Dīn Bākharzī," *EI3*, ed. Kate Fleet et al., <http://referenceworks.brillonline.com/entries/encyclopaedia-of-islam-2/sayf-al-di-n-ba-k-h-arzi-SIM_6683>, last accessed 20 November 2014.

63 On the Maḥbūbīs see, e. g., al-Qurashī, *Jawāhir*, 1: 196; 2: 94, 490, 492; 3: 74, 101, 102, 337, 464; 4: 310, 357, 404; C. E. Bosworth, "Ṣadr in Transoxania," *EI2*, ed. P. Bearman et al., http://referenceworks.brillonline.com/entries/encyclopaedia-o-islam/s-adr-COM_0961, accessed 10 December 2014.

64 On Ḥāfiẓ al-Dīn al-Kabīr, see e. g. al-Dhahabī, *Taʾrīkh*, 60: 178–9; al-Birzālī, *Muqtafā*, 2: 366; Maria E. Subtelny, "The Making of *Bukhārā-yi sharīf*: Scholars and Libraries in Medieval Bukhara (The Library of Khwāja Muḥammad Pārsā)," in *Studies on Central Asian History in Honor of Yuri Bregel*, ed. Devin DeWeese (Bloomington, : Indiana University Press, 2001), 79–111, esp. 80–81.

65 Al-Sakhāwī, *Ḍawʾ*, 2: 194–201;-al Sakhāwī, *al-Tuḥfa al-laṭīfa fī taʾrīkh al-Madīnah al-sharīfa* (Beirut: Dār al-kutub al-ʿilmīyya, 1993), 1: 147–153. By the end of his travels al-Akhawī settled in Medina, becoming a leading scholar. Most of his sons and grandsons as well as some students followed him in remaining in the city and becoming renown scholars appreciated by al-Sakhāwī, who also spent much time in Medina and wrote its history in *al-Tuḥfa*. See *al-Tuḥfa*, 1: 67, 83, 109, 130, 191; 2: 15, 77, 86, 117, 184, 223, 292, 295, 306, 308, 403, 430, 431, 434, 454, 456, 488, 504, 524, 561.

(1319–1401), a Hanafi lawyer, Sufi and traveler, was born in the city of Khujand, in Farghāna (modern day Tajikistan), to a scholarly family. When he was six or seven his father took him to a local teacher who taught him Qurʾān as well as Arabic language and grammar, and basic Hanafi law according to the (still popular) abridgement of the manual of al-Qurdūrī (d. 1037 in Baghdad), as well as according to local authorities. He then moved to study with the famous teachers of the city, simultaneously continuing learning with his relatives, his training including also algebra, medicine (an abridgment of Ibn Sīnā's *al-Qānūn fī al-ṭibb)*, poetry, and literature like *Maqāmāt al-Ḥarīrī.* In 1340, when he was 22, he traveled to Samarqand, visiting its major shrines and taking part in the classes of leading scholars. After a short while, he continued to Bukhara where he stayed for more than a year studying in Madrasat al-Khānī, the college founded by Tolui's widow, Sorqaqtani Beki, in the 1250s,[66] and defined as an old and flourishing institution. There he met *Ṣadr al-Sharīʿa*, the head of the Hanafi community, and various other scholars, later moving to a college in the Bukharan suburb of Wabkant, where there were only 80 students. Among the scholars he met in Bukhara was the preacher al-Ḥusām al-Yāghī, whom Ibn Baṭṭūṭa described as one of the closest councilors of the Mongol khan Tarmashirin.[67] Al-Akhawī also visited the tombs of thirteenth-century luminaries – al-Kardārī, Ḥāfiẓ al-Dīn Kabīr, al-Bākharzī – thereby attesting that by the mid-fourteenth century they had already become the subject of veneration and pilgrimage.[68] From Bukhara he moved to Khwārazm, where he stayed for eleven years continuing his training in law but also in medicine and the sciences. His description of the Khwārazmian colleges, where one college instructed 1000 students, strongly suggests that in the 1340s Bukhara was marginal in comparison to the learned community of Khwārazm, in the Golden Horde.[69] This is not surprising when we remember that the Golden Horde was then at its height under the Khans Özbeg (r. 1313–41) and Janibeg (r. 1242–1353), while the Chaghadaid Khanate was having another period of instability and succession struggles.[70] Al-Akhawī's

66 Juwaynī/Boyle, 108.

67 Ibn Baṭṭūṭa, *Voyages*, 3: 38; tr. Gibb, 3: 560.

68 Al-Sakhāwī, *Ḍawʾ*, 2: 194–5; idem, *al-Tuḥfa*, 147–8.

69 Al-Sakhāwī, *Ḍawʾ*, 2: 195–6; idem, *al-Tuḥfa*, 148–9.

70 On Chaghadaid political history in that period, see Biran, "Central Asia," 58–60; on Özbeg's reign see, e.g., Vasary, "The Jochid Realm," 78–79. Al-Akhawī's continued travels brought him to various locations in the Golden Horde (Sarai, Crimea, Caffa), al-Shām (Damascus, Jerusalem, Hebron), Iraq (Baghdad, where he met the son of Nūr al-Dīn al-Isfraʾinī, the famous Sufi sheikh, and joined his disciples), and the Hijaz (Mecca and Medina). Around 1365 he settled in Medina, but continued to be in touch with his family in Khujand (al-Sakhāwī, *Ḍawʾ*, 2: 197–201; idem, *al-Tuḥfa*, 149–153); and see Or Amir, "Islamic Learning on the Silk Roads: The Career of Jalāl al-Dīn al-Akhawī (d. 1400)," forthcoming in *Along the Silk Roads in Mongol Eurasia: Generals, Merchants, Intellectuals*, ed. M. Biran, J. Brack and F. Fiaschetti (Berkeley: California University Press, 2019).

biography also makes clear that most of his education – in Transoxania as well as in Khwārazm – was based on an "Eastern"curriculum, mainly works originating in Transoxania and, to a lesser extent, in Iran and Iraq.[71]

It is hard to evaluate the scholarly production of Mongol Central Asia in terms of either quality or quantity, but Mamluk and Ottoman sources retained a long and impressive list of books that were authored by the contemporaneous Central Asian scholars mainly in the fields of law, prophetic traditions, grammar and Qurʾān exegesis.[72] While this can give the impression of a productive academic environment, the Mongol period was not exactly a bed of roses for Central Asia even before the 1340s, and this is certainly also reflected in the Mamluk sources, at least in connection to Bukhara. They describe "the three disasters of Bukhara:" the Mongol conquest of 1220; the Ṭarabī rebellion of 1238; and the Ilkhanid retaliation campaign of 1273, following the Chaghadaid attempt to conquer Khurasan.[73] Recovery after the two first calamities seems to have been rather quick: al-Dhahabī, abridging Sayf al-Dīn al-Bākharzī's biography in Ibn al-Fuwaṭī's dictionary, cited the sheikh saying that he came to Bukhara at the order of Najm al-Dīn Kubrā, soon after it was burned by the Mongols (in Chinggis Khan's time), when there was not a place to stay in the city. Gradually he assembled a crowd and in 1225 read to them from *Ṣaḥīḥ al-Bukhārī*, after the reading of Jamāl al-Dīn al-Maḥbūbī (d. 1232–3), the famous local authority.[74] Also important for the restoration were Mongol administrative measures, such as the census conducted by the Mongol administrator Maḥmūd Yalāwach, and the new taxes he imposed: *qalān*, a head tax of one dinar levied according to the census, and a trade tax of ten percent. After Ṭarabī's rebellion, al-Bākharzī was instrumental in securing the people from the avenging Mongols, due to the prestige he enjoyed among them. The Mongols marked those who asked for al-Bākharzī's protection with a burn on their foreheads to ensure that they would not be harmed. Later he also restored the mausoleum of al-Bukhārī, author of the *Ṣaḥīḥ*. The wealth that al-Bākharzī soon amassed – villages and orchards, cattle and horses, slaves, mamluks and peasants, as well as various luxury items – suggests a rapid recovery by the city. Moreover, the various gifts that al-Bākharzī allegedly received from

71 Al-Sakhāwī, *Ḍawʾ*, 2: 194–197.

72 See e.g. Ḥājjī Khalīfah, *Kashf al-ẓunūn ʿan asāmī al-kutub wal-funūn* (n.p.: Wikālat al-Maʿārif, 1943), 74, 146, 410, 417, 1246, 1395, 1515, 1634, 1640, 1749, 1799, 1803, 1823, 1849, 1871, 1997, 2033, 2034; also al-Qurashī, *Jawāhir*, e.g., 2: 204, 225, 294, 490; 3: 334, 350, 351.

73 For the conquest of Bukhara and the Ṭarabī rebellion, see e.g. Juwaynī/Boyle, 97–115; for the 1270s, see Biran, "The Battle of Herat," 175–220.

74 Al-Dhahabī, *Siyar*, 23: 365. This biography is based on *Sīrat Bākharzi*, written by Sayf al-Dīn's disciple Minhāj al-Dīn al-Nasafī, who migrated to Baghdad following his master's death. It reached al-Dhahabī via Ibn al-Fuwaṭī, but is not included in the partial abridgement of Ibn al-Fuwaṭī's biographical dictionary that has reached us, and is unattested in other sources (or studies, as far as I can tell).

the last Abbasid Caliph, and from the rulers of Shiraz, Mosul, Azerbaijan, Delhi and Sind, as well as from quite a few Mongol khans, attest that Bukhara retained a certain amount of centrality despite its marginal political role.[75]

The 1273 attack and its repercussions were harder to offset. They resulted in significant emigration from Bukhara,[76] and while Ḥāfiẓ al-Dīn al-Kabīr, al-Maḥbūbī and their students, still led the city's academic circles, its importance declined. As I have shown elsewhere,[77] Mamluk interest was mainly limited to Transoxania. Despite the presence of migrants from further east in the Sultanate and the availability of materials about them, e. g. in Ibn al-Fuwaṭī's dictionary, the Mamluks were much less interested in Turkestan or the eastern part of the Khanate and hardly referred even to its (albeit newly) Muslim parts (e. g. Almaliq). Moreover, as most of the materials originated from migrants who left Transoxania in 1273 or beforehand, namely before the consolidation of Qaidu's and the Chaghadaid power in Central Asia, they hardly contributed information about this Mongol branch. By Tarmashirin's times, the improved commercial and diplomatic relations enabled al-ʿUmarī to reconstruct Chaghadaid genealogy and provide information on its armies and process of islamization. Chaghadaid islamization was of great interest to the Mamluks, and their reports can elucidate this little known process. I have dealt elsewhere with their information on the conversion of Tarmashirin Khan and will not repeat it here.[78] But the biography of Sayf al-Dīn al-Bākharzī (d. 1261) mentioned above informs us that already in his lifetime he had managed to convert a considerable number of rank and file Mongols, including a certain Amīr, who became the sheikh's gatekeeper (*bawwāb*) and upon whom al-Bākharzī conferred a new name: Muʾmin (believer). The respect the sheikh enjoyed from "both Muslim and infidels" was probably also instrumental in his appeal to the Mongol rank and files. Known as *Ulugh Shaykh*, the Great Sheikh (in Turkish), he was respected not only by Berke, who was converted by him – together with many of his followers – but also by Berke's brothers Batu and Berkechar, by Hülegü and Möngke, as well as by the Mongol administrators Maḥmūd Yalawach and his son Masʿūd Beg, and the Juwaynīs Bahāʾ al-Dīn and his son, the historian ʿAlāʾ al-Dīn. Interestingly, no Chaghadaid prince is recorded among the sheikh's Mongol admirers, nor is he credited for the early conversion of the Chaghadaid princes (e. g. princess Orghina, r. 1251–9), despite the fact that the Chaghadaids' respect for al-Bākharzī's family is attested in Central Asian sources.[79] Perhaps the author preferred to

75 Al-Dhahabī, *Siyar*, 23: 364–6; Biran, "Mental Maps," 35–36.

76 E. g. A. K. Muminov, *Rol' i mesto khanafitskikh 'ulamā' v zhizni gorodov tsentral'novo mavarannakhra (II–VII/VIII–XIII vv.)* (Tashkent: n.p., 2003), 30–4.

77 Biran, "Mental Maps," 31–51.

78 Biran, "The Chaghadaids and Islam," 742–52.

79 Olga D. Chekhovich, *Bukhariskie dokumenty XIV veka* (Tashkent: Nauka, 1965), 36.

mention more distinguished Mongols, not the lesser-known Chaghadaid names. As noted by al-ʿUmarī, and emphasized by Devin DeWeese, the ample presence of religious scholars in Chaghadaid Transoxania – imāms and sheikhs – advanced the islamization of the Mongol rank and file, even before their rulers.[80] Moreover, the highly islamized landscape of Mongol Central Asia, which was dotted with shrines, mausoleums, colleges, Sufi lodges and mosques, often venerated by both Mongols and Muslims, must also have been instrumental in attracting the Mongols to Islam.[81]

As explained before, Mamluk sources retained a much greater amount of information on Tamerlane and the Timurids. Unlike the Chaghadaids, however, Temür and his descendants employed their own historians and their whereabouts are well documented. I suspect, though, that systematically going over Timurid-related information in the Mamluk sources (beyond Ibn ʿArabshāh's and Ibn Khaldūn's accounts) is a very deserving mission that will be able shed new light even on the well-documented Timurids.[82]

Conclusion

Mongol Central Asia was of marginal importance to the Mamluk Sultanate up to the rise of Tamerlane, but certain diplomatic, commercial and cultural ties existed between the two polities, not least due to the presence of Transoxanian migrants in the Sultanate. The common parts of the curriculum that these migrants brought to the Mamluk (and Ilkhanid) realms might have facilitated later scholarly connections between the Mamluks and the Timurids, who succeeded the Chaghadaids. Moreover, Mamluk sources are of great value for reconstructing certain aspects of the poorly documented history of Mongol Central Asia and can potentially contribute even to the study of Timurid history.

80 ʿUmarī/Lech, 38–41; Devin Deweese, "Islamization in the Mongol Empire," in *The Cambridge History of Inner Asia: The Chinggisid Age*, 131.

81 For tomb veneration in Central Asia see al-Sakhāwī, *Daw'*, 2: 194–5; for common veneration by Mongols and Muslims of Qutham b. ʿAbbās's tomb in Samarqand (also part of al-Akhawī's itinerary), see Ibn Baṭṭūṭa 3: 54; tr. Gibb, 3: 568; for the Islamized landscape of the eastern realm of Chaghadaid Central Asia see Jamāl Qarshī, *al-Mulkhakāt bi-l-ṣurāḥ*, in *Istorija Kazakhstana v persidskikh istochnikakh*, ed. A.K. Muminov (Almaty: Institut Vostokovedenija, 2005), 1: CLXXXII–CCXI (Arabic text), 138–60 (Russian translation).

82 Cf. Amitai's works on the well-documented Ilkhanate.

Bibliography

Algar, Hamid. "Sayfal-Dīn Bākharzī," in *Encyclopaedia of Islam, Three*, eds. Kate Fleet et al., <http://referenceworks.brillonline.com/entries/encyclopaedia-of-islam-2/sayf-al-din-bakharzi-SIM_6683>.

Amitai, Reuven. "Whither the Ilkhanid Army? Ghazan's First Campaign into Syria (1299–1300)," in *Warfare in Inner Asian History (500–1800)*, ed. Nicola Di Cosmo. Leiden-Boston-Köln: Brill, 2002, 221–264.

Amitai-Preiss, Reuven. *Mongols and Mamluks: The Mamluk-Ilkhanid War 1260–1281.* Cambridge: Cambridge University Press, 1995.

Baybars al-Manṣūrī, Rukn al-Dīn al-Dawādār. *Zubdat al-fikra fi taʾrīkh ahl al-hijra*, ed. D.S. Richards. Beirut and Berlin: Orient-Institut der Deutschen Morgenländischen Gesellschaft and "Das Arabische Buch," 1998.

Biran, Michal. *Qaidu and the Rise of the Independent Mongol State in Central Asia.* Richmond, Surrey: Curzon Press, 1997.

–. "The Battle of Heart (1270): A Case of Inter-Mongol Warfare," in *Warfare in Inner Asian History (500–1800)*, ed. Nicola Di Cosmo. Leiden-Boston-Köln: Brill, 2002, 175–220.

–. "The Chaghadaids and Islam: The Conversionof Tarmashirin Khan (1331–34)." *Journal of the American Oriental Society* 122 (2002): 742–52.

–. *The Empire of the Qara Khitai in Eurasian History: Between China and the Islamic World.* Cambridge: Cambridge University Press, 2005.

–. "Chaghadaid Diplomacy and Chancellery Practices: Some Preliminary Remarks." *Oriente Moderno* 88 (2008): 369–92.

–. "The Mongols in Central Asia from Chinggis Khan's Invasion to the Rise of Temür: The Ögödeid and Chaghadaid Realms," in *The Cambridge History of Inner Asia: The Chinggisid Age*, eds. Nicola Di Cosmo, Allen J. Frank and Peter B. Golden. Cambridge: Cambridge University Press, 2009, 46–66.

–. "The Mental Maps of Mongol Central Asia as Seen from the Mamluk Sultanate." *Journal of Asian History* 49 (2015): 31–51.

–. "Libraries, Books, and Transmission of Knowledge in Ilkhanid Baghdad," *Journal of the Economic and Social History of the Orient* 62/2–3 (2019).

Al-Birzālī, al-Qāsim b. Muḥammad. *Taʾrīkh al-Birzālī (al-Muqtafā ʿalā kitāb al-rawḍatayn)*. Beirut: al-Maktaba al-ʿaṣriyya, 1427/2006.

Bosworth, C.E. "Ṣadr in Transoxania," in, *Encyclopaedia of Islam, Second Edition*, eds. P. Bearman et al., http://referenceworks,brillonline.com/entries/encyclopaedia-of-islam-2/sadr-COM_0961.

Broadbridge, Anne F. *Kingship and Ideology in the Islamic and Mongol Worlds.* Cambridge: Cambridge University Press, 2008.

Chekhovich, Ol'ga Dmitrievna. *Bukhariskie dokumenty XIV veka.* Tashkent: Nauka, 1965.

DeWeese, Devin A. (ed.). *Studies on Central Asian History in Honor of Yuri Bregel.* Bloomington, IN: Indiana University, 2001.

–. "Cultural Transmission and Exchange in the Mongol Empire: Notes from the Biographical Dictionary of Ibn al-Fuwaṭī," in *Beyond the Legacy of Genghis Khan*, ed. Linda Komaroff. Leiden: Brill, 2006, 11–29.

–. "Islamization in the Mongol Empire," in *The Cambridge History of Inner Asia: The Chinggisid Age*, eds. Nicola Di Cosmo, Allen J. Frank and Peter B. Golden. Cambridge: Cambridge University Press, 2009, 120–35.

Al-Dhahabī, Shams al-Dīn Muḥammad b. Aḥmad. *Siyar aʿlām al-nubalāʾ*. 25 vols. Beirut: Muʾassasat al-risāla, 1982–88.

–. *Taʾrīkh al-islām*, vols. 53–62, ed.ʿUmar ʿAbd al-Salām Tadmurī. Beirut: Dār al-kitāb al-ʿarabī, 1995–2004.

Di Cosmo, Nicola, Allan J, Frank, and Peter B. Golden (eds.). *The Cambridge History of Inner Asia: The Chinggisid Age*. Cambridge: Cambridge University, 2009.

Encyclopaedia of Islam, Second Edition [EI2] Leiden: Brill, 1960–2007 [online reference: http://referenceworks.brillonline.com/entries/encyclopaedia-of-islam-2/].

Encyclopaedia of Islam, THREE [EI3]. Leiden: Brill, 2007- [online reference: http://referenceworks.brillonline.com/entries/encyclopaedia-of-islam-3/].

Fischel, Walter J. *Ibn Khaldūn and Tamerlane: Their Historic Meeting in Damascus, 1401 A.D. (803 A.H.)*. Berkeley: University of California Press, 1952.

Gibb, Hamilton Alexander Rosskeen (trans.). *The Travels of Ibn Baṭṭūṭa, A.D. 1325–1354.* 5 vols. Cambridge: The Hakluyt Society, 1958–2000.

Guo, Li, "Baybars al-Manṣūrī," in *Encyclopaedia of Islam, THREE* eds. Kate Fleet et al., <http://referenceworks.brillonline.com/entries/encyclopaedia-of-islam-3/baybars-al-mansuri>.

Ḥājjī Khalīfah. *Kashf al-ẓunūn ʿan asāmī al-kutub wal-funūn.* [Istanbul]: Wikālat al-maʿārif, 1943.

Het'um (Hayton/Hetoum). "La Flor des estories de la Terre d'Orient," in *Receuil des historiens des croisades, documents armeniens* (Paris: L'ImprimérieNationale, 1869–1906), 2: 111–253.

Holt, Peter M. *The Age of the Crusades: the Near East from the Eleventh Century to 1517.* London: New York: Longman, 1986.

Ibn ʿArabshāh, Aḥmad b. Muḥammad. *ʿAjāʾib al-maqdūr fī nawāʾib Tīmūr*, text available at http://www.al-mostafa.info/data/arabic/depot/gap.php?file=001405-www.al-mostafa.com.pdf, last accessed July 20, 2016.

–. *Tamerlane; or Timur the great amir*, tr. J.H. Sanders. London: Luzac, 1936.

Ibn Baṭṭūṭa, Muḥammad b. ʿAbd Allāh. *Voyages d'Ibn Baṭṭūṭa*. ed. and trans. Ch. Defrémery and B. R. Sanguinetti. 4 vols. Paris: L'Imprimérie Nationale, 1853–58 [rpt.: Paris: Édition Anthropos, 1969].

Ibn al-Dawādārī, Sayf al-Dīn Abū Bakr b. ʿAbdallāh. *Kanz al-durar wa-jāmiʿ al-ghurar*, eds. Hans Robert Roemer et al. 9 vols. Cairo: Deutsches Archäologisches Institut Kairo (in cooperation with various publishers in Germany and Egypt), 1960–94.

Ibn al-Furat, Nāṣir al-Dīn ʿAbd al-Raḥmān ibn Muḥammad. *Taʾrīkh al-duwal wa-l-muluk*, vol. 8. Eds. K. Zurayk and N. Izzedin. Beirut: American University Press, 1939.

Ibn al-Fuwaṭī, Kamāl al-Dīn Abū al-Faḍl. *Talkhīṣ majmaʿ al-ādāb fī muʿjam al-alqāb.* Tehran: Muʾassasat al-ṭibāʿa wal-nashr, 1995.

Ibn Ḥajar al-ʿAsqalānī. *Al-Durar al-kāmina.* Cairo: Dār al-kutub al-ḥadītha, 1966; Beirut: Dār al-jīl, 1993; searchable online edition: http://www.al-mostafa.com (last accessed July 7, 2013).

–. *Inbāʾ al-ghumr bi-anbāʾ al-ʿumr*, ed. Ḥasan Ḥabashī. Cairo: s.n., 1969.

Ibn Khaldūn. *Kitāb al-ʿibar.* 7 vols. Beirut: Dār al-kitāb al-lubnānī, 1957.

–. *The Muqaddimah: An Introduction to History*, tr. Franz Rosenthal. 2nd edition. 3 vols. Princeton: Princeton University Press, 1967.

Ibn Rāfiʿ al-Sulāmī. *Tārīkh ʿulamāʾ Baghdād al-musammā muntakhab al-mukhtār.* Baghdad: Maṭbaʿat al-Ahālī, 1938.

Ibn Rajab, ʿAbd al-Raḥmān b. Aḥmad. *Al-Dhayl ʿalā ṭabaqāt al-ḥanābila*, ed. ʿAbd al-Raḥmān b. Sulaymān al-ʿUthaymīn. Riyadh: Maktabat al-ʿUbaykān, 2005.

Ibn Taghrī Birdī, Jamāl al-Dīn Abū al-Maḥāsin Yūsuf. *al-Nujūm al-zāhira fī mulūk miṣr wa-l-qāhira.* 16 vols. Cairo: Dār al-kutub al-miṣriyya, 1929–72.

–. *Al-Manhal al-ṣāfī wa-l-mustawfā baʿd al-wāfī.* 13 vols. Cairo: al-Hayʾa al-miṣriyya al-ʿāmma lil-kitāb, 2005. [Rpr. of 1984 ed.]

Jackson, Peter. "Chaghatayid Dynasty," *Encyclopedia Iranica*, http://www.iranicaonline.org/articles/chaghatayid-dynasty.

Jamāl Qarshī. *Al-Mulkhakāt bi-l-ṣurāḥ*, in *Istorija Kazakhstana v persidskik histochnikakh*, ed. A.K. Muminov. Almaty: Institut Vostokovedenija, 2005.

Al-Jazarī. *Taʾrīkh ḥawādith al-zamān wa-anbāʾihā wa-wafayāt al-akābir wa-l-aʿyān min abnāʾihā*, ed. ʿU.ʿA. Tadmūrī. 3 vols. Beirut and Sidon: al-Maṭbaʿa al-baṣariyya, 1998

Juwaynī, ʿAlāʾ al-Dīn ʿAṭā Malik. *The History of the World-Conqueror*, tr. J.A. Boyle. 2 Vols. Cambridge, MA: Harvard University Press, 1958 [rpt. In 1 vol. Manchester: Manchester University, 1997].

Kortantamer, Samira (ed. and trans.). *Ägypten und Syrien zwischen 1317 und 1341 in der Chronik des Mufaḍḍal b. Abī l'Faḍāʾil.* Freiburg im Breisgau: Klaus Schwarz, 1973.

Lech, Klaus, ed. and trans. *Das Mongolische Weltreich: Al-ʿUmarī's Darstellung der mongolischen Reiche in seinem Werk Masālik al-abṣār fī mamālik al-amṣār.* Wiesbaden: Harrassowitz, 1968.

Levanoni, Amalia, "The Mamlūks in Egypt and Syria: the Turkish Mamlūk Sultanate (648–784/1250–1382) and the Circassian Mamlūk Sultanate (784–923/1382–1517)," in *The New Cambrisge History of Islam.* Vol. 2, ed. Maribel Fierro. Cambridge: Cambridge University Press, 2010, 237–284.

al-Maqrīzī, Taqī al-Dīn Aḥmad n. ʿAlī. *Al-Mawāʿiẓ wa-l-iʿtibār bi-dhikr al-khiṭaṭ wa-l-āthār fī miṣr wa-l-qāhira*, ed. M. Q. al-ʿAdawī. 2 vols. Bulaq: Dār al-ṭibāʿa al-miṣriyya, 1854.

–. *Kitāb al-suluk li-maʿrifat duwal al-muluk*, eds. M. M. Ziyāda and ʿA. ʿĀshūr. Cairo: Maṭbaʿat dār al-kutub, 1934–73.

Mazor, Amir. *The Rise and Fall of a Muslim Regiment: the Mansụriyya in the First Mamluk Sultanate, 678/1279–741/1341.* Göttingen: V&R unipress, 2015.

McChesney, R. D. "A Note on the Life and Works of Ibn ʿArabshāh," in *History and Historiography of Post-Mongol Central Asia and the Middle East: Studies in Honor of John E. Woods*, eds. Judith Pfeiffer and Sholeh A. Quinn. Wiesbaden: Harrassowitz Verlag, 2006, 205–249.

Melchert, Christopher. "al-Bukhārī," in: *Encyclopaedia of Islam, THREE*, eds. Kate Fleet et al., <http://referenceworks.brillonline.com/entries/encyclopaedia-of-islam-3/al-bukhari-COM_24024>.

Mufaḍḍal b. Abī al-Faḍāʾil, *al-Nahj al-sadīdwa-l-durr al-farīd fī mā baʿda ibn al-ʿamīd (Histoire des sultans mamlouks)*, ed. and trans. E. Blochet (*Patrologia orientalis* 12 (1919) 343–550; 14 (1920), 373–672: 20 (1928), 1–217). Paris: Firmin Didot, 1919–28. [See also under Kortantamer]

Muminov, Ashirbek Kurbanovich. *Rol' i mesto khanafitskikh 'ulamā' v zhizni gorodov tsentral'novo mavarannakhra (II–VII / VIII–XIII vv.).* Tashkent 2003.

(ed.). *Istorija Kazakhstana v persidskikh istochnikakh*, vol. 1. Almaty: Institut Vostokovedenija, 2005.

Navā'ī, ʿAbd al-Ḥusayn. *Asnād wa mukātabāt-i ta'rīkhī-i Īrān az Tīmūr tā Shāh Ismāʿīl.* Ṭehrān: Bungāh-i tarjamah wa nashr-i kitāb,1341/1962.

Northrup, Linda. *From Slave to Sultan: The Career of Al-Manṣūr Qalāwūn and the Consolidation of Mamluk Rule in Egypt and Syria (678–689 A.H./1279–1290 A.D.).* Stuttgart: F. Steiner, 1998.

Al-Nuwayrī, Shihāb al-Dīn. *Nihāyat al-arab fī funūn al-adab*, vol. 27 [of 31 vols.], ed. Saʿīd ʿAbd al-Fattāḥ ʿĀshūr. Cairo: Dār al-kutub al-miṣriyya, 1985.

Pritsak, Omeljan. "Āl-i Burhān." *Der Islam* 30 (1950): 81–96 [rpt. In his *Studies in Medieval Eurasian History* (London: Variorum, 1981), Art. XX].

Qāshānī, Abū al-Qāsim ʿAbdallāh b. ʿAlī. *Ta'rīkh-i Ūljāytū,* ed. M. Hambly. Tehran: Bangah-i tarjumah wa-nashr-i kitāb, 1969.

Al-Qalqashandī, Aḥmad b. ʿAlī. *Ṣubḥ al-aʿshā fī ṣināʿat al-inshā'.* 14 vols. Cairo: al-Maṭbaʿa al-amīriyya, 1913–19.

Al-Qurashī, ʿAbd al-Qādir b. Muḥammad. *Al-Jawāhir al-muḍiyya fī ṭabaqāt al-ḥanafiyya,* ed. ʿA. M. al-Ḥilw. 5vols. Cairo: Hajar, 1993.

Rosenthal, Franz. "Ibn al-Fuwaṭī,", in *Encyclopaedia of Islam, Second Edition,* ed. P. Bearman et al., <http://dx.doi.org/10.1163/1573-3912_islam_SIM_3165>.

Al-Ṣafadī, Khalīl b. Aybak. *Al-Wāfī bi-l-wafayāt,* ed. Helmut Ritter. 32 vols. Beirut: Orient-Institut, 2008.

–. *Aʿyān al-ʿaṣr wa-aʿwān al-naṣr,* ed. ʿAlī b. Abū Zayd. 6 vols. Beirut: Dār al-fikr al-muʿāṣir, 1998.

Al-Sakhāwī, Muḥammad b. ʿAbd al-Raḥmān. *al-Daw' al-lāmiʿ li-ahl al-qarn al-tāsiʿ.* 12 vols. in 6. Cairo: Maktabat al-Quds, 1353–5/1934–36.

–. *Al-Tuḥfa al-laṭīfa fī ta'rīkh al-Madīnah al-sharīfa.* Beirut: Dār al-kutub al-ʿilmīyya, 1993.

Shabībī, Muḥammad Riḍā. *Mu'arrikh al-ʿIrāq Ibn al-Fuwaṭī.* Baghdād: al-Majmaʿ al-ʿilmī al-ʿirāqī, 1950.

al-Shujāʿī, *Ta'rīkh al-malik al-nāṣir Muḥammad b. Qalāwūn al-ṣāliḥī wa-awlādihi,* ed. B. Schäfer. Wiesbaden: Franz Steiner, 1985.

Subtelny, Maria Eva. "The Making of *Bukhārā-yi Sharīf:* Scholars and Libraries in Medieval Bukhara (The Library of Khwāja Muḥammad Pārsā)," in *Studies on Central Asian History in Honor of Yuri Bregel,* ed. Devin DeWeese. Bloomington, IN: Indiana University, 2001, 79–111.

– and Anas B. Khalidov. "The Curriculum of Islamic Higher Learning in Timurid Iran in the Light of the Sunni Revival under Shāh-Rukh." *Journal of the American Oriental Society* 115:2 (1995), 210–36.

al-ʿUmarī, Ibn Faḍlallāh. *al-Taʿrīf bi-l-muṣṭalaḥ al-sharīf.* Beirut: Dār al-kutub, 1988.

–. *Masālik al-abṣār wa-mamālik al-amṣār.* Beirut: Dār al-kutub al-ʿilmiyya, 2010.

Vásáry, István. "The Jochid Realm: The Western Steppe and Eastern Europe," in *The Cambridge History of Inner Asia: The Chinggisid Age,* eds. Nicola Di Cosmo, Allen J. Frank and Peter B. Golden. Cambridge: Cambridge University Press, 2009, 67–85.

Cihan Yüksel Muslu (University of Houston)

Patterns of Mobility between Ottoman and Mamluk Lands[1]

Prominent Mamluk scholars al-Maqrīzī (766–845/1364–1442) and Ibn Ḥajar al-ʿAsqalānī (773–852/1371–1448) note in their annals that Mollā Şemseddīn Muḥammed b. Ḥamza al-Fenārī (751–834/1351–1431) from Anatolia (*Bilād al-Rūm*) appeared in Cairo on 4 Rabīʿ I 823/19 March 1420 while returning from pilgrimage. They introduced the visitor as the chief qadi of the Ottoman ruler Meḥmed I (r. 816–824/1413–1421). Known in Ottoman sources as Mollā Fenārī, he had in Cairo an audience with the Mamluk sultan at the request of Mamluk sultan al-Malik al-Muʾayyad Shaykh al-Maḥmūdī (r. 815–824/1412–1421). Well-known for his high regard of scholars,[2] Shaykh al-Maḥmūdī questioned his guest regarding conditions in Ottoman lands;[3] it was common for sovereigns to use travelers for intelligence.[4] Neither author records Mollā Fenārī's response, yet they emphasize that the Mamluk sultan honored the scholar with gifts and ordered his staff to host him properly. Unlike a typical traveler who could have gone

1 I acknowledge my debts to the participants of the conference *The Mamluk Sultanate and Its Neighbors: Economic, Social, and Cultural Entanglements, Bonn, December 18–20, 2015* and Professor Nikolas Jaspert (University of Heidelberg) for invaluable comments. I am particularly grateful to Nikolas Jaspert who kindly shared his (at the time) unpublished work with me.

2 İsmail Yiğit, "Şeyh el-Mahmûdî," *Türkiye Diyanet Vakfı İslam Ansiklopedisi* (henceforth *DİA*) 39 (2010): 59–60. For a comprehensive treatment of this Mamluk sultan's reign see Kâzım Yaşar Kopraman, *Mısır Memlükleri Tarihi: Sultan Melik el-Müeyyed Şeyh el-Mahmûdî Devri (1412–1421)* (Ankara: Kültür Bakanlığı, 1989).

3 Sultan Shaykh al-Maḥmūdī regularly corresponded with his peer Meḥmed I and undertook multiple campaigns against Anatolian powers such as the Karamanids. See Kopraman, *Mısır Memlükleri Tarihi*; Cihan Yüksel Muslu, *The Ottomans and the Mamluks: Imperial Diplomacy and Warfare* (London: I.B. Tauris, 2014), 90–94.

4 For an example from the late fifteenth century see Arnold von Harff, *The Pilgrimage of Arnold von Harff: Knight from Cologne, through Italy, Syria, Egypt, Arabia, Ethiopia, Nubia, Palestine, Turkey, France and Spain, Which He Accomplished in the Years 1496 to 1499*, trans. Malcolm Letts (London: Hakluyt Society, 1946), 239–241. For older but still useful articles on Arnold von Harff's time in Ottoman lands see Semavi Eyice, "II. Bayezid Devrinde Davet Edilen Batılılar," *Belgelerle Tarih Dergisi* 4 (1939): 23–30; idem, "Arnold von Harff," *Türk Yurdu* 254 (1956): 690–694.

to a khān, Mollā Fenārī was instead housed in the mansion of a dignitary.[5] A few days later the Mamluk sultan invited Mollā Fenārī to the celebrations of the Prophet's birthday (*mawlid*) on 7 Rabīʿ I/22 March. The lavish banquet was attended by both local and foreign dignitaries including an Ottoman ambassador.[6] On 22 Rabīʿ I/6 April Mollā Fenārī started his return journey. During his brief sojourn of less than twenty days in Cairo he spent time with fellow scholars and judges, gave lectures and tutored students, and was showered with generous gifts. He was not only recognized by the Mamluk sultan and the ruling elite, but also by his peers and colleagues.[7]

Despite their detailed descriptions, al-Maqrīzī and Ibn Ḥajar's narratives fail to fully illustrate the intricacy of Mollā Fenārī's ties with the lands of Egypt and Greater Syria. Additional passages expand Mollā Fenārī's image from that of a typical pilgrim-scholar who happened to pass through Mamluk lands like thousands of others did every year into that of a former resident-student and scholar who had spent almost two decades in Mamluk cities. Both al-Maqrīzī and Ibn Ḥajar recount the vicissitudes of the scholar's career within Ottoman lands (i.e. his temporary relocation to Karamanid territory), his interest in Sufism (particularly in the writings of the famous Ibn al-ʿArabī who died in 638/1240), and his scholarly works in a thorough manner that seems surprising to our 21st century minds that separate the Ottoman and Mamluk worlds. They provide further details regarding his aforementioned pilgrimage in 822/1418, his subsequent one in 832/1429, and his death in 834/1431.[8] Ibn Ḥajar concludes the detailed obituary of this well-known scholar with a personal note that he skillfully saves for the end: "[H]e composed a certificate (*ijāza*) for me with his own

5 Taqī al-Dīn Aḥmad b. ʿAlī Al-Maqrīzī, *Kitāb al-Sulūk li-maʿarifa duwal al-mulūk*, ed. Saʿīd ʿAbd al-Fattāḥ ʿĀshur, vols. 3 and 4 (Cairo: Dār al-Kutub, 1972), 4/1: 524. According to al-Maqrīzī, Mollā Fenārī's host was Qadi Zayn al-Dīn ʿAbd al-Bāsiṭ, who was Nāẓır al-Khizāna (the controller of the royal depository of robes). For translation of this terminology see Carl F. Petry, *The Civilian Elite of Cairo in the Later Middle Ages* (Princeton, New Jersey: Princeton University Press, 1981), 398.

6 For the Ottoman ambassador Ḳaçḳar al-Çağatay's formal audience with the Mamluk sultan on 28 Ṣafar 823/14 March 1420 see al-Maqrīzī, *Kitāb al-Sulūk*, 4/1: 519. For this ambassador and his mission see Yüksel Muslu, *Imperial Diplomacy and Warfare*, 207–208.

7 Al-Maqrīzī, *Kitāb al-Sulūk*, 4/1: 523–525; Ibn Ḥajar al-ʿAsqalānī, *Inbāʾ al-Ghumr bi-Anbāʾ al-ʿUmr*, ed. Ḥasan Ḥabashī, 4 vols., (Cairo, 1969), 3:216. There are some inconsistencies between these two accounts that are not discussed in this paper (i.e. Mollā Fenārī's dates of departure and arrival, etc.).

8 Taqī al-Dīn Aḥmad b. ʿAlī Al-Maqrīzī, *Durar al-ʿUqūd al-Farīda fī Tarājim al-Aʿyān al-Mufīda*, ed. Maḥmūd al-Jalīlī, 4 vols., (Bairut: Dār al-Gharb al-Islāmī, 2002), 3: 349–350; Ibn Ḥajar, *Inbāʾ al-Ghumr*, 3: 57–64 (in passing), 464–465. For a reference to Mollā Fenārī in another Mamluk source see Shams al-Dīn Muḥammad b. ʿAbd al-Raḥman al-Sakhāwī, *Wajīz al-Kalām fī Zayl ʿAlā Duwal al-Islāmī*, ed. Bashshār ʿAwwād Maʿrūf, 4 vols. (Beirut: Muassasa al-Risala, 1995), 2: 516.

handwriting when he was in Cairo."[9] Ibn Ḥajar was apparently among the students who were privy to spend time with Mollā Fenārī during one of the scholar's stays in Cairo.

The fact that a significant part of Mollā Fenārī's biography, albeit with gaps, can be based on two Mamluk authors' works alone displays the familiarity of these scholars with Mollā Fenārī's life.[10] This familiarity is a consequence of dense cultural and intellectual ties between the Ottoman and Mamluk lands. The mobility of both celebrated and ordinary individuals as well as the connectedness of the Muslim world manifest themselves in almost every time and age as shown in other studies.[11] In this historical context the case of Mollā Fenārī presents a typical yet still fascinating instance of exchange and networking, exemplifying the most common and often overlapping patterns of Muslim travel motivations ranging from pilgrimage to education. Mollā Fenārī's journeys into Mamluk lands were among the few examples written down out of the numerous individuals who similarly moved between these two regions over the centuries. Despite the frequency of such travel, the impact of these travelers' ready movement between what are often considered fully separate societies has not been fully explored. A strong focus on Ottoman-Mamluk military conflicts and the Ottoman conquest of Mamluk lands currently dominates the historiography of Ottoman-Mamluk relations.[12]

This prosopographical inquiry focuses on a selection of case studies and is organized around individuals' motivations for travel from education to pilgrimage. Although a comprehensive treatment of individual mobility and its impact on Ottoman and Mamluk societies is beyond the scope of this paper, a

9 Ibn Ḥajar, *Inbāʾ al-Ghumr*, 3: 465.

10 For studies on Mollā Fenārī's life see the bibliography in İbrahim Hakkı Aydın, "Molla Fenârî," *DİA* 30 (2005): 246–247.

11 For a brief sample of numerous studies on travel within the Muslim world see: Ross E. Dunn, "International Migrations in the Later Middle Period: The Case of Ibn Battuta," in *Golden Roads: Migration, Pilgrimage, and Travel in Medieval and Modern Islam*, ed. Ian Richard Netton (Richmond: Curzon Press, 1993); Dale F. Eickelman and James Piscatori, (eds.), *Muslim Travellers: Pilgrimage, Migration, and the Religious Imagination* (Berkeley: University of California Press, 1990); Houari Touati, *Islam and Travel in the Middle Ages*, tr. Lydia G. Cochrane (Chicago: University of Chicago Press, 2010); Roxanne Euben, *Journeys to the Other Shore: Muslim and Western Travelers in Search of Knowledge* (Princeton: Princeton University Press, 2006); Amira Bennison, "Muslim Universalism and Western Globalism," in *Globalization in World History*, ed. A.G. Hopkins (New York: Norton, 2002); Engseng Ho, *The Graves of Tarim: Genealogy and Mobility across the Indian Ocean* (Berkeley: University of California Press, 2006); Halil İnalcık, "The Socio-Political Effects of the Diffusion of Firearms in the Middle East," in *War Technology and Society in the Middle East*, ed. V.J. Parry and M.E. Yapp (London: Oxford UP, 1975).

12 For a similar criticism of the historiography regarding Ottoman-Venetian relations, see Eric Dursteler, *Venetians in Constantinople: Nation, Identity, and Coexistence in the Early Modern Mediterranean* (Baltimore: John Hopkins University Press, 2006), 2–10.

quick glance at the primary sources makes it clear that interactions between the Ottoman and Mamluk societies were in part buttressed and fostered by the individuals who circulated between these two geographies whether of their own free will or at the orders of their rulers. While these travelers may not be the immediate policy-makers on either side of the borders, they nonetheless played their parts as agents of cultural and social exchanges against the backdrop of Ottoman-Mamluk relations. These regional guests possessed overlapping motives in the form of scholars, students, royal tutors, judges, merchants, traveling mystics, pilgrims, refugees, captives, spies, envoys, and others. Regardless of their origins or ultimate residences, these travelers and sojourners made an impact on the social memory wherever they passed by contributing to the evolution of mutual perceptions. Their identities as well as their allegiances presented porous and multi-layered characteristics as was commonly the case in those centuries.[13]

While this flow of human traffic moved easily between both empires, individuals traveling from the Mamluk lands in particular played critical roles both in the formation of Ottoman institutions and the evolution of Ottoman intellectual trends as the Ottomans consolidated their presence along the fringes of the Muslim world.[14] Regardless of individual motivations, these travelers brought

13 For a limited list of studies on identity formation in the Ottoman world see Dursteler, *Venetians in Constantinople*, especially chaps. 1, 4, and 5; Cemal Kafadar, *Between Two Worlds: The Construction of Ottoman State* (Berkeley: University of California Press, 1995); idem, "A Rome of One's Own: Reflections on Cultural Geography and Identity in the Lands of Rum," *Muqarnas* 24 (2007): 7–25; Ulrich Haarmann, "Ideology and History, Identity and Alterity: The Arab Image of the Turk from the Abbasids to Modern Egypt," *International Journal of Middle Eastern Studies* 20 (1988): 175–196; Salih Özbaran, *Bir Osmanlı Kimliği: 14.–17. Yüzyıllarda Rûm/ Rûmî Aidiyet ve İmgeleri* (İstanbul: Kitap Yayınevi, 2004).

14 There are two major exemptions in this paper: non-Muslims (either residents of these regions or those arriving from the West such as merchants) and Muslims coming from other parts of the larger Muslim world (i.e. Timurid Lands). Individuals who belonged to both categories contributed equally significantly to mobility within these lands. Both regions received incoming individuals from the East at least since the eleventh century, particularly following the thirteenth-century Mongol attacks when immigrants settled in different parts of Anatolia, Egypt, and Greater Syria. The famous founder of *Mevlevī* Sufi tariqa, Celāleddīn al-Rūmī (d. 672/1273) and his family are among the most well-known examples of this phenomenon. Likewise, İhsanoğlu and Şeşen point out that Turkish-speaking people who were not necessarily from Anatolia but instead from regions such as Transoxiana had been coming to Egypt and Greater Syria for education as early as the twelfth century. See Ekmeleddin İhsanoğlu and Ramazan Şeşen, "Araplarla Türkler'in İlk Temasları," in *İki Tarafın Bakış Açısından Türk-Arap Münasebetleri* (Istanbul: IRCICA, 2000), 43–47. However, this paper does not deal with the extended population movement but instead focuses on population movements between the Ottoman and Mamluk lands. For an example of incoming immigrants to the Ottoman lands see, Hanna Sohrweide, "Dichter und Gelehrte aus dem Osten im osmanischen Reich (1453–1600)," *Der Islam* 46 (1970): 263–302.

their expertise and educational backgrounds into their new homes within the expanding Ottoman lands.[15]

Historical Precedence of Mobility: Arriving Scholars and Returning Students

Exchange between the Ottoman and Mamluk lands has both historical and geographical precedence as the continuation of a long-lasting contact pattern between *Bilād al-Rūm* and *Bilād al-Miṣr wa'l-Shām* through the centuries. Commerce, while the least researched factor in this paper, significantly contributed to this consistent pattern; for example, the Mamluk sultan Qalāwūn (r. 678–689/1279–1290) signed treaties with the Byzantine emperor in order to ensure the flow of trade between their lands long before the Ottomans replaced the Byzantines in this region. The campaign by Mamluk sultan Baybars (r. 658–676/1260–1277) to Anatolia in 675–676/1266–1277 during the period of Ilkhanid vassalage must have also strengthened these ties since this campaign brought parts of *Bilād al-Rūm* into the Mamluk sphere of influence. This region subsequently took its place within the peripheries of the Mamluk domain, while members of Anatolian political factions and ruling dynasties (i.e. Karamanids, Ramazanids, Dulkadirids, and others) frequently visited Cairo in order to reaffirm ties with their Mamluk overlords.[16]

The residents of Egypt and Greater Syria were accordingly not strangers to the people who arrived from *Bilād al-Rūm*,[17] assigning the nisba "al-Rūmī" to many

15 For a recent treament of the Samarkand influence on early Ottoman *tafsīr* training see Susan Günaştı, "Political Patronage and the Writing of Qur'ān Commentaries among the Ottoman Turks," *Journal of Islamic Studies* 24 (2013): 335–357. For an old but still useful treatment of parallels between Ottoman administrative and bureaucratic practices and those of other Muslim regimes see İsmail Hakkı Uzunçarşılı, *Osmanlı Devleti Teşkilâtına Medhal: Büyük Selçukîler, Anadolu Selçukîleri, Anadolu Beylikleri, İlhanîler, Karakoyunlu ve Akkoyunlularla Memlûklardaki Devlet Teşkilatına Bir Bakış* (Ankara: TTK, 1941).

16 For the vassalage ties between parts of Anatolia and Mamluk sultans see Reuven Amitai-Preiss, "Northern Syria between the Mongols and Mamluks: Political Boundary, Military Frontier, and Ethnic Affinities," in *Frontiers in Question: Eurasian Borderlands, 700–1770*, ed. Daniel Power and Naomi Standen (New York, NY: St.Martin's Press, 1999), 128–152; Faruk Sümer, "Ḳaramān-og͟hullari," *EI*[2] 4 (1950): 619–630; Şehabettin Tekindağ, "Karamanlılar," *İslam Ansiklopedisi* 6: 316–330; Faruk Sümer, "Ramazanoğulları," *DİA* 34 (2007): 442–447; Refet Yınanç, *Dulkadir Beyliği* (Ankara: TTK, 1989) Margaret Venzke, "The Case of a Dulgadir-Mamluk Iqṭāʿ: A Reassessment of the Dulgadir Principality and Its Positions within the Ottoman-Mamluk Rivalry," *Journal of Economic and Social History of the Orient* 43 (2000): 399–474.

17 David Ayalon, "Names, Titles, and 'Nisbas' of the Mamlūks," *Israel Oriental Studies* 5 (1975): 196–200; Michel Balivet, *Şeyh Bedreddin: Tasavvuf ve İsyan*, trans. Ela Güntekin (İstanbul: Tarih Vakfı Yurt Yayınları, 2000), 41–44; idem, "Gens du Pays de Rûm en Égypte sous les

of these incoming individuals from Anatolia as a reference to Anatolia's history as a former Roman province.[18] Search for knowledge has always been among the most prominent motivations for travel, particularly following the rise of local Muslim principalities in Anatolia. Many students beginning their training in fourteenth- and fifteenth-century Anatolia (and later from the extended Ottoman lands) were drawn to prominent scholars residing in Mamluk lands. Having been under the rule of various Islamic powers since the eighth century, Egypt and Greater Syria had become home to numerous advanced learning institutions within the Islamic world. The Mamluk sovereigns, other members of the ruling elite, and wealthy upper class individuals became generous benefactors to scholars, authors, artists, and poets while also adding new *madrasas* and endowments to the existing collection of charities supported within the Mamluk domain.[19] Ambition for learning and knowledge made the Mamluk domain a melting pot for students from different parts of the known world.

Similarly, Anatolia was no stranger to people from older Islamic lands. Individuals trained in Mamluk territories (as well as those trained in Timurid lands) left a permanent impact by consolidating Muslim learning traditions and legal practices used by the new Anatolian Muslim magnates who emerged during the post-Seljuk period. Although this impact was not limited to the spheres of learning and legal practices, it is the most visible one in sources.[20] The ruling elite in Anatolian principalities – from established ones such as Karamanids and Hamidoğulları to relative newcomers such as the Ottomans – proffered new lives, careers, and wealth which were likely not readily available in the great Muslim metropolises due to the surplus of skilled individuals. They particularly welcomed incoming individuals whether returning or emigrating as they settled

Premiers Sultans Circassiens," *Turcica* 41(2009):199–206; Ekmeleddin İhsanoğlu, "Osmanlı Devleti'nin Arap Topraklarına Yayılışı," in *İki Tarafın Bakış Açısından Türk-Arap Münasebetleri* (İstanbul: IRCICA, 2000), 83–87; Özbaran, *Bir Osmanlı Kimliği*, 58–62; Petry, *The Civilian Elite of Cairo*, 68–72.

18 For what the Mamluk society understood from al-Rūmī's identity markers see Haarmann, "Ideology and History," 177. For the evolving definition of this attribute within the Ottoman context, see Kafadar, "A Rome of One's Own"; Özbaran, *Bir Osmanlı Kimliği*, esp. 50–51, 61. For a recent discussion of the concept of Rum regarding Byzantine images of the Seljuks of Rum see Adem Tülüce, *Bizans Tarih yazımında Öteki: Selçuklu Kimliği* (Ankara: Doğubatı, 2016).

19 For scholarly patronage of the Mamluk ruling elite see Jonathan Berkey, *Transmission of Knowledge in Medieval Cairo* (Princeton: Princeton University Press, 1992), esp. Introduction and Ch. 5. For patronage and charity in general among the Mamluk elites, see Adam Sabra, *Poverty and Charity in Medieval Islam* (Cambridge: Cambridge University Press, 2001), esp. Chp. 4.

20 For the influence of craftsmen from Mamluk lands on Anatolian edifices constructed under the Anatolian emirates, see Sara Nur Yıldız, "From Cairo to Ayasuluk: Ḫācı Paşa and the Transmission of Islamic Learning to Western Anatolia in the Late Fourteenth Century," *Journal of Islamic Studies* 25 (2014): 271–272, notes 30–33.

along the frontiers between the Byzantine Empire and its peers. These frontiers represented territory with limited or no prior experience of Islamic rule that additionally lacked the human resources and infrastructure required to sustain a Muslim sovereign's rule.[21] The well-known account of the Muslim pilgrim and jurist Ibn Baṭṭūṭa (d. 770/1368–1369) from North Africa who visited Anatolia in 730–732/1331–32 successfully captures these regional characteristics.[22] Among many Anatolian towns he visited he counts Eğridir (north of today's Isparta in southern Turkey) where he was hosted by "a pilgrim and sojourner" called Muṣliḥ al-Dīn in a *madrasa*.[23] Ibn Baṭṭūṭa particularly praised his host Muṣliḥ al-Dīn's scholarly talents, oratory skills, manners, and impeccable hospitality. Muṣliḥ al-Dīn's scholarly pedigree brought together three core areas of the Muslim intellectual world, Egypt, Greater Syria, and Iraq.

In addition to these immigrants who made Anatolian towns their homes, numerous natives such as Mollā Fenārī had naturally opted for a return to either their hometowns or the vicinity after completing their training. For instance, the aforementioned scholar Muṣliḥ al-Dīn was employed under the auspices of a local overlord Isḥāḳ Bey from the Hamidoğulları ruling family who died sometime between 730/1331 and 734/1335 (Ibn Baṭṭūṭa gives his name as Abū Isḥāq Bey). Complimented by Ibn Baṭṭūṭa for his piety, Isḥāḳ Bey was among those who opted to return to his homelands.[24] While he was not necessarily a student, he had stayed in Egypt during his father's lifetime and completed his pilgrimage before returning to fill his father's position.[25] Although his sojourn in Mamluk lands must be evaluated within the ties of vassalage and lordship between his family and the Sultans of Cairo, it nonetheless proves one aspect of the networks between the center and peripheries of Mamluk authority. At the time of Ibn Baṭṭūṭa's visit the town was a flourishing center under Isḥāḳ Bey's control.

Isḥāḳ Bey does not present an altogether unique profile among these returning individuals. The background of Qāḍı Burḥān al-Dīn closely resembles Isḥāḳ Bey's because he combined the skills of a political leader, warrior, and legal

21 Regarding the openness of frontier sovereigns toward accepting or demanding the services of skilled individuals from Muslim metropolitan regions see Dunn, "International Migrations," 77–79.

22 Ibn Baṭṭūṭa, *The Travels of Ibn Battuta*, ed. H.A.R. Gibb (London, 1956–1961), 422–423. For other examples in Ibn Baṭṭuṭa see pp. 418, 451, 453–454; for discussion of travelers with no reference to their origins see pp. 457–458, 460–461, 462–463. Additional references to travelers as well as scholars who were presumably from other parts of the Muslim world are not included in this footnote because Ibn Baṭṭūṭa does not identify their origins.

23 For the identity of this scholar see Esat Coşan, "XV. Asır Türk Yazarlarından Muslihu'd-din, Hamid-oğulları ve Hızır Bey," *Vakıflar Dergisi* 13 (1981): 109; for the college where this scholar hosted Ibn Baṭṭūṭa see Sait Kofoğlu, "Hamîdoğulları," *DİA* 15 (1997): 472–473.

24 Ibn Baṭṭūṭa, 422–423.

25 Kofoğlu, "Hamîdoğulları," 472–473.

scholar. Born in Kayseri to a family of legal scholars and judges, Qāḍı Burḥān al-Dīn (745–798/1345–1398) completed his education in Egypt, Damascus, and Aleppo. His successful and stormy career first began as a judge in his hometown Kayseri and then continued with his vizierate under the ruler of Eretna. Qāḍı Burḥān al-Dīn was able to establish his own rule in Sivas following the death of his patron (783/1381), where he ruled until his death in 800/1398. During the eighteen years he remained in power he fought against adversaries such as the Karamanids, Ottomans, and even Mamluks. However, he also sought help at least from two of these powers, the Ottomans and the Mamluks, against Tīmūr (or Temür, d. 807/1405). He was later killed by the leader of the Akkoyunlu confederation, Ḳarāyülük ʿO<u>s</u>mān (d. 839/1435). As a successful ruler of Sivas he was not only a prominent figure in fourteenth-century Anatolian political history, but also contributed to its cultural and intellectual history through his poetry and work in legal studies.[26]

During the fourteenth century or post-Seljuk period the multiplicity of possibilities that Anatolia offered to those who sought patrons was particularly impressive. Although a statistical study has yet to be done on the patterns of patronage within *Bilād al-Rūm*, the Ottomans appeared merely among the humbler patrons at least for the greater part of the fourteenth century at this moment of political diversity. For instance, Aḥmedī (d. 816/1413) who was presumably a native of Germiyanid lands (centered in modern Kütahya in Western Anatolia) had completed his education in Mamluk territory.[27] He returned Anatolia at a time when the Ottomans were particularly distinguishing themselves with their expansion into the Balkans and their extending domination over their Anatolian peers. This geographic growth was also accompanied by generous patronage to learning, art, and architecture. Nonetheless, Aḥmedī preferred the Aydınid dynasty in Western Anatolia as his benefactor.

On the one hand, Aḥmedī's career reveals the comparatively lesser status of Ottoman patronage vis-à-vis other principalities. On the other hand, it also proves the extremely dynamic and shifting regional political dynamics because at an unknown later date Aḥmedī established ties with the Ottoman dynasty. He first sought the protection of Ottoman ruler Süleymān who controlled in the

26 Yaşar Yücel, *Kadı Burhaneddin Ahmed ve Devleti (1344–1398)* (Ankara: Ankara Üniversitesi, 1970); Abdülkadir Ozaydın ve Hatice Tören, "Kadı Burhaneddin," *DİA* 24 (2001): 74–77.

27 For the possibility of Sivas (a central-eastern Anatolia town) as Aḥmedī's hometown see Günay Kut, "Ahmedî," *DİA* 1 (1988):165. For Aḥmedī in general, see Aḥmedī, *İskender-nāme: İnceleme, Tıpkıbasım*, ed. İsmail Ünver (Ankara: TTK, 1983); Aḥmedī, *Tevārīḫ-i Mülūk-i Āl-i ʿOsmān Ġazv-i İşān Bā Küffār*, ed. Kemal Sılay (Harvard Üniversitesi: Yakın Doğu Dilleri ve Medeniyetleri Bölümü, 2004); Pal Fodor, "Aḥmedī's Dāsitān as a Source of Early Ottoman History," *Acta Orientalia Academiae Scientiarum* Hungaria 38 (1984): 41–54; Halil İnalcık, *Has-Bağçede ʿAyş u Tarab: Nedîmler, Şâirler, Mutrîbler* (Istanbul: İş Bankası Yayınları, 2010), 112–140.

Balkan lands under the Ottoman domain sometime between 804/1402 and 813/1411, and then continued this protection under Süleymān's younger brother Meḥmed I.[28] This period was a moment of intense Ottoman political instability that historians typically call the Interregnum in post-Timurid Anatolia. Among Aḥmedī's peers in Cairo, Hācı Paşa (b. after 740/1339–d. 823s/1420s) presents a similar case for the rich venues of patronage that Anatolia proffered during the fourteenth century and the concomitant rise of the Ottomans. Born in the old Seljuk and subsequent Karamanid capital Konya, Hācı Paşa came to Mamluk urban centers including Cairo and Damascus in order to study medicine. Remarkably, he had already gained recognition in Mamluk territory and was consequently appointed to various positions at Mamluk endowed institutions. Similar to Aḥmedī, Hācı Paşa also entered the service of the Aydınid dynasty on his return to Anatolia in 771/1370.[29] He remained in Aydınid lands at least until 792/1390 when his protector submitted to the Ottoman ruler Bāyezīd I (r. 791–804/1389–1402). His whereabouts between 792/1390 and 827/1424 (the likely year of his death) are not known. Some evidence suggests he might have gone to his Karamanid homelands, while others indicate that he might have also applied to the Ottoman ruler Murād II (r. 824–848 and 850–855/1421–1444 and 1446–1451) protection once the political chaos in post-Timurid Anatolia had calmed to the Ottoman advantage.[30] The results of this attempt are not known. Nonetheless, both of these biographies indicate that the Ottomans were gaining recognition towards the end of the fourteenth century.

The paths of Aḥmedī and Hācı Paşa who were concomitantly present in Mamluk lands also overlapped with those of the aforementioned Mollā Fenārī. These three students who originated from different corners of Anatolia shared at least one professor in Mamluk lands: Akmal al-Dīn Bābartī (d. 786/1384). It is a telling fact that of these three scholars Mollā Fenārī was the only one who both originated from Ottoman lands and entered the service of the Ottoman ruler on his return during the 792s/1390s – approximately the same time that Hācı Paşa came to Aydınid lands.[31] This further proves the idea that the Ottoman ruling

28 For Süleyman's controversial reign and the Interregnum, see Dimitris Kastritsis, *The Sons of Bayezid: Empire Building and Representation in the Ottoman Civil War of 1402–1413* (Leiden: Brill, 2007).

29 For a recent and comprehensive treatment of Hācı Paşa's biography, oeuvre, and legacy, see Yıldız, "From Cairo to Ayasuluk." For his return to Anatolia in 1370 see Yıldız, "From Cairo to Ayasuluk," 273. Also see Cemil Akpınar, "Hacı Paşa," *DİA* 14 (1996): 492–496; J. Walsh, "Ḥādjdjī Pasha, Djalāl al-Dīn Khıḍr b. ʿAlī," *EI*[2] 3 (1971): 45.

30 Yıldız, "From Cairo to Ayasuluk," 288.

31 There are conflicting claims regarding Mollā Fenārī's birthplace. However, he completed his early education in İznik which was conquered by the Ottomans in 723/1324. In this paper he is therefore considered as originating from Ottoman lands. Aydın claims that Bāyezīd I ap-

elite was gradually establishing themselves as potential patrons. Although the practical need for trained staff to serve local political actors was a major motivation in accommodating immigration and travel, it was not the only consideration. Both pre-Ottoman and Ottoman examples of the universal genre "Mirror for Princes" frequently invoked offering protection to visitors.[32] Becoming the patron of scholars, poets, and artists was also depicted as one of the qualities of a generous and just ruler.[33] The patronage rulers offered to these incoming individuals even caused occasional competition between sovereigns; if a person of significance (in knowledge, science, law, etc.) departed one ruler's lands for another's territory this preference for a new placement was humiliating for the former patron.[34] Ibn Baṭṭūṭa's notes suggest the existence of this sentiment

pointed Mollā Fenārī to the judgeship of Bursa in 795/1393. See Aydın, "Mollā Fenārī," *DİA* 30 (1995): 245.

32 For a concise treatment of this genre in the Islamic world see the introduction by Robert Dankoff in Yūsuf Khāṣṣ Ḥājib, *Wisdom of Royal Glory (Kutadgu Bilig): A Turko-Islamic Mirror for Princes,* trans. Robert Dankoff (Chicago: Chicago University Press, 1983), 1–35. Also see Hasan Hüseyin Adalıoğlu and Coşkun Yıldırım, "Siyâset-nâme," *DİA* 37 (2009): 304–308.

33 For example, Yūsuf Ḥāṣṣ Ḥājib (d. 469/1077) emphasizes the significance of generosity and patronage for a good ruler in his *Kutadgu Bilig.* Similarly, Niẓām al-Mulk (d. 485/1092) listed the act of "patronizing men of learning and wisdom" among the qualities of a good ruler as early as in the first chapter of his *Siyāset-nāme.* Three centuries later Şeyhoğlu (741-after 803/1340-after 1401) repeats the importance of generosity and patronage for a good ruler in his work entitled *Kenzü'l-Küberâ*t hat he composed in Turkish for the Ottoman ruler Bāyezīd I. Muṣṭafā ʿĀlī (948–1008/1541–1599), the Ottoman intellectual who wrote his *Counsel for Sultans* substantially later than the aforementioned works, brought an additional dimension to this discussion of patronage by describing how a monarch should treat an individual coming from another ruler's land. Although Muṣṭafā ʿĀlī lived long after the period this paper focuses on, his description is helpful in understanding the attitudes of Ottoman rulers toward the scholars who arrived from Mamluk lands. See Yūsuf Khāṣṣ Ḥājib, *Wisdom of Royal Glory,* 180 and 183; Niẓām al-Mulk, *The Book of Government or Rules for Kings: The Siyar al-Muluk or Siyat-nama of Nizam al-Mulk,* trans. Hurbert Darke, 3rd ed. (London: Curzon, 2002), 10; Şeyhoğlu Mustafa, *Kenzü'l-Küberâ ve Mehekkü'l-ulemâ: İnceleme, Metin, İndeks,* ed. Kemal Yavuz (Ankara: Atatürk Kültür Merkezi, 1991), 56, 66, 70–71; Muṣṭafā ʿĀlī, *Mustafā ʿĀlī's Counsel for Sultans of 1581: Edition, Translation, Notes,* ed. Andreas Tietze (Vienna: Österreichische Akademie der Wissenschaften, 1979–1982), 2: 62. For Şeyhoğlu's reference to the Ottoman ruler Bāyezīd I, see p. 73; for his acknowledgement of his patron Paşa Ağa who was formerly under Germiyanid authority yet offered his allegiance to Bāyezīd I following the death of Süleymān Şāh, see p. 152.

34 Muṣṭafā ʿĀlī's narrated reaction that Meḥmed II showed on Mollā Gürānī's (his former teacher) departure from Ottoman territory reveals how rulers valued their roles as patrons: "...vilāyetümden böyle bir fāẓıl ḳalḳub gitmek ve aḫaruñ memleketinde mütemekkin itmek nāmūs-ı salṭanata ḫalel virmiştir..." See Muṣṭafā ʿĀlī, *Künhü'l-Aḫbār,* 5 vols. (İstanbul: Takvimhane-i Amire, 1277/1877 or 1878), 5: 227. When Sinān Paşa was imprisoned by Meḥmed II the scholars of the time intervened on behalf of Sinān Paşa, threatening Meḥmed II that they would leave Ottoman lands if Sinān Paşa is not freed. According to Muṣṭafā ʿĀlī's report Meḥmed II gave in and freed Sinān Paşa after receiving this threat. See

among the lords of Anatolian principalities. On one occasion he specifically speaks highly of the generosity of rulers in the Anatolian town of Kastomunu toward "visiting scholars," while in another he narrates that a scholar called al-Kharazmī invoked Ibn Baṭṭūṭa's help to save him from the wrath of his patron. His patron, the current ruler of Menteşe principality in Western Anatolia, had felt offended when al-Kharazmī preferred the patronage of the Aydınid dynasty over his.[35] Rulers arriving from humble origins and attempting to consolidate their authorities within these newly conquered lands cultivated a preference for their lands and patronage by individuals educated and trained in older Islamic lands as a source of prestige, legitimization, and power. This mentality gave hope to individuals that they could also find generous patrons in other lands. The search for a patron therefore became a primary impetus for individuals to circulate between the courts of upcoming powers along the fringes of the Muslim world.

Patronage: Identities and Allegiances

The Ottomans were not initially considered impressive when compared to their peers in Anatolia, nor did they inherit the venerable traditions of the Mamluk sultans. Nonetheless, as early as the 1330s Ottoman rulers and administrators initiated the construction of learning institutions and endowments within their newly conquered lands as well as readily embracing the historical pattern of accepting immigrants who yearned for a protector. Settling in frontier lands brought some advantages to the Ottomans. Despite examples such as Aḥmedī and Hācı Paşa who initially preferred alternative patrons in Anatolia, the biographies of scholars and bureaucrats in the service of early Ottoman rulers reveals that most individuals were primarily trained in either Mamluk or Timurid lands while others joined the Ottoman polity from its immediate neighbors.[36] During the early decades of Ottoman growth administrators specifically acknowledged the necessity of hiring individuals trained in various branches of Islamic law and learning. As Ottoman borders expanded into the Balkans the Ottomans required judges to administer cities and towns which had no pre-existing Islamic institutions or personnel. They hired scholars from established Islamic lands in order to employ them in these recently founded colleges. Dāvūd-i Ḳayserī, the

Muṣṭafā ʿĀlī, *Künhü'l-Aḫbār: Cilt II, Fâtiḥ Sulṭān Meḥmed Devri 1451–1481*, ed. M. Hüdai Şentürk (Ankara: TTK, 2003), 202–203.

35 Ibn Baṭṭūṭa, 427 and 429.

36 For example, Aḥmedī, Aḥmed-i Dāʿī (d. after 824/1421), Şeyhoğlu (d. 807/1414), and Şeyhī (d. after 832/1429) were among the intellectuals and poets who came to Ottoman lands from Germiyanid ones along with the aforementioned patron of Şeyhoğlu, Paşa Ağa. For individuals joining the Ottomans from the Germiyanids see İnalcık, *Has-Bağçede*, 93–151.

first professor appointed to the first known Ottoman *madrasa* founded by an Ottoman ruler, is a particularly suitable example for this profile.[37] Originating from the Karamanid lands, Dāvūd spent years in Egypt in order to excel in his studies before traveling widely – including through Iran and visiting his hometown Kayseri.[38] When the earliest known Ottoman *madrasa* in Iznik was completed he was appointed as the first *mudarris* a few years after the visit Ibn Baṭṭūṭa paid to the Ottoman towns of Bursa and Iznik. He remained in this position until he died in 751/1350. As a scholar trained in both a prominent Anatolian center such as Kayseri and then in Mamluk *madrasas* he left his mark on Ottoman higher learning during its earliest stages.

Among the natives returning to Ottoman lands Şeyh Bedreddīn (760–819/1358–1416 or d. 823/1420) was by far the most controversial.[39] Born and raised in Thrace (conquered for the first time by the Ottomans), Bedreddīn found his way to Cairo where he studied under scholars such as Akmal al-Dīn Bābartī who had also trained Bedreddīn's contemporaries Aḥmedī, Hācı Paşa, and Mollā Fenārī.[40] This successful scholar later became the tutor of Barqūq's son Faraj (r. 801–808/1399–1405 and 808–815/1405–1412) who was to become the Mamluk sultan. Thanks to his position as the young prince's preceptor Bedreddīn spent considerable time in social gatherings that the Mamluk sultan convened. During such an occasion the young scholar met also Ḥusayn al-Akhlātī, who played a major role in Bedreddīn's later spiritual life. Under the influence of Ḥusayn's charismatic personality Bedreddīn became attracted to Sufism. Ḥusayn eventually returned to Anatolia and entered the service of Mūsā, Bāyezīd I's son who was killed in 816/1413 during the Interregnum by his brother Meḥmed I. Following the death of his patron Bedreddīn became involved in a rebellion and appeared as its ideological leader. Finally, he was captured by Meḥmed I's men as the Ottoman sovereign gradually reclaimed former Ottoman territories, and was executed following a biased trial. However, his works continued to circulate within the Ottoman world despite the author's execution.[41]

As a growing political entity required to correspond regularly with other political powers, the Ottoman polity was also faced with the challenge of organizing the bureaucracy and resources they had seized. These diplomatic and administrative tasks demanded scribes who specialized in organizing the chan-

37 Mehmet Bayrakdar, *Kayserili Dâvûd: Dâvûdu'l-Kayserî* (Ankara: Kültür ve Turizm Bakanlığı, 1988).

38 Bayrakdar, *Kayserili Dâvûd*, 11.

39 H.J. Kissling, "Badr al-dīn b. Ḳāḍī Samāwnā," *EI*[2] 1 (1958): 869–70; Bilal Dindar, "Bedreddin Simâvî," *DİA* 5 (1992): 331–334.

40 For Bedreddīn's *Rūmī* qualities see Balivet, *Tasavvuf ve İsyan*, 39; Özbaran, *Bir Osmanlı Kimliği*, 57.

41 See Muṣṭafā ʿĀlī, *Künhü'l-Aḫbār*, ed. M. Hüdai Şentürk, 194.

cery as well as composing diplomatic letters in multiple languages. Shams al-Dīn ibn al-Jazarī (751–833/1350–1429) was a celebrated scholar of Qur'anic reading *(qirā'āt)* and the art of composition *(inshā')* who had occupied prominent positions under Mamluk sultans.[42] He became estranged from the Mamluk regime after his property was confiscated, and thereafter came to the court of Bāyezīd I where he was welcomed with utmost respect. The treatment Ibn al-Jazarī received in his new home was so generous that Ṭūlū, the Mamluk ambassador to the Ottoman court, gave a detailed report to the Mamluk sultan Barqūq (r. 790–799/1390–1399) regarding Ibn al-Jazarī's conditions of stay and salaries.[43] Despite Ibn al-Jazarī's controversial departure from Mamluk lands Bāyezīd must have perceived Ibn al-Jazarī's arrival as a sign of the Ottoman court's increasing prestige within the region, and so he treated this celebrated scholar accordingly.[44]

The support that Ottoman rulers offered to these incoming scholars was repaid in a multitude of ways. For instance, Ibn al-Jazarī became a major influence in the development of Qur'anic reading in Ottoman lands.[45] He also remained in Bāyezīd I's court as a major scribe until 804/1402 (the battle of Ankara). Having witnessed the memorable battle of Nicopolis, Ibn al-Jazarī composed the victory proclamation (now lost) sent by Bāyezīd to the Mamluk sultan Barqūq in 798/1396. He also became a teacher to Bāyezīd I's sons. Although Ibn al-Jazarī left Ottoman lands with Tīmūr, one of his sons was later employed in Meḥmed I's court as a *nişāncı* (head of the chancery)[46] and penned some of the correspondence sent from the Ottoman ruler to his contemporary sultan Shaykh al-Maḥmūdī.[47] Another scholar who moved freely between at least three regions of the Muslim world is Ibn ʿArabshāh (791–854/1389–1450), who also substantially contributed to the Ottoman chancery and diplomatic correspondence. Born in Mamluk lands, Ibn ʿArabshāh spent majority of his education in Timurid lands and beyond where he also learned Turkish. During the reign of Meḥmed I he came to the Ottoman capital, serving as the tutor of Meḥmed I's sons and head of the Ottoman chancery. He translated multiple Arabic and Persian works into Turkish under Meḥmed I patronage, as well as composed some diplomatic

42 For a recent and thorough treatment of this scholar see İlker Evrim Binbaş, "A Damascene Eyewitness to the Battle of Nicopolis: Shams al-Dīn Ibn al-Jazarī (d. 833/1429)," in *Contact and Conflict in Frankish Greece and the Aegean, 1204–1453,* ed. Nikolaos G. Crissis and Mike Carr (Surrey: Ashgate, 2014), 153–175.

43 Ibn al-Furāt, *Ta'rīkh al-Duwal wa'l-Mulūk,* ed. Costi K. Zurayk and Nejla Izzeddin, vols. 8 and 9 (Beirut, 1936–1942), 9: 457; Ibn Ḥajar, *Inbā' al-Ghumr,* 1: 510 and 524–525.

44 For the allegations of Ibn al-Jazarī's dubious financial transactions regarding his appointments see Binbaş, "A Damascene Eyewitness."

45 Tayyar Altıkulaç, "İbnü'l Cezerî," *DİA* 20 (1999): 551–557.

46 Ibid.

47 See Yüksel Muslu, *Imperial Warfare and Diplomacy,* 35 and relevant footnotes in this work for additional sources.

correspondence for the Ottoman ruler to the Mamluk ruler Shaykh al-Maḥmūdī (the Mamluk sultan who hosted Mollā Fenārī in Cairo).[48]

The presumable impact of Mamluk institutions and intellectual traditions most remarkably manifests itself in three of the eight scholars believed to have occupied the post of *Şeyhülislām* – the most prestigious position a scholar of law could attain in the fifteenth century Ottoman state: Mollā Fenārī, Mollā Gürānī (813–883/1410–1488), and Mollā ʿArab (d. 901/1495–96).[49] While Mollā Fenārī's background has been briefly mentioned, Mollā Fenārī's two successors Mollā Gürānī and Mollā ʿArab present substantially different cases.[50] Mollā Gürānī's career within Ottoman lands was closely associated with the cultural significance of pilgrimage and phenomenon of patronage. Sources do not agree on the details of Mollā Gürānī's early life. He was likely born in a town called Gürān in northern Iraq. After his early education, possibly in Baghdad, he visited the Mamluk cities of Damascus and Jerusalem. He finally came to Cairo and completed his studies under the guidance of various Mamluk scholars such as Ibn Ḥajar (who was among Mollā Fenārī's students). He quickly gained recognition in *fiqh* and joined the social gatherings of the Mamluk sultan Jaqmaq (r. 842–854/1438–1453). However, around 840/1440 he lost the sultan's favor and was dismissed as a result of a quarrel with another scholar. Mollā Gürānī was brought to Ottoman lands in a state of extreme poverty by the former Ottoman *Şeyhülislām* Mollā Yegān (d. appr. 865/1461). Even after giving up his position Mollā Yegān remained a prominent scholar during both Murād II and Meḥmed II's (r. 848–850 and 855–886/1444–1446 and 1451–1481) reigns. In 844/1441 he made a pilgrimage during which he was entrusted with Murād II's annual gifts to Mecca and Medine. He met Mollā Gürānī during one stop (likely in Aleppo) after Mollā Gürānī had already lost the Mamluk sultan's favor.[51] According to Ottoman chroniclers Mollā Yegān brought Mollā Gürānī to Murād II as, "a gift of *ḥajj*."[52]

48 Ibid., 35–36 and relevant footnotes in this work for additional sources.

49 For Mollā Fenārī see R.C. Repp, *The Müfti of İstanbul: A Study in the Development of the Ottoman Learned Hierarchy* (London: Ithaca Press, 1986), 73–98.

50 For Mollā Gürānī, see Ahmet Ateş, "Mollā Gürānī (1416–1488)," *İA* 8: 406–408; Repp, *The Müfti*, 166–74; J.R. Walsh, "Gūrānī, Sharaf al-Dīn," *EI*² 2 (1965): 1140–41, M. Kamil Yaşaroğlu, "Molla Gürânî," *DİA* 30 (2005): 248–250. In his book *The Müfti of İstanbul*, Repp argues that the inception of the position *Şeyhülislām* (or the *müftī* of the capital) is obscure. Before the sixteenth century the Ottomans used the words of *müftī* and *Şeyhülislām* interchangeably; in later centuries the usage of *Şeyhülislām* became more widespread. Despite Repp's convincing arguments the present study uses the title *Şeyhülislām* for the sake of clarity. See Repp, *The Müfti*, xix–xxi; J.H. Kramers, R.C. Repp, and R.W. Bulliett, "Shaykh al-Islām," *EI*² 9 (1996): 399–402.

51 For the reason of his dismissal by the Mamluk sultan see Ibrāhīm b. Ḥasan al-Biqāʿī, *ʿInwān al-Zamān bi-Tarājim al-Shuyūḥ wa'l-Aqrān*, ed. Ḥasan Ḥabashī, vols. 5 (Cairo: Dār al-Kutub, 2001), 1: 61–62.

52 Repp, *The Müfti*, 101.

The fact that Ottoman chroniclers presented Mollā Gürānī as a gift of *ḥajj* from Mollā Yegān to Murād II shows the value that the Ottoman world attached both to the incoming Mollā and the pilgrimage. Already a celebrated scholar within Mamluk territory, the Mollā was worthy of being presented to the Ottoman ruler as a gift commemorating another scholar's pilgrimage. He immediately became subject to the generosity of Murād II, and except for short intervals spent the rest of his life in Ottoman lands. The multitude of positions held by Mollā Gürānī and works he produced confirm his successful career as a scholar who circulated between the Ottoman and Mamluk lands. He taught in a variety of Ottoman institutions of high learning, produced works in Islamic sciences, and served as a judge in a number of towns including Bursa.

Yet at least by the Ottoman authors this scholar was mostly remembered as the tutor of the future Meḥmed II, who succeeded his father Murād II and later conquered Constantinople. By the time Mollā Gürānī arrived in Ottoman lands Murād II had been receiving unsatisfactory reports regarding the training of his son. Disappointed with his son's teachers and likely with his son as well, Murād II decided to appoint Mollā Gürānī as the young prince's teacher. This was the beginning of a complex relationship between Meḥmed and Mollā Gürānī that oscillated between extremes. Mollā Gürānī reportedly managed to "convince" young Meḥmed to become serious about his studies with the help of a stick.[53] The alleged improvement in his son's education pleased Murād II so much that he expressed his appreciation to the successful tutor with lavish gifts. The manner by which Mollā Gürānī tamed the young prince gave almost a legendary quality to Gürānī's reputation as he was described in Ottoman sources. According to Repp, Mollā Gürānī remained in the post of "Hoca" until Meḥmed II's second accession to the throne in 855/1451. He remained an influential figure in Meḥmed II's rule even after his ascension to power;[54] his former position as the Sultan's teacher opened the road for high positions such as vizierate, which he rejected. The Mollā instead preferred to remain a member of the legal profession.

Mollā Gürānī's presence in the Ottoman court was an opportunity for the Ottoman ruler to advertise his role as a patron of scholars within the region, and Meḥmed II knew how to use this opportunity. For example, he asked his former teacher to compose the *fatḥnāme* (proclamation of victory) for Constantinople which he sent to Mamluk lands. Mollā Gürānī's competence in Arabic literature was well known, and Meḥmed II wished to benefit from his teacher's eloquence in this language in order to impress his counterpart in Cairo. This letter also allowed

53 Ateş, "Mollā Gürānī," *İA* 8: 406–408.

54 For instance, Mollā Gürānī argued for the continuation of this surge before Constantinople; Repp, *The Müfti*, 170.

Meḥmed II to send the implicit message that Mollā Gürānī, who had once been in the service of the Mamluk sultan, was now in his service instead.[55]

No matter how closely Mollā Gürānī became involved with Ottoman institutions he remained associated with his former patrons and homeland, at least in the minds of Ottoman authors. Soon after Mollā Gürānī composed the *fatḥ-nāme* he became the leading actor in an incident between the Ottomans and Mamluks.[56] The incident, which is said to have occurred around the year 859/1454–1455, also revealed that patronage might cause rivalry between two sovereigns. Mollā Gürānī left Ottoman holdings for Mamluk lands after falling out with his former pupil Meḥmed II regarding a legal matter. According to Taşköprülüzāde (d. 968/1561) and Muṣṭafā ʿĀlī (d. 1008/1600), Mollā Gürānī went to

55 Yüksel Muslu, *Imperial Warfare and Diplomacy,* 110–111.

56 This anecdote was available first in Taşköprülüzāde, and then narrated by later generations such as Muṣṭafā ʿĀlī. It is also mentioned by the Mamluk author Ibrāhīm b. Ḥasan al-Biqāʿī (809–885/1406–1480). Ahmed Ateş's article discussing Mollā Gürānī concludes that this story was a later fabrication by Ottoman authors. His arguments were two-fold. First, Qāytbāy (whose name was given by Taşköprülüzāde as the Mamluk sultan in question) did not come to the Mamluk throne until 872/1468. Second, al-Sakhāwī included a detailed chronology in the biography of Mollā Gürānī. The information he gave regarding the whereabouts of Mollā Gürānī within Mamluk lands during these years excludes the possibility of an additional visit to Cairo. John Walsh agrees with Ateş. Repp also accepts the idea that this incident (if it ever happened) could not have taken place during the 860s/1455s. However, Repp suggests that Mollā Gürānī might have gone to Egypt after 872/1467–68 as a result of a quarrel with Meḥmed II since little is known of Mollā Gürānī's activities between 870/1465–1466 and 886/1481; this would also explain why Taşköprülüzāde named Qāytbāy as the Mamluk sultan. However, Repp does not present an explanation for either the presence of Mollā Gürānī in Mamluk lands or for his pilgrimage between 858/1454 and 862/1457. However, in light of the information that al-Biqāʿī presents in two of his works we must revise our information regarding Mollā Gürānī's life. This anecdote is likely not completely a later fabrication. Al-Biqāʿī provides detailed discussion regarding a quarrel between Mollā Gürānī and Meḥmed II manner, as well as Mehmed II's reconciliation efforts between 859/1455 and 861/1457. Although he does not say anything regarding the Mamluk sultan's involvement in this affair, he does mention that the Mamluk sultan Īnāl (r. 857–865/1453–1461) showed great respect to Mollā Gürānī who had been dismissed by the previous Mamluk sultan (also narrated in detail by al-Biqāʿī). It is likely that multiple quarrels prompted Mollā Gürānī to leave the Ottoman lands more than once, and Ottoman authors might be confusing the details and dates of these incidents. Although detailed analysis by Ateş and Repp excludes the possibility that this anecdote took place during Mollā Gürānī's trip between 858/1454 and 862/1457, we must reexamine Mollā Gürānī's life in light of the evidence al-Biqāʿī offers. For primary sources on Mollā Gürānī see al-Biqāʿī, *ʿInwān al-Zamān,* 1: 60–66; idem, *Iẓhār al-ʿAṣr li-Asrār Ahl al-ʿAṣr: Tārīkh al-Biqāʿī,* ed. Muḥammad Sālim b. Shadīd al-ʿAwfī, 3 vols. (al-Muhandisin, Jizah: Hajar, 1992), 2: 137 and 293; Taşköprülüzāde, *Eş-Şeḳāʾiḳu n-Nuʿmānīye fī ʿUlemāʾi d-Devleti l-ʿOsmānīye,* ed. Ahmed Subhi Furat (İstanbul: Edebiyat Fakültesi Basımevi, 1985), 83–90; Mecdî Mehmed Efendi, *Şakaik-ı Nuʿmaniye ve Zeyilleri: Hadaiku'ş-Şakaik,* ed. Abdülkadir Özcan (İstanbul: Çağrı Yayınları, 1989), 1: 102–111; Muṣṭafā ʿĀlī, *Künhü'l-Aḫbār,* 5: 226–228. For scholarly studies see Ateş, "Mollā Gürānī"; Repp, *The Müfti,* 166–174; J.R. Walsh, "Gūrānī, Sharaf al-Dīn"; Yaşaroğlu, "Molla Gürânî."

the court of the Mamluk sultan Qāytbāy (r. 872–901/1468–1496), who these sources mistakenly name as the Mamluk sultan at the time. Mollā Gürānī was well received by Qāytbāy; however, Meḥmed II looked for a way to bring his teacher back in regret over their falling-out. He wrote a letter to Qāytbāy asking him to send Mollā Gürānī back, and the Mamluk sultan passed this message to Mollā Gürānī even though he did not want the scholar to leave. In response Mollā Gürānī said that no matter what happened between him and Meḥmed II they were like father and son; if he did not return then the two sultans would become enemies. Mollā Gürānī then returned to Ottoman lands loaded with gifts he received from Qāytbāy. He and Meḥmed reconciled once Mollā arrived at Constantinople either in 861/1456–1457 or 862/1457–1458, and he was soon after appointed to the judgeship of Bursa. Some modern scholars question the authenticity of this anecdote. However, despite the controversy this anecdote remains significant in showing that Ottoman writers continued to associate Mollā Gürānī with Mamluk lands and possibly with patronage of the Mamluk sultan. Mollā Gürānī ultimately rose to the position of *Şeyhülislām*, and clearly continued to be respected by the state cadres even after Meḥmed's death since he maintained his positon as a *Şeyhülislām* until his own death in 1488.

One episode that took place during Mollā Gürānī's tenure as *Şeyhülislām* but after the death of his pupil Meḥmed II proves that the Ottoman sources might not be off track in their assessments regarding this scholar's lingering sympathies toward the Mamluk regime. The Mamluk ambassador Jānibak al-Ḥabīb al-ʿAlay al-Īnālī was granted an audience by the Ottoman ruler Bāyezīd II (r. 886–918/1481–1512) during carefully choreographed series of ceremonies and audiences held on a plain called Çöke near Edirne.[57] He arrived at the Ottoman court following a defeat that the Ottoman forces suffered against the Mamluk troops near Malatya in 889–890/1485. His task was to mend relations between the two courts; however, a question posed by a member of Bāyezīd II's entourage made it clear that that there was little hope for Jānibak to complete this mission successfully: "[W]ho are you [the Mamluks] to rule over the Two Protected Sanctuaries, you sons of Infidels? This rule (or land) is more proper for our sultan, [since] he is the son of the sultans and the sultans."[58] This rhetorical question targeted the Mamluk sultan's slave background as contrasted with the dynastic lineage of Bāyezīd II, as well as the Mamluk sultan's recent conversion to Islam versus the Muslim background of Bāyezīd II's (male) ancestors. Jānibak as the representative of the Mamluk sultan could not stand silent when challenged by

57 For a detailed study of this mission see Yüksel Muslu, *Imperial Diplomacy and Warfare*, 1–2, 134–136, 138–141, 147, and 249–250.

58 Ḥusayn b. Muḥammad al-Ḥusaynī, "Kitāb Nafāʾis al-Majālis al-Sulṭāniyya," in *Majālis al-Sulṭān al-Ghawri*, ed. ʿAbd al-Wahhāb ʿAzzām (Cairo, 1941), 134.

this humiliating question. However, for the purposes of this paper Mollā Gürānī's response is more relevant than Jānibak's. The aged scholar who was the *Şeyhülislām* at the time was also present in the audience and in fact seated to the right side of the sultan, indicating the respect that Bāyezīd II showed to both his *Şeyhülislām* and his late father's tutor. Addressing the individual who asked the humiliating question he said, "[D]on't speak about the rulers of Egypt, you dishonored yourself." In light of this episode it is possible, albeit speculative, to think that Mollā Gürānī did not approve of armed conflict between the Ottomans and the Mamluks. It is telling that even after spending years in Ottoman service as well as occupying the highest position within the Ottoman learning and legal system Mollā Gürānī still did not hesitate to intervene and aid the Mamluk ambassador in front of his Ottoman patron. When Mollā Gürānī passed away in 883/1488 the Ottoman ruler Bāyezīd was not only present in the funeral procession, but also paid the scholar's accumulated debts. Clearly Bāyezīd continued to value the scholar and did not necessarily perceive Mollā Gürānī's intervention as anti-Ottoman.

The case of Mollā ʿArab, Mollā Gürānī's student and successor as *Şeyhülislām*, also exhibits the continuation of ties among these highly valued individuals within Ottoman lands.[59] Born in Aleppo, Mollā ʿAlā al-Dīn ʿAlī al-ʿArabī (known as Mollā ʿArab) completed his early education in his hometown and then came to Bursa in order to study under Mollā Gürānī. During Bāyezīd II's reign he began to climb the ranks of *ʿilmiyye*. Upon his tutor's death he was brought to his position as *Şeyhülislām* in 893/1488 during the intense days of the Ottoman-Mamluk war, maintaining his position until 901/1496.[60] Both Ottoman and Mamluk sources indicate that Mollā ʿArab actively pursued conclusion of the peace between the Ottomans and Mamluks. He appears to be the person who spoke against the war on the Ottoman council and played a critical role in convincing Bāyezīd not to pursue another campaign season against the Mamluks.[61] The following quotation from an Ottoman chronicle summarized Mollā ʿArab's possible argument for

59 For example, about intellectual networks in the Muslim world, see İlker Evrim Binbaş, *Intellectual Networks in Timurid Iran: Sharaf al-Dīn ʿAlī Yazdī and the Islamicate Republic of Letters* (New York: Cambridge University Press, 2016); Judith Pfeiffer, *Politics, Patronage, and the Transmission of Knowledge in 13th–15th Century Tabriz* (Leiden: Brill, 2014). Unfortunately, I was not able to see Binbaş's book before the completion of this paper.

60 Repp, *The Müfti*, 128.

61 Muṣṭafā ʿĀlī clearly states that Mollā ʿArab was the only person courageous enough to speak against the war, while the rest of the congregation kept silence out of fear. İbn Kemāl does not give the name of Mollā ʿArab, but he also described how prominent administrators, governors, and commanders were seeking a convenient moment to express their opposition. See İbn Kemāl, *Tevârîḫ-i Âl-i O̱sman: VIII. Defter*, ed. Ahmed Uğur, (Ankara: TTK, 1997), 123; Muṣṭafā ʿĀlī, *Künhü'l-Aḫbār*, Süleymaniye Library MS. Fatih 4225, 162a; Muṣṭafā ʿĀlī, *Kayseri Raşid Efendi Kütüphanesindeki 901 ve 920 no.'lu nüshalara gore Kitābü't-târīḫ-i Künhü'l- Aḫbār*, ed. Ahmed Uğur et all. (Kayseri: Erciyes Üniversitesi Yayınları, 1997), 2: 864.

peace: "[i]t has been a long time since your ancestors and you have been occupied with fighting against the non-Muslims for the sake of faith(.) It is not a good sign that now Your Highness has been fighting against the Muslim brethren..."[62] This argument particularly highlights the fact that the two sovereigns shared the same faith – a statement which one would naturally expect from a scholar of Islamic religion and law. Due to his prestigious position as a *Şeyhülislām* it is not surprising that he had close contacts with many members of the Ottoman administration, first and foremost with the Ottoman sultan. Mollā ʿArab also facilitated the peace efforts by sending his personal delegates to prominent governors of the Mamluk regime in order to accelerate the process; the Mollā had reportedly never ceased to correspond with acquaintances in his homeland.[63] These networks seemed to have helped in his efforts for peace and his active role as a facilitator paid off; Bāyezīd followed the advice of Mollā ʿArab and his fellows within the Ottoman divan by agreeing to sign the peace treaty in 896/1491.[64]

In light of Mollā Gürānī's defensive comments concerning the Mamluk sultan during the Mamluk ambassador Jānibak's audience with the Ottoman court it is possible to say that Mollā Gürānī would have agreed with his pupil regarding the Ottoman-Mamluk war.[65] Moreover, judging from his earlier position during the siege of Constantinople in 857/1453 Mollā Gürānī would have likely become an ardent supporter of the *ghazā* argument presented by Mollā ʿArab to Bāyezīd II. Both İdrīs-i Bidlīsī (d. 926/1520) and Hoca Saʿdeddīn (d. 1008/1599) (likely citing İdrīs-i Bidlīsī) emphasized that Mollā Gürānī, whom they called the tutor (*hoca*) of the sultan Meḥmed II, had spoken for the continuation of the siege despite the

62 Bihiştī, *Die Chronik des Ahmed Sinân Čelebi Genannt Bihišti: Eine Quelle zur Geschichte des osmanischen Reiches unter Sultan Bāyezid II*, ed. Brigitte Moser (Munich: Dr. Rudolf Trofenik, 1980), 34v: "bunca müddetdir ki abā ʿan cedd işüñüz kāfire cezā ve gazāʾdur şimdi müslümānlar ile muʿādāt ve muḥāṣama ʿalāmet-i saʿādet degildür."

63 Hoca Saʿadeddīn, *Tācü't-tevārīḫ* (İstanbul: Matbaa-yi Amire, 1862–63), 2: 67.

64 Without providing a source for this information Repp also states that Mollā ʿArab continued to have contact with Mamluk rulers. Relying on Ibn Ṭūlūn, Tekindağ states Mollā ʿArab sent his own envoy to the Mamluk sultan in order to convince him to accept peace. See Repp, *The Müfti*, 182; Şehabettin Tekindağ, "II. Bayezid Devrinde Çukurova'da Nüfuz Mücadelesi," *Belleten* 31 (1967): 370–71.

65 The relationship between Mollā ʿArab and his tutor Mollā Gürānī requires further investigation. Taşköprülüzāde supplements this biography with anecdotes from his father who was a former student of Mollā ʿArab. According to Taşköprülüzāde's father, Mollā Gürānī liked his student. Taşköprülüzāde, *Eş-Şeḳāʾiḳ*, ed. Furat, 150–55. Contrary to Taşköprülüzāde, Repp thinks that Mollā Gürānī disliked his student or at least later grew to dislike him. Repp bases his argument on a letter in the Topkapı Palace archive belonging to Mollā Gürānī. Repp thinks that Mollā Gürānī sent this letter to the sultan (either Bāyezīd or Meḥmed II), complaining about his former student's lack of qualities in teaching and practicing law. However, Mollā Gürānī did not cite the name of this individual in the letter. I believe that Taşköprülüzāde provides an accurate assessment, and that in the letter Repp refers to Mollā Gürānī is discussing another contemporary scholar from the same region.

opposition of a strong group who spoke against the war with the Byzantines, including the grand vizier Çandarlı Ḥalil Paşa (d. 857/1453).[66]

The examples of Mollā Gürānī and Mollā ʿArab suggest that despite their long and successful careers within the Ottoman empire the sensitivities of both individuals accommodated both pro-Ottoman and pro-Mamluk sympathies. Mollā Gürānī's pro-Mamluk stance in front of a predominantly Ottoman audience as well as Bāyezīd II's reaction or lack of reaction to this stance remind us that dual loyalties were possible during the sixteenth century. Numerous studies on identity formation have shown that this flexibility was not unique to Ottoman-Mamluk exchanges; identities as well as allegiances were both flexible and porous within the medieval and early-modern Mediterranean basin. However, this identity plasticity does not mean that there were no personal qualities that would be perceived as distinguishing marks of one polity over another. Religion, regional provenance, familial relations, and education were likely the prime delineators for such categories.[67] The existence of such category markers did not necessarily preclude the permeability of loyalties, including that between individuals from different religious backgrounds.[68] The fact that substantial portions of both the Ottoman and Mamluk populations shared the same religion (Sunni Islam) while their ruling classes both shared both a language (Turkish) and a general preference toward the same school of law (Ḥanafī) likely created a broader canvas on which dual loyalties and allegiances were easily accommodated. Networks or connected lives could also be easily maintained since a complete and absolute transfer of loyalties was not the norm when individuals moved between these lands. It is interesting to further contemplate whether Mollā ʿArab or Mollā Gürānī was ever approached by the Mamluk administration in order to either pursue or protect Mamluk interests within the Ottoman court. Nor did this elasticity prevent a general sense of competition between the Ot-

66 Repp, *The Müfti.*

67 For this definition of identity formulation by early-modern Venetians see Dursteler, *Venetians in Constantinople.* For another study on connected lives as well as medieval and early-modern identities see Sanjay Subrahmanyam, *Three Ways to be Alien* (Waltham, MA: Brandeis University Press, 2011). For the argument that a general sense of regional variations and distinctive community characteristics existed as forerunners of national identities in medieval and early modern societies (in response to Benedict Anderson's approach) see Simon Forde, Lesley Johnson, and Alan Murray, *Concepts of National Identity in Middle Ages* (Leeds: University of Leeds, 1995).

68 For the possibility of Muslim military men serving under the Catholic rulers of the Iberian Peninsula or vice versa (with some limitations) see Nikolas Jaspert, "Zur Loyalität Interkultureller Makler im Mittelmeerraum: Christliche Söldnerführer im Dienste Muslimischer Sultane," in *Loyalty in the Middle Ages: Ideal and Practice of a Cross-Social Value*, edited by Jörg Sonntag and Coralie Zermatten (Brepols: Turnout, 2016), 235–274; idem, "Military Orders at the Border: Permeability and Demarcation," in *Military Orders 6: Culture and Conflict*, ed. Jochen Schenk and Mike Carr (Oxford: forthcoming).

toman and Mamluk ruling elite. This rivalry found its voice in patronage in addition to other fields such as diplomatic engagements.[69] Patronage for the production of works in Turkish might have been also an aspect of this same rivalry alongside the aforementioned competition for the patronage of scholars and other skilled immigrants.[70] Although the Ottomans attempted to counter the supremacy and prestige of the Mamluk regime, the Mamluks had a solid presence in the Muslim world.

The presence of such scholars in Ottoman lands and the investments of Ottoman rulers in patronage led gradually to a slight shift in the intellectual network patterns between the two lands. The Ottoman sovereigns, first and foremost Meḥmed II, expended significant effort in order to attract prominent scholars of the Islamic world to their fledgling educational institutions. The construction of Meḥmed II's complex in Constantinople was completed in 875/1471. In addition to a mosque and a hospital the complex included *madrasa*s called *Ṣaḥn-ı S̱emān* or *Medāris-i S̱emāniyye*.[71] As a result of Meḥmed II's codification efforts these institutions of higher learning ranked first within the Ottoman system of learning. The professors appointed to *Medāris-i S̱emāniyye* were selected carefully and received the highest salaries. Meḥmed II further contributed to this process by inviting prominent scholars of the Islamic world such as ʿAlī Kuşçu (d. 879/1474) to teach and conduct research under his patronage. Students from other parts of the Islamic world were naturally attracted to the important names of the Islamic intellectual world. In fact, the aforementioned Mollā ʿArab arrived in Ottoman lands as a young student in order to study with Mollā Gūrānī. The biography of Mollā ʿArab exemplifies a gradual transformation in the direction of this scholarly circulation – formerly students flowed into Mamluk lands before leaving as scholars, while now potential students and established scholars traveled instead into Ottoman lands to fulfill their needs. Similarly, during subsequent centuries the ranks of the Ottoman legal system and higher education institutions began filling with scholars trained in colleges within the borders of its own empire.[72]

However, this change was neither abrupt nor absolute. Although the Ottoman patronage and scholars residing within these lands became attractive options

69 For an assessment of Ottoman-Mamluk rivalry in diplomacy see Cihan Yüksel Muslu, "Attempting to Understand the Language of Diplomacy between the Ottomans and the Mamluks," *Archivum Ottomanicum* 30 (2013): 247–269.

70 Yüksel Muslu, *Imperial Diplomacy and Warfare*, 336 n37 and n. 38. The rise of the Safavids during the early sixteenth century can be also a factor in this rivalry for the production of Turkish works and the translation of existing works into Turkish.

71 M. İpşirli, "Ṣaḥn-i Thamān or Medāris-i Thamāniyye," *EI*[2] 8 (1995): 842–43; Repp, *The Müfti*, 27–72.

72 For instance, Ömer Faruk Akün, "Alaeddin Ali Çelebi," *DİA* 2 (1989): 315–319.

for curious minds, the patronage efforts of the Ottoman ruling elite could not surpass the scholarship and reputation that the *madrasas* and libraries in Mamluk lands had accumulated over centuries. Some natives of Anatolia who came to Mamluk lands for study never left their new residence. No place or patron in Anatolia could compete with the prestige of establishments located within Mamluk lands, and their homelands remained only as a place of origin.[73] While ʿAlī Kuşçu accepted Meḥmed II's offer, his colleague Mollā Jāmī (817–898/1414–1492) remained in Harat despite also receiving an attractive offer from Meḥmed II.[74] Likewise, the Mamluk *madrasas* remained prominent centers of learning within the Islamic world long after the Ottoman conquest of Mamluk territories. For instance, the personal physician of Murād IV (r. 1032–1049/1623–1640) Emīr Çelebi was trained in Cairo. He remained there as head physician in the Qalāwūnid Hospital until he entered into the service of the Ottoman sultan.[75]

Sufis and Pilgrims

Most students and scholars completed their pilgrimages while interacting with prominent mystics of the Muslim world along their paths whenever and wherever the opportunity arose, so that most travel motivations overlapped. The search for

73 For example, see Hasan Gökbulut, "Kafiyeci," *DİA* 24 (2001): 154–155. The famous Akmal al-Dīn al-Babartī might have been one of those individuals, although the claim that his origins were from Anatolia are disputed in some sources; İsmet Mirioğlu, "Bayburt", *DİA* 5 (1992): 225–228; Arif Aytekin, "Bâbertî," *DİA* 4 (1991): 377–378. For a recent treatment of his origins see Yıldız, "From Cairo to Ayasuluk," 267, n. 14. For the terminologies regarding "a place of return" versus "a place of origin", see Ho, *Graves of Tarim*, 97.

74 See H. Massé, "Djāmī," *EI*² 2 (1962): 421–422; Ömer Okumuş, "Câmî, Abdurrahman," *DİA* 7 (1993): 94–99; H. Ritter and Zeki Velidi Togan, "Câmî," *İA* 3:15–20. An Ottoman envoy came to Aleppo in order to invite Mollā Jāmī to Constantinople. However, Mollā had left the city and gone to Diyarbakır before this envoy arrived at Aleppo. It is not clear whether or not Mollā Jāmī left Aleppo in order to avoid the Ottoman envoy. Meḥmed II later sent a second envoy to this scholar and commissioned him to compose a scholarly study. However, Meḥmed passed away before he saw the product of his patronage. Following the death of Meḥmed the contact between the Ottoman court and this scholar continued; for example, Bāyezīd II exchanged letters with him.

75 Miri Shefer, "Physicians in Mamlūk and Ottoman Courts," in *Mamlūks and Ottomans: Studies in Honor of Michael Winter*, ed. David J. Wasserstein and Ami Ayalon (London and New York: Routledge, 2006), 117. Focusing on the court physicians, Shefer argues that the direction of individuals flowing from Anatolia to Egypt did not change: "…we can note a difference between the Mamlūk and Ottoman physicians. Scholars from Egypt, it seems, rarely made long travels outside Egypt. … Physicians from Anatolia, on the other hand, were more willing to invest time and effort to travel outside their regions in order to study with renowned teachers. This difference may reflect the different degree of self-importance which Muslims in Anatolia and Egypt attached to themselves and their position in the Muslim cultural hierarchy…" This argument requires further investigation.

spiritual guidance prompted many mystics to circulate from region to region.[76] Both core and peripheral Mamluk lands were natural targets for these Sufis, and most Mamluk sultans proved generous patrons for these charismatic personalities of Islamic spirituality.[77] Many Sufis from both the Eastern and Western lands of Islam roamed Anatolia in order to settle in this newly conquered region. The idea of settling along the frontiers of the Muslim world had become prevalent among the mystics[78] so that Sufis of different brands frequently circulated between Ottoman and Mamluk lands. Factors such as famine and Mongol attacks further propelled population movements among the common populace along with the pilgrims, scholars, and mystics typically found on the roads.[79]

The journeys of Eşrefoğlu Rūmī (754 or 779–874/1353 or 1377–1469) between Iznik and Hama show how deeply travel was embedded in the lives of Sufis living within the Ottoman and Mamluk territories.[80] His case is significant not only because of his deep influence on Anatolian Sufi culture, history, and literature, but also his and his family's ties with the Mamluk city of Hama. Eşrefoğlu's family had presumably emigrated from Greater Syria, likely during the thirteenth century, before settling in Iznik. His ancestors were already presumed to be closely involved with Islamic mysticism by the time they came to Anatolia.[81] Born in Ottoman Iznik, Eşrefoğlu Rūmī received his early education in Ottoman *madrasas*. He became a disciple of Emīr Sulṭān (d. 833?/1429?), the prominent Sufi of Bursa (the Ottoman capital at the time) who was also the son-in-law of Ottoman ruler Bāyezīd I. In order to complete his spiritual training Eşrefoğlu Rūmī traveled from Ankara to Hama – then under Mamluk control.[82] He sub-

76 An earlier example is Ṣadreddīn Ḳonevī (605–673/1207–1274) and his father. Originally from an Arab family of Malatya, his father went on pilgrimage. His son Ṣadreddīn later traveled extensively for education and spiritual training, becoming a follower of Ibn ʿArabī's teaching. He also visited Cairo and finally settled in Konya. He left behind theoretical writings on Sufism and in particular on Ibn al-ʿArabī's teachings. W.C. Chittick, "Ṣadr al-Dīn Muḥammad b. Isḥāḳ b. Muḥammad b. Yūnus b. Al-Ḳūnawī," *EI²* 8 (1994): 753–755; Ekrem Demirli, "Sadreddin Konevî," *DİA* 35 (2008): 420–425.

77 Jonathan Berkey, "Mamluk Religious Policy," *MSR* 13 (2009): 18–22; Leonor Fernandes, *The Evolution of a Sufi Institution in Mamluk Egypt: Khanqah* (Berlin: Klaus Schwarz Verlag, 1988); Helena Hallenberg, "The Sultan who loved Sufis," *MSR* 4 (2000): 147–166.

78 Nile Green, *Sufism: A Global History* (Chichester: Wiley-Blackwell, 2012), esp. Chp. 3.

79 For instance, Celāleddīn Rūmī's family came from Iran while escaping Mongol attacks.

80 Necla Pekolcay and Abdullah Uçman, "Eşrefoğlu Rumi," *DİA* 11 (1991): 480–483. Mustafa Güneş, *Eşrefoğlu Rûmî: Hayatı, Eserleri ve Dîvânı'ndan Seçmeler* (Ankara: Kültür Bakanlığı, 1999). However, the dates that Güneş provides for Eşrefoğlu's life are controversial. Fahir İz does not give a date for Eşrefoğlu's death, but believes that the poet died in 874/1469. See Fahir İz, "Eshrefoğlu ʿAbd Allāh," *EI²* 12 (2004): 282–83.

81 For this claim see Güneş, *Eşrefoğlu Rûmî*, 29–31.

82 Mustafa Güneş, *Eşrefoğlu Rûmî*, 36–58. According to one tradition Emīr Sulṭān sent Eşrefoğlu Rūmī to Ḥacı Bayram Velī in Ankara in order to complete his disciple's spiritual training. After spending time under Hacı Bayram's guidance Eşrefoğlu was sent to Hama, in order to

sequently returned to Anatolia and established his own convent in his hometown Iznik.

Most mystics along with many other Muslims traversed Mamluk lands for pilgrimage. Most yearned for this experience not only as a religious duty but also as a step in their spiritual development. Pilgrimage, like every other pattern of travel, also functioned as a social experience as pilgrims entered into contact with local people. Some like Ḳaygusuz Abdāl (742–845/1341–1441?) who was a Sufi and poet from Teke (ancient Lycia, a peninsula in southern Anatolia), left vivid memories in both Ottoman and Mamluk memories.[83] This significant figure of Turkic folklore and Sufi literature grew up in the mountainous region of Teke which was located along the northern Mamluk frontier and often visited by the semi-nomadic tribes affiliated with various confederations, first and foremost the Dulkadirids. Ḳaygusuz Abdāl's homeland was witness to many battles between the Ottoman and Mamluk armies between 890/1485 and 896/1491. Most of the information regarding Ḳaygusuz Abdāl's life comes from a half-legendary hagiography or *menāḳıbnāme.* During his early twenties Ḳayghusuz Abdāl became a disciple of Abdāl Mūsā (?) who was a follower of Ḥācı Bektāş Velī (d. 669/1271?). His early years as a mystic were spent at Abdāl Mūsā's shrine in Elmalı, in Teke.[84] After receiving Abdāl Mūsā's permission Ḳaygusuz Abdāl went on a pilgrimage with "forty companions." On their way to the pilgrimage the group stayed in Cairo. The same source narrates that Ḳaygusuz miraculously restored the eyesight of the Mamluk sultan. Out of gratitude the Mamluk sultan not only proffered gifts, but also built a palace as a residence for Ḳaygusuz and his friends.[85] Some details of the story are unrealistic. However, a Mamluk sultan's seeking healing from a sojourning Sufi and subsequent generosity to his healer may reflect the ties between the Mamluk ruling elite and charismatic figures of Islamic spirituality who often came from the Eastern Lands and were fluent in Turkish or Persian - or both.[86] This general biographical information also corresponds with later findings concerning the life of Ḳaygusuz. Ḳaygusuz Abdāl

find another shaykh called Ḥusayn Ḥamawī. We do not know whether or not Eşrefoğlu performed the pilgrimage during his stay in Hama.

83 Abdurrahman Güzel, *Kaygusuz Abdal Menâkıbnâmesi* (Ankara: TTK, 1999).

84 During the fourteenth century Teke had not yet been conquered by the Ottomans and was ruled by a faction of the Karamanid family. See Barbara Flemming, *Landschaftsgeschichte von Pamphylien, Pisidien und Lykien im Spaetmittelalter* (Wiesbaden: F. Steiner, 1964), 93–120. Although the region of Teke became subject to Ottoman attacks during the reign of Bāyezīd I it was incorporated into the Ottoman lands only after 827/1423. See G. Leiser, "Teke-Og̱hullari", *EI*² 10 (1999): 412–13.

85 For Ḳaygusuz's stay in Egypt and pilgrimage see Güzel, *Kaygusuz Abdal Menâkıbnâmesi,* 105–27.

86 Berkey, "Mamluk Religious Policy," 18–22; Fernandes, *The Evolution of a Sufi Institution in Mamluk Egypt*; Helena Hallenberg, "The Sultan who loved Sufis."

reportedly spent some years in Cairo and founded the Bektāşī convent in Cairo. After returning from his extended journey he roamed the Ottoman territories as well as visiting the newly conquered Balkan regions.

Ḳaygusuz Abdāl's legendary pilgrimage to Mecca and his stay in Cairo suggest that he left a significant legacy for the cultural and social worlds of both the Ottomans and the Mamluks. Rumors regarding the location of Ḳaygusuz's tomb also corroborate this notion. Among the two locations shown as possible burial spots for Ḳaygusuz Abdāl one is not surprisingly located in Teke in the vicinity of Abdāl Mūsā's shrine, which was central to Ḳaygusuz's spiritual training. The other possible location was neither in the Balkan cities nor in western Anatolia – both of which were within fifteenth-century Ottoman borders and visited by Ḳaygusuz. Instead, some reports place the tomb of Ḳaygusuz Abdāl at the heart of Mamluk world, namely at the mountain of al-Muqaṭṭam in the vicinity of the Mamluk capital Cairo. Many other Anatolian Muslims also observed the annual practice of pilgrimage, although no Ottoman ruler was known to fulfill this religious obligation.[87] However, sources do identify prominent members of both the Ottoman army and the learned class as having completed their pilgrimages. Evranos Bey (d. 820/1417) is among the earliest examples of an Ottoman warlord who went on pilgrimage (likely sometime between 786/1385 and 791/1389). According to the Ottoman chronicler Neşrī's (d. after 926/1520?) reports he was received well by Murād I (r. 763–791/1362–1389) following his return from pilgrimage.[88] Considering the historical importance of Evranos it is also sensible to ask whether or not he went to pilgrimage of his own account, since on his way to Mecca he might have assumed some ambassadorial duties for which we have no written evidence. Likewise, İsḥāḳ Bey (?) another fifteenth century Balkan warlord went on pilgrimage after asking for Murād II's permission to do so.[89] The famous chronicler ʿĀşıḳpaşazāde (d. after 889/1484) accompanied İsḥāḳ Bey on pilgrimage.[90]

Pilgrims' presentations of these observations to people at home must have influenced Ottoman-Mamluk mutual perceptions. For instance, according to ʿĀşıḳpaşazāde the tension that developed between Meḥmed II and Khushqādam

87 Although some female members of this dynasty completed their pilgrimages, the Princes Cem and Ḳorḳud are the only known examples among the male members.

88 Neşrī, *Kitâb-ı Cihan-nümâ: Neşrī Tarihi,* ed. Faik Reşit Unat and Mehmed A. Köymen (Ankara: TTK, 1949), 257.

89 ʿĀşıḳpaşazāde, *Die altosmanische Chronik des ʿĀşıḳpaşazāde,* ed. F. Giese (Leipzig: Otto Harrasowitz, 1929), 114. Ḥacı ʿIvaż Paşa, the famous vizier of Meḥmed I and Murād II, also made the pilgrimage.

90 Necdet Öztürk writes that ʿĀşıḳpaşazāde stayed in Egypt while he was returning from pilgrimage; however, he does not cite his source for this information. ʿĀşıḳpaşazāde's chronicle also does not state anything regarding his stay in Egypt. See Necdet Öztürk, ed., *XV. Yüzyıl Tarihçilerinden Kemâl: Selâtin-nâme (1299–1490)* (Ankara: TTK, 2001), XXIII.

(r. 865–872/1461–1467) during 862/1458 was triggered by the words of a pilgrim[91] who complained about the conditions of the water wells along the pilgrimage routes.[92] Apart from the fact that it epitomized the ideological challenge that Meḥmed II formed against the Mamluks, this anecdote demonstrates that even the observations of pilgrims who traveled for a holy reason figured into rulers' decision-making processes.

A Brief Remark on Commerce

Commerce is one persistent mode of communication that has connected Egypt, Greater Syria, and Anatolia to each other for centuries, yet it will be treated only briefly in this paper.[93] Commerce has always attracted merchants from multiple regions and faiths. While the Ottomans were still only a small power in the northwest corner of Anatolia merchants from Mamluk lands conducted business transactions with Anatolian principalities (i.e. Aydınoğulları and Menteşeoğulları). During the latter half of the fifteenth century Jewish merchants in Ottoman lands were frequently involved in business transactions with merchants from Aleppo and Alexandria.[94] At least two cities under Ottoman rule, Bursa and Antalya, simultaneously served both as direct and transitional trade centers between the Ottoman and Mamluk lands. Records from the city of Bursa indicate the presence of Mamluk merchants who likely stayed in this city as the agents of long-distance Ottoman-Mamluk trade networks. For instance, fur and sable from

91 ʿĀşıḳpaşazāde, ed. Giese, 221–22. This anecdote contains additional details, but only the relevant sections are given here. Tekindag thinks that the pilgrim was Mollā Gūrānī. Neither Ahmet Ateş nor J.R.Walsh discusses this possibility. See Ateş, "Mollā Gürānī"; Şehabettin Tekindağ, "Fatih Devrinde Osmanlı Memluklü Münasebetleri," *İstanbul Üniversitesi Edebiyat Fakültesi Tarih Dergisi* 30 (1976): 77; J.R. Walsh, "Gūrānī, Sharaf al-Dīn."

92 ʿĀşıḳpaşazāde, ed. Giese, 221.

93 R. Stephen Humphreys, "Egypt in the World System of the Later Middle Ages," in *Cambridge History of Egypt*, vol.1, ed. C.F. Petry (Cambridge: Cambridge UP, 1998), 445–462. For older but still useful discussions on Egypt's commercial connections with the rest of the world see Eliyahu Ashtor, *The Levant Trade in the Later Middle Ages* (Princeton: 1983); Subhi Labib, *Handelsgeschichte Ägyptens im Spätmittelalter, 1171–1517* (Wiesbaden: Steiner, 1965). For trade relations between Anatolia and Egypt, see Kate Fleet, *European and Islamic Trade in the Early Ottoman State: The Merchants of Genoa and Turkey* (Cambridge: Cambridge University Press, 1999); Halil İnalcık, "Bursa and the Commerce of the Levant," *Journal of Economic and Social History of the Orient* 3 (1960): 131–147; idem, "Bursa: XV. Asır Sanayi ve Ticarat Tarihine Dair Vesikalar," *Belleten* 24 (1960): 45–102; E. A. Zachariadou, *Trade and Crusade, Venetian Crete and the Emirates of Mentesche and Aydın 1300–1415* (Venice: Istituto Ellenico di Studi Bizantini e Postbizantini, 1983).

94 Halil İnalcık, "Jews in the Ottoman Economy and Finances, 1450–1500," in *The Islamic World from Classical to Modern Times: Essasys in Honor of Bernard Lewis*, ed. C. E. Bosworth et al. (Princeton: Darwin Press, 1988), 516–517.

the Black Sea region were transported via Bursa and/or Antalya to Mamluk lands. Spices arriving from Aleppo were occasionally taken by Italian merchants to Europe (the role of Bursa as a transit center for the spice trade between Aleppo and Italian city states never totaled to a substantial amount, but was present). Meanwhile, lumber and timber abundant in the Taurus Mountains region were exported from Antalya to Alexandria.[95]

However, the volume of this trade showed fluctuations through the centuries. For instance, commercial activity receded between the city of Bursa and the lands of Egypt and Greater Syria during the war of 890–896/1485–1491.[96] Nonetheless, the Ottomans and Mamluks generally enjoyed consistent commercial interaction. Both Ottoman and Mamluk rulers acknowledged the significance of commerce in their relations; correspondence expressed their shared concerns regarding both the security of merchants and the flow of trade in general; the earliest Ottoman-Mamluk diplomatic exchanges from the fourteenth century concerned the well-being of Mamluk and Ottoman merchants.[97] Nearly two decades later Bāyezīd I's son Meḥmed I expressed his hope that commerce between the Ottoman and Mamluk domains would prosper.[98] Likewise, during Murād II's reign a judge from Ottoman lands arrived Cairo on behalf of his wife in order to handle the properties of her father who died in Tripoli. He was armed with a letter to the Mamluk sultan from the Ottoman ruler Murād II who implored the sultan's assistance. We must conduct further research in order to establish the volume of this trade and its significance for both societies' economic lives since the human agents of this particular pattern are visible in the sources.

The relative silence from sources regarding the social and cultural impact of merchant travel, despite continuous circulation between Ottoman and Mamluks lands, presents an irony. For instance, the consequences of a correspondence regarding the well-being of Mamluk and Ottoman merchants remain unknown.[99] Another significant question is how significantly the ruling classes invest their personal fortunes into these economic networks. Likewise, how substantial was the deceased businessman's inheritance that it prompted his son-in-law to face

95 For the role of these two cities in commerce see İnalcık, "Bursa and the Commerce of the Levant"; idem, "Bursa: XV. Asır Sanayi ve Ticaret Tarihine Dair Vesikalar." Antalya has been an important center for commerce with Egypt and Greater Syria at least since the twelfth century; see Claude Cahen, *The Formation of Turkey: The Seljukid Sultanate of Rūm: Eleventh to Fourteenth Century*, trans. P. M. Holt (New York: Longman, 2001), 91–96.

96 İnalcık, "Bursa and the Commerce of the Levant"; idem, "Bursa: XV. Asır Sanayi ve Ticarat Tarihine Dair Vesikalar."

97 Aḥmed Ferīdūn Bey, ed., *Münşe'ātü's-Selāṭin*, 2 vols. (İstanbul, 1274–1275/1857–1859), 1: 114–115 and 115–116.

98 Ibid., 1: 145.

99 Ibid., 1: 114–115 and 115–116.

the Mamluk sultan in Cairo?[100] How should we understand this marriage between a travelling businessman's daughter and a member of Ottoman legal system within the larger context of Ottoman-Mamluk diplomacy?

Although there is no information regarding the social and cultural encounters these merchants initiated, evidence suggests that they too acted as sources of intelligence. The intelligence report that an İskender sent to Bāyezīd II stated clearly that merchants of Antalya returning from their trip to Mamluk territory brought news, including the story that the Mamluk sultan had fallen from his horse and was severely wounded.[101]

Sojourners: Refugees, Ambassadors, Spies, and Captives

During the late thirteenth century military refugees flowed into Mamluk lands from power centers in Anatolia as well as other parts of the world. The Mongol attacks and sack of Baghdad essentially forced a substantial population movement on the residents of Eastern Lands. The collapse of the central authority in Anatolia and subsequent instability within the Ilkhanid world led to the dispersal of the elite into the Seljuks of Rum.[102] Refugees were relatively few when compared to the numerous pilgrims, scholars, and students who roamed within these territories. However, they were often people of political significance such as the members of various ruling families (Ottoman, Karamanid, Dulkadirid, etc.) as well as members of the Mamluk military and administrative cadres.[103] As the Ottomans became an integral part of regional politics these influential individuals began considering Ottoman lands as a safe haven. Among the remarkable examples of the late fourteenth century we must count Sulṭān Aḥmad (r. 784–813/1382–1410) from the Jalayirid dynasty along with his peer and fellow-refuge Qara Yūsūf who controlled the Karakoyunlu confederation between 791/1389 and 823/1420. Both sought refuge in both Mamluk (twice) and Ottoman courts while escaping from Tīmūr's attacks. Reportedly, one of the reasons Tīmūr attacked the Ottoman lands was Aḥmad and Qara Yūsūf, when Tīmūr

100 Ibid., 1: 145.

101 Topkapi Palace Archive Document (henceforth T.E.) 5900.

102 David Ayalon, "The Wafidiyya in the Mamlūk Kingdom," *Islamic Culture* 25 (1951): 89–104; Nakamachi Nobutaka, "The Rank and Status of Military Refugees," *MSR* 10 (2006): 55–83. For Ayalon's claim discussing the arrival of refugees from the Ottoman army (based on Ibn Iyās) see Ayalon, "The Wafidiyya in the Mamlūk Kingdom," 102.

103 For refugees from Akkoyunlu to the Ottoman court see Tayyib Gökbilgin, "XVI. Asır Başlarında Osmanlı Hizmetindeki Akkoyunlu Ümerāsı," *Türkiyat Mecmuası* 9 (1946–1951): 35–46.

requested that Bāyezīd to return these two refugees. Unsurprisingly, Bāyezīd did not accept this request and instigated Tīmūr's wrath.[104]

Members of neighboring ruling families such as the Karamanids and Dulkadirids who had close vassalage ties with the Mamluks also frequently appear in either territory depending on changing times and needs.[105] The sensitive politics of handling political refugees had also serious repercussions for the local populations who often caught between the fires of these imperial conflicts. The cases of Prince Cem (d. 900/1495) and Ḳorḳud (d. 919/1513) stand apart among these episodes because of their respective strong claims to the Ottoman throne. It is well-known that Cem caused substantial tension between the Ottoman and Mamluk courts, although the reason for this tension was explained in different ways by different sources.[106] Despite his eventual return to his father Bāyezīd II's domain, Ḳorḳud likely gave headaches to his father when forced to deal first with his own brother Cem and then his son Ḳorḳud during his reign. Ḳorḳud's eventual return and reappointment as a prince-governor presents a successful case of negotiation in part because both the Ottoman sultan Bāyezīd II and the Mamluk sultan Qāytbāy (along with their agents) had learned their lessons from Cem's unfortunate end, devoting substantial energy during multiple rounds of mediation.[107] While less notorious, provincial Mamluk governors created lesser-known but nonetheless significant episodes of Ottoman-Mamluk interactions. At least two Mamluk governors sought refuge in the Ottoman court: Jānibak and Dawlatbāy. Both episodes presented substantial challenges to the contemporary

104 For the refuge sought by these two figures see Faruk Sümer, *Karakoyunlular* (Ankara: TTK, 1967), 60–68; Patrick Wing, *The Jalayirids: Dynastic State Formation in the Mongol Middle East* (Edinburgh: Edinburgh University Press, 2016), 172–182. For references to this incident from an anonymous Ottoman source see Anonymous, *Anonim Osmanlı Kroniği*, ed. Necdet Öztürk (İstanbul: Türk Dünyası Araştırmaları Vakfı, 2000), 49.

105 For the refuge sought by various Dulkadirid princes and rulers in the Mamluk and Ottoman courts see Yınanç, *Dulkadir* Beyliği; Venzke, "The Case of a Dulgadir-Mamluk *Iqṭā* ". For the refuge of Karamanid Kasım Bey, see Yüksel Muslu, *Imperial Diplomacy and Warfare*, 132–133.

106 For Cem see Aḥmad Darrāj, "Jem Sulṭān wa'l-diblūmāsiyya al-duwaliyya," *Al-Majalla al-Tarikhiyya al-Misriyya* 8 (1959): 201–242; Ralph S. Hattox, "Qaytbay's Diplomatic Dilemma Concerning the Flight of Cem Sultan (1481–1482)," *MSR* 6 (2002): 177–90; Halil İnalcık, "A Case Study in Renaissance Diplomacy: The Agreement between Innocent VIII and Bāyezīd II on Djem Sultan," *Journal of Turkish Studies* 3 (1979): 209–30; Nicolas Vatin, *Sultan Djem* (Ankara: TTK, 1997).

107 For Ḳorḳud see Nabil Al-Tikriti, "The Ḥajj as Justifiable Self-Exile: Şehzade Korkud's Wasīlat al-Aḥbāb (915–916/1509–1510)," *Al-Masāq* 17 (2005): 125–46; idem, "Kalam in the Service of State: Apostasy and the Defining of Ottoman Islamic Identity," in *Legitimizing the Order: The Ottoman Rhetoric of State Power*, ed. Hakan K. Karateke and Maurus Reinkowski (Leiden: E.J. Brill, 2005); idem, "Şehzade Korkud and the Articulation of Early 16th Century Ottoman Religious İdentity." PhD diss., Chicago University, 2004; Yüksel Muslu, *Imperial Diplomacy and Warfare*, 168–171. For other dynasty members see Gaston Wiet, "Deux Princes Ottomans à la Cour d'Égypte," *Bulletin de l'Institue d'Égypte* 20 (1938):137–150.

Mamluk sultan's authority while also prompting intense traffic between the two capitals.[108]

The impact of diplomatic representatives on these Ottoman-Mamluk exchanges is often underestimated. However, of all these travelers only ambassadors were specifically asked to both impress and observe the other court and audience. Naturally, this process of telling and retelling observations was tainted by their personal upbringings, prejudices, and particularly personal interests. The lives of these ambassadors oscillated between extremes both at the other's and at their own sovereign's courts. Depending on the success of their missions they might enjoy extreme honors or suffer deep humiliations, as well as risking imprisonment and even death. Despite these caveats ambassadors remained indispensable agents of communication. Amir Ḥusām al-Dīn al-Kujkūnī who was among the confidants of the Mamluk sultan Barqūq was sent to Bursa as an ambassador. Following his return he shared his observations of the Ottoman court with his friend al-Maqrīzī in a rare account.[109] Later, Amir Jānibak's impressions of the Ottoman court during the Ottoman-Mamluk war took place (albeit briefly) in a manuscript produced for the Mamluk sultan Qānsūh al-Ghawrī (r. 906–922/1501–1516) who dealt with the Ottomans following his predecessor Qāytbāy.[110] An unforgettable example is the Mamluk governor of Aleppo Hayr (Khāyr) Bey (d. 928/1522). He changed sides during the Ottoman ruler Selīm's (r. 918–926/1512–1520) campaigns to Mamluk lands. Afterward he was appointed governor of Egypt and remained in this position until his death. It is highly likely that his change of heart first took place during his visit to the Ottoman capital as an ambassador in 903–904/1497–1498. During his embassy he observed a procession of victory in the Ottoman palace where the famous sea captain Kemāl Reis (d. 916/1510) and prominent frontier lord Malkoçoğlu Bāli Bey (d. 916/1510?) simultaneously presented their spoils to Bāyezīd II. The Mamluk ambassador was also granted slaves from these spoils in a grandiose gesture and likely negotiation of loyalty.[111]

In contrast to the cases discussed so far, captives and spies were probably most elusive in the records. Some individuals were caught spying; others were imprisoned because they broke local law and regulations. Members of the military

108 Aḥmed Ferīdūn Bey, ed., *Münşe'āt*, 1: 354–356. For Janibak seeking refuge during Murād II's reign see Yüksel Muslu, *Imperial Diplomacy and Warfare*, 101. For Dawlatbāy seeking refuge during Bāyezīd II's reign see Yüksel Muslu, *Imperial Diplomacy and Warfare*, 166 and 261–262.

109 Al-Maqrīzī, *Durar al-ʿUqūd*, 1: 439–453.

110 Al-Ḥusaynī, "Kitāb Nafā'is al-Majālis al-Sulṭāniyya," 133–135.

111 The first scholar who draws our attention to the Mamluk governor's early contacts with Bāyezīd II is the late Fuad Mutawalli. See Fuad Mutawalli, *Al-Fatḥ al-ʿUthmanī li'l-Shām wa-Miṣr wa-Muqaddimātuhu min Wāqiʿ al-Wathā'iq wa-l-Maṣādir al-Turkiyyah wa-l-ʿArabiyyah al-Muʿāṣirah* (Cairo, 1976); Yüksel Muslu, *Imperial Diplomacy and Warfare*, 160–162.

and nobility were captured in battle and kept in prison until they either found an opportunity to escape or were exchanged or ransomed as the result of a truce. The Ottoman-Mamluk war between 890/1485 and 896/1491 before the two campaigns by Ottoman ruler Selīm I in 922/1516 and 923/1517 produced a substantial number of captives and spies. Among the most remarkable captives was Hersekzāde Aḥmed Paşa (d. 932/1517).[112] Yet even under their severely restricted conditions captives were noted among the agents of communication and interaction between powers. This impact of this intriguing collage from political refugees to envoys to captives should be also considered in addition to more regular intellectual networks.

Manifestations of Networks

Undoubtedly these networks had an infinite number of manifestations within every sphere of life, some of which have been mentioned only in a preliminary manner in this paper. Among these cases the Mamluk scholar al-Biqāʿī (809–885/1406–1480) deserves a particular treatment. Although he is among the lesser known cases for modern scholars of Ottoman history, al-Biqāʿī includes multiple and interesting references to the Ottomans in at least two of his works: his chronicle and his biographical dictionary.[113] The interest he shows in the Ottomans can in part be explained by the geopolitical realities of his lifetime. Al-Biqāʿī's life coincides with the reconsolidation of the Ottoman power during the post-Interregnum period and the reign of Meḥmed II. When the Ottoman ruler Murād II inundated the Mamluk capital with a series of diplomatic missions announcing his victories in the Balkans with diligent respect to the Mamluk sovereignty al-Biqāʿī was a young student witnessing the arrivals and receptions of these missions. When Murād II's son and successor Meḥmed II and the Mamluk sultan Ināl (d. 865/1461) exchanged consecutive embassies for the conquest of Istanbul (among others) al-Biqāʿī had reached his years of maturity as a scholar and social observer. His attention to Ottoman lands and society is accordingly different than that paid by his predecessors al-Maqrīzī[114] and İbn Ḥajar who had observed both the growth of the Ottoman domain and the chaos

112 For this incident see Yüksel Muslu, *Imperial Diplomacy and Warfare,* 141–143, 152–153.

113 I acknowledge both Prof. Dr. Frédéric Bauden and Dr. Malika Dekkiche who brought this scholar to my attention. For example, see al-Biqāʿī, *ʿInwān al-Zamān,* 1: 60–66, 139; 2: 107–110; 3: 110–112, 121–122, 154–156; idem, *Taʾrīkh al-Biqāʿī,* 1: 373–380; 2: 293–294; 3: 103, 131, 177, 199, 257, 364–65. This list presents a random and limited selection.

114 It is necessary to acknowledge one of al-Maqrīzī's works in specific with its closer attention to the Ottomans and people from *Bilād al-Rūm* as compared to his other works; al-Maqrīzī, *Durar al-ʿUqūd.*

Tīmūr had inflicted on Ottoman lands. The Ottomans would accordingly hold a definitely grander and more remarkable position in al-Biqāʿī's worldview.

Another reason for his special interest in the Ottomans can be al-Biqāʿī's well-known yet occasionally questioned personal interest in *ghazā* and *jihād.*[115] Presumably he accompanied the Mamluk armies in their two campaigns to Rhodes during the Mamluk sultan Jaqmaq's reign. While in his chronicle al-Biqāʿī gives special place to incidents highlighting this particular aspect of Ottoman identity, in his biographical dictionary he celebrates at least one individual who visited the Ottoman lands because he wanted to join the *ghazā*. This focus of al-Biqāʿī corroborates the tone of the Ottoman-Mamluk correspondence exchanged between the two courts during these decades which particularly emphasized Ottoman success in the Balkans.[116] Al-Biqāʿī's focus further suggests that the Ottoman entity might have lured a particular group of individuals who were interested in either observing or participating in *ghazā*, yearning to visit Ottoman lands as the new bastion of *ghazā* and *jihād*. However, this conclusion also raises the question of whether or not he in fact represented a new profile among people from Mamluk lands who slightly admired the Ottoman entity for their growth within the Balkans. The existence and volume of this phenomenon deserves further research.[117]

Conclusion

As these cases of exchange accumulate they lead us to question the meaning and place of these rich networks within Ottoman-Mamluk historiography. This vibrant circulation of individuals from students to captives casts light on a general phenomenon concerning these societies. Despite the contemporary conditions of transportation and communication these societies did not live in seclusion. They had ways, although limited, of keeping informed regarding each other and the surrounding world. The mobility that members of both societies enjoyed helped sustain these information channels. They also clearly represent the continuation of the already well-known and well-documented connectedness of the Muslim world via patterns of travel and mobility. While metropolitan centers such as Cairo lured people with their prestige, wealth, and establishment, newly rising centers along the fringes of the Muslim world attracted people with the promise

115 Li Guo, "Al-Biqāʿī's Chronicle: A Fifteenth Century Learned Man's Reflections on his Time and World," in *Historiography of Islamic Egypt*, ed. Hugh Kennedy (Leiden: Brill, 2001), 121–148.

116 Yüksel Muslu, *Imperial Diplomacy and Warfare,* Conclusion.

117 For an example of Ottoman chroniclers who show a special interest in Mamluk affairs see Oruç Bey, *Oruç Beğ Tarihi,* ed. Necdet Öztürk (Istanbul: Çamlıca, 2007).

of advancement and opportunity. These networks survived and proved to become more resilient as political regimes changed, patrons disappeared, or other instabilities from famine to military attacks imposed chaos and instability on the worlds of these individuals.[118] For example, the role that Mollā ʿArab played in the Ottoman-Mamluk peace process not only shows the scope of the intellectual and cultural networks between these two realms, but also provides an alternative picture of Ottoman-Mamluk relations. The Ottoman and Mamluk rulers were not only the two leading sovereigns competing for leadership of the Sunni Muslim world, but also two political leaders whose territories were parts of a larger Mediterranean system. These territories and their sovereigns were accordingly connected to each other and the rest of the Mediterranean world through vibrant commercial, political, and social networks. These existing ties were reinforced by the mutual exchange between both the ruling classes and a considerable portion of their subjects who shared the same faith and the same language. The fluid understanding of identity and the possibility of dual loyalties fostered the pattern of travel. Numerous cases proving the porousness of these societies indicate a particular profile of people who were, "strangers nowhere in the world."[119] Markers of distinct identities did exist; people became increasingly aware of their differences or unique cultural qualities as they travelled and spent time in other parts of the Muslim world.[120] Nonetheless, these differences did not necessarily construct fractured worldview according to the nineteenth century understanding of national identity. A broader framework must therefore be formulated that accommodates these ties along with episodes of competition and warfare in order to capture this richness of Ottoman-Mamluk relations within the study of both Muslim societies and the larger Mediterranean basin.

118 I owe this interpretation regarding the post-Timurid world to the comments of Evrim Binbaş and Jo Van Steenbergen at the Conference in Bonn (December 2015).

119 For this phrase see Margaret Jacob, *Strangers Nowhere in the World: The Rise of Cosmopolitanism in Early Modern Europe* (Philadelphia: University of Pennsylvania Press, 2006).

120 Abderrahmane El Moudden, "The Ambivalence of ʿRihla': Community Integration and Self-Definition in Moroccan Travel Accounts," in Eickelman and James Piscatori (eds.), *Muslim Travellers*, 69–84.

Bibliography

Abbreviations

DİA – *Türkiye Diyanet Vakfı İslam Ansiklopedisi.* İstanbul: Diyanet Vakfı, 1988–2013.
EI² – *Encyclopaedia of Islam: Second Edition.* Leiden: Brill, 1960–2007.
İA – *İslam Ansiklopedisi.* Istanbul: Maarif Matbaasi, 1940–1988.
IJMES – *International Journal of Middle Eastern Studies*
MSR – Mamlūk Studies Review
T.E. – Topkapi Palace Archive Document

Primary Sources

Aḥmedī. *İskender-nāme: İnceleme, Tıpkı basım.* Edited by İsmail Ünver. Ankara: Türk Tarih Kurumu, 1983.

–. *Tevārīḫ-i Mülūk-i Āl-i ʿOsmān Ġazv-i İşān Bā Küffār.* Edited by Kemal Sılay. Harvard Üniversitesi: Yakın Doğu Dillerive Medeniyetleri Bölümü, 2004.

ʿĀlī, Muṣṭafā. *Künhü'l-Aḫbār.* 5 vols. İstanbul: Takvimhane-i Amire, 1277/1877 or 1878.

–. *Mustafā ʿĀlī's Counsel for Sultans of 1581: Edition, Translation, Notes.* Edited by Andreas Tietze. Vienna: Österreichische Akademie der Wissenschaften, 1979–1982.

–. *Künhü'l-Aḫbār.* Süleymaniye Library MS. Fatih 4225.

–. *Kayseri Raşid Efendi Kütüphanesindeki 901 ve 920 no.'lu nüshalara gore Kitābü't-târīḫ-i Künhü'l- Aḫbār.* Edited by Ahmed Uğur et al. Kayseri: Erciyes Üniversitesi Yayınları, 1997.

–. *Künhü'l-Aḫbār: Cilt II, Fâtiḥ Sulṭān Meḥmed Devri 1451–1481.* Edited by M. Hüdai Şentürk. Ankara: Türk Tarih Kurumu, 2003.

Anonymous. *Anonim Osmanlı Kroniği.* Edited by Necdet Öztürk. İstanbul: Türk Dünyası Araştırmaları Vakfı, 2000.

ʿĀşıḳpaşazāde. *Die altosmanische Chronik des ʿĀşıḳpaşazāde.* Edited by F. Giese. Leipzig: Otto Harrasowitz, 1929.

Bihiştī. *Die Chronik des Ahmed Sinân Čelebi Genannt Bihišti: Eine Quelle zur Geschichte des osmanischen Reiches unter Sultan Bāyezid II.* Edited by Brigitte Moser. Münich: Dr. Rudolf Trofenik, 1980.

Al-Biqāʿī, Ibrāhīm b. Ḥasan. *ʿInwān al-Zamān bi-Tarājim al-Shuyūkh wa'l-Aqrān.* Edited by Ḥasan Ḥabashī. 5 vols. Cairo: Dār al-Kutub, 2001.

–. *Iẓhār al-ʿAṣr li-Asrār Ahl al-ʿAṣr: Taʾrīkh al-Biqāʿī.* Edited by Muḥammad Sālim b. Shadīd al-ʿAwfī. 3 vols. Al-Muhandisin, Jizah: Hajar, 1992.

Ferīdūn Bey, Aḥmed, ed. *Münşeʾātü's-Selāṭin.* 2 vols. İstanbul, 1274–1275/1857–1859.

von Harff, Arnold. *The Pilgrimage of Arnold Von Harff: Knight from Cologne, through Italy, Syria, Egypt, Arabia, Ethiopia, Nubia, Palestine, Turkey, France and Spain, Which He Accomplished in the Years 1496 to 1499.* Translated by Malcolm Letts. London: Hakluyt Society, 1946.

Ḥājib, Yūsuf Khāṣṣ. *Wisdom of Royal Glory (Kutdagu Bilig): A Turko-Islamic Mirror for Princes.* Translated by Robert Dankoff. Chicago: Chicago University Press, 1983.

Al-Ḥusaynī, Ḥusayn b. Muḥammad. "Kitāb Nafāʾis al-Majālis al-Sulṭāniyya." In *Majālis al-Sulṭān al-Ghawri*, edited by ʿAbd al-Wahhāb ʿAzzām. Cairo, 1941.
Ibn al-Furāt. *Taʾrīkh al-Duwal wa-l-Muluk*. Edited by Costi K. Zurayk and Nejla Izzeddin. Vols. 8 and 9. Beirut, 1936–1942.
Ibn Ḥajar al-ʿAsqalānī. *Inbāʾ al-Ghumr bi-Anbāʾ al-ʿUmr*. Edited by Ḥasan Ḥabashī. 4 vols. Cairo, 1969.
İbn Kemāl. *Tevârîḫ-i Âl-i Osman: VIII. Defter*. Edited by Ahmed Uğur. Ankara: Türk Tarih Kurumu, 1997.
Al-Maqrīzī, Taqī al-Dīn Aḥmad b. ʿAlī. *Kitāb al-Sulūk li-Maʿrifat Duwal al-Mulūk*. Edited by Saʿīd ʿAbd al-Fettāḥ ʿĀshur. Vols. 3 and 4. Cairo: Dār al-Kutub, 1972.
–. *Durar al-ʿUqūd al-Farīda fī Tarājim al-Aʿyān al-Mufīda*. Edited by Maḥmūd al-Jalīlī. 4 Vols. Bairut: Dār al-Gharb al-Islāmī, 2002.
Mehmed Efendi, Mecdî. *Şakaik-ı Nu'maniye ve Zeyilleri: Hadaiku'ş-Şakaik*. Edited by Abdülkadir Özcan. İstanbul: Çağrı Yayınları, 1989.
Mustafa, Şeyhoğlu. *Kenzü'l-Küberâ ve Mehekkü'l-ulemâ: İnceleme, Metin, İndeks*. Edited by Kemal Yavuz. Ankara: Atatürk Kültür Merkezi, 1991.
Neşrī, Mehmed. *Kitâb-ı Cihan-nümâ: Neşrī Tarihi*. Edited by Faik Reşit Unat and Mehmed A. Köymen. Ankara: Türk Tarih Kurumu, 1949.
Niẓām al-Mulk. *The Book of Government or Rules for Kings: The Siyar al-Muluk or Siyasat-nama of Nizam al-Mulk*. Translated by Hurbert Darke. 3rd ed. London: Curzon, 2002.
Oruç Bey. *Oruç Beğ Tarihi*.Edited by Necdet Öztürk. Istanbul: Çamlıca, 2007.
Saʿdeddīn, Hoca. *Tācü't-tevārīḫ*. İstanbul: Matbaa-yi Amire, 1862–63.
Al-Sakhāwī, Shams al-Dīn Muḥammad b. ʿAbd al-Raḥmān. *Wajīz al-Kalām fī Zayl ʿAlā Duwal al-Islāmī*. Edited by Bashshār ʿAwwād Maʿrūf. 4 vols. Bairut: Muassasat al-Risāla, 1995.
Taşköprülüzāde. *Eş-Şeḳāʾiḳu n-Nuʿmānīye fī ʿUlemāʾi d-Devleti l-ʿOsmānīye*. Edited by Ahmed Subhi Furat. İstanbul: Edebiyat Fakültesi Basımevi, 1985.

Modern Studies

Adalıoğlu, Hasan Hüseyin, and Coşkun Yıldırım. "Siyâsetnâme." *DİA* 37 (2009): 304–308.
Akpınar, Cemil. "Hacı Paşa." *DİA* 14 (1996): 492–496.
Akün, Ömer Faruk. "Alaeddin Ali Çelebi." *DİA* 2 (1989): 315–319.
Altıkulaç, Tayyar. "İbnü'l Cezerī." *DİA* 20 (1999): 551–557.
Amitai-Preiss, Reuven. "Northern Syria between the Mongols and Mamluks: Political Boundary, Military Frontier, and Ethnic Affinities." In *Frontiers in Question: Eurasian Borderlands, 700–1770*, edited by Daniel Power and Naomi Standen, 128–152. New York, NY: St. Martin's Press, 1999.
Ashtor, Eliyahu. *The Levant Trade in the Later Middle Ages*. Princeton: Princeton University Press, 1983.
Ateş, Ahmet. "Mollā Gürānī (1416–1488)." *İA* 8: 406–408.
Ayalon, David. "Names, Titles, and 'Nisbas' of the Mamlūks." *Israel Oriental Studies* V (1975): 196–200.
–. "The Wafidiyya in the Mamlūk Kingdom" *Islamic Culture* 25 (1951): 89–104.

Aydın, İbrahim Hakkı. "Molla Fenârî." *DİA* 30 (2005): 245–247.
Aytekin, Arif. "Bâbertî." *DİA* 4 (1991): 377–378.
Balivet, Michel. *Şeyh Bedreddin: Tasavvuf ve İsyan*. Translated by Ela Güntekin. İstanbul: Tarih Vakfı Yurt Yayınları, 2000.
–. "Gens du Pays de Rûm en Égypte sous les Premiers Sultans Circassiens." *Turcica* 41 (2009): 199–207.
Bayrakdar, Mehmet. *Kayserili Dâvûd: Dâvûdu'l-Kayserî*. Ankara: Kültür ve Turizm Bakanlığı, 1988.
Bennison, Amira. "Muslim Universalism and Western Globalism." In *Globalization in World History*, edited by A.G. Hopkins, 73–98. New York: Norton, 2002.
Berkey, Jonathan. *Transmission of Knowledge in Medieval Cairo*. Princeton: Princeton University Press, 1992.
–. "Mamluk Religious Policy." *MSR* 13 (2009): 18–22.
Binbaş, İlker Evrim. "A Damascene Eyewitness to the Battle of Nicopolis: Shams al-Dīn Ibn al-Jazarī (d. 833/1429)." In *Contact and Conflict in Frankish Greece and the Aegean, 1204–1453*, edited by Nikolaos G. Crissis and Mike Carr, 153–175. Surrey: Ashgate, 2014.
–. *Intellectual Networks in Timurid Iran: Sharaf al-Dīn ʿAlī Yazdī and the Islamicate Republic of Letters*. New York: Cambridge University Press, 2016.
Cahen, Claude. *The Formation of Turkey: The Seljukid Sultanate of Rūm: Eleventh to Fourteenth Century*. Translated by P.M. Holt. New York: Longman, 2001.
Chittick, W.C. "Ṣadr al-Dīn Muḥammad b. Isḥāḳ b. Muḥammad b. Yūnus b. al-Ḳūnawī." *EI*[2] 8 (1994): 753–755.
Coşan, Esat. "XV. Asır Türk Yazarlarından Muslihu'd-din, Hamid-oğulları ve Hızır Bey." *Vakıflar Dergisi* 13 (1981): 101–111.
Darrāj, Aḥmad. "Jem Sulṭān wa'l-diblūmāsiyya al-duwaliyya." *Al-Majalla al-Taʾrīkhiyya al-Miṣriyya* 8 (1959): 201–242.
Demirli, Ekrem. "Sadreddin Konevî." *DİA* 35 (2008): 420–425.
Dindar, Bilal. "Bedreddin Simâvî." *DİA* 5 (1992): 331–334.
Dunn, Ross E. "International Migrations in the Later Middle Period: The Case of Ibn Battuta." In *Golden Roads: Migration, Pilgrimage, and Travel in Medieval and Modern Islam*, edited by Ian Richard Netton, 75–85. Richmond: Curzon Press, 1993.
Dursteler, Eric. *Venetians in Constantinople: Nation, Identity, and Coexistence in the Early Modern Mediterranean*. Baltimore: John Hopkins University Press, 2006.
Eickelman, Dale F., and James Piscatori, eds. *Muslim Travellers: Pilgrimage, Migration, and the Religious Imagination*. Berkeley: University of California Press, 1990.
Euben, Roxanne. *Journeys to the Other Shore: Muslim and Western Travelers in Search of Knowledge*. Princeton: Princeton University Press, 2006.
Eyice, Semavi. "II. Bayezid Devrinde Davet Edilen Batılılar." *Belgelerle Tarih Dergisi* 4 (1939): 23–30.
–. "Arnold von Harff." *Türk Yurdu* 254 (1956): 690–694.
Fernandes, Leonor. *The Evolution of a Sufi Institution in Mamluk Egypt: Khanqah*. Berlin: Klaus Schwarz Verlag, 1988.
Fleet, Kate. *European and Islamic Trade in the early Ottoman State: The Merchants of Genoa and Turkey*. Cambridge: Cambridge University Press, 1999.
Flemming, Barbara. *Landschaftsgeschichte von Pamphylien, Pisidien und Lykien im Spaetmittelalter*. Wiesbaden: F. Steiner, 1964.

Fodor, Pal. "Aḥmedī's Dāsitān as a Source of Early Ottoman History." *Acta Orientalia Academiae Scientiarum Hungaria* 38 (1984): 41–54.

Forde, Simon, Lesley Johnson, and Alan Murray, eds. *Concepts of National Identity in Middle Ages.* Leeds: University of Leeds, 1995.

Gökbilgin, Tayyib. "XVI. Asır Başlarında Osmanlı Hizmetindeki Akkoyunlu Ümerāsı." *Türkiyat Mecmuası* IX (1946–1951): 35–46.

Green, Nile. *Sufism: A Global History.* Chichester: Wiley-Blackwell, 2012.

Guo, Li. "Al-Biqāʿī's Chronicle: A Fifteenth Century Learned Man's Reflections on his Time and World." In *Historiography of Islamic Egypt,* edited by Hugh Kennedy, 121–148. Leiden: Brill, 2001.

Günaştı, Susan. "Political Patronage and the Writing of Qur'ān Commentaries among the Ottoman Turks." *Journal of Islamic Studies* 24 (2013): 335–357.

Güneş, Mustafa. *Eşrefoğlu Rûmî: Hayatı, Eserleri ve Dîvânı'ndan Seçmeler.* Ankara: Kültür Bakanlığı, 1999.

Güzel, Abdurrahman. *Kaygusuz Abdal Menâkıbnâmesi.* Ankara: Türk Tarih Kurumu, 1999.

Haarmann, Ulrich. "Ideology and History, Identity and Alterity: The Arab Image of the Turk from the Abbasids to Modern Egypt." *IJMES* 20 (1988): 175–196.

Hallenberg, Helena. "The Sultan who loved Sufis." *MSR* 4 (2000): 147–166.

Hattox, Ralph S. "Qaytbay's Diplomatic Dilemma Concerning the Flight of Cem Sultan (1481–1482)." *MSR* 6 (2002): 177–90.

Ho, Engseng. *The Graves of Tarim: Geneaology and Mobility across the Indian Ocean.* Berkeley: University of California Press, 2006.

Humphreys, Stephen R. "Egypt in the World System of the Later Middle Ages." In *Cambridge History of Egypt,* edited by C. F. Petry, vol.1, 445–462. Cambridge: Cambridge University Press, 1998.

İhsanoğlu, Ekmeleddin. "Osmanlı Devleti'nin Arap Topraklarına Yayılışı." In *İki Tarafın Bakış Açısından Türk-Arap Münasebetleri,* 49–98. İstanbul: IRCICA, 2000.

İhsanoğlu, Ekmeleddin and Ramazan Şeşen. "Araplarla Türkler'in İlk Temasları." In *İki Tarafın Bakış Açısından Türk-Arap Münasebetleri,* 3–47. İstanbul: IRCICA, 2000.

İnalcık, Halil. "The Socio-Political Effects of the Diffusion of Fire-arms in the Middle East." In *War Technology and Society in the Middle East,* edited by V.J. Parry and M.E. Yapp, 175–211. London: Oxford UP, 1975.

–. "Bursa and the Commerce of the Levant." *Journal of Economic and Social History of the Orient* 3 (1960): 131–147.

–. "Bursa: XV. Asır Sanayi ve Ticaret Tarihine Dair Vesikalar." *Belleten* 24 (1960): 45–102.

–. "Jews in the Ottoman Economy and Finances, 1450–1500." In *The Islamic World from Classical to Modern Times: Essasys in Honor of Bernard Lewis,* edited by C.E. Bosworth et al., 513–531. Princeton: Darwin Press, 1988.

–. "A Case Study in Renaissance Diplomacy: The Agreement between Innocent VIII and Bāyezīd II on Djem Sultan." *Journal of Turkish Studies* 3 (1979): 209–30.

–. *Has-Bağçede ʿAyş u Tarab: Nedîmler, Şâirler, Mutrîbler.* İstanbul: İş Bankası Yayınları, 2010.

İpşirli, Mehmet. "Ṣaḥn-i Thamān or Medāris-i Thamāniyye." *EI²* 8 (1995): 842–43.

İz, Fahir. "Eshrefoğlu ʿAbd Allāh." *EI²* 12 (2004): 282–83.

Jacob, Margaret. *Strangers Nowhere in the World: The Rise of Cosmopolitanism in Early Modern Europe.* Philadelphia: University of Pennsylvania Press, 2006.

Jaspert, Nikolas. "Zur Loyalität Interkultureller Makler im Mittelmeerraum: Christliche Söldnerführer im Dienste Muslimischer Sultane." In *Loyalty in the Middle Ages: Ideal and Practice of a Cross-Social Value,* edited by Jörg Sonntag and Coralie Zermatten, 235–274. Brepols: Turnout, 2016.

–. "Military Orders at the Border: Permeability and Demarcation." In *Military Orders 6: Culture and Conflict,* edited by Jochen Schenk and Mike Carr. Oxford: forthcoming.

Kafadar, Cemal. *Between Two Worlds: The Construction of Ottoman State.* Berkeley: University of California Press, 1995.

–. "A Rome of One's Own: Reflections on Cultural Geography and Identity in the Lands of Rum." *Muqarnas* 24 (2007): 7–25.

Kastristis, Dimitri. *The Sons of Bayezid: Empire Building and Representation in the Ottoman Civil War of 1402–1413* .Leiden: Brill, 2007.

Kissling, H.J. "Badr al-Dīn b. Ḳāḍī Samāwnā." *EI*[2] 1 (1958): 869–70.

Kofoğlu, Sait. "Hamîdoğulları." *DİA* 15 (1997): 471–476.

Kopraman, Kâzım Yaşar. *Mısır Memlükleri Tarihi: Sultan Melik el-Müeyyed Şeyh el-Mahmûdî Devri (1412–1421).* Ankara: Kültür Bakanlığı, 1989.

Kramers, J.H., R.C. Repp, and R.W. Bulliett. "SHaykh al-Islām," *EI*[2] 9 (1996): 399–402.

Kut, Günay. "Ahmedî." *DİA* 1 (1988): 165.

Labib, Subhi. *Handelsgeschichte Ägyptens im Spätmittelalter, 1171–1517.* Wiesbaden: Steiner, 1965.

Leiser, Gary. "Teke-Og̲h̲ullari." *EI*[2] 10 (1999): 412–13.

Massé, H. "D̲j̲āmī." *EI*[2] 2 (1962): 421–422.

Mirioğlu, İsmet. "Bayburt." *DİA* 5 (1992): 225–228.

El-Moudden, Abderrahmane. "The Ambivalence of 'Rihla': Community Integration and Self-Definition in Moroccan Travel Accounts." In *Muslim Travellers: Pilgrimage, Migration, and the Religious Imagination,* edited by Dale F. Eickelman, and James Piscatori, 69–84. Berkeley: University of California Press, 1990.

Mutawallī, Fuʾād. *Al-Fatḥ al-ʿUthmanī li'l-Shām wa-Miṣr wa-Muqaddimātuhu min Wāqiʿ al-Wathāʾiq wa-l-Maṣādir al-Turkiyya wa-l-ʿArabiyya al-Muʿāṣira.* Cairo, 1976.

Nobutaka, Nakamachi. "The Rank and Status of Military Refugees." *MSR* 10 (2006): 55–83.

Okumuş, Ömer. "Câmî, Abdurrahman." *DİA* 7 (1993): 94–99.

Özaydın, Abdülkadir, and Hatice Tören. "Kadı Burhaneddin," *DİA* 24 (2001): 74–77.

Özbaran, Salih. *Bir Osmanlı Kimliği: 14.–17. Yüzyıllarda Rûm/Rûmî Aidiyet ve İmgeleri.* İstanbul: Kitap Yayınevi, 2004.

Öztürk, Necdet, ed. *XV. Yüzyıl Tarihçilerinden Kemâl: Selâtin-nâme (1299–1490).* Ankara: Türk Tarih Kurumu, 2001.

Pekolcay, Necla, and Abdullah Uçman. "Eşrefoğlu Rumi." *DİA* 11 (1991): 480–483.

Petry, Carl F. *The Civilian Elite of Cairo in the Later Middle Ages.* Princeton, New Jersey: Princeton University Press, 1981.

Pfeiffer, Judith, ed. *Politics, Patronage, and theTtransmission of Knowledge in 13th–15th Century Tabriz.* Leiden: Brill, 2014.

Repp, R.C. *The Müfti of İstanbul: A Study in the Development of the Ottoman Learned Hierarchy.* London: Ithaca Press, 1986.

Ritter, H. and Zeki Velidi Togan, "Câmî." *İA* 3: 15–20.

Sabra, Adam. *Poverty and Charity in Medieval Islam.* Cambridge: Cambridge University Press, 2001.

Shefer, Miri. "Physicians in Mamlūk and Ottoman Courts." In *Mamlūks and Ottomans: Studies in Honor of Michael Winter*, edited by David J. Wasserstein and Ami Ayalon, 114–122. London and New York: Routledge, 2006.

Sohrweide, Hanna. "Dichter und Gelehrte aus dem Osten im Osmanischen Reich (1453–1600)." *Der Islam* 46 (1970): 263–302.

Subrahmanyam, Sanjay. *Three Ways to be Alien*. Waltham, MA: Brandeis University Press, 2011.

Sümer, Faruk. *Karakoyunlular*. Ankara: Türk Tarih Kurumu, 1967.

–. "Ḳaramān-og̲h̲ullari." *EI²* 4 (1950): 619–630.

–. "Ramazanoğulları," *DİA* 34 (2007): 442–447.

Tekindağ, Şehabettin. "II. Bayezid Devrinde Çukurova'da Nüfuz Mücadelesi." *Belleten* 31 (1967): 345–375.

–. "Fatih Devrinde Osmanlı Memluklü Münasebetleri." *İstanbul Üniversitesi Edebiyat Fakültesi Tarih Dergisi* 30 (1976): 73–98.

–. "Karamanlılar." *İA* 6: 316–330.

Al-Tikriti, Nabil. "Şehzade Korkud and the Articulation of Early 16th Century Ottoman Religious İdentity." PhD diss., Chicago University, 2004.

–. "The Ḥajj as Justifiable Self-Exile: Şehzade Korkud's Wasīlat al-Aḥbāb (915–916/1509–1510)." *Al-Masāq* 17 (2005): 125–46.

–. "Kalam in the Service of State: Apostasy and the Defining of Ottoman Islamic Identity." In *Legitimizing the Order: The Ottoman Rhetoric of State Power*, edited by Hakan K. Karateke and Maurus Reinkowski, 131–151. Leiden: E.J. Brill, 2005.

Touati, Houari. *Islam and Travel in the Middle Ages*. Translated by Lydia G. Cochrane. Chicago: University of Chicago Press, 2010.

Tülüce, Adem. *Bizans Tarihyazımında Öteki: Selçuklu Kimliği*. Ankara: Doğubatı, 2016.

Uzunçarşılı, İsmail Hakkı. *Osmanlı Devleti Teşkilâtına Medhal: Büyük Selçukîler, Anadolu Selçukîleri, Anadolu Beylikleri, İlhanîler, Karakoyunlu ve Akkoyunlularla Memlûklardaki Devlet Teşkilatına Bir Bakış*. Ankara: Türk Tarih Kurumu, 1941.

Vatin, Nicolas. *Sultan Djem*. Ankara: Türk Tarih Kurumu, 1997.

Venzke, Margaret. "The Case of a Dulgadir-Mamluk Iqṭāʿ: A Reassessment of the Dulgadir Principality and Its Positions within the Ottoman-Mamluk Rivalry." *Journal of Economic and Social History of the Orient* 43 (2000): 399–474.

Yaşaroğlu, M. Kamil. "Molla Gürânî." *DİA* 30 (2005): 248–250.

Yıldız, Sara Nur. "From Cairo to Ayasuluk: Hacı Paşa and the Transmission of Islamic Learning to Western Anatolia in the Late Fourteenth Century." *Journal of Islamic Studies* 25 (2014): 263–297.

Yınanç, Refet. *Dulkadir Beyliği*. Ankara: Türk Tarih Kurumu, 1989.

Yiğit, İsmail. "Şeyh el-Mahmûdî." *DİA* 39 (2010): 58–60.

Yücel, Yaşar. *Kadı Burhaneddin Ahmed ve Devleti (1344–1398)*. Ankara: Ankara Üniversitesi, 1970.

Yüksel Muslu, Cihan. *The Ottomans and the Mamluks: Imperial Diplomacy and Warfare*. London: I.B. Tauris, 2014.

–. "Attempting to Understand the Language of Diplomacy between the Ottomans and the Mamluks." *Archivum Ottomanicum* 30 (2013): 247–269.

Walsh, J. "Hād̲j̲d̲j̲ī Pas̲h̲a, D̲j̲alāl al-Dīn K̲h̲ıḍr b. ʿAlī," *EI²* (1971) 3:45.

–. "Gūrānī, S̲h̲araf al-Dīn," *EI²* (1965) 2: 1140–41.

Wiet, Gaston. "Deux Princes Ottomans à la Cour d'Égypte." *Bulletin de l'Institue d'Égypte* 20 (1938): 137–150.

Wing, Patrick. *The Jalayirids: Dynastic State Formation in the Mongol Middle East.* Edinburgh: Edinburgh University Press, 2016.

Zachariadou, E.A. *Trade and Crusade, Venetian Crete and the Emirates of Mentesche and Aydın 1300–1415.* Venice: Istituto Ellenico di Studi Bizantini e Postbizantini, 1983.

Albrecht Fuess (Philipps University, Marburg)

Three's a Crowd. The Downfall of the Mamluks in the Near Eastern Power Struggle, 1500–1517

Introduction

The present study discusses the power struggle between the Mamluks, Ottomans and Safavids in the Near East in the years 1500–1517, in order to understand why the Mamluk Empire vanished so quickly after several centuries of rule whereas the other Muslim states in the region thrived and survived. Previous scholarship has emphasized Mamluk arrogance towards the adaptation of new military technologies such as firearms as a key cause for the downfall of the Mamluks, but this study argues for the existence of a broader range of structural and geographic reasons which undermined the Mamluk Empire. It shows how the empire in the long term became the victim of its own initial success of establishing itself as the Muslim state that defeated the Mongols and Crusaders, and yet failed to perceive the potential challenge emerging from the Ottomans, which had turned themselves into an aggressive Muslim military land and sea power. The paper first describes the military conflict between the three powers, then it assesses the impact of warfare on the three states, and finally it discusses the causes why the Mamluk Empire disappeared in 1517.

The Mamluks were the oldest of the three Muslim dynasties involved in the power struggle of the early sixteenth century. Early military successes against Crusaders and Mongols in the second half of the thirteenth century had shaped the high prestige the Mamluks enjoyed in the Muslim world.[1] As overlords of the holy cities of Mecca and Medina, they claimed the leading role in the Islamic realm. Moreover, they had been the undisputed masters of Egypt and Syria for two hundred and fifty years. When the Mamluks established themselves in the year 1250 the Ottomans were still a marginal force, if any force at all. First signs of a small Ottoman principality can be traced to the early fourteenth century and to a tiny Ottoman dominion not exceeding North-western Anatolia. However, soon

1 Ulrich Haarmann, "Der arabische Osten im späten Mittelalter 1250–1517" in *Geschichte der arabischen Welt,* ed. Ulrich Haarmann (Munich: C. H. Beck ^{4}2001), 236–241.

thereafter it expanded considerably in Europe and Anatolia. By the end of the fourteenth century it seemed that the Ottomans presented a real military menace to the Mamluks. But a direct fight was postponed, as the army of Timur (Tamerlane), the famous ruler of Samarqand, thrashed the Ottoman army at the battle of Ankara in 1402. The Ottomans needed time to reorganize. After a phase of consolidation, they managed to regain their territories and expand even further conquering the old Byzantine capital of Constantinople in 1453. Having achieved this victory, they challenged the Mamluks militarily and ideologically. The question was: Who would take up the role of the leading Muslim power?

Surprisingly at the beginning of the sixteenth century, a third party vied for this position as well, which brings us to the Safavids. Originally the Safavids were a family of sheikhs of a religious order from Ardabil in Azerbaijan. The Safavid Shah Ismāʿīl I (r. 1501–1524) then transformed the Sufi movement into a powerful political force. He defeated Alwand, the ruler of the Turcoman tribal confederation of the Aq Qoyunlu ("White Sheep") in 1501 and conquered Tabrīz, which he chose as his capital. This incident is often regarded as the moment of birth of the Safavid Empire. Ismāʿīl proclaimed under the banner of the Shia the advent of a new era for the region. Very soon he entered in a conflict with the Ottomans as many Turcoman followers of the Ṣafavīya order, which were also known as Qizilbash "Redheads" because of their typical red headgear, who happened to live in Eastern Anatolia on Ottoman soil

Always a Quarrel in Eastern Anatolia

In Eastern Anatolia the interests of Mamluks, Safavids and Ottomans overlapped. The Mamluks, who wanted to keep the status quo, had the oldest claim to the region. Shortly after the expulsion of the Mongols from Syria they had turned against the Kingdom of Lesser Armenia of Cilicia in South-eastern Anatolia which was finally conquered in 1375.[2] In order to secure this newly acquired territories in the North the Mamluks subdued the neighbouring Turcoman principalities of Ramaḍān and Dulkadir (Dhū l-Qadr) and installed them as dependent buffer state.[3] When the Ottomans regained strength in the course of

2 Shai Har-El, *Struggle for Domination in the Middle East. The Ottoman-Mamluk War 1485–1491* (Leiden: Brill, 1995), 39.

3 Ibid., 39–41; For the Turkoman dynasty of the Dulkadir, see: Margaret L Venzke, "Dulkadir", in: Encyclopaedia of Islam, THREE, Edited by: Kate Fleet, Gudrun Krämer, Denis Matringe, John Nawas, Everett Rowson. Consulted online on 13 August 2018 <http://dx.doi.org/10.1163/1573-3912_ei3_COM_27743>; For the less known principality of Ramaḍān, see: Franz Babinger, "Ramaḍān Og̲h̲ullari̊", in: Encyclopaedia of Islam, Second Edition, Edited by:

the fifteenth century occasional tensions broke out about the question of lordship over these principalities. They resulted in a full-scale war in 1485. The Ottomans invaded under Sultan Bāyezīd II (r. 1481–1512) the Mamluk interest sphere in Cilicia. Although the Mamluks managed to win the major battles of this war, the conflict itself remained unsettled. When a truce was concluded in 1491 the Ottomans handed back all places that they had conquered during the conflict, while the Mamluks were obliged to transform these localities into religious endowments (*awqāf*), whose income should be devoted to the holy cities of Mecca and Medina.[4] It is important to keep in mind that according to Har-El this war had been a secondary issue for the Ottomans, whereas the Mamluks had to push their forces almost beyond their limits.[5]

For the time being the Mamluks and Ottomans settled for the status quo, but the emerging Safavids were soon to disturb the balance of power in the region, as there was a growing fear in the Ottoman Empire concerning the Turcoman followers of the Safavids. In order to cut the links of the Qizilbash to the Safavid Empire, the Ottomans resorted to a policy of Qizilbash-chasing in Anatolia. During these persecutions 30,000 Safavid supporters are said to have been marked in the face and to have been deported to the Peloponnese.[6] However, these harsh measures could not bring to an end the Qizilbash unrest. Shah Ismāʿīl aggravated the situation, when he campaigned in 1507 against ʿAlāʾ al-Dawla, the ruler of the South-eastern Anatolian principality of Dulkadir thereby passing through Ottoman territory during his campaign. In any case, Ismāʿīl provoked the Mamluks as well as they were officially the overlords of ʿAlāʾ al-Dawla. But the Mamluks preferred to wait, rather than to take action. Troop contingents deployed by the Mamluk Sultan Qānṣawh al-Ghawrī (r. 1501–1516) to northern Syria did not move.[7]

Further Safavid campaigns against Mamluk border states were widely feared in the Mamluk Empire.[8] The Venetians in the Mamluk Empire sensed this atmosphere of fear. Zuan Moresini wrote in 1508 from Damascus and informed the

---

P. Bearman, Th. Bianquis, C.E. Bosworth, E. van Donzel, W.P. Heinrichs. Consulted online on 13 August 2018 <http://dx.doi.org/10.1163/1573-3912_islam_SIM_6209>.

4 Her-El, *Struggle*, 211.

5 Ibid., 192.

6 Adel Allouche, *The Origins and Development of the Ottoman-Safavid Conflict (906–962/1500–1555)* (Berlin: Klaus Schwarz, 1983), 85; Marino Sanuto (d. after 1533): *Šāh Ismāʿīl I nei "Diarii" di Marino Sanudo*, ed. by Biancamaria Scarcia Amoretti, vol. 1 (Rome: Istituto per l'Oriente, 1979), 141.

7 Allouche, *The Origins*, 90. Ibn Ṭūlūn (d. 1546), *Mufākahat al-khillān fī ḥawādith al-zamān*, ed. by Mohamed Mostafa, vol. 1 (Cairo: Wizārat al-Thaqāfa wal-Irshād al-Qawmī, 1962), 316, 318; Ibn Iyās (d. around 1524), *Badāʾiʿ al-zuhūr fī waqāʾiʿ al-duhūr*, ed. by Mohamed Mostafa vol. 4 (Wiesbaden: Franz Steiner, 1960), 118–119.

8 David Ayalon, "The End of the Mamluk Sultanate. Why did the Ottomans spare the Mamluks of Egypt and wipe out the Mamluks of Syria?," *Studia Islamica* 65 (1987), 128.

Serenissima that Shah Ismāʿīl could certainly be a match for even the mighty Turks.[9] From all the Europeans the Venetians had the strongest bonds to the Mamluks due to trade relations, but apparently the Venetian confidence in the Mamluk capability to prevail against external enemies was increasingly waning.[10] Therefore Venetian embassies were sent to Iran, when Safavid power asserted itself in the region. Unfortunately though, these emissaries were caught in 1510 by the Mamluks on their way back from Shah Ismāʿīl.[11] According to Ibn Iyās the returning envoys were to have proposed to the kings of the Franks on behalf of Shah Ismāʿīl to fight the Mamluks side by side with the Safavids. The Safavids would thereby attack by land and the Franks would invade the coast from the seaside.[12] This episode led to a temporary severe chill in Mamluk-Venetian relations and shows that the Safavid ruler pursued a deliberate diplomatic policy in order to obtain his aims of subjugating the Mamluks and that he would have liked to be perceived as the new powerful Muslim ruler on the block. In this respect he sent an ambassador to Cairo in the year 1511, whose task was to challenge the Sunni Mamluk authority as the main Muslim power. The envoy brought with him a poem, which stated that the Safavids would deeply love the cousin of the Prophet ʿAlī ibn Abī Ṭālib and if there were people who would blame the Safavids for this, then God would curse them. A similar letter arrived at the Ottoman court. Moreover, the envoy handed over a precious box with the head of Uzbek Khān, Muḥammad Shaybanī. This head, so the accompanying message, presented now a cup for drinking the blood of the enemies of the Shah.[13] Similar affronts

---

9 Marino Sanuto, *I Diarii*, ed. by Rinaldo Fulin et al., vol. 7 (Venice: Fratelli Visentini, 1882), 529.

10 Already in 1472 the Venetians had sent embassies to Uzun Ḥasan (r. 1457–1478), then the ruler of the Turkmen confederation of the Aq Qoyunlu in Iran, in order to found a mutual alliance by land and sea against the Ottomans. It was part of the plan that the Aq Qoyunlu would be helped to conquer Mamluk territory. Moreover, ships were equipped which contained ammunition for Uzun Ḥasan. Although these plans came to a halt after the Ottomans defeated Uzun Ḥasan at the battle of Bashkent in 1473, it did not prevent the Venetians to look for other partners for a possible alliance, see therefore: Barbara von Palombini, *Bündniswerben abendländischer Mächte um Persien 1453–1600* (Wiesbaden: Franz Steiner, 1968), 26–27. David Morgan, *Medieval Persia 1040–1797* (London: Longman [5]1997), 105.

11 Ibn Iyās, *Badāʾiʿ*, vol. 4, 191; von Palombini, *Bündniswerben*, 45–47.

12 Ibn Iyās, *Badāʾiʿ*, vol. 4, 191.

13 Ibn Iyās, *Badāʾiʿ*, vol. 4, 219–221; Ibn Ṭūlūn, *Mufākahat*, vol 1, 357. According to Morgan the skull of Muḥammad Shaybanī ("set in gold and fashioned into a drinking cup") had been sent to the Ottoman sultan, see: Morgan, *Medieval Persia*, 115. Given Ismāʿīl's attitude towards the Ottomans and the Mamluks it is quite likely that he sent both of them a skull drinking cup, claiming that it had been the head of the Uzbek Khān before. The question remains though who got the real one. It is quite improbable, that Ismāʿīl just sent one head to the Mamluk sultan urging him to send it to the Ottoman sultan once he had looked at it.

followed.[14] Apparently, Shah Ismāʿīl thought he could intimidate the Ottomans and Mamluks. Well, he was wrong.

The Decisive Years: 1511–1517

In 1511 a massive rebellion broke out among the Qizilbash in Anatolia. The leading Ottoman military men forced Sultan Bāyezīd II to abdicate in favour of his son Selīm I (r. 1512–1520). Meanwhile a Safavid governor raided far into Ottoman territory to support the rebels. Once Selīm I had firmly established himself as sultan, he turned towards the Qizilbash menace, quelled the rebellion and stabilized the situation. Many Qizilbash were executed, others imprisoned. Selīm then started a military campaign in March 1514, marching against his Safavid foe. He inflicted a crushing defeat on Shah Ismāʿīl in August 1514 at the battle of Chāldirān at the north eastern edge of Lake Van.[15] The usual explanations for the Ottoman victory are that the Ottomans outnumbered the Safavids by far and that the Ottomans employed field artillery and handled their guns far more professionally. Apparently, so goes the storyline of this explanation, the Safavids were reluctant to adopt these techniques, as they preferred the chivalrous art of fighting as cavalry archers.[16] This resembles in fact the argument given for the subsequent defeat of the Mamluks. But in the case of the Safavids it is nowadays contested as well. David Morgan writes in this context:

> … the superiority of the guns ought not, at this date, to be pressed too far. It may well be that what was really dangerous to the Safawids about the Ottoman field artillery was not so much what came out of the gun's barrel as the fact that, chained together, they formed an effective barrier to cavalry charges and a safe refuge behind which the Janissary musketeers could shelter while loading and firing.[17]

The cavalry of the Safavids just did not come round the Ottoman *Wagenburg*, which they encountered here for the very first time. Having understood the functioning of the *Wagenburg* they tried to build it themselves as will be shown in

14 In the same year he sent envoys through the Mamluk territory who carried the *kiswa* (ritual covering) for the Kaʿba in Mekka, which was usually sent by the Mamluks. In 1512 Ismāʿīl sent a document to the Mamluks proving that Ismāʿīl' was a direct descendant of the Prophet Muḥammad and that he should rule the Muslim world., Ibn Ṭūlūn, *Mufākahat*, vol 1, 362; Ibn Iyās, *Badāʾiʿ*, vol. 4, 265–266, 271; Sanuto, *I Diarii*, vol. 14, 202, 356; W.W. Clifford, "Some Observations on the Course of Mamluk-Safavi Relations (1502–1516/908–922)," *Der Islam*, 70 (1993), 264–265.

15 Hans-Robert Roemer, *Persien auf dem Weg in die Neuzeit. Iranische Geschichte von 1350–1750* (Beirut: Institut der Deutschen Morgenländischen Gesellschaft, 1989), 258–263.

16 Morgan, *Medieval Persia*, 116; Monika Gronke, *Geschichte Irans. Von der Islamisierung bis zur Gegenwart* (Munich: C.H. Beck, 2003), 70.

17 Morgan, *Medieval Persia*, 117.

the following. For the time being, the Safavids retreated to the Iranian High Plateau and resorted to a scorched earth policy which kept the Ottomans effectively away. However, after this battle Anatolia was definitely lost for the Safavids. The Qizilbash of the Ottoman territories were for ever separated from Shah Ismāʿīl and his successors. The Mamluks had stayed out of this conflict altogether. In May of 1514 an Ottoman envoy had arrived in Cairo to ask for support, but the Mamluks refused and their troops in Syria had the order to only fight if one of the two fighting sides would invade Syria.[18]

Ibn Iyās tells the story about the immediate reaction of the Mamluk side after the battle of Chāldirān. When the first rumours spread, the Mamluk sultan had Koran recitation read in the mosques to commemorate the event, but when a little bit later false news arrived that even Ismāʿīl had been killed, Qānṣawh had, apparently contrary to normal custom, not had the drums beaten and it was said that the Mamluk emirs started now to be afraid of the might and energy of the Ottoman sultan.[19] There was reason for such fear. In recent years the Mamluk had appeared less vigorous than the Ottomans, as the Mamluks already had to ask the Ottomans for help in the conflict with the Portuguese in the Red Sea and the Indian Ocean. When in 1497/1498 the Portuguese navigator Vasco da Gama sailed around the Cape of Good Hope he literally turned the Mamluk world view upside down. Europeans came now from a direction were they were least expected.[20] The Portuguese threatened not only to undermine the successful spice trade of the Mamluks with India, but presented a real menace for the holy cities of Mecca and Medina. Since 1507 the Ottomans therefore sent the Mamluks (via Alexandria) timber and other materials on a regular basis needed for the construction of ships to fight the Portuguese. Later on the Ottomans even helped out with seamen in order to fight the Portuguese.[21] In the course of their naval help policy, the Ottomans must have realized the weak points in the Mamluk defence system.[22] As late as the summer of 1515 a joint Mamluk-Ottoman navel expedition with 20 ships went on its way to India.[23]

18 Ibn Iyās, *Badāʾiʿ*, vol. 4, 372–373, 376; James B. Evrard, *Zur Geschichte Aleppos und Nordsyriens im letzten halben Jahrhundert der Mamlukenherrschaft (872–921 AH)* (München: Rudolf Trofenik, 1974), 121–122.

19 Ibn Iyās, *Badāʾiʿ*, vol. 4, 393, 398.

20 Ibn Iyās tells that the Franks had tried for ages to perforate the dam, which Alexander the great had once built until they finally succeeded, see: Ibid., vol. 4, 109.

21 Sanuto, *I Diarii*, vol. 7, 12–13, 128; Palmira Brummet, *Ottoman Seapower and Levantine Diplomacy in the Age of Discovery* (Albany: State University of New York Press, 1994), 114.

22 Albrecht Fuess, *Verbranntes Ufer. Auswirkungen mamlukischer Seepolitik auf Beirut und die syro-palästinensische Küste in mamlukischer Zeit (1250–1517)* (Leiden: Brill 2001), 51–63.

23 Ibn Iyās, *Badāʾiʿ*, vol. 4, 467. The joint fleet returned in the summer of 1517. When the Ottoman captain Salmān Ra'īs heard of the Ottoman victory against the Mamluks, he let his Mamluk co-captain Ḥusayn drown, ibid., vol. 5, 190; Besides joint naval efforts it seems that there had been Mamluk-Ottoman expeditions against the Safavids. Apparently in the early

However, at the time of Chāldirān the Mamluks stopped cooperating with the Ottomans. Sultan Selīm now decided to occupy southeastern Anatolia once and for all, despite the Mamluks vested interest in the region. He occupied the Turcoman principality of Dulkadir in Cilicia in 1515, which the Mamluks had always regarded as their vassal.[24] Another box was sent to the Mamluk sultan in 1515, this time from the Ottoman ruler. Inside, one could find the heads of the Dulkadir ruler ʿAlāʾ al-Dawla and some of his nobles. Apparently Qānṣawh al-Ghawrī was upset and exclaimed: "What is he sending me these heads for? Are these perhaps heads of Christian kings, who he has defeated and now he wants to show them to me?"[25] One might sympathize with the Mamluk sultan being fed up with the fact that everybody was sending him heads. It was clear now what the Ottoman sultan was heading at. In the fall of 1515 rumours spread in the Mamluk Empire that the Ottoman Sultan had equipped 400 ships against Egypt, while his land army was marching towards Aleppo. As a result from such hearsay Sultan Qānṣawh al-Ghawrī ordered the sending of 200 canons for the security of Alexandria in February of 1516.[26] In these circumstances it remains unclear why the Mamluks rebuked an offer of alliance of Shah Ismāʿīl at the end of 1514.[27] Maybe because of his recent insults, he was not deemed a trustworthy ally.

Mamluks and Ottomans finally clashed in Northern Syria. The Mamluk army still left a deep impression when it set out for the battle. Ibn Iyās praised them and states that the Mamluks had looked like shining stars with their horses and their weaponry. Each of these cavalrymen, so he states, was equal to at least 1000 infantrymen of the Ottoman army.[28] But the shining stars should twinkle not for much longer. On the 24th of August 1516 the Mamluk army suffered a crushing and complete defeat by the Ottomans at Marj Dābiq north of Aleppo.[29] According to Ayalon the defeat was a consequence of Mamluk arrogance, as they had refused to carry artillery and hand guns with them, although they possessed them. Such fighting style was apparently not the chivalrous manner they

summer of 1511 a joint Mamluk-Ottoman military operation had driven back Qizilbash, who were raiding the west bank of the Euphrates River; see therefore: Anonymous, *Tārīkh al-Jarākisa*, MS. Biblioteca Vaticana, Vat. Arabo 273, fol. 100b, here cited after: Clifford, "Some Observations," 270.

24 Peter Malcolm Holt, *The Age of the Crusades. The Near East from the Eleventh Century to 1517* (London: Longman, [8]1997), 200.

25 Ibn Iyās, *Badāʾiʿ*, vol. 4, 462.

26 Ibn Iyās, *Badāʾiʿ*, vol. 4, 471; vol. 5, 14; Brummet, *Ottoman Seapower*, 109.

27 Jean-Louis Bacqué-Grammont, *Les Ottomans, les Safavides et leurs voisins. Contribution à l'histoire des relations internationales dans l'Orient Islamiques de 1514 à 1524* (Istanbul: Nederlands Historisch-Archaeologisch Instituut te Istanbul 1987), 191–192.

28 Ibn Iyās, *Badāʾiʿ*, vol. 5, 86–87.

29 Ibid., 68–70.

preferred.[30] The might and power of the modern Ottoman army did indeed impress the contemporaries and found its expression in Egyptian folk literature. The Egyptian author Ibn Zunbuls writes concerning effects of the Ottoman artillery at the battle of Marj Dābiq: "Each Canon killed 50 or 60 or even 100 souls. And the steppe resembled a slaughterhouse because of the blood."[31] Sultan Qānṣawh al-Ghawrī himself died in the course of the battle and his nephew and successor Ṭūmān Bāy (r. 1516–1517), who hastily tried to organize the defence of Egypt, was defeated by the Ottomans at al-Raydānīya near Cairo in January of 1517.[32] The last Mamluk sultan was caught and hanged at the Bāb al-Zuwayla in Cairo in April of 1517.[33] The Mamluk Empire was history.

Ottomans and Safavids in the Aftermath of the Tripartite Struggle

After their successive victories the Ottomans were the strongest power of the Near and Middle East. The Safavid Empire was thrown back to Iran and the Mamluk Empire annihilated. The efficiency of the Ottoman administration, a powerful economy and the tight organisation of their military sector is often given as main reason for the Ottoman military advance.[34] According to Matuz, military expansion constituted a vital element of the Ottoman Empire. The Ottomans depended on military campaigns as the goods, which were produced by their subjects, did not suffice to support the needs of the huge military sector and the Ottoman bureaucracy.[35] In order to appease the *Landhunger* of the Empire, the Ottomans had 250,000 soldiers at arms at the time of Marj Dābiq. The campaign against the Safavids was apparently undertaken by 140,000 men.[36] The Ottomans dominated their Near Eastern enemies in the military sector just by sheer size. And they were quite innovative as well. After the capture of Constantinople in 1453, the Ottomans decided to become a naval power, in fact the first Muslim naval power since Fatimid times. With the help of their ships they could undertake warfare in the Mediterranean over long distances, a capability

30 David Ayalon, *Gunpowder and Firearms. A Challenge to a Medieval Society* (London: Frank Cass ²1978), 48–49, 62–64.
31 Ibn Zunbul (d. after 1553), *Ākhirat al-mamālīk aw wāqiʿat al-sulṭān al-ghawrī maʿa Selīm al-uthmānī*, ed. by ʿAbd al-Munʿim Amīr (Cairo: al-Hayʾa al-Miṣrīya al-ʿĀmma lil-Kitāb, 1997), 101.
32 Ibn Iyās, *Badāʾiʿ*, vol. 5, 87, 145–148.
33 Ibid., 176.
34 See for example: Josef Matuz, *Das osmanische Reich. Grundlinien seiner Geschichte* (Darmstadt: Wissenschaftliche Buchgesellschaft, ³1994), 84–114.
35 Ibid., 98.
36 Ibid., 101.

that helped defeat the Mamluks.[37] For the first time in centuries the leading role of the Europeans in the Mediterranean was challenged and in the course of the sixteenth century at least the Eastern Mediterranean became a veritable Ottoman "mare nostrum". The funds for military campaigns were partly provided by the "unfriendly takeover" of the Mamluk Empire, as the annual remittance from Cairo to Istanbul started according to Italian sources at 400,000 ducats a year in 1525 and went up dramatically afterwards.[38] The Ottomans became therefore the undisputed Muslim power of the Near East.

Despite this development, the Safavids managed to hold on to their Empire, although immediately after the battle of Chāldirān they had appeared doomed. The Ottomans had occupied the Safavid capital Tabrīz. Moreover, Sultan Selīm was ready to chase the fleeing Shah Ismāʿīl. But his troops were more than reluctant to spend the winter in Tabrīz and to push forward towards the Iranian High Plateau. The climatic conditions in Eastern Anatolia and Azerbaijan were harsh and the line of communication was very long and vulnerable.[39] The powerful Ottoman fleet had its natural limits in this mountainous land area and could not operate at all. Still, the defeat of Chāldirān meant for the Safavids the end of large scale expansion. Now, in the time of crises the newly reconstituted Safavid realm proved its stability. And it is quite remarkable how quick the Safavid Empire recovered. The argument that Shah Ismāʿīl fell in complete agony after the defeat and let everything slip into decay is not persuasive. Even though he now refrained from participating personally in military campaigns, he tried intensively to bring together an anti-Ottoman alliance by sending envoys to European powers and the Mamluks and he modernized his army.[40] He tried to purchase and to fabricate fire arms for his armies in different ways. A Safavid spy, who was caught by the Ottomans, told them that the Ottoman army lost a chariot with a canon in the Araks river during their Iranian campaign in 1514. Shāh Ismāʿīl had it pull out, and built fifty canons with chariots after the Ottoman model.[41] Having learned from the Chāldirān experience, the Safavids did not engage the Ottomans in open battles anymore. Instead, they opted for a scorched earth policy when numerically superior Ottoman armies approached Iranian territory. The Safavids were expecting the Ottomans to return by wintertime. By doing so, the Safavids could minimize their territorial losses in the first half of the sixteenth century. Maybe the most important long term consequence of the battle of Chāldirān lies in the fact, that the Turcoman element became less

37 Andrew C. Hess, "The Ottoman Conquest of Egypt (1517) and the Beginning of the Sixteenth Century World War," *International Journal of Middle East Studies*, 4 (1973), 62.

38 Ibid., 74.

39 Roemer, *Persien*, 263–264.

40 Bacqué-Grammont, *Les Ottomans*, 73–127, 146–186.

41 Ibid., 165–166.

important in the Safavid Empire as the contact to the Eastern Anatolian Qizilbash was cut off. In the long run this meant an increasing Iranisation of the Empire in terms of its military and administration.[42]

Possible Reasons for the Mamluk Disappearance

Contemporary Europeans remarked that the late Mamluks had no military ambitions towards their neighbours. The Italian Andrea Cambini states that in the sixteenth century the Mamluk Sultan would never initiate a military campaign unless someone attacked the Mamluk realm. According to him, the Mamluks had maintained this policy for three hundred years and had never tried to expand their frontiers.[43] The Cypriote Historian Makhairas noticed similar Mamluk behaviour at the beginning of the fifteenth century, when Frankish corsair aggressions on the Mamluk shore represented a common nuisance. He said that the Mamluks would endure foreign aggressions without reaction for a long time and they would never take revenge without warning their enemies at least two or three times in advance.[44] Both these statements show the outward perceptions of the Mamluks as a defensive and peaceful regime. And indeed the Mamluks had ceased military expansion once the wars against the Crusaders and Mongols had been successfully fought in the first decades of their reign. The strategy deployed by the early sultans was to defend their state rather than expanding it, thereby building a "fortress-state" as Humphreys calls it.[45] It seems that they simply lacked the manpower for further expansions and the lives of the imported and then highly trained military slaves represented a too precious good to be wasted in a hazardous campaign. The recruitment of new Mamluks was a difficult task as their import had to be done in parts through enemy territory. Moreover, maintaining the Mamluk armies was expensive, without having a direct positive effect on the economy. Therefore, the number of Mamluks depended on the economic situation of the whole empire. As a result of the long term economic slump the number of Mamluks decreased from 12,000 in

42 Roemer, *Persien*, 267; Andrew J. Newman, *Safavid Iran. Rebirth of a Persian Empire* (London: I.B. Tauris, 2006), 22, 34–38.

43 Andrea Cambini (d. 1550), *Andrea Cambini della origine de Turchi et delli Ottomani* (Florence, 1529), here cited after: Har-El, *Struggle for Domination*, 27.

44 Leontios Makhairas (d. after 1432), *Recital Concerning the Sweet Land of Cyprus*, ed, and transl. by R.M. Dawkins, vol. 1 (Oxford: The Clarendon Press, 1932), § 645, § 646.

45 Stephen R Humphreys, "Egypt in the World System of the Later Middle Ages," in Carl Petry (ed.), *The Cambridge History of Egypt*, Vol. I: *Islamic Egypt, 640–1517* (Cambridge: Cambridge University Press, 1998), 460.

the middle of the fourteenth century to 4–6000 at the end of the fifteenth century.[46]

The shrinking of their military manpower coincided luckily with the lack of a serious outside threat until the campaign of Timur at the beginning of the fifteenth century, which only ended fortunately for the Mamluks because Timur retreated with his army back to the East instead of marching towards Cairo. The shock from Timur, however, was not strong and lasting enough to reverse long-term Mamluk neglect of their military strength. The Mamluks desired to maintain the status quo from the fourteenth century and succeeded in this endeavour for more than two hundred years. But their empire more or less followed according to Humphreys the patterns of outer defence, interior organisation and sources of income, which "had been constructed in and for the world of the late thirteenth century,"[47] thereby they failed to keep up with developments in neighbouring countries. However, this traditional view on the Mamluk state has been seen differently in recent years as it seems that the Mamluks did in fact try to adjust actively to the challenges of the fifteenth century by introducing military and fiscal reforms. It is still a matter of debate, if these reform initiatives were so strong as to alter the current academic view on the later Mamluk period altogether.[48]

Still, the circumstances with which they were confronted with at the beginning of the sixteenth century represented a very demanding and unprecedented challenge for which they had not been prepared. They now had to cope with the Portuguese in the Red Sea to the South, the Safavid Empire in the East and the Ottomans from the north. Their multiple military reforms were not enough to increase their military strength to the level required. Despite the lack of the will for transformation, the most common explanation for the decline and fall of the Mamluk Empire is that the Mamluk military elite was the reluctance to fight with firearms, which they considered unchivalrous and contrary to their code of honor. This thesis was especially supported by Ayalon in his classical study "Gunpowder and Firearms."[49] He based his affirmation especially on the Egyptian author of the sixteenth century Ibn Zunbul, who died in 982/1574. Ibn Zunbul cites for example the Mamluk emir Kurtbāy who says to Sultan Selīm

46 Haarmann, "Der arabische Osten," 226.

47 Humphreys, "Egypt in the World System," 461.

48 See for example: Daisuke Igarashi, *Land Tenure, Fiscal Policy, an Imperial Power in Medieval Syro-Egypt* (Chicago: Middle East Documentation Center, 2015); Francisco Javier Appellániz Ruiz de Galarreta, *Pouvoir et finance en Méditerranée pré-moderne: le deuxième état mamelouk et le commerce des épices (1382–1517)* (Barcelona: Consejo Superior de Investigaciones Científicas 2009); Albrecht Fuess: "Mamluk Politics," in *Ubi sumus? Quo vademus? Mamluk Studies – State of the Art*, ed. Stephan Conermann (Göttingen: Bonn University Press, 2013), 95–117.

49 Ayalon, David, *Gunpowder.*

after his capture: "If we had decided to shoot with firearms, you would have never become better in using them. But we are people who do not ignore the rules of our Prophet Muḥammad. You should be ashamed! How could you dare to shoot with fire at those who profess the unity of god and the sending of Muḥammad." Later on after his capture the Mamluk sultan Ṭūmān Bāy delivered according to Ibn Zunbul a similar speech towards the Ottomans.[50]

With his literary motives about the rejection of firearms by the noble Mamluks Ibn Zunbul has influenced decisively the explanations of the Ottoman victories to be found by later Arab and modern authors like David Ayalon.[51] However, Robert Irwin has already challenged the Ayalon thesis based on the fact that Ibn Zunbul is more of an literary than a historical source. Moreover, Ayalon had ignored or downplayed the frequent mentioning of firearms in Mamluk sources at the beginning of the sixteenth century.[52] And in fact there are enough reasons to critizise Ayalon's view. He argues that fighting with firearms was not prestigious enough for a Mamluk soldier and therefore you never find a high ranking Mamluk in the list of those who fight with firearms.[53] Here I would argue that nowhere in the known world you will find horse riders fighting with firearms on a horse back at the beginning of the sixteenth century. These arms were exclusively reserved for the infantry. Guns are simply not suited to be carried and loaded on horses at that time. It would constitute a considerable waste of money and manpower to have these highly trained professional cavaliers leaving their bows, descending from their horses just to take up firearms which any men could cope with after some initial training. When horsemen fought at the beginning of the sixteenth century they did not use firearms.[54] It is unclear however, if and to what extent the new arms were used by the Mamluk elite cavalry corps, or if they were only used by auxiliary forces. Nevertheless, the Mamluk sultans knew about the importance of fire weapons.[55] Although previous attempts to introduce fire arms

50 Ibn Zunbul, *Ākhirat al-mamālīk*, 139–140, 217. For Ibn Zunbul as an author, see: Andrea Moustafa-Hamouzova, "The Ottoman Conquest of Egypt through Egyptian Eyes. Ibn Zunbul's Wāqiʿat as-Sulṭān Selim Khān maʿa s-Sulṭān Ṭūmānbāy," *Archiv Orientální*, 69/2 (2001), 187–206.

51 Ayalon, *Gunpowder.*

52 Robert Irwin, "Gunpowder and Firearms in the Mamluk Sultanate Reconsidered," in *The Mamluks in Egyptian and Syrian Politics and Society*, ed. Michael Winter and Amalia Levanoni (Leiden: Brill, 2004), 117–139; see as well: Carl Petry, *Protectors or Praetorians? The Last Mamlūk Sultans and Egypt's Waning as a Great Power* (Albany: State University of New York Press, 1994), 195.

53 Ayalon, *Gunpowder*, 69, 73.

54 Kenneth Chase, *Firearms a Global History to 1700* (Cambridge: Cambridge University Press, 2003), 1, 24.

55 See for a more thorough discussion on this topic: Albrecht Fuess: "Les Janissaires, les Mamlouks et les armes à feu. Une comparaison des systèmes militaires ottoman et mamlouk à partir de la moitié du quinzième siècle, " *Turcica,* 41 (2009), 209–227.

were not always successful,[56] Sultan Qānṣawh al-Ghawrī initiated the so-called "fifth corps" in his struggle with the Portuguese. The fifth corps was composed out of *awlād al-nās,* Turcomans, Persians and mariners. They were especially trained to fight with firearms, but no leading Mamluks were among them. It seems that their sole purpose was to fight the Portuguese as their name is not mentioned at all in the historical accounts of the Marj Dābiq.[57] In any case, the Mamluks did use fire arms and artillery. The Venetian consul in Alexandria reported, for example, how the Mamluks brought with them around 25–30 pieces of artillery to Syria.[58] Furthermore, as was already mentioned, Sultan Qānṣawh al-Ghawrī ordered the sending of 200 canons for the security of Alexandria in February of 1516, when rumours about an Ottoman naval attack circulated.[59]

There is also evidence that the Mamluks utilized firearms and purchased them from abroad. Soon after their defeat at Marj Dābiq the Mamluks hastily established contact with the Knights of St. John of Rhodes. Prisoners were released by the Mamluks and a treaty was concluded, by which the Knights would provide the Mamluks with naval assistance against the Ottomans. Integral part of these new relations was Rhodian help concerning firearms. In January 1517 there were rumours that Sultan Ṭūmān Bāy received substantial aid by the Knights of St. John of Rhodes, who send around 40 artillerist experts and arms.[60] The real problem therefore seems not to be the reluctance of the Mamluk soldiers to fight with fire arms, but the incapability of the Mamluk sultans to obtain a sufficient number of them or to produce them on their own. What rendered things even more complicated for the Mamluks was that they had to import the key raw materials for canons and fire arms like copper, saltpetre, sulphur, timber, iron, etc. from Europe or from the Ottomans. It would have been a task for titans to overcome the inequality of resource distribution in comparison to the Ottomans.[61] The Ottomans had therefore far more guns at their disposal and another decisive factor is that they outnumbered the Mamluks on the battlefield.[62] With this military advantage on their side the Ottomans are reported to have won four decisive battles, Bashkent in 1473 against the Aq Qoyunlu,

56 The Mamluk Sultan al-Nāṣir Muḥammad (r. 1496–1498) equipped a military unit of harquebusiers out of black slaves, but was apparently killed for that by his own emirs, see: Holt, *The Age of the Crusades,* 198. See as well: Fuess," Les Janissaires, les Mamlouks et les armes à feu."

57 Ibn Iyās, *Badāʾiʿ,* vol. 4, 308, 331, 335; 369, 458, 466. Petry, *Protectors or Praetorians?,* 195; Ayalon, *Gunpowder,* 71–83.

58 Irwin, "Gunpowder," 133.

59 Ibn Iyās, *Badāʾiʿ,* vol. 4, 471; vol. 5, 14; Brummet, *Ottoman Seapower,* 109.

60 Ibn Iyās, *Badāʾiʿ,* vol. 5, 139; Bacqué-Grammont, *Les Ottomans,* 145–146.

61 See for the resource situation: Albrecht Fuess, "How to Cope with the Scarcity of Commodities? The Mamluk's Quest for Metal," also in this volume.

62 Irwin, "Gunpowder," 128, 136.

Chāldirān against the Safavids in 1514, Marj Dābiq in 1516 and al-Raydanīya in 1517 against the Mamluks, due to a large extent because of their superior fire power. Maybe we can see here more a sign of general dominance and modern armoury on the side of the Ottomans than reluctance to fight with fire arms on the other side. The Ottomans were at the top of the game concerning numbers, weaponry and military logistics.

As already mentioned above, one of the main innovations of the Ottomans was the invention of the *Wagenburg* which they had brought from Central European battle fields and used with great success against the Safavids at the battle of Chāldirān in 1514. The Ottomans used the same tactics at Marj Dābiq against the Mamluks. Their carts were chained together and formed almost invincible *Wagenburgs*.[63] The Damascene chronicler Ibn Ṭūlūn himself witnessed thirty wagons (*ʿaraba*) and twenty wheeled fortresses (*qalʿa ʿalā ʿajal*) when Sultan Selīm entered Damascus in the fall of 1516. He remarked that they were chained together thereby resembling a fortified wall. For him they represented a remarkable sign of the power of the Ottoman sultan. And when they fired once, the people of Damascus felt as if the heaven had come down on them.[64] Apparently the Mamluks had no similar weapons and especially wagons in their arsenal. And as soon as they experienced their effects in battle, Sultan Ṭūmān Bāy copied them as good as he could and brought a considerable number of them (Ibn Iyās speaks of hundred) to the battleground at al-Raydānīya (although without success).[65] Therefore one might assume, that the Mamluks decided not to bring artillery and firearms in large numbers with them to the Syrian battleground, although they possessed them;[66] this might have had nothing to do with presumed chivalry at all. Maybe the Mamluks just simply lacked the infrastructure, men and horsepower for the transport of large numbers of mobile field artillery. And it was only at the battle of Marj Dābiq where they were confronted with the tactics of the Ottoman *Wagenburgs* in a large-scale military encounter for the first time.

Naval policy is certainly another aspect which marked the difference. The main aim of Mamluk naval policy had always been to prevent the return of the Crusaders. Thus they resorted to a "scorched shore" policy. Towns and fortresses along the Syro-Palestinian coast were razed. This policy was designed to hinder the Crusaders from capturing a fortified town on the coast and using it as a base for further operations in Syria. From the Mamluk point of view this policy worked, as the Crusaders never came back. On the other hand, it left the coast open to raids by European pirates. Only on few occasions did the Mamluk

63 Irwin, "Gunpowder," 133.
64 Ibn Ṭūlūn, *Mufākahat*, vol. 2, 30, 31, 34.
65 Ibn Iyās, *Badāʾiʿ*, vol. 5, 134.
66 Ayalon, *Gunpowder*, 48–49.

cavalrymen embark on ships, for example when they subdued Cyprus in the years 1424–26 and transformed the island into a form of protectorate. But these ships were troop transports and not battleships and never heard of again, once the campaigns were over. As in the case of firearms, the Mamluks had the problem to obtain appropriate building material for ships. But they had two hundred years to develop a naval policy, which would have contained war ships, etc. Had they shown more effort, like in the case of the firearms, the Eastern Mediterranean might have been theirs. The main reason why they did not become a naval power was that their anti-Crusader policy worked very successfully in their eyes. On a more psychological level on might argue that there was no prestige to be gained for proud Central Asian horse riders on the decks of ships.[67] Be that as it may, without the resistance of a Mamluk fleet, the Ottoman advance on Egypt was easily supported through naval assistance. The Ottoman Sultan Selīm had resumed extensive construction works in his arsenals once Anatolia was under his control. The Galata and Gallipoli harbours housed two hundred ships in 1514 and even more were constructed, even though Selīm was campaigning in the East against the Safavids. This action suggests that Selīm had already ambitious plans regarding the Eastern Mediterranean. An embassy from Rhodes told the Pope in March of 1516 about the fact that the Ottomans prepared an armada "such no one had ever seen before."[68]

Although the attack finally came by land, it was assisted by the Ottoman fleet, which could provision the Ottoman troops on their advance to Egypt unhampered by the Mamluks such as a convoy of thirteen Ottoman ships passing Beirut on their way to Cairo in the spring of 1517.[69] How helpless the Mamluks were in naval affairs can be seen by the fact that they relied heavily on Ottoman assistance, when they faced the Portuguese challenge in the Red Sea.[70] The fact that the Ottomans could fully employ their navy against the Mamluks might also be an explanation why they vanished; whereas the Safavid land empire survived the Ottoman attacks. On top of these aspects, the Mamluk Sultanate witnessed considerable internal problems at the beginning of the sixteenth century. There had been a general decrease of the population due to recurring plagues which haunted the Mamluk Empire since the first outbreak of the Black Death in the

67 See for the naval policy of the Mamluks: David Ayalon, "The Mamluks and Naval Power: A Phase of the Struggle between Islam and Christian Europe," in: *Proceedings of the Israel Academy of Sciences and Humanities*, 1/8 (1967), 1–12; Fuess, *Verbrannte Ufer*; Albrecht Fuess, "Rotting Ships and Razed Harbours: The Naval Policy of the Mamluks, " *Mamlūk Studies Review*, 5 (2001), 45–71.

68 Brummet, *Ottoman Seapower*, 109–110.

69 Ibn Ṭūlūn, *Mufākahat*, vol 2, 59.

70 Fuess, "Rotting Ships" 57–60; Jean-Louis Bacqué-Grammont and *Anne* Kroell, *Mamlouks, Ottomans et Portugais en Mer Rouge. L'affaire de Djedda en 1517* (Cairo: Institut Français D'Archéologie Orientale, 1988), 2–3.

Middle of the fourteenth century. The plagues took an especially high toll among the freshly imported Mamluks as they were living close together in barracks.[71] The economic system as a whole suffered from the decline in population. The income of the Egyptian agricultural sector for example decreased considerably from 9 million *dinar* to 2 million *dinar*. The monetary system collapsed. Gold and silver coins were replaced by copper coins, which heralded the decline of the economy[72] Long distance trade could not replace the downturn in the agricultural sector, as Borsch tells it:

> Although Egypt bordered the Mediterranean, it did not have a Mediterranean economy. Unlike the Italian city states and other small Mediterranean countries that relied heavily upon long-distance trade, Egypt derived almost all of its GNP from agrarian revenue. Total annual exports to the northern Mediterranean accounted for less than two percent of Egypt's GDP … Long-distance trade played a subordinate role in the overall development of Egypt's economy.[73]

Above all the traditional system of payment for the professional Mamluk soldiers was altered by the sultans in the fifteenth century also. The *iqṭāʿ*-system, whereby soldiers were granted the tax income of a certain land portion in exchange for military service (*khidma*) had been undermined profoundly by the practise of many Mamluk nobles and especially the sultans to transform *iqṭāʿ* land into religious endowments (*awqāf*), whose income should be to the benefit of the offspring of the founder. Therefore, a considerable portion of land income was controlled by the *awlād al-nās* and their families. The privatisation of the land proceeded quickly and at the beginning of the sixteenth century around 40 % of the overall cultivable land was already transformed into *waqf* property, thereby leaving less and less land for the *iqṭāʿ*-system of the Mamluk state.[74] While the process in itself is undisputed, the legitimate question has to be asked, if this was not done on purpose by the sultans? Direct taxation of agricultural products of *waqf* land meant more direct cash for the sultans whereas through the *iqṭāʿ*-system less cash was generated for the royal treasury as the income went to the Mamluk emirs and not the sultan. Moreover the treasury profited in the short run from the selling of *iqṭāʿ* land, because an owner had to possess the land before turning it into *waqf*. By the mid-fifteenth century Mamluk sultans would know that the successful Ottoman army was paid very much directly and not indirectly. Financial reforms were mainly undertaken by the last two important sultans

71 David Ayalon, "The Plague and its Effects upon the Mamluk Army", *Journal of the Royal Asiatic Society* (1946), 67–73.

72 Haarmann, "Der arabische Osten," 247.

73 Stuart J Borsch, *The Black Death in Egypt and England. A Comperative Study* (Austin: University of Texas Press, 2005), 19.

74 Lucian Reinfandt, *Mamlukische Sultansstiftungen des 9./15. Jahrhunderts. Nach den Urkunden der Stifter al-Ašraf Īnāl und al-Muʾayyad Aḥmad Ibn Īnāl* (Berlin: Schwarz, 2003), 32–36.

Qāytbāy (r. 1468–1496) and Qānsūh al-Ghawrī (r. 1501–16) at a time when the Ottoman threat became virulent. Daisuke Igarashi has shown in a 2009 article on "the Financial Reforms of Sultan Qāytbāy", how Qāytbāy tried to increase his cash reservoir by getting all unproductive people from the payroll, for example by letting them draw a bow to prove their military abilities.[75]In his 2009 book Francisco Appelaniz has argued as well that Qāytbāy was looking for alternative funding for the military as the *iqṭāʿ*-system seemed less and less appropriate for his military needs. He wanted a better direct influence on the army and needed more cash for new arms like canons and firearms.[76]

However, to the ordinary Mamluks it meant that his life circumstances and his economical bases were severely threatened. The still remaining *iqṭāʿāt* were hotly disputed among Mamluks and to obtain them they resorted sometimes to violent acts. For example in the year 1506 one of the old *Qarāniṣa*[77] Mamluk became severely ill. The sultan promised the *iqṭāʿ* to some *Julbān*[78] Mamluks in case of the death of the Mamluk. Upon hearing that the *Qarāniṣa* Mamluk had recovered the *Julbān* stabbed the old man to death at the time of the morning prayer out of frustration and then claimed the *iqṭāʿ*.[79] Tensions between the *Qarāniṣa* and the *Julbān,* where also to play a vital role in the defeat of Marj Dābiq, as the *Qarāniṣa* were not pleased by the fact that the Sultan held the *Julbān* back at first and restrained them from engaging in the fight, therefore the *Qarāniṣa* apparently slowed down their own efforts considerably.[80] Much of the energy of the Mamluk Empire was taken up by such inner Mamluk fractional rivalries. These developments might also explain why a considerable part of the Mamluks deserted at the battle of Marj Dābiq and defected with the Mamluk governor of Aleppo, Khāyrbak, to the Ottomans.[81] Finally, I would like to introduce a further reason for the Mamluk downfall which, I would like to call the "age factor." Mamluk sultans usually had a long career in various functions in the army before obtaining the supreme post of the Empire. The sultans of the sixteenth century were on average around seventy years old when they climbed up to the throne.[82] The age structure and the vulnerability to disease among the members of the high command in the late Mamluk Empire resemble strikingly the Soviet Politburo before the fall of the Iron Curtain. In both cases, the will for major changes and

75 Daisuke Igarashi, "The Financial Reforms of Sultan Qāytbāy," *Mamlūk Studies Review,* 13/1 (2009), 27–51.

76 Apellániz, *Pouvoir et Finance*, 172.

77 The veteran Mamluks of previous sultans.

78 The Mamluks bought, trained and emancipated by a reigning sultan in the Circassian period.

79 Ibn Iyās, *Badāʾiʿ*, vol. 4, 107.

80 Ibid, vol. 5, 69; Irwin, "Gunpowder," 128.

81 Ibn Iyās, *Badāʾiʿ*, vol. 5, 69; Petry, *Protectors,* 25. For his treason Khāyrbak was awarded with the governorship of Egypt by the Ottomans.

82 Fuess, *Verbrannte Ufer*, 250.

reforms was weakly developed since it had taken such a long time to climb the career ladder as a brave servant of the system. Once at the top, there was little incentive to question the complete structure of the Empire. Keeping this age factor in mind it is quite symptomatic that Sultan Qānṣūh al-Ghawrī died from apoplexy due to excitement at the decisive battle at Marj Dābiq.[83] The generally younger age of Ottoman and Safavid rulers may have encouraged more innovative approaches in conducting the affairs of the state. According to Haarmann at the end of the fifteenth century, "the capability of following through reforms within the Mamluk system was apparently exhausted." The Mamluks were no longer fit to react to the challenges of the Age of Discovery. Therefore the Mamluks disappeared, whereas Ottomans and Safavids adjusted better to the tasks posed by the sixteenth century.

Bibliography

Allouche, Adel, *The Origins and Development of the Ottoman-Safavid Conflict (906–962/ 1500–1555)* (Berlin: Klaus Schwarz, 1983).

Appellániz Ruiz de Galarreta, Francisco Javier: *Pouvoir et finance en Méditerranée pré-moderne: le deuxième état mamelouk et le commerce des épices (1382–1517)* (Barcelona: Consejo Superior de Investigaciones Científicas 2009).

Ayalon, David, "The End of the Mamluk Sultanate. Why did the Ottomans spare the Mamluks of Egypt and wipe out the Mamluks of Syria?," *Studia Islamica* 65 (1987), 125–148.

–, *Gunpowder and Firearms in the Mamluk Kingdom. A Challenge to a Medieval Society*, (London: Frank Cass ^{2}1978).

–, "The Mamluks and Naval Power: A Phase of the Struggle between Islam and Christian Europe," *Proceedings of the Israel Academy of Sciences and Humanities*, 1/8 (1967), 1–12.

–, "The Plague and its Effects upon the Mamluk Army," *Journal of the Royal Asiatic Society* (1946), 67–73.

Babinger, Franz, "Ramaḍān Og͟hullari̊", in: *Encyclopaedia of Islam*, Second Edition, ed. P. Bearman, Th. Bianquis, C.E. Bosworth, E. van Donzel, W.P. Heinrichs. Consulted online on 13 August 2018 <http://dx.doi.org/10.1163/1573-3912_islam_SIM_6209>.

Bacqué-Grammont, Jean-Louis, *Les Ottomans, les Safavides et leurs voisins. Contribution à l'histoire des relations internationales dans l'Orient Islamiques de 1514 à 1524* (Istanbul: Nederlands Historisch-Archaeologisch Instituut te Istanbul 1987).

Bacqué-Grammont, Jean-Louis, and Anne Kroell, *Mamlouks, Ottomans et Portugais en Mer Rouge. L'affaire de Djedda en 1517* (Cairo: Institut Français D'Archéologie Orientale 1988).

83 Ibn Iyās, *Badāʾiʿ*, vol. 5, 69; According to Ibn Ṭūlūn, he became suddenly unconscious and died from an intestinal colic, see: Ibn Ṭūlūn, *Mufākahat*, vol. 2, 24.

Borsch, Stuart J, *The Black Death in Egypt and England. A Comperative Study* (Austin: University of Texas Press 2005).

Brummet, Palmira, *Ottoman Seapower and Levantine Diplomacy in the Age of Discovery* (Albany: State University of New York Press, 1994).

Chase, Kenneth, *Firearms a Global History to 1700* (Cambridge: CUP 2003).

Clifford, W.W, "Some Observations on the Course of Mamluk-Safavi Relations (1502–1516/908–922)," *Der Islam*, 70 (1993), 264–265.

Evrard, James B., *Zur Geschichte Aleppos und Nordsyriens im letzten halben Jahrhundert der Mamlukenherrschaft (872–921 AH)* (Munich: Rudolf Trofenik, 1974).

Fuess, Albrecht, "How to Cope with the Scarcity of Commodities? The Mamluk's quest for Metal," in *The Mamluk Sultanate and its Neighbors: Economic, Social and Cultural Entanglements*, ed. Reuven Amitai and Stephan Conermann. (Göttingen: Bonn University Press 2018), (this present volume).

–, "Les Janissaires, les Mamlouks et les armes à feu. Une comparaison des systèmes militaires ottoman et mamlouk à partir de la moitié du quinzième siècle," *Turcica,* 41 (2009), 209–227.

–, "Mamluk Politics," in *Ubi sumus? Quo vademus? Mamluk Studies – State of the Art*, ed. Stephan Conermann, Göttingen: Bonn University Press 2013, 95–117.

–, *Verbranntes Ufer. Auswirkungen mamlukischer Seepolitik auf Beirut und die syro-palästinensische Küste in mamlukischer Zeit (1250–1517),* (Leiden: Brill 2001).

–, "Rotting Ships and Razed Harbours: The Naval Policy of the Mamluks," *Mamlūk Studies Review* 5 (2001), 45–71.

Gronke, Monika, *Geschichte Irans. Von der Islamisierung bis zur Gegenwart* (Munich: C.H. Beck, 2003).

Moustafa-Hamouzova, Andrea, "The Ottoman Conquest of Egypt through Egyptian Eyes. Ibn Zunbul's Wāqiʿat as Sulṭān Selim khān maʿa s-Sulṭān Ṭūmānbāy," *Archiv Orientální* 69/2 (2001), 187–206.

Haarmann, Ulrich, "Der arabische Osten im späten Mittelalter 1250–1517," in: *Geschichte der arabischen Welt,* ed. Ulrich Haarmann (Munich: C. H. Beck [4]2001), 236–241.

Har-El, Shai, *Struggle for Domination in the Middle East. The Ottoman-Mamluk War, 1485–1491* (Leiden: Brill, 1995).

Hess, Andrew C., "The Ottoman Conquest of Egypt (1517) and the Beginning of the Sixteenth Century World War," *International Journal of Middle East Studies*, 4 (1973), 55–76.

Humphreys, Stephen R., "Egypt in the World System of the later Middle Ages," in: *The Cambridge History of Egypt, Vol. I: Islamic Egypt, 640–1517*, ed. Carl F. Petry (Cambridge: Cambridge University Press, 1998), 445–461.

Holt, Peter Malcolm, *The Age of the Crusades. The Near East from the Eleventh Century to 1517* (London: Longman, [8]1997).

Ibn Iyās, *Badāʾiʿ al-zuhūr fī waqāʾiʿ al-duhūr*, ed. by Mohamed Mostafa, 5 vols. (Wiesbaden: Franz Steiner, 1960–1975).

Ibn Ṭūlūn, *Mufākahat al-khillān fī Ḥawādith al-zamān,* ed. by Mohamed Mostafa, 2 vols. (Cairo: Wizārat al-Thaqāfa wal-Irshād al-Qawmī, 1962).

Ibn Zunbul, *Ākhirat al-mamālīk aw wāqiʿat al-Sulṭān al-ghawrī maʿa Selīm al-ʿuthmānī,* ed. ʿAbd al-Munʿim Amīr (Cairo: al-Hayʾa al-Miṣrīya al-ʿĀmma lil-kKitāb, 1997).

Igarashi, Daisuke, "The Financial Reforms of Sultan Qāytbāy," *Mamlūk Studies Review*, 13/1 (2009), 27–51.

–, *Land Tenure, Fiscal Policy, an Imperial Power in Medieval Syro-Egypt* (Chicago: Middle East Documentation Center, 2015).

Irwin, Robert, "Gunpowder and Firearms in the Mamluk Sultanate Reconsidered," in: *The Mamluks in Egyptian and Syrian Politics and Society*, ed. Michael Winter and Amalia Levanoni (Leiden: Brill 2004), 117–139.

Makhairas, Leontios (d. after 1432), *Recital Concerning the Sweet Land of Cyprus*, ed. and transl. by R.M. Dawkins, 2 vols. (Oxford: The Clarendon Press, 1932).

Matuz, Josef, *Das osmanische Reich Grundlinien seiner Geschichte* (Darmstadt: Wissenschaftliche Buchgesellschaft, [3]1994).

Morgan, David, *Medieval Persia 1040–1797* (London: Longman [5]1997).

Newman, Andrew J., *Safavid Iran, Rebirth of an Empire* (London: I.B. Tauris, 2006).

von Palombini, Barbara, *Bündniswerben abendländischer Mächte um Persien 1453–1600* (Wiesbaden: Franz Steiner, 1968).

Petry, Carl, *Protectors or Praetorians? The Last Mamlūk Sultans and Egypt's Waning as a Great Power,* (Albany: State University of New York Press 1994).

Reinfandt, Lucian, *Mamlukische Sultansstiftungen des 9./15. Jahrhunderts. Nach den Urkunden der Stifter al-Ašraf Īnāl und al-Mu'ayyad Aḥmad Ibn Īnāl* (Berlin: Schwarz 2003).

Roemer, Hans-Robert, *Persien auf dem Weg in die Neuzeit. Iranische Geschichte von 1350–1750* (Beirut: Institut der Deutschen Morgenländischen Gesellschaft, 1989).

Sanuto, Marino, *I Diarii,* sous la dir. de Rinaldo Fulin et al., 58 vols., (Venice: Fratelli Visentini, 1879–1902).

–, *Šāh Ismāʿīl I nei "Diarii" di Marino Sanudo*, ed. Biancamaria Scarcia Amoretti, vol. 1 (Rome: Istituto per l'Oriente, 1979).

Venzke, Margaret L., "Dulkadir," in: *Encyclopaedia of Islam*, THREE, ed. Kate Fleet, Gudrun Krämer, Denis Matringe, John Nawas, Everett Rowson. Consulted online on 13 August 2018 <http://dx.doi.org/10.1163/1573-3912_ei3_COM_27743>.

V. The Red Sea and Beyond

John Meloy (American University of Beirut)

Mecca Entangled

This paper examines some of the "mechanisms, linkages, and movements" of a region centered on Mecca and the Hijaz during the late medieval period, a period when the Cairo Sultanate achieved its political apogee. Mecca may seem a rather well-trodden topic: of course, the connections of the faith are already well-known; naturally, these movements of pilgrims, pious sojourners, and palanquins played an important role in representing the city and its place within the Islamic world. While one should not forget the moral value invested in a holy city, its sacred character all too often eclipses more mundane dimensions of social and economic life that are essential to understand the city as a place where people lived and the connections it had with its regions. My use of regions in the plural here is deliberate: Mecca, together with its port of Jedda, may be seen as a single node within overlapping regions, each defined by its sets of relations. My goal here is to understand in more detail the place of Mecca within a space defined by the multivalent interactions of Mecca with other places undertaken by people who did not see it as simply a sacred place. In an effort to achieve a more contextual view of Mecca, this paper borrows from, and modifies, some of the ideas of relational geography as well as the archaeological notion of entanglement.

My approach here is shaped by urban geographer Ash Amin's notion of a place as "the city, region, or rural area – as a site of intersection between network topologies and territorial legacies."[1] One benefit of this view is to illustrate how connectivity is constructed, even at a distance, so that the city "becomes the sum of its spatial interactions," requiring that we look for "the multiple registers of urban formation."[2] In this approach, community and connectivity consist of

1 Ash Amin, "Re-thinking the Urban Social," *City*, 11:1 (2007): 100–114, citing 103. Also see his "Regions Unbound: Towards a New Politics of Place," *Geografiska Annaler* 86B (2004): 33–44; and Eric Sheppard, "Thinking Geographically: Globalizing Capitalism and Beyond," *Annals of the Association of American Geographers*, 105/6 (2015): 1113–34.

2 Amin, "Re-thinking," 102, 104.

processes and interactions.[3] In what follows I will argue that these relations can engender dependence and dependency, a distinction that leads us to consider Ian Hodder's entanglement. Hodder has proposed entanglement to subvert the prevailing "anthropocentric view" within archaeology of people living within the material world. His goal is "to examine the relationship between people and material things from the point of view of things."[4] There is no need here to sift through the details of Hodder's theory, and I am not interested in the social evolutionary significance of entanglement theory.[5] However, it can be said that by leveling the relative positions of people and things, and by compiling the permutations of their interactions, one can begin to determine the extent to which they are mutually interdependent so that one can see "the dialectic of dependence and dependency" among people and things.[6] Here, I would like to use this notion of the dialectic of dependence and dependency with regard to places, in order to understand more accurately how, through their connections – usually via people – a place (and the people in it) can become dependent on, or benefit from, another place. In this context, dependence is a means of empowerment that, however, is not static. Thus, dependence can easily slip into dependency, that is to say exclusive reliance, when that external relation becomes vitally and uniquely essential for a place's existence, thus exposing its vulnerability.

Broadly conceived, I intend to examine Mecca's multifarious connections, often, but not always, through its port of Jedda, within a broader region to illuminate aspects of its social and economic history: connections of subsistence and status; intellectual, philanthropic, and institutional relations; and commercial and diplomatic contact. This survey is necessarily tentative since the sum of relational connections and their resultant dependences and dependencies, which need to be surveyed, is far greater than can be covered in a single article, even if one is restricted to material from the fourteenth and fifteenth centuries. However, as an exercise it is useful to consider this approach when thinking about this most important neighbor of the Cairo Sultanate – a place that was simultaneously central to the Sultanate's ideological world, yet peripheral to it geographically. Together these relational features are yet another illustration of the cosmopolitan vitality of the later Middle Periods of the Islamic world; however,

3 Stephan Conermann. "Networks and Nodes in Mamluk Times: Some Introductory Remarks." In *Everything is on the Move: The Mamluk Empire as a Node in (Trans-)Regional Networks*, ed. Stephan Conermann, 9–26, Bonn: Bonn UP, 2014.

4 Susan Pollock et al., "Entangled Discussions: Talking with Ian Hodder about his book *Entangled*," *Forum Kritische Archäologie*, 3 (2014): 151–161, citing 151.

5 Ian Hodder, *Entangled: An Archaeology of the Relationships of Humans and Things* (Malden, MA: Wiley-Blackwell, 2012); idem, "The Entanglements of Humans and Things: A Long-Term View," *New Literary History*, 45:1 (2014): 19–36.

6 Hodder, "Entanglements," 20.

beyond that, these features show how the connections of the Cairo Sultanate's apparent domination of Mecca and Mecca's connections elsewhere could expose the vulnerability of Cairo's imperial reach. In general, Mecca's entanglements, and by extension, Cairo's, seem to have shifted eastward to the extent that we discern an emerging dependency on southern Asia as well.[7]

Sacred Status and Material Subsistence

Of course, because Mecca's sacred aura and its barren setting are constants in the history of the city, its ties of status and subsistence form the necessary backdrop for a number of other connections. That this relationship was one of dependency, and not merely dependence, has not gone unnoticed: in 1985, Richard Mortel published an excellent survey of Mecca's food supply and argued that Egypt's provision of nourishment, particularly with regard to the annual influx of pilgrims, when the city's population could easily double or treble, enabled Cairo to establish its control over Mecca (as well as Medina) through the conventional symbols of Islamic sovereignty, whether the invocation of the sultan's name in the *khuṭba* or the sending of the *maḥmal*.[8] Since then, the publication of Jār Allāh ibn Fahd's brief account of the wadis of Mecca has provided local knowledge about its food supply.[9] However, the evidence to ascertain the extent of external reliance remains largely anecdotal, and it is still difficult to escape obvious assumptions about the comparative agricultural productivity of the fertile Nile Valley versus the barren mountain valleys and coastal plains of the Hijaz. This contrastive view is seemingly corroborated in the accounts of European travelers who, although they offer useful information, also assert categorically, as the early sixteenth century traveler Ludovico di Varthema did, that nothing could grow in Mecca. In his view, this was due to divine retribution: "The curse of God has been laid upon the said city, for the country produces neither grass nor trees nor any one thing."[10] However, we know from local, contemporary descriptions of the Hijaz that a surprising variety of agricultural products were available in the vicinity of Mecca.

7 From the perspective of Egypt, one might in the future want to explore this dependency in relation to Egypt's emerging dependency on Europe; see Jean-Claude Garcin, "The Mamluk Military System and the Blocking of Medieval Moslem Society," in *Europe and the Rise of Capitalism*, ed. Jean Baechler et al. (Oxford: Basil Blackwell, 1988), 113–130.

8 Richard Mortel, "Maṣādir al-Tamwīn al-Ghadhīʾī li-Imārat Makka (358 H./969 M.–923 H./1517 M.)," *Majallat Kulliyyat al-Ādāb, Jāmiʿat al-Malik Saʿūd* 12:1 (1985): 193–219, citing 210.

9 Jār Allāh Muḥammad ibn Fahd, *Ḥusn al-Qirā fī Awdiyat Umm al-Qurā*, ed. ʿAlī ʿUmar (Cairo: Maktabat al-Thaqāfa al-Dīniyya, 2001).

10 Ludovico di Varthema, *The Travels*, trans. J. W. Jones and ed. G. P. Badger (The Hakluyt Society, no. 32 [first series], 1863; republished: New York: Burt Franklin, n.d.), 37.

Jār Allāh ibn Fahd's small book on the wadis of Mecca expands on bits of information that can be gleaned from al-Qalqashandī and other compendia. The upland districts of al-Ṭāʾif, Ibn Fahd writes, were an important source of foodstuffs for the residents of Mecca, who "relish and enjoy" them, including a variety of fruits – "grapefruit, grapes, berries, figs called *al-ḥimāṭ*, plums known as *al-farsak*, apples, some apricots" – as well as barley and a grain called *luqayma*.[11] These highlands were the Jibāl al-Sāra, the mountain range within the region of the Hijaz that separates the coastal Tihama from the Najd in the interior, identified by Mortel as "the most important source of food for the people of Mecca."[12] Ibn Fahd also mentions the produce of fishermen who sailed from the port of Jidda in their local craft (*jilāb*) to catch numerous varieties of fish.[13] More interesting is Jār Allāh's report that market gardens, fed by wells and springs, of villages in the Wadi Marr and Wadi Nakhla offered a variety of products. The wadi villages provided "bananas, green melons called *habhab*, yellow melons called *khazbar*, cucumbers, dates of all kinds, eggplant, squash called *al-dabāʾ*, colocasia, okra, carrots, turnips, radishes, mallow, leeks, garlic, coriander, *laym* (?), and lemons". The wadi al-Ḥadda, also known as Ḥaddat Banī Jābir, supplied four types of grain: wheat (*hinta*), barley, millet (*dukhn*), sorghum (*dhurra*), and *daqsa*, which, Ibn Fahd explains, "is among the products of Mecca, and Bilād al-Sūdān, and Hadramawt, and Yemen, and, so it is said, India."[14] In addition, the wadis supplied alluvial soil that could be brought in to supplement the vegetable gardens in Mecca itself.[15] Undoubtedly, the productivity of the wadi gardens must have been precarious, as Mortel noted,[16] susceptible not only to the region's harsh climate but also the destructive power of flash floods. Be that as it may, Ibn Fahd's local view allows us to see how the indigenous population was able to survive, in part on local goods but also on a region of supply that extended to adjacent localities, partly evident in the regional distribution of the *daqsa* grain, which connected Mecca to a region that did not necessarily include the Nile valley, but rather extended southwest across the Red Sea, to southern Arabia, and possibly even south Asia.

However, the challenge in Mecca was to feed the pilgrims, who could easily overwhelm the city's indigenous population. As long-distance travel became

11 Jār Allāh Muḥammad ibn Fahd, *Ḥusn al-Qirā*, 44; Shihāb al-Dīn Aḥmad al-Qalqashandī, *Ṣubḥ al-Aʿshā fī Ṣināʿat al-Inshāʾ* (Cairo: Dār al-Kutub al-Khidīwiyya, 1913–20; reprinted 1963), 4: 248, 258.

12 Mortel, "Maṣādir," 200.

13 Jār Allāh ibn Fahd, *Ḥusn al-Qirā*, 31–32.

14 Jār Allāh ibn Fahd, *Ḥusn al-Qirā*, 50 (both quotations).

15 Ruqayya Ḥusayn Saʿd Nujaym, *al-Bīʾa al-Ṭabīʿiyya li-Makka al-Mukarrama: Dirāsa fī al-Jughrāfiyya al-Ṭabīʿiyya li-Minṭaqat al-Ḥaram al-Makkī al-Sharīf* (Mecca: Muʾassasat al-Furqān, 2000), 296–297.

16 Mortel, "Maṣādir," 200.

more reliable, no doubt these numbers grew, increasing also Mecca's reliance on external sources of nourishment. Documentary evidence recovered from excavations at Quseir, the Red Sea port, includes mention of a transaction involving 43 *irdabbs* (about 3,000 kgs.) of wheat, sufficient to feed four or five medium-sized households for a year, or as many as one hundred adult pilgrims for one month. This record represents what was probably a steady stream of grain transactions that supplied Mecca from the Nile valley,[17] and reinforces our view of Mecca's close connections to Upper Egypt, where the sharifs held substantial endowments,[18] which helped to support their patronage system. Other residents of Mecca had holdings in the Nile valley as well, like Najm al-Dīn Muḥammad ibn Fahd (d. 811/1408–9) who, after the death of his mother, Khadīja bt. Najm al-Dīn ʿAbd al-Raḥmān al-Qurashī al-Makhzūmī (d. 770/1368–9), moved to Aṣfūn al-Jabalayn, a village near the upper Egyptian town of Asnā, to claim the benefits from a *waqf*, constituting houses and hamlets originally established by his maternal grandfather, which his mother had inherited.[19] Najm al-Dīn Muḥammad later returned to Mecca, where his descendants became notable for recording the city's history. The narrative sources from Cairo provide the most vivid evidence of large shipments of foodstuffs from the Nile valley. Jean-Claude Garcin concluded that these consignments were made for a variety of reasons, ranging from efforts by politically prominent pilgrims to enhance their prestige to emergency measures adopted to alleviate famine.[20] Compared to the transaction documented above, the episodic shipments cited in the narrative sources were significantly greater in volume – no doubt the reason that they were noteworthy – but the laconic nature of these reports makes it difficult to estimate the volume of foodstuffs that were transported to the Hijaz annually. At times, one cannot help but wonder about the reliability of these anecdotes. For example, a report in 722/1322–23 of 3,000 *irdabbs* of wheat sent by sultan al-Nāṣir Muḥammad and others, due to drought-induced shortage, stands in marked contrast to a report in

17 Li Guo, *Commerce, Culture, and Community in a Red Sea Port in the Thirteenth Century* (Leiden: Brill, 2004), 28, 36; Guo offers the kilogram equivalent based on S.D. Goitein.

18 Jean-Claude Garcin, *Un centre musulman de la haute-Égypte medieval: Qus* (Cairo: IFAO, 1976), 134, 208.

19 Taqī al-Dīn Muḥammad al-Fāsī, *al-ʿIqd al-Thamīn fī Taʾrīkh al-Balad al-Amīn* (Cairo: Maṭbaʿat al-Sunna al-Muḥammadiyya, 1959–69), 2: 333, no. 436; Najm al-Dīn ʿUmar ibn Fahd, *al-Durr al-Kamīn bi-Dhayl al-ʿIqd al-Thamīn fī Taʾrīkh al-Balad al-Amīn* (Mecca: Maktabat al-Asadī, 2004), 1: 385–395, no. 280; the author, Najm al-Dīn ʿUmar, was the grandson of Najm al-Dīn Muḥammad; on Aṣfūn as a source of educated men, see Garcin, *Qus*, esp. p. 308, note 3).

20 Garcin, *Qus*, p. 203; Taqī al-Dīn Aḥmad al-Maqrīzī, *Kitāb al-Sulūk li-Maʿrifat Duwal al-Mulūk* (Cairo: Lajnat al-Taʾlīf wa-al-Tarjama wa-al-Nashr, 1956–73), 1: 917; also see 1: 954; and 2: 238, 702.

747/1346–47 of 150,000 *irdabb*s of barley sent by sultan al-Nāṣir Ḥasan out of his concern for the pilgrimage.[21]

Notwithstanding questionable details, there seems to have been a relatively small scale but steady supply of grains passing through Quseir which could be supplemented by occasional large shipments driven by emergency, piety, or prestige. Many of the latter may well have supplied the charitable institutions in Mecca that supplied indigent pilgrims with the *dashīsha*, a type of porridge made from wheat and fat, produced in the city's hospices (*ribāṭ*s) and soup kitchens, which must have constituted a valuable source of nourishment for the impoverished.[22]

With regard to Mecca's supply of foodstuffs, the Nile valley was not the only option, as we see more clearly in the Meccan sources. In ʿIzz al-Dīn ʿAbd al-ʿAzīz ibn Fahd's occasional reports about the grain market in Mecca, one gets the impression – and it isn't much more than that – that entrepots like Zaylaʿ, Yemen, and Barbara were as significant as Egypt in moderating grain prices.[23] This impression may be confirmed by the account of Ludovico di Varthema. While he clearly did not have sufficiently accurate local knowledge to understand the suppliers of Mecca's markets, his account does provide a broader view that situates Mecca in a region that includes not only the Nile valley but also territories south: "A great part of their provisions comes from Cairo, that is, from the Red Sea. There is a port called Zida [Juddah], which is distant from the said city forty miles. A great quantity of food also comes there from Arabia Felix, and also a great part comes from Ethiopia."[24] Ludovico's rather dismal opinion of Mecca and its port of Jidda stands in contrast to his opinions of other Red Sea ports. Noteworthy is Jīzān, a Red Sea town about 650 km. south of Jedda, which:

> has a very fine port; and we found there forty-five vessels belonging to different countries. This city is situated on the sea shore, and is subject to a Moorish lord, and is a district very fruitful and good, like Christian countries. Here there are very good grapes and peaches, quinces and pomegranates, very strong garlic, tolerable onions, excellent nuts, melons, roses, flowers, nectarines, figs, gourds, citrons, lemons, and sour oranges, so that it is a paradise. The inhabitants of this city go almost naked, and live after the manner of the Moors. There is here abundance of flesh, grain, barley, and white millet, which they call dora, and which makes very good bread. We remained here three days in order to lay in provisions.[25]

21 Al-Maqrīzī, *Kitāb al-Sulūk*, 2: 238 and 702.

22 Doris Behrens-Abouseif, "Qaytbāy's Foundation in Medina, the Madrasah, the Ribāṭ, and the Dashīshah," *Mamluk Studies Review*, 2 (1998): 61–71, citing 65–66; she has suggested that *dashīsha* might be similar to Syrian *harīsa*.

23 See, for example, ʿIzz al-Dīn ʿAbd al-ʿAzīz ibn Fahd, *Bulūgh al-Qirā fī Dhayl Itḥāf al-Warā bi-Akhbār Umm al-Qurā* (Cairo: Dār al-Qāhira, 2005), 1: 422, 487, 624–5; 2: 776, 832.

24 Varthema, *Travels*, 37–38.

25 Varthema, *Travels*, 55–56.

He also notes the port of Zaylaʿ, in the far north part of Somalia: "In this city people live extremely well, and justice is excellently administered. Much grain grows here and much animal goods, oil in great quantity, made not from olives but from zerzalino [sesame], honey and wax in great abundance."[26]

Thus we can conclude that Mecca imported foodstuffs from a range of locations, within the peninsula and beyond: the highland town of al-Ṭāʾif, the Sāra mountains to its south, the Yemeni Tihama, as well as African ports of the Red Sea and the Gulf of Aden. Mortel's reconstruction of Mecca's nutritional history during the Mamluk period argues for the holy city's dependency, and not merely dependence, on Egypt. But one might specify that it was the pilgrims' dependency on external foodstuffs that defined the relationship, rather than that of the permanent inhabitants of the city, although this is not to diminish the precariousness of their livelihood. However, as agriculturally rich as the Nile valley was, the Sultanate does not seem to have discovered the mechanism to assure a constant supply of food for pilgrims; as long as Mecca had recourse from year to year to a number of sources of staples, its reliance on Cairo was not exclusive. One can surmise that the Cairo sultans' symbolic reliance on Mecca was perhaps even more exclusive than the Meccan sharifs' nutritive reliance on Egypt: thus the sultans' dependency on Mecca's holy status afforded the sharifs a certain amount of leverage over their overlords in Cairo. The intertwined connections of status and subsistence constituted a kind of co-dependency, asymmetrical weaknesses that not only formed the backdrop to Mecca's other types of connections, but also remind us that Mecca had intimate connections to destinations south in the Arab peninsula and southwest across the Red Sea.

Intellectual Connections

When we examine other dimensions of life in Mecca it becomes clear that the city's external connections were equally diffuse. Many of Mecca's residents lived there temporarily, as "pious sojourners," *mujāwirūn*, who pursued their spiritual devotions and studied and taught in the holy city. Mecca, as well as Medina, thus became important centers of religious instruction thanks to the scholars, whether native to the Hijaz, or foreign. In this regard, they were much like other cities at the time that benefited from the geographical mobility of the religious elite and the *madrasa* system which could accommodate them – these are hallmarks, of course, of medieval Islamic society, fundamental to the era's cosmopolitanism. Najm al-Dīn ʿUmar ibn Fahd, the grandson of Najm al-Dīn Muḥammad, mentioned above, compiled in his *al-Durr al-Kamīn* biographies that provide

26 Varthema, *Travels*, 86–87.

glimpses into these intellectual connections, through the reported journeys of scholars. Najm al-Dīn the elder was the progenitor of a well-known scholarly family active in Mecca. His son, Taqī al-Dīn, became a well-known *muḥaddith*, who studied with the likes of Ibn Ḥajar al-ʿAsqalānī, al-Maqrīzī, and Ibn al-Jazarī, and who in turn taught al-Sakhāwī. Taqī al-Dīn was also highly regarded in scholarly circles for making his personal library a *waqf*, open to scholars in Mecca. He was born in Upper Egypt during his father's sojourn to claim the family *waqf*, but the family subsequently returned to Mecca, where Taqī al-Dīn completed his education and his descendants continued their scholarly pursuits. Taqī al-Dīn's son, Najm al-Dīn ʿUmar, was an established *muḥaddith* himself and the author of an annalistic history and a biographical dictionary that continued al-Fāsī's compilation, the first major work by a Meccan scholar since the tenth century.[27] Najm al-Dīn ʿUmar's son, ʿIzz al-Dīn ʿAbd al-ʿAzīz, continued his chronicle, a work continued in turn by Najm al-Dīn's grandson, Jār Allāh ibn Fahd, who also authored the book on Mecca's wadis, referred to earlier.[28] These men focused their intellectual efforts on the religious sciences and the history of Mecca, but their horizons extended far beyond the confines of their hometown.

Najm al-Dīn's biographical entries in *al-Durr al-Kamīn* allow us to trace the intellectual connections of these men and women when he relates their travels in order to study, which seem to extend further afield with each generation and which, for some, extended into commerce. His father, Taqī al-Dīn (d. 871/1466–7), born in Upper Egypt in 787/1385–6, had studied in Mecca, Medina, and Yemen; perhaps noteworthy is that he did not, apparently, go to Cairo, but was able to study with a number of Cairene scholars in Mecca. Najm al-Dīn noted that his father was also able to obtain *ijāza*s for his son from scholars hailing from Alexandria, Jerusalem, Hebron, Damascus, Aleppo, Hims, Hama, and Baalbek.[29] Najm al-Dīn ʿUmar (d. 885/1480–1) himself studied in Cairo, as well as in Jerusalem, Baalbek, Damascus, and Aleppo. Najm al-Dīn ʿUmar's son, ʿIzz al-Dīn ʿAbd al-ʿAzīz (d. 922/1516–7), travelled to Cairo four times and visited also Jerusalem, Hebron, Damascus, and Aleppo. Jār Allāh ibn ʿIzz al-Dīn ibn Fahd travelled to Yemen, and at least twice to Egypt, Syria, and Anatolia.[30] Taqī al-Dīn's

27 Najm al-Dīn ʿUmar ibn Fahd, *al-Durr al-Kamīn bi-Dhayl al-ʿIqd al-Thamīn fi Taʾrikh al-Balad al-Amīn* (Mecca: Maktabat al-Asadī, 2004); idem, *Itḥāf al-Warā bi-Akhbār Umm al-Qurā* (Mecca: Jamiʿat Umm al-Qurā, 1983–90).

28 ʿIzz al-Dīn ʿAbd al-ʿAzīz ibn Fahd, *Bulūgh al-Qirā fī Dhayl Itḥāf al-Warā bi-Akhbār Umm al-Qurā* (Cairo: Dār al-Qāhira, 2005).

29 Najm al-Dīn ʿUmar ibn Fahd, *al-Durr al-Kamīn*, 1: 385–395, no. 280; also see: Shams al-Dīn Muḥammad al-Sakhāwī, *al-Ḍawʾ al-Lāmiʿ li-Ahl al-Qarn al-Tāsiʿ* (Cairo: reprint, Dār al-Kitāb al-Islāmī, n.d.), 9: 231, no. 570.

30 Muḥammad Ḥabīb al-Hīla, *al-Taʾrīkh wal-Muʾarrikhūn bi-Makka* (London and Mecca: Muʾassasat al-Furqān, 1994), 137–145, no. 60; 147–159, no. 62; 170–178, no. 72; 195–212, no. 81.

brother, Abū Bakr Aḥmad (d. 890), visited Egypt, where he studied with Ibn Ḥajar al-ʿAsqalānī, as well as all the major cities of Syria. He also made the journey to India twice, for "amusement," going to Calicut in 840, where his son ʿAbd al-Raḥmān was born, and to Cambay in 847.[31] Other members of the family travelled for business, as will be noted subsequently.

Another view of these linkages may be achieved from statements about authorizations, *ijāza*s, to relate texts issued to *ḥadīth* scholars, both male and female, from other localities. Here I will confine my discussion to *ijāza*s issued to women – this allows us to see a sector of the population that is all too often overlooked. A more thorough study of *ijāza*s would demonstrate that the geographical range of these connections is not much different than that of their male counterparts. An unusual example is that of Kamāliyya bint Najm al-Dīn Muḥammad (d. 866/1461–2), also known as Umm Kamāl, the sister of Taqī al-Dīn (the founder of the library), who was trained in *ḥadīth.*[32] Like many of her male kinfolk, she also studied al-Azraqī's (d. 244/858) history of Mecca. Umm Kamāl was married for some time to the Ḥanafī chief judge of Mecca, Abū Ḥāmid Muḥammad ibn Aḥmad ibn Ḍiyāʾ (d. 858/1454). She later married a prominent merchant, Khawājā Kamāl al-Dīn Ibrāhīm al-Shaybānī (d. 848/1444–5), and traveled with him to Cairo, Gaza, Hebron, Ramla, Jerusalem, and Damascus, which allowed her to broaden her scholarly contacts. The renowned scholar al-Sakhāwī reported that he obtained an *ijāza* from her not long before her death. Most women, we might assume, would not have enjoyed this degree of geographical mobility. In place of this, they had to resort to *ijāza*s requested from afar, often solicited through their fathers or brothers, who used their scholarly connections to boost their daughters' or sisters' intellectual reputations.

Noteworthy about Najm al-Dīn ʿUmar ibn Fahd's biographies is that he shows the geographical connectedness, a kind of virtual mobility, of his subjects by listing the issuers of their *ijāza*s arranged by city. He does not explain why he uses this format, and it seems to be an idiosyncratic approach – al-Sakhāwī, for example, who compiled biographies for many of the same women, does not organize his information in this way. One clear benefit of this format is that the reader can fully appreciate the distribution of the individual's intellectual contacts and one cannot help but conclude that this was Najm al-Dīn ʿUmar's intention. A good example is that of his sister, Umm Rīm (d. 891/1486–7).[33] Twenty-four scholars, all named, from Cairo issued Umm Rīm *ijāza*s; sixteen

31 Najm al-Dīn ʿUmar, *al-Durr al-Kamīn*, 1: 545–553, no. 470; for his son, see *al-Durr al-Kamīn*, 2: 795–798, no. 750.

32 Najm al-Dīn ʿUmar, *al-Durr al-Kamīn*, 3: 1538–41, no. 1628; al-Sakhāwī, *al-Ḍawʾ al-Lāmiʿ*, 12: 121–122, no. 741, but numbered 841.

33 Najm al-Dīn ʿUmar ibn Fahd, *al-Durr al-Kamīn*, 3: 1595–97, no. 1702; al-Sakhāwī, *al-Ḍawʾ al-Lāmiʿ*, 12: 146–147, no. 910.

from Damascus; at least nine from Aleppo; at least five from Baalbek; at least six from Jerusalem; one from Hebron; at least nine from Mecca; at least seven from Medina; and one from Shiraz. Umm Rīm's connections are rather typical in terms of extent, but not in terms of frequency, since most of her authorizations came from Cairo.

Another example is that of another of Najm al-Dīn ʿUmar's sisters, Fāṭima, better known by her *laqab*, Sitt Quraysh (d. 879/1474).[34] Through the requests of her father, the *ḥāfiẓ* Jamāl al-Dīn Muḥammad ibn Mūsā al-Marrākushī, and others, Sitt Quraysh received *ijāza*s from thirty-five identified authorizers in the following localities: in Egypt, Cairo (10 names) and Alexandria (3); in Syria, Damascus (11), Hama (2), Baalbek (2), Aleppo (1), Jerusalem (1), noting also, without names, Homs, Hebron, Tripoli, Gaza, and Ramla; in the Hijaz, Mecca (at least 5) and Medina; and in Yemen, Zabid, and Taʿizz.

When we take into consideration all the women Najm al-Dīn ʿUmar described in this way, we see that most *ijāza*s were issued from scholars in Mecca and Medina, followed by Syria and then Egypt; Yemen and Fars are far behind (see Table 1). One hesitates to use Najm al-Dīn's figures in any more than an impressionistic manner – as echoes of Mecca's intellectual networks. However, the predominance of the Hijazi cities (38.5% of the total) is an obvious reflection of accessibility: 122 authorizations were issued from scholars in Mecca and 47 were granted from scholars in Medina. Cairo, at 99, comes second to Mecca, but Syrian authorizers outnumbered those from Egypt, 157 (35.8%) to 103 (23.5%). In Syria, Damascus predominated as a source of *ijāza*s, with 63; Jerusalem produced about half of that number, with 32; and Aleppo, about half that again, with 17; with other cities trailing behind. Were we to include men, we could also add places as diverse as Damanhur in northern Egypt and Khurasan. All of these scholars depended on each other and, of course, prized those individuals who could minimize the links in the chains of transmission. Connections embodied in the *ijāza* entailed mutual obligation. One's status could not exist without these connections. In contrast to Mecca's nutritive connections, what we see here is that this dimension of Meccan society was intensively connected to the cities of Syria and Egypt, constituting a kind of scholarly archipelago, with a few connections to other intellectual centers, such as Yemen and more tenuously to localities across the distant Mashriq.

34 Najm al-Dīn ʿUmar ibn Fahd, *al-Durr al-Kamīn*, 2: 1463–1464, no. 1534.

Philanthropic and Institutional Connections

Mecca's institutional history provides yet another perspective on the city's connections abroad. The patronage of institutions and donations of voluntary alms (*ṣadaqāt*) from foreign rulers show substantial monetary flows that supported a variety of people from various social classes in Mecca.[35] The foundation of institutions like colleges (*madrasas*) and hospices (*ribāṭs*) represents an infusion of resources into Meccan society insofar as they would support the well-being of a range of individuals, from custodial staff to well-known scholars and judges, whose reputations circulated through the intellectual networks we have just looked at. With regard to these institutions, over the course of the Mamluk period, most of their patrons came from Cairo or from the Hijaz itself. While the Nile valley played an important role in sustaining pilgrims to Mecca, patronage and donations indicate that the Egyptian Sultanate was by no means exclusively dominant in the holy city's economic life.

The large numbers of transients who passed through the city, whether pilgrims attending to the *ḥajj* rituals or pious sojourners residing for longer periods of time, were able to find accommodation in Mecca's relatively numerous hospices. Of the 59 hospices Richard Mortel documented from the medieval period, the earliest dating to sometime before 395/1005, 21 were endowed during the Mamluk period (see Table 2). In the period prior to the middle of the seventh/thirteenth century, especially before and during the sixth/twelfth century, patrons from the more distant parts of the Mashriq – Anatolia, Iraq and Iran – dominated this form of philanthropy in Mecca, with a total of ten institutions founded, just slightly more than all those established by patrons from the Maghrib, Egypt, and Yemen, as well as those that remain unattributed. After the Mamluk takeover, patrons from Egypt and Syria dominate. Of the sixteen hospices founded in the fifteenth century, thirteen may be associated with patrons from identifiable regions. Noteworthy is the relatively large number (six) of Hijazi patrons in the ninth/fifteenth century, along with five patrons from Egypt and Syria, and one from India.

The foundation of colleges shows a similar trend, although with a more distinct geographical twist toward India in the fifteenth century. The documented number of colleges is considerably fewer than the number of hospices, since they were presumably more costly to endow: twenty-four *madrasas* were founded in Mecca during the medieval period, fifteen of which were established during the

35 On colleges and hospices, see Richard Mortel, "Madrasas in Mecca during the Mamluk Period," *Bulletin of the School of Oriental and African Studies*, 30 (1997): 236–52; idem, "Ribats in Mecca during the Medieval Period," *Bulletin of the School of Oriental and Asian Studies*, 31 (1998): 29–50. The following is based on Mortel's study, with some additions of data.

Mamluk period (see Table 3).[36] Initially, colleges founded by patrons from the Yemen or the Mashriq dominated the Meccan landscape. However, during the fourteenth century, in rough parallel to the situation with hospices, the balance started to shift with *madrasas* being founded by Egyptian and Syrian or local Hijazi patrons as the Yemeni donors became less financially robust. In the fifteenth century, the number of Mamluk institutions continued to increase – the most famous being the madrasa founded by Sultan Qaytbāy. In the thirteenth and early fourteenth centuries, the Rasulid madrasas played a major role in the scholarly life of Mecca.[37] However, by the fifteenth century, with the weakening of the Rasulid state and the diminished role of the Tahirids, Yemen no longer held much weight in the Hijaz. Furthermore, in the fifteenth century, it is especially noteworthy that we also see Indian colleges being established: the Bangaliyya, the Gulbargiyya, the Khaljīya, and the *madrasa* of the ruler of Cambay, representing a considerable infusion of cash into Mecca from the Indian subcontinent.[38]

In spite of the slight preponderance of the Cairo institutions, and the significant role that Cairo played in Meccan politics by virtue of its proximity, the Indian colleges, especially the Bengal institution, carried considerable status locally. The Bangaliyya Madrasa supported four professorships in the Sunni legal *madhhabs*, from the time of its foundation.[39] At the beginning of the eighth/fourteenth century, the only chief judge of Mecca was Shāfiʿī and it was only from the time of al-Nāṣir Muḥammad that the chief judge was appointed from Cairo; prior to this time the chief judge of Mecca was appointed by the Rasulid sultan. In good measure due to concern about Ilkhanid interests in Mecca, Sultan al-Nāṣir Muḥammad arrogated the right to make these appointments, excluding the Yemeni sultans from their prerogative in the Hijaz, and extending the Mamluk state structure more firmly into western Arabia.[40] The Cairo state apparatus was further extended when Sultan Faraj ibn Barqūq (r. 801–808/1399–1405) increased the number of chief judges four-fold, by making similar appointments in the remaining three *madhhabs*. With the establishment of the Bangaliyya Madrasa, these chief judges, who owed their authority to the Cairo Sultanate, became partly beholden as well to their Indian patron. Mecca's administrative relations to Cairo

36 Mortel, "Madrasas," 236–52; and for an additional example, the madrasa of the ruler of Malwa in India, see John Meloy, "'Aggression in the Best of Lands': Mecca in Egyptian-Indian Diplomacy in the Ninth/Fifteenth Century," *Mamluk Cairo: Crossroads for Embassies*, ed. F. Bauden and Malika Dekkiche (Leiden: Brill, forthcoming).

37 Mortel, "Madrasas," 239–242.

38 Meloy, "Aggression."

39 Founded in 813 AH/1410 by Ghiyāth al-Dīn Aʿẓam Shāh (r. 792–813 AH/1390–1410), the sultan of Bengal, it was also known as the Ghiyāthiyya.

40 John Meloy, "The Judges of Mecca and Mamluk Hegemony," paper delivered at the conference "Whither the Early Modern State? Fifteenth-Century State Formations across Eurasia," at Ghent University, September 2014, submitted for publication.

were now complicated by powerful ties to the Indian subcontinent. Cairo's judicial appointees, it would appear, fell into a relation of dependency on the fiscal power of the Bengali ruler.

In this cursory examination of Mecca's institutional connections to other places, we can also include the donation of voluntary alms. ʿIzz al-Dīn ʿAbd al-ʿAzīz ibn Fahd scrupulously recorded these donations as they arrived in Mecca.[41] Whether in the form of cash or in kind, alms arrived in Mecca throughout the year, although about one-third of the recorded gifts were received and distributed during the month of the pilgrimage, in Dhū al-Ḥijja. These donations came from a variety of lands, like India (most often Cambay and Calicut), Anatolia (al-Rūm), or West Africa (Takrūr); from particular rulers, like those of Gujarat, of Dabul, or of Yemen; or, less often, from wealthy individuals. The gifts were traditionally distributed by the Shāfiʿī chief judge of Mecca to officials of various ranks, those of higher ranks receiving a higher share and those of lower ranks receiving less. I have speculated elsewhere that ʿIzz al-Dīn's attention to this matter was probably due to the fact that he often received a sum, usually not very large, but something nevertheless. In the seventeen-year period from 885/1480–1, when his chronicle starts, to the beginning of 903/1497–8, when Sharif Muḥammad died, ʿIzz al-Dīn ibn Fahd recorded the delivery and distribution of alms on 51 occasions, 39 of which he reported the origin of the donation. India and Anatolia were clearly the principal sources of these funds: fifteen donations came from Calicut, Dabul, Gujarat, Cambay, and Bengal. Thirteen donations arrived from Anatolia (Bilād al-Rūm). Five donations came from Iraq, four from Yemen, and one each from West Africa (Bilād al-Takrūr) and Morocco. These donations ranged in value from a couple hundred dinars to as many as 60,000 for a period of two years from Anatolia and 60,000 dinars from India.[42] Given this admittedly rough measure of this form of foreign donations, India and Anatolia seem to have played a relatively outsized role in the financial support of officials and scholars in Mecca.

Donations from Egypt are more problematic: no doubt donations were sent from Egypt, but Ibn Fahd does not record them with the same care, possibly in part because subventions from Cairo were more a regular occurrence or came in the form of grain to be distributed in the form of the *dashīsha*, which fed Mecca's poor and indigent. It would seem, however, that the members of the religious hierarchy were the principal beneficiaries of the alms coming from further afield

41 On this topic generally, see John Meloy, *Imperial Power and Maritime Trade: Mecca and Cairo in the Later Middle Ages* (Chicago: Middle East Documentation Center, 2015), 191–197.

42 ʿIzz al-Dīn ibn Fahd, *Bulūgh al-Qirā*, 2:926; 3:2019; the latter sum dwindled through embezzlement to a mere 2,100 by the time it got to Mecca when it was heard that the donor, the "Habashi" ruler of Bengal, probably Nāṣir al-Dīn Maḥmūd Shāh b. Aḥmad Fīrūz Shāh (r. 895–896/1490–1491), had died.

in the Islamic world. Thus we can see here the way these donations connected Meccans, ranging from the sharif at the top, down through the ranks of the judicial and religious officials to its lowliest members. The livelihoods of all of these individuals, whether as employees in endowed institutions or as recipients of alms, were thus connected to foreign sources of wealth from the farthest parts of the Maghrib to the distant Mashriq, but especially to Anatolia and India.

Commercial Connections

Mecca's commercial entanglements were as extensive as its scholarly entanglements, a parallel that follows quite naturally from the religious education that many businessmen received.[43] After all, business travel could enable unique opportunities to meet new scholars, and scholarly travel might be funded by commercial transactions. More significantly, in the fifteenth century we see new categories of traders entering the commercial fray in the western Indian Ocean, displacing the apparently previously dominant Kārimī merchants. In 1400, in al-Maqrīzī's *Kitāb al-Sulūk*, for example, references to the Kārimī merchants dominate, appearing as a monolithic source of exotic goods from the east who conduct their business with considerable clout. In contrast, one hundred years later, in ʿIzz al-Dīn's Ibn Fahd's *Bulūgh al-Qirā*, we read of Indian ships coming from a variety of ports: Calicut, Dabul, Cambay; as well as others coming from Hormuz, Zaylaʿ, Sawakin, and Aden. For the period from 887/1482–3 to 908/1502–3 (see Table 4), the vast majority of ships (93.5%) recorded arrived from Indian ports: Calicut (124), Cambay (29), and Dabul (20), along with another 11 noted as "Indian." More minor ports of origin were Hormuz (7), two from Sawakin, and one each from Zaylaʿ, Barbara, Quseir, and Aden.[44] Of course these figures may be considered impressionistic, perhaps reflecting ʿIzz al-Dīn's bias to exotic locales, but his keen interest betrays the powerful attraction of south Asia to a resident in Mecca during the last decades of the ninth/fifteenth century. Certainly his reports sharpen our view of the western Indian Ocean, a contrast perhaps due to the vantage points of authors in Cairo versus those in Mecca. Clearly the latter had more reason to be more informed about Indian Ocean

43 Jean Aubin, "Merchants in the Red Sea and Persian Gulf at the Turn of the Fifteenth and Sixteenth Centuries," in *Asian Merchants and Businessmen in the Indian Ocean and the China Sea*, ed. D. Lombard and J. Aubin (New Delhi: Oxford University Press, 2000), 86; originally published as "Marchands de Mer Rouge et du Golfe Persique au tournant des 15e et 16e siècles," *Marchands et hommes d'affaires asiatiques dans l'Ocean Indien et al Mer de Chine*, ed. Denys Lombard and Jean Aubin (Paris, 1988), 83–90.

44 These data may be found in Meloy, *Imperial Power*, Appendix C, pp. 249–254, with sources noted there.

commerce – although it must be added that Ibn Fahd's father did not bother to distinguish between all these commercial emporia.

Who broke into this trading world? For long, our view of long-distance commerce has been dominated by the activities of business magnates, like the Kārimīs, who were powerful enough to attract the attention of chroniclers. Given their role in power politics, the Kārimī merchants are said to have been driven from business by the monopolies of Sultan Barsbāy – a view, in my opinion, that is too simplistic.[45] But it was not just the Mamluks, Rasulids, and powerful merchants – like the Kārimīs and later the Khawājās – who were interested in commerce in the Hijaz. The growing commercial wealth of Jedda and Mecca, and of course, the religious significance of Mecca, attracted the attention of foreign powers. A number of Indian rulers – the sultans of Gujarat and of Bengal – sent embassies to the sharifs in the first three decades of the ninth/fifteenth century.[46] Finally, perhaps the most well-known example of foreign engagement in the region was the series of commercial expeditions undertaken by the Chinese from 1406 to 1433.[47] Indeed, the scale of the Chinese missions may have impressed upon the newly rising Indian states the importance of undertaking their own diplomatic efforts.

Given that interest in Red Sea commerce came from a variety of far-flung quarters, it is perhaps not surprising that yet another group of merchants appeared on the scene. The Kārimīs may have been the major players in the eastern trade, but even their kind of commercial control may have left room for other, less prominent, businessmen who were willing to take risks. Thus, commercial activity in the western Indian Ocean may be seen as the entanglement of a variety of merchants from a variety of places through the act of *tajwīr*, interloping.[48] What does interloping mean in this context? We can attribute to the practice of *tajwīr* a number of characteristics. First, it was a commercial technique in which traders, operating evidently singly, or at least without the security of a trading

45 On this issue, see Meloy, "Imperial Strategy and Political Exigency: The Red Sea Spice Trade and the Mamluk Sultanate in the Fifteenth Century," *Journal of the American Oriental Society* 123:1 (2003): 1–19. For recent views on the Kārimī merchants, also see Francisco Javier Apellániz, *Pouvoir et finance en Méditerranée pré-moderne* (Barcelona: Consejo Superior de Investigaciones Cientificas, 2009); and Eric Vallet, *L'Arabie marchande: état et commerce sous les sultans Rasulides du Yémen* (Paris: Publications de Sorbonne, 2010).

46 Al-Fāsī, *al-ʿIqd al-Thamīn*, 4: 104, 105, 108; Ibn Fahd, *Itḥāf al-Warā*.

47 J. V. Mills, "Notes on Early Chinese Voyages," *Journal of the Royal Asiatic Society* (1951): 3–25.

48 I first proposed these ideas in a paper entitled "Fifteenth Century 'Interlopers' in the Red Sea," presented at the 40th Annual Meeting of the Middle East Studies Association, Boston, November, 2006, and mentioned them briefly in my *Imperial Power*, 71, 76–78, 180, 191. My paper was inspired by an article by R. B. Serjeant, "Fifteenth Century 'Interlopers' on the Coast of Rasulid Yemen," *Itineraires d'Orient: Hommages a Claude Cahen*, "Res Orientales," 6 (Bures-sur-Yvette: Groupe pour l'étude de la civilisation du Moyen-orient, 1994), 83–91.

network as the Kārimīs, for example, enjoyed, intrepidly sought out new markets for their wares – making connections in new places. The Indian Nākhudhā Ibrāhīm is a good example in the 820s/1420s. Ibrāhīm was from Calicut, on the Malabar coast of southwest India. Over a period of successive trading seasons, he sailed to different destinations and found inhospitable markets: in Jedda, then in Sawakin and Dahlak on the Sudan coast, then Yanbuʿ, and finally back to Jedda, where the situation had improved. He was treated so favorably that he returned to Jedda with a larger number of vessels, bearing goods.[49] It would seem that the interlopers were willing to expend considerable effort, from one trading season to the next, to find suitable ports governed by amenable political authorities. A second characteristic is that interloping was an "international" activity: traders from a variety of places (by the way, none of whom are referred to as Kārimīs) engaged in interloping. In fact, incidents of *tajwīr* are documented from before this time, when Yemeni merchants by-passed Jedda for Yanbuʿ, as occurred in 821/1418. Later on, in 833/1430, we learn of an interloper from Sumatra.[50] These examples illustrate the seamless movement of navigators from the Indian Ocean into the Red Sea that conforms to the depiction of Ibn Mājid, who in his navigational handbook depicted the southern Red Sea and the Indian Ocean as a discrete maritime unit.[51] Furthermore, ground-breaking documentary testimony from the Venetian State Archives of these connections binding the Mediterranean, the Red Sea, and the farthest reaches of the Indian Ocean, and even to the South China Sea, has recently been published by Francisco Apellániz.[52] Finally, the term "interloper" does not necessarily imply that the merchant evaded authorities or taxation; rather, it means that the traders simply did not have prior license to trade in a particular port – that is, they could not assume the protection of the port's political authorities.[53] The translation of *mujawwir* as "interloper," in the Anglo-Indian sense of the term, of trading without permission, is thus appropriate.[54] In a particular place, the interlopers and the political authorities

49 Al-Maqrīzī, *Kitāb al-Sulūk*, 4: 680–681; cf. Serjeant, "Interlopers," 84. Also reported in Najm al-Dīn ibn Fahd, *Itḥāf al-Warā*, 3: 588.

50 Al-Fāsī, *al-ʿIqd al-Thamīn*, 4: 128; on Sumatra, see *A Chronicle of the Rasulid Dynasty of Yemen from the Unique MS Paris No. Arabe 4609*, ed. Hikoichi Yajima, Monograph Series No. 7 (Tokyo: Study of Languages and Cultures of Asia and Africa, 1976), 128; cf. Serjeant, "Interlopers," 87.

51 Aḥmad ibn Mājid, *Arab Navigation in the Indian Ocean before the Coming of the Portuguese*, ed. G. R. Tibbets (London: Royal Asiatic Society, 1971).

52 The document offers a "global" view of the Indian Ocean trading world; Francisco Apellániz, "News on the Bulaq: A Mamluk-Venetian Memorandum on Asian Trade, AD, 1503" (European University Institute, Working Paper HEC 2016/01).

53 This is observed also by Apellániz, "News from the Bulaq," 11.

54 Henry Yule and A. C. Burnell, *Hobson-Jobson: A Glossary of Colloquial Anglo-Indian Words and Phrases, and of Kindred Terms, Etymological, Historical, Geographical, and Discursive* (London: Routledge, 1968), 438.

engage in a process of negotiation – the reports about Nākhudhā Ibrāhīm note that the authorities were at times severe, and at other times lenient – in which each side tried to extract benefit from commerce, whether from profit or from taxation. But, of course, the interlopers were not the only ones engaged in this trade and their approach to commerce stands in contrast to that of more powerful merchants, who used political connections and networks to boost their commercial power. While the Kārimī merchants do seem to gradually disappear from the historical record over the course of the fifteenth century, their niche may simply have been filled by the merchants who went by the epithet Khawājā. Francisco Apellániz has also demonstrated that the *khawājākiyya*, who retained their status as private merchants, were loosely connected to the Mamluk state and received recognition from it. In other words, having a kind of official status, they were exempted from the need to negotiate with state authorities upon arrival at a particular destination, unlike the interlopers, the *mujawwirūn*.[55] In effect, these two types of merchants filled two different niches in the commercial ecosystem, as it were, the interlopers apparently willing to operate with the risk that came without a network of contacts implied by the license to trade. The Khawājā merchants of Mecca, as documented by Richard Mortel, came from across the lands of the Mashriq to take advantage of the business opportunities it could offer. Nearly half hailed from Iran and Syria (24 percent and 23 percent, respectively). Eighteen percent were from Egypt. But these merchants came from other parts of the region as well: Khawājās from Iraq and Yemen numbered 7.5 percent each, and five percent of the Khawājā merchants came from Anatolia.[56]

In sum, taking Mecca as a long-distance commercial epicenter of the western Indian Ocean, our sources show that commerce was diversified in two ways: first, merchants of recognized status, like the Kārimīs and the Khawājās (and, perhaps, the Kazarūnīs further to the east), who plied known routes, enjoyed secure and extensive commercial networks, and dealt with familiar authorities. The second group consisted of merchants of an apparently lesser, informal, status who adopted riskier, more free-wheeling, commercial strategies. Both groups came from diverse backgrounds: the formally established groups, however, who obviously had extensive commercial dealings with India, do not appear to actually have been from there. In contrast, the interlopers, one surmises, hailed from ports from the full breadth of the Indian Ocean. As a commercial destination, Mecca was hardly dependent on the established commercial groups. To be sure, our commercial data are sketchy, but it would appear that the diminution of Kārimī activity, and the interventions of Sultan Barsbāy, did not necessarily

55 On this, see Apellániz, *Pouvoir et finance en Méditerranée pré-moderne.*

56 Richard Mortel, "The Mercantile Community in Mecca during the Late Mamluk Period," *Journal of the Royal Asiatic Society*, 3rd ser., 4:1 (1994): 15–35.

entail a downturn in commerce in the western Indian Ocean. If anything, commercial activity with Mecca and its port of Jedda became more competitive and interlinked with businessmen and traders from across the Indian Ocean. Nākhudhās like Ibrāhīm ventured westward to Jedda, while members of the Banū Fahd family, who preferred commerce to scholarship, like Yaḥyā ibn ʿAbd al-Raḥmān (d. 843/1439–40) and perhaps even Abū Bakr Aḥmad, mentioned earlier, ventured eastward. In 830/1426–7, Yaḥyā ibn ʿAbd al-Raḥmān travelled to Cambay for business, staying there for some time before moving on to Gulbarga, where he died.[57] Mecca's commercial range extended as far as its philanthropic range, opening up long-distance trade to a broader range of commercial actors, for whom there seems to have been a powerful gravitational pull to the east.

Diplomatic Connections

What might have been the consequences of this shift to the east? An exchange of diplomatic correspondence between Maḥmūd Shāh Khaljī (r. 839–873/1436–1469), the Sultan of Malwa, in central India, who was the founder of one of Mecca's Indian colleges mentioned earlier, and the Cairo Sultanate in the late 1460s speaks to the increasing influence of India in Mecca and the diplomatic pressure that could be brought to bear on the rulers of Cairo through their dependency on Mecca. The first of these two letters was sent to the Mamluk Sultan al-Ẓāhir Khushqadam (r. 865–872/1461–1467), shortly before his death. A response, dated nearly two years later, was sent from Sultan al-Ashraf Qaytbāy (r. 872–901/1468–1496), Khushqadam's main successor, arriving in Malwa after Maḥmūd Shāh died, and was received by his son and successor, Ghiyāth al-Dīn Shāh (r. 873–906/1469–1501).[58] The episode addressed in the correspondence started in 870/1466, when Maḥmūd Shāh sent his emissary, Malik Sunbul al-Sulṭānī, with funds to establish a college in Mecca, which was duly built on purchased land near a gate to the Ḥaram Mosque. Malik Sunbul oversaw the construction and then departed, learning later that the senior Mamluk official in Jedda, Jānibak al-Ẓāhirī, had expelled its residents "by force," destroyed the building, and erected his own.[59] When Maḥmūd Shāh had heard about this "aggression in the best of lands" (*al-ʿudwān fī khayr al-buldān*), he sent a second mission of emissaries with 50,000 Ashrafī dinars worth of gifts for the Mamluk sultan, the caliph in Cairo, the sharif of Mecca, and alms (*ṣadaqāt*) for the judges

57 Najm al-Dīn ʿUmar, *al-Durr al-Kamīn*, 2: 1241–1244, no. 1286; al-Sakhāwī, *al-Ḍawʾ al-Lāmiʿ* 10: 233.

58 For a more detailed study of this episode, see Meloy, "Aggression."

59 BnF 4440, fol. 181a; Aḥmad Darrag, "Risālatān bayna Sulṭān Malwa wal-Ashraf Qaytbāy," *Majallat Maʿhad al-Makhṭūṭāt al-ʿArabiyya*, 4 (1958): 97–123, citing 112–113.

and officials.[60] The delegation met a worse fate than their predecessor; they were beaten and robbed of the sultan's gifts. In his letter to the Mamluk sultan in Cairo, Maḥmūd Shāh complained of the treatment that his representatives had received and expressed his derision by invoking a passage from the Quran (Sūrat Āl ʿImrān, 97):

> So this is what happened in the Sanctuary of God Almighty in the days of the Just King, and God Almighty says, "He who enters it is safe." So the security they had hoped for there is replaced with intimidation?[61]

In brief, the Indian ruler brought to bear on the Mamluk ruler the moral force of their common faith, invoking the Prophet Muḥammad,[62] stating that such actions could possibly lead to disastrous political consequences, echoing Prophetic injunction to urge the Mamluk ruler to his duty.[63] Maḥmūd Shāh's letter was ultimately effective since it elicited a very favorable response from Sultan Qaytbāy. Given the principled language of Maḥmūd Shāh, it is no surprise that at the outset the Cairo sultan asserted the basis of his rule, "to command right and to forbid wrong, to eliminate injustices and to rescue (*akhadha*) the oppressed from the oppressor."[64] More specifically, Qaytbāy recognized the illegal nature of Jānibak's seizure of the property and he ordered that the Indians could build there.[65] The sultan also forbade collection of illegal taxes, posted the decree on the gate of the Jedda customs house and in the Ḥaram mosque, appointed a new deputy to Jedda, and assured the safety of the Indian ruler's emissaries.[66] Cordial communications followed: three years after the second letter was sent, in 876 (1472–1473), Najm al-Dīn ibn Fahd reported that Qaytbāy sent a message to his officials in Jedda asking them to forward to India decrees and a robe of honor to Ibn al-Khaljī, the ruler of Malwa.[67] Thus the Mamluk protector of the Caliphate, who claimed to be the Servitor of the Two Holy Sanctuaries, was held responsible for crimes perpetrated in Mecca against a distant Indian ruler who had previously depended on Cairo for political recognition.

60 BnF Ar. 4440, 181a-b, 183b: Darrag, "Risālatān," 113, 115.

61 BnF Ar. 4440, fol. 181b; Darrag, "Risālatān," 113–114: "Would the officials have leave to treat them as they please, no one to hold them accountable for what they perpetrate? God protect you and us from their evil deeds and benefit you and us with their just actions."

62 BnF Ar. 4440, fol. 181b; Darrag, "Risālatān," 114.

63 BnF Ar. 4440, fol. 182a-b; Darrag, "Risālatān," 114–115.

64 BnF Ar. 4440, fol. 192a; Darrag, "Risālatān," 119.

65 BnF Ar. 4440, fol. 193a-b; Darrag, "Risālatān," 121.

66 BnF Ar. 4440, fol. 192a, 193a; Darrag, "Risālatān," 120, 121; Najm al-Dīn Ibn Fahd, *Itḥāf al-Warā*, 4: 483; also see Meloy, *Imperial Power*, 173.

67 Najm al-Dīn ʿUmar ibn Fahd, *Itḥāf al-Warā*, 4: 537.

Concluding Remarks

A variety of mechanisms, linkages, and movements of people and products entangled Mecca, often through its port of Jedda, with disparate places across the Islamic world. Mecca's connections to Cairo and the Nile valley were important, but not exclusive. My approach here, grappling as it does with often sketchy data, highlights the manifold dimensions of social life in Mecca, a site of intersecting entanglements, whether near or far, that could oscillate between dependence and dependency. As a pilgrimage city located in a barren landscape, its nutritive dependency on other localities was heightened. Conversely, its sacredness imbued the city with unassailable attractive power, fueling multiple dependencies, manifested yearly in the arrival of pilgrims and donations. As a locus of commerce and scholarship, Mecca depended on other localities as they depended on it.

Three additional remarks can be offered as well: about the wider historical context of the forces at play here, concerning the vulnerability of entanglement, and on cosmopolitanism. First, this approach to understanding Mecca, as a very important neighbor of Cairo, has led us to consider a variety of connections to India and thus it may be appropriate to start these tentative concluding remarks from there. Jean Aubin wrote that the political, social, and economic changes that affected the northern Indian subcontinent – what he called "the second expansion of Islam" – resulted in a positive impact on the establishment of new ports and new interest groups.[68] In this context, he referred to the emergence of prominent classes of merchants, noting in particular the Khawājā and Kazarūnī businessmen. It seems to me that we can posit the *mujawwirūn* as part of this phenomenon. Descriptions from the fifteenth and sixteenth centuries of port cities of the Asian maritime rim portray ports that were not only commercially vibrant, but also extremely cosmopolitan. Calicut, Malacca, and Quanzhou were "merchant cit[ies] made up of ethnically and culturally diverse communities, all or nearly all involved in large-scale international trade."[69] During the late medieval period, the maritime trading community on the Malabar coast was nearly always Muslim, but it seems likely that there may have been a shift towards

68 Aubin, "Movements," 83–90.

69 Denys Lombard, "Introduction" to *Asian Merchants and Businessmen in the Indian Ocean and the China Sea*, ed. D. Lombard and J. Aubin (New Delhi: Oxford University Press, 2000), 5, and the following articles in the same volume: Chen Dasheng and Denys Lombard, "Foreign Merchants in Maritime Trade in Quanzhou ("Zaitun"): Thirteenth and Fourteenth Centuries," 19–23; Luis Felipe F. R. Thomaz, "Melaka and its Merchant Communities at the Turn of the Sixteenth Century," 25–39; Geneviève Bouchon, "A Microcosm: Calicut in the Sixteenth Century," 40–49. See also Richard Eaton, "Multiple Lenses: Differing Perspectives of Fifteenth-century Calicut," *Essays on Islam and Indian History* (New Delhi: Oxford University Press, 2000), 76–93.

including communities that, though also Muslim, were not exclusively from Arabic and Persian-speaking areas. Furthermore, Burton Stein has suggested that the foundation of the Vijayanagara Empire in the middle of the fourteenth century triggered a transformation in the Muslim trading communities of western India.[70] Itinerant merchants who had worked in southern India, he proposes, were excluded from the patronage networks established by the Nayakas, the landed military elite, and consequently entered maritime trade. Thus, if there were socio-economic transformations on the Malabar coast among traders who plied the western Indian Ocean, one would expect to see similar transformations in the Arabian ports of call – like Mecca and Jedda. Our view of commerce in the Islamic later Middle Ages has been inordinately populated by the merchant elite, the Kārimīs and the Khawājās; perhaps the interloping *mujawwirūn* offer us a glimpse of a less influential, but no less aggressive, class of traders.

Second, Aubin's "second expansion of Islam," it would seem, engendered the entanglement of Cairo in Mecca, producing multiple interconnections there, a place already intimately connected to other parts of the Islamic world, creating something similar to Hodder's notion of entanglement as a dialectic of dependence and dependency, the precarious dynamic that can shift from empowerment to vulnerability. Cairo's dependence on Mecca, whether as a source of political and religious legitimacy or as a source of wealth, was nonetheless a source of empowerment. However, with Mecca's interconnections to other places, through status, scholarship, philanthropy, commerce, or even as a moral space, Cairo became vulnerable and lost its autonomy, as evident in the epistolary rebuke of the sultan of Malwa.

Finally, these multiple entanglements of places and people energized the social and economic life of Mecca and infused it with a cosmopolitan character that mirrored those other ports of call elsewhere in the Indian Ocean. Quite a wide variety of people, men, women, merchants, both powerful and not so powerful, prominent shaykhs and humble custodial staff, *fuqahā*ʾ and *fuqarā*ʾ, depended on distant sources of revenue. To what extent their dependence shifted to dependency might vary from person to person and year to year, and within a city most notable for its holiness. But beyond that sacred status, and like many other places, the city can also be defined by its connections to other localities. My suggestion here is that Mecca, as a cosmopolitan locale, appears also as a site of multivalent dependence and dependency.

70 Burton Stein, "South India: Some General Considerations of the Region and its Early History," 14–42, esp. 18–19, and see also Simon Digby, "The Maritime Trade of India," 125–160, both in *Cambridge Economic History of India, c. 1200 to c. 1750*, vol. 1, ed. T. Raychaudhuri and I. Habib (Cambridge: Cambridge University Press, 1982).

Table 1: *Ijāzas*, identified by authorizer, issued to women *ḥadīth* scholars in Mecca, by region and city, as reported by Najm al-Dīn ʿUmar ibn Fahd in his *al-Durr al-Kamīn* (sample of 438 reports).

Region	Number of ijāzas	%age	City	Number of ijāzas
Hijaz	169	38.5		
			Mecca	122
			Medina	47
Syria	157	35.8		
			Damascus	63
			Jerusalem	32
			Aleppo	17
			Hebron	11
			Baalbakk	7
			Hamah	3
			Hums	2
			Ramla	2
			Tripoli	1
			Gaza	1
Egypt	103	23.5		
			Cairo	99
			Alexandria	4
Yemen	8	1.8		
			Zabid	3
			Taʿizz	3
			Yemen	2
Fars	1	0.2		
			Shiraz	1

Table 2: *Ribāṭs* founded in Mecca by origin of patron and date of foundation (59 total); based on the compilation of Richard Mortel, "Ribats in Mecca during the Medieval Period," BSOAS, 31 (1998): 29–50.

Origin of patron	Before 395/1005 through $6^{th}/12^{th}$ c.	Pre-658/1260	Post-658/1260	$8^{th}/14^{th}$ c.	$9^{th}/15^{th}$ c.	Unknown date
Unknown	3	6	0	1	2	4
Maghrib	1	1	0	0	0	0
Egypt/ Syria	3	2	0	2	5	0
Hijaz	1	1	0	1	6	0
Yemen	1	0	0	2	1	0

(Continued)

Origin of patron	Before 395/1005 through 6th/12th c.	Pre-658/ 1260	Post-658/1260	8th/14th c.	9th/15th c.	Unknown date
Iran/Iraq/ Rum	10	2	0	2	0	0
India/Af-ghan	0	1	0	0	1	0

Table 3: *Madrasas* founded in Mecca by origin of patron and date of foundation (24 total); supplementing the compilation of Richard Mortel, "Madrasas in Mecca during the Mamluk Period," *BSOAS*, 30 (1997): 236–52.

Origin of patron	6th/12th c.	Pre-1260	Post-1260	8th/14th c.	9th/15th c.
Unknown	0	2	0	0	0
Egypt/Syria	1	0	0	1	4
Hijaz	0	0	0	2	1
Yemen	1	2	1	2	0
Iran/Iraq	1	2	0	0	0
India	0	0	0	0	4

Table 4: Shipping to Mecca by port of origin, from 887/1482–3 to 908/1502–3 (197 total), as recorded by ʿIzz al-Dīn ʿAbd al-ʿAzīz ibn Fahd in his *Bulūgh al-Qirā.*

Region of origin	Number of ships	%age	Port of origin	Number of ships
India	184	93.5		
			Calicut	124
			Dabul	20
			Cambay	29
			"Indian"	11
Iran	7	3.5		
			Hormuz	7
Sudan/East Africa	4	2.0		
			Sawakin	2
			Zaylaʿ	1
			Barbara	1
Yemen	1	0.5		
			Aden	1
Egypt	1	0.5		
			Quseir	1

Bibliography

Amin, Ash. "Regions Unbound: Towards a New Politics of Place," *Geografiska Annaler* 86B (2004): 33–44.

Amin, Ash. "Re-Thinking the Urban Social." *City* 11/1 (2007): 100–114.

Apellániz, Francisco Javier. "News on the Bulaq: A Mamluk-Venetian Memorandum on Asian Trade, AD, 1503." European University Institute, Working Paper HEC 2016/01. Florence: EUI, 2016.

Apellániz, Francisco Javier. *Pouvoir et finance en Méditerranée pré-moderne.* Barcelona: Consejo Superior de Investigaciones Cientificas, 2009.

Aubin, Jean. "Merchants in the Red Sea and Persian Gulf at the Turn of the Fifteenth and Sixteenth Centuries." In *Asian Merchants and Businessmen in the Indian Ocean and the China Sea*, ed. D. Lombard and J. Aubin, 79–86. New Delhi: Oxford University Press, 2000.

Behrens-Abouseif, Doris. "Qaytbay's Foundation in Medina, the Madrasah, the Ribat, and the Dashishah." *Mamlūk Studies Review* 2 (1998): 61–71.

Bouchon, Geneviève. "A Microcosm: Calicut in the Sixteenth Century." In *Asian Merchants and Businessmen in the Indian Ocean and the China Sea*, ed. D. Lombard and J. Aubin, 40–49. New Delhi: Oxford University Press, 2000.

Stephan Conermann. "Networks and Nodes in Mamluk Times: some introductory remarks." In *Everything is on the Move: The Mamluk Empire as a Node in (Trans-) Regional Networks*, ed. Stephan Conermann, 9–26, Bonn: Bonn UP, 2014.

Darrag, Ahmad. "Risālatān bayna Sulṭān Malwa wa-al-Ashraf Qaytbāy." *Majallat Maʿhad al-Makhṭūṭāt al-ʿArabiyya* 4 (1958): 97–123.

Dasheng, Chen, and Denys Lombard. "Foreign Merchants in Maritime Trade in Quanzhou ('Zaitun'): Thirteenth and Fourteenth Centuries." In *Asian Merchants and Businessmen in the Indian Ocean and the China Sea*, ed. D. Lombard and J. Aubin, 19–23. New Delhi: Oxford University Press, 2000.

Digby, Simon. "The Maritime Trade of India" In *Cambridge Economic History of India, c. 1200 to c. 1750*, vol. 1, ed. T. Raychaudhuri and I. Habib, 125–160. Cambridge: Cambridge University Press, 1982.

Eaton, Richard. "Multiple Lenses: Differing Perspectives of Fifteenth-Century Calicut." In *Essays on Islam and Indian History*, 76–93. New Delhi: Oxford University Press, 2000.

al-Fāsī, Taqī al-Dīn Muḥammad. *Al-ʿIqd al-Thamīn fi Taʾrīkh al-Balad al-Amīn*, ed. M. H. Fiqī, et al. 8 vols. Cairo: Maṭbaʿat al-Sunna al-Muḥammadiyya, 1959–69.

Garcin, Jean-Claude. *Un centre musulman de la haute-Égypte medieval: Qus.* Cairo: IFAO, 1976.

Garcin, Jean-Claude. "The Mamluk Military System and the Blocking of Medieval Moslem Society." In *Europe and the Rise of Capitalism*, ed. Jean Baechler, et al., 113–130. Oxford: Basil Blackwell, 1988.

Guo, Li. Commerce, *Culture, and Community in a Red Sea Port in the Thirteenth Century.* Leiden: Brill, 2004.

al-Hīla, Muḥammad Ḥabīb. *Al-Taʾrīkh wa-al-Muʾarrikhūn bi-Makka.* London and Mecca: Muʾassasat al-Furqān, 1994.

Hodder, Ian. *Entangled: An Archaeology of the Relationships of Humans and Things.* Malden, Massachusetts: Wiley-Blackwell, 2012.

Hodder, Ian. "The Entanglements of Humans and Things: A Long-Term View." *New Literary History* 45:1 (2014): 19–36.

Ibn Fahd, ʿIzz al-Dīn ʿAbd al-ʿAzīz. *Bulūgh al-Qirā fī Dhayl Itḥāf al-Warā bi-Akhbār Umm al-Qurā*, ed. S. Ibrāhīm. 4 vols. Cairo: Dār al-Qāhira, 2005.

Ibn Fahd, Jār Allāh Muḥammad. *Ḥusn al-Qirāfī Awdiyat Umm al-Qurā*, ed. ʿAlī ʿUmar. Cairo: Maktabat al-Thaqāfa al-Dīniyya, 2001.

Ibn Fahd, Najm al-Din ʿUmar. *Al-Durr al-Kamīn bi-Dhayl al-ʿIqd al-Thamīn fī Taʾrīkh al-Balad al-Amīn*, ed. A Duhaysh. 3 vols. Mecca: Maktabat al-Asadī, 2004.

Ibn Fahd, Najm al-Din ʿUmar. *Itḥāf al-Warā bi-Akhbār Umm al-Qurā*, ed. F. M. Shaltūt. 5 vols. Mecca: Jāmiʿat Umm al-Qurā, 1983–90.

Ibn Mājid, Aḥmad. *Arab Navigation in the Indian Ocean before the Coming of the Portuguese*, ed. G. R. Tibbets. London: Royal Asiatic Society, 1971.

Lombard, Denys, and Jean Aubin, eds., *Asian Merchants and Businessmen in the Indian Ocean and the China Sea.* New Delhi: Oxford University Press, 2000; originally published as *Marchands et hommes d'affaires asiatiques dans l'Ocean Indien et al Mer de Chine.* Paris: Editions de l'Ecole des hautes étudies en sciences sociales, 1988.

Lombard, Denys. Introduction to *Asian Merchants and Businessmen in the Indian Ocean and the China Sea*, ed. D. Lombard and J. Aubin, 1–9. New Delhi: Oxford University Press, 2000.

al-Maqrīzī, Taqī al-DīnAḥmad. *Kitāb al-Sulūk li-Maʿrifat Duwal al-Mulūk*, ed. S. A. ʿĀshūr. 4 vols. Cairo: Lajnat al-Taʾlīf wa-al-Tarjama wa-al-Nashr, 1956–73.

Meloy, John L. "'Aggression in the Best of Lands': Mecca in Egyptian-Indian Diplomacy in the Ninth/Fifteenth Century." In *Mamluk Cairo: Crossroads for Embassies*, ed. F. Bauden and Malika Dekkiche. Leiden: Brill, forthcoming.

Meloy, John L. "Fifteenth Century 'Interlopers' in the Red Sea." Paper presented at the 40th Annual Meeting of the Middle East Studies Association, Boston, November, 2006.

Meloy, John L. *Imperial Power and Maritime Trade: Mecca and Cairo in the Later Middle Ages.* Revised paperback edition. Chicago: Middle East Documentation Center, 2015.

Meloy, John L. "Imperial Strategy and Political Exigency: The Red Sea Spice Trade and the Mamluk Sultanate in the Fifteenth Century." *Journal of the American Oriental Society* 123:1 (2003): 1–19.

Meloy, John L. "The Judges of Mecca and Mamluk Hegemony." Paper presented at the conference "Whither the Early Modern State? Fifteenth-Century State Formations across Eurasia," at Ghent University, September 2014. Submitted for publication.

Mills, J.V. "Notes on Early Chinese Voyages." *Journal of the Royal Asiatic Society* (1951): 3–25.

Mortel, Richard. "Madrasas in Mecca during the Mamluk Period." *Bulletin of the School of Oriental and African Studies* 30 (1997): 236–52.

Mortel, Richard. "Maṣādir al-Tamwīn al-Ghadhīʾī li-Imārat Makka (358 H./969 M.–923 H./1517 M.)." *Majallat Kulliyat al-Ādāb, Jāmiʿat al-Malik Saʿūd* 12:1 (1985): 193–219.

Mortel, Richard. "The Mercantile Community in Mecca during the Late Mamluk Period." *Journal of the Royal Asiatic Society* (3rd ser.) 4:1 (1994): 15–35.

Mortel, Richard. "Ribats in Mecca during the Medieval Period." *Bulletin of the School of Oriental and African Studies* 31 (1998): 29–50.

Nujaym, Ruqayya Ḥusayn Saʿd. *Al-Biʾa al-Ṭabīʿiyya li-Makka al-Mukarrama: Dirāsa fī al-Jughrāfiyya al-Ṭabīʿiyya li-Minṭaqat al-Ḥaram al-Makkī al-Sharīf.* Mecca: Muʾassasat al-Furqān, 2000.

Pollock, Susan Pollock, et al. "Entangled Discussions: Talking with Ian Hodder about his book *Entangled.*" *Forum Kritische Archäologie* 3 (2014): 151–161.

al-Qalqashandī, Shihāb al-Dīn Aḥmad. *Ṣubḥ al-Aʿshā fī Ṣināʿat al-Inshāʾ*. 14 vols. Cairo: Dār al-Kutub al-Khidiwiyya, 1913–1920; reprinted 1963.

al-Sakhāwī, Shams al-Dīn Muḥammad. *al-Ḍawʾ al-Lāmiʿ li-Ahl al-Qarn al-Tāsiʿ*. Bulaq/Cairo reprint: Dar al-Kitāb al-Islāmī, n.d.

Serjeant, Robert B. "Fifteenth Century 'Interlopers' on the Coast of Rasulid Yemen." *Itineraires d'Orient: Hommages a Claude Cahen*, ed. R. Curiel and R. Gyselen, 83–91. Res Orientales, 6. Bures-sur-Yvette: Groupe pour l'étude de la civilisation du Moyen-orient, 1994.

Sheppard, Eric. "Thinking Geographically: Globalizing Capitalism and Beyond." *Annals of the Association of American Geographers* 105:6 (2015): 1113–34.

Stein, Burton. "South India: Some General Considerations of the Region and its Early History." In *Cambridge Economic History of India, c. 1200 to c. 1750*, vol. 1, ed. T. Raychaudhuri and I. Habib. Cambridge: Cambridge University Press, 1982.

Thomaz, Luis Felipe F.R. "Melaka and its Merchant Communities at the Turn of the Sixteenth Century." *Asian Merchants and Businessmen in the Indian Ocean and the China Sea*, ed. D. Lombard and J. Aubin, 25–39. New Delhi: Oxford University Press, 2000.

Vallet, Eric. *L'Arabie marchande: état et commerce sous les sultans Rasulides du Yémen.* Paris: Publications de Sorbonne, 2010.

Varthema, Ludovico di. *The Travels*, trans. J. W. Jones and ed. G. P. Badger. The Hakluyt Society, no. 32 (first series), 1863; republished: New York: Burt Franklin, n.d.

Yajima, Hikoichi, ed. *A Chronicle of the Rasulid Dynasty of Yemen from the Unique MS Paris No. Arabe 4609*, Monograph Series No. 7. Tokyo: Study of Languages and Cultures of Asia and Africa, 1976.

Yule, Henry and A.C. Burnell. *Hobson-Jobson: A Glossary of Colloquial Anglo-Indian Words and Phrases, and of Kindred Terms, Etymological, Historical, Geographical, and Discursive.* London: Routledge, 1968.

Anne Regourd (CNRS, UMR 7192, Paris)
with the collaboration of Fiona Handley (University of Brighton)

Late Ayyubid and Mamluk Quṣayr al-Qadīm: What the Primary Sources Tell Us

1. Introduction

The economic activity of the Red Sea zone will be considered from the perspective of the anchorage of Quṣayr al-Qadīm on the Egyptian side of the Sea. This paper looks at Quṣayr from the end of the Ayyubid era to the start of the Mamluk period, which, according to the documents discovered at the site, was a time of busy economic activity.

The Bonn Conference of 2015 showed us how Mamluk power was exercised and structured, from the centre via a multitude of links, some of them of allegiance, without regard for frontiers, recognized by local rulers delivering in turn their own networks of agreements and allegiances in their areas of influence, reaching east to west from China to Spain, and south to Ethiopia. It invites us to consider the flow of goods over long distances, and to talk about "big commerce."[1] The trade links between Quṣayr al-Qadīm and Cairo, which involve the Mediterranean to the north and India to the east, will be examined here as an example of these links and the flow of goods.

A portion of the goods arriving at Quṣayr were not, however, intended to be dispatched very far, a fact consistent with the "solar" model of the Mamluk Empire. This article will explore other destinations of the goods arriving at Quṣayr, highlighting local networks and even some links so far undocumented. The model developed by Romain Bertrand, one of "histoire à parts égales"[2] thus makes sense here. It proposes a disengagement from the historical view of the past as a reconstruction from the viewpoint of the West, or any hegemonic centre. In our case, we could say that if history was seen exclusively from the viewpoint of the "metropolis" (Cairo) we would have to deal with a story which was, in both senses of the word, partial, and which ignored the importance of the peripheral trades and markets beyond the sight of the center. In order to bring to light this

1 See the paper by Jo van Stenbergen in this volume.
2 Romain Bertrand, *L'histoire à parts égales* (Paris: Le Seuil, 2011).

aspect of the activity of Quṣayr, we will consider textiles and clothing. This point of departure allows us to offer a synthetic study based on written documents, artifacts, and new evidence.

There are two sources that can be used in investigating this, existing narrative sources, and the finds from two campaigns of archaeological excavation, conducted first by the University of Chicago, then by the University of Southampton, which uncovered buildings, artifacts and written documents from both the Greco-Roman and Islamic periods. The Chicago documents written in Arabic were published separately by Li Guo (84 pieces) and Andreas Kaplony (25 business letters and process slips). These were found in the so-called Shaykh's House.[3] The University of Southampton's excavations uncovered a major quantity of documents, ca. 1000 pieces, mostly, but not all, found in what were rubbish dumps.[4] It has been assumed that all documents found at Quṣayr were related to Quṣayr in one way or another. The Chicago finds illustrate the trade activity of a company, that of Abū Mufarrij and sons.[5]

2. Comparison of Sources

The narrative sources and the finds from the Islamic period do not tell us the same story. The narrative sources describe activity in Quṣayr going back to the Fatimid period and give the beginning of the Ottoman period as a *terminus ad quem* for its activity.[6] In contrast, the physical remains at Quṣayr are mainly Ayyubid and Mamluk, with a peak at the end of the fifteenth century, and show

3 Li Guo, *Commerce, Culture and Community in a Red Sea Port in the Thirteenth Century: The Arabic Documents from Quseir* (Leiden: E.J. Brill, 2004); Andreas Kaplony, *Fünfundzwanzig arabische Geschäftsdokumente aus dem Rotmeer-Hafen al-Quṣayr al-Qadīm (7./13. Jh.) [P. Quseir Arab. II]* (Leiden: E.J. Brill, 2015).

4 Anne Regourd, "Report," in *Myos Hormos – Quseir al-Qadim: A Roman and Islamic Port on the Red Sea Coast of Egypt. Interim Report 2003*, ed. David P.S. Peacock, Lucy Blue, and S. Moser (Southampton: University of Southampton), 2003; idem, "Trade on the Red Sea during the Ayyubid and the Mamluk Period: The Quṣeir Paper Manuscript Collection 1999–2003, first data," *Proceedings of the Seminar for Arabian Studies* 34 (2003), 277–292; idem, "Arabic Language Documents on Paper," ch. 24 in *Myos Hormos – Quseir al-Qadim. Roman and Islamic Ports on the Red Sea.* Vol. 2: *Finds from the excavations 1999–2003*, ed. David P.S. Peacock and Lucy Blue (Oxford: Oxbow, 2011), 339–344.

5 Guo, *Commerce, Culture and Community*, Chap. 1, p. 1sq.

6 Jean-Claude Garcin, "Ḳuṣayr," *Encyclopaedia of Islam*, 2nd edition (Leiden: E.J. Brill, 1979); Andrew Peacock "Jeddah and the India Trade in the Sixteenth Century: Arabian Contexts and Imperial Policy," in *Human Interaction with the Environment, Past and Present in the Red Sea*, ed. Dionisius A. Agius, Emad Khalil, Eleanor M.L. Scerri, and Alun Williams (Leiden: Brill, 2017), 290–322.

dwellings, artisan workshops, a company storehouse, a possible caravanserai and a cemetery.[7]

Southampton document PA0278[8] (unpublished) bears the latest date known to us at the time, 10 Rajab 700/21 of March 1301. Dates collected by Guo take us back to the late Ayyubid, the period of the Sultans al-Malik al-ʿĀdil (d. 1217) and his son al-Malik al-Kāmil (d. 1238).[9] As PA0278 is a legal document (the release of a debt [*istiqāla*]), the date mentioned in the text applies to the document as a whole, as it corresponds to the date of the act as part of a performative formula. PA0278 was found in a building which has been identified as Mamluk by the archaeologists, and which shows signs of occupation throughout a long period. The analysis carried out in the field suggested that it was found in a re-occupied part of the Mamluk building, and that the material was "recovered from one of the late deposits in the sequence," but nonetheless "was related to the occupation of the building."[10] The very early date of the fragment in the Mamluk period may allow us to confirm the length of time the building was occupied, but suggests that this occupation possibly started during the late Ayyubid period. The presence of such an unusual item, a document on paper, supports the hypothesis that the building was "an important structure perhaps for administration," particularly when combined with other evidence, i. e. "the prominent situation of the building, the temporal dimension to the occupation of the building, the quality of the construction, the stone floors, the evidence for decoration in some of the rooms, traces of painted plaster and a carved screen."[11] But the paper, being a legal document that claims the release of a debt after some goods have been sold, refers to commercial activity, and to an agreement between two individuals, without the implication either of a *qāḍī*, or of officials. Nor does any Quṣayri document known to us so far mention taxes.[12] The building could therefore be the house of a very rich merchant. Unfortunately, the man mentioned in the text, i. e. Muḥammad b. ʿAlī b. ʿAbd Allāh, is not the person who is making the claim, and thus he remains unidentifiable.

7 Peacock and Blue, *Finds from the Excavations 1999–2003.*
8 Written documents shelf marked "PA" belong to Southampton's finds. Other pieces from Southampton's finds are under "QAQ."
9 Guo, *Commerce, Culture and Community*, 3–4.
10 David P.S. Peacock and Lucy Blue, *Myos Hormos – Quseir al-Qadim. Roman and Islamic Ports on the Red Sea.* Vol. 1: *Survey and Excavations 1999–2003* (Oxford: Archeopress 2006), 171–172.
11 Ibid.
12 By "known to us" we mean Chicago's published written documents and Southampton's written documents.

3. Trade as Pictured in the Documents of Quṣayr

The remains leave the strong impression that trade was flourishing during this period and that it was neither a seasonal activity nor informally organized, whereas the narrative sources, as well as the Geniza documents, suggest that ʿAydhāb was the big port of the Red Sea, at least during the eleventh-twelfth centuries.[13] For this reason, Quṣayr's secondary activities directly linked to trade, for example boat repair, or household items such as food and textiles, must not to be forgotten as the possible final destination of commodities mentioned in the documents or uncovered. The type of documents, which support this include: 1) legal documents (not very numerous) of an administrative nature; 2) inventories, often check marked; 3) day-to-day work records; 4) miscellanies, of which the Sufi poem mentioned below is part; and, 5) folios of codices. The bulk of these documents are: letters (merchant, private, official, semi-official) and shipping notes.[14]

a. Evidence of International Trade

In terms of imported commodities, we have evidence for international trade through Quṣayr during the late Ayyubid period, with goods identified for the first time at Quṣayr in documents uncovered during the University of Southampton excavations.[15] Two documents shed light on this matter. One letter refers, amongst other things, to a consignment of coral (PA0428). It is mentioned here exclusively as a trade item, a coral of a particular type *al-marjān al-rūmī*, and of a very good quality, passing through Quṣayr. We learn from different sources, that during the eleventh to the thirteenth centuries, coral came from the West (i. e. from the western coast of the Mediterranean), and went to Yemen or India. The second document (PA0456), in two parts, records several commodities, among them:

13 Ibn Jubayr (d. 614/1217), *Riḥlat Ibn Jubayr* (Beirut, 1964); al-Kutubī (1235–1318), *Mabāhij al-fikar*, ms. f. 216, in: Garcin, *Un centre musulman de la Haute-Égypte médiévale: Qūṣ* (Cairo: Institut Français d'Archéologie Orientale, 1976), 228, n. 4; al-Qalqashandī (d. 821/1418), *Ṣubḥ al-aʿshā fī ṣināʿat al-inshāʾ*, ed. Muḥammad ʿAbd al-Rasūl Ibrāhīm (Cairo: Dār al-Kutub al-Ḫadīwiyya, 1963, 14 vols.), 4:27; al-Maqrīzī (d. 845/1442), *Kitāb al-sulūk li-maʿrifat duwal al-mulūk*, Vol. 2: ed. Muḥammad Ziyāda (Cairo: Maktabat Lağnat al-Taʾlīf wal-tarjama wal-Našr, 1958), 2:194; Garcin, "Ḳuṣayr"; Shelomo D. Goitein, *Mediterranean Society* (Berkeley: University of California Press. 1983), 1:269 (henceforth *MS*); Guo, *Commerce, Culture and Community*, 62.

14 A publication of Southampton's written documents on paper is in preparation by Regourd.

15 Anne Regourd, "Arabic Language Documents on Paper," 339–344.

- brazilwood or sappan wood (*baqqam*) used mainly as a dyestuff, a commodity coming from the East, from India/the East Indies; pepper, in the eleventh-twelfth centuries, when the routes goes to ʿAydhāb through Aden, then to Fusṭāṭ, then sold to Rūm in Mediterranean ports;
- ebony (*abnūs* or *abanūs*), numerous references in late thirteenth century *Nūr al-maʿārif*, a Rasūlid collection of administrative archives, where the Aden pricing system shows that it comes from the Zanj coast through Maqdishū;
- a kind of glass bottle (*makhzān*), in another positive reference to Yemen;
- spears from India (*rumḥ*) were reputed to be of very good quality in Yemen, both again in the *Nūr al-maʿārif*[16].

Other key trade items which appear in both the documentary and archaeological records at Quṣayr are textiles. Luxury textiles would have passed through Quṣayr from East to West, supplying the European textiles market. The traditional overland routes of the Silk Road across Central Asia had been disrupted in the tenth century, and the sea routes through the Gulf and the Red Sea had became more popular.[17] Small pieces of these rich silks surviving from this period have been found in liturgical garments and objects in Europe.[18] However, few examples of textiles of this high quality survive from the Islamic occupation of Quṣayr. Only one example of an imported high quality textile, a *mulham* (silk on a cotton warp) survives, which would have come from Persia or Central Asia.[19] In contrast, Quṣayr has a rich selection of imported poorer quality textiles, including 142 examples of Indian trade textiles, 73 found during the Southampton's excavations[20] to join the 69 found by the Chicago expedition.[21] Some of these Indian textiles emulate the higher quality silk *ṭirāz* fabrics by being decorated with writing, albeit resist dyed or printed onto cotton, rather than sewn or woven into silk. These brightly colored cotton fabrics would have been destined for the markets of Cairo for use in both clothing and furnishings as documented in the

16 For full references, see Regourd "Arabic Language Documents on Paper," 342–343.

17 Patricia L. Baker, *Islamic Textiles* (London: British Museum Press, 1995), 14.

18 Anna Muthesius, "Byzantine Silks," in *5000 Years of Textiles*, ed. Jennifer Harris (London: The British Museum Press, 1993).

19 Fiona J.L. Handley, "'I have brought cloth for you and will deliver it myself': Using Documentary Sources in the Analysis of the Archaeological Textile Finds from Quseir al-Qadim, Egypt," in *Textiles and Text: Re-establishing Links between Archival and Object-based Research*, ed. Maria Hayward, and Elizabeth Kramer (London: Archetype, 2007), 10–17, 13.

20 Fiona J.L. Handley and Anne Regourd, "Textiles with Writing from Quseir al-Qadim: Finds from the Southampton Excavations 1999–2003," in *Connected Hinterlands: Proceedings of the Red Sea Project IV*, ed. Lucy Blue, John Cooper, Ross Thomas, and Julian Whitewright (Oxford: Archaeopress, 2009), 141–153.

21 Gillian M. Vogelsang-Eastwood, *Resist Dyed Textiles from Quseir al-Qadim* (Paris: AEDTA, 1990).

Geniza documents,[22] and are well known through entering European museum collections.[23] Some ended up staying in Quṣayr, and the good preservation of some of the examples suggests that Quṣayr itself was a market for these textiles[24] as well as being a transit point for the textiles before they were traded further north. These examples offer further evidence of trade between Quṣayr and India, through Yemen. And we are also able to infer trade along the same route, but in the other direction from India to Quṣayr through Yemen (Aden), thence to Alexandria or other Mediterranean ports through Cairo/Fusṭāṭ.

b. Connections to the Nile

As Li Guo pointed out, names of the expeditors normally do not appear on shipping notes and letters. This means that "the direct textual evidence one may use to pin down the itinerary of these merchants and their merchandise is thin."[25] In other words, we have almost all of the names of the receivers, who are normally based at Quṣayr, although exceptions do appear in the Southampton documents: Letter PA0369 is addressed to Qifṭ, on the East bank of the Nile to the north of Qūṣ, to Muḥammad b. al-Qāsim al-Qifṭī. Letter PA0221 (not pictured) was to be delivered to the south, to Aswān. And in Chicago document RN 1004b, published recently, to Karākūsh/Qarākūsh, south of Qūṣ, where goods were sent to Abū Mufarrij.[26] In the text of the documents as well, we see toponyms which evidence the link between Quṣayr and the Nile as part of trade routes, and to cities which are known as market places or to be at the crossing point of different routes, like Qūṣ. "Quṣayr, natural port of Qūṣ" is Jean-Claude Garcin's expression, who pointed out its pivotal role.[27]

In the Southampton documents, the connection between Quṣayr and Qūṣ through Dishnā, a small city downstream of Qinā, which is itself downstream of Qifṭ and Qūṣ, on the Eastern bank of the Nile (see Map 1), is illustrated by letter PA0457.[28] In shipping note PA0463, ʿAbd al-Salām al-Qifṭī states that someone

22 *MS*, 4:160.

23 E.g. Albert F. Kendrick, *Catalogue of Muhammaden Textiles of the Medieval Period* (London: HM Stationery Office, 1924); R. Pfister, *Les toiles imprimées de Fostat et l'Hindoustan* (Paris: Les Éditions d'Art et d'Histoire, 1938).

24 Handley, "'I have brought cloth for you and will deliver it myself'," 10–17, 13.

25 Guo, *Commerce, Culture and Community*, 58.

26 Kaplony, *Fünfundzwanzig arabische Geschäftsdokumente*, no. 12, 89–94, address, v.1.

27 Garcin, *Un centre musulman*, 6, note 1.

28 In the Quṣayrī documents, Qinā appears with its final letter rendered either by an *alif ṭawīla* or by an *alif maqṣūra*. Yāqūṭ, *Muʿjam al-buldān*, ed. Farīd ʿAbd al-ʿAzīz al-Jundī (Beirut: Dār al-Kutub al-ʿIlmiyya, 1410/1990, 7 vols.), 2:520, no. 4812, with *alif maqṣūra*, a city well-known

called Muqbil sent some flour and other goods. Moreover in shipping note PA0220 (not pictured), where goods are to be delivered to the storehouse (*šūna*) of Shaykh Abū Mufarrij, the head of the company studied by Li Guo, he appears for the first time with his *nisba* of al-Qinā'ī, showing definitely his own link to the river Nile through the city of Qinā. Let us now look to the southern part of Qūṣ district: letter PA0597 mentions somebody who came to Quṣayr from al-Ṭawd, a city in the district of Qūṣ, south of Luxor. Al-Ṭawd appears in its *nisba* form in another letter, PA061, where somebody called al-Ḥājj al-Ṭawdī is in relation with a Abū al-Naṣr Qayyūm (?) al-Nārī, resident at Quṣayr ("*sāḥil al-Quṣayr*"). Further north, in letter PA0428, already mentioned, which deals with good species of coral, i.e. from the Mediterranean, appears a merchant named al-Marsāwī.

Among the Chicago documents, "new" connections become apparent, between Quṣayr and other places, still in the Ṣa'īd, through *nisbas*: in the region of al-Bahnasā, al-Ṭambuḍayyī from Ṭambudā, and al-Shanqurī; al-Iṭṣā[wī], from Iṭṣā in the region of Qifṭ; and al-Shanhūrī, south of Qūṣ.[29] Another document, where a delivery of grain to the author of the letter was ordered by the *dīwān* of Qūṣ, leads us to understand that he went down the Nile up to Cairo (al-Qāhira) with a cargo.[30]

Commodities coming from inland mentioned in our documents are grains, flour and high quality flour (*daqīq mumtāz*), rice, chickpeas, fenugreek (?, *ḥalbān*),[31] oil and pure oil (*zayt ṭayyib*), bread, biscuits (*ka'k*), honey, sugar, sugar molasses, wine, vinegar, milk (*laban*), clarified butter, cheese, coriander, dates, dried dates, apple, watermelon (*biṭṭīḫ*), grapes, carob, starch (*nishā'*), soap (?), lighting oil (*zayt ḥārr*), linen, clothes.[32]

---

for its gardens and its sugar-press; Qift in Colloquial Arabic means "vegetable garden" (*mabqala, mabqula*).

29 Al-Ṭambuḍayyī, *nisba* of Ṭambudā/Ṭambuḍā/Ṭambuday/Ṭambaḍā, RN 983a; al-Shanhūrī, same doc., and RN 1092b; al-Shanqurī RN 1001a; Iṭṣā[wī], same doc.; RN 983a. Kaplony, *Fünfundzwanzig arabische Geschäftsdokumente*, no. 10, 79–82, l. 4, and l. 3; no. 17, 123–125, l. 1; no. 11, 81–88, l. 3, and l. 2.

30 RN, ibid.: no. 8, 65–69, v. It is damaged in its upper and lower part, so that it is uncertain to connect both deliveries, although it is the same person.

31 R Dozy, *Supplément aux dictionnaires arabes* (Leiden: E.J. Brill), 2 vols, 1:314a: حلبانة, *storax*.

32 For plant remains dating to the Islamic Quṣayr, see Marijke Van der Veen, Alison Cox, and Jacob Morales "Plant Remains - Evidence for Trade and Cuisine," ch. 18, in Peacock and Blue, *Finds from the Excavations 1999–2003*, 227–234, especially, section 18.4, on seeds of watermelon, which were consumed by humans at the place. Apart from these "snacks," various cereals were found (hulled barley and hard wheat at a first place, sorghum and pearl millet, all cultivated in Egypt in our period), rice, chickpeas, coriander, dates, grapes, and carob. Rice (*Oryza sativa*) is an interesting item brought into discussion: originating almost certainly in China and/or South East Asia and being first domesticated there, the point in time it became a crop cultivated in Egypt, rather than imports from India, is still being discussed; see ibid., 228a, 229a. As for textual sources, the thirteenth-century traveler Ibn al-Mujāwir mentions "rice" in his list of main exports from Egypt to Yemen, together with wheat, flour, soap, dried

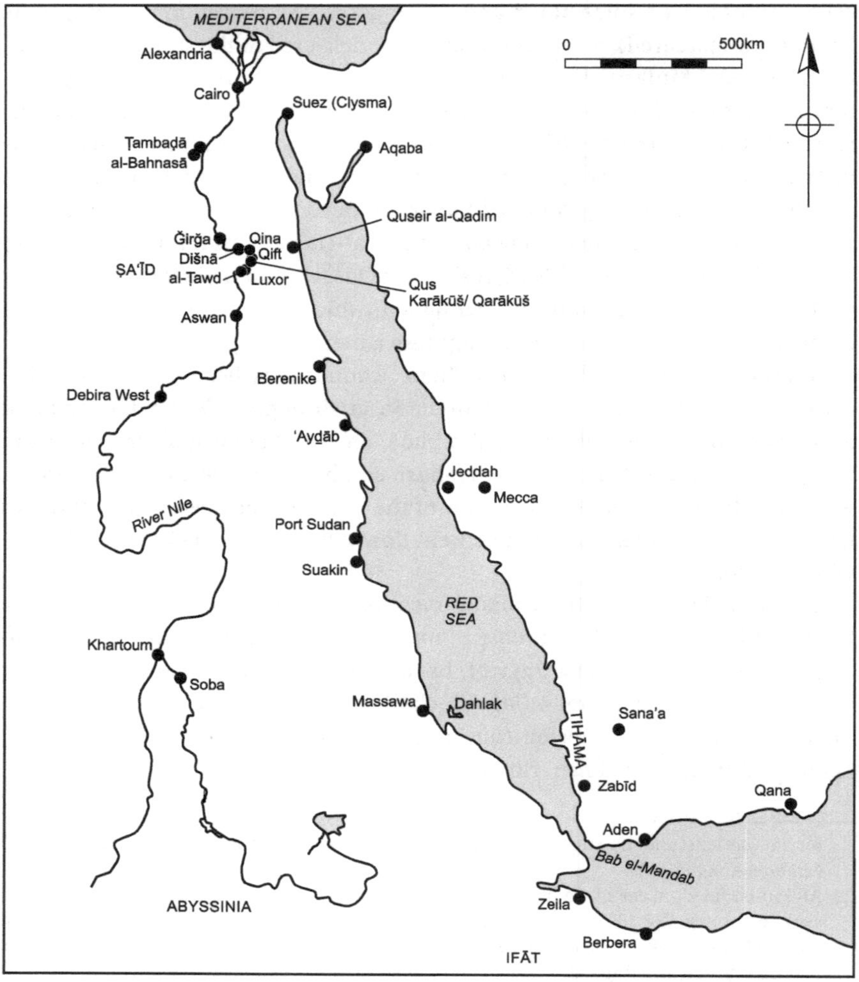

Map 1. Map showing location of Qusayr al-Qadim and its regional connections. Drawn by Penny Copeland, University of Southampton.

fruits, and lighting oil (*zayt al-ḥārr*); Ibn al-Mujāwir, *Ṣifat bilād al-Yaman wa-Makka wa-baʿḍ al-Ḥijāz al-musammā taʾrīḫ al-mustabṣir*, ed. O. Löfgren (Leiden: Brill, 1951), 142–143; G. Rex Smith, *A Traveller in Thirteenth Century Arabia. Ibn al-Mujāwir's Taʾrīkh al-Mustabṣir* (London: Ashgate/The Hakluyt Society, 2008), 133; Guo, *Commerce, Culture and Community*, 38, n. 34.

c. Relations with Mecca

Relations with Mecca were referred to in the Chicago documents: numerous pilgrims embarked for Mecca, expressing their need for grain. Also some petitions seem to show that the people in charge at Mecca also needed grain.[33] Those petitions suggest that the Abū Mufarrij business and Quṣayr were in correspondence with institutions like the Ayyubid court in Cairo or Qūṣ, or the Sultan. Among the Southampton documents is a Sufi poem written using "Maghrebian script" (PA0518). It has been interpreted as an item possibly left behind by somebody on his way to Mecca. Beyond this, it shows *ipso facto* a connection between Quṣayr and the Maghreb at least for the purpose of the pilgrimage. However, in a document where the writing has been struck through, we have a delivery of grains or flour for or to Ibn Ayyūb Yaḥyā al-Tūnisī (PA0433), which may indicate that Maghrebian traders were involved in the trade at Quṣayr. As previously discussed above in section a, there are additional links to the West.

The archaeological material includes textiles from a tailor's workshop established in Quṣayr that indicate that quantities of simple *ṯawb* garments were produced from low quality cotton and linen fabrics. The very low prestige value of these items in northern Egypt[34] and their appropriateness for the constrained attire for the Hajj,[35] suggests that these garments were made to supply pilgrims, either passing through Quṣayr or even being exported to supply that market. The remnants include a range of offcuts of pristine cloth in white and blue patterns, from neck holes, seam trimming and underarm darts (QAQ03T126–134, figure 1 and Appendix B.). The large number of similar cut pieces (over 150), often folded in a distinctive pattern to identify them as waste products rather than the right shape and size to be reused, would suggest this deposit was made in a relatively short period of time, perhaps as short as one season.

33 Gladys Frantz-Murphy, "The Red Sea Port of Quseir. Arabic Documents and Narrative Sources," in *Quseir al-Qadim 1980. Preliminary Report*, ed. Donald S. Whitcomb, and Janet H. Johnson (Malibu: Undena Pubications, 1982), 267–283; Guo, *Commerce, Culture and Community*, 27–28, 60–61; texts of petitions, no. 74, RN 1057, 295–297; no. 75, RN 1060b, 297–300. For major grain suppliers of Mecca during the Mamluk period, see Richard Mortel "Prices in Mecca during the Mamlūk Period," *Journal of the Economic and Social History of the Orient* 32 (1989): 279–334, 290*sq.*, among them, Egypt, 292–293, who also gives a brief account of the political ties between Egypt and the Hijaz during Ayyubid and Mamluk times in the first part of his study.

34 *MS*, 4:165, p. 174.

35 Baker, *Islamic Textiles*, 16.

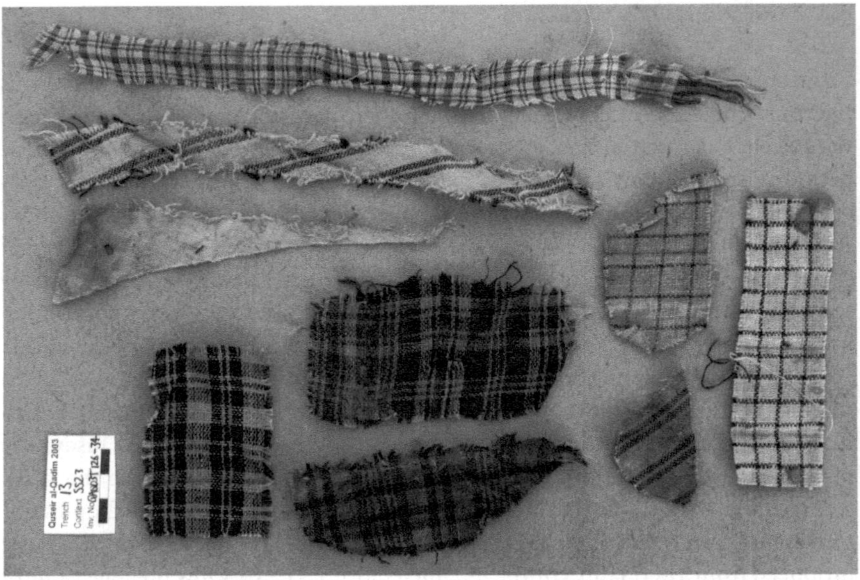

Figure 1 QAQ03T126–134. Waste offcuts from garment making

d. Quṣayr-Yemen: A Taste for *fuwaṭ*

Trade relations with Yemen and further east to India were also evidenced in the Chicago documents: traffic on the Red Sea coast and Aden, and Yemen as a stopover for traffic headed from the Indian Ocean. The commodities mentioned are pepper and perfumes coming from India and the Far East passing through Yemen,[36] and also textiles, especially *fūṭa* (plur. *fuwaṭ*) or waist-wrappers, which are a common item in the Chicago and Southampton documents. These are particularly interesting given our examination of local markets, tastes and clothing customs.

In 2004, Li Guo emphasized that if the Geniza documents from the twelfth century illustrated trade heading from the Indian Ocean to Egypt and the Mediterranean, the contribution of the Quṣayr documents was to point out the link to Yemen. Among the commodities from which he draws his conclusions were *fuwaṭ*. The letter Southampton-PA090 (not pictured; text ed.: Appendix A.) is addressed to a certain ʿAṭāʾ Allāh. The sender, Abū al-Faḍl, uses the formula "*mawlāʾī*" when writing to ʿAṭāʾ Allāh, and designates himself as his servant "*al-ʿabd*". He explains he was selling *fūṭa* and *kaʿk*, a kind of dry biscuit which was

36 Guo, *Commerce, Culture and Community*, 62–63.

produced in many parts of the Arab world, in Quṣayr as well, probably during the Ayyubid or Mamluk period.[37] The *ka'k* appears here as a commodity sold in a *zinğīla*, a "usual kitchen implement," "canister" or "spice box" that is ubiquitous in trousseau lists and inventories. ʿAṭāʾ Allāh is obviously at the heart of a network of people working with or for him, and is attempting to extend its reach to the inland markets of Egypt. This is slightly unusual as normally the direction of trade for *fūṭa* would be from Egypt to Yemen or elsewhere through Aden. But Qūṣ is described as a common place where Indian, Ethiopian or Arabian traders gathered before stepping up to Aswān, Nubia and the Upper Nile route or the route to Suākin.[38] Here the *fūṭa*-type is not detailed, but silk *fuwaṭ* were available in the Rasūlid Yemen, as a well-known complementary payment by Indian merchants involved in the horse trade.[39] On the basis of Geniza documents (published in *The India Book*), expensive *fūṭa*s made of silk or a weave of silk and linen or of high quality linen were sent from Egypt to India via Aden. The places of their production were: Miṣr (Fusṭāṭ), "where one manufacturer seems to have enjoyed particular fame"; Sūsa, Tunisia; Spain; and, perhaps Sicily.[40] In those texts, we also came across the expression "sari-like cloth," and that *fūṭa* were bought for children in the first third of the twelfth century, i.e. it is not only an item of men's clothing.[41] In our document, the price of the *fūṭa*, "8," without any specification of currency, is difficult to interpret, but seems anyway low, and was probably made of cotton.[42]

Moreover, there was a distinct area where *fuwaṭ* were popular and worn in thirteenth century, which included India, Yemen and Abyssinia. Passing merchants and travelers could find *fūṭa*s in market places, including Qayrawān,

37 See PA0248, a bakery account, unpublished, image in: Regourd, "Arabic Language Documents on Paper," 341, Fig. 24.1.

38 Garcin, *Un centre musulman*, 229, quoting Ibn Fāḍl Allāh al-ʿUmarī, *Kitāb al-ta'rīf*, and *Masālik al-abṣār*. Yasuyuki Kuriyama assumes that textiles were produced in Qūṣ. See "Egyptian Fabrics and Their Distribution as Seen in the Red Sea Trade during the Thirteenth to Fifteenth Centuries," *Takahashi Tsuguo Kyouju Koki Kinen Toyo Daigaku Touyoushi Ronshu* (Tokyo: Toyo Daigaku, 2016), 429–451. [In Japanese, transl. into English in: *Chroniques du manuscrit au Yémen*, 23 (January 2017), 89–102]).

39 Anonymous (13th c.), *Nūr al-ma'ārif fī nuẓum wa-qawānīn wa-a'rāf al-Yaman fī 'ahd al-muẓaffarī wa-wārif. Lumière de la connaissance: Règles, lois et coutumes du Yémen sous le règne du sultan rasoulide al-Muẓaffar*, ed. Muḥammad ʿAbd al-Raḥīm Jāzim (Ṣanʿāʾ: Centre français d'archéologie et de sciences sociales, 2005), 1:504.

40 S.D. Goitein, and Mordechai A. Friedman, *India Traders of the Middle Ages: Documents from the Cairo GenizaIndia Book* (Leiden: E.J. Brill, 2008), 175, 176 (now *India Book*). Goitein adds that: "Goat's hair *fūṭa*s have been noted"; ibid., 176, 178, and n. 22.

41 Reference in Appendix A, and more details on customers by gender, age, and social stratum.

42 Goitein and Freidman, *India Book*, 177. A market of second hand *fūṭa*s seems to have existed, see the case of this Alexandrian merchant, who, on his way to the East, bought a *fūṭa* in the Red Sea port of ʿAyḏāb, for one third of a dinar; ibid.

Palermo, Cairo, ʿAydhāb, Dahlak, and Aden.[43] Goitein underlined that expensive *fūṭas* exported to India "were destined for the Westerners living or sojourning in India, who adapted themselves to the clothing habits of their environment, but wished to be distinguished from it by the special types of *fūṭas* they wore."[44] Cairo did not really have a taste for those items, and it was not fashionable to wear them,[45] although document PA090 edited here may suggest an interest in them in the Ṣaʿīd (see Appendix A.). Clothing habits in Ifāt (*Awfāt*), and probably in the six other Muslim kingships of Abyssinia in the second half of the thirteenth century and later, show a tradition of wearing *fūṭas*, as well as other unsewn pieces of cloth from India.[46] Sometimes *fūṭas* were produced on the spot: Ibn al-Mujāwir, a thirteenth-century traveler to Yemen and Mecca, noticed *fūṭas*, among other types of cloths, were produced and sold in Zabīd, on the coastal plain of the Tihāma, along the Red Sea coast.[47] References to as *fuwaṭ maqdishī*, suggest that *fūṭas* were being produced in Maqdishū in the second half of the thirteenth century and later.[48] There is also evidence for the production of *fūṭas* made of cotton in India.[49]

43 *India Book*, 177–178.

44 *Appendix to I, 1–2, India Book*, 176.

45 *India Book*, 179.

46 Al-ʿUmarī, Ibn Faḍl Allah al-ʿOmarī, *Masālik el abṣār fi mamālik el amṣār*. I. *L'Afrique, moins l'Égypte*, transl. annotated by Gaudefroy-Demombynes (Paris: Geuthner, 1927); reprinted by Publications of the Institute for the History of Arabic-Islamic Science, ed. Fuat Sezgin, Islamic Geography, vol. 142 (Frankfurt: Johann Wolfgang Goethe University, 1993), transl., chap. on Ifāt (*Awfāt*), p. 5, where al-ʿUmarī underlines that it is the closest region to Egypt and Coastal Sea facing Yemen and that imports are more considerable, precisely because of the proximity. Its King reigns on Zeilaʿ, the port where merchants who wish to enter this Kingdom arrive (p. 5). Then, al-ʿUmarī describes the usual cloths of emirs and soldiers, pp. 6–7, and notices: "Rares sont ceux qui ont une chemise ou un vêtement cousu, et ils s'enveloppent d'ordinaire dans des pagnes", i. e. note (4): "*Yattazirūna wazarāt:* plur. de *wazra:* voir Reinhart Dozy, *Suppl.* II, 799, et le texte de Muqaddessi où se joignent *wazra* et *ʿizār*, pour s'opposer à *qamiṣ*, comme dans notre texte: il s'agit d'ailleurs de Yéménites"; "Parmi les savants et les gens aisés, il y en a qui portent des chemises, mais en général, on s'habille de deux pagnes, l'un sur l'épaule en bandoulière, l'autre autour de la ceinture." Further, he says, in a general final description: "Abyssinie [Northern and Eastern?] Le costume des habitants de ce pays est le même, été comme hiver; les grands et les soldats portent des étoffes de soie, des tissus de laine de l'Inde, et autres semblables; la masse de la population a des vêtements tissés en coton, non cousus; chaque personne porte deux de ces vêtements, l'un pour se serrer le milieu du corps, l'autre pour s'envelopper le buste. Les grands s'enveloppent donc la ceinture et la poitrine avec de la soie et de l'indienne, tissée et non cousue.", p. 25.

47 Ibn al-Muǧāwir: ed. Löfgren, p. 89, transl. Smith, 115; *Nūr al-maʿārif*, 1:82–83, and note 620, where the editor sends readers to the index of his text edition to have an idea of the kinds, places of production, fabrics, and to the related footnotes; p. 663 of the index, one can find no less than 43 entries under "*fuwwaṭ*." In a document of the Geniza, it is reported that an Egyptian lady possessed many Yemenite items, among them, a silk *fūṭa* from Zabīd; "Her father seems to have been an India trader." See *India Book*, 179.

48 Al-Sharīf al-Ḥusaynī, al-Ḥasan b. ʿAlī, *Mulakhkhaṣ al-fiṭan* (815/1412), 25v–13.

At Quṣayr there is one example of a textile that can be traced to Yemen, through its distinctive construction and pattern. It is a cotton *ikat* textile, with a pattern of red, white and blue chevrons (QAQ99T561, see figure 2 and Annex C.). *Ikat* fabrics have patterns dyed into their warp, which are then showcased in warp-faced fabrics, and Yemen during this time period produced high quality cotton *ikats* with *ṭirāz* embroidery.[50] The Quṣayr example has no embroidery and is not of the highest quality of cotton, but is probably a Yemeni piece. However, the remnants of a seam would suggest that this was not a *fūṭa,* which presumably would not have been a fitted garment.

Figure 2 QAQ99T561. Cotton *ikat* textile

A more likely candidate for a *fūṭa* is QAQT146 (figure 3 and Annex D.), a larger piece of surviving fabric (19 x 22 cm), with a blue border and two blue stripes running along the longer edge. The slightly open weave and simple decorative pattern make this distinctive from the more densely striped and checked examples of fabrics that dominate the garment fabrics at Quṣayr. It is still a humble cloth however, suitable for the *fūṭa* worn by "the camel drivers and Arabs of the desert and the servants and people of the lowest sort."[51]

49 *India Book,* 176 and n. 8, with quotations of al-ʿUmarī and al-Qalqashandī; "*fuwaṭ maʿbarī*" from South-East India, *Nūr al-maʿārif,* 1:447/11, 470/11.

50 Lisa Golombek, and Veronika Gervers, "Tiraz Fabrics in the Royal Ontario Museum," in *Studies in Textile History in Memory of Harold B. Burnham,* ed. V. Gervers (Toronto: Royal Ontario Museum, 1977), 82–125.

51 S. Muhammed Husayn Nainar, cited in Robert B. Serjeant, "Material for a History of Islamic Textiles up to the Mongol Conquest," *Ars Islamica,* 13 (1948), 83.

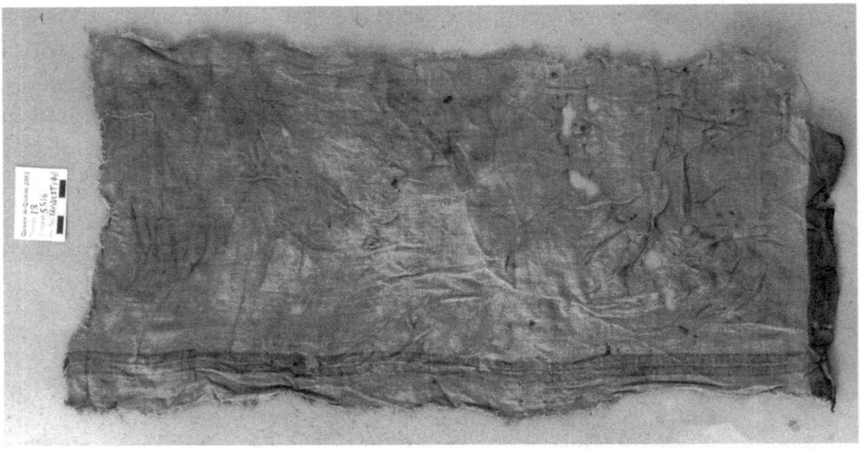

Figure 3 QAQ03T146

4. Conclusion

The effect of traditional Western historical perspectives regarding this time period and in this region has been to prioritize research into the trading routes of luxury goods from the East to the Mediterranean. While this serves to bolster large scale historical narratives centered on Europe, this partial account leaves little scope for historical explanation of local and regional trade. This case study of Quṣayr begins to address some of these issues by contrasting the narrative documentation about Quṣayr which has typically been interpreted to show its role from a European perspective, to a local reinterpretation of this documentation in the light of the rich documentary and artifact resources uncovered during the archaeological excavations.

What this has revealed is the variety of local trading networks, both in terms of the types of goods, their provenance and destination, and the people involved. Whether providing grain for Mecca, clothing for pilgrims, or detailing the supply of day to day necessities such as oil, bread and dried dates from the Nile Valley, heads of companies, merchants, wives, or port workers were all beneficiaries of trading networks.

Some of these activities may have related to the long distance East to West trade routes, but the local evidence clearly shows the importance of other trading activities that are distinct from this, based, for instance, on movements of people and goods for the *ḥajj*, and on markets for commodities such as *fuwaṭ* which centered on the Indian Ocean and the Red Sea. As document PA090 shows, beyond a general taste for Indian cloth, which was confirmed by multiple finds in

Quṣayr, we should not ignore local and regional markets, as well as tastes to which local production responded.

Appendices

A: PA090

Letter about the Receipt of a *fūṭa* and a Box of Biscuits (*kaʿk*)

Inv. no. PA090; 1999; trench, context undefined (reg. 78); not photographed during the excavation campaign

Physical description under glass

Yellow brown laid paper, remains of laid lines, vertical/writing; 9 x 8.5 cm, *basmala:* 3.2 x 1.5 cm; black ink; the sheet was turned from right to left by the scribe; traces of folds, but these do not seem original; conservation status: good, tearing at top, traces of sand, a few small holes.

Introduction

Undated, almost complete. The *fūṭa* brings to mind here a trade extending its branches to the west of Egypt. The verb *nādā ʿalā* (recto l. 6) leads us to consider a sale of the goods in the streets, or at the souk – and more precisely in the space of the souk, a place where the clothing merchants congregate – or a sale from premises such as a *khān*. Therefore, in the place where the goods were sent, there is in the broad sense a "market." The price the *fūṭa* was sold by the author of the letter is given, but without the currency.

Text

Recto

1. خـ<ـا>دمــها ابو الفضل
2. بسم الله الرحمن الرحيم
3. الى حضر<ة> مولاي الشيخ عطا الله
4. وفقه الله تعالى وسوا ذلك
5. يا مولاي قد وصلني فوطة
6. وزنجيلة كعك وناديت
7. على الفوطة جابت ثمانية و
8. [..]

Verso, address

1. يصل هذا لجر[جة ؟] يسلم <لـ>ـعطا الله
2. دامت سعادته

Textual notes

Recto

3. ʿAṭā Allāh for ʿAṭāʾ Allāh.
6. *Zinjīla:* the dot of the *zayn* is apparent and there is no diacritical dot under the third letter; reading as *zanjala* presents a problem because there is an indentation between *jīm* and *lām* with, below, an oblique stroke for a *yāʾ*: hence the proposed variation in *zinjīla*. There is also a stroke between the *lām* and the *hāʾ* below the line, but that might instead be a stain. Another possible reading would be *raḥīla*, referring to something like a quantity transported, but no evidence for the term was found. It would also entail ignoring the dot of the *zayn* and would not make more account of the stroke between the *lām* and the *hāʾ*.

Translation

Recto

1–2. In the name of God, the Merciful, the Compassionate. [In] his servant Abū al-Faḍl,
3. to the Shaykh ʿAṭāʾ Allāh, my master
4. – That God Transcendent ensures his success! – and so forth. [Now to the topic:]
5. O my master, the *fūṭa* has reached me,
6. and a box of biscuits (*kaʿk*). I began the public sale

7. of the *fūṭa*, it brought in 8, and
8. [..]

Verso, address

1. This <letter> is to be delivered to Jir[ǧa (?)] to ʿAṭā Allāh
2. — may his happiness last forever!

Commentary

Recto

1. *Kh<ā>dimuhā:* the angular part of the *khāʾ* is prolonged to the right by a slight stroke, suggesting a reading of *bi-khidma<t>ihā*, but it was not ultimately chosen because it is in the *tarjama*, cf. Guo 2004: 7, 149, recto l. 3, and comment. The pronoun is feminine, agreeing with *ḥaḍrat mawlāʾī*, cf. Guo 2004: 181–182, 20, address l. 1; in Diem, for instance, *DAA1:* 61, 392, l. 3–4, 5. Abū al-Faḍl is not identified in the known corpus from Quṣayr.

3. ʿAṭā Allāh: in the document PA0372, verso. l. 6, an ʿAṭāʾ Allāh is mentioned, who seems to live in Quṣayr; an ʿAṭāʾ Allāh appears in the documents published by Guo, this is a client of Abū Mufarriǧ, Guo 2004: 44, 236–237; the second ʿAṭāʾ Allāh attested by Guo is identifiable only as a sender of a letter to the market inspector (*muḥtasib*) of Quṣayr, Guo 2004: 27.

4. "*Wa-siwā ḏālika*," cf. Guo 2004: 6, 146–147, recto l. 3; 14, 168, recto l. 2; 20, 180–181, the recto l. 5; 24, 193–194, recto l. 5; 28, 204–205, recto l. 4.

5. *Fūṭa:* piece of cloth with which men in this region, and especially in Yemen, gird the loins; Guo 2004: 42, 62–63, and note 87, 68, 206, *waist-wrapper*. The following references shows potential users as being of various genders, ages or social conditions: *MS:* 4: 403, note 143, "sari-like cloth," the father of a bride native of Aden ordered two *fūṭa*s, either bearing silk decorations on silk, or linen decorations on silk (ref. Westminster College, Frag. Cairens, 9, *India Book* 50); *LMJT:* "sari," two occurrences of *fūṭa*s for children in chap. V, "the India traders", 196, *fūṭa*s in linen, Letter from Aden dated from the late 1130s, and 226, Letter of an Indian trader to his wife, dated approx. 1204. *Fūṭa*s appear in a list of clothing for the poor at Fusṭāṭ, *MS:* 2, 448, note 33; but the price varies considerably according to the material used, ibid.: 2, 131 and 4, 155. In fact, in l. 7, it is unclear whether "8" refers to the quantity of *fūṭa*s that the client wanted to buy or to an amount that he wanted to pay, expressed as 8 units of a currency (*dirhams?*).

6. *Zanjala* or *zinjila:* box, cf. *MS:* 6, 21 (index) and ibid.: 4, 143, appears in lists of "usual kitchen implements," "canister" or "spice box," "is as ubiquitous in trousseau lists and inventories as it is absent from Arabic dictionaries"; however, it is difficult to understand what exactly its function was, as many very different

types are mentioned in the documents of the Geniza; some, eg., are earthenware (note 31). *Nāda ʿalā* + thing: "*crier*, proclamer pour vendre ou retrouver quelque chose, *vendre à l'encan*" (Dozy, 2:662); "to cry one's wares, hawk (*ʿalā* s.th. to be sold)" (Wehr: 952); "To cry (wares)", ex. "he's hawking chicks through the streets" (*DEA:* 856); "to proclaim a. th. to" (Hava: 760).

Verso, address

1. Jirğa?: the reading is hypothetical since part of the word is missing; in the wording of an address, we expect here the name of the place where the letter should be delivered; *yaṣil hadhā al-kitāb li-makān yusallam ilā fulān:* same formula here in PA028, and in Guo 2004: 199–200, 26, verso (address) l. 1; Jirğa is a locality situated north of Qinā, on the left bank of the Nile, at the northern end of the "zone of influence" of Qūṣ, and which took the political leadership on this the ninth/fifteenth century (Garcin 1976: XVI, according to al-Udfuwī and 486sq; Jirğa however, is not among the place names most often cited in the province of Qūṣ in the Mamluk era, according to the same source, 607–608; Yāqūṭ, 2:138–139, entry 3023, Jargā); attempts to identify with the names of other places in the province of Qūş yielded nothing, especially due to the estimated length of the word; nor can other locations in Egypt be excluded.

2. This is a recurring concluding formula in the addresses of documents of Quṣayr, cf. PA028 here, and Guo 2004: 149–150, 7, verso l. 1–2; 157, 10, verso (address) l. 2; 197, 25, verso (address) l. 2.

B: QAQT126-T134

Pieces of Cloth from a Tailor's Workshop

Cut pieces of cotton and bast tabby fabrics in white, and blue and white combined. Warps mostly 's' spun, circa 18 warps per cm. Wefts mostly 's' spun, circa 18 warps per cm. Found in trench 13 5523. Figure 1.

These are a representative sample of the dozens of offcuts found in one context which was the rubbish dump for a tailor's workshop. The roundish pieces are from cutting neck holes in garments, the triangular pieces from shaping garments, for examples under the arms, while the long thin pieces were from trimming down seams.

C: QAQ99T561

Ikat Textile

Slightly warp-faced weave in cotton with *ikat* design in blue and red on a white ground. Warp 's' spun, 32 threads per cm. Weft 's' spun, 24 threads per cm. Longest length of warp = 11.5 cm, longest length of weft = 25 cm. Found in trench 2C context 1019. Figure 2.

This medium sized fragment of *ikat* cloth has been used and reused several times. It is well worn, and was once part of a seamed garment judging by the remains of a run-and-fell seam. A rectangular section has been cut from it, leaving this piece. There is a pattern of red "chevrons" along one edge, with an aligned pattern of red and blue chevrons along the other. It is probably of Yemeni origin. Comparators include "Tiraz Fragment Accession Number 29.179.9 The Metropolitan Museum of Art," which is of slightly higher quality and earlier date.

D: QAQ146

Cotton Textile with Border Stripes

Slightly open weave tabby in medium weight cotton with border stripes. Warp 'z' spun, 17 warps per cm. Weft 'z' spun, 22 warps per cm. Longest length of warp 19 cm, longest length of weft 40 cm. Found in trench 13 context 1566. Figure 3.

This is a fairly large piece of fabric for Quṣayr, which would suggest it was fairly low status as it was not reused. The dark blue weft selvedge is formed by thinner dark blue warp threads creating a warp faced blue border, while the stripes along the longer edge are simple weft stripes. Its similarity to current Yemeni waist wrappers and disposal when relatively complete, suggest that this may be an example of a Yemeni *fūṭa* worn by working people at the port.

Abbreviations

DAA1 = Werner Diem, *Arabische Geschäftbriefe des 10. bis 14. Jahrhunderts aus der Österreichischen Nationalbibliothek in Wien.* (Wiesbaden: Otto Harrassowitz, 1995), 2 vols.

DEA = Martin Hinds, and El-Said Badawi, *A Dictionary of Egyptian Arabic* (Beirut: Librairie du Liban, 1986).

Dozy = Reinhart Dozy, *Supplément aux dictionnaires arabes* (Leiden: E.J. Brill, 1881), 2 vols.

Garcin 1976 = Jean-Claude Garcin, *Un centre musulman de la Haute-Égypte médiévale: Qūṣ* (Cairo: Institut Français d'Archéologie Orientale, 1976).

Guo = Li Guo, *Commerce, Culture and Community in a Red Sea Port in the Thirteenth Century: The Arabic Documents from Quseir* (Leiden: E.J. Brill, 2004).

Hava = J.G. Hava, *Arabic-English Dictionary for the Use of Students* (Beirut: Catholic Press, ca. 1915).

India Book = S.D. Goitein, and Mordechai A. Friedman, *India Traders of the Middle Ages: Documents from the Cairo Geniza India Book* (Leiden: E.J. Brill, 2008).

LMJT = Shelomo D. Goitein, *Letters of Jewish Merchant Traders* (Princeton: Princeton University Press, 1973).

MS = Goitein, Shelomo D. *A Mediterranean Society* (Berkeley: University of California Press, 1967–1986), 6 vols.

Wehr = Hans Wehr, *A Dictionary of Modern Written Arabic* (London: McDonald & Evans / Beirut: Librairie du Liban, 1980 [reprint]).

Yāqūṭ, *Buldān* = Yāqūt ibn ʿAbd Allāh al-Ḥamawī, *Muʿǧam al-buldān*, ed. Farīd ʿAbd al-ʿAzīz al-Ǧundī (Beirut: Dār al-Kutub al-ʿIlmiyya, 1410/1990), 7 vols.

Bibliography

Anonymous (13th c.), *Nūr al-maʿārif fī nuẓum wa-qawānīn wa-aʿrāf al-Yaman fī ʿahd al-muẓaffarī wa-wārif. Lumière de la connaissance: Règles, lois et coutumes du Yémen sous le règne du sultan rasoulide al-Muẓaffar*, ed. Muḥammad ʿAbd al-Raḥīm Jāzim (Ṣanʿāʾ: Centre français d'archéologie et de sciences sociales, 2005).

Baker, Patricia L. *Islamic Textiles* (London: British Museum Press, 1995).

Diem, Werner. *Arabische Geschäftsbriefe des 10. bis 14. Jahrhunderts aus der Österreichischen Nationalbibliothek in Wien* (Wiesbaden: Otto Harrassowitz, 1995). 2 vols.

Dozy, Reinhart. *Supplément aux dictionnaires arabes* (Leiden: E.J. Brill, 1881). 2 vols.

Frantz-Murphy, Gladys. "The Red Sea Port of Quseir. Arabic Documents and Narrative Sources." In *Quseir al-Qadim 1980. Preliminary report*, ed. Donald S. Whitcomb, and Janet H. Johnson (Malibu: Undena Publications, 1982), 267–283.

Garcin, Jean-Claude. *Un centre musulman de la Haute-Égypte médiévale: Qūṣ* (Cairo: Institut Français d'Archéologie Orientale, 1976).

Garcin, Jean-Claude. "Ḳuṣayr." *Encyclopaedia of Islam*. 2nd edition (Leiden: E.J. Brill, 1979).

Goitein, Shelomo D. *Letters of Jewish Merchant Traders, Princeton* (Princeton: Princeton University Press, 1973).

Goitein, Shelomo D. *A Mediterranean Society* (Berkeley: University of California Press. 1967–1986). 6 vols.

Goitein, Shelomo D., and Mordechai A. Friedman, *India Traders of the Middle Ages: Documents from the Cairo Geniza India Book* (Leiden: E.J. Brill, 2008).

Golombek, Lisa, and Veronika Gervers. "Tiraz Fabrics in the Royal Ontario Museum." In *Studies in Textile History in Memory of Harold B. Burnham*, ed. V. Gervers (Toronto: Royal Ontario Museum, 1977).

Guo, Li. *Commerce, Culture and Community in a Red Sea Port in the Thirteenth Century: The Arabic Documents from Quseir* (Leiden: E.J. Brill, 2004).

Handley, Fiona J.L. "'I have brought cloth for you and will deliver it myself': Using Documentary Sources in the Analysis of the Archaeological Textile Finds from Quseir al-Qadim, Egypt." In *Textiles and Text: Re-establishing Links between Archival and Object-based Research*, ed. Maria Hayward, and Elizabeth Kramer (London: Archetype, 2007). 10–17.

Handley, Fiona J.L., and Anne Regourd. "Textiles with Writing from Quseir al-Qadim: Finds from the Southampton Excavations 1999–2003." In *Connected Hinterlands: Proceedings of the Red Sea Project IV*, ed. Lucy Blue, John Cooper, Ross Thomas and Julian Whitewright (Oxford: Archaeopress, 2009), 141–153.

Hava, J.G. *Arabic-English Dictionary for the Use of Students* (Beirut: Catholic Press, ca. 1915).

Hinds, Martin, and El-Said Badawi. *A Dictionary of Egyptian Arabic* (Beirut: Librairie du Liban, 1986).

Ibn Jubayr. *Riḥlat Ibn Jubayr* (Beirut, 1964).

Kaplony, Andreas. *Fünfundzwanzig arabische Geschäftsdokumente aus dem Rotmeer-Hafen al-Quṣayr al-Qadīm (7./13. Jh.) [P. Quseir Arab. II]* (Leiden: E.J. Brill, 2015).

Kendrick, Albert F. *Catalogue of Muhammaden Textiles of the Medieval Period* (London: HM Stationery Office, 1924).

Kuriyama, Yasuyuki. "Egyptian Fabrics and its Distribution in the Red Sea Trade during the Thirteenth and Fifteenth Centuries." *Takahashi Tsuguo Kyouju Koki Kinen Toyo Daigaku Touyoushi Ronshu* (Tokyo: Toyo Daigaku, 2016), 429–451. In Japanese, translation into English in: *Chroniques du manuscrit au Yémen*, 23 (January 2017), 89–102.

al-Maqrīzī. *Kitāb al-sulūk li-maʿrifat duwal al-mulūk*, Vol. 2: ed. Muḥammad Ziyāda (Cairo: Maktabat Lağnat al-Taʾlīf wal-tarjama wal-Našr, 1958).

Mortel, Richard T. "Prices in Mecca during the Mamlūk Period," *Journal of the Economic and Social History of the Orient* 32 (1989), 279–334.

Ibn al-Mujāwir. *Ṣifat bilād al-Yaman wa-Makka wa-baʿḍ al-Ḥijāz al-musammā taʾrīḫ al-mustabṣir*. Ed. O. Löfgren (Leiden: E.J. Brill, 1951–1954). Reprinted Beirut, 1407/1986.

Muthesius, Anna. "Byzantine Silks." In *5000 Years of Textiles*, ed. Jennifer Harris (London: The British Museum Press 1993).

Peacock, Andrew. "Jeddah and the India Trade in the Sixteenth Century: Arabian Contexts and Imperial Policy." In *Human Interaction with the Environment, Past and Present in the Red Sea*, ed. Dionisius A. Agius, Emad Khalil, Eleanor M.L. Scerri and Alun Williams (Leiden: Brill, 2017), 290–322.

Peacock, David P.S., and Lucy Blue. *Myos Hormos – Quseir al-Qadim Roman and Islamic Ports on the Red Sea.* Vol. 1: *Survey and Excavations 1999–2003* (Oxford: Archeopress, 2006), 171–172.

Peacock, David P.S. and Lucy Blue. *Myos Hormos – Quseir al-Qadim Roman and Islamic Ports on the Red Sea.* Vol. 2: *Finds from the Excavations 1999–2003* (Oxford: Archeopress, 2011).

Pfister, R. *Les toiles imprimées de Fostat et l'Hindoustan* (Paris: Les Éditions d'Art et d'Histoire, 1938).

al-Qalqashandī. *Ṣubḥ al-aʿshā fī ṣināʿat al-inshāʾ*. Ed. Muḥammad ʿAbd al-Rasūl Ibrāhīm (Cairo: Dār al-Kutub al-Ḫadīwiyya, 1963). 14 vols.

Regourd, Anne. "Report." In *Myos Hormos – Quseir al-Qadim: A Roman and Islamic Port on the Red Sea coast of Egypt. Interim Report 2003*, ed. David P.S. Peacock, Lucy Blue and S. Moser (Southampton: University of Southampton, 2003).

Regourd, Anne. "Trade on the Red Sea during the Ayyubide and the Mamluk Period: The Quṣeir Paper Manuscript Collection 1999–2003, First Data." *Proceedings of the Seminar for Arabian Studies* 34 (2003): 277–292.

Regourd, Anne. "Arabic Language Documents on Paper," Ch. 24 in *Myos Hormos – Quseir al-Qadim. Roman and Islamic Ports on the Red Sea.* Vol. 2: *Findings 1999–2003*, ed. David P.S. Peacock and Lucy Blue (Oxford: Oxbow, 2011), 339–344.

Serjeant, Robert B. "Material for a History of Islamic Textiles up to the Mongol Conquest." *Ars Islamica*, 13 (1948): 29–85.

al-Sharīf al-Ḥusaynī, al-Ḥasan b. ʿAlī. *Mulakhkhaṣ al-fiṭan* (815/1412), manuscript.

Smith, G. Rex. *A Traveller in Thirteenth Century Arabia. Ibn al-Mujāwir's Taʾrīkh al-Mustabṣir* (London: Ashgate/The Hakluyt Society, 2008).

al-ʿUmarī. *Ibn Faḍl Allah al-ʿOmarī. Masālik el abṣār fi mamālik el amṣār.* I. *L'Afrique, moins l'Égypte.* Translation and annotation by Maurice Gaudefroy-Demombyne (Paris: Geuthner, 1927); reprinted by Publications of the Institute for the History of Arabic-Islamic Science, ed. Fuat Sezgin, "Islamic Geography," vol. 142 (Frankfurt: Johann Wolfgang Goethe University, 1993).

Van der Veen, Marijke, Alison Cox, and Jacob Morales. "Plant Remains – Evidence for Trade and Cuisine." Ch. 18 in *Myos Hormos – Quseir al-Qadim Roman and Islamic Ports on the Red Sea.* Vol. 2: *Finds from the Excavations 1999–2003*, ed. David P.S. Peacock and Lucy Blue (Oxford: Archeopress, 2011), 227–234.

Vogelsang-Eastwood, Gillian M. *Resist Dyed Textiles from Quseir al-Qadim* (Paris: AEDTA, 1990).

Wehr, Hans. *A Dictionary of Modern Written Arabic* (London: McDonald & Evans/Beirut: Librairie du Liban, 1980 [reprint]).

Yāqūṭ. *Muʿjam al-buldān.* Ed. Farīd ʿAbd al-ʿAzīz al-Jundī (Beirut: Dār al-Kutub al-ʿIlmiyya, 1410/1990). 7 vols.

Contributors

Reuven Amitai (PhD, Hebrew University, 1990) is Eliyahu Elath Professor for Muslim History at the Hebrew University of Jerusalem. His areas of research include the Mamluk Sultanate, the Mongols in the Middle East, processes of Islamization, and medieval Palestine. From 2010 to 2014, he was dean of the Faculty of Humanities at the Hebrew University, and from 2014 to 2016, he was a senior fellow at the Annemarie Schimmel Kolleg in Bonn. His recent publications include *Holy War and Rapprochement: Studies in the Relations between the Mamluk Sultanate and the Mongol Ilkhanate (1260–1335)* (Brepols, 2013); co-edited with Michal Biran: *Nomads as Agents of Cultural Change: The Mongols and Their Eurasian Predecessors* (University of Hawaii Press, 2015); and co-edited with Christoph Cluse: *Slavery and the Slave Trade in the Eastern Mediterranean, 11th to 15th Centuries*, published in late 2017 at Brepols. In 2018, he received the degree of *doctor honoris causa* from the National University of Mongolia.

Amar S. Baadj (Ph.D. University of Toronto, 2012) is a post-doctoral researcher at Bonn University and Trier University. His areas of research are the medieval Maghrib, medieval Egypt, and Arabic historiography. His publications include *Saladin, the Almohads and the Banū Ghāniya: The Contest for North Africa (12th and 13th centuries)* (Leiden: Brill, 2015); "The Term *Zawāwa* in the Medieval Sources and the Zawāwī Presence in Egypt and Syria during the Ayyubid and Mamluk Periods," in *History and Society during the Mamluk Period (1250–1517): Studies of the Annemarie Schimmel Institute for Advanced Study II*, ed. Stephan Conermann, (Bonn & Göttingen: Bonn University Press and V&R Unipress GmbH, 2016), 107–124; "The Political Context of the Egyptian Gold Crisis during the Reign of Saladin," *International Journal of African Historical Studies*, Vol. 47, No. 1 (2014), 117–134.

Michal Biran (PhD Hebrew University 2000) is a historian of Inner Asia and a member of the Israeli Academy of Science and Humanities. She is the Max and Sophie Mydans Foundation Professor in the Humanities at the Hebrew University of Jerusalem, where she led the ERC-funded project "Mobility, Empire and Cross-Cultural Contacts in Mongol Eurasia." She has published extensively on Mongol and Pre-Mongol Central Asia (10th–14th centuries), including the Qara Khitai, the Qarakhanids and the Chaghadaids; the Mongol Empire; cross-cultural contacts between China and the Islamic world; nomadism; conversion; and Ilkhanid Baghdad. Her books include *Qaidu and the Rise of the Independent Mongol State in Central Asia* (Curzon, 1997), *The Empire of the Qara Khitai in Eurasian History: Between China and the Islamic World* (Cambridge University Press, 2005, 2008) and *Chinggis Khan* (Oxford: OneWorld Publications, 2007). She has edited and co-edited several volumes, the most recently published is *In the Service of the Khans: Elites in Transition in Mongol Eurasia*, published in *Asiatische Studien* 71/4 (2017), 1051–1245. She is currently working on two book projects and, together with Hodong Kim, is editing *The Cambridge History of the Mongol Empire* for Cambridge University Press.

Georg Christ (PhD Basel, 2006) is senior lecturer for medieval and early modern history at the University of Manchester. His recent publications include "Collapse and Continuity: Alexandria as a Declining City with a Thriving Port (13th–16th centuries)," in *The Routledge Handbook of Maritime Trade Around Europe, 1300–1600: Commercial Networks and Urban Autonomy*, ed. Wim Blockmans and Justyna Wubs-Mrozewicz (London: Routledge, 2017); "A King of Two Seas? Mamluk Maritime Trade Policy in the Wake of the Crisis of the 14th Century," *Ulrich Haarmann Memorial Lecture* (Berlin: EB-Verlag, 2017); "Differentiated Legality: Venetian Slave Trade in Alexandria," in *Slavery and the Slave Trade in the Eastern Mediterranean (c.1000–1500 CE)*, ed. Reuven Amitai and Christoph Cluse (Turnhout: Brepols, 2017). He is currently working on a book on Venetian and Mamluk entanglements in the fourteenth century.

Stephan Conermann (PhD University of Kiel, 1996) is Vice Rector of the University of Bonn, where he has been professor of Islamic Studies since 2003. He is also director of the Department of Near Eastern History and Languages. He is series editor of "Bonner Islamstudien" (BIS), "Bonner Asienstudien" (BAS), "Bonner islamwissenschaftliche Hefte" (BiH), "Narratologia Aliena" and "Mamluk Studies." His research interests include narrative strategies in historiographic texts, transition periods, mobility and immobility, global history, and rule and power. He focuses on the Mamluk and Delhi Sultanates, the Mughal Empire and the Crossroads Area "Transottomanica." His latest publications include *Mamlukica – Studies on the History and Society during the Mamluk Era/Studien zu Geschichte* *und Gesellschaft der Mamlukenzeit* (Göttingen: V&R unipress, 2013); (ed.) *Everything is on the Move: The 'Mamluk Empire' as a Node in (Trans-)Regional Networks* (Göttingen: V&R unipress, 2014); (ed.) *Kulturspezifische Erzählstrategien in "nicht-abendländischen" Lebensdarstellungen* (Göttingen: V&R unipress, 2015); (ed.) *Innovation oder Plagiat? Kompilationstechniken in der Vormoderne* (Göttingen: V&R unipress, 2015); (ed., with Gül Şen) *The Mamluk-Ottoman Transition Continuity and Change in Egypt and Bilād al-Shām in the Sixteenth Century* (Göttingen: V&R unipress, 2017).

Marie Favereau (PhD University of Paris IV-Sorbonne and Università degli Studi di San Marino, 2004) is research associate at the University of Oxford and member of the ERC project "Nomadic Empires: A World-Historical Perspective" (2014–19). She specializes in the history of the Golden Horde and her current research investigates trade and diplomacy between the Mongol Empire, Europe, and the Middle East. Among her publications, she edited *Les Conventions diplomatiques dans le monde musulman: L'Umma en partage (1258–1517)* (Cairo: Ifao, 2008) and *The Golden Horde and the Islamisation of the Eurasian Steppes* (Aix-en-Provence: MMSH-IREMAM, 2018). She has also co-edited, *The Golden Horde in World History* (Kazan: Sh.Marjani Institute of History, 2016), and she is the author of *La Horde d'Or. Les héritiers de Gengis Khan* (Lascelles: La Flandonnière, 2014) and *La Horde d'or et le sultanat mamelouk: naissance d'une alliance* (Cairo: Ifao, 2018).

Yehoshua Frenkel (PhD Hebrew University, 1992) is professor emeritus at the University of Haifa, and investigates the history of the Islamicate world in the late Middle Islamic Period. Among his recent publications are: "In Search of Consensus: Conflict and Cohesion among the Political Elite of the Late Mamlūk Sultanate," *The Medieval History Journal*, 19/2 (2016): 253–284; "Slave-Girls and Rewarded Teachers: Women in Mamlūk Sources," in Yuval Ben-Bassat (ed.), *Developing Perspectives in Mamluk History: Essays in Honor of Amalia Levanoni* (Leiden: Brill, 2017), 158–176; "Islam as a Peacemaking Religion: Self-Image, Medieval Theory, and Practice," Yvonne Friedman (ed.), *Religion and Peace: Historical Aspects* (London: Routledge, 2018), 84–97; "Some Notes Concerning the Trade and Education of Slave-Soldiers during the Mamluk Era," in Reuven Amitai and Christoph Cluse (eds.), *Slavery and the Slave Trade in the Eastern Mediterranean (11th–15th Centuries)* (Turnhout: Brepols, 2018), 187–212; "Mamluk Historiography Revisited: Narratological perspectives in Damascene Chronicles," in Stephan Conermann (ed.), *Mamluk Historiography Revisited – Narratological Perspectives* (Göttingen: V&R unipress and Bonn University Press, 2018), 27–50; "Mamluk Soundscape. A Chapter in Sensory History," *ASK Working Paper 31* (Bonn, July 2018).

Albrecht Fuess (PhD Cologne, 2000) studied History and Islamic Studies at the University of Cologne and Cairo University. His PhD dissertation was on the history of the Syro-Palestinian coast in the Mamluk era (1250–1517). In 2002 he became an Assistant Professor for Islamic Studies at the University of Erfurt. From 2007 to 2009 he was a fellow at *"Le Studium," the Institute of Advanced Studies of the University of Tours (France), where he worked on a project comparing the system of governance of the Mamluks, Safavids, and Ottomans in the 15th and 16th centuries.* Since 2010 he has beenProfessor of Islamic Studies at the Center for Near and Middle Eastern Studies (CNMS) at the Philipps-University Marburg. Among his recent publications are: co-edited with Bernard Heyberger and Phillipe Vendrix, *La frontière méditerranéenne (15e–17e siècles). Échanges, circulations, et affrontements*, "Etudes Renaissantes" 12 (Turnhout: Brepols, 2014); and, co-edited with Stefan Weninger, *Life with the Prophet? Examining Hadith, Sira and Qur'an in Honor of Wim Raven*, "Bonner Islamstudien" 36 (Berlin: EB Verlag, 2017).

Fiona Handley (PhD University College, London, 2004) is a Senior Lecturer in Learning and Teaching at the University of Brighton. An archaeologist by training, she currently works mainly in academic development, but retains a research interest in Islamic and Roman textiles from Egypt, and has researched and published textile and/or basketry finds from the sites of Quṣayr al-Qadīm/ Myos Hormos and Mons Porphyrites. Recent publications include "What Did People Wear at Myos Hormos? Evidence for Clothes from the Textile Finds," *HEROM: Journal on Hellenistic and Roman Material Culture* 6/2 (2017); (with Anne Regourd) "A Name of a Private Factory (or Workshop) on a Piece of Textile: The Case of the Document A.L.18 (Vienna)," in Salvatore Gaspa, Cécile Michel and Marie-Louise Nosch (eds.), *Textile Terminologies from the Orient to the Mediterranean and Europe, 1000 BC to 1000 AD* (Lincoln, NE: Zea E-Books, 2017), 374–382; "The Textiles: An Overview," in David Peacock and Lucy Blue (eds.) Quseir al-Qadim, vol. 2: *The Finds* (Oxford: Oxbow, 2010), 321–328; "The Matting, Basketry and Cordage," in David Peacock and Lucy Blue (eds.) Quseir al-Qadim, vol. 2: T*he Finds* (Oxford: Oxbow, 2010), 289–320; "The Textilesm," in David Peacock and Valerie Maxfield (eds.), *Excavations at Mons Porphyrites*, vol. 2: *The Finds* (London: Egypt Exploration Society, 2007), 355–371.

Robert Irwin was formerly a lecturer in the Department of Mediaeval History of the University of St Andrews. He is currently a Senior Research Associate of the Department of Middle Eastern Languages and Literatures of London University's School of Oriental and African Studies (which awarded him a Doctorate of Literature, Honoris Causa in 2016). He is the author of various books on Middle Eastern history and culture, including *For Lust of Knowing: The Orien-*

talists and Their Enemies and *Ibn Khaldun: An Intellectual Biography*, as well as seven novels.

Nikolas Jaspert (PhD Free University, Berlin, 1995) is Professor for Medieval History at Heidelberg University (since 2013) and Co-Director of the Centre of Excellence "Asia and Europe in a Global Context" (Heidelberg University). He is co-editor of the journal "Zeitschrift für Historische Forschung" (ZHF) and series editor of "Geschichte und Kultur der Iberischen Welt," "Spätmittelalterstudien," "Mittelmeerstudien," "Outremer. Studies in the Crusades and the Latin East", "Heidelberger Abhandlungen zur Mittleren und Neueren Geschichte, Neue Folge," and "Heidelberger Forschungen." Jaspert is a member of the Institut d'Estudis Catalans and was president of the Société Internationale des Historiens de la Méditerranée from 2013–2017. His academic work is centred on the medieval Mediterranean, the history of the Iberian Peninsula, the crusades, medieval religious orders and urban history. His latest publications include: (edited with Matthias Bley and and Stefan Köck): *Discourses of Purity in Transcultural Perspective (300–1600)* (Leiden: Brill 2015); (edited with Stefan Tebruck): *Die Kreuzzugsbewegung im römisch-deutschen Reich (11.–13. Jahrhundert)* (Ostfildern: Thorbecke 2016); (edited with Sebastian Kolditz): *Entre mers – Outre-mer. Spaces, Modes and Agents of Indo-Mediterranean Connectivity (3rd Century BCE-18th Century)* (Heidelberg: Heidelberg University Publishing 2018); (edited with Christian Neumann/Marco di Branco): *Ein Meer und seine Heiligen. Hagiographie im mittelalterlichen Mediterraneum* (Paderborn-München: Schöningh-Fink 2018).

Nimrod Luz (PhD Hebrew University, 2001) is professor at Kinneret College on the Sea of Galilee, Israel. A cultural geographer specializing in Islamic and Middle Eastern Studies, his interdisciplinary research and interests are the multiple and reflexive relations among society, culture, politics, and the built environment of the Middle East, past and present. His publications range over a wide variety of themes including cities and urbanism in the Middle East, Islamization and transformations of the cultural landscape, religion and the politics of sacred landscapes. His book, *Mamluk City of the Middle East* (Cambridge University Press, 2014), theorizes these issues and suggests a methodology of exploring and engaging past landscapes. His current research focuses on the infrastructures of urban *religiocity* in Acre – a comparative analysis of religion and urbanism. He has held numerous research positions and fellowships in international institutions, among which: Fulbright Scholar in Residence at Indiana University South Bend 2007–8; the Max Planck for the History of Science, Berlin; Topoi, Berlin; Erasmus at University College Dublin; and, recently at the Department of Religious Studies at Masaryk University in Brno (Czech Republic).

John L. Meloy (PhD University of Chicago, 1998) is Professor of History in the Department of History and Archaeology at the American University of Beirut, where he has also served as Director of the Center for Arab and Middle Eastern Studies and Associate Dean of the Faculty of Arts and Sciences. His research interests have always been rather eclectic, currently ranging from the medieval Hijaz and the Mamluk Sultanate of Egypt and Syria to the development of the field of Middle East studies in the twentieth century. Publications include: *Imperial Power and Maritime Trade: Mecca and Cairo in the Later Middle Ages* (Chicago: Center for Middle Eastern Studies/Middle East Documentation Center), re-issued in 2015 in a revised paperback edition; and, "Arab and Middle East Studies at AUB: Between Local Concerns and Global Pressures," in *One Hundred and Fifty*, ed. N. El-Cheikh, et al. (Beirut: AUB Press) in 2016. Forthcoming articles include: "'Aggression in the Best of Lands': Mecca in Egyptian-Indian Diplomacy in the Ninth/Fifteenth Century," in *Mamluk Cairo, a Crossroads for Embassies*, ed. F. Bauden and M. Dekkiche (Leiden: Brill); and "The Judges of Mecca and Mamluk Hegemony," in *Trajectories of State Formation across Fifteenth-Century Muslim West-Asia – Eurasian Parallels, Connections, Divergences*, ed. J van Steenbergen (Leiden: Brill).

Anne Regourd (PhD University Paris-Sorbonne) is an Associate of the CNRS in Paris. She has published Arabic texts with descriptions of their material and physical aspects, particularly the paper upon which they are written, so that they can be used by scholars as primary sources in their own right. Studies of this type include "Quinze mémos de transport de la collection Rémondon (musée du Louvre) datés de 957/1550," *The Arabist*, 35 (2015), 33–72, and the volume that she initiated and edited, *The Trade in Papers Marked with Non-Latin Characters.* "Documents and History," 2 (Leiden: Brill, 2018), where papers of Islamic manuscripts were taken as primary sources for the history of trade. Other recent publications include "Une requête (petition) au calife fatimide al-Ḥākim bi-amr Allāh (Rémondon 1, musée du Louvre)," *Bulletin of the School of Oriental and African Studies*, 80/3 (2017), 465–471; "Les documents Denise Rémondon conservés au Louvre: identification et inventaire d'une collection," *The Arabist*, 32 (2013), 117–126; "Arabic Documents from the Cairo Geniza in the David Kaufmann Collection in the Library of the Hungarian Academy of Sciences – Budapest," *Journal of Islamic Manuscripts*, 3/2 (2012), 1–19. She has published the Arabic documents of Quseir al-Qadim found between 1999 and 2003 by a team of archaeologists from Southampton University, for which see "Arabic Language Documents on Paper," in David Peacock and Lucy Blue (eds.), *Myos Hormos-Quseir al-Qadim. Roman and Islamic Ports on the Red Sea*, Volume 2: *The Finds from the 1999–2003 Excavations* (Oxford: Archaeopress, 2011), 339–344 (chapter 24), and has published various studies on Quseiri textiles with Fiona Handley.

Jo Van Steenbergen (PhD KU Leuven [Belgium], 2003) is a professor of Arabic and Islamic Studies at Ghent University (Belgium). His research interests cover various aspects of the social and cultural history of the pre-modern Islamic world, with a particular focus on Egypt and Syria in the later Islamic middle period (ca. 1200–1500), on the practices, discourses and structural appearances of power elites in the Sultanate of Cairo (ca. 1200–1517), on the de/construction of grand narratives in Mamluk/Islamic history, and on the development of new analytical and digital tools. He is the author of *Order Out of Chaos. Patronage, Conflict, and Mamluk Socio-Political Culture. 741–784/1341–1382* (Brill, 2006), of *Caliphate and Kingship in a Fifteenth-Century Literary History of Muslim Leadership and Pilgrimage. Al-Ḏahab al-masbūk fī ḏikr man ḥaǧǧa min al-ḫulafāʾ wa-l-mulūk. Critical Edition, annotated translation, and study* (Brill, 2016), and of various chapters and articles on 14th-century Qalāwūnid and 15th-century Mamluk history. He has been the recipient of a European Research Council Starting Grant (2009–14) and of a European Research Council Consolidator Grant (2016–21), for research projects on the intersection of political, social and cultural history in 15th-century Egypt and Syria. He is currently PI of the latter project ("The Mamlukisation of the Mamluk Sultanate-II. Historiography, political order, and state formation in 15th-century Egypt and Syria") as well as of a digital humanities project funded by the Flemish Research Foundation (FWO) ("Mamluk Prosopography Project. From a project-specific database to an open access digital humanities database for prosopographical research of late medieval Syro-Egyptian elites, practices, and networks"). Among his current publications in preparation are a pre-modern Islamic history textbook, a general history of the Mamluk Sultanate (with Patrick Wing), and a collective volume on the dynamics of 15th-century state formation in Muslim West-Asia.

Bethany Walker (PhD University of Toronto, 1998) came to the University of Bonn in 2013 from Missouri State University, where she was a Full Professor of Middle Eastern History. She currently holds the Chair of Mamluk Studies as a Research Professor in the Department of Islamic Studies and directs the Research Unit of Islamic Archaeology. Walker is a historically trained archaeologist and directs three long-term field projects in Israel and Jordan. She received her PhD in Islamic art and archaeology from the Department of Middle Eastern Studies at the University of Toronto in 1998 and held professorships for thirteen years in the United States before moving to Bonn. Committed to professional service, she is a long-term Board member of the American Center of Oriental Research in Amman) and has served as the liaison between the Jordanian Department of Antiquities and American and Canadian archaeologists since 2001. Among her many publications is *Jordan in the Late Middle Ages: Transformation of the*

Mamluk Frontier. "Chicago Studies on the Middle East Monograph Series" (Chicago: Middle East Documentation Center, University of Chicago, 2011).

Koby Yosef (PhD Tel Aviv University, 2011) is a lecturer in the Department of Arabic at the Bar-Ilan University. His research interests include the history and historiography of the Mamluk Sultanate. Currently, he is working on a monograph on the transformation of the family of *mamlūks* during the Mamluk Sultanate. He published several articles on the social ties of *mamlūks*, among them most recently "Usages of Kinship Terminology during the Mamluk Sultanate and the Notion of the '*Mamlūk* Family'," in Yuval Ben-Bassat (ed.), *Developing Perspectives in Mamluk History: Essays in Honor of Amalia Levanoni* (Leiden: Brill, 2017), pp. 16–75.

Cihan Yüksel Muslu (PhD Harvard University, 2007) is an associate professor of history at University of Houston (Texas, USA). Her research interests include the social and cultural history of the Ottoman Empire, interactions between medieval and early-modern Islamic empires, and Mediterranean history. In 2009–2010, she was a senior fellow at ANAMED at Koç University (Istanbul, Turkey). She has published articles in *Archivum Ottomanicum* and has edited volumes. Her book *The Ottomans and the Mamluks: Imperial Diplomacy and Warfare* came out in 2014; the Turkish translation of her book was published in 2016. Her most recent project concerns networks between the Ottoman and Mamluk worlds.

List of Illustrations

Fuess

Table	Resource Situation around the Turn of the 16th Century in the Middle East	72

Luz

Map 1	Mamluk Jerusalem – Layout of Monumental-Public Buildings and Vernacular Components	131
Picture	A Luxurious House Located on one of the Main Thoroughfares of Mamluk Jerusalem	137
Map 2	Layout of Pious Buildings in Jerusalem	143

Yosef

Table A	*Mamlūks* Labeled "Tatar" who Arrived in the Sultanate after the 1320s	175–77
Table B	*Mamlūks* Originating from the East after the 1320s	178
Table C	"Persian" (*'Ajam*) *Mamlūks* and Envoys to the Timurids	179–80

Christ

Fig. 1	Beachhead and Landing Areas (schematic)	220
Fig. 2	Arsuf Castle (plan)	221
Fig. 3	Arsuf Castle (aerial photograph)	221
Fig. 4	Fortifications of Chania, Venetian Crete	222
Fig. 5	ʿAtlīt	222
Fig. 6	Lines of Coastal Defence	223
Fig. 7	Burj as-Sulṭān	234

Meloy

Table 1	*Ijāzas*, identified by authorizer, issued to women *ḥadīth* scholars in Mecca, by region and city, as reported by Najm al-Dīn ʿUmar ibn Fahd in his *al-Durr al-Kamīn* (sample of 438 reports)	474
Table 2	*Ribāṭs* founded in Mecca by origin of patron and date of foundation (59 total); based on the compilation of Richard Mortel, "Ribats in Mecca during the Medieval Period," BSOAS, 31 (1998): 29–50	474–5
Table 3	*Madrasas* founded in Mecca by origin of patron and date of foundation (24 total); supplementing the compilation of Richard Mortel, "Madrasas in Mecca during the Mamluk Period," BSOAS, 30 (1997): 236–52	475
Table 4	Shipping to Mecca by port of origin, from 887/1482–3 to 908/1502–3 (197 total), as recorded by ʿIzz al-Dīn ʿAbd al-ʿAzīz ibn Fahd in his *Bulūgh al-Qirā*	475

Regourd / Handley

Map 1	Map showing location of Qusayr al-Qadīm and its regional connections. Drawn by Penny Copeland, University of Southampton	486
Figure 1	QAQ03T126–134. Waste Offcuts from Garment Making	488
Figure 2	QAQ99T561. A Cotton *ikat* Textile with a Pattern of Red, White and Blue Chevrons	491
Figure 3	QAQ03T146. A Larger Piece of Surviving Fabric with a Blue Border and Two Blue Stripes Running along the Longer Edge	492

Index

Note: The definite article in Arabic (al-) has been ignored in the alphabetical order of the index.

Abaqa (Ilkhan) 69, 136, 275
ʿAbbasids 347, 427
ʿAbd al-Bāsiṭ b. Khalīl al-Malaṭī, see: al-Malaṭī
ʿAbd al-Salām al-Qifṭī 484
Abdāl Mūsā (Sufi) 414
Abdala Abenxando 330, 331
Abdalwadids 24, 314, 315
al-ʿAbdarī (Maghrebi traveler) 282, 283, 300, 304
Abkhaz, Abkhazes 114, 116, 118, 120
Abu Lughod, Janet 18, 27, 32
Abū al-Fidāʾ (Ayyūbid prince and historian) 157–159, 163, 164, 184, 193, 196, 205, 206
Abū Ḥamīd Muḥammad ibn Aḥmad ibn Ḍiyāʾ 461
Abū Ḥammū (Zayānid ruler) 284
Abū Madyān (Sufi saint) 294
Abū Mufarrij (merchant in Quseir) 480, 484, 485, 487
Abū Saʿīd (Ilkhan) 150, 358
Abū Thābit (Merinid ruler) 284
Abū Yaʿqūb Yūsuf (Merinid ruler) 284
Abulustayn (Elbistan, in Anatolia) 157, 164
Abulustayn, battle of 157, 164
Abyssinia 489, 490, see also: Ethiopia 48, 49, 458, 479, 489
Acre 189, 215–219, 227, 228, 230–235, 238, 249, 251–254, 281, 368, 505
Ada Pazar (in Turkey) 117
al-ʿĀdil, al-Malik (Ayyubid ruler) 481
Ādar (in Transjordan) 273
Aden 30, 59, 459, 466, 475, 483, 484, 488–490, 495
- Gulf of 459
adhān (call to prayer) 328, 330, 331
Adorno, Anselm 111, 119
Afghanistan 368
Africa, Africans 9, 18–20, 22, 26, 30, 32, 40, 47, 48, 53, 55, 60, 63, 64, 66, 70, 74, 89, 109, 111, 120, 146, 161; see also: East Africa, Maghreb, West Africa
Age of Discovery 121, 448, 449
Agoston, Gabor 68, 73
Aḥmad I (Ottoman sultan) 418
Aḥmad b. Īnāl, al-Muʾayyad (Mamluk sultan) 98–99, 446, 450
Aḥmad b. Uways (Jalāyirid ruler) 373
Aḥmad, Ḥasan 305
Aḥmedī (Anatolian scholar) 398–99, 401–02
Ahwānī, Dr. 289
ʿajāʾib (fantastic stories) 50
Ajdābiya 283
ʿAjlūn (in Jordan) 83–84, 266–67, 273–74
akābir al-dawla ("leading men of the regime") 97
al-Akhawī, Aḥmad b. Muḥammad al-Khujandī al-Madanī (Central Asian scholar) 381–382, 385
al-Akhlāṭī, Ḥusayn (Sufi) 402
ʿAlāʾ al-Dawla (Dulkader ruler) 433, 437
Alarcón Santón, Maximiliano A. 309, 332
Alans 118–119, 151, 356
Albania, Albanians (in Balkans) 111–113
Alemany, Ramon 317

Aleppo 9, 69, 71, 110, 136, 158, 173, 201, 228, 238, 379, 398, 404, 408, 416–17, 420, 437, 447, 449, 460, 462, 474
Alexander the Great 48, 51–52, 59, 436
Alexandria 9, 29, 30, 33, 64, 67, 71, 92, 98, 99, 102, 111, 189–191, 215–219, 226–230, 233–236, 238–241, 243, 245, 247, 250–254, 280–288, 290–294, 296–300, 303, 308, 318, 334, 416, 417, 436, 437, 443, 470, 462, 474, 484, 489, 502
Alfonso III (king of Aragon) 312, 326
Alfonso V the Magnificent (king of Aragon, etc.) 314, 318, 341
Algeria 109, 121, 282, 285, 286, 325
Algiers 109, 282, 285, 287, 294
Alí Benxarnit 325
ʿAlī ibn Abī Ṭālib 51, 434
ʿAlī Jurjānī (Central Asian scholar) 379
ʿAlī Kuşçu (Ottomanscholar) 411, 412
ʿAlī Pādshāh 82, 84, 100
ʿAlībāy min Amīr ʿAlam 200
Almaliq 384
Almeria 283, 286, 287, 292
Almohad 296, 300, 321, 332, 333, 501
Almoravids 382
Almuñecar (al-Munakkab, in Spain) 291
Alṭun Khujā al-Ibrāhīmī al-Ẓāhirī 177
Alwand (Aq Qoyunlu ruler) 432
Alwīn Bughā (supposed son of Qaidu) 370
amān (grant of safety) 369
ambassadors and envoys ; see also: diplomacy 39, 59, 70, 284, 289–291, 299, 303, 310, 311, 316, 352, 357, 360, 418, 420
Americas 19, 26
Amin, Ash 476
Amin, Samir 27
Amīr (commander, "emir") 43, 64, 104, 116, 219, 236, 238, 239, 240, 245, 353, 436, 441, 446
amīr al-ʿarab (chief of the Bedouin) 93
Amman 141, 146, 186, 206, 262, 269, 273, 507
al-Amshāṭī 47, 57
Anaṣ (father of sultan Barqūq) 196
Anatolia 24, 43, 49, 62, 68, 80–82, 84, 101, 106, 130, 146, 156, 185, 189, 213, 271, 274, 345, 354, 359, 391–399, 401, 402, 412–416, 418, 429, 431–440, 445, 460, 463, 465, 466, 469; see also: Asia Minor, Bilād al-Rūm
al-Andalus 49, 279, 282–284, 293, 295, 306, 314, 320, 322, 323, 332, 333, 341; see also: Iberia, Spain
Andi River in Caucasia 117
Angevins 9, 328
Ankara 273, 391, 395, 396, 398, 400, 401, 402, 403, 408, 413, 414, 415, 419, 424, 425, 426, 427, 428, 429, 432
– battle of 403, 432
Annaba 282–285, 287, 288
Antalya 416–418
Antioch 368
Appelániz Ruiz de Galarretain, Francisco Javier 28
Āqbardī (Great-Dawadar) 70
AqbirdīṬaṭar al-Ẓāhirī 177
Aqbirdī al-Ẓāhirī al-Khāṣṣakī 177
AqQoyunlu/Akkoyunlu 95
Aqqūsh al-Mawṣilī 201
Aqṭuwah al-Mūsāwī 180
ʿArab, Mollā (ʿAlā al-Dīn al-ʿArabī) 408
Arabia, Arabians 54, 68, 456, 458, 464.40, 473, 489
Arabian Nights, see: *One Thousand and One Nights* 54
Arabia Felix 458, see also: Yemen
Arabian Sea 42, 190
Arabic language, literature and sources 168, 169, 172, 201, 382, 110, 156, 182, 279, 280, 298, 303, 359, 367
Arabs 24, 47, 48, 52, 53, 60, 83, 93, 103, 110, 115, 157, 192, 205, 215, 282, 284, 285, 295, 300, 316, 372, 378, 379, 385, 387, 388, 403, 409, 410, 491; see also: Bedouin
Aragon 6, 24, 29, 245, 297, 307–341
– Royal Archives in, see: Archivo de la Corona de Aragón
Aranbughā al-Yūsufī al-Nāṣirī 177, 180
Arbel, Benjamin 166, 185, 195, 196–198, 211, 232, 249
Archeology 10

architecture, vernacular 123, 126–129, 132, 133, 144, 146, 147
Archivo de la Corona de Aragón (Arxiu de la Corona d'Aragó) 309, 317, 324, 325, 332, 336, 339, 341, 342
Arci (Caucasian language) 117
Ardabil (in Azerbaijan) 432
Arghun (Ilkhan) 313, 351, 364
Arghūn Shāh al-Baydamurī al-Ẓāhirī 180
Ariqṭāy 160
Aristotle 47
Armenia, Armenians 9, 24, 45, 47, 110, 113, 116, 119, 188, 189, 192, 194, 195, 196, 198, 201, 359, 369, 432; see also: Cilicia
Arkas (Circassian tribe) 115
Arrān/Arran 347, 351–353
Arsūf (on Palestinian coast) 219, 221
Artillery 71, 229, 236, 244, 435, 437, 438, 443, 444; see also: cannons
As (Ossetes) 115, 116
Asanbāy al-Zardakāsh al-Ẓāhirī 174, 176, 179
Asanbughā al-Dawādārī 179
Asanbughā min Ṣafar Khujā 177
Asanbughā al-Sharābī 181
Asanbughā al-Yashbakī al-Nāṣirī 177
Asandamur Kurjī 198
Aṣfūn al-Jabalayn (Upper Egypt) 457
Ashdod 224
Ashkelon 219
Ashlūn bint Sutatāy 152
Ashrafi dinars 64, 470
Ashtor, Eliyahu 9, 170, 209, 228, 232, 250, 416, 425
Asia 6, 19, 20, 25–27, 30–34, 37, 40, 44, 49–53, 55, 58, 63, 64, 68, 70, 74, 79–82, 85, 86, 87, 88, 91, 99–104, 106, 111, 113, 114, 120, 121, 156, 165, 166, 181, 186–188, 192, 197, 202, 208, 210–215, 232, 244, 249, 250, 289, 293, 314, 333, 345, 348, 351, 361, 363, 364, 367, 368, 369–389, 445, 446, 448, 455, 456, 463, 466–469, 472, 476, 477, 478, 483, 485, 502, 505–507
Asia Minor 64, 68, 114, 188, 218, 289, 293; see also: Anatolia
ʿĀşıḳpaşazāde (Ottoman historian) 415
Asnā 457
Astrakhan 345
Aswān 484, 489
Atiya, Aziz 308, 329
Atlantic Ocean 20, 76
ʿAtlīt (Château des Pèlerins in Palestine) 219, 222, 235, 244
Aubin, Jean 348, 466, 472, 477
Avars 119
Awlād al-Nās (sons of Mamluks) 183, 187, 212
Ayalon, David 9, 69, 113, 139, 150, 151, 169, 183, 186, 203, 215, 346, 395, 418, 433, 438, 442, 445, 446
Ayas in Cilicia 189, 359
Aydhāb 482, 483, 490
Aydınids 398, 399, 401
ʿAyn Tāb 289
al-ʿAynī, Badr al-Dīn (Mamluk-era writer) 44, 175, 178, 205
Aydughdī al-Khwārizmī (Mamluk ambassador) 284
Aydughdī al-Talīlī (Mamluk ambassador) 284
Aytamush al-Ashrafī 159, 165, 166
Ayyūbids 93, 141, 149, 150, 211, 240, 347
Azerbaijan/Azerbeidjan 95, 345, 347, 348, 353, 384, 432, 439
al-Azmeh, Aziz 26, 48
al-Azraqī (Meccan historian) 461

Baalbek 460, 462
Bāb al-Silsila (Jerusalem) 70
Bāb al-Zuwayla (Cairo) 438
Bacharach, Jere 64, 73
Baghdad 82, 84, 139, 147, 174, 313, 348, 376, 377, 382, 383, 386, 388, 404, 418, 502
Bahādur Ḥalāwa 169
Bahādur al-Manṣūrī, al-Ḥājj 162
Baiju (Mongol commander) 349
al-Bākharzī/Bāḫarzī (Sufi shaykh) 485
al-Bakrī (Arabic geographer) 280, 282, 302
Baktamur al-Abūbakrī al-Ashrafī 177
Baktamur Jilliq 178
Balabān al-Manṣūrī 160

al-Balawī (Magrhebi traveler) 286, 287, 297, 302, 306
Balearic Islands 282
Balkans 65, 67, 68, 156, 214, 398, 401, 421, 422
Baltic Sea 18
Banū Faḍl Bedouins 110
Banū Fahd in Mecca 470, see also under: Ibn Fahd
Banū Ḥusayn Bedouins 284
Banū Juhma region of Jordan 264
Banū Khāṣṣ Bak 96, 97, 99
Banū Māza, see: Burhān Family
Banū Sāsān 54
Banū Sulaym Bedouin 300
Banū Thābit 300
Baraq (Chaghadaid khan) 368, 372
Barbary 109, 120, 121, 235 see also: Maghreb, North Africa
al-Bābartī, Akmal al-Dīn (Mamluk scholar) 399, 402
Barbara (in Somalia) 54, 59, 81, 116, 121, 158, 207, 312, 328, 335, 342, 414, 426, 434, 450, 458, 466, 475
Barcelona 19, 25, 29, 30, 33, 34, 67, 73, 216, 249, 307–315, 317–320, 322–327, 333–336, 339–342, 441, 448, 467, 476
Barghūtī, ʿAbd al-Laṭīf 300
Barker, Hannah 165, 200, 209
Barkey, Karen 88–90, 96, 98, 102
Barqa (=Cyrenaica) 282, 283, 287, 292, 295, 297, 300
Barsbāy, al-Ashraf (Mamluk sultan) 81, 101, 112, 170, 174, 177, 190
Basel 111, 112, 502
Bashkent, battle of 434, 443
Bashqurd 193
Bashtāk al-Nāṣirī 168
basmala 83, 493
Basna (Circassian tribe) 115
Basṭa (Baza) 291, 292
al-Baṭḥā' 294
Batu 384
Bavaria 111, 120
Baybars, al-Ẓāhir (Mamluk sultan) 153
Baybars al-Jāshankīr, al-Muẓẓafar (Mamluk sultan) 198
Baybars al-Manṣūrī (Mamluk historian) 153, 284, 285, 303, 304, 369, 374, 376, 386, 387
Baybughā al-Muẓaffarī al-Ẓāhirī 174, 176
Baybughā Rūs 94
Baydarā al-Manṣūrī 159
Bāyezīd I (Ottoman sultan) 399, 402, 403, 413, 417
Bāyezīd II (Ottoman sultan) 62, 407–10, 418–20
Bayly, John 18, 19, 31, 33, 86, 102
bayt (Ar. house, residential unit) 194
Bayt Ramah (in Jordan Valley) 262
Bedouin 84, 85, 102, 238, 261, 284, 285, 295, 300
beglerbeg (chief Mongol commander) 352
Behrens-Abouseif, Doris 58, 209, 363
Beirut 7, 41–43, 46–50, 57–59, 63, 69, 72, 73, 81, 82, 93, 97, 103, 105, 106, 115, 119, 135, 146, 151–154, 157–162, 168, 170, 175, 177, 178, 179, 182, 183, 186, 188, 190, 192, 193, 199, 201, 205–208, 210–212, 216, 218, 225, 228, 235, 238, 241, 243, 251, 252, 254, 281, 283–285, 288, 291, 293, 296, 300, 304–306, 312, 318, 319, 337, 339, 352, 359, 362, 363, 369–372, 377, 381, 386–389, 392, 403, 425, 435, 436, 445, 449, 450, 453, 482, 484, 497–500, 506
Bejaia (in Algeria) 325; see also Bijāya
Bektāşī Sufi movement 432
Bengal 464, 465, 467
Berbers 47, 295
Berenice (Barnīq) 283
Berke (khan of Golden Horde) 34, 55, 58, 64, 73, 78, 82, 86, 103, 105, 151, 170, 202, 209, 213, 346–350, 359, 361, 372, 382, 384, 387, 393, 394, 396, 413, 414, 426–428, 482, 498
Berkechar 384
Bertrand, Romain 110, 111, 119, 479
Bible 52
Bijāya 281–285, 287, 288, 292, 294, 295; see also Bejaia
Bilād al-Qatrān ("Land of Pitch") 288

Bilād al-Rūm 188, 192, 210, 391, 395, 398, 465; see also Anatolia, Asia Minor
Bilād al-Shām, see: Syria
Bilād al-Sūdān, see: Sudan
Bilyāna 285
al-Biqāʿī (Mamluk historian) 203, 404, 406, 421, 422, 424
Black Death 34, 102, 262, 445, 446, 449
Black Sea 9, 114, 166, 185, 345, 352, 354–356, 360, 364
Blake, Stephen 86, 89
de Boateriis, Nicola 185
Bohemia 66
de Bonnesmains, Guillaume 318
Borsch, Stuart 446
Bosphorus 348, 359
de Boucicault, Jean (Genoese admiral) 190, 230, 249
Braudel, Fernand 73
von Breydenbach, Bernhard 111, 119
Britain, British
- navy 241
Broadbridge, Anne 210, 233
de la Brocquière, Bertrandon 111, 119
Brunschvig, Robert 293
Buddhism 20
Bukhara 44, 349, 368, 376, 378, 380–384, 389
al-Bukhārī (Ḥadīth scholar) 97, 378, 383, 388
Būlāq (port of Cairo) 228, 242–244, 248
Bulgarians 110, 111, 113
bullion 63, 67
Burbank, Jane 87
Burdbak al-Ẓāhirī Jaqmāq al-Mashṭūb 201
Bureaucracy 86, 87, 154, 402, 438
Burgoyne, Michael 142
Burgundians 111
Burhān al-Dīn, Qāḍī 135, 397, 398
Burhān family (leaders of Bukhara) 380
Burj al-Sulṭān (in Acre) 234 n.
Burjiyya regiment 165, 167, 197
Bursa 46, 402, 405, 407, 408, 413, 416, 417, 420, 427
Byzantine Empire, Byzantines 9, 24, 188, 192, 362, 397
Bzedux (in Caucasia) 117

Caesarea (in Palestine) 219
Caffa (in Crimea) 113, 114, 185, 354, 356, 360
Cagliari (in Sardinia) 285
Cairo 5, 9, 31, 36, 39–41, 43–45, 48–50, 55–57, 59, 64, 66, 70, 73, 75–77, 80–84, 91, 93–98, 100–105, 110, 112, 118–120, 134, 146, 174, 205–207, 209, 212–214, 217–18, 226, 228–29, 238–241, 246, 251–52, 255, 262, 264–65, 272–73, 279, 285, 288–89, 291–92, 296, 305–06, 318, 320, 326–328, 333–335, 348, 350, 357, 362–364, 376, 387–389, 391–393, 395, 397, 399, 402, 404–05, 412, 414–415, 417–18, 422, 424–426, 428–29, 434, 436, 438–39, 441, 445, 448–49, 453–455, 457–466, 470–474, 476–479, 483–485, 487, 490, 498–99, 500, 503–04, 506–07
Citadel 39, 43, 49, 56, 70, 75–77, 82, 118, 269
Calicut/Calcutta 30, 56, 205, 372, 461, 465–66, 468, 472, 475–76
Caliphs, caliphate 9, 346–47, 363, 471, 507 see also: ʿAbbasids, Umayyads, Hafsids
Cambay 461, 464–466, 470, 475
Cambini, Andrea (Italian writer) 440
Candia (in Crete) 291
Çandarlı Ḫalīl Paşa (Ottoman grand wazir) 410
Cannons 68; see also: artillery
Cantoria (Qantūra) 286–87
Cape of Good Hope 436
Cape St. Mark (in Sardinia) 281
Capetians 327
Cartagena 282
Carthaginians 238
Casablanca 140
Caspian Sea 348
Castile 24, 191, 275, 313, 335
Catalonia, Catalans 60, 285, 314, 320, 326, 331
- Royal Archives of, see: Archivo de la Corona de Aragón
Cathay 368, 375

Caucasus, Caucasians 9, 82, 114, 117–121, 185, 187–88, 196, 345, 348, 353–54; see also: Armenia, Georgia, Circassia
- languages of 110, 113
Cefalu (in Sicily) 282
Cem (Ottoman prince) 419, 425, 427
Central Asia 6, 20, 25, 30, 40, 49, 53, 55, 187, 214, 345, 364, 367, 368, 369, 370, 372, 374, 375, 376, 377, 378, 379, 380, 383, 384, 385, 386, 388, 483, 502
Ceuta (Sabta) 281
Ceylon 9, 53
Chaghadai (son of Chinggis Khan) 367, 380
Chaghadaids/Chaghatayids/Chaghatayid Khanate 368, 370, 372, 373, 375, 384, 385, 386, 502
Chāldirān, battle of 435, 436, 439, 444
Changshi (Chaghadaid khan) 372
Chania/Chanea 219, 222
Chapar (Mongol khan in Central Asia) 51, 370
Chapoutot-Remadi, Mounira 102, 305
Chase-Dunn, Christopher 27, 33
China, Chinese 19, 20, 26, 49, 54, 55, 56, 63, 68, 110, 156, 345, 351, 364, 375, 386, 467, 468, 476, 477, 478, 479, 502
Chinese language 110
Chinggis Khan 78, 345, 347, 351, 367, 368, 370, 372, 383, 386, 502
Chinggisids 370, 372
Chios 114
Christ, Georg 6, 29, 74, 215, 250, 251, 252, 334, 502
Christians, Christianity 20, 24, 42, 53, 68, 109, 110, 111, 113, 141, 189, 191, 194, 195, 196, 197, 198, 201, 204, 210, 213, 235, 282, 290, 297, 305, 320, 321, 322, 325, 326, 327, 328, 331, 332, 333, 340
- apostates from 109
- Oriental Christians 326
- violence against 327
Cilicia 62, 432, 433, 437
Circassia, Circassians 47, 112, 113, 115, 117–120, 183, 185, 188, 189, 196, 200–203, 209
Circassian language 113, 118
Circassian period of Mamluk rule 28, 55, 109, 112, 117, 119, 120, 155
college, Muslim, see: madrasa 141, 164, 262, 264, 272, 273, 382, 396, 397, 402, 411, 412, 413, 459, 463, 464, 475, 477
Colley, Linda 109
commerce, see: trade 28, 33, 34, 67, 73, 74, 101, 114, 210, 245, 249, 250, 254, 279, 311, 319, 325, 334, 335, 337, 338, 365, 395, 416, 417, 427, 448, 460, 467, 469, 470, 472, 473, 476, 478, 479, 498, 499
Comoro Islands 52
Conermann, Stephan 5, 11, 17, 58, 59, 80, 91, 102, 105, 211, 251, 252, 275, 276, 334, 341, 449, 476, 501, 502, 503
Consell de Cent 317
Constantine (Qusanṭīna) 254, 282, 285, 287, 288, 294
Constantinople 95, 113, 214, 348, 405, 407, 409, 411, 426, 432, 438 see also: Istanbul
Contarini, Thomà 71
conversion to Islam 210, 349, 357, 364, 407
Cook, Michael 26, 27
Cooper, Frederick 87
Çöke, plain of (near Edirne) 407
copper 87, 102, 499
Copts 24, 194, 326, 335
Corsica 315
cotton 228, 231, 232, 483, 487, 489, 490, 491, 496, 497
Coulon, Damien 28, 29, 334, 335, 336, 342
courtyards, courtyard houses 130, 132, 133, 134, 135, 136, 145
Crete 120, 198, 222, 247, 252, 281, 286, 291, 430
Crimea 9, 114, 180, 181, 214, 345, 346, 348, 352, 354, 359
Crusaders, Crusades 19, 27, 75, 112, 150, 191, 211, 218, 220, 224, 225, 250, 254, 348, 368, 431, 440, 444/20, 25, 27, 59, 103, 190, 191, 208, 209, 210, 211, 338, 387, 449, 505 see also: Franks
Cumans 185, 214; see also Qipchaqs
Custodia di Terra Sancta 327, 328

Cyprus, Cypriotes 64, 70, 72, 73, 102, 189.190, 208, 209, 210, 213, 218, 231, 238, 242, 243, 244, 253, 273, 286, 288, 445, 450/64
Cyrenaica, see: Barqa 285, 295, 300, 301

Dabbāb Bedouin 300
Dabul 465, 466, 475
Dahlak 468, 490
Dajjāl (Anti-Christ) 52, 53
Damanhur 462
Damascus 9, 40, 44, 46, 49, 83, 92, 93, 94, 97, 98, 101, 105, 110, 113, 121, 163, 174, 179, 201, 206, 208, 211, 218, 226, 228, 238, 249, 274, 288, 304, 306, 363, 369, 373, 374, 376, 379, 387, 398, 399, 404, 433, 444, 460, 461, 462, 474
Damietta 30, 229, 239
Damurdāsh al-Iqrīṭishī 198
Danzig 112
dār (house, residence) 46
Dār al-Ḥarb (Abode of War) 41
Dār al-Islām (Abode of Islam) 41, 314, 315, 320, 323, 329, 349
darb (Ar. quarter) 140, 141
Darwin, John 20
Datini accounts 232
David, king of Georgia 118
Dāvūd-i Ḳayseri (Ottoman scholar) 426
dawla (dynasty, regime, state) 83, 84, 97, 105, 115, 122, 172, 187, 206, 433, 437
Dawlat Khujā al-Ẓāhirī 174, 176
Dawlat al-Atrāk ("The Turkish State," i. e. the Mamluk Sultanate) 115, 122, 214
Dawlatbāy (Mamluk governor) 419
defters (tax registers), Ottoman 259
Delhi 37, 58, 348, 375, 384, 476, 477, 478, 502
Delhi Sultanate 348, 375, 502
Denmark 112
Derbent 352, 353
DeWeese, Devin 210, 364, 385, 386, 389
al-Dhahabī (Mamluk historian) 155, 205, 376, 377, 383, 387
dhimmi, dhimmīs 246
Dhū al-Qarnayn, see: Alexander the Great
Dido (Caucasian language) 117, 388
dīnār 54, 64, 73, 243, 294, 357, 358, 359, 383, 446, 465, 470
diplomacy 39, 41, 55, 58, 59, 208, 209, 311, 312, 314, 315, 317, 318, 319, 320, 326, 329, 335, 337, 357, 361, 363, 364, 386, 418, 427, 429, 449, 477, 503, 506, 508; see also: ambassadors and envoys
dirham 63, 65, 66, 67, 92, 135, 495
Dishnā (in Upper Egypt) 484
dīwān al-inshā' (chancery) 361
dīwān al-khāṣṣ (sultan's private fisc) 239
Diyarbakr 81
Dniester 352
Dnieper 352
Dodecanese 286
Dolfin, Biago 29
Dome of the Rock 325
Dominicans 327
Doumerc, Bernard 280, 303, 305
Doyle, Michael 87
Du'a (Mongol khan) 351
Ducat 63, 64, 65, 73, 113, 439
Dulkadirids/Dhū 'l-Qadrids 395, 414, 419
al-Duqayr (in Transjordan) 267
Dusay, Pere 318

East Africa 70, 475
East Asia 20, 26, 27, 50, 104
Eastern Europe 345
East India 483
Edigü 184
Edirne 68, 407
Edward I (king of England) 368
Egypt 5, 9, 19, 24, 29, 30, 34, 40, 45, 49, 52, 58–60, 63, 64, 66, 69, 70, 73–76, 78, 79, 84, 91, 92, 98, 100–105, 110–121, 132, 145, 149, 152, 154, 155, 161, 174, 179, 180, 182–184, 186, 187, 194, 195, 200, 205, 208–214, 228, 237–239, 241, 250, 253, 254, 260, 263, 267, 274, 276, 279–285, 288, 291–298, 300–305, 310, 311, 313–319, 322, 324, 326, 328, 329, 331, 332, 335, 340, 342, 345, 346, 348, 358, 360, 365, 369, 374–378, 380, 387–389, 392, 395–398, 402, 408, 416, 417, 420, 424, 426, 427, 430,

431, 437, 438, 445, 446, 448, 449, 450, 455, 457–463, 465, 469, 474–476, 487–489, 493, 496, 498–501, 503–507
Upper Egypt 293, 457, 460
Eğridir 397
Eickelman, Dale 140, 146, 426, 428
Eisenstadt, Shmuel 86, 87
Elmalı (in Teke, Anatolia) 414
emir, see: amīr 43, 64, 104, 116, 219, 236, 238, 239, 240, 245, 353, 436, 441, 446
Emīr Çelebi (Ottoman physician) 412
Emīr Sulṭān (Sufi) 413
endowment, see: waqf
England, Englishmen 19, 270, 275, 368, 449/109, 121
enslavement, see: slaves and slave trade 91, 170, 187, 196
envoys, see: ambassadors 70, 71, 179, 311, 313, 319, 348, 350, 352, 353, 357, 359, 369, 394, 421, 434, 439
Eretna 398
Escorial 289
Esen Boqa (Chaghadaid khan) 370
espionage, see: spies
Eşrefoğlu Rūmī (Sufi) 427, 428
ethnicity 45
ethnography 115
Ethiopia, Ethiopians 48, 49, 424, 458, 479/489, 490/see also: Abyssinia
Euphrates 81, 348, 373
Eurasia 9, 10, 18, 20, 26, 32, 37, 53, 55, 89, 102, 208, 210, 211, 213, 250, 345, 346, 351, 363, 364, 386, 389, 425, 477, 501, 502, 503, 506
Europe, Europeans 19, 20, 25–27, 30–34, 63–66, 68, 74, 113, 120, 121, 156, 184–186, 188, 190, 191, 193, 195, 209, 218, 238, 249–251, 254, 258, 259, 270, 290, 303, 310, 315, 320, 322, 328, 331, 334–338, 342, 345, 352, 389, 417, 427, 432, 443, 448, 476, 483, 492, 502–505/42, 63, 65, 110, 112, 150, 195, 196, 434, 436, 439, 440
Evranos Bey (Ottoman commander) 415

Fabri, Felix 111, 119
factionalism 99, 104
Famagusta 185, 253, 288
Far East, see: East Asia 215, 238, 488
al-Faraḍī, ʿAlāʾ al-Dīn (scholar and Sufi) 376
Faraj (Mamluk sultan), see: al-Nāṣir Faraj 94, 97, 177, 180, 183, 189, 195, 200
Farghāna (in Tajikistan) 382
Fars 462, 474
al-Fāsī (Meccan historian) 460, 467, 476
fatḥnāme (letter proclaiming victory) 405, 406
Fāṭima bint ʿAlī b. Khāṣṣ Bak 96
Fatimids 304
fatwā (legal opinion) 208, 232, 249, 250
Feldbauer, Pete 24, 26, 33
Fenārī, Mollā Şemseddīn Muḥammad b. Ḥamza 391
Ferrer, Rafael 317
Ferrer i Mallol, María Teresa 336
Fez 284, 286
Fiqh (Muslim jurisprudence) 57, 83, 146, 404
firāsah (physiognomy) 46, 47, 57
Firdawsī 116
firearms 67, 73, 103, 229, 250, 252, 431, 441, 442, 443, 444, 445, 447, 448, 449, 450 see also: artillery, cannons, handguns
Flanders 295, 298
Florence, Florentines 185, 250, 255, 339, 362, 476
Formont, Marie-Christine 146
fortifications 217, 220, 222, 225, 229, 230, 231, 290
France, French 19, 24, 67, 231, 249, 251, 254, 306, 313, 317, 332, 335, 335, 336, 337, 340, 351, 362, 424, 504/28, 61, 62, 68, 112, 190, 210, 247, 252, 313, 318
Franciscans 327, 328, 355
Frank, Andre Gunder 27
Franks 9, 37, 42, 47, 59, 64, 180, 182, 188, 191, 193, 195, 196, 198, 201, 209, 244, 316, 364, 368, 434
Frankish merchants 171; see also Genoa, Venice, etc
Freitag, Ulrike 23
Frescobaldi, Lionardo 112

Fuess, Albrecht 5, 6, 61, 73, 103, 209, 210, 213, 215, 226, 251, 252, 337, 431, 449, 504
fuqahā' (legal experts) 473
fuqarā' (Sufi mendicants) 473
Fusṭāṭ 483, 484, 489, 495
fūṭa (pl. fuwaṭ, "waist-wrappers") 134, 206, 229, 377, 383, 384, 386, 387, 389, 488, 489, 490, 492

Galata 445
Galen 47
Gallipolli 445
Galtung, Johan 34
García de Linares, Ramón 309, 332
Garcin, Jean-Claude 103, 146, 476, 484, 498
Gaza 97, 111, 226, 249, 250, 254, 461, 462, 474
Gedik Ahmed Pasha 114
Genghis Khan, see: Chinggis Khan 212, 386
Geniza of Cairo 296, 301, 482, 484, 488, 489
Genoa, Genoese 19, 24, 25, 27, 29, 30, 63, 74, 185, 233, 252, 297, 313, 426/112, 114, 190, 208, 238, 280, 281, 282, 288, 291, 295, 296, 298, 299, 303, 313, 318, 319, 346, 348, 354, 355, 356, 358, 359, 360, 363/
geographers, Arab 196, 275
Georgians 82, 114, 118, 188, 189, 192, 198; see also: Gurjastan
Germany, Germans 10, 61, 112, 118, 387/ 111
Germiyanids 398
al-Ghālib Billāh Muḥammad IX "el Zurdo" (Nasrid ruler) 289
Ghānim al-Ghazāwī 83
Ghassanids 115, 116
Ghazan (Ilkhan) 208, 352, 353, 369, 376, 386
ghazā (raid for Holy War) 83, 409, 422
ghāzī (raider for Holy War) 229, 230
Ghazna 208, 352, 353, 369, 376, 386
van Ghistele, Joos 112, 119
Ghiyāth al-Dīn Shāh (ruler of Malwa) 470
Ghuzz (Oghuz) Turks 118
Gibraltar 298
Gills, Barry K. 27, 32, 34
Gog and Magog 53
Goitein, S.D. 305, 498
gold 30, 63, 64, 65, 66, 72, 73, 199, 246, 290, 446, 501
Golden Horde 6, 9, 19, 41, 150, 151, 157, 159, 160, 171, 180, 181, 183, 184, 185, 186, 187, 210, 345, 346, 347, 348, 350, 351, 352, 354, 355, 356, 358, 359, 360, 361, 362, 364, 365, 368, 369, 373, 374, 375, 382, 503
Goldstone, Jack 87, 103
Golubovich, Gịrolamo 308, 337, 362
Golvin, Lucien 146
Goths 119
Granada 214, 289, 291, 292, 294, 295, 297, 299, 315, 323, 338, 339
Great Khan 347, 348, 351
Greco-Roman period in Egypt 480
Greece, Greeks 112, 257, 273, 276, 426/47, 111, 119, 188, 211, 356; see also: Byzantine Empire
Greek Church 24
Greek language 240
Gruzinski, Serge 22
Gujarat 465, 467
Gulbarga 470
Gunpowder 67, 68, 69, 73, 103, 250, 252, 441, 448, 450
Guo, Li 211, 387, 427, 476, 480, 484, 485, 498, 499
Gürān (in Iraq) 429
Gürānī, Mollā 429
Gurjistan (Georgia) 353

Haarmann, Ulrich 10, 112, 116, 121, 194, 207, 209, 211, 212, 252, 337, 427, 449, 502
Ḥabīb, Shawqī 306
Ḥācı Bektāş Velī (Sufi saint) 414
Ḥācı Paşa (Anatolian Scholar) 425, 429
Ḥadīth (Prophetic tradition) 504
Hadramawt 456
Ḥāfiẓ al-Dīn al-Kabīr (Central Asian scholar) 381, 384
Hafsids 19, 24, 299, 300, 303, 314, 315
Ḥaḥa (in Morocco) 282
ḥajj 332, 487; see also: pilgrimage
al-Ḥajjī, Ḥayāt Nāṣir 332

Ḥalab 95, see: Aleppo
Haldon, John 87, 103
Halland, Thomas D. 27
Ḥalqa formation 164, 165
Ḥamā/Hama 93, 288, 413, 460, 462, 474
Hamburg 33, 73, 229, 252, 253
Hamidoğulları 396, 397, 428
Ḥanafīs 97, 202, 203, 367, 376, 380, 381, 382, 410, 461
Ḥanbalīs 57, 116, 138, 147, 182
Hand guns 437
ḥāra (Ar. neighborhood) 141
al-Ḥaram al-Sharīf (Ar. "The Noble Sanctuary"/Temple Mount) 135, 138, 141, 142, 146
Ḥaram Mosque 470, 471
Har-El, Shai 103, 449
harem 97
al-Ḥarīrī (Arabic writer) 382
von Harff, Arnold 112, 119, 424, 426
Harhār 264
al-Ḥasan b. Khāṣṣ Bak, Badr al-Dīn 97
Ḥasan Bak b. ʿAlī Bak b. Qarā Yuluk, see: Uzun Ḥasan 82
Hassan Veneziano 109
Hausberger, Bernd 24, 35
Ḥawrān 271
al-Haytamī, Ibn Ḥajar 44, 57
Hebron (al-Khalīl) 111, 139, 358, 371, 460, 461, 462, 474
Hejaz/Ḥijāz 30, 31/49, 64, 81, 238, 239, 272, 279, 282, 291, 453, 455, 456, 457, 459, 462, 463, 464, 467, 474, 475, 506; see also: Mecca, Medina
Herat/Harat 347, 368/412
Hersekzāde Aḥmed Paşa 421
Hetʿum (Armenian historian) 369, 387
Heyd, Uriel 233, 252
Ḥijāz, see: Hejaz 49, 64, 81, 238, 239, 272, 279, 282, 291, 453, 455, 456, 457, 459, 462, 463, 464, 467, 474, 475, 506
Hilla (in Iraq) 352
Hillenbrand, Carole 191, 211
Ḥimṣ, see: Homs 460
– battle of Ḥimṣ 164
Hindu Kush 76
Ḥisbān (in Jordan) 260, 275, 276
hoca 405, 409, 425
Hoca Saʿdeddīn 409
Hodder, Ian 454, 477, 478
Hodgson, Marshall G.S. 27, 35
Hohenstaufens 9
Holt, Peter M. 9, 59, 103, 211, 308, 312, 337, 387, 426, 449
Holy Land 120, 250, 252, 254, 322, 325; see also: Palestine
Holy Sepulchre 325, 327, 328
Homs 462
Hormuz 40, 466, 475
Horn of Africa 48
Hospitallers 71, 189, 314
household 45, 86, 87, 102, 105, 140, 153, 182, 194, 214, 457, 482
Howe, Stephen 87
al-Ḥujāwī, Sharaf al-Dīn 42, 57
Hülegü (founder of Ilkhanate) 157, 158, 347, 348, 349, 384
Humphreys, R. Stephen 75, 103, 211, 427, 449
Hunayn (in Algeria) 286, 287
Hungary, Hungarians 24, 112/111, 112, 193
Hurgronje, C. Snouck 31
al-Ḥusām al-Yāghī (Central Asian scholar) 382
al-Ḥusaynī, Ḥusayn b. Muḥammad 115

Iberia 28, 29, 313–315, 317, 320–324, 331, 505; see also al-Andalus, Portugal, Spain
Ibiza 281
Ibn ʿAbd al-Ẓāhir, Muḥyī al-Dīn (Mamluk-era official historian) 155, 205, 289, 349
Ibn al-Akfānī 47, 57
Ibn al-ʿArabī (Sufi) 392
Ibn ʿArabshāh (historian) 205, 378, 379, 385, 387, 388, 403
Ibn Ayyūb Yaḥyā al-Tūnisī (merchant) 487
Ibn Baṭṭūṭa (Maghrebi traveler) 55, 58, 59, 60, 69, 73, 205, 279, 285, 297, 301, 304, 371, 382, 397, 400–402, 426

Ibn al-Dawādārī (Mamluk-era historian) 154, 171, 179, 205, 362, 386, 387
Ibn Fahd ʿAbd al-Raḥmān b. Abū Bakr Aḥmad (scholar) 457
Ibn Fahd Abū Bakr Aḥmad b. Najm al-Dīn Muḥammad (merchant) 205, 206, 304, 461, 470
Ibn Fahd ʿIzz al-Dīn ʿAbd al-ʿAzīz b. Najm al-Dīn ʿUmar (Meccan writer) 458, 465, 466, 475, 477
Ibn Fahd Jār Allāh (Meccan writer, grandson of above) 455, 456, 460, 477
Ibn Fahd Kamāliyya bint Najm al-Dīn Muḥammad (Ḥadīth scholar) 461
Ibn Fahd Najm al-Dīn Muḥammad (Meccan scholar) 457, 459, 460, 461, 471, 474, 477
Ibn Fahd Najm al-Dīn ʿUmar b. Najm al-Dīn Muḥammad (Meccan writer) 459, 460, 461, 474, 477
Ibn Fahd Sitt Quraysh Fāṭima bint Najm al-Dīn Muḥammad (scholar) 462
Ibn Fahd Taqī al-Dīn b. Najm al-Dīn Muḥammad (Meccan traditionalist) 460, 477
Ibn Fahd Umm Rīm bint Najm al-Dīn Muḥammad (scholar) 461, 462
Ibn Fahd Yaḥyā ibn ʿAbd al-Raḥmān (merchant) 57, 206–208, 470, 487
Ibn al-Fuwaṭī (Ikhanid scholar) 206, 377, 383, 384, 386, 387, 389
Ibn Ḥajar al-ʿAsqalānī (Mamluk-era scholar) 57, 203, 206, 210, 287, 391, 425, 460, 461
Ibn Ḥabīb (Mamluk-era historian) 476, 478
Ibn Ḥawqal (Arabic geographer) 280, 302
Ibn Ḥijjī (Mamluk-era historian) 200, 206
Ibn Iyās (Mamluk-era historian) 57, 64, 71, 73, 199, 200, 201, 206, 434, 436, 437, 444, 449
Ibn al-Jazarī, Shams al-Dīn (Syrian scholar) 379, 403, 426
Ibn Jubayr (Maghrebi traveler) 281, 282, 283, 298, 302, 304, 305, 499
Ibn Kathīr (Mamluk-era historian) 155, 176, 206
Ibn Khaldūn (historian, philosopher and statesman) 48, 57, 115, 119, 150, 156, 157, 183, 206, 209, 210, 235, 239, 279, 287, 288, 303, 304, 372, 379, 380, 385, 387, 505
Ibn al-Khaljī 471, see also: Maḥmūd Shāh Khaljī
Ibn al-Layth 116
Ibn al-Liḥyānī (Hafsid prince) 285
Ibn Mājid 468, 477
Ibn Manjlī, Muḥammad 186, 206
Ibn Mibrad 45
Ibn al-Mujāwir (traveler) 490, 499, 500
Ibn al-Nafīs (Mamluk-era physician and writer) 48
Ibn Naqūla, ʿAbd al-Ghanī b. ʿAbd al-Razzāq al-Armanī al-Qibṭī (Mamluk wazir) 194
Ibn Rushayd (Maghrebi traveler) 283, 284, 304
Ibn al-Saʿīd al-Maghribī (geographer) 157
Ibn Shaddād al-Ḥalabī (Ayyubid and Mamluk-era official and writer) 155, 161
Ibn Sīnā 382
Ibn Taghrī Birdī (Mamluk-era historian) 63, 64, 73, 97, 103, 120, 168, 173, 174, 178, 180, 183, 194, 206, 213, 388
Ibn Ṭūlūn (Mamluk-era historian) 444
Ibn al-Wardī (Mamluk-era historian) 50, 57, 155
Ibn Zunbul (Mamluk-era writer) 438, 441, 442, 449
Ibrāhīm al-Tāzī 239
İdrīs-i Bidlīsī 409
al-Idrīsī (Arab geographer) 302
Ifrīqiya (Tunisia) 308, 315, 321
Igarashi, Daisuke 274, 447, 450
ijāza (certificate of learning) 377, 392, 460–462, 474
ikat cloth 497
Ilkhanids, Ilkhans, Ilkhanate 352, 353, 356, 358, 360, 362/150–153, 158, 161, 163, 171, 187, 192, 211, 212, 369, 377/19, 81, 105, 110, 150, 153, 157, 160, 171, 173, 212,

214, 345, 348, 351, 353, 354, 367–369, 371, 375, 501
Ilkhanid historians; see also: Rashīd al-Dīn
Ilkhanid-Mamluk peace of 352, 353, 356, 358, 360, 362/150, 151, 152, 153, 158, 161, 163, 171, 187, 192, 211, 212, 369, 377/19, 81, 105, 110, 150, 153, 157, 160, 171, 173, 212, 214, 345, 348, 351, 353, 354, 367, 368, 369, 371, 375, 501
imām (prayer leader) 41
al-ʿImāra 287, 292
Imerethi (in Caucasia) 118
Īnāl al-Ajrūd, al-Ashraf (Mamluk sultan) 97
Īnāl Bāy al-Nawrūzī 177
India, Indians 9, 19, 20, 27, 40, 44, 48, 49, 51, 52, 54, 55, 58, 59, 60, 66, 68, 86, 102, 215, 227, 238, 345, 456, 461, 463, 465, 466, 468, 469, 470, 471, 472, 473, 475, 476, 478, 479, 482, 483, 484, 488, 489, 490, 495, 498/ 10, 18, 26, 28, 30, 31, 33, 47, 49, 50, 51, 55, 56, 59, 75, 78, 190, 244, 247, 248, 249, 251, 305, 375, 386, 389, 427, 436, 464, 465, 466, 467, 468, 469, 470, 471, 472, 473, 475, 476, 477, 483, 488, 489, 492, 495, 505, 506/20, 30, 32, 456, 466; see also: South Asia
- madrasas in Mecca founded by Indians 396, 402, 411, 412, 413, 463, 464, 475, 477
Indian Ocean 10, 18, 20, 26, 28, 30, 31, 33, 49, 50, 51, 56, 59, 60, 75, 78, 244, 248, 249, 251, 305, 427, 436, 466, 467, 468, 469, 470, 473, 476, 477, 478, 488, 492
Inner Asia 156, 210, 211, 212, 386, 387, 389, 502
inshā' (composition) 73, 207, 361, 389, 403, 478, 500
ipsimission 109
iqṭāʿ (land allocation) 164, 262, 263, 447
Iran 43, 65, 68, 73, 75, 81, 105, 345, 348, 364, 369, 371, 373, 383, 389, 402, 426, 434, 438, 449, 450, 463, 469, 475
Iranians, see: Persians 28, 436, 439
Iranisation 440
Iraq 82, 84, 345, 358, 373, 375, 376, 377, 383, 397, 404, 463, 465, 469, 475
Irishman 110
Iron 68, 69, 71, 72, 142, 241, 269, 417, 443, 447
Iron Age 269
Iron Curtain 447
Irwin, Robert 5, 10, 99, 103, 109, 195, 211, 212, 252, 442, 450, 504
al-Iṣfahānī, Abū Rashīd al-Ghazzāl (Central Asian scholar) 381
Isḥāḳ Bey (from Hamidoğulları family) 397, 415
Isḥāḳ Bey (Ottoman commander from Balkans) 397, 415
al-Isʿirdī, Badr al-Dīn Ḥasan (trader) 374
Islam 19, 20, 24, 27, 32, 33, 34, 35, 37, 42, 43, 49, 53, 58, 59, 60, 76, 77, 102, 109, 110, 111, 114, 121, 122, 130, 132, 141, 146, 149, 170, 171, 181, 182, 183, 184, 189, 191, 193, 194, 199, 200, 202, 208, 209, 210, 211, 213, 214, 230, 240, 250, 251.253, 273, 305, 321, 329, 331, 332, 333, 334, 337, 340, 341, 349, 357, 364, 373, 385, 386, 387, 388, 389, 407, 410, 413, 424, 426, 428, 429, 448, 449, 450, 472, 473, 476, 498, 503
Islamization, see: conversion to Islam 181, 183, 184, 186, 187, 193, 210, 364, 367, 370, 380, 384, 385, 387, 501, 505
Ismāʿīl, Shah (Safavid ruler) 65, 71, 389, 432, 433, 434, 435, 436, 437, 439, 450
Isparta (in southern Turkey) 397
Istanbul 109, 206, 249, 251, 273, 274, 341, 387, 421, 424, 425, 439, 448, 508; see also: Constantinople
Italian language 242
Italy, Italians 41, 71, 103, 112, 185, 212, 424; see also: Genoa, Pisa, Venice
Iṭṣā (in Upper Egypt) 485
Iyās al-Muḥammadī al-Nāṣirī 199
Iyāz al-Jurjāwī 200
Iznik 402, 413, 414

Jackson, Peter 156, 212, 337, 364, 388
Jaffa 225, 228, 252
Jāmī, Mollā 412
James II (king of Aragon) 312, 313, 314, 315, 316, 317, 326, 328, 330

Jānī Bek/Janibeg (Golden Horde khan) 382
Jānibak (Mamluk governor) 407
Jānibak al-Ḥabīb al-ʿAlay al-Īnālī (Mamluk ambassador) 407
Jānibak al-Nāṣirī 200
Jānibak al-Ẓāhirī 470
Janissaries 73, 435, 449
Jānim al-Ashrafī 95
Janus (Cypriot king) 64, 254
Jaqmaq, al-Ẓāhir (Mamluk sultan) 177, 194, 195, 201, 289, 291, 404, 422
Jaraktamur al-Ashrafī 178
al-Jarīrī (Maghrebi traveler) 291, 299
Jarkas (=Circassians, and a Circassian tribe) 115, 116, 182, 197
Jarmak al-Nāṣrī 159
Jaspert, Nikolas 6, 24, 35, 251, 307, 334, 337, 338, 342, 428, 505
Jalāyrids 373, 418, 430
Jazira (today: north Iraq, southeast Turkey and northeast Syria) 147, 354
Jedda, see: Jidda 49, 57, 60, 448, 453, 454, 458, 467, 468, 470, 471, 472, 473, 499
Jehel, George 306
Jerusalem 6, 9, 10, 11, 111, 119, 122, 123, 126, 127, 128, 129, 130, 134, 135, 136, 137, 138, 139, 131, 142, 143, 144, 145, 146, 147, 209, 214, 226, 250, 253, 254, 259, 263, 275, 288, 312, 322, 325, 326, 327, 329, 331, 335, 337, 338, 358, 359, 365, 367, 371, 404, 460, 461, 462, 474, 501, 502
Jews, Jewish merchants 53, 110, 194, 209, 332, 338, 339, 427
Jibāl al-Sāra 456
Jidda 30, 31, 456, 458
jihād (holy war) 251
jinn 52, 54, 56
jins (ethnic group, race) 159, 161, 171, 174, 180, 181, 182, 193, 197, 201
Jirba (in Tunisia) 285, 292, 294
Jirja (in Upper Egypt) 496
Jīzān (on Red Sea) 458
jizya (poll tax) 42
Joachimsthal (in Bohemia) 66
John of Sulṭāniyya 118
Jordan 257, 259, 260, 262, 263, 264, 265, 266, 267, 268, 269, 270, 272, 273, 274, 275, 276, 507; see also Transjordan
Jordan River/Valley 260/41, 228, 260, 262, 263, 264, 268, 274, 455, 456, 457, 458, 459, 463, 472
Jöchi (founder of Golden Horde) 345, 346, 347, 348, 349, 350, 351, 352, 353, 354, 355, 356, 357, 358, 360, 361, 362, 389
Jöchids 345, 346, 347, 348, 349, 350, 351, 353, 354, 356, 357, 360, 361, 362
judges, Muslim, see: qāḍī 45, 138, 392, 394, 398, 401, 407, 463, 464, 470, 477, 406
julbān (recently bought Mamluks of sultan) 170, 447
jumaqdāriyya (mace-bearers) 197
jundī (common soldier) 97, 207, 234, 500
Juwaynī family 376
– ʿAlāʾ al-Dīn (historian and administrator) 384

Kafr Lām (Habonim, in Israel) 224
Kafrīn (in Jordan Valley) 264
al-Kāmil, al-Malik (Ayyubid ruler) 94, 481
Kaplony, Andreas 480, 499
Karak 263, 264, 265, 266, 272
Karakoyunlu, see: Qara Qoyunlu 418, 429
Karākūsh/Qarākūsh (in Upper Egypt) 484
Karamanids 395, 396, 398, 419
Karatāy 160
Ḳarāyülük ʿOsmān (Akkoyunlu leader) 398
al-Kardārī, Shams al-A'imā (Central Asian scholar) 381
Kārimī merchants 466, 467, 469
Karmuk (Circassian tribe) 115
Karpathos (near Crete) 286
Kasa (Circassian tribe) 115
Kashgar 54, 376
Kastomunu (in Anatolia) 401
Ḳaygusuz Abdāl (Sufi) 427
Kayseri 398, 402, 424, 426
Kazakhstan 345
Kazarūnī merchants 469, 472
Kazikumyks (in Caucasia) 119
Kemāl Reis (Ottoman admiral) 420

Kenney, Ellen 91, 93
Khalafallāh, Ibtisām 306
Khalīl, Ṣalāḥ al-Dīn, b. Khāṣṣ Bak 97
Khalilieh, Ḥasan 223, 253
khān (caravanserai) 34, 78, 212, 254, 263, 275, 345, 346, 347, 348, 349, 350, 351, 352, 353, 354, 355, 356, 357, 358, 359, 360, 361, 364, 367, 368, 370, 372, 373, 374, 382, 383, 384, 386, 502, 503
khānqāh (Sufi lodge) 426
Khans, Great 157
al-Kharazmī (Anatolian scholar) 401
Kharbandā, see: Öljeitü 353
Khāṣṣ Bak/Turk 96, 97, 98, 99
khāṣṣakiyya (sultan's bodyguard) 375
Khawājā merchants 469, 472
Khāyirbak (Hayr Bey) al-Jārkasī 95
al-Khiḍr 57
Khitai/Khita'i 115, 376, 347, 386, 502
Khorasan/Khurāsān 348, 349, 352/368, 369, 376, 383, 462
Khotan 376
Khujand 376, 382
Khushqadam, al-Ẓāhir (Mamluk sultan) 95, 470
khuṭba (Friday sermon) 59
Khwārazm, Khwārizm 346, 349
Khwārazmshāhs 347
Kitbughā, al-ʿĀdil (Mamluk sultan) 162, 186
von Klaproth, Julius 118
Knights of St. John, see: Hospitallers 290, 443
KoissouRiver (in Caucasia) 117
Koran, see: Qur'ān 436
Ḳorḳud 429
Krämer, Gudrun 27, 35, 250, 450
Kubrā, Najm al-Dīn (Sufi saint) 383
Kubrāwiyya (Sufi order) 378, 381
al-Kujkūnī, Ḥusām al-Dīn (Mamluk ambassador) 420
Kūkāy min Ḥamza al-Ẓāhirī 177, 182
Kurdish language 116
Kurds 115, 138, 139
Kuri (in Caucasia) 117
Kurjī al-Ashrafī 159
Kurtbāy (Mamluk amir) 441
Kütahya 398
kuttāb (secretaries) 361
Kuvendik al-Sāqī 160, 161
Kuzul al-Muḥammadī al-Ẓāhirī 180

Labib, Subhi 27, 35, 74, 428
Labna (city in Barqa) 295
Lafi, Nora 23
Lājīn al-Manṣūrī (Mamluk sultan) 197, 200
Land tenure 261, 267, 268, 270, 272, 274, 258, 450, 103
Landscape, "liquid" 257, 273, 275
Landscape, urban 6, 123, 127, 133, 138, 140, 141, 144
Languedoc 112
de Lannoy, Ghillelbert 111, 120
de Laranda, Pedro 111
Latakia 228, 238
Latin America 22
Latin language 217, 239, 240, 310
Latins, see: Franks 41, 211
law, Muslim, see: Sharīʿa 41, 58, 64, 131, 274, 342, 375, 401
lead 17, 18, 20, 23, 29, 53, 56, 62, 68, 69, 72, 76, 170, 229, 261, 268, 369, 373, 380, 422, 454, 471, 485, 493
Lebanon 105, 225, 226
Lehners, Jean-Paul 24, 34, 35, 37
Leks (people in Caucasia) 119
Leo VI (Byzantine emperor) 241, 251
Leo Africanus 118, 300
Levanoni, Amalia 10, 99, 101, 104, 208, 212, 214, 249, 251, 252, 338, 388, 450, 503, 508
Levant 19, 27, 29, 30, 59, 66, 145, 189, 208, 209, 215, 218, 250, 274, 275, 299, 308, 318, 320, 337, 364, 425, 427
Libya 215, 282, 283, 292, 293, 300, 301
Liebermann, Viktor 80
Liedl, Gottfried 25, 26, 33, 34, 35
Liguria 233
Lirola-Delgado, Jorge 303, 306
Little, Donald P. 116, 121, 146, 154, 212
Lleida 324, 340

London 5, 32, 34, 35, 37, 58, 59, 60, 73, 103, 109, 119, 120, 121, 145, 146, 147, 207, 208, 209, 210, 211, 212, 213, 229, 250, 251, 254, 274, 322, 333, 363, 364, 387, 389, 424, 425, 427, 428, 229, 448, 449, 450, 476, 477, 478, 498, 499, 500, 502, 503, 504
Lübeck 229
de Lucena Paredes, Luis Seco 289, 305
Lusignans of Cyprus 189, 235, 313
Luxor 485

Madaba Plains (in Jordan) 269, 270
madhhab (Muslim legal school) 464
madrasa (Muslim college) 141, 164, 262, 264, 272, 273, 382, 396, 397, 402, 411, 412, 413, 459, 463, 464, 475, 477
Madrasat al-Khānī 382
Maghāriba (people from the Maghreb) 138, 279, 280–1, 286, 301–2
Maghreb/Maghrib 24, 28, 63, 235, 305, 315, 321, 332, 338, 487
Maḥbūbī family (leaders of Bukhara) 380–1, 384
al-Mahdiyya 283, 284
maḥmal (symbolic litter for ḥajj) 455
Maḥmūd of Ghazna 116
Maḥmūd Shāh Khaljī (ruler of Malwa) 470–1
Mājid (in Banū Juhma region of Jordan) 266
Makhairas (Cypriote historian) 440
Majorca 281
Malabar 44, 468, 472–3
Malaga 284, 295
al-Malaṭī, ʿAbd al-Bāsiṭ b. Khalīl b. Shāhīn al-Ẓāhirī 168, 173, 175–83, 186, 187, 194, 197–201, 293–5, 299, 301
Malaṭya (Melitene in Anatolia) 292, 407
Malik Sunbul al-Sulṭānī (Indian envoy) 470
Mālikīs 301
Malkā (in Transjordan) 264
Malkoçoğlu Bāli Bey (Ottoman frontier lord) 420
Mallorca 307
Malta 286
Malwa (in India) 470, 471, 473, 476
Mamluk, Mamluks, passim, but for specific matters:
- Mamluk diplomacy 59, 308, 337, 418
- Mamluk treasury 266
- Mamluks, education of 118
- Mamluks, names and naming 112, 161, 195, 196, 209, 214, 425
- Mamluks, trade in 280, 301, 374, 416
manāqib (praise) literature 349
Mandū 163, 164
Manklībughā al-Ṣalīḥī 179
Mann, Michael 187
Mansā al-Mūsā 63
al-Manṣūra (in Algeria) 284
Manṣūriyya complex (in Cairo) 160
al-Manūfī 51
Maqdishū 483
al-Maqdisī, Abū Ḥāmid (Mamluk historian) 170
al-Maqrīzī (Mamluk-era writer) 41, 97, 118, 200, 203, 210, 212, 391–2, 420, 421, 460
Marçais, George 130
Mardin (in Turkey) 354
al-Marghīnānī (Central Asian scholar) 378
Maria of Lusignan 314
Marinids, see: Merinids 314, 315
Marj Dābiq 71, 437–38, 443–4, 447–48
al-Marrākushī, Jamāl al-Dīn Muḥammad ibn Mūsā (scholar) 462
Marsā Hawwāra (Qaṣr Aḥmad) 283
Marsā al-ʿImāra 287
Martyrdom, Muslim 330, 331
Marw (in Sawād region of Jordan) 264
al-Mashaddālī (Maghrebi traveler) 298
Mashriq (Islamic East) 279, 281, 292, 296, 301, 302, 304, 462–64, 466, 469
Masià de Ros, Àngles 310
Maslāta 285
Masrāta 285
Matar, Nabil 109
al-Māturīdī, Abū Manṣūr 45
Matuz, Joseph 438
Māzūna 286, 294

McChesney, Robert 378
Mecca 7, 9, 30–31, 36, 57, 63, 81, 97–98, 104, 113, 263–4, 289, 324–5, 329, 350, 371, 404, 415, 431, 433, 436, 453–73, 487
Medāris-i Semāniyye 411
Medina/Medine 9, 263, 264, 291, 329, 350, 371, 381, 404, 431, 433, 436, 455, 459, 460, 462, 474, 476
Mediterranean 5, 6, 9, 10, 17–32, 40, 42, 49, 62, 65, 75, 77, 78, 130, 229, 238, 241, 260–3, 272–5, 281–303, 307–331, 345, 348, 410, 423, 439–1, 445–6, 468, 479, 482–5, 488, 492
Meḥmed I (Ottoman sultan) 391, 399, 402, 403
Mehmed II (Ottoman sultan) 114, 404, 407, 409, 411, 412, 415, 416, 421
Meloy, John L. 30–31, 81
menāḳibnāme (hagiography) 414
Menteşe (principality in western Anatolia) 401, 416
mercenaries 320–2
merchants (and traders) 9, 18, 28–9, 40, 64, 166, 171, 229, 241, 250, 267, 281, 285–6, 287, 294, 295–7, 297–299, 302–5, 312, 308, 314, 318, 320, 327, 347–51, 351, 354–58, 360, 362, 366–67, 374, 394, 416–18, 461, 466–70, 472–75, 479–82, 484–85, 479, 490, 492, 495
Merinids 19, 24, 284, 303
Messina 281
de Mignanelli, Bertrando 110
Michael Palaiologos (Byzantine emperor) 348
Middle East 20, 30, 34, 53, 54, 62, 63, 72, 73, 102, 103, 104, 123, 130–1, 136–7, 144–5, 210, 212, 252, 373, 431, 473, 475, 438–9
al-Midīya 281
migration 19, 25, 36, 211, 260, 261, 271, 272, 275, 296, 324, 336, 338, 341, 368, 384, 400, 426, 428
milk (private property) 262
Milyāna 282, 284
Ming dynasty 110, 345
Mingrelia, Mingrelians 110, 113, 114, 118
Minorca 281
"Mirror for Princes" 192, 198, 400, 424
Miṣr (here: Old Cairo) 64
Misrāta 284, 295
Mitjavila, Pere 317, 318
Moguls (dynasty in India) 26, 86
Mojacar 287
Möngke (Mongol Great Khan) 347, 384
Möngke-Temür (khan of Golden Horde) 350, 355, 368
Mongol names 113
Mongol Peace, see: Pax Mongolica 6, 345, 346, 347, 353, 361, 362
Mongolia 345
Mongolian language and culture 116, 159, 179–1
Mongols 9, 18, 25–26, 75, 78, 81, 93, 110, 113, 115, 149–4, 156–60, 163–74, 178, 185–6, 188, 192, 196–7, 202, 240, 293, 313, 329, 345–62, 431–2, 440
Moors 458
Morea 113
Moresini, Zuan (Venetian merchant) 433
Morgan, David 156, 208, 212, 435, 450
Morocco 140, 282, 304, 306, 465
Mortel, Richard 455–6, 459, 463, 469, 474–5, 477, 499
mosques 259, 266, 328, 329, 385, 436
Mosul 354, 384
Motyl, Alexander 88–89, 90, 104
muda 298, 299
Muda al Trafego 298–299, 303
mudéjares (Muslims in Christian Iberia) 323–4, 328, 332, 335, 336, 337, 341
muftī/mufti (Muslim legal consultant) 350
Mughals (dynasty in India), see: Moguls
Mughul (term for Mongol) 156–59, 162
muḥadddith (Muslim traditionalist) 462
Muḥammad (Prophet of Islam) 253, 255, 273
Muḥammad b. ʿAlī b. ʿAbd Allāh (from Quseir) 481
Muḥammad b. al-Qāsim al-Qifṭī (merchant) 484
Muḥammad Parsā (Sufi) 378
Muḥammad Shaybanī (Uzbek ruler) 434

Muhannā, amīr al-ʿArab 93
muḥtasib ("market inspector") 44, 495
mujāwirūn ("pious sojourners" in Mecca) 459
mujawwir ("interloper") merchants 468–9, 472–3
Mumford, Lewis 138, 146
muqaddam al-mamālīk al-sulṭāniyya (commander of royal mamluks) 97
Muqaṭṭam Hills (near Cairo) 415
Murād I (Ottoman sultan) 415
Murād II (Ottoman sultan) 404–5, 415, 417, 421
Murād IV (Ottoman sultan) 412
Murad Ali 109
Mūsā b. Bāyezīd I 402
Mūsā b. Samūyal b. Yahūdā al-Mālaqī (Jewish physician) 294
Mūsā, ʿUmar 306
Musʿad, Sāmiya 306
Muslim/Muslims 9, 10, 26, 30, 39, 40, 41, 42, 43, 47, 48, 49, 50, 52, 53, 54, 58, 59, 60, 65, 76, 86, 87, 88, 91, 95, 97, 100, 102, 104, 109, 120, 130, 132, 141, 142, 145, 146, 151, 152, 161, 162, 163, 164, 167, 170, 171, 172, 174, 175, 176, 177, 178, 180, 181, 182, 183, 188, 190, 191, 192, 193, 194, 197, 198, 199, 200, 201, 208, 209, 210, 211, 212, 213, 214, 235, 246, 249, 253, 255, 259, 272, 281, 281, 282, 284, 285, 286, 287, 289, 290, 291, 292, 293, 294, 295, 297, 299, 304, 306, 307, 308, 312, 314, 315, 318, 319, 321, 322, 323, 324, 325, 326, 328, 329, 330, 331, 332, 333, 335, 337, 338, 339, 341, 342, 347, 349, 355, 373, 375, 376, 378, 379, 380, 384, 385, 388, 393, 394, 396, 397, 401, 403, 407, 409, 411, 412, 413, 414, 415, 422, 423, 426, 428, 431, 432, 434, 438, 439, 472, 473, 490, 501, 506, 507
- in Christian Iberia 314, 320
Muṣṭafā ʿAlī 407
Mustaghānim 286
muwādaʿa (ceasefire, truce) 42

Nadrūma 286
nāʾib (governor) 92, 95, 97
Najd 456
Nākhudhā Ibrāhīm 468–470
Nākhudhā merchants 469
naphta (Greek fire) 229
Naples 313
Napoleonic Wars 118
Naqshandī Sufi order 378
Nart cycle (Circassian folklore) 117
Nasaf 376
al-Nashw, Sharaf al-Dīn 92
al-NāṣirFaraj (Mamluk sultan) 94, 97, 111–2, 177, 180, 189, 196, 201, 373–4, 402, 464
al-Nāṣir Ḥasan b. Muḥammad b. Qalāwūn (Mamluk sultan) 332, 264, 458
al-Nāṣir Muḥammad II (Mamluk sultan) 70
al-Nāṣir Muḥammad b. Qalāwūn (Mamluk sultan) 91–93, 95, 98, 150, 152–4, 162, 164–6, 171–3, 173, 183, 188–9, 192–5, 201, 204, 264, 316–7, 328–1, 346–7, 352–4, 356–61, 371, 457, 464
Nasrids 24, 289, 292, 295, 314
Naumakhia 241
navy 6, 215, 218, 235, 237–39, 243–45, 248, 250, 445
- Mamluk 215–50, 297, 431, 444–5
- Ottoman 438–9, 442, 443, 445
- see also: British navy
Nawrūz al-Ḥāfiẓī 177
Naxos 110
Nayakas (landed elite in southern India) 473
Near East, see: Middle East
Negüder (Mongol general) 348
Neşrī (Ottoman historian) 415
Nestorian Church 24
networks 5, 18, 30, 32, 59, 75, 80, 91, 94, 95, 99, 100, 102, 105, 140, 250, 257, 258, 271, 308, 311, 314, 331, 334, 335, 345, 356, 409, 410, 416, 417, 421–3, 426, 462, 463, 469, 473, 476, 479, 492, 502, 503, 507, 508
Nicophorus, Gregoras (Byzantine historian) 356
Nicopolis 112, 403, 426
- Battle of 403

Nile 41, 51, 53, 229, 236, 239, 242, 291, 427, 429, 455, 456, 457, 458, 459, 463, 472, 484–5, 489, 492, 496
Nimrīn (in Jordan Valley) 264
nişâncı (head of the chancery) 403
Nogay (Mongol general) 352
North Africa 26, 30, 89, 109, 243, 296, 297, 298–9, 303, 306, 320–1, 339, 397, 501 see also: Maghreb
noyan (senior Mongol commander) 348
Nuʿayr (Bedouin leader) 110
Nubia 41, 489
Nuʿmān Khwārazmī, shaykh (physician from Golden Horde) 358–9, 361
al-Nuwayrī (Mamluk-era historian) 102, 240, 370

Ögödei (Mongol Great Khan) 351
Ögödeids 368, 370, 373, 386
Oirat Mongols 159, 162–3, 186
"Old World" 18
Olivera, Gerart 317
Öljeitü 186, 351, 353–4, 357, 364
One Thousand and One Nights 54
von Oppen, Achim 23, 34
Oppenheim 111
Oran 291, 292, 294, 295, 298
orders, monastic military 42; see also: Templars, Hospitallers
Orghina (Chaghadaid princess) 384
Orhan, Sultan (Ottoman) 66
Orientalists 26
Orontes 228
ortaq (Mongolian trading partnership) 354
Orthodox Church, see: Greek Church
Ossetes 118
Osterhammel, Jürge 20
Ottoman Empire 24, 65, 67, 68, 72, 73, 74, 88, 102, 120, 270, 274, 410, 433, 438, 508
Oubykh (Caucasian language) 117
Oxus 367
Özbek, see: Uzbak 200

Pact of ʿUmar 141
paganism 113
Palermo (in Sicily) 282, 337, 490
Palestine 29, 110, 119, 120, 145, 146, 207, 223, 228, 234, 249, 252, 253, 254, 271, 273, 275, 281, 501
Palmer, Carol 267
Pantellaria (Qawsara) 286
Papacy 313
paqṭ 41
Pax Mongolica 18, 28, 375
Pax Romana 345
Pegolotti, Francesco di Balducci 231, 254
Peloponnese 433
People of the Book (ahl al-kitāb) 42
pepper 228, 483, 488
Persia, see: Iran 26, 68, 151, 353, 450, 483
Persian Gulf 30, 40, 476
Persian language, culture and literature 44
Persianization, see: Iranization 178, 184, 187
Persians 174, 178, 179, 184, 186, 443
Peter (brother of King Alfonso III of Aragon) 312, 9, 24, 26, 33, 59, 66, 74, 121, 156, 189, 191, 210, 324, 325
Peter of Castile 191
Peter I of Lusignan (king of Cyprus) 190, 236
Peter IV, the Ceremonious (king of Aragon) 324, 325
Petry, Carl 74, 98, 96, 274, 275, 450
philanthropy 473, 463; see also: waqf
Philip II of Spain 23
Philip the Fair (French king) 351
pilgrims, pilgrimage 9, 30–1, 63, 112, 227, 229, 263, 281, 383–88, 290, 292–3, 296, 299–2, 312–3, 322–7, 331, 350, 380, 391, 37–4, 397, 404–5, 413–18, 453–59, 487, 492
Piloti, Emmanuel 110, 112, 113, 120, 242, 254
pirates, piracy 62, 109, 190, 215, 216, 227, 235, 238, 246, 290, 444
Pirenne, Henri 24
Pīrī Reis 233
Pisa 24
plague, see: Black Death 19, 25, 27, 114, 187, 234, 445, 446, 448

Popper, Karl 362
population, see: demography
Portugal, Portuguese 26, 28, 31, 49, 64, 69, 70, 111, 190–2, 220, 246, 251, 313, 436, 441, 443, 445
pre-Ottoman period 250
prisoners-of-war, see: captives 112

qāḍī/qadi (Muslim judge, also spelled cadi) 350, 358, 391
Qāḍī Khān (Central Asian scholar) 380, 378
Qaidu (Mongol ruler in Central Asia) 351, 369–2, 374–5, 384
qalān (Mongol head tax) 383
al-Qalaṣādī (Magrebi traveler) 291–2, 297, 302
Qalāwūn, al-Manṣūr, Sultan (Mamluk) 104, 152–154, 161, 163, 164, 188, 213, 340, 389
Qalāwūnids 154, 204
al-Qalqashandī (Mamluk-era writer) 73, 207, 254, 315, 373, 389, 456, 478, 500
Qānṣūh/Qānṣawh/Qāniṣawh al-Ghawrī, Sultan (Mamluk) 274
Qapuci (Caucasian language) 117
Qāqūn (in Palestine) 225
Qara Qoyunlu 373
Qarā Yūsuf (Qara Qoyunlu ruler) 418
Qara-Khitai 347
qarāniṣa (Mamluks of former sultans) 447
Qarāsunqur al-Manṣūrī 94
Qarāṭāy al-Khāzindārī (Mamluk historian) 154, 164, 193
Qardum al-Ḥasanī 175
Qaṣr Aḥmad 295
Qaṣr Barṣīṣ 285
Qaṣr Hawwāra 295
Qaṭyā 110
Qāyitbāy/Qāytbāy, al-Ashraf (Mamluk sultan) 64, 96–98, 111, 116, 196, 232, 266, 407, 419–20, 447, 464, 470–71
Qayrawān 282, 291, 294, 489
Qibjaq/Qipchaq al-Manṣūrī, Sayf al-Dīn 159, 163–64
Qifṭ (in Upper Egypt) 484
Qilī 163, 164
Qinā (in Upper Egypt) 484–5, 496
Qipchaq Turks 111–2, 113, 115, 118, 150–1, 155, 158, 161, 165, 168, 169, 181–2, 185, 187–99, 197, 293, 295, 346, 348, 355
- Land (Bilād) or Steppe (Dasht) of Qipchaqs (al-Qifjaq) 171, 346, 359
- language (maybe referring to Mongolian) 160
- sultanate, see: Baḥrīperiod
- Turkish 10, 43, 53, 112–8, 150, 295
Qizilbash 62, 432–3, 435–6, 440
Quanzhou 472
Qubbat Salām 285
Qubilai (Great Khan) 348, 370, 374
Qujqār al-Baktamurī 179
Qujqār al-Qardumī 173–75
Qujuq al-Shaʿbānī al-Ẓāhirī 175
Qulzum 241, see also: Suez Canal 240, 241
Qumārī al-Manṣūrī 160
Qur'ān 60, 131, 378, 382–3, 403, 436, 471, 504
al-Qurdūri (Baghdadi scholar) 382
Qūṣ 165, 484–5, 487, 489, 496, 327, 337, 476
Qusanṭīna, see: Constantine 284
Quṣayr/Quseir 457–59, 466, 475, 486–90
Qūṣūn (merchant, then Mamluk amir) 358
Quṣūr Sirt 285
Quṭlūbak 160
Qutluq Qocha (Chaghataid prince) 369

al-Rabwah, Shaykh 46–7, 50, 53, 58
Raḍī al-Dīn Ibn al-Ḥanbalī 183
Ragusa 24
Raḥba (in Syria) 369
Ramazanids, Ramāḍānids 395, 432
Ramla 225, 461, 462, 474, 254
Rashīd al-Dīn (statesman and historian) 252, 253
Rasulids 239, 467
rawk (cadastral survey) 262
Raydāniyya 438, 444
Raymond, André 133
al-Rāzī, Fakhr al-Dīn 46

Red Sea 7, 30–1, 49, 50, 52, 69, 70, 104, 190, 237, 239, 249, 251, 253, 436, 441, 445, 451, 456–59, 467–69, 479, 482–83, 488, 492
Reinfandt, Lucian 96, 98
Reinhard, Wolfgang 77–80, 85–86, 89–90, 105
Relics 44, 328
Renaissance 25
Repp, R.C. 405, 428
Reynolds, Susan 87
Rhodes 71, 189, 190, 192, 210, 238, 244, 249, 250, 254, 255, 289, 290, 291, 294, 297, 314, 422, 443, 445
ribāṭ (frontier fortification or urban hospice) 221, 227–9, 233–4, 243, 460, 465, 476, 477
Richardson, Kristina 192, 213
riḥla (travel) books 333, 428
Ritter, Helmut 45
Robert of Anjou (king of Sicily) 327–28
Rodinson, Maxime 27
Roman Church 315
Roman Empire, Romans 24, 229, 240, 244, 271–2, 396
Romano, David 324
Rosetta 229, 291
royal mamluks 162, 263
Rūm, see: Asia Minor, Bilād al-Rūm, Anatolia 418, 426, 428, 475
Rūm, Sultanate of 348, 418; see also Saljuqs
Rumelia 271
Rūmīs ("Greeks," "Anatolians") 427, 428
Russia, Russians (Rus) 108, 111–113, 118, 119, 182, 186, 345
Rut'ul (in Caucasia) 117

Sabta, see: Ceuta 281, 283, 284
Saclosa, Francesc 317
ṣadaqāt (alms) 463, 470
Ṣafad, Safed 133, 226, 234
al-Ṣafadī, Khalīl b. Aybak (Mamluk-era writer) 92, 154–5, 159, 164, 168
Safāqus 286, 287
Safavids 9, 26, 62, 65, 67, 69, 72, 431–39, 444, 445, 448, 504
Ṣafavīya/Ṣafawiyya Sufi order 432
Sahara 9, 26, 30, 55, 282
Ṣaḥīḥs of al-Bukhārī and Muslim 97, 378, 383
al-Ṣa'īd 293, 457, 460 see also: Upper Egypt
al-Sa'īd Muḥammad Berke Khan b. al-Ẓāhir Baybars (Mamluk sultan) 169
Saint Catherine's Monastery (in Sinai) 259, 265, 266, 273
al-Sakhāwī (Mamluk-era writer) 58, 194, 203, 207, 288, 305, 389, 425, 460, 461, 478
Saladin 141, 142, 501
Salār al-Manṣūrī 159, 163, 164
al-Ṣāliḥ Ayyūb (Ayyubid sultan) 152, 188
al-Sakkākī (Central Asian scholar) 378
Saljuqs 43, 364; see also: Rūm, Sultanate of
Salonica, Salonika 111
Saltpeter 67–69, 71–2, 443
Salvaygo, Segurano (Sakrān, Genoese merchant) 358, 359, 360, 364
Samarkand/Samarqand 19, 178/373–6, 378–80, 382, 432
de Sambuceto, Lamberto 185
Sanderson, Stephan K. 27
Sanjar al-Shujā'ī 164–5
Sardinia 199, 281–2, 285, 315
Sarkand 19
Sarandīb Island 51, 53; see also: Ceylon
Sarāy/Saray (in Golden Horde) 346, 355, 358
Sarban (Qaidu's son) 369
Sarghatmish 262
sarraïns 323–5, 328, 336
Sauveget, Jean 113
Sawād region of Jordan 266
Sawakin (on East African coast) 466, 468, 475
Schäber, Birgit 25
Scheidel, Walter 87, 90
Schiltberger, Johannes 111, 117
Schlögel, Karl 61–2, 74
scholars, Muslim, see: 'ulamā' 145, 154–58, 161, 169, 170, 187, 195, 202, 261, 279, 280, 302, 310, 376, 377, 379
Schulze, Reinhard 27

Schwats (in Tirol) 66
Sclavonia, Sclavonians 111
Selīm I, Sultan (Ottoman) 95, 449
Seljuks, see: Saljuqs
Semeonis, Simon 110
Semites 116
Serenissima (Venice) 434
Seville 19
Şeyh Bedreddīn (Ottoman scholar) 426
Şeyhülislām 404, 407–409
Sha'ban, al-Ashraf (Mamluk sultan) 178, 265, 267
Sha'bān, al-Kāmil (Mamluk sultan) 200
Shādhiliyya (Sufi order) 99
Shāfi' b. 'Alī (Mamluk historian) 155
Shāfi'īs 155, 203, 464–5
al-Shāghūr 273
Shāh Rūkh (Timurid ruler) 374, 389
Shāhnāmah 116
al-Shām, Bilād, see: Syria 260, 275, 276, 58
shamanism 355
Shanhūr 485
Shanqūr (in Upper Egypt) 485
Shaqḥab, battle of 163
Sharifs of Mecca 457, 459, 467
Sharī'a (Muslim law) 147, 375
Shawbak 264, 265
al-Shaybanī, Khawājā Kamāl al-Dīn Ibrāhīm 461
shaykh (Sufi leader) 94, 95, 99, 115, 135, 294, 384, 473, 480, 485, 494
- Ulugh Shaykh (Turkish Great Shaykh) 384
Shaykh al-Maḥmūdi, al-Mu'ayyad (Mamluk sultan) 94, 96, 179, 391, 404, 428, 429
Shi'a, Shi'is 198, 199, 432
Ships 30, 36, 70, 225, 231–2, 237–41, 244, 282–5, 287–299, 302–3, 313, 317–18, 348, 356, 434–7, 438–39, 445, 466, 475
- Cogs 229
- galleys 229, 236, 241, 294, 298, 299, 303
- jafn 284, 298
- navi 229
- qaraqūra 298
- shūna/shawānī 294, 295, 298
- ṭarā'id 239
shipwrecks 296
Shiraz 384, 462, 474
Siberia 345
Sicilian Vespers 313, 340, 327
Sicily, Sicilians 9, 24, 112, 281, 283, 312, 315, 327, 489
Siena 110
Sievert, Henning 99, 105
Sighnāq 376
sijill (Ar. archive, registration) 135, 147 ; see also: defter
silāḥdāriyya ("arms-bearers") 167, 197
Silk 18, 30, 316, 325, 345, 483, 489, 495
Silk Road 18, 30, 483
silver 30, 63, 65–68, 71–73, 269, 446
Simmel, Georg 17, 34, 37
Sinai 119, 259, 265, 273
Sind 384
Ṣīnī (Arabic: "Chinese") 375
Sirt 282, 284–5, 300
Sirvent, Lluis 317
Sivas 398
slaves and slave trade 9, 22, 39, 46–7, 56, 109, 112–4, 117–18, 152–3, 163, 166, 170, 181, 183–88, 196–8, 199, 303, 355–6, 374
slave girls 45, 346, 352, 355, 357, 358, 503
slave traders 356, 359, 303
Slavs 111, 188
Slovania 112
Solkhat (Crimea) 359
Somalia 459
Sorqaqtani Beki (Tolui's widow) 382
South Asia 20, 30, 32, 456, 466; see also: India
South China Sea 49, 56, 468
South-east Asia 50, 54
Soviet Union 447
Spain, Spanish 22–24, 111, 192, 283, 292, 479; see also: Iberia
spices 20, 28, 66–7, 230, 241, 417, 436
spies 174, 394, 418–421
Sri Lanka, see: Ceylon
Staufens 9, see also: Hohenstaufens
Stein, Burton 473
Steiner, George 117

Suākin 489
Subrahmanya, Sanjay 22
von Suchem, Ludolph 111
Sudan, Bilād al-Sūdān (sub-Saharan Africa) 43, 53, 468, 475
Suez Canal 238
Sufis, Sufism 43–4, 99, 138–9, 141, 293, 295, 350, 367, 376, 378, 383, 385, 392, 402, 413, 432, 482, 487, 326, 335
Sufyānī 83–5, 91, 100
sugar 264, 268, 485
Süleymān (Ottoman sultan) 398–9, 424
sulphur 52, 68–9, 72, 443
Sultanate of Cairo, nature of 75–76, 91, 100, 101, 255, 507
Sultanate of Ḥamā 93
Sumatra 468
Sunnī, Sunnism 75, 97, 146, 149, 171, 389, 410, 423, 434, 464
Sunqur al-Ashqar 94, 160, 161
Sūsa (Tunisia) 285, 489
Suwaysa 285
Syria 9, 19, 24, 30, 40, 45, 52, 58, 64, 69, 70, 76, 78, 79, 81, 83, 84, 92, 93, 94, 98, 100, 101, 102, 103, 104, 105, 110, 118, 119, 121, 132, 133, 147, 149, 154, 161, 164, 173, 189, 230, 242, 259, 261–74, 281, 291, 346, 350, 353, 360, 368, 373, 375, 392, 395, 410, 416, 432, 436, 444, 462–4, 469, 474–5
Syrian Church 24

Tabriz 347–48, 352, 353, 356, 428
Taftāzānī (Central Asian scholar) 379
Tafur, Pero 110, 111, 113
Taghrībirdī (dragoman) 120, 73, 97, 71, 70, 63, 64, 70, 103, 168, 173, 174, 177, 178, 180, 182, 183, 194, 198, 199, 201, 206, 210, 213, 388
Taghrībirdī al-Armanī al-Manṣūrī 189
Taghrībirdī al-Maḥmūdī al-Rūmī 202
Taghrībirdī al-Mu'dhī al-Baklamushī 22
Taghrībirdī al-Sayfī Lājīn 200
Taghrībirdīal-ShamsīṬaṭar al-Ẓāhirī 177, 182
Tahirids (Yemenite dynasty) 464
al-Ṭā'if 456, 459
Ta'izz (Yemen) 452, 474
Tajikistan 382
Ṭajūra 286
tajwīr ("interloping") 467, 468
Talu Sea 351
Tamar, queen of Georgia 118
al-Ṭambudā (in Upper Egypt) 485
Tamerlane, see: Timur 34, 121, 367, 371, 372–79, 385, 387, 432
Tamurbughā, al-Ẓāhir (Mamluk sultan) 198
Tana 114, 185
Tangier (Ṭanja) 286
Tankiz al-Ḥusāmī al-Nāṣirī, Sayf al-Dīn 91, 103
al-Takrūr, Bilād 30, 63–4, 465
Tamīm al-Dārī 52
Tamurbāy min Ḥamza Ṭaṭar al-Nāṣirī 177
Tamurtāsh 110
Tanzimat era 1270
Ṭarabī rebellion in Bukhara 383
tarjumān (translator) 110, 112
Tarmashirin (Chaghadaid khan) 370–72, 374, 375, 382, 384, 386
Tatars 111, 118, 156–59, 169, 173, 179–87, 212, 214, 372; see also: Mongols
al-Ṭawd (in Upper Egypt) 485
Ṭaynāl al-Ẓāhirī 160
Tāzā 287
Tāza Gap 284
Teke (ancient Lycia, peninsula in Anatolia) 414–5, 428
Temür, see: Tamerlane 34, 121, 432, 351, 368, 372, 373, 374, 379, 385, 386, 398
Temür Qa'an (Great Khan) 351
Tengri (the heavens, and also God) 351
Termini (in Sicily) 283
textiles 231, 232, 295, 302, 316, 357, 480, 482–5, 488, 498, 499, 500, 504, 506
thaghr (frontier, pl. thughūr) 230, 240
Thats (people in Caucasia) 119
Thenaud, Jean 112
Thrace 402
Thulā 132
Tibet 345
Tihama 456

Tilimsān 284–7, 289, 293, 295, 283, 282, 292, 294, 295
Timur, Temür, Tamerlane 110, 114, 173–4, 176, 179, 367, 371–5, 377, 385, 396, 398, 419, 432, 441
Timurids 19, 173, 178, 180, 184–5, 187, 378, 379, 385, 399, 401, 403–4
tin 68, 72, 69
Tinis (in Algeria) 287
ṭirāz fabrics 483, 497, 498
Tirol 66
Tokta/Toqta (khan of Golden Horde) 347/ 350, 352, 353, 354, 355, 356, 357, 360
Tolui/Tului (Chinggis Khan's youngest son) 382
Toluids 370
Toqtamish (khan of Golden Horde) 346
trade in foodstuffs 9, 18–19, 20, 22, 26–29, 39, 42, 49, 67, 69, 70, 75, 114, 217, 226, 227, 229, 241, 247–50, 260, 273, 281, 294, 298, 307, 317–20, 325, 345–49, 351–59, 360–2, 374–5, 377, 382, 383, 395, 416, 434, 446, 465, 472, 475, 479, 455–59, 485, 487, 492
traders, see: merchants
Trafego shipping route 299, 303
Transcaucasia 352
Transjordan 259, 257, 274, 267, 263, 260; see also: Jordan
Transoxania 367, 370, 372, 374, 377, 378, 380, 383–6
Trapini (in Sicily) 283
travelers 40, 69, 195, 241, 265, 283, 286, 296, 300, 302, 324–5, 51, 382, 391–4, 418, 420, 455, 489
Trebizond, Trabzon 70, 113
trebuchets 229
Tripoli (Libya) 282–88, 285, 287–8, 292, 294, 295, 297–300, 302
Tripoli (Syria) 133, 200, 228, 230, 290, 417, 462, 474
Tripolitania 300
Ṭubruq 285, 288
Ṭughjī al-Ashrafī 159
Ṭulmaytha 286
Ṭūlū (Mamluk ambassador) 403
Ṭulunbāy (Jöchid princess) 358, 361
Ṭūmān Bāy (Mamluk sultan) 71, 438, 442–444
Ṭūmāntamur al-Yūsufī al-Ẓāhirī 175
tümen (Mongol military division) 349
Tunis 303, 354, 284–88, 292, 294, 295, 297, 298, 299, 300, 303, 304, 305, 364, 280, 282
Tunisia 489 see also: Ifrīqiya
Ṭuqṣubā al-Ashrafī 160
al-Ṭūr (in Sinai) 267
Turkestan 26, 384
Turkification 182
Turkish language and culture 20, 116–19, 160, 169, 180, 182, 201–2, 295, 384, 403, 410–11, 414–5
Turkish names 113
Turkish period; see: Baḥrī period 154, 155, 157, 158, 188, 189, 196, 200, 202, 203, 204, 172, 173, 181
Turkomans/Turcomans/Turkmens 9, 83, 183, 202, 227, 356, 432–33, 437, 439, 443
Turks 43, 45, 47, 53, 83, 109, 111–114, 118, 149, 154, 165, 171–72, 174, 175–78, 185–89, 193, 195, 201–3, 367, 334
al-Turra (in Transjordan) 263, 267
Tuscany 118, 121, 233
Tyre 227, 281

Ubykhs 118, 119, 120
Ughurlū al-Sayfī (Mamluk officer) 198
Uj Ali 109
Ukek (in Golden Horde) 355
ʿulamāʾ, ulema (Muslim scholars) 244, 301, 367, 376–85, 391–413, 279, 302, 425
Ulmās al-Ḥājib al-Nāṣirī 170
ulus (patrimony of Mongol ruler or prince) 351
al-ʿUmarī, Ibn Faḍl Allāh 48, 57, 155, 207, 282, 302, 315, 346, 371–2, 374, 384–5
Umayyads 83, 226, 374
umma (community of Muslim believers) 349
University of Chicago 480, 249, 253, 274, 275, 336, 429, 506, 508
University of Southampton 480, 482, 486, 500

urban landscape, see: landscape, urban 6, 123, 127, 133, 138, 140, 141, 144, 146
ʿUthmān Beg Qarā Yulūk 80
Uzbak/Uzbek/Özbek/Özbeg (khan of Golden Horde) 158, 181, 184, 346–7, 357–61, 382
Uzbeks 434
Uzbak al-Nāṣrānī 200
Uzun Ḥasan 82

Valencia 281, 307, 315, 322, 325, 330, 333, 339–41
van den Bent, Josephine 156
Van, Lake 347, 435
di Varthema, Lodovico 113, 121, 455, 458
Vásáry, István 156, 186
Vasco de Gama 436
Velérian, Dominique 282
Venice, Venetians archives in 9, 19, 24–5, 27, 29, 63, 65, 69–71, 110, 112, 114, 185, 218, 221, 224, 233, 240–3, 245, 247–50, 282, 292, 294, 298, 303, 319, 346, 354, 356, 360, 433–4, 443, 297, 302, 468
vernacular architecture, see: architecture, vernacular 123, 126–33, 144
vernacular language 310
Vienne, Church Council 330
Vijayanagara Empire 473
Vlachs 112
Volaks (people in Caucasia) 119
Volga 345, 348, 357

Wabkant (suburb of Bukhara) 382
Wādī al-ʿAlāqī 63
Wādī al-Ḥadda 466
Wādī al-Khaznadār 369
Wādī Marr 456
Wādī Nakhla 476
Wāfidiyya (Mongol refugees) 152–3, 156, 161–2, 169, 186, 418
Wagenburg 435, 444
Wallachia, Wallachians 113, 111
waqf (religious endowment, pl. awqāf) 142, 143, 262, 263, 266, 267, 272, 275, 359, 446, 457
"waqfization" 264, 265
waqfiyyāt (waqf documents) 261, 265, 267, 272, 273, 259, 263, 264, 267, 270
Wāq-Wāq Island 52, 60
Weber, Max 86
Werner, Michael 22, 37
West Africa 9, 63–4, 465, 280
West Asia 63, 82, 86–88, 91, 100–1, 506, 507
White Horde 370
Wing, Patrick 80, 60, 214, 430, 507
wood 62, 106, 133, 134, 215, 235, 237, 238, 241, 363, 388, 483

Xàtiva 330–1, 340
Xwarsi (Caucasian language) 117

Yalāwach, Maḥmūd (Mongol administrator) 383–4
Yalāwach, Masʿūd Beg (son of above) 384
Yalbughā al-Khāṣṣikī 236, 239
Yalbughā al-Sālimī al-Ẓāhirī 178, 179
yam (Mongol postal system) 351
Yanbuʿ 469, 468
Yaʿqūb b. Uzun Ḥasan 99, 82, 84, 85, 91, 95, 98, 100
Yasa (Mongol law) 168, 368
Yashbak al-Aʿraj 177
Yashbak min Mahdī 98, 116
Yashbak al-Yūsufī al-Jarkasī 182
Yegān, Mollā 404–5
Yemen 50, 52, 146, 456, 458–460, 462–5, 468, 469, 478, 482, 483, 484, 488–491, 495, 497–499

al-Zaʿāfiyya 289, 285
Zabid (Yemen) 462, 474
al-Zamakhsharī (Arabic lexicographer) 193, 192
Zanj coast 483
Zarrāʿa (in Jordan Valley) 266, 264
Zawāgha 282
Zawāra 282
al-Zawāwī (Maghrebi Sufi traveler) 288, 292, 296, 306
zāwiya (Sufi center) 139
Zayla' (in Somalia) 458–59, 466, 475
Zaynab bint Ḥasan b. Khāṣṣ Bak 96, 97